International Intellectual Property

RESEARCH HANDBOOKS IN INTELLECTUAL PROPERTY

Series Editor: Jeremy Phillips, *Intellectual Property Consultant, Olswang, Research Director, Intellectual Property Institute and co-founder, IPKat weblog*

Under the general editorship and direction of Jeremy Phillips comes this important new *Handbook* series of high quality, original reference works that cover the broad pillars of intellectual property law: trademark law, patent law and copyright law – as well as less developed areas, such as geographical indications, and the increasing intersection of intellectual property with other fields. Taking an international and comparative approach, these *Handbooks*, each edited by leading scholars in the respective field, will comprise specially commissioned contributions from a select cast of authors, bringing together renowned figures with up-and-coming younger authors. Each will offer a wide-ranging examination of current issues in intellectual property that is unrivalled in its blend of critical, innovative thinking and substantive analysis, and in its synthesis of contemporary research.

Each *Handbook* will stand alone as an invaluable source of reference for all scholars of intellectual property, as well as for practicing lawyers who wish to engage with the discussion of ideas within the field. Whether used as an information resource on key topics, or as a platform for advanced study, these *Handbooks* will become definitive scholarly reference works in intellectual property law.

Titles in the series include:

Copyright Law
A Handbook of Contemporary Research
Edited by Paul Torremans

Trademark Law and Theory
A Handbook of Contemporary Research
Edited by Graeme Dinwoodie and Mark D. Janis

Patent Law and Theory
A Handbook of Contemporary Research
Edited by Toshiko Takenaka

Research Handbook on the Future of EU Copyright
Edited by Estelle Derclaye

The Law and Theory of Trade Secrecy
A Handbook of Contemporary Research
Edited by Rochelle C. Dreyfuss and Katherine J. Strandburg

Research Handbook on Intellectual Property Licensing
Edited by Jacques de Werra

Criminal Enforcement of Intellectual Property
A Handbook of Contemporary Research
Edited by Christophe Geiger

Research Handbook on Cross-border Enforcement of Intellectual Property
Edited by Paul Torremans

Research Handbook on Human Rights and Intellectual Property
Edited by Christophe Geiger

International Intellectual Property
A Handbook of Contemporary Research
Edited by Daniel J. Gervais

International Intellectual Property

A Handbook of Contemporary Research

Edited by

Daniel J. Gervais

Professor of Law, Vanderbilt University Law School, USA

RESEARCH HANDBOOKS IN INTELLECTUAL PROPERTY

EE Edward Elgar PUBLISHING

Cheltenham, UK • Northampton, MA, USA

Published by
Edward Elgar Publishing Limited
The Lypiatts
15 Lansdown Road
Cheltenham
Glos GL50 2JA
UK

Edward Elgar Publishing, Inc.
William Pratt House
9 Dewey Court
Northampton
Massachusetts 01060
USA

A catalogue record for this book
is available from the British Library

Library of Congress Control Number: 2014947019

This book is available electronically in the **Elgar**online
Law subject collection
DOI 10.4337/9781782544807

MIX
Paper from responsible sources
FSC www.fsc.org FSC® C013056

ISBN 978 1 78254 479 1 (cased)
ISBN 978 1 78254 480 7 (eBook)

Typeset by Columns Design XML Ltd, Reading
Printed and bound in Great Britain by T.J. International Ltd, Padstow

Contents

Contributors

Philippe Baechtold was recently appointed as the Acting Director of the PCT Operations Division at the World Intellectual Property Organization (WIPO). Prior to this, he was the Director of the Patent Law Division at WIPO, where his area of supervision covered legal questions related to patent and utility model law, the development of international patent law, and legislative and policy advice to WIPO Member States. Before joining WIPO, he was employed by the Swiss Federal Intellectual Property Institute, where he occupied different functions, including heading the Patent Department. He is a Swiss national and an attorney-at-law.

Irene Calboli is a Professor of Law at Marquette University Law School, a Visiting Professor at the Faculty of Law of the National University of Singapore, and a Transatlantic Technology Law Forum Fellow at Stanford Law School. Her research interests focus on trademark law and policy, overlapping intellectual property rights, and the protection of geographical indications of origin. She is an active member of the Academic Committee of the International Trademark Association (INTA), the International Association for the Advancement of Teaching and Research in Intellectual Property (ATRIP), the Association Littéraire et Artistique Internationale USA (ALAI-USA), and the Executive Committee of the Section on Law and Arts of the Association of American Law Schools.

Katharina de la Durantaye is a Junior Professor of private law, private international law and comparative law at Humboldt University in Berlin (Germany). Her research focuses, among other things, on questions of comparative copyright law. She has published several articles on orphan works as well as a book on limitations for education and research purposes (*Allgemeine Bildungs- und Wissenschaftsschranke*, 2014). Before coming to Humboldt University, she taught at Columbia Law School, St. John's University School of Law, and Boston University School of Law. She studied at the University of Bologna (Italy), at Humboldt University and at Yale Law School.

Graeme B. Dinwoodie is the Professor of Intellectual Property and Information Technology Law at the University of Oxford, Director of the Oxford Intellectual Property Research Centre, and a Professorial Fellow of St. Peter's College. He was elected to membership in the American Law Institute in 2003, and served as President of the International Association for the Advancement of Teaching and Research in Intellectual Property (ATRIP) from 2011–13.

Rochelle C. Dreyfuss is the Pauline Newman Professor of Law at New York University School of Law and the Co-Director of the Engelberg Center on Innovation Law and Policy. She holds B.A. and M.S. degrees in Chemistry and spent several years as a research chemist before entering Columbia University School of Law, where she served as articles and book review editor of the Law Review. After graduating, she was a law clerk to Chief Judge Wilfred Feinberg of the U.S. Court of Appeals for the Second Circuit and to Chief Justice Warren Burger of the U.S. Supreme Court. She is a member of the American Law Institute and served as a Reporter for its Project on Intellectual Property: Principles Governing Jurisdiction, Choice of Law, and Judgments in Transnational Disputes. She also sits on the National Academy of Science's Committee on Science, Technology and Law.

Susy Frankel is a Professor of Law and Director of the New Zealand Centre of International Economic Law at Victoria University of Wellington. She is Chair of the New Zealand Copyright Tribunal. She was Consultant Expert to the Waitangi Tribunal on the WAI 262 flora, fauna, and indigenous intellectual property claim. Susy's scholarship focuses on international intellectual property law, including the nexus of intellectual and international trade law, and the protection of indigenous peoples' innovation and knowledge as a global issue.

Christophe Geiger is Associate Professor, Director General, and Director of the Research Department of the Centre for International Intellectual Property Studies (CEIPI) at the University of Strasbourg (France). In addition, he is affiliated senior researcher at the Max Planck Institute for Innovation and Competition in Munich (Germany). He specializes in national, European, international and comparative intellectual property law, has drafted reports for the European institutions and acts as external expert for the European Parliament and the Office for Harmonization in the Internal Market (OHIM). He is also General Editor of the Collection of the CEIPI published by Litec (LexisNexis), co-editor of the EIPIN series, and member of the editorial board of several journals on IP law. He has published numerous articles as well as authored and edited many volumes in this field.

Daniel J. Gervais is Professor of Law and Director of the Intellectual Property Program at Vanderbilt University Law School. He is a former

Legal Officer at the WTO, Head of Section at WIPO, and Acting Dean at the University of Ottawa (Common Law Section).

Jane Ginsburg is the Morton L. Janklow Professor of Literary and Artistic Property Law at the Columbia Law School. She also directs the law school's Kernochan Center for Law, Media, and the Arts. She holds degrees from the University of Chicago, Harvard Law School, and the University of Paris. At Harvard, she served as an editor of the Harvard Law Review. After law school, she clerked for Judge John Gibbons of the United States Court of Appeals for the Third Circuit. In 2011, she was elected to the British Academy.

Sam F. Halabi is a Scholar at the O'Neill Institute for National and Global Health Law at Georgetown University and an Associate Professor at the University of Tulsa College of Law. He is a member of the Editorial Advisory Board of the Food and Drug Law Journal as well as the American Society of Law, Medicine, and Ethics. Before joining O'Neill, he was an associate at Latham & Watkins, LLP. He earned his J.D. from Harvard Law School and an M.Phil. from the University of Oxford (St. Antony's College).

Thomas Henninger currently serves as a Legal Information Officer at WIPO in the PCT Legal Division, PCT Knowledge Management Section. Before joining WIPO in the Patent Law Division, he practiced in the private sector as an attorney, and worked as a research and teaching assistant at the University of Geneva. He holds a bar exam in Munich, a law degree from the University of Berlin, and a master and a PhD in comparative law from the University of Geneva.

Elizabeth F. Judge is Professor of Law at the Faculty of Law at the University of Ottawa, where she specializes in intellectual property, law and literature, and privacy. She is a member of the Centre for Law, Technology and Society, an affiliate member of the Institute for Science, Society and Policy, and holds a cross appointment with the Department of English. Prior to joining the Faculty of Law, she practiced law in Washington DC, and she served as a law clerk to the Honourable Mr Justice Ian Binnie at the Supreme Court of Canada.

Tomoko Miyamoto is the Head of the Patent Law Section, Patent Law Division, in the World Intellectual Property Organization (WIPO). She joined WIPO in 1997, and has worked on various issues with respect to patent policy, law, and practice, including the development of the international patent system and the promotion of patent-related treaties. Prior to working for WIPO, she was a patent examiner at the Japan

Patent Office (JPO), and later worked in the International Affairs Division of the JPO. She holds a Master degree in electronic engineering and an LLM in IP law and management.

Cees A.M. Mulder studied Physics and Chemistry at the University of Utrecht (the Netherlands). After completing his PhD in Physics at the University of Leiden (1982), Cees joined Philips Electronics as a researcher. Later on he worked in the Philips Patent Department. In 1999, he qualified as a European patent attorney. In 2001, he was one of the founding partners of DeltaPatents (Eindhoven, the Netherlands). In 2009, Cees resigned from partnership and since then he has been Assistant Professor of Intellectual Property Law at the Faculty of Law of the University of Maastricht (the Netherlands). He is vice-director of the post-doc curriculum "Advanced Masters in Intellectual Property Law and Knowledge Management" (LLM/MSc) at Maastricht University.

Cees is a senior lecturer in many courses and seminars relating to the European Patent Convention, the Patent Cooperation Treaty, the Paris Convention and the Patent Law Treaty. He is a CEIPI and epi tutor. Since 2003, Cees is the author of the book *The Cross-Referenced Patent Cooperation Treaty* (published yearly). In 2011, he successfully defended at Maastricht University a PhD thesis (this time not in physics but in law) entitled: "On the Alignment of the European Patent Convention and the Patent Cooperation Treaty with Requirements of the Patent Law Treaty".

Lisa P. Ramsey is a Professor of Law at the University of San Diego School of Law, where she is a founding member of the Center for Intellectual Property Law and Markets. She teaches and writes in the areas of trademark law, intellectual property, and international intellectual property. Her current scholarship focuses on the potential conflict between trademark rights and free expression in national and international laws. Her most recent works include publications in the Yale Journal of International Law and the International Review of Intellectual Property and Competition Law. Before joining the University of San Diego law faculty, she was an intellectual property attorney in San Diego, California.

Sam Ricketson is a Professor in the Law School of the University of Melbourne who has written widely and taught in all areas of intellectual property law. He also practiced part-time at the Victorian Bar until mid 2012, principally in intellectual property. He holds degrees from the Universities of Melbourne and London, and is a Fellow of the Academy of Social Sciences of Australia. Prior to his appointment to the University of Melbourne in November 2000, Sam was the Sir Keith Aickin

Professor of Commercial Law at Monash University. Before this, he had held positions at the University of Melbourne (1977 to 1991) and in the Centre for Commercial Law Studies, Queen Mary and Westfield College, London (1984–86).

Geoffrey R. Scott is a professor at Penn State Law School. He possesses a wide range of teaching and scholarly interests, but his focus is in intellectual property and on the intersection of the worlds of artistic and scientific expression and the law. He has given particular pragmatic attention to the protection of cultural properties in Europe, Asia, and Australia, to domestic and international entertainment issues with an emphasis on music, and to the representation of the individual professional athlete. Scott received a Fulbright Scholar award in 2004–05 for his research in the protection of cultural and ethnographic properties in Asia, and he has been a visiting professor and scholar at the University of Delaware Graduate College of Marine Studies in the fields of biotechnology and intellectual property law. Professor Scott has taught intellectual property courses and given lectures in London and other European capitals as well as Kyoto, Beijing, Seoul, Sydney, and Melbourne. He has been a Fellow at the Institute of Advanced Legal Studies in London, and is the founder and supervisor of a clinic that provides pro bono services to innovative persons and allied organizations.

Martin Senftleben is Professor of Intellectual Property and Head of the Private Law Department at the VU University Amsterdam, and of Counsel at Bird & Bird, The Hague. His activities focus on the reconciliation of private intellectual property rights with competing public interests of a social, cultural or economic nature. He studied law at the University of Heidelberg and worked as a researcher at the Institute for Information Law of the University of Amsterdam and the Max Planck Institute for Innovation and Competition in Munich. Prior to his appointment in Amsterdam, he worked as a legal officer at the WIPO.

Haochen Sun is Assistant Professor of Law at the University of Hong Kong Faculty of Law. He has been a visiting professor at the University of California, Davis, School of Law. He teaches and writes in the areas of intellectual property and property. His scholarship draws on social, cultural and political thought to explore the theoretical foundations of intellectual property and property law. Haochen's recent research has focused on the intellectual property protection of luxury goods, the ideas of social responsibility and justice in intellectual property law, and the reconceptualization of the nature of fair use in copyright law. Before joining the University of Hong Kong, Professor Sun worked as a research fellow at the Berkman Center for Internet & Society and the Max Planck Institute for Innovation and Competition.

Peter K. Yu holds the Kern Family Chair in Intellectual Property Law and is the founding director of the Intellectual Property Law Center at Drake University Law School. He has served as Wenlan Scholar Chair Professor at Zhongnan University of Economics and Law in Wuhan, China and as visiting professor of law at the University of Haifa, the University of Hong Kong, the University of Strasbourg, and Washington and Lee University.

Preface

The purpose of this book is twofold. First, it aims to provide researchers and practitioners of international intellectual property law with the necessary tools to understand the latest debates in this incredibly dynamic and complex field. Second, the book can be used by students of international intellectual property to obtain useful knowledge of major institutions and instruments, and to gain an understanding of ongoing discussions. The book thus contains both doctrinal analyses and ground-breaking theoretical research by many of the most recognized leading experts in the field.

The book is divided into four main parts. The first part begins with an analysis of the origins, structure and content of the two instruments that can undoubtedly be considered historically as the most important intellectual property treaties, namely the Berne Convention on the Protection of Literary and Artistic Works and the Paris Convention on the Protection of Industrial Property.

The first chapter, on the Berne Convention, was co-authored by the two most prominent commentators on the Convention, namely Professors Jane Ginsburg and Sam Ricketson. They anchor the origins of the Convention solidly in human rights waters, explain the major features of the Convention, and turn to events since its last revision in 1971 and in particular since 1986, the year at which they situate the high-water mark for authors' rights' protection, adding that in "the years since 1986, there has been increasing awareness of other human rights that are competing for attention along with those of authors." In spite of a very rapid increase in its geographical coverage (the Convention had 168 Member States as of November 2014), however, the authors suggest that:

> when its broader context is considered, the real story of the Berne Convention in recent years is rather different, and its successes have been more formal than substantive, with countervailing currents and pressures that have led to its reduced relevance since 1986. At the symbolic level, the institutional importance of the Berne Union now also appears diminished.

The following chapter, on the Paris Convention and other major patent-related instruments, was co-authored by three experts from the Patent Law Division at the World Intellectual Property Organization (WIPO) including its director, Dr Philippe Baechtold, with Tomoko Miyamoto and Thomas Henninger. The chapter explores the emergence of the Paris Convention (176 Member States as of November 2014), but also the role of other instruments such as the Patent Cooperation Treaty (PCT) (on which there is a separate chapter by Dr Cees Mulder – see below), the Patent Law Treaty, and the interface with the TRIPS Agreement. The chapter also discusses the role of major regional organizations (including the European Patent Office) and others in achieving a greater degree of patent law harmonization (that is, beyond existing instruments). Future harmonization, to the extent that it does happen, is likely to emerge not (just) as a set of new multilateral norms, but also as administrative practice, especially of major examining entities, which new technological tools make much easier and cost-effective.

In Chapter 3, Professor Peter Yu considers the different fora in which international intellectual property norms have been or are being negotiated. The chapter then focuses in particular on the recent move away from the multilateral institutions such as WIPO, and towards a regional or a "like-minded" fora, such as the Trans-Pacific Partnership discussions. The chapter offers several important insights on the back-and-forth between smaller (regional or like-minded) groups and multilateral institutions, concluding that if:

> the many diverse, and at times conflicting, normsetting activities that take place in the non-multilateral era would eventually lead to norm consolidation through the multilateral process, such as the development of TRIPS II, non-multilateral activities will benefit the international intellectual property regime. By contrast, if those activities further fragment the existing international intellectual property regime or polarize the global community, those activities will greatly undermine the regime.

In the final chapter of Part I, Professors Graeme Dinwoodie and Rochelle Dreyfuss discuss a key emerging issue namely the existence of an *acquis* in international intellectual property. They define this *acquis* as "a set of basic principles that form the background norms animating the intellectual property system." They note that there indeed exist:

> principles that constitute the backdrop to all international and national intellectual property lawmaking. The international intellectual property system has been 150 years in the making; comprehensively fleshing out its underlying principles will also take time and will require the efforts of numerous scholars and policy makers. However, the benefits are potentially vast. As the *acquis* grows, so too will its significance. Retrospectively, it can be used interpretively, to bring coherence to the international system, and to

> fill gaps. Prospectively, it would create a template for crafting new intellectual property instruments.

Part II is devoted to copyright and related rights. Copyright is of course mentioned in most of the chapters of Part I. Here, the book presents two major substantive issues that have caused a significant degree of difficulty and disagreement among scholars and policy makers alike and illustrate ongoing difficulties in defining an optimal set of copyright rules. The first chapter of this part, co-authored by Professors Christophe Geiger and Martin Senftleben and the Editor, explains the origins of the three-step test in Article 9(2) of the Berne Convention and recent debates concerning the interpretation of the test. As the chapter explains, the test has become the key norm guiding lawmakers and negotiators crafting domestic exceptions and limitations to copyright rights but also to other rights, including industrial designs and patents in Articles 26.2 and 30 of the TRIPS Agreement. Beyond Berne and TRIPS, the test is also used in the WIPO Copyright Treaty, the WIPO Performances and Phonograms Treaty, the Beijing Treaty on Audiovisual Performances and the Marrakesh Treaty to Facilitate Access to Published Works for Persons who are Blind, Visually Impaired or Otherwise Print Disabled. Interestingly, "a significant concern follows from the fact that the language of the test changes, sometimes quite significantly, each time it appears somewhere new."

In the next chapter, Professor Katharina de la Durantaye, explores options to ameliorate the fate of "orphan works," that is, works that are still protected by copyright but are "without an owner to negotiate with." There is no uniform international solution or policy response. Current proposals can be grouped in three main categories: licensing; expansion or recognition of a greater role for exceptions and limitations; and limitations on remedies (e.g. statutory or predetermined damages). The chapter explains that another approach would be to work to reduce the size of the problem.

> The most elegant way of dealing with the orphan works problem, at least prospectively, would be to prevent orphanage and the market failure associated with it. The orphan works problem is mainly an information problem. It comes in three forms: a work may have never contained any ownership information, ownership information may have gotten lost, or the information may be outdated, either because the author has died or because ownership has changed for other reasons.

While copyright remains extremely important, as debates in national courts, WIPO, and legal literature illustrate, much of the research and policy focus in recent years have been on patents due mostly to two issues: the interface between patents and pharmaceutical research (and access thereto), and generally the desire in many countries around the world to develop a better innovation policy. In parallel, efforts are afoot to implement easier mechanisms to obtain a patent in multiple jurisdictions. These are the themes explored in Part III.

The part begins with a chapter by Professor Susy Frankel on "Traditional Knowledge and Innovation as a Global Concern." Using a number of Māori examples from Aotearoa/New Zealand, the chapter demonstrates the importance of the protection of certain knowledge assets for indigenous peoples and also several developing countries, explaining that the "tension over what sort of intellectual property is protected and what is not is also a concern for indigenous populations of both developing and developed countries, and particularly minority populations in developed countries with high levels of intellectual property protection." After a discussion of the (considerable) definitional difficulties in this area, the chapter shows the overlap and disjuncture of traditional knowledge and intellectual property rules, including those contained in the TRIPS Agreement. It concludes that "some agreed minimum standards are necessary."

The next chapter examines the limits of patents. The co-authors, Professor Elizabeth Judge and the Editor, explain that, at times perhaps too much is expected of the patent system. It does not always deliver. At times, it may indeed be counterproductive – either systemically or because of the specific way in which some people use it – if measured in terms of impact on net innovation outcomes. Among the issues mentioned in the chapter are: the one-size-fits-all way in which patentable inventions are typically defined domestically and internationally; relatedly, the possible need to factor in industry-specific impacts of patents; low quality of patents issues in certain jurisdictions at least; the fact that patents are rights to exclude; and finally the fact that patents are seldom compared to other forms of incentives (such as prizes). The chapter then examines the applicable provisions of the TRIPS Agreement. It also considers the latest research on whether patents help or hinder, in which circumstances and why, and how patents interface with human rights. The last part provides a detailed account of research on the role that patents play, with other policy levers, in developing a coherent innovation policy.

Asking whether patents – in aggregate or at least by type of invention or industry – help or hinder research and innovation presupposes that there are convincing ways to measure such impact. This is the subject of the next chapter by Professor Geoffrey Scott, which provides a detailed account of how information is generated, including in the "open source" context, and disseminated, based on various and often cultural factors, which are reflected, inter alia, in the existence of different legal systems. The chapter offers a broad historical and geographic *tour d'horizon,* concluding that "[m]isunderstanding, whether through failure of inquiry, failure to truly appreciate the presumptions and perspectives of others in the dialogue, or nondisclosure of assumptions or expectations, seems to often punctuate discussion and has led to considerable tension and unsatisfactory outcomes in the global IP community."

The last chapter of Part III presents the PCT: the poster child for internationally integrated application systems for intellectual property that can or must be registered with or granted by governmental authorities, given that intellectual property rights are largely territorial in nature. One of the world's foremost experts on the PCT, Dr Cees Mulder presents the PCT: its history, structure, and its principal features (process and procedures). While formal harmonization of substantive patent law has been an elusive target, much progress has been made on the administrative side as the PCT and instruments adopted since (including the PLT) amply demonstrate. The chapter presents a complete picture of the PCT application, examination, and publication process, one of the very few publications to do so comprehensively.

The last part of the book (Part IV) deals with the protection of two types of trade symbols, namely trademarks and geographical indications. Trademarks are a major influence in the daily lives of billions of people. They guide the hand of the buyer. People wear them proudly (sometimes) on everything from t-shirts to designer handbags. They function as symbols from the grocery store to fancy soirees and even among various countercultural movements. Their interface with free expression is, therefore, an essential area of study. It is also the topic of the first chapter of this part, authored by Professor Lisa Ramsey. The chapter explains how trademark can be speech-restrictive, describes the major applicable rules including those contained in the TRIPS Agreement, and discusses the role of model laws. Important "external" limits on trademark rights to further expressive interests can be found in a number of constitutional laws and human rights treaties. Countries can also internalize free speech principles within their trademark laws, however. The chapter thus includes a call to "develop a global soft law instrument that contains specific, speech-protective model trademark laws that comply with international obligations to protect trademarks in TRIPS and the Paris Convention."

The following chapter, by Professor Sam F. Halabi, offers a path to reconcile trademarks with a somewhat different normative concern, namely international rights and obligations to protect health. After setting the stage by offering useful examples of the interface between trademarks and public health (such as the ban or limitations on the use of trademarks on cigarette packaging), the chapter proceeds to explain the expansion of trademark rights in international intellectual property. After a brief discussion of speech-related issues, the chapter then turns to its central thesis, namely that seeing trademarks as a "form of property with narrow rights to exclude and alienate" would allow "regulators to tailor their protective scope to their commercial function." It suggests in this context that "[n]ational authorities and international arbitrators enjoy sufficient flexibility to craft an expropriation proceeding that balances the state's duty to protect individual and public health with the trademark holder's legitimate interest in the distinguishing characteristics of its mark."

The penultimate chapter, by Professor Haochen Sun, focuses on a particular form of expansion of trademark right – domestically but increasingly internationally as well – namely anti-dilution protection, in particular when applied to luxury brands. The chapter draws a clear picture, illustrated by several examples, of the arguments surrounding the emergence of anti-dilution protection for global brands, the (limited) role of dilution in the TRIPS Agreement, and divergences among major players, especially the European Union and the United States on the best way to define and implement anti-dilution rules. The chapter then considers the regime of protection of well-known marks in China. It suggests a path forward: amend the TRIPS Agreement to include an explicit requirement about anti-dilution protection; rely on an expansive application of the national standard to link the fragmented domestic anti-dilution laws together; consider the limitations that should be carved out in anti-dilution protection to avoid overzealous trademark protection; and continue research to ascertain the appropriate level of anti-dilution law in protecting brands.

Last but not least, Professor Irene Calboli's chapter "Of Markets, Culture, and *Terroir*", discusses the unique economic and culture-related benefits of geographical indications (GIs). GIs are mentioned in the TRIPS Agreement, where a distinction is made between GIs on wines and spirits (high level of protection); other GIs (lower, trademark-like level in that it requiring a likelihood of confusion); and an obligation to negotiate a possible system of notification and registration for GIs on wines (and spirits as was added by the Doha Declaration in 2001). There is also renewed interest as of this writing (early 2014) in a renovated Lisbon system. The chapter presents the economic and cultural advantages of GIs, but also relevant critiques and counterarguments. Among the key economic arguments is that GIs can incentivize "the creation and conservation of niche-markets," but also "provide consumers with a unique set of information about the products that are identified by the GIs, namely with respect to the physical location and the methods of production of the GI-denominated products." The chapter ends with a suggestion that the GI issue is ripe for consideration multilaterally, which would allow the development of better and clearer rules and exceptions.

Daniel J. Gervais

Table of cases

United Kingdom

European Union

European Court of Human Rights

International

Australia

Canada

China

France

Germany

New Zealand

South Africa

Spain

Switzerland

United States of America

WTO Reports

Table of legislation

European Union

International Treaties and other Instruments

National Legislation

Albania

Australia

Brazil

Canada

PART I

HISTORICAL AND INSTITUTIONAL ASPECTS

1. The Berne Convention: Historical and institutional aspects

*Sam Ricketson and Jane Ginsburg**

INTRODUCTION

Declarations, let alone 'solemn declarations', are grand things. They have a tradition that goes back at least as far as the US Declaration of Independence and are exemplified, in the twentieth century, by various declarations in the international sphere, beginning with the Universal Declaration of Human Rights at the end of World War II. Other more contemporary declarations of rights have proliferated in specific areas of concern, for example, the rights of indigenous peoples,[1] the human genome[2] and human genetic data,[3] and bioethics.[4]

Authors' rights, too, have been the subject of a 'solemn declaration', although one that is perhaps less well known. This declaration was made by members of the Berne Union at the celebration of the centenary of the Berne Convention for the Protection of Literary and Artistic Works meeting in formal assembly in Geneva on 11 September 1986. Reaffirming their commitment to protect the rights of authors in 'as effective and uniform manner as possible', these states went on to:

> *Solemnly declare* that copyright is based on human rights and justice and that authors, as creators of beauty and learning, deserve

* The authors thank Dr Silke von Lewinski and Shira Perlmutter for their comments and suggestions.

1 United Nations Declaration on the Rights of Indigenous Peoples (adopted 13 September 2007) UNGA Res 61/295 (DRIP).

2 Universal Declaration on the Human Genome and Human Rights (adopted 11 November 1997) UNESCO 29 C/Res 31 (DHGHR).

3 International Declaration on Human Genetic Data (adopted 16 October 2003) UNESCO 32 C/Res 15 (IDHGD).

4 Universal Declaration on Bioethics and Human Rights (adopted 19 October 2005) UNESCO 33 C/Res 15 (DBHR).

> that their rights in their creations be recognized and effectively protected both in their own country and in all other countries of the world,
> *Solemnly declare* that the law of copyright has enriched and will continue to enrich mankind by encouraging intellectual creativity and by serving as an incentive for the dissemination throughout the world of expressions of the crafts, learning and information for the benefit of all people,
> *Solemnly declare* that international respect for the law of copyright opens paths across frontiers for works of the mind, this contributing to a better international understanding and to the cause of peace,
> *Solemnly declare* that the Berne Convention for the Protection of Literary and Artistic Works, by providing an outstanding, comprehensive and harmonized codification of the rights of authors, has guaranteed for a hundred years the most effective international protection of those rights.[5]

It then ended with the exhortation that members:

> *Pledge* themselves to continue to work together to safeguard the rights of authors against all forms of piracy and other unlawful acts and to ensure the effective application of those rights in the framework of new opportunities for communication between authors and the public created by economic, social, scientific and technological progress,
> *Urge* all States that so far have not done so to join them by adhering to the Berne Convention for the Protection of Literary and Artistic Works.[6]

While lofty, and even self-congratulatory in tone, this document provides a good vantage point from which to look both backwards and forwards – to the origins and development of the Berne Convention, and to what has happened in the more immediate past as the Convention entered its second century. The year 1986, in fact, was a watershed year, the point at which the 'old' Berne Union had reached its fullest bloom before entering the brave new world of personal computers, digital media,

---

[5] The text of the Declaration appears in [1986] *Copyright* 373.

[6] Adopted by 'acclamation' by Berne members at a meeting of the Berne Assembly convened in the same place where the Convention was signed 100 years previously.

online communications and trade negotiations (to mention only some of the significant post-1986 developments).

The solemn declarations set out above provide a perfect reflection of the 'old' Berne Union as an agreement between states with a largely Euro-centric focus. While there was a significant membership of countries with common law systems, this membership had not had a large influence on the development of the Convention; a similar lack of influence was true for both the small bloc of 'socialist countries' and the larger and steadily increasing group of developing-country members.[7] In 1986, however, many large and economically important countries – namely, the United States (US), the Union of Soviet Socialist Republics and the People's Republic of China – still remained outside the Berne Union. The same was true of many emerging economies, such as Malaysia, Indonesia, the Republic of Korea and a large swathe of South American, African and other Asian countries. The Union was far from universal and the world was divided into two almost equal blocs of Berne and non-Berne countries.

Within a decade, this picture had changed substantially. By 1996, each of the countries mentioned above were members of the Berne Union and the overall membership of the Union had expanded to 121.[8] At the time of writing, this number had increased to 168.[9] Throughout this period, the actual text of the Berne Convention has remained unchanged from its last revision in 1971, but the legal and wider context within which the Convention applies has changed radically. At the international level, this includes the advent of the World Trade Organization, with its annexed Agreement on Trade-Related Intellectual Property Rights 1994 ('TRIPS Agreement')[10], followed in 1996 by the WIPO-sponsored negotiation of two special agreements linked to Berne (the WIPO Copyright Treaty and

---

7 Although the demands of developing countries had caused a near crisis in the Berne Union over the issue of compulsory licenses in the period 1967–71. For a detailed account, see Sam Ricketson and Jane C Ginsburg, *International Protection of Copyright and Neighbouring Rights: The Berne Convention and Beyond* (OUP 2006) Ch 14.

8 *Industrial Property and Copyright* (WIPO 1997) 12.

9 For a list of current members, see WIPO, 'Contracting Parties > Berne Convention' <http://www.wipo.int/treaties/en/ShowResults.jsp?lang=en&treaty_id=15> accessed 19 October 2014. The 168th member is Kuwait, which acceded on 2 September 2014. This accession will come into effect on 2 December 2014.

10 Agreement on Trade-Related Aspects of Intellectual Property Rights (adopted 15 April 1994, entered into force 1 January 1996) 1869 UNTS 299 (TRIPS Agreement).

the WIPO Performances and Phonograms Treaty).[11] Two other WIPO treaties have followed in the past two years: the 2012 Beijing Treaty on Audiovisual Performances,[12] and the Marrakesh Treaty to Facilitate Access to Published Works for Persons who are Blind, Visually Impaired or otherwise Print Disabled (the VIP Treaty)[13] signed on 27 June 2013. At the broader technological, cultural and economic levels, the rapid shift into the online environment has radically changed the modes of creation and dissemination of works, while the re-emergence of developing countries as a major and potent factor has brought about a significant change in the setting of international norms, including a heightened awareness of human rights issues. All of these matters will be taken up in the succeeding chapters of this volume. Our present task, however, is to step back from these immediate concerns, and to provide a reflection upon the history and development of the Berne Convention, both up to and after these changes. The 1986 solemn declaration, with its powerful exhortation, furnishes a good starting point for such reflection.

HUMAN RIGHTS AND JUSTICE

While the first Act of the Berne Convention adopted in 1886 was a very limited and pragmatic document that was chiefly directed at obtaining protection for authors in their literary and artistic works in members' territories through application of the principle of national treatment, there was nonetheless a background to it that we would now describe as a 'human rights' one. English translations of the original French text may serve to blur this humanistic dimension given that 'copyright' is an imperfect reflection of the French expression 'droit d'auteur' or the German or Italian equivalents. Nevertheless, even in common law copyright traditions, there was a natural rights focus, beginning with the United Kingdom's Statute of Anne, in which authors were made the starting point for protection. Although a more cynical view may be that

---

[11] WIPO Copyright Treaty (adopted December 20, 1996, entered into force 6 March 2002), 2186 UNTS 121 (WCT); WIPO Performers and Phonograms Treaty (adopted December 20, 1996, entered into force May 20, 2002), 2186 U.N.T.S. 203 (WPPT).

[12] Beijing Treaty on Audiovisual Performances (adopted 24 June 2012) AVP/DC/20 (Beijing Treaty).

[13] Marrakesh Treaty to Facilitate Access to Published Works for Persons who are Blind, Visually Impaired or Otherwise Print Disabled (adopted 27 June 2013) VIP/DC/8 Rev (VIP Treaty).

'authors' in this context were simply stalking horses for publishers (in this view, the real beneficiaries of the new statutory rights), the Statute of Anne endeavored to ensure that authors in fact benefited from the rights with which the statute vested them. This was because section 11 of the Act provided that, at the expiration of the 14-year term of protection, if the author was still living, then '[t]he sole right shall return to the Author' for another 14 years.[14]

Writing more than 150 years later, a leading British commentator, WA Copinger, argued that the claims of authors were based on the principles of natural rights. Copinger traced this claim back to the writings of John Locke, who had significantly set the bounds of political and philosophical discourse in late-seventeenth and early-eighteenth century England.[15] Similar thinking underlies the adoption of colonial and early state copyright acts in the US and, more significantly, was embodied by the Framers of the US Constitution, who sought to promote the 'progress of science and useful arts by securing for limited times to authors and inventors the exclusive right to their respective writings and discoveries'.[16] The term 'copyright' may therefore serve to mask the natural rights origins of these new rights, placing them in a more utilitarian and functional light (the rights of those who exploit the protected works, rather than those of the actual creators).[17] Nonetheless, authors and their concerns were in the forefront in the debates over the extension of

---

[14] For an extensive discussion of Section 11 and its successors, see Lionel Bently and Jane C Ginsburg, '"The Sole Right … Shall Return to the Author": Anglo-American Authors' Reversion Rights from the Statute of Anne to Contemporary U.S. Copyright' (2011) 25 *Berkeley Technology LJ* 1475.

[15] WA Copinger, *The Law of Copyright in Works of Literature and Art* (Stevens & Haynes 1870) 1. See also R Deazley, 'Commentary on Copinger's *Law of Copyright* (1870)' in L Bently and AM Kretschmer (eds) *Primary Sources on Copyright, 1450–1900* at <www.copyrighthistory.org> accessed 18 November 2014; Laura Moscati, 'Un "Memorandum" di John Locke tra *Censorship* et *Copyright*' (2003) 76 Rivista di storia del diritto italiano 69.

[16] Consistent with James Madison's *Federalist Papers* (No. 43) observation that 'the copyright of authors has been solemnly adjudged, in Great Britain, to be a right of common law', US pre-Constitutional state copyright statutes adopted natural rights rhetoric. Jane C Ginsburg, 'A Tale of Two Copyrights: Literary Property in Revolutionary France and America' in B Sherman and A Strowel (eds), *Of Authors and Origins* (OUP 1994) pp 138–9.

[17] The 'masking' may also result from a misapprehension of the meaning of 'copyright' as a right over the production of physical copies; in fact, for the drafters of the Statute of Anne, the meaning of the 'copy' was the incorporeal 'work'. Properly understood, 'copyright' means the right in the work of authorship, not merely in its physical instantiations. John Locke, 'Memorandum'

copyright protection that occurred in the UK during the nineteenth century.[18] These concerns were also reflected in the scholarly and professional commentary on copyright that occurred on both sides of the Atlantic during this period.[19]

Understandably, natural rights justifications were more explicit in France, beginning with the recognition in two French revolutionary decrees of 1791 and 1793 of authors' and artists' rights to perform and reproduce their works. While such thinking quickly spread to other continental European countries in the first part of the nineteenth century,[20] the notion of these rights as universal (i.e., extending beyond national boundaries) was much slower to evolve. As a consequence of this asymmetric progression, 'free riding' problems frequently arose, particularly in countries with a common language. The case of the UK and the US is well known and has attracted some distinguished scholarly writing,[21] but the same phenomenon was present in French- and German-speaking countries,[22] particularly in the period before unification of the German states (and, likewise, in the Italian

(against the renewal of the Licensing Act) in ES de Beer (ed.), *The Correspondence of John Locke*, vol 5 (Clarendon Press 1979) pp 785–91. On Locke's 'Memorandum', see Moscati (n 15).

[18] Notably in the parliamentary debates that occurred in 1841 and 1842 in relation to the proposals of Serjeant Talfourde to extend the term of copyright protection in the UK: see *House of Commons Debates*, 29 January 1841, pp 146–7; 4 February 1841, pp 1250–8; 5 February 1841, pp 342–60; 6 April 1841, pp 1348–402. See also C Seville, *Literary Copyright Reform in Early Victorian England: The Framing of the 1842 Literary Copyright Act* (CUP 1999), and R Deazley. "Commentary on Copyright Amendment Act 1842" in Bently and Kretschmer (eds), *Primary Sources in Copyright* (n 15).

[19] Copinger (n 15), 1–5. See also A Birrell, *Seven Lectures on the Law and History of Copyright in Books,* (Cassell & Co 1899) pp 9–24; WA Briggs, *The Law of International Copyright* (Stevens & Haynes 1906) pp 2–33 ('The Nature and Origin of Copyright'). In relation to US law, see George Ticknor Curtis, *Treatise on the Law of Copyright* (CC Little & J Brown 1847) pp 1–25 ('Theory of the Rights of Authors'); Eaton S Drone, *A Treatise on the Law of Property in Intellectual Productions in Great Britain and the United States: Embracing Copyright in Works of Literature and Art, and Playwright in Dramatic and Musical Compositions* (Little, Brown & Co 1879 pp 1–16 ('The Origin and Nature of Literary Property').

[20] Ricketson and Ginsburg (n 7) 5ff.

[21] For example, see C Seville, *The Internationalisation of Copyright Law: Books, Buccaneers and the Black Flag in the Nineteenth Century* (CUP 2006); JJ Barnes, *Authors, Publishers and Politicians: The Quest for an Anglo-American Copyright Agreement 1815–1854* (Routledge & Kegan Paul 1974).

[22] For example, see Alfred Villefort, *De la propriété littéraire et artistique au point de vue international: Aperçu sur les législations étrangères* 11

states). Bilateral treaties provided some safeguards as between some important markets for authors and publishers, but the coverage was incomplete and inconsistent as to the level of protection granted, the term of such protection, and the conditions under which protection was available.

Hence, by the second part of the nineteenth century, the time was ripe for some multilateral initiative, particularly if it could bring the US into some kind of international arrangement. More broadly, this was the beginning of an era of multilateralism, as states began to seek common and uniform solutions for a range of practical problems arising in relation to such matters as international communications, standards of measurement, trade relations, and humanitarian aid. Significant milestones were the establishment of the International Red Cross (1863), the International Telegraph Union (1865), the Universal Postal Union (874), and the Metrics Convention (1875). In the case of industrial property, moves towards the adoption of a multilateral agreement had begun with the calling of a patents congress at the time of the Vienna International Exhibition in 1873[23] and a further congress dealing with patents, trademarks and designs during the Paris Universal Exhibition of 1878.[24] These last-mentioned initiatives led, within a short space of time, to the drafting and adoption of the Paris Convention for the Protection of Industrial Property in 1883 (Paris Convention).

The Paris Convention was clearly a model for what might be achieved in the sphere of authors' rights, particularly with its somewhat amorphous concept of a 'Union'.[25] But the seeds for such a union in the case of authors' rights had already been sown some years previously. Against the patchwork coverage of national laws and bilateral treaties, there was a growing recognition that authors' rights were peculiarly vulnerable in the cross-border context in the absence of some overarching system of protection. Authors' groups, publishers, academics and lawyers from

---

(Imprimérie et Librairie Générale de Jurisprudence 1851) (French lawyer complaining of Belgian practice of copying French books and exporting them back to France: 'There is a country at our gates, whose territory is separated from ours only by the imaginary line drawn in treaties, and whose name is in effect synonymous with piracy.').

[23] Thomas Webster, QC, 'International Patent Congress' in WP Blake and Henry Pettit, *Reports on the Vienna Universal Exhibition, 1873,* pt IV, C.1072-IV (Eyre & Spottiswoode 1874) pp 333ff.

[24] See further *Congrès international de la Propriété Industrielle tenu à Paris du 5 au 17 septembre 1878, Comptes-rendus sténographiques, No 24 de la série* 1879, Paris imprimerie nationale.

[25] Paris Convention for the Protection of Industrial Property (adopted 20 March 1883) 828 UNTS 305 (Paris Convention) art 1.

different European countries had articulated the need for such protection as early as 1858 during a congress in Brussels. A series of resolutions was passed calling for the adoption of a universal copyright law, in particular declaring that the 'principle of the international protection of the property of authors in their literary and artistic works should be enshrined in the legislation of all civilized peoples'.[26] A subsequent conference of over 1,000 practicing artists in Antwerp in 1861 gave its support to these resolutions and called for efforts by governments to negotiate between themselves for the protection of artistic property.[27] Following these early meetings, it appears that there were no more international meetings of this kind, but there were some important national meetings, notably in France and Germany, that continued to agitate for more comprehensive protection.[28] Interest in international protection for authors' rights was also taken up by two important non-governmental associations of international lawyers that were founded in the early 1870s: the UK-based Association for the Reform and Codification of the Law of Nations (later the International Law Association) and the Ghent Institute of International Law. In the case of the International Law Association, Draft Outlines of an International Code that were prepared and discussed in several conferences in the early 1870s referred to the need to accord international protection to patents, trademarks and copyrights.[29] More immediate impetus for international action, however, came at the time of the Paris Universal Exhibition in June 1878, where a parallel international literary congress – organized by the French *Société des gens de lettres* and presided over by Victor Hugo, the preeminent French literary figure of his day – was held. This Congress passed a number of resolutions calling for enhanced protection of authors' rights; for this to be available in all other countries on the

[26] See further E Romberg (ed.), *Compte rendu de Travaux du Congrès de la Propriété Littéraire et Artistique*, vol 1 (E Flatau 1859) pp 175ff.

[27] See further Ricketson and Ginsburg (n 7) pp 44ff.

[28] See further E Röthlisberger, *Die Berner Übereinkunft zum Schutze von Werken der Literatur und Kunst und die Zusatzabkommen geschichtlicht und rechtlich beleuchtet und kommentiert* (Franke, Berne 1906) pp 4–5; A Darras, *Du Droits des auteurs et des artistes dans les rapports internationaux* (Arthur Rousseau 1887) p 275.

[29] The work of these bodies is discussed further by L Duncan, 'From Privileges to the Paris Convention: The Role of Theoretical Debate in the Evolution of National and International Patent Protection' (1997) Monash University unpublished PhD thesis (Monash Law Library, Victoria, Australia) pp 377–80. See also T Webster, 'Reform and Codification of the Law of Nations' [1874] *L Magazine & Rev* 1016, pp 1017–21.

basis of national treatment, free of formalities other than those imposed in the country of origin; and to be available in perpetuity, subject to a system of paying public domain at a fixed time after the author's death.[30] The most concrete achievement of this meeting was the establishment of the International Literary Association.[31] This Association was open to literary societies and authors from all countries and adopted the following objects: (1) the protection of the principles of literary property; (2) the organization of regular relations between the literary societies and writers of all countries; and (3) the initiation of all enterprises possessing an international literary character.[32]

A parallel congress on artistic property was held at the same time, and, while passing similar resolutions, also called for the constitution between the different states of Europe and elsewhere of 'a General Union which would adopt a uniform law in relation to artistic property'.[33] A similar call was made by the literary congress, which requested the French Government to undertake the summoning of a diplomatic conference to establish such an agreement.[34] This request was not taken up by the French Government (perhaps because it was then in the throes of revising its own national law[35]), but the International Literary Association met regularly after its foundation in 1878 and became a strong advocate for the adoption of some kind of international agreement on authors' rights, ultimately adopting a resolution calling for the preparation of a draft convention at its Congress in Rome in 1882.[36] In the following year, the Association extended its membership to include artists, and the present

---

[30] For the resolutions of the Congress, see *Congrès littéraire international de Paris 1878 : présidence de Victor Hugo: comptes rendus in extenso et documents* (hereinafter termed *Congrès littéraire 1878*), Société des gens de lettres de France, Paris (1879) p 369–70.

[31] Ibid., 370. See also *Association littéraire et artistique internationale, son histoire, ses travaux, 1878–1889* (Bibiliothèque Chacornac, Paris, 1889) (hereinafter termed *Histoire*) pp 3ff.

[32] Article 2 of the Resolution passed by the Congress on 28 June 1878. *Histoire*, p 4.

[33] *Congrès international de la propriété artistique tenu à Paris du 18 au 21 septembre 1878* (hereinafter termed *Congrès artistique 1878*), Exposition universelle, 1878, Paris, 117 (resolution 20).

[34] *Congrès littéraire 1878*, 370 (fourth 'wish'). A similar wish was expressed by the Artistic Congress: *Congrès artistique 1878*, 117.

[35] The suggestion of Numa Droz, a Swiss Federal Councillor, who was himself instrumental in the Swiss Government undertaking this role some years later. *Histoire* (n 30) 130–1.

[36] Ibid, p 123.

name, International Literary and Artistic Association was adopted (or ALAI, as it is more commonly known, from the French 'Association littéraire et artistique internationale').[37] In that same year, ALAI also adopted a draft of an international convention, which it then presented to the Swiss Government as the likely international sponsor of such a project.[38] The Swiss Government responded favorably and took the next vital step, which was the convoking of a diplomatic conference in Berne in 1884. The role of ALAI as the catalyst for the calling of the diplomatic conference is akin to that of the Congress on Industrial Property that was held at the same time as the Paris Universal Exhibition in 1878.[39] The Congress was essentially a private initiative that also provided draft treaty provisions that were then taken up by the French Government, which convoked a diplomatic conference in Paris in 1880.[40] This meeting led, in turn, to the adoption of the Paris Convention for the Protection of Industrial Property at a further conference in 1883.

The history of the Berne drafting conferences – two substantive ones in 1884 and 1885 respectively, and then a final conference for formal signature and adoption in 1886 – has been well documented and analyzed elsewhere;[41] accordingly, there is little point in retracing such ground here. Still, there are some generally relevant points that should be made about the process that led to the final adoption of the Convention in 1886.

- Even though the ALAI draft of 1883 and the Swiss Federal Council's draft program of 1884 were relatively limited documents as compared to more ambitious previous projects, there was still considerable debate among delegates as to the scope of the proposed

---

[37] This happened at the International Literary Association Conference in Berne from 10–17 September 1883, although the formal name change did not occur until the following year in Rome. *Histoire* (n 30) pp 129ff.

[38] Ibid, pp 135ff, 182ff.

[39] See generally: *Congrès international de la Propriéte Industrielle tenu a Paris du 5 au 17 septembre 1878, Comptes-rendus stenographiques, No 24 de la serie*1879, Paris imprimerie nationale.

[40] For an account of the steps leading to this, see *Journal du Droit internationale privé et du la jurisprudence comparée*, vol 7 (1880) 628–9. A number of draft treaties, based on the resolutions of the Congress, were prepared after the Congress by the Permanent Committee appointed by the Congress.

[41] For example, see S Ricketson, 'The Birth of the Berne Union' (1986) 11 *Columbia-VLA J L & Arts* 9, 23–9; Ricketson and Ginsburg (n 7) Ch 2. For more contemporary accounts, see Darras, *Du Droits des auteurs et des artistes dans les rapports internationaux* (Arthur Rousseau 1887) pp 518ff; WA Briggs, *The Law of International Copyright*, pt III (Stevens & Haynes 1906) pp 230ff.

convention. In this regard, it is notable that there was a strongly worded proposal from the German delegates that asked delegates to consider seriously the question of aiming for a codification, in the framework of a convention, to regulate copyright protection in a uniform manner.[42] This document, in turn, had a significant effect on subsequent discussions, flowing over to the next conference of 1885.

- While the final text adopted was very far removed from the ideal of a universal codification, it nonetheless was an instrument that had authors at its heart and was directed, through the application of national treatment, at securing the same level of protection for foreign and local claimants in each member state. The significance of this achievement in a multilateral instrument cannot be underestimated. In addition, the language of 'rights' was highlighted in the first article of the 1886 text, which constituted a 'union' of the contracting states for the protection of 'the rights of authors in their literary and artistic works' ('des droits des auteurs dans leurs oeuvres littéraires et artistiques'). At a textual level, this contrasts with the wording of the corresponding article of the Paris Convention text of three years earlier, in which contracting governments constituted themselves in a 'Union for the Protection of Industrial Property'.[43] While the preamble of that Convention did refer in passing to the rights of inventors, there was also a more overtly commercial tone in its provisions (the protection of the 'fairness [loyalty] of commercial transactions').[44] The Berne text, however, was quite unambiguous in its focus on authors and continues to be so today in its latest iteration in the Paris revision of 1971.
- While specific substantive norms of protection were largely absent from the 1886 text (the particular case of translations remaining a point of contention between member states), some of its provisions

---

[42] See further *Actes de la Conférence internationale pour la protection des Droits d'auteur réunie à Berne du 8 au 19 septembre 1884*, International Office, Berne (1884), p 24 (first session, 8 September 1884).

[43] Paris Convention, art 1.

[44] Ministère des affaires étrangères, *Conférence internationale pour la protection de la propriété industrielle*, Paris, (1883) p 51. Importantly, the preamble of this text did refer specifically to the 'rights of inventors': 'Egalement animés du désir d'assurer, d'un commun accord, une complète et efficace protection à l'industrie et au commerce des nationaux de leurs Etats respectifs, et de contribuer à la garantie des droits des inventeurs et de la loyauté des transactions commerciales, ont résolu de conclure une Convention à cet effet et ont nommé pour leurs Plénipotentiaires.'

were prescient in pointing to permissible limits on the scope of the protection to be granted. This is reflected in the oft-quoted statement of Numa Droz in his closing speech to the 1884 Conference that 'limits to absolute protection are rightly set by the public interest'.[45] At an early stage, therefore, this was a reminder of something that we have now come to recognize in modern human rights discourse – namely, that rights may come into conflict with each other, and that there will be a need to strike a balance between them in given circumstances.

- Quite apart from its multilateral character,[46] the Berne text of 1886, like that of the Paris text in 1883, was seen as a 'work in progress', a text that would be revised and upgraded at regular intervals.[47] In this regard, its success throughout its first century, particularly when contrasted with that of the Paris Convention, was notable.
- An important (though unnecessary) corollary to the multilateral character of the new instrument was that it was open to membership by any state, old world or otherwise.[48] Indeed, its initial membership of nine masked its vast potential territorial reach: six of these

---

[45] *Actes de la Conférence internationale pour la protection des Droits d'auteur réunie à Berne du 8 au 19 septembre 1884*, International Office, Berne (1884), p 67. Examples of such articles in the Berne Act of 1886 were Article 7 ('news of the day') and Article 8 ('the making of extracts of works for educational or scientific purposes'). At the same time, it should be noted that the Berne Act did require some limited recognition, in addition to national treatment, of certain exclusive rights that were to be accorded to Convention claimants – notably, translation rights for ten years from first publication of the original work (Article 5); public representation of published or unpublished dramatic or dramatico-musical works and public performance of published musical works where rights had been expressly reserved (Article 9); and protection against certain kinds of 'illicit reproductions' (Article 10).

[46] To claim that this was the first multilateral copyright convention would go too far: as early as 1840, such a convention already existed between Austria and Sardinia, and this convention was extended over time to include the other Italian states. The Convention of 22 May 1840 concluded between His Majesty the King of Sardinia and the Emperor of Austria in favor of property rights in and against infringement of scientific, literary and artistic works. On the Austro-Sardinian treaty, see generally Laura Moscati, 'Il caso Pomba-Tasso e l'applicazione della prima convenzione internazionale sulla proprietà intellettuale' in *Mélanges en l'honneur d'Anne Lefebvre-Teillard* (Panthéon-Assas 2009) pp 747, 754–7.

[47] Berne Convention for the Protection of Literary and Artistic Works (adopted 9 September 1886, as revised at Paris 24 July 1971) 828 UNTS 221 (hereinafter termed Berne Convention) art 17.

[48] Berne Convention, art 18.

signatories had significant colonial possessions and dependencies[49] and were generally, over time, to extend the application of the Convention to these territories.[50] At a later stage, this colonial past served to extend individual state membership, as newly independent countries would usually choose to continue the Berne membership of their metropolitan state.

- The continental Euro-centric character of this first text of 1886 cannot be denied. Indeed, although the UK – the sole common law country represented – was involved in all stages of the negotiations, little (if any) UK influence is to be seen in the text that was adopted (though the UK delegates were generally in support and recommended adoption to their government). But the real reason for this apparent lack of influence may have been that the UK's interest in the negotiations was a more strategic one, focused on achieving a multilateral instrument that might succeed in finally bringing the US into the web of international copyright relations. But while the US delegates themselves were favorably inclined towards accession,[51] this was ultimately not the view of Congress, and the US remained outside the new Union for the next century (this isolation was to become more marked after the Berlin revision of 1908).[52] Notwithstanding the absence of the US, the British Government remained part of the negotiations in Berne, directing its efforts principally towards ensuring that any text that was adopted would require minimal readjustments to its own disorganized national

---

49 Namely, France, Italy, Spain, Germany, Belgium and the UK.

50 Berne Convention, art 19.

51 The issues here were well-summarized in the report of the UK delegates (FO Adams and JHG Bergne) to the Marquis of Salisbury (Foreign Secretary as well as Prime Minister) on the conclusion of the 1885 Conference: report dated 25 September 1885, in *Correspondence Respecting the Formation of the International Copyright Union (Switzerland, no 1, 1886)* C-4606 (January 1886) (hereinafter termed *Correspondence 1886*) 55:

> In fact, from the friendly interest in the objects of the Conference which has been expressed by the United States' Delegate, we are justified in anticipating that when once the Union has been formed, and has been acceded to by the more important European countries, the United States will before long feel it difficult to abstain from becoming a party to it also.

52 See, for example, Arpad Bogsch, 'Study No 32: Protection of Works of Foreign Origin' (June 1959) in *Copyright Law Revision: Studies Prepared for the Subcommittee on Patents, Trademarks and Copyrights of Committee on the Judiciary of the United States Senate, 86th Congress, Second Session, Pursuant to S. 240* (Government Printing Office 1961) pp 1–8.

laws.[53] For better or worse, however, it was now part of an international framework of protection that gradually came to affect its domestic legislation in an increasingly substantive manner.

- It is worth noting that, compared with today's diplomatic conferences, the Convention was discussed and drafted in terms of comparative intimacy and informality.[54] Only ten countries were ultimately represented at the 1884 sessions, and only 16 persons were present at its opening session. The common language was French, and there was clearly a commonality of assumptions – both cultural and legal – between the participants. Even though many of the delegates were career diplomats accredited to Switzerland, there were also some delegates experienced in copyright matters, such as Ullbach (the president of ALAI) from France, d'Orelli from Switzerland, and Dambach from Germany. Furthermore, some of the diplomatic delegates, such as Adams from the UK, Arago (France) and Reichardt (Germany) already had considerable familiarity with the issues raised by international copyright protection. In such an environment, agreement can be more readily expected.

Hence, it must be concluded that the first paragraph of the 1986 solemn declaration does resonate with the history of the Convention and its adoption. Even with just nine founding members, the 1886 text was a very considerable advance on the protection of authors' rights, with a clear mechanism for extension of this protection in the coming years.

---

[53] Adams and Bergne, the UK delegates, expressed their desire for a wholesale codification of UK copyright law in keeping with the recommendations of the Copyright Commission of 1878, arguing in their report to the Foreign Secretary that this would enhance accession to the new multilateral agreement. They went on to say that if 'Her Majesty's Government should not think proper to undertake the complete reform of British Copyright Law which we suggest, it might be possible to allow Great Britain to enter the Union by a simple amendment of the existing International Copyright Acts'. *Correspondence 1886* (n 48) p 56. This was duly done in the International Copyright Act 1886 (England). For a commentary on the background of this Act, including the attitudes of the British Government during the Berne Conferences, see R Deazley, 'Commentary on International Copyright Act 1886' in Bently and Kretschmer (eds) *Primary Sources on Copyright,* (n 15).

[54] See further Ricketson and Ginsburg (n 7) s 2.22ff.

ENRICHMENT AND INCENTIVE

Theories of authors' rights protection differ greatly from one national system to another and from one legal tradition to another. How does one test the assertion that the law of copyright has 'enriched and will continue to enrich mankind by encouraging intellectual creativity and by serving as an incentive for the dissemination throughout the world of expressions of the crafts, learning and information for the benefit of all people'? If one accepts the general proposition that people are 'enriched' by having access to the products of intellectual creativity of all kinds, and the more arguable assertion that intellectual property protection provides an incentive for authors to engage in this kind of activity, the successive revised texts of Berne have been notably successful in achieving these objects. Consider, for example, the following:

- *Works protected*: Beginning with an impressive and inclusive list of specific categories of literary and artistic works of the kinds current in 1886, the definition of this term in the Berne Act 1886 concluded with the following general residual formulation: 'in fact, every production whatsoever in the literary, scientific, or artistic domain which can be published by any mode of impression or reproduction'.[55] This definition was reshaped in the Berlin Act 1908, with the general formulation coming first, followed by the inclusive list of examples introduced by the words '… such as'.[56] The Berlin and subsequent revisions have expanded this list of examples to include choreographic works and entertainments in dumb show (Berlin, 1908), derivative works (translations, Berne 1886, and then adaptations and the like (Berlin 1908), cinematographic works produced by a process analogous to cinematography (Brussels 1948, although these had previously received protection under separate provisions

---

55 Berne Act 1886, art 4. This provided in full as follows:

The expression 'literary and artistic works' shall include books, pamphlets, and all other writings; dramatic or dramatico-musical works, musical compositions with or without words; works of drawing, painting, sculpture and engraving; lithographs, illustrations, geographical charts; plans, sketches, and plastic works relative to geography, topography, architecture, or science in general; in fact, every production whatsoever in the literary, scientific, or artistic domain which can be published by any mode of impression or reproduction.

56 Berlin Act 1908, art 2.1.

of the Berlin 1908[57] and Rome 1928 texts[58]), photographic works and works produced by a process analogous to photography (Brussels 1948, although these had also received protection under separate provisions going back to Paris 1896[59]), collections of works (a sub-category of compilation, Berlin 1908) and works of applied art (Brussels 1948, although limited protection had been required under Rome 1928[60]). While these steady accretions to the categories of protected works kept pace with changing modes of cultural production, some claimants failed to make the cut at successive revision conferences – namely, performers, phonogram producers and broadcasters – notwithstanding some clearly 'literary' or 'artistic' aspects of their activities.[61] Overall, in a conceptual sense, this was a Convention for the hard copy, print environment; the challenges of the computer age, let alone the virtual environment of the Internet, were far ahead.

- *Exclusive rights accorded*: the extension of protection for exclusive rights accorded under national laws to Berne claimants, regardless of national treatment, was equally impressive, reflecting changing technologies in the context of reproduction and dissemination of works. Alongside public representations of dramatic or dramatic-musical works,[62] translation rights (albeit in a limited form) were first recognized in Berne 1886;[63] and adaptation rights, mechanical reproduction rights and cinematographic reproduction and public representation rights were adopted at Berlin in 1908.[64] Protection for the following was then adopted in subsequent revisions: broadcasting and limited wired public communication rights (Rome 1928[65]); full public performance and representation rights and public recitation rights (Brussels 1948[66]); and a broadly framed

[57] Berlin Act 1908, art 4.1.

[58] Rome Act 1928, art 4(2).

[59] Paris Additional Act 1896, art 2.I.B.

[60] Rome Act 1928, 2(4).

[61] See further Ricketson and Ginsburg (n 7) ss 8.109–8.114. See also the comparative table of works protected under different Acts of the Convention. Ibid, s 8.134.

[62] Berne Act 1886, art 9.

[63] Berne Act 1886, art 5.

[64] Berlin Act 1908, arts 10, 13.1 and 14.1. There have also been adaptations to the Berne Act 1886, art 10.

[65] Rome Act 1928, art 11*bis*(1).

[66] Brussels Act 1948, arts 11 and 11*ter*.

reproduction right (Stockholm 1967[67]). Equally significant was the requirement to protect the moral rights of attribution and integrity at Rome 1928[68] – an unfamiliar concept for common law countries, and one that took them many years properly to digest and apply within the context of their own national laws.[69]

- *Formalities*: A significant step taken in the Berlin revision of 1908 was the abolition of formalities conditioning protection,[70] thereby affirming the principle that the rights accorded under the Convention did not require state endorsement or authentication after the points of attachment (nationality or place of first publication) required under the Convention were made out. Together with the principle of the independence of protection, also adopted in Berlin in 1908,[71] authors' rights in a work vest automatically throughout the Berne Union upon the work's creation (or first publication), without regard as to whether the work's country of origin would protect the work. This universal and immediate character of Berne Convention rights stands in stark contrast to the industrial property rights protected under the Paris Convention, where territorial registrations usually play a critical role in ensuring entitlement, most notably through the right of priority following first filing in a Paris Convention country.[72]
- *Duration of protection*: Finally, the general rule as to duration, again adopted in Berlin 1908,[73] underlines the attachment of the rights the Convention secures to the person of the author: with rare exceptions (the most significant being cinematographic works), the term of protection is tied to the life of the author. This is in sharp contrast to the Paris Convention (which does not contain any stipulations as to duration) or the TRIPS Agreement (which provides finite minimum terms of protection for patents,[74] designs[75] and trademarks,[76] respectively (but not for copyright).

---

[67] Stockholm Act 1967, art 9(1).

[68] Rome Act, art 6*bis*.

[69] For example, see Copyright, Designs and Patents Act 1988 (UK) ch IV; Copyright Act 1968 (Australia) pt IX. To date, US law recognizes these rights only to a limited extent: Copyright Act 1976 (US) s 106A.

[70] Berlin Act 1908, art 4.2.

[71] Ibid.

[72] See generally Paris Convention, art 4A–H.

[73] Berlin Act 1908, art 7.1.

[74] TRIPS Agreement, art 33.

[75] Ibid, art 26.3.

[76] Ibid, art 18 (albeit renewable indefinitely).

INTERNATIONALIZATION AND WORLD PEACE

For most (if not all) of its first century, it may be said that the Berne Convention has opened 'paths across frontiers for works of the mind'. The steady increase of membership, first across continental Europe and then into significant Asian and South American countries, reveals a consistent upwards trajectory. Berne membership in the period before World War I extended to all of Western Europe, and the post-war years saw the entry of a number of newly created states in Eastern Europe, including the former Yugoslavia and the Baltic states. Non-European members during the first 50 years were outliers, but included Japan (1899), Brazil (1922), Thailand (1931) and a number of self-governing dominions of the British Empire that had become members of the Union in their own right by the time of Rome in 1928.[77] From the end of World War II to 1986, membership increased again in Africa and Asia as many former colonies opted either to declare their continuing adherence to the Convention or to accede anew. Of particular significance here (in territorial terms) were India, Pakistan, the Congo, the Philippines (following independence from the US) and, for a brief time, Indonesia.[78] In the years following 1986, the accessions of the US, Russian Federation and China have brought in their wake a slew of other states, including the emerging Asian 'tigers' such as Malaysia, Singapore, the Republic of Korea, and Indonesia (again), the new States that have sprung up from the dissolution of the former Soviet Union and Republic of Yugoslavia, the various countries of Central and South America that had been outside the Berne Union, and sundry other African and Asian-Pacific countries.

At a purely conceptual and textual level, this continuing extension of membership has enabled literary and artistic works to move freely across borders without formality, thereby creating the 'paths' referred to in the solemn declaration. Whether this has inured to the benefit of authors and owners in a practical sense across all of these territories is quite another question. The negotiation of the TRIPS Agreement in the early 1990s was a direct response to this insofar as it provided, for the first time,

---

[77] Notably, Australia, New Zealand, South Africa, Ireland and Canada.

[78] The Rome Act (1928) was applied to the Dutch East Indies by the Netherlands on 27 June 1931 and came into force on 1 August 1931. Following independence from the Netherlands in 1949, there was a declaration of continued application by Indonesia, which was adopted 23 February 1956 and entered into force on 27 December 1949. Indonesia denounced this declaration of continued application on 19 February 1959, and the denouncement became effective on 19 February 1960. Indonesia ultimately rejoined in a new act of accession in 1997.

substantive norms for enforcement. Even more significantly, it contained a mechanism for state-to-state enforcement through incorporation of the WTO dispute resolution process (albeit also shifting the focus of protection from 'authors' to 'rightholders'). But it cannot be denied that the Berne Convention has provided a common text to which almost all states now adhere, and has done so in terms that continue to enshrine the central importance of authors and their works. At an abstract level, therefore, the continuity of Berne norms must contribute to 'a better international understanding' (to quote the solemn declaration). Whether it has further served 'the cause of peace' is a much less certain proposition, even at the level of abstraction, but the following observations may be made in relation to this issue:

- Despite the occurrence of two major world conflicts during the twentieth century (to say nothing of dozens of smaller conflicts both between and within member states), the Berne Union has remained intact and has continued to grow.
- It should not be surprising that this is so, given that the Convention is a multilateral instrument that is unaffected by the addition of new members or the departure of existing ones. In the case of war, there is no cessation of relations between belligerent and non-belligerent states. Even between belligerents, there is often only a temporary suspension of relations, which are resumed upon the making of peace. The obligations under the Convention for each member state are to protect the works of authors from other member states. So long as this is done, there is no breach of the Convention. An example of this occurred during the First World War where the UK vested the literary and artistic property of enemy aliens in the official custodian; this property was restored to its rightful owners after the war, and the works continued to receive protection throughout this time as required by the Convention.[79] Obviously, these are issues for each belligerent state to work out for itself. The Berne Convention does not deal with issues of ownership,[80] but rather with what is to be protected and the scope of this protection.

---

[79] See the *Trading with the Enemy (Copyright) Act 1916* and the Order in Council of 9 February 1920 (made under the *Termination of the Present War (Definition) Act 1918*) revesting these rights: discussed further in *Copinger on the Law of Copyright* (6th ed, 1927), pp 296–297. See further [1920] *Droit d'Auteur* 38 and [1939] *Droit d'Auteur* 109.

[80] Because the Berne Convention does not concern issues of ownership, it does not address wartime expropriations of the sort described above.

Accordingly, it will only be where a belligerent state completely extinguishes the literary or artistic property of enemy aliens that any question of breaching the Berne Convention will arise. So far as we are aware, this has not happened at any point during the history of the Convention.

- The member states of the Berne Union have generally had a very open attitude towards questions of membership; indeed, political and/or ideological considerations have not usually played a role here. There is only one clear instance of refusal of a purported application for membership (that of Turkey in 1931), and the reason for this is more correctly described as legal (the making of a reservation as to translation rights that was not allowed under the relevant Berlin text of 1908) rather than political.[81] The reference in later texts to 'countries' rather than 'states' has also allowed for the accession of various territorial entities that did not strictly meet the full requirements of statehood, such as protectorates, mandated territories of the League of Nations, the Free City of Danzig, and the Holy See, to say nothing of microstates such as Monaco, Liechtenstein and Andorra. Oddities in the history of the Convention are also to be found, such as the accession of the puppet state of Slovakia in 1944 (extinguished in 1945 and reabsorbed into the reconstituted Czechoslovakia, more recently reconstituted as the Slovak Republic – and as a sovereign state – following the 'velvet divorce' from the Czech Republic in 1992). More significantly, for over 40 years the Federal Republic of Germany and the Democratic Republic of Germany maintained separate memberships of the Convention,[82] and the same is true of the two Koreas today (although Taiwan – the Republic of China – remains outside). Likewise, although the State of Israel does not have diplomatic relations with many of its surrounding Arab neighbors, all are

---

[81] See further Ricketson and Ginsburg (n 7) s 17.18.

[82] Due to this division, both countries were called upon to celebrate the centenary of Germany's accession to the Berne Convention in the special studies that were published in *Le Droit d'Auteur/Copyright* in 1986. E Ulmer, 'The Federal Republic of Germany and the Berne Union' [1986] *Copyright* 82 (writing for the FRG) and H Püschel, 'The International Union of the Berne Convention and the National Copyright Law of the Member States, with Particular Reference to the Legislation of the German Democratic Republic' [1986] *Copyright* 144 (writing for the GDR).

Berne members. If world peace is advanced by common membership of a treaty such as Berne, this is clearly an achievement of sorts.

- A related explanation for the continuity of the Berne Convention is also to be found in the notion of 'Union' that was adopted at the outset. The Berne Convention is not simply a multilateral instrument – by its establishment of a Union of states for the protection of the right of authors, it is a separate international legal entity that has its own 'organs' and finances. This was the case from its inception, when an international office of the Union was established, and the constitution of more formal deliberative bodies of an Executive Committee and Assembly following the Stockholm Revision of 1967.
- Throughout the history of the Berne Union, the role of the International Office has been critical in providing a central point of reference for member states, and has been an impressive source of information and intelligence, as well as a general clearing house. It has done this, not only through its liaison role with the relevant hosting state in the preparations for each revision conference, but also through its central record-keeping functions and the comparative and other studies provided in its monthly publication *Le Droit d'Auteur* (from 1887 to 1997) and its English version *Copyright* (from 1964 to 1997). While these functions have now been taken over by the much larger World Intellectual Property Organization and the monthly journal is no longer published, for most of its first century the International Office had a small coterie of skilled legal professionals who did much to add to the systematic understanding of the national and international laws relating to authors' rights. They also played a considerable intellectual role in its development.[83]
- The concept of 'Union' also provides a basis for a legal link between members, where they are not bound by a common text of the Convention: until recently, at least, there was a particular problem where there were members who continued to be bound by earlier texts of the Convention (for example, Rome or Brussels) but had not acceded to the Stockholm/Paris revision. Where both had once been bound by the earlier text, it was possible to say that their relations *inter se* should be on the basis of the earlier text by which they were bound. Problems arose, however, when a state from

83 See further Ricketson and Ginsburg (n 7) s 16.34ff.

outside the Union acceded to the latest text, such as Paris, without ever having been bound by any of the earlier texts. This problem yields no strictly legal solution, but common membership of the overall Union provided a basis for the practice that each member should apply to other members the latest text by which it was bound.[84] This problem has now receded, as almost all members have now acceded to the Stockholm/Paris Act, but several countries at the time of this writing still remain bound by earlier Acts of the Convention (for example, Fiji, Lebanon, Madagascar, New Zealand and Zimbabwe[85]).

CODIFICATION AND HARMONIZATION

Self-congratulation was clearly to the fore when Berne members in 1986 solemnly declared that the Convention had provided 'an outstanding, comprehensive and harmonized codification of the rights of authors'. If 'outstanding' means that there had been nothing like it before, such a statement was certainly true, but the adjectives 'comprehensive' and 'harmonized' need careful qualification:

- As noted above, successive revisions of the Convention have achieved a high degree of comprehensiveness as to the subject matter and scope of what must be protected, the level of protection to be given, conditions for its availability, and its duration. In other respects, in 1986 as today, there were significant gaps in coverage notably with respect to issues of entitlement and ownership, which, apart from enunciating a presumption regarding the identity of the work's author,[86] Berne leaves to member states to regulate. With respect to enforcement and remedies, the Berne Convention itself mandates no remedies other than border seizures of infringing

---

[84] See further Article 32 of the Paris Act, which requires signatories to accept that countries bound by an earlier Act may apply to such signatories the provisions of the Paris Act. There can, of course, be no obligation of this kind imposed on the non-member states. See also Ricketson and Ginsburg (n 7) 17.69–17.76.

[85] See the list of members at WIPO, 'Contracting Parties > Berne Convention' <http://www.wipo.int/treaties/en/ShowResults.jsp?lang=en&treaty_id=15> accessed 10 October 2014.

[86] Berne Convention, art 15.

copies,[87] but instead leaves it to member states to supply the 'means of redress'.[88] That said, while Berne does not specify remedies, it does impose detailed conditions on the availability of compulsory licenses. A member state may not substitute an equitable compensation remedy for actual damages or injunctive relief unless, with respect to the reproduction right, the remedy passes the 'three-step test'[89] or, with respect to certain communications to the public, meets the criteria of Article 11*bis*(2). One may infer that Berne anticipates that member states' 'means of redress' will include at least actual damages and injunctive relief.

- Furthermore, Berne says little about private international law issues. While Article 5(2) directs that 'the extent of protection, as well as the means of redress afforded to the author to protect his rights, shall be governed exclusively by the laws of the country where protection is claimed', ambiguity remains concerning the identification of that country, particularly where, as occurs frequently on the Internet, an alleged infringement may originate from one country but have an impact in many others. In addition, whatever the 'country where protection is claimed', matters of authorship and ownership remain beyond the scope of Berne by virtue of its delegation of them to national law.
- Even at the level of substantive norms (for example, the exclusive rights to be protected), Berne does not 'codify' these matters in the sense of providing a strict template to be applied by all member states. State practice has long established that members possess a high degree of flexibility in giving effect to their obligations under the Convention; indeed, the Convention is concerned with questions of 'whether' rather than questions of 'how'. An example here is to be seen in the different ways in which member states protect public recitation and broadcasting rights – some doing this through the grant of specific exclusive rights and others doing it through extensions of the public performance or representation right. By the same token, determining the scope of the Conventional right of 'communication to the public' requires synthesizing the piecemeal provisions of Articles 11(1)(ii), 11*bis*(1)(ii), (iii), 11*ter*(1)(ii) and 14(1)(ii) to ascertain what gaps may exist. In a number of other instances, such as limitations and exceptions, Berne refers these

87 Ibid, art 16.
88 Ibid, art 5(2).
89 Ibid, art 9(2).

> matters back to member states, subject to certain broad parameters.[90]

As these observations suggest, it can fairly be said that Berne, in its first 100 years, had, in terms of formal conventional obligations, thereby 'guaranteed [for authors] … the most effective international protection of those rights.' At the level of enforcement and state compliance, however, much was to be desired – hence the story of TRIPS and subsequent developments in the post-1986 period. We now turn to these matters.

FUTURE DEVELOPMENTS – THE PLEDGE AND EXHORTATION

In this regard, the 'pledge' that came at the end of the 1986 solemn declaration was prescient and, at one level, can be seen as having been fully redeemed, both by those states that were Berne members in 1986 and by post-1986 adherents. In this respect, the following can be said:

- While lacking enforcement standards and effective means of ensuring member compliance, Berne has provided the basic corpus of substantive norms to be protected under the TRIPS Agreement. In legal drafting terms, this was certainly efficient. The substantive effect of the TRIPS Agreement has been to bolt on the Berne requirements (except for moral rights) as the baseline standards for copyright in the revised international trading system inaugurated under the World Trade Organization. These standards also come into play in the bilateral free trade agreements that have become an increasing part of the post-TRIPS environment.
- Berne has also leapt into the digital era, as special agreements in the shape of the WIPO Copyright Treaty (WCT) have been negotiated. Once again, Berne provides the starting point for the new obligations, even in the (unlikely) event that an adherent to the WCT is not actually a Berne member.[91]

The years since the making of the solemn declaration have also borne out its final exhortation for non-members to join. Indeed, the increase in membership of the Convention in this period has been highly impressive,

---

[90] For example, see Articles 10, 10*bis* and 9(2).

[91] WIPO Copyright Treaty (adopted 20 December 1996, entered into force 6 March 2002) 2186 UNTS 121 (WCT) art 1(4).

at least in purely numerical terms – from 76 in 1986 to 168 in 2014. While some of this increase can be attributed to the creation of new states in the 1990s, only a handful of states now remain outside the Union.[92]

In 1986, however, there was still a large and very significant group of non-Berne states, with the link between them and Berne members being provided, at least in part, by the Universal Copyright Convention (UCC). The speed with which Berne obtained new member state adherences in the post-1986 period was extraordinary, but it is probably the case that few present at the 1986 centenary foresaw this happening. In retrospect, it may all appear to have been obvious, with the linking of intellectual property rights to trade and enforcement providing the obvious vehicle with Berne being a ready-made garment of standards that could instantly be used as a starting point. In immediate terms, however, US adherence to Berne was a critical turning point, leading to the rapid atrophying of the UCC as other large states, such as China and the Russian Federation, followed suit. In consequence, the Berne Union, in its second century, has had quite a different complexion and appearance than in its first.

THE STORY GOES ON – MORE OF THE SAME OR IS THERE A NEED FOR A RE-TELLING?

In light of the preceding account, it might fairly be said that the Berne Convention has been a great success in achieving its object of protecting the rights of authors. In terms of geographical spread, subject matter, and scope of protection accorded, this is certainly correct. But is this the whole story? Is there another narrative that can be constructed about this history, particularly in its recent years?

In our view, when its broader context is considered, the real story of the Berne Convention in recent years is rather different, and its successes have been more formal than substantive, with countervailing currents and pressures that have led to its reduced relevance since 1986. At the symbolic level, the institutional importance of the Berne Union now also appears

---

92 That 188 states are members of the WIPO Convention means that 20 of those 186 remain outside the Berne Union (to say nothing of the few states that remain outside WIPO entirely). Of present non-Berne members, Iran (77 million), Burma (53 million), Ethiopia (86 million) and the Republic of China (Taiwan) (23 million) appear to be the most significant in terms of population and economic development. Population figures derived from 'List of Countries by Population' (*Wikipedia*, 29 January 2014) <http://en.wikipedia.org/wiki/List_of_countries_by_population> accessed 18 November 2014.

diminished. While much of this development is simply a consequence of the more complex world we now inhabit, the matters listed below have operated to make the Convention more contested and less relevant than was the case in 1986; certainly, they have created an environment that would not have been in the minds of the delegates who made the solemn declaration in that year. Some illustrations of what has changed:

- As a charter of authors' rights, Berne 1886–1971 was premised on a unilateral conception of authorship, with the flow going one way, from creator to consumer. The advent of Internet communications has enriched this paradigm: creativity increasingly is an interactive process where users themselves become 'authors' as part of a continuing and expanding activity with many participants. So far as 'authors' rights' are concerned, this has obvious implications for the questions of who is an author and whether the traditional formulations of exclusive rights require modification or reconsideration. The dispersal of authorship activity may also call for wider formulations of exceptions and limitations in order to enable 'downstream' contributors to borrow from or elaborate on prior works. At the same time, the disaggregation of authorial activities may require concentration of ownership in persons or entities that coordinate or assemble diverse contributions, lest the exploitation of the ensemble prove unmanageable. Understandably, given its age, the current Berne text directly addresses none of these issues, and even the 'special agreement' embodied in the WCT does so only to a very limited extent. Much creative practice and usage therefore now lies outside the formal structure of Berne and its derivatives. That said, we should not exaggerate the significance of these new practices and usages. Not all interactive authors seek compensation or control over their works, but we should not assume that the arrival of disinterested amateurs has substantially displaced professional creators, for whom copyright remains a necessary means to earn a living.
- In the years since 1986, there has been increasing awareness of other human rights that are competing for attention along with those of authors. While recognition of creators' rights now finds a place in international human rights instruments beyond the Berne Convention,[93] so too do other important human rights, such as

[93] For example, see the Universal Declaration of Human Rights (adopted 10 December 1948) UNGA Res 217 A(III) (UDHR), art 27(2), and the International

rights to free speech, education, health and development. Recognizing and giving effect to these other rights may therefore come into collision with those of authors. At present, this conflict is seen in relation to the new treaty concerning access to work by visually handicapped persons (the VIP treaty of which more below). How to accommodate these claims with continued protection of the rights enshrined in Berne is therefore a major challenge (this is not confined to Berne, of course, as similar challenges arise with respect to other intellectual property rights protected under the international conventions, such as Paris).

- Linked to the discourse on human rights is the growing influence of developing countries in international forums concerned with intellectual property rights, including those of authors. In the history of Berne, this is nothing new – the debates over compulsory educational and development licenses almost brought an end to the Convention in the late 1960s. But the concerns and views of developing countries have now moved more fully to the center in the various forums of the WIPO, the WTO and other international agencies, providing a weighty backing to the human rights arguments referred to immediately above. Balancing these concerns is a difficult process in the case of an international agreement such as Berne, given that its roots are still strongly anchored in the intellectual and cultural traditions of the late nineteenth century. Again, this development may point to the sidelining of Berne.
- Institutionally, the Berne Union has suffered the fate of many older institutions, both national and international: it has become subsumed into the framework of a larger international organization, the WIPO, and has now lost much of its former identity. Thus, its administrative functions are all carried out by WIPO and its finances are part of the larger block contributions made by WIPO members. While the Assembly still meets in a formal sense, this is now part of the series of regular meetings of assemblies of all the 'unions' administered by WIPO and is really a matter of formality rather than substance. No longer is there the monthly journal of record and informed commentary dedicated to authors' rights that

---

Covenant on Economic, Social and Cultural Rights (opened for signature 16 December 1966, entered into force 3 January 1976) 993 UNTS 3 (ICESCR), art 15(1)(c).

> was published from 1888 until 1997.[94] Finally, the activities of the Executive Committee are now subsumed into those of a broader Standing Committee that deals generally with copyright and related rights. Participation in the Standing Committee no longer requires Berne membership, and widespread observer participation from intergovernmental and non-governmental interest groups have shifted the character of these meetings from discrete assemblies of experts to occasionally boisterous gatherings of strong-willed (if not always technically proficient) advocates. All these developments are readily understandable in administrative terms and may certainly be said to make these processes more transparent, if not more time consuming. Furthermore, the deliberations of the Standing Committee, which is now more than 15-years old, have led to some significant initiatives, such as the protection of audiovisual performers[95] and, most recently, access to published works for visually handicapped persons.[96] However, there has been the loss of a distinct institutional identity for the Berne Union, which means the Convention is now simply a text, albeit a foundational one, that no longer has the iconic importance that it had for its founders in 1886 or even for those celebrating its centenary in 1986.

These are the realities, then, in any contemporary account of the Berne Convention: it is an ancient text that retains high formal importance but is under significant challenges from all directions.

IF 1986 WAS THE HIGH-WATER MARK, IS BERNE NOW IN DECLINE? SOME CONCLUDING REFLECTIONS

If the preceding analysis is correct, one might inquire whether Berne's emphasis on the effective 'protection of the rights of authors in their literary and artistic works' has become a quaint relic of a time when national legislatures and international institutions honored authorship. To parody the 'grand declaration', some today would maintain that 'copyright is antithetical to human rights and justice and that authors, as

[94] There is now a twice-yearly journal carrying some scholarly and other commentary generally in relation to intellectual property matters. This is the WIPO Journal: http://www.wipo.int/about-wipo/en/wipo_journal/.

[95] Beijing Treaty, *supra* n 12.

[96] VIP Treaty, *supra* n 13.

alleged creators of beauty and learning, have no greater claim to rights in their creations than does the society at large which is the ultimate source of authors' creativity in any event'. Calls to redress Berne's perceived imbalance and indifference (or even hostility) to users' rights[97] have garnered political acceptance among WIPO member states, leading most recently to the conclusion on 27 June 2013 of the VIP Treaty.[98] Some WIPO member states have urged further treaties designed to limit the scope of copyright protection.[99]

Whatever these treaties' socially laudable substantive objectives, it is appropriate to step back from the particular issues confronting their beneficiaries and to consider more broadly an institutional quandary: Are copyright-limiting treaties in fact consistent with the Berne Convention? The VIP treaty asserts in its first article that '[n]othing in this treaty shall derogate from any obligations that Contracting Parties have to each other under any other treaties'. But such declarations do not necessarily make this so.

Careful examination of the structure and policies underlying the Berne Convention suggests a fundamental tension between that Convention's norms and the norms of treaties whose explicit goal is to limit the scope of copyright. Article 20 of the Berne Convention allows member states

---

[97] Of course, one may take issue with the characterization of Berne as 'unbalanced'. Berne and the TRIPS Agreement already include 'balancing' features such as exclusions from the subject matter of copyright; a panoply of permissible exceptions (most notably the 'three-step test', which allows member states broad leeway to allow copying 'in certain special cases, provided that such reproduction does not conflict with a normal exploitation of the work and does not unreasonably prejudice the legitimate interests of the author'); and the Article 10(1) requirement that member states permit 'quotations from a work which has already been lawfully made available to the public, provided that their making is compatible with fair practice, and their extent does not exceed that justified by the purpose, including quotations from newspaper articles and periodicals in the form of press summaries'. As such, the Berne-TRIPS package, while designed primarily to further the international circulation of works of authorship by ensuring effective protection, nonetheless takes into account countervailing considerations of free expression and access to culture. One of the original Framers of the Berne Convention, Swiss jurist Numa Droz, recognized this in 1884 when he emphasized that 'limits to absolute protection are rightly set by the public interest'. *Actes du Congrès de Berne de 1884*, 67.

[98] VIP Treaty, *supra* n 13.

[99] See treaty proposals on exceptions and limitations for libraries and archives, discussed in WIPO, 'Standing Committee on Copyright and Related Rights, Twenty-Third Session' (21–25, 28 and 29 November and 2 December 2011) SCCR/23/REF/CONCLUSIONS, p 1.

'to enter into special agreements among themselves, in so far as such agreements grant to authors more extensive rights than those granted by the Convention, or contain other provisions *not contrary to this Convention*'.[100] Agreements among member states therefore must not establish a level of protection inferior to that set by the Convention.

If the new treaty's mandatory exceptions are compatible with the 'three-step test' framework for exceptions to the reproduction right set out in Article 9(2) of the Berne Convention and with other Berne exceptions or limitations on that right or other rights, then, at first blush, there would seem to be no problem with making obligatory those exceptions that are already permissible. For example, under this view, it would not be contrary to the Convention to enter into an agreement requiring member states to subject foreign literary or artistic works to free use 'by way of illustration in publications, broadcasts or sound or visual recordings for teaching', under the conditions set out in Berne Article 10(2).

The argument that 'those exceptions which Berne permits, another instrument may make mandatory' nonetheless encounters the following objections:

1. The substantive aspects of the Berne Convention (covering subject matter, minimum rights, permissible exceptions and limitations) apply only to foreign works. Article 5(3) provides that '[p]rotection in the country of origin is governed by domestic law'. Thus, Berne does not affect the domestic treatment of local works. Any new agreement that purports to make Berne exceptions mandatory will not, without more, impose those exceptions on member states' own works. Berne's explicit forbearance from interfering in domestic law gives rise to the first problem: If member states impose the exceptions only on foreign works, member states will violate the Berne Articles 5(2) and 19 principle of national treatment, which forbids member states from according less protection to foreign-member-state works than to local works. Of course, if the exceptions and limitations already applied to local authors, then to apply them to foreign works would create no imbalance between local and foreign works with respect to national treatment. But if a Berne-compatible exception were made mandatory for foreign works, without imposing a corresponding exception on local works,

100 Berne Convention art 20 (emphasis supplied).

then foreign works would receive worse treatment than local works. This would be inconsistent with the principle of national treatment.

2. Mandatory exceptions unaccompanied by equivalent exceptions for country of origin works are thus contrary to the spirit and structure of the Berne Convention, and therefore are 'contrary to th[e Berne] Convention' within the meaning of Article 20. To avoid impermissible disparities in treatment, member states would need to enact equivalent domestic copyright exceptions. (And, indeed the VIP Treaty, in Article 4, directs signatories to enact the requisite limitations as part of their national law.) But in that event, there would be no need for mandatory exceptions at the multilateral level because the principle of national treatment would require member states to apply their Berne-compatible domestic exceptions to foreign works without any additional instrument. The following consequences therefore arise: (1) Without concomitant limitations in domestic law, mandatory exceptions to the protection of foreign works are ineffective under Articles 5(1) and 19; and (2) with concomitant limitations in domestic law, mandatory (Berne-compatible) limitations on the protection of foreign works are unnecessary.

3. Perhaps treaties requiring member states to incorporate mandatory exceptions into their domestic law are, even if unnecessary, desirable nonetheless. Arguably, if member states would not on their own provide such limitations, an international obligation should do the job, although one might wonder why a member state unwilling on its own to implement publicly beneficial domestic exceptions would in fact change its laws if faced with the requisite treaty obligation (which, at least within the Berne model, lacks enforcement measures). Even assuming the factual basis prompting the adoption of mandatory exceptions, their implementation through a treaty ignores a key feature of the Berne structure. As we have seen, by virtue of Article 5(3) Berne declines to intervene in domestic copyright norms as applied to local authors. By leaving domestic protection to the country of origin, Berne preserves the local lawmaking autonomy of its member states. So long as they extend Berne-minimum protection to Union works, member states remain free to determine the scope of their own cultural policies. (Indeed, preservation of local lawmaking authority with respect to domestic rightholders is a hallmark of many other multilateral intellectual property treaties, including, most notably, the TRIPS Agreement.) In the realm of limitations on copyright, member states may gauge

the level of protection their own authors require in light of countervailing local needs and changing situations in the future.

4. Treaties binding member states to implement internally a supranational, worldwide standard of copyright limitations would thus deprive those states of the autonomy and flexibility (otherwise built into Berne) subsequently to modify or eliminate those exceptions should local experience prove them unwarranted; any change to domestic law would require revising the international agreement, or a withdrawal from the treaty, which is in fact both extremely unlikely and politically difficult. Of course, if the treaty text is sufficiently vague and general it will not impose real constraints on member states' local flexibility, but such an outcome is problematic for two reasons. First, the instrument will lack the bite some member states claim to require to enact the aspired exceptions, and second, if the standards are in fact meaningless, all that will remain will be the symbolism of treaties dedicated to the diminution of authors' rights.

In light of these concerns, does the VIP Treaty foretell the eclipse of the Berne era? This chapter is not the occasion for detailed analysis of the VIP Treaty, but a few general remarks are appropriate. In an exceptional departure from Berne and its Paris Appendix (and the WCT and TRIPS Agreement), the treaty mandates enactment of domestic exceptions or limitations: it states that Contracting Parties:

> shall provide in their national copyright laws for a limitation or exception to the right of reproduction, the right of distribution, and the right of making available to the public as provided by the WIPO Copyright Treaty (WCT), to facilitate the availability of works in accessible format copies for beneficiary persons.[101]

But:

> [i]n adopting measures necessary to ensure the application of this Treaty, a Contracting Party may exercise the rights and shall comply with the obligations that that Contracting Party has under the Berne Convention, the Agreement on Trade-Related Aspects of Intellectual Property Rights and the WCT, including their interpretative agreements.[102]

---

[101] VIP Treaty, art 4(1)(a). Articles 2 and 3 define 'works', 'accessible format' and 'beneficiary persons'.

[102] Ibid, art 11.

Thus, to the extent that the exceptions or limitations on the rights of reproduction, distribution, making available or public performance apply to the works of foreign authors, contracting parties must ensure that they confine them 'to certain special cases which do not conflict with a normal exploitation of the work and do not unreasonably prejudice the legitimate interests of the rightholder'.[103] With respect to the cross-border exchange of accessible format copies – a pressing issue in light of less developed countries' limited capacity to create accessible formats domestically – the treaty enacts a compromise: accessible format copies made pursuant to an exception in Country A may be distributed or made available in Country B,[104] but Country B may not further export those copies unless it adheres to the three-step test.[105]

Perhaps the most reassuring indication that the VIP Treaty should not herald an onslaught of copyright-diminishing international accords derives from comparing the final text with its predecessors. Most tellingly, the penultimate version of the VIP Treaty was titled, 'Draft Text of an International Instrument/Treaty on Limitations and Exceptions for Visually Impaired Persons/Persons with Print Disabilities'.[106] The final version forgoes proclaiming itself a 'treaty on exceptions and limitations' in favor of the more modest 'treaty to facilitate access'. Of course, it facilitates access through imposing exceptions and limitations, so the difference may primarily be rhetorical. Because, however, the rhetoric of copyright cutbacks long seemed to propel the VIP initiative,[107] the shift

---

[103] TRIPS Agreement, art 13.

[104] 'Contracting Parties shall provide that if an accessible format copy is made under a limitation or exception or pursuant to operation of law, that accessible format copy may be distributed or made available by an authorized entity to a beneficiary person or an authorized entity in another Contracting Party.' VIP Treaty, art 5(1). The reference to 'that copy' raises the question whether the 'accessible format' copies must be hard copies (including fixations of digital formats) given that digital communication entails the creation of new copies rather than the distribution of 'that copy'. See, for example, *Capitol Records, LLC v ReDigi Inc* 934 F Supp 2d 640 (SDNY 2013). On the other hand, the reference to 'made available' suggests that digital communication of a file of any accessible format is intended to be covered.

[105] Ibid, art 5(4).

[106] (Drafted 20 April 2013) VIP/DC/3 REV (Draft VIP Treaty).

[107] See further Silke von Lewinski, 'Report on the 24th Session of the Committee of Copyright and Related Rights (SCCR) in Geneva, July 16–25, 2012' <http://www.alai.org/assets/files/infos-internationales/wipo-2012.pdf> accessed 18 November 2014.

in tone suggests that further international instruments to shrink the scope of copyright may not loom after all.

Seen in the broader international IP perspective, moreover, the VIP Treaty may be a small but important step in healing some of the rancor that has beset relations between developed and developing countries for over four decades. The latter mounted a strong campaign to revise Berne in order to achieve enhanced access to published works for educational and developmental purposes at Stockholm in 1967. This campaign, however, was unsuccessful – the compromise Appendix achieved in Paris four years later was still tilted in favor of the developed countries.[108] Similar efforts to obtain greater access to patented technology through changes to the non-voluntary licensing provisions of the Paris Convention in the early 1980s foundered in the marshes of mutual misunderstanding and distrust.[109] The same tensions have continued to resonate within the forums of the WTO and WIPO, particularly with the adoption of the WIPO Development Agenda and the continuing debates occurring within that body about disclosure requirements with respect to access to the genetic resources of developing countries and the protection of traditional knowledge and expressions. Developed and developing countries are locked in contest across the whole range of intellectual property rights, and there has been much bad blood in relation to many of these encounters. Given the significance of the VIP Treaty's provisions for persons in developing and less developed countries, it may therefore represent a significant achievement in the promotion of cooperation and reduction of tension: a text that can sit comfortably alongside the mother ship of Berne, doing justice to the legitimate concerns of developing countries (and providing real assistance to the visually impaired whatever their countries of residence) while maintaining the respect for authorship that was central to the declaration made in 1986 on the centenary of that Convention.

---

[108] See further Ricketson and Ginsburg (n 7) Ch 14.

[109] The sad story of four successive sessions of a diplomatic conference that met between 1980 and 1984 is revealed in the bare accounts of their proceedings in *Industrial Property*: [1980] *Industrial Property* 144 (first session); [1981] *Industrial Property* 309-310 (second session); [1983] *Industrial Property* 100 and 87 (third session); and [1984] *Industrial Property* 196 (fourth session). See further MK Kirk, 'The 1982 Geneva Diplomatic Conference on the Revision of the Paris Convention' [1983] *Intellectual Property L Rev* 139,; FK Beier, 'One Hundred Years of International Cooperation – the Role of the Paris Convention in the Past, Present and Future' (1984) 15 *Intl Rev Industrial Property* 1, 14–16.

2. International patent law: Principles, major instruments and institutional aspects

Philippe Baechtold, Tomoko Miyamoto and Thomas Henninger[1]

I. INTRODUCTION

The search for more innovation for the benefit of the human condition has always driven the human mind, and one early attempt to achieve innovative results was to create incentives encouraging private initiative. Against this background, patent systems were created and developed, and today, some of the most important systems at the international level include the Paris Convention for the Protection of Industrial Property (Paris Convention), the Patent Cooperation Treaty (PCT), the Patent Law Treaty (PLT), and a number of regional patent systems. But while these systems have been – and still are – very useful, there are also questions about the social and economic impact of patent systems and of their possible harmonization, which have led to exploring ways to improve those systems without necessarily imposing further obligations or restrictions on states. The present contribution gives a (necessarily incomplete) overview of both harmonization measures that have been taken at the normative level, as well as of other, more practical, efforts aiming at making the international patent system more user-friendly, more efficient, and also more adapted to respond to developing countries' needs, without removing the existing policy space of governments.

[1] The statements and views expressed in the article are solely those of the authors and do not represent any official position of the World Intellectual Property Organization (WIPO).

II. HARMONIZATION OF LAWS: UNIFICATION, ASSIMILATION, CONVERGENCE, AND FLEXIBILITY

The evolution of international law may take different forms. Harmonization of laws is one form among others that has been utilized regularly. Since the mid 2000s, discussions at the World Intellectual Property Organization (WIPO) with respect to the normative development of patent law have shown contrasting views toward harmonization. For some, harmonization is a general objective, or a goal, to be pursued in general terms for the progressive development of law. For others, it is a general concept that should be opposed as a direction of international work.[2] However, it has rarely been clarified in those debates exactly what "harmonization" means in terms of the development of the international patent system.

The literal meaning of the term "harmonization", which relates to the terms "harmonize" and "harmony", suggests a state of forming a consistent whole,[3] or a congruent arrangement of parts.[4] The notion and characteristics of harmonization are well explained by Boodman,[5] using the analogy of "harmony" in the sphere of music. According to Boodman, harmonization implies the following features: (i) it presupposes and preserves the diversity of the objects harmonized; (ii) its components, while retaining their individuality, form a new and more complex musical sound; and (iii) it is often perceived as involving consonance in the subjective sense, but objectively, it could involve both consonance and dissonance (the same music could be a sound from heaven for some but mere noise for others). Regarding the third feature, Boodman writes that, in its relative sense, harmonization is the creation of a relationship between diverse things, without any value judgment.

Applying this notion of harmonization to the legal sphere, and in the context of the present chapter on patent law, harmonization of law necessarily involves diverse national/regional laws. The process of harmonization seeks an environment which, as a whole, may be complex yet rich with diverse national/regional laws. Harmonization processes are

---

2 For example, the Reports of the discussions within the WIPO Standing Committee on the Law of Patents (SCP) show divergent views on harmonization of patent law, in particular since 2005.

3 *Oxford Dictionary* <http://www.oxforddictionaries.com>.

4 *Merriam Webster Dictionary* <http://www.merriam-webster.com>.

5 M Boodman, "The Myth of Harmonization of Law" (1991) 39(4) *American J. Comp. L.* 699–724.

sought when the differences create "dissonance" at the regional or international level involving multiple jurisdictions. The dissonance may be based on the low level of legal certainty and predictability, or on discriminatory treatment. It can be spurred by strong ethical or moral sentiments or the economic interests of particular parties involved. The harmonization process, therefore, cannot be considered in the abstract sense. The nature and level of harmonization of law required in a particular situation depend entirely on the specific circumstances of that situation: i.e., what problems exist, what differences are found in the laws, and how to achieve harmony. In some cases, uniformity of certain elements could be an appropriate solution. In other cases, diversity of certain elements is required for the harmony of the system as a whole.

Further, the instruments for attaining harmony can be numerous, again depending on the specific situation. It is not limited to legally binding instruments (treaties), but includes other forms (for example, soft law instruments) that allow co-existence in concordance. In addition, one cannot disregard the effect of an international forum that allows parties to discuss their legal provisions for a better understanding of each other's laws, clarifying the existing differences and the effects perceived by each party that result from such differences.

When it comes to the harmonization of patent law, the term "harmonization" has often been used as a synonym for "unification" of national patent laws,[6] and consequently, an antonym for "flexibility".[7] However, harmonization and flexibility are not conflicting notions. Rather, the notion of flexibility is another necessary part of creating and managing a relationship within a world of diversity. The development of international norms is thus a history of seeking a harmony that necessarily includes convergence and divergence. In other words, the elements of both convergence and divergence are regulated and managed by the international community as two sides of the same coin. Therefore, the characteristics of flexibility also mirror the features of harmonization, and flexibility in international law cannot be discussed in the abstract, but can be only examined in specific sets of circumstances.

International norms have been developed in order to deal with areas which are impossible or impracticable to handle solely under the national

---

6 D Chun, "Patent Law Harmonization in the Age of Globalization: The Necessity and Strategy for a Pragmatic Outcome" (2011) *Cornell Law School Inter-University Graduate Student Conference Paper*.

7 SRW Rajec, "Evaluating Flexibility in International Patent Law" *Hastings L. J.* (forthcoming) <http://papers.ssrn.com/sol3/papers.cfm?abstract_id=2248398>.

legislation or national implementation of international law. Drawing from the commonly shared principal objectives of the patent system, such as encouraging innovation, promoting the development of technology, and fostering dissemination of innovative knowledge to the public,[8] a number of common aims for sovereign states to establish international patent norms can be observed. They include: (i) increase legal certainty and ensure fair and equitable protection at the international level; (ii) establish an accessible and affordable international patent system for the granting, maintenance, and enforcement of patents; and (iii) facilitate global access to patent information by the public.[9] To achieve these general goals, progressive development of patent law has taken place by identifying the "discords" and seeking "harmonization" against the backdrop of specific technical, political, or economic circumstances.

The purpose of this chapter is neither to examine whether a global uniform patent law is desirable or feasible, nor to analyze the appropriate level of flexibility and convergence in international patent law. Instead, the process of harmonization using various instruments will be reviewed, with a particular focus on the specific context in which harmony had been established and re-established at each point in time. By understanding this dynamism and learning to value variety and harmony, we may be able to reflect on future opportunities for the international development of patent law, and enrich the international patent system.[10]

III. SHARING COMMON UNDERSTANDING THROUGH INTERNATIONAL TREATIES

(1) Paris Convention for the Protection of Industrial Property (Paris Convention)

By the second half of the nineteenth century, recognizing the value of industrial property as a tool for national technological and commercial

---

8 Article 7 of the Agreement on Trade-Related Aspects of Intellectual Property Rights (TRIPS Agreement).

9 T Miyamoto, "International Treaties and Patent Law Harmonization: Today and Beyond" in Toshiko Takenaka (ed.), *Patent Law and Theory: a Handbook of Contemporary Research* (Edward Elgar Publishing 2008).

10 J Duffy, "Harmony and Diversity in Global Patent Law" (2002) 17 *Berkeley Tech. L. J.* 685.

development, many countries introduced a national system for protecting industrial property, including the protection of inventions.[11]

Since no international conventions existed at that time, bilateral agreements were the instruments that were used by states to protect the interests of their nationals and overcome a number of hurdles when protecting their industrial property abroad.[12] Nevertheless, with the development of a more internationally oriented flow of technology and the increase in international trade, certain provisions found in some national laws are seen to make it difficult for foreigners to obtain, maintain, and enforce their rights at the international level.[13]

When the Government of the Empire of Austria-Hungary announced the hosting of an international exhibition of inventions in Vienna in 1873, it faced great unwillingness on the part of foreign inventors to exhibit their inventions, because the legal protection offered to exhibited inventions by Austrian law was considered inadequate.[14] In the area of patents, there were mainly two issues. First, under Austrian law at that time, patents were invalidated if the patented inventions had not been manufactured in Austrian territory within 12 months from the date of patent grant. This meant that many patents obtained by foreigners were forfeited after 12 months. There were countries that did not impose a local working requirement and forfeiture,[15] while among those countries that did impose such a requirement,[16] the conditions for working a patent and the time period within which a patented invention had to be locally worked varied significantly. Many felt that such treatment discriminated against foreign inventors and restricted their rights.[17]

Second, the absolute novelty requirement based on the filing date was one of the patentability criteria in many European countries. This requirement prevented applicants from obtaining patents if there was any prior foreign patent or publication that had disclosed the same invention. As a consequence, the applicant had to file patent applications in various countries at roughly the same time in order to avoid destroying the

---

[11] Ibid.

[12] Prior to the Paris Convention, among the 69 bilateral treaties on industrial property, only two related to patents. *See* S Ladas, *Patents, Trademarks and Related Rights* (Harvard University Press, 1979) 45–6.

[13] *WIPO Intellectual Property Handbook: Policy, Law and Use* 241 http://www.wipo.int/about-ip/en/iprm/.

[14] Ibid.

[15] For example, the United States of America and the United Kingdom.

[16] For example, Germany, Belgium, and France.

[17] *Scientific American* (23 December 1871) 25(26) 407.

novelty of the invention. The problem was exacerbated by different publication rules. In many countries, the description of the invention was kept secret until the grant of a patent, whereas the laws of Germany and the United Kingdom (UK), for example, allowed public inspection of the description of the invention before the grant of a patent.[18] On the one hand, earlier access to information on new inventions might have the positive effect of stimulating innovation by inventors in those countries, but on the other hand, when they sought patent protection abroad, such disclosure made it impossible for them to obtain patents in foreign countries.

The first international conference on industrial property, the Congress of Vienna for Patent Reform, was held in Vienna in 1873. In response to a series of resolutions adopted by the Congress of Vienna and the subsequent conference, the French Government suggested the establishment of a permanent international union for the protection of industrial property in 1880. This proposal eventually led to the adoption of the Paris Convention for the Protection of Industrial Property in 1883, which was signed by 11 states.[19] Since then, the Paris Convention has been revised periodically, and includes 175 Contracting States as at 5 August 2013.

The principle of "national treatment" under Articles 2 and 3 of the Paris Convention is one of the cornerstone provisions of the Convention. In effect, the Paris Convention replaced a number of bilateral reciprocity agreements with a single international treaty by way of the reciprocity obligation entailed by adherence to the Convention.[20] Articles 2 and 3 provide that each Contracting State of the Convention must apply to nationals of other Contracting States (and nationals of non-Contracting States who are domiciled or have real and effective industrial or commercial establishment in the territory of one of the Contracting States) the same treatment as it gives to its own nationals. The Paris Convention, however, provides limited exceptions to the principle of national treatment. Specifically, each country is free to provide different treatments between nationals and non-nationals with respect to judicial

---

[18] FA Seely, "History of the International Union for the Protection of Industrial Property" *Washington Government Printing Office* (1887).

[19] The following countries signed the Paris Convention upon its adoption in 1883: Belgium, Brazil, El Salvador, France, Guatemala, Italy, the Netherlands, Portugal, Serbia, Spain, and Switzerland. Great Britain, Tunisia, and Ecuador joined the Paris Convention when it entered into force in July 1884.

[20] GHC Bodenhausen, *Guide to the Paris Convention for the Protection of Industrial Property* (WIPO 1969).

and administrative procedure and jurisdiction, and to the designation of address for service or the appointment of a representative, which may be required by the laws on industrial property.[21] Those limited exceptions take into account practical difficulties that the national administration or courts may face when dealing with parties who are non-nationals, particularly when they are living abroad. It is a known fact that, even today, a number of countries require a foreign applicant to be represented by a recognized national professional representative, whereas such representation is not mandatory for national applicants.

At the same time, the sovereign right of the Contracting States to decide on granting or refusing patent protection can be understood to be confirmed by Article 4*bis* of the Paris Convention, whereby the independence of patents obtained for the same invention in different countries is ensured.

In addition to the above principles, the Paris Convention provides certain common rules that are either required or permitted to be implemented under national legislation. In the field of patents, the tension regarding the forfeiture of patents that are not worked locally is addressed in Article 5A – failure to work the patented invention and compulsory licenses. Article 5A(1) clarifies that importation by the patentee into the country of articles manufactured in other member countries of the Paris Convention should not entail forfeiture of the patent. However, "failure to work" is one example of the abuses which might result from the exercise of the exclusive patent rights, and each country has the right to take legislative measures for the grant of compulsory licenses to prevent such abuses.[22] Since it is practically impossible for a patentee to work the patented invention immediately after the grant of the patent, Article 5A(4) stipulates that a compulsory license may not be applied for on the ground of failure to work or insufficient working before the expiration of a period of four years from the filing date of the patent application or three years from the date of the grant of the patent, whichever period expires last. The two possible time periods are provided so that a patentee will have an appropriate time to work the patented invention in a particular country, which may grant patents with or without substantive examination.[23] Furthermore, a compulsory license on the ground of failure to work or insufficient work is refused if the patentee justifies his inaction by legitimate reasons. It shall

---

21 Paris Convention, art 2(3).

22 *See* ibid., art 5A(2).

23 Bodenhausen (note 20 above), at 72.

be non-exclusive and non-transferable, even in the form of the grant of a sub-license, except with that part of the enterprise or goodwill which exploits such license. As regards forfeiture of patents, it is limited to cases where the grant of compulsory licenses would not have been sufficient to prevent abuses by the patentee, and proceedings for the forfeiture or revocation of a patent may not be instituted before the expiration of two years from the grant of the first compulsory license.[24] The Paris Convention does not define what constitutes "abuses" by a patentee, and Contracting States may provide compulsory licenses on grounds other than failure to work or insufficient working. Furthermore, the interpretation of the terms "failure to work" and "insufficient working" are left to Contracting States. The question as to whether the term "work" in Article 5A is limited to local working or also encompasses importation by the patentee of a patented product or a product obtained by a patented process has been put in the spotlight recently, since Article 27.1 of the Agreement on Trade-Related Aspects of Intellectual Property Rights (TRIPS Agreement) states that patent rights shall be enjoyable without discrimination as to whether products are imported or locally produced.[25]

The difficulties in obtaining patents under a strict novelty criterion, and also the issue of the early publication of inventions, were addressed by the introduction of the right of priority under Article 4 of the Paris Convention.[26] Before the conclusion of the Paris Convention, a similar right of priority was recognized between Austria and Germany, where an application was filed within three months from the publication in the other country.[27] By developing such a mechanism to be applicable at the international level, the Paris Convention significantly put national and foreign applicants on an equal footing, taking into account the costs and

---

[24] *See* Paris Convention, art 5A(3).

[25] T Cottier, S Lalani, and M Temmerman, "Use it or lose it? Assessing the Compatibility of the Paris Convention & TRIPS with respect to Local Working Requirements" (NCCR Trade Working Paper No. 2012/11 June 2013).

[26] Article 4 of the Paris Convention states that, if an applicant, on the basis of a regular first application filed in one of the Member States, applies for industrial property protection in any of the other Member States within a certain period of time (12 months for patents and utility models, and six months for industrial designs and marks), these subsequent applications shall not be invalidated by reason of any acts accomplished in the interval, in particular, another filing the publication, or the exploitation of the invention.

[27] Actes de la Conférence international pour la protection de la propriété industrielle, réunie à Paris du 4 au 20 novembre 1880, BIRPI, at 49.

additional work involved in preparing and filing applications in foreign countries.

Similarly, under Article 11, the Paris Convention obliges Contracting States to grant temporary protection to industrial property in respect of goods exhibited at official or officially recognized international exhibitions held in any Contracting State. The Convention, however, leaves the states to decide the ways and means for providing the temporary protection under their respective legislation.[28]

Other common rules that are required to be implemented under national legislation with respect to patents include the right of the inventor to be mentioned in the patents,[29] a grace period for the payment of the maintenance fee,[30] and the limitation of patent rights where the patented invention is on a means of transportation temporarily entering the territory.[31]

The Paris Convention leaves its Contracting States free to decide on a number of fundamental issues concerning substantive patent law, such as the patentability criteria, the term of protection, rights conferred by a patent, and enforcement of rights. As the very first international treaty in the field of industrial property, the Paris Convention achieved the establishment of fundamental principles and of a permanent Union for the protection of industrial property, under which further development of international industrial property law became possible.

(2) Patent Cooperation Treaty (PCT)

Until the adoption of the PCT in 1970, the Paris Convention had been the only truly multilateral treaty in the field of patents. Even if the Paris Convention had facilitated access to foreign patent rights, national

---

[28] In the United States of America, disclosure of an invention exhibited at an official or officially recognized international exhibition is covered by a broad grace-period provision, while the term "official or officially recognized international exhibition" is interpreted strictly under the European Patent Convention, which considers the public disclosure of the invention through such exhibition as non-prejudicial to the determination of novelty with respect to the exhibitor's subsequent application. The national laws of, for example, Georgia, Slovenia, the Former Yugoslav Republic of Macedonia, and Turkey grant a right of priority similar to Article 4 of the Paris Convention for the temporary protection of exhibited inventions. The period of temporary protection also varies from six to 12 months, depending on the applicable national law.

[29] *See* Paris Convention, art 4*ter*.

[30] *See* ibid., art 5*bis*.

[31] *See* ibid., art 5*ter*.

procedural and substantive patent laws and practices continued to be significantly different. The PCT was adopted with a view to streamlining the patent filing procedures at the global level. Since the start of its operations in 1978, the PCT has been responsive to applicants' needs and has become one of the most successful treaties in the field of intellectual property with 148 Contracting States. More than half (54.9 percent) of world-wide non-resident filings use the PCT system in order to obtain patents abroad, amounting to around 194,400 international applications filed by 45,134 applicants in 2012 and 205,300 applications in 2013.[32]

One of the objectives of the PCT is to "simplify and render more economical the obtaining of protection for inventions where protection is sought in several countries".[33] The PCT established an operational framework, and a unique and common procedure for filing international patent applications, with publication of the applications and prior art search and optionally also preliminary examination, and harmonization of the form and contents of international applications.[34] It is called a "cooperation" treaty, since national IP offices and the "International Bureau (IB)" of WIPO play distinct but coordinated roles in the filing and prosecution of international patent applications. The PCT, however, explicitly ensures the freedom of the Contracting States to prescribe substantive conditions of patentability,[35] such as the definition of prior art, novelty, and inventive step. Consequently, the results of the international search and preliminary examination do not have a binding effect.

As the detailed PCT procedures will be described in Part III of this book,[36] for the purpose of the present chapter it will suffice to indicate that the PCT system consists of two phases: the international phase and the national phase. The procedures in the international phase include (i) filing and formality examination of a single international application, filed with the "Receiving Office" (RO); (ii) preparation of an international

---

[32] PCT Yearly Report (2013). PCT applicants refer to the first-named applicants in published PCT applications<http://www.wipo.int/export/sites/www/freepublications/en/patents/901/wipo_pub_901_2013.pdf>.

[33] *See* Preamble of the Treaty.

[34] Article 27(1) of the PCT states that "no national law shall require compliance with requirements relating to the form or content of the international application different from or additional to those which are provided for in this Treaty and the Regulations".

[35] *See* PCT, art 27(5).

[36] CAM Mulder, The Patent Cooperation Treaty, Ch 10 this volume.

search report by the "International Searching Authority" (ISA);[37] and (iii) optional international preliminary examination of the International Preliminary Examining Authority (IPEA). The international application, together with its search report, will be published, regularly after 18 months from the priority date, on the WIPO PATENTSCOPE database.[38]

After reviewing the results of the prior art search and preliminary examination, the applicant decides whether, and in respect of which states, he wishes to continue the procedure in the national phase. If he does wish to continue, he will have then to pay the national fees and appoint a local patent attorney and, in some cases, file a translation of the application, in each country in which he seeks patent protection.[39] In the national phase, each patent office is responsible for granting a patent or refusing the international application, in accordance with its national or regional patent law.

While there is no immediate plan to amend the treaty provisions of the PCT, there is a continual process of amendment and updating of the Regulations under the PCT, the PCT Administrative Instructions, and the Guidelines for International Authorities and Offices.[40] In particular, in 2009, the PCT Roadmap was proposed by the International Bureau of WIPO so as to enable the PCT to fulfill its role as a work-sharing tool of the international patent system.[41] The current discussions on further improvement of the operation of the PCT system focus on: (i) improved quality of products and services during the international phase; (ii) improved efficiency and timeliness of the procedure; and (iii) better access to the international PCT filing system, particularly for applicants from developing countries and small- and medium-sized enterprises.[42]

---

37 International Searching Authorities are appointed by the PCT Assembly to carry out the international searches. They shall meet the requirements prescribed in PCT Article 16.

38 *See* <http://patentscope.wipo.int/search/en/search.jsf>.

39 PCT, art 22.

40 The PCT Receiving Office Guidelines and PCT International Search and Preliminary Examination Guidelines are used by the Receiving Offices and International Searching and International Preliminary Examining Authorities, respectively.

41 WIPO document PCTWG/2/3.

42 Reports of the sessions of the PCT Working Group are found at <http://www.wipo.int/meetings/en/topic.jsp?group_id=238>.

(3) Budapest Treaty on the International Recognition of the Deposit of Microorganisms for the Purposes of Patent Procedure

Around 1950, in order to secure his patent application, an American scientist by the name of Dr. Benjamin Duggar deposited a microorganism, called actinomycete, with the United States Department of Agriculture's research laboratory.[43] Since the actinomycete was not generally available and it was doubtful that the description of the invention in the patent application satisfied the enabling disclosure requirement, Dr. Duggar took this extra step to supplement the written disclosure in the patent application. That practice was followed by other inventors,[44] and by the end of the 1950s, a number of patent offices required deposit of microorganisms in similar cases. The courts started to confirm such requirements in the 1960s.[45] As more countries introduced a deposit requirement, when an applicant sought protection of inventions involving microorganisms in multiple jurisdictions, he/she was obliged to deposit samples of the same microorganism in each country in which he/she sought patent protection. Consequently, the Budapest Treaty on the International Recognition of the Deposit of Microorganisms for the Purposes of Patent Procedure was negotiated and adopted in 1977 with a view to simplifying the procedures.

The main feature of the Treaty is that a Contracting State that allows or requires the deposit of microorganisms for the purposes of patent procedure must recognize, for such purposes, the deposit of a microorganism with any "international depositary authority", irrespective of whether that authority is on or outside the territory of the said state.[46] In other words, the Treaty established mutual recognition of the deposit made with international depositary authorities among the Contracting States. A country can become a member of the Budapest Treaty without having a depositary authority within its territory. What the Treaty calls an "International Depositary Authority" is a scientific institution, which is typically a culture collection capable of storing microorganisms. An institution acquires the international depositary authority status through the furnishing, by the Contracting State of the territory in which it is located, of assurances to the Director General of WIPO to the effect that

---

[43] J Straus and R Moufang, *Deposit and Release of Biological Material for the Purpose of Patent Procedure* (Nomos Verlagsgesellschaft Baden-Baden 1990).

[44] Ibid.

[45] Ibid.

[46] Budapest Treaty, art 3.

said institution complies and will continue to comply with the requirements of the Treaty.[47]

The term "microorganism" is not defined in the Treaty. In practice, biological material that has to be deposited for the purposes of an enabling disclosure, such as bacteria, fungi, yeasts, algae, tissue cultures, and plasmids, may be deposited with international depositary authorities, as long as they accept the deposit of biological material that may not be covered by the strict interpretation of the term "microorganism". While the Budapest Treaty simplifies the procedure for depositing biological material for the purpose of obtaining patents in Contracting States, it falls short of providing uniform rules on important substantive requirements concerning deposit, most notably the latest date by which the biological material must be deposited.

(4) Patent Law Treaty

Despite the fact that the PCT greatly simplified the filing of patent applications at the international level, substantive patentability requirements varied significantly in different jurisdictions. Further, considerable numbers of applications are filed abroad not using the PCT system. In the mid 1980s, starting from the discussion on harmonizing a grace-period provision, the negotiation of a new treaty, a draft "Treaty Supplementing the Paris Convention as Far as Patents Are Concerned" (draft 1991 Patent Harmonization Treaty), was started. The draft Treaty covered a wide range of both procedural and substantive issues under patent law, including provisions related to patent applications and examination procedures, patentability requirements, rights conferred by a patent, and available remedies, as well as post-grant procedures.[48] That draft Treaty was never adopted, because it failed to resolve two major issues, i.e., the worldwide introduction of a grace period and the "first-to-file" principle.

In conjunction with the launch of the GATT Uruguay Round in 1986, another negotiation on the broad harmonization of intellectual property law, namely the TRIPS Agreement, was taking place under the framework of the General Agreement on Tariffs and Trade (GATT). In the early 1990s, with the prospect of a successful conclusion of the TRIPS Agreement, countries decided to transfer a number of provisions regarding substantive patent law from the draft Patent Harmonization Treaty to

47 Ibid., arts 6 and 7.

48 WIPO document PLT/DC/3 (reproduced in WIPO document SCP/4/3).

the draft TRIPS Agreement. Thus, after the adoption of the TRIPS Agreement, it was a natural course of development that the WIPO Member States agreed to pursue another approach by limiting the scope of the negotiation to formalities of national and regional patent applications. The idea of simplifying formality requirements under national/regional patent systems was also inspired by the successful conclusion of the Trademark Law Treaty (TLT) in 1994.

The discussion on the draft Patent Law Treaty (PLT) started in 1995 and was concluded in June 2000. In expressly excluding substantive requirements,[49] the PLT confined itself to a simplification of formality requirements set by national and regional offices and the streamlining of the procedures for obtaining and maintaining national and regional patents.[50] The PLT deals with formality issues such as requirements for obtaining the filing date and belated claims of priority. It also includes other matters such as representation, signatures, changes in names and addresses, changes in ownership, and conditions for the extension of time limits and restoration of rights.

As a general rule, the PLT regulates the maximum set of requirements that an office of a Contracting Party may apply. In other words, the PLT does not establish a completely uniform procedure for all Contracting Parties, but a Contracting Party is, in principle, free to impose fewer, or more user-friendly, requirements than those prescribed in the Treaty.[51] Another general principle of the PLT is its close proximity to the requirements under the PCT. Since the PCT already regulates formality requirements with respect to international applications in detail, creating a new and different set of international standards applicable to national and regional applications does not make sense. Therefore, the requirements relating to the form or content of international applications under the PCT, for both the international phase and the national phase, are incorporated by reference into the PLT, with minor exceptions. Thus, with respect to national and regional applications, no PLT Contracting Party may apply requirements relating to form or contents different from, or additional to, those of international applications under the PCT.[52] The expression "form or contents of an application" is to be construed in the same way as the corresponding expression in PCT Article 27(1). The PLT incorporates by reference not only the relevant PCT treaty provisions but

---

[49] PLT, art 2(2).

[50] *See* <http://www.wipo.int/patent-law/en/plt.htm>.

[51] In accordance with PLT, art 2(1), a notable exception is the application of PLT, art 5 (filing date).

[52] PLT, art 6(1).

also the relevant provisions of the Regulations and the Administrative Instructions under the PCT. In order to maintain consistency between the PCT and the PLT, where the relevant PCT provisions are amended or modified, the PLT Assembly has to decide on the applicability of the amendments or modifications to the PLT.

Because of the importance of the filing date for the determination of the patentability of the invention and of the term of protection, one of the main achievements of the PLT is the standardization of the filing date requirement.[53] The PLT requires that the office of any Contracting Party must accord a filing date to an application upon submission of three simple elements: (i) an indication that the elements received by the office are intended to be an application for a patent for an invention; (ii) indications that would allow the office to identify or to contact the applicant (however, a Contracting Party is allowed to require indications on both); and (iii) a part which appears to be a description of the invention.[54] No additional elements can be required for according a filing date. In particular, a Contracting Party cannot include one or more claims or a filing fee in a filing date requirement. The underlying consideration behind such a simple requirement is that as long as an invention is described in the application in a part which appears to be a description, there is no doubt that the applicant was in possession of the invention at the time the application was submitted. Therefore, it would be justified to accord a filing date on that date, and to claim priority based on that date. The submission of claims and the payment of a fee are, like the submission of a translation, requirements that can be complied with after the accordance of the filing date.

Another main pillar of the PLT is to provide procedures for avoiding the unintentional loss of substantive rights resulting from the failure to comply with time limits, taking into account the legal certainty and predictability for third parties and the administrative burden on offices. To that end, the PLT sets out: (i) relief in respect of time limits established by the patent office in the form of an extension and/or continued processing;[55] (ii) reinstatement of rights where an applicant or owner has failed to meet a time limit and, as a consequence, has lost his rights with respect to an application or patent unintentionally or in spite

---

[53] The filing date requirement under PLT, art 5 is an absolute requirement, not a maximum or minimum requirement, although the provisions in art 5 provide limited options for Member States in implementing that article.

[54] PLT, art 5(1).

[55] Ibid., art 11.

of all due care required by the circumstances;[56] (iii) correction or addition of a priority claim after the filing date;[57] and (iv) a remedy for the loss of a priority right due to innocent non-compliance with related time limits, for example, restoration of a priority right where a subsequent application claiming priority is filed after the expiration of the 12-month priority period in spite of the required due care having been taken by the applicant, or where the delay was unintentional.[58] Considering its effects on *bona fide* third parties, the provisions regarding restoration or reinstatement of the expired rights are designed in such a way that they can be granted only under exceptional circumstances. In particular, it was clarified that the restoration of a priority right by no means extends the 12-month priority period prescribed in the Paris Convention.[59]

Formality requirements under patent law are as important as substantive patentability requirements, since non-compliance with the former requirements also results in the refusal of a patent application. However, the complexity of the preparation and prosecution of patent applications in various jurisdictions mainly derives from the differences found in the substantive requirements, rather than the formality requirements. Therefore, although the simplification of the procedure achieved by the PLT was generally appreciated by users of the patent system,[60] the effects of the PLT are rather limited.

(5) TRIPS Agreement[61]

The TRIPS Agreement, which came into effect on 1 January 1995, is to date the most comprehensive multilateral agreement on intellectual property. The general goals of the TRIPS Agreement are contained in the Preamble, which include the reduction of distortions and impediments to international trade, promotion of effective and adequate protection of intellectual property rights, and ensuring that measures and procedures to enforce intellectual property rights do not themselves become barriers to legitimate trade. These objectives should be read in conjunction with Article 7, entitled "Objectives", according to which the protection and

56 Ibid., art 12.

57 Ibid., art 13(1).

58 Ibid., art 13(2), (3).

59 Records of the Diplomatic Conference for the Adoption of the Patent Law Treaty (PLT), WIPO (2002).

60 WIPO document SCT/27/4.

61 See <http://www.wto.org/english/tratop_e/trips_e/intel2_e.htm>.

enforcement of intellectual property rights should contribute to the promotion of technological innovation and to the transfer and dissemination of technology, to the mutual advantage of producers and users of technological knowledge and in a manner conducive to social and economic welfare, and to a balance of rights and obligations. Article 8, entitled "Principles", recognizes the rights of Members of the World Trade Organization (WTO) to adopt measures for public health and other public interest reasons and to prevent the abuse of intellectual property rights, provided that such measures are consistent with the provisions of the TRIPS Agreement.

For the purpose of this chapter, only the notable characteristics of the Agreement compared with the patent-related treaties administered by WIPO and its contribution to the development of international patent law will be mentioned.

First, the TRIPS Agreement is unprecedented in term of its broad coverage. It covers a wide range of intellectual property rights within a single agreement, i.e., copyright and related rights, trademarks, geographical indications, industrial designs, patents, the layout-designs of integrated circuits, and undisclosed information, including trade secrets and test data. The obligations under the Agreement apply equally to all Members of the WTO, provided that developing countries and least developed countries have longer periods to prepare themselves for implementing the Agreement.[62] In contrast, treaties administered by WIPO stem from the two distinctive treaties, the Paris Convention for the Protection of Industrial Property (already discussed) and the Berne Convention for the Protection of Literary and Artistic Works (Berne Convention), which laid foundations in international industrial property law and international copyright law, respectively. The subsequent treaties have been developed around specific narrower areas which are not addressed by the Paris Convention or the Berne Convention. The obligations under each treaty bind WIPO Member States only where they have acceded to or ratified that treaty. The TRIPS Agreement, however, is also built on the foundation of the intellectual property treaties that existed at the time of its adoption. With the exception of the provisions of the Berne Convention on moral rights, all the main substantive provisions of the Paris Convention and the Berne Convention are incorporated by reference in the TRIPS Agreement, and thus become obligations among the WTO Members.[63] The TRIPS Agreement also incorporates by

[62] TRIPS, arts 65 and 66.

[63] Ibid., arts 2.1 and 9.1.

reference a WIPO treaty which has never entered into force, namely the Treaty on Intellectual Property in Respect of Integrated Circuits, adopted at Washington on 26 May 1989.

Second, by virtue of Article 3.1, the national treatment principle under Articles 2 and 3 of the Paris Convention applies to WTO Members as well. In addition, the TRIPS Agreement has introduced the principle of the most-favored-nation (MFN) treatment in the context of the international intellectual property law. The MFN principle laid down in Article 4 forbids discrimination between the nationals of other Members. These obligations cover not only the substantive standards of protection but also matters affecting the availability, acquisition, scope, maintenance, and enforcement of intellectual property rights, as well as matters affecting the use of intellectual property rights specifically addressed in the Agreement. The TRIPS Agreement provides certain limited exceptions to the MFN obligation. Procedures provided in treaties administered by WIPO relating to the acquisition or maintenance of intellectual property rights are not covered by the national treatment and MFN obligations.

Third, the TRIPS Agreement adds additional minimum obligations on matters where the pre-existing conventions administered by WIPO are silent. For example, the Agreement deals with domestic procedures and remedies for the enforcement of intellectual property rights, including civil and administrative procedures and remedies, provisional measures, special requirements related to border measures, and criminal procedures. In respect of each of the main areas of intellectual property, the subject matter to be protected, the rights to be conferred and permissible exceptions to those rights, and the minimum duration of protection are defined in the Agreement. Regarding patents, the TRIPS Agreement requires Members to make patents available for any inventions, whether products or processes, in all fields of technology without discrimination, subject to the normal tests of novelty, inventiveness, and industrial applicability. It is also required that patents be available and patent rights enjoyed without discrimination as to the place of invention and whether products are imported or locally produced.[64] There are three permissible exceptions to the basic rule on patentability: (i) inventions, the prevention of the commercial exploitation of which is necessary to protect *ordre public* or morality;[65] (ii) diagnostic, therapeutic, and surgical methods for

---

[64] Ibid., art 27.1.

[65] Ibid., art 27.2 explicitly includes protection of human, animal, or plant life, health, or avoiding serious prejudice to the environment.

the treatment of humans or animals; and (iii) plants and animals other than microorganisms and essentially biological processes for the production of plants or animals other than non-biological and microbiological processes. However, any country excluding plant varieties from patent protection must provide an effective *sui generis* system of protection.[66] Members shall require that an applicant for a patent shall disclose the invention in a manner sufficiently clear and complete for the invention to be carried out by a person skilled in the art, and may require the applicant to indicate the best mode for carrying out the invention known to the inventor at the filing date or, where priority is claimed, at the priority date of the application.[67] In addition, Members may also require an applicant to provide information concerning the applicant's corresponding foreign applications and grants.[68] The exclusive rights that must be conferred by a product patent are the ones of making, using, offering for sale, selling, and importing for these purposes. Process patent protection must give rights not only over use of the process but also over products obtained directly by the process. Patent owners shall also have the right to assign, or transfer by succession, the patent, and to conclude licensing contracts.[69] However, Members may provide limited exceptions to the exclusive rights conferred by a patent, provided that such exceptions do not unreasonably conflict with a normal exploitation of the patent and do not unreasonably prejudice the legitimate interests of the patent owner, taking account of the legitimate interests of third parties.[70] Compulsory licensing and government use without the authorization of the right holder are allowed, but are made subject to conditions aimed at protecting the legitimate interests of the right holder.[71] The term of protection available shall not end before the expiration of a period of 20 years counted from the filing date.[72] Where the infringement of a patent is litigated, if the subject matter of a patent is a process for obtaining a product, the judicial authorities shall have the authority to order the defendant to prove that the process to obtain an identical product is different from the patented process, where certain conditions indicating likelihood that the protected process was used are met.[73] Members shall

[66] Ibid., arts 27.2 and 27.3.
[67] Ibid., art 29.1.
[68] Ibid., art 29.2.
[69] Ibid., art 28.
[70] Ibid., art 30.
[71] Ibid., art 31.
[72] Ibid., art 33.
[73] Ibid., art 34.

also provide an opportunity for judicial review of any decision to revoke or forfeit a patent.

Fourth, the Agreement makes consultations and the settlement of disputes under the TRIPS Agreement between WTO Members subject to the WTO's dispute settlement procedures by referring to Articles XXII and XXIII of GATT 1994 (except subparagraph 1(b) and 1(c) of Article XXIII), as elaborated and applied by the WTO Understanding on Rules and Procedures Governing the Settlement of Disputes. This means that benefits enjoyed in another trade area may be withdrawn in retaliation for the violation of the TRIPS Agreement (so-called cross-retaliation).

(6) Summary: Harmonization Landscape by International Treaties

The international intellectual property treaties have gradually formed an international legal framework that facilitates sharing of common principles and legal frameworks among the adhering parties. On the one hand, those treaties, in particular the TRIPS Agreement, undoubtedly contributed to the significant consolidation of national patent laws, including the substantive patent law. On the other hand, they are not able and will not be able to regulate the entire sphere and the full depth of intellectual property law, regulations, ministerial orders, and National Office instructions and guidelines. In order to reach an agreement, international treaties are often concluded with deliberately ambiguous wording.[74] Consequently, any treaty leaves its Contracting Parties a certain space for interpretation of its provisions. With that in mind, it would be interesting to look at the landscape of harmonization achieved by international treaties so far.

Entitlement: Who is entitled to acquire, maintain, and enforce patent rights?

Interestingly, there is no international agreement that answers this fundamental question. However, the rule applied all over the world *de facto* is that the inventor, the person who has directly contributed to the advancement of technology, and his successor in title, are those who are entitled to acquire patents and enforce the rights. While that principle may be universal, when it comes to patent protection of inventions made in conjunction with the employment contract (i.e., employee's inventions), inventions created in universities and public research institutions,

[74] A Taubman, *What TRIPS is and What it is not: A Practical Guide to Working with TRIPS* (Oxford University Press 2011); AA D'Amato, *International Law Studies* (Kluwer Law International 1997).

or inventions created with the support of public funding, various rules are applied in national laws with respect to entitlement as well as the conditions attached to it.

In principle, national treatment and MFN treatment have ensured non-discriminatory treatments among intellectual property owners for the enjoyment of their intellectual property rights at the international level. The exceptions to those principles, for example, the exceptions to the national treatment obligation under Article 2(3) of the Paris Convention,[75] have been widely applied under the national laws even today, and there does not seem to have been much development since the time when the Paris Convention was adopted.[76]

Geographical coverage: What are the geographical boundaries of patent rights?

In principle, independence of patents obtained for the same invention in different countries, as stipulated in Article 4*bis* of the Paris Convention, has been widely maintained. While regional patent offices that grant patents on behalf of its Member States consolidate patent granting procedures within their respective regions, the effect and status of regional patents in the Member States continue to be independent in most of the regional systems.[77]

Even if there are some initiatives that aim at mutual recognition of patents granted on the same invention by different countries,[78] thus far, each country maintains its right to grant patents and revoke them, where appropriate. It is one thing to harmonize the legal provisions of national patent laws and another thing to automatically recognize the actions and decisions made by foreign patent authorities. In that sense, the automatic recognition among the Contracting Parties of the Budapest Treaty of the deposit of microorganisms at the International Depositary Authorities is a rare example of mutual recognition in the area of patents. However, it

---

75 Article 2(3) of the Paris Convention states that the national law provisions relating to judicial and administrative procedure and to jurisdiction, and to the designation of an address for service or the appointment of an agent, which may be required by the laws on industrial property are expressly reserved.

76 Article 7(2) of the PLT slightly narrowed down this exception to the national treatment by allowing foreign applicants and patent owners to act for themselves before the office in respect of a limited number of procedures under certain conditions.

77 *See* Section IV for the regional systems. The notable exceptions are the patents granted by the African Intellectual Property Organization (OAPI) and the proposed unitary patents under the European Union.

78 *See* Vancouver Group's initiatives in Section VII.

should be noted that while these deposits are recognized by the Contracting Parties, the applicant has to convince each patent authority that the national requirement on sufficient disclosure of the claimed invention has been met.

Scope and duration of the rights: What are the rights conferred by patents?

The type of exclusive rights that a patent confers on its owner is stipulated in the TRIPS Agreement.[79] Although that Agreement provides the general principles for WTO Members in providing limited exceptions to exclusive patent rights,[80] Members are free to shape the exact scope of the exclusive rights under their jurisdictions as long as they comply with a three-step test under Article 30, which is akin to the three-step test that has been developed in the field of copyright law.[81]

The compulsory license mechanism is a limitation to exclusive rights in the sense that a patent owner must non-voluntarily provide a license to a third party against appropriate financial or other forms of remuneration. Compared with any other area of substantive patent law, both the Paris Convention (art 5) and the TRIPS Agreement (art 31), supplemented by a decision by Members in 2003 to establish the Paragraph 6 System and the Protocol amending the TRIPS Agreement adopted in 2005, provide extremely detailed international rules regarding the conditions for granting compulsory licenses. At the same time, both treaties keep it open for their members to decide on the grounds on which compulsory licenses may be requested by third parties.

Article 33 of the TRIPS Agreement provides a minimum statutory term of protection, which is 20 years from the filing date. As it is a minimum requirement, Members of the WTO are free to provide any protection that goes beyond the minimum 20-year term, as they consider appropriate. Indeed, a number of countries provide extension of patent protection, or additional protection, in order to compensate a patent owner for the period during which he was not able to exploit his patent, because, for example, the patent office failed to examine a patent application in time or a patentee has to wait for approval from a competent regulatory authority for putting a patented product on the market.

---

[79] TRIPS, art 28.

[80] Ibid., art 30.

[81] *See* Berne Convention for the Protection of Literary and Artistic Works, art 9(2), and TRIPS Agreement, art 13. *See* WIPO document SCP/18/3 for various exceptions and limitations to the patent rights under national laws.

One area which has not been regulated by any international treaty is the exhaustion of patent rights. Article 6 of the TRIPS Agreement and the Doha Declaration on TRIPS and Public Health explicitly give leeway for WTO Members to introduce an exhaustion mechanism as they see fit in their countries.[82]

Conditions for patent protection, revocation, and enforcement

Many, but not all, the formal and substantive requirements for obtaining patents are regulated in the PLT and the TRIPS Agreement, respectively. Because of the nature of the formality requirements, the PLT had to prescribe detailed formalities that applicants have to follow, for example, time limits and contents of a form to be submitted for a specific purpose. In contrast, the TRIPS Agreement leaves out the definition of key terms regarding the substantive conditions of patentability, such as "invention", "novelty", "inventive step", and the scope of "prior art" for determining novelty and inventive step. In particular, even if Articles 27.2 and 27.3 determine the subject matter excluded from patentability, the lack of a definition of the term "invention" allows Members to effectively exclude other subject matter from patent protection. Further, although the Paris Convention in Article 11 obliges Member States to introduce temporary protection of inventions at certain international exhibitions in their domestic laws, neither the Paris Convention nor the TRIPS Agreement regulates the matter of which kinds of public disclosure made before the filing date could be disregarded for the determination of novelty/inventive step – the so-called grace period. Although the America Invents Act (AIA) brings the US practice closer to the first-to-file system applied in the rest of the world, because of the unique grace-period provision under US law, the US system after the AIA is effectively a "first-inventor-to-file" system.

No international treaty regulates the substantive grounds for revocation of patents, although Article 10 of the PLT provides that, in principle, formal requirements may not be a ground for revocation or invalidation of a patent, except where the non-compliance with the formal requirement occurred as a result of a fraudulent intention. Administrative opposition during the pre- or post-grant stage is another area where almost no provision[83] is found in the existing international agreements.

---

[82] Consequently, various exhaustion mechanisms are found in national laws. *See* WIPO document SCP/18/3.

[83] With respect to formality requirements, a number of provisions in the PLT exclude *inter partes* procedures from their applicability. As to the administrative revocation and *inter partes* procedures, Article 62.4 of the TRIPS

The substantive law on enforcement is predominantly a matter for each country to decide upon. Part III of the TRIPS Agreement ensures that the judicial authorities of its Members have the authority to order provisional measures, injunctions, payment of damages, or other appropriate remedies. However, doctrines relating to, for example, equivalents, calculation of damages, and the availability of injunctive relief or provisional measures are developed and applied by the judicial authorities of the jurisdiction concerned.

Procedures: How to obtain, maintain, and enforce patent rights

Perhaps the most important harmonization with respect to the procedures for obtaining patents is the procedure laid down in Article 4 of the Paris Convention for claiming the priority of an earlier application in subsequent applications. Beyond that, the PLT provides certain procedures before the offices of the Contracting Parties for obtaining national/regional patents, such as time limits for the prescribed actions by an applicant or a patent holder and a procedure for restoring the priority right. As the requirements under the PLT are, in principle, the maximum requirements, different ways to implement the PLT under national patent systems are possible. The PCT prescribes detailed procedures to be followed by applicants, offices, and the International Bureau with respect to international filing, international search, international publication, international preliminary examination, and other actions during the international phase of PCT international applications. Evidently, in order for such an international filing system to be operational, the PCT provides a unique procedural rule that parties concerned must follow, although in certain instances they are given options.

Apart from the above, the procedures for obtaining patents vary from one country to another. For example, since the amount of patenting activity differs from one country to another according to the overall resource allocation within the country and its economic efficiency, there is no uniformity with regard to whether and how the prior art search and substantive examination are carried out by the patent offices in the various countries. Further, many aspects of the administrative procedures before patent offices are regulated under the general administrative law and procedural law of the respective countries. For that reason, when it comes to the procedures for the revocation of patents or procedures for

Agreement states that they shall be governed by the general principles laid down in art 41.2 and 41.3. For example, the procedures shall be fair, equitable, and not unnecessarily complicated, costly, or delayed.

enforcing patents, seeking a uniform international rule is very difficult. In particular, significant differences in court proceedings can be observed. While the TRIPS Agreement prescribes certain provisions regarding administrative, civil, and criminal procedures with respect to intellectual property, the provisions mostly state principles, and the implementation of those principles is largely left to the discretion of the Members.

IV. SHARING COMMON PRINCIPLES THROUGH REGIONAL TREATIES AND BY INSTITUTIONS

In addition to international treaties, regional treaties have significantly contributed to the progressive development of international patent law. In general, there are two types of regional agreement. The first consists of establishing a regional patent system. The second aims at harmonizing national patent laws within the region. Examples of the latter include: (i) Decision No. 486 of 14 September 2000 – Common Regime on Industrial Property, adopted by the Andean Community;[84] (ii) Directive 2004/48/EC of the European Parliament and of the Council of 29 April 2004 on the enforcement of intellectual property rights; and (iii) Directive 98/44/EC of the European Parliament and of the Council of 6 July 1998 on the legal protection of biotechnological inventions. As regards the regional agreements establishing regional patent systems, most of them create a regional patent office that grants regional patents for its Member States. However, more recently, a regional organization for the provision of search and examination services was established among the Nordic countries.

(1) Regional Patent Organizations Granting Regional Patents

The first regional agreement to create a common patent office with a centralized procedure for granting patents on behalf of its Member States was concluded among a number of French-speaking African countries in 1962 – known as the Libreville Agreement. A regional patent office pools financial and human resources of its member states in patent matters in order to increase the efficiency gain in the region. While their primary function is to grant regional patents for their member states, their objectives may go well beyond that, depending on the mandates given by

---

[84] The Andean Community is a customs union comprising Bolivia, Colombia, Ecuador, and Peru.

the governing regional conventions.[85] Although regional agreements of this kind do not oblige member states to enact a uniform national patent law, since a regional patent granted by a regional office on behalf of a particular country has the same effect and rights as a national patent granted by the patent office of that country, the countries belonging to a regional organization would be inclined to avoid, as much as possible, applying different standards and conditions for the grant of regional and national patents. Therefore, the creation of a regional patent office and grant of a regional patent indirectly promote the convergence of the substantive patent law, at least with respect to the patentability criteria.

At present, there are five regional patent organizations/offices that grant regional patents: the African Intellectual Property Organization (OAPI), the African Regional Intellectual Property Organization (ARIPO), the Eurasian Patent Office (EAPO), the European Patent Office (EPO), and the Gulf Cooperation Council (GCC) Patent Office.

African Intellectual Property Organization[86]

The African Intellectual Property Organization was established following the adoption of the Bangui Agreement[87] on 2 March 1977. The Bangui Agreement was revised on 24 February 1999 in order to comply with the TRIPS Agreement. OAPI has 16 French-speaking African countries as its members. One of the characteristics of this regional system is that there are no parallel national patent granting systems in the member states. OAPI, located in Yaoundé, Cameroon, serves as the common intellectual property office for its member states, which apply the Bangui Agreement and its Annexes as their national laws. The filing of a regional OAPI patent application has the same effect as the filing of a patent application in each OAPI member state, and a patent granted by OAPI is effective in all member states of OAPI. However, infringement of intellectual property rights is a matter dealt with by the courts of each member state.

---

[85] For example, Article III of the Agreement on the Creation of the African Regional Intellectual Property Organization (ARIPO) states that the objectives of ARIPO include organizing conferences, seminars and other meetings on intellectual property matters and assisting its members, as appropriate, in the acquisition and development of technology relating to intellectual property matters.

[86] See <http://www.oapi.int/>.

[87] The full title of the Bangui Agreement is the "Bangui Agreement Relating to the Creation of an African Intellectual Property Organization, Constituting a Revision of the Agreement Relating to the Creation of an African and Malagasy Office of Industrial Property". *See* <http://www.wipo.int/wipolex/en/other_treaties/details.jsp?group_id=21&treaty_id=227>.

Regarding the validity of the regional patents, the final judicial decision of a court of one member state has authority over all other member states, except with respect to the question of validity based on the ground of *ordre public* and morality.

African Regional Intellectual Property Organization[88]

The history of the African Regional Intellectual Property Organization goes back to the Agreement on the Creation of the Industrial Property Organization for English-speaking Africa (ESARIPO) concluded on 9 December 1976. In December 1982, the Administrative Council of ARIPO adopted the Harare Protocol, which empowered ARIPO to receive and process patent and industrial design applications on behalf of states party to the Protocol. Seventeen English-speaking African countries are the Contracting States to the Protocol.

In a regional patent application, the applicant designates the Contracting States in which he wishes his invention to be protected. If the application complies with the substantive patentability requirements, each designated Contracting State receives a notification of that fact from ARIPO. Within six months from the notification, the designated states have the possibility to deny the effect of the regional patent in its territory, based on the grounds that are specified in the Protocol.[89] Disputes regarding the validity and enforcement of regional patents are handled by national courts of each country. Further, a regional patent is subject to the provisions of the applicable national law on compulsory licenses, forfeiture, and the use of patented inventions in the public interest.

Eurasian Patent Office

The Eurasian Patent Convention (EAPC) was signed on 9 September 1994 by the heads of the Governments of the CIS countries, and entered into force on 12 August 1995.[90] The main purpose of the EAPC is to strengthen cooperation in the field of protection of inventions and to create an inter-state system for obtaining legal protection on the basis of a single patent valid in the territory of the Contracting States. Nine CIS countries are the Contracting Parties to the EAPC.

---

88 *See* <http://www.aripo.org/index.php/about-aripo>.

89 The permissible grounds are: (i) the invention is not patentable in accordance with the provisions of the Protocol; or (ii) because of the nature of the invention, a patent cannot be registered or granted or has no effect under the national law of the designated State.

90 *See* <http://www.eapo.org/en/history.html>.

When a Eurasian patent application is filed, EAPO conducts a prior art search. The applicant may submit a request for substantive examination within six months from the publication of a search report. Once a regional patent is granted, the applicant chooses the EAPC Contracting Parties in which the patent shall be maintained. Any dispute arising from the validity or the infringement of a Eurasian patent in a given Contracting State shall be resolved by the national courts or other competent authorities of that State, the decision of which has effect only in the territory of that Contracting State. Similarly, compulsory licenses for the use of a Eurasian patent by third parties may be granted by the competent authority of a Contracting State with effect in the territory of that State.

European Patent Office

The European Patent Convention (EPC), which provided the legal basis for establishing the European Patent Office, entered into force on 7 October 1977. All 27 European Union (EU) Member States, as well as 11 other European countries, are parties to the EPC. A European patent is a "bundle" of individual national patents having effect in the Contracting States chosen by the patentee. A European patent shall, in each of the Contracting States for which it is granted, have the effect of, and be subject to the same conditions as, a national patent granted by that state, unless otherwise provided in the EPC.[91] In particular, any Contracting State may require that a translation of a European patent be submitted within a certain time period. In the event of failure to comply with such requirement, the European patent may be deemed to be void *ab initio* in that state. Further, the EPC provides a centralized post-grant opposition procedure and an administrative appeal procedure before the Boards of Appeal. However, disputes regarding the validity of European patents and infringement of such patents are settled by the competent court of each Contracting State in which the European patents have been validated.

Although the EPC significantly simplified the procedures for obtaining patents in a number of countries in Europe, the submission of translations of European patents in the prescribed languages upon validation in each Contracting States has raised costs for obtaining patents in Europe.[92] Furthermore, the fact that national courts and authorities are competent to decide on the infringement and validity of European patents gives rise to a number of difficulties where enforcement or revocation of European

---

[91] *See* <http://www.epo.org/applying/european/validation.html>.

[92] According to the European Commission, an average of €36,000 is required to obtain a patent in the EU countries, in comparison to €2000 in the United States of America and €600 in China.

patents is sought by a patentee or a third party, respectively, in several countries. These include high costs, risk of diverging decisions by national courts, lack of legal certainty, and forum shopping. Consequently, a single European patent having effect in all EU countries with a single court having jurisdiction over litigation relating to such a patent has been sought for decades. Finally, on 11 December 2012, the European Parliament voted positively on the regulation creating a unitary patent and the regulation establishing a language regime applicable to the unitary patent.[93] Further, on 19 February 2013, an International Agreement setting up a single and specialized patent jurisdiction (the "Unified Patent Court", UPC) was signed by 24 EU Member States.[94] The two regulations will apply from 1 January 2014, or from the date of the entry into force of the Agreement on a UPC, whichever is later. The UPC Agreement will enter into force once 13 EU Member States have ratified the package, including France, Germany, and the UK.

When the unitary patent system is operational, it will create another option for applicants in addition to the already existing national patents and regional European patents granted by the EPO. If requested by a patentee, a patent granted by the EPO in accordance with the EPC will have a unitary effect for the territory of all the 25 participating states. The EPO will additionally be in charge of centrally administering the unitary patents, collecting the annual renewal fees, and distributing the fees to the participating EU Member States. It is expected that a coherent unitary system of patent protection in the EU internal market will contribute to reducing competitive disadvantages vis-à-vis other markets.[95]

Gulf Cooperation Council Patent Office

Since 3 October 1998, the Gulf Cooperation Council (GCC)[96] Patent Office has received applications for regional patents in the Gulf Region. The objectives of the Office are not limited to the granting of patents, but

---

[93] During the European Council meeting held 28–29 June 2012, an agreement was reached on the regulation implementing enhanced cooperation in the area of the creation of unitary patent protection among 25 of the 27 Member States of the EU (except Italy and Spain).

[94] Bulgaria signed the Agreement on 5 March 2013. Spain and Poland did not sign the Agreement.

[95] *See* <http://www.europarl.europa.eu/news/en/pressroom/content/20121205BKG57397/html/The-new-EU-unitary-patent-QA>.

[96] The GCC comprises Bahrain, Oman, Qatar, Saudi Arabia, and the United Arab Emirates.

extend to, for example, encouragement of scientific and technical research, facilitating technology transfer, and boosting economic growth in the region. Patents granted by the GCC Patent Office, located in Riyadh, Saudi Arabia, secure legal protection for inventions in all member states upon prompt validation of the regional patents in the member states as of the date of grant.[97] Compulsory licenses may be issued by the Board of Directors of the GCC Patent Office on the grounds of, for example, failure to work or insufficient working of the invention. Any decision issued by the Office may be appealed before the Grievance Committee, the decision of which may be appealed before the competent authority in accordance with the applicable regulations of the host country. The competent authorities of each member state examine all disputes pertaining to infringement of a regional patent.

(2) Nordic Patent Institute[98]

The Nordic Patent Institute was established by the governments of Denmark, Iceland, and Norway, and has been operational since 1 January 2008. The aim of the Institute is to stimulate innovation and economic growth in those states by providing improved and enhanced patent-related services from patent authorities at local level. Specifically, the Nordic Patent Institute serves as the International Searching and Preliminary Examining Authority under the PCT for residents of the above Contracting States. In that capacity, it conducts supplementary international searches and international-type searches in connection with national patent applications. In addition, the Institute offers the prior art search service for other government authorities and private customers. Therefore, it is not an intergovernmental body that grants regional patents, but rather a regional prior art search and substantive examination service provider for users in the region and beyond, covering both public and private customers. In that sense, the Nordic Patent Institute is a unique intergovernmental organization that operates in a niche in the global patent demands.

---

[97] *See* <http://www.gccpo.org/AboutUSEn.aspx>.

[98] *See* <http://internationalcooperation.dkpto.org/nordic-patent-institute.aspx>.

V. FREE TRADE AGREEMENTS AND MFN TREATMENT

As thoroughly examined by Professor Peter K Yu,[99] plurilateral and bilateral agreements between states also form part of the international norm. In particular, since the entry into force of the TRIPS Agreement, the number of Free Trade Agreements (FTAs) containing provisions on intellectual property protection and enforcement has risen.[100] While many FTA provisions merely reaffirm the principles of the TRIPS Agreement, requiring adequate and effective protection of intellectual property in accordance with the minimum standards set down in that Agreement, some FTA provisions require the parties to implement more extensive protection and enforcement of IPRs than provided for in the TRIPS Agreement. The following FTA provisions are examples of the latter in the field of patents:

- *Patentability*: Article 14.8 of the US-Bahrain FTA states that each Party shall make patents available for plant inventions.
- *Grace period*: Article 15.8 of the US-Oman FTA provides for a 12-month grace period for the public disclosure made or authorized by, or derived from, the applicant with respect to the determination of novelty and inventive step.
- *Patent-term extension*: Article 2(b) in Annex XIII of the European Free Trade Association (EFTA)-Republic of Korea FTA provides for a compensatory term of protection for pharmaceuticals of up to five years for curtailment of the term of patent protection as a result of the delay caused by the marketing approval process.
- *Exhaustion*: Article 15.9 of the US-Morocco FTA states that each Party shall provide that the exclusive right of the patent owner to prevent importation of a patented product, or a product that results from a patented process, without the consent of the patent owner shall not be limited by the sale or distribution of that product outside its territory (a Party may limit application of this paragraph

---

99 PK Yu, "ACTA and Its Complex Politics" (2011) 3 WIPO J. 1 – 16. See also D Gervais, "Country Clubs, Empiricism, Blogs and Innovation: The Future of International Intellectual Property Norm-Making in the Wake of ACTA," in M Burri and Th Cottier (eds), *Trade Governance in the Digital Age* (Cambridge University Press 2012) 323–43.

100 WIPO, WHO, & WTO, *Promoting Access to Medical Technologies and Innovation – Intersections between Public Health, Intellectual Property and Trade* (2012) 186.

to cases where the patent owner has placed restrictions on importation by contract or other means).

Since the entry into force of the TRIPS Agreement which introduced the MFN principle in the field of intellectual property, the international effect of plurilateral and bilateral agreements has changed. Except for the limited exemptions from the MFN obligation expressly prescribed in Articles 4 and 5 of the TRIPS Agreement, a WTO Member that grants any advantage, favor, privilege, or immunity to the nationals of an FTA partner country must accord the same to the nationals of all other WTO Members. In particular, in accordance with Article 4(d) of the TRIPS Agreement, only those bilateral or plurilateral agreements that entered into force before 1995, i.e., before the entry into force of the WTO Agreement, and that are notified to the Council for TRIPS, can escape from the application of the MFN.[101]

VI. INTERNATIONAL NORMS AND NATIONAL PRACTICES AT A CROSSROADS: CHANGING LANDSCAPE AND THE RATIONALE FOR INCREASINGLY ADDRESSING PRACTICAL – RATHER THAN NORM-SETTING – MEASURES

More than ten years ago, the World Bank wrote that "[k]nowledge is like light. Weightless and intangible, it can easily travel the world, enlightening the lives of people everywhere. Yet billions of people still live in the darkness of poverty – unnecessarily."[102] These words could imply that there is something out there that prevents knowledge from traveling, since otherwise poverty would not exist, or at least not to the extent we witness today. It could, however, also be understood in the sense that it is poverty that prevents knowledge from traveling, or that knowledge, while traveling and enlightening the lives of people, has no influence on the

[101] Article 4(d) of the TRIPS Agreement also requires that in order to be exempted from the MFN, the agreements shall not constitute an arbitrary or unjustifiable discrimination against nationals of other Member States. The examples of the regional treaties notified under art 4(d) include the North America Free Trade Agreement (NAFTA), the Treaty Establishing the European Economic Community (Treaty of Rome), and the Andean Subregional Integration Agreement (Cartagena Agreement).

[102] The World Bank, *World Development Report 1998/99 – Knowledge for Development – Summary* (Washington 1998–1999).

level of poverty. And indeed, many different interpretations have emerged around the notion and role of knowledge, and with it, the question of how to inspire and boost its creation and diffusion for the sake of improving welfare: while some are of the opinion that a system of limited exclusive rights, such as patents or trade secrets, is required to act as an incentive for the creation of knowledge and as a framework to ensure its diffusion, others believe that the creation of knowledge will occur with or without the existence of a protection system, and that the more freely knowledge can flow, the more easily it will develop. Against this backdrop, among other influencing factors, the debate over IP rights, and more specifically patent rights, has in the past decade reached unprecedented levels of controversy, not infrequently characterized by a remarkable absence of rationality and wisdom.

Those defending the necessity of a system for the protection of rights claim, with Mark Twain, that "[a] country without a patent office and good patent laws is just a crab and can't travel any way but sideways and backwards."[103] The defenders of a less rights-oriented understanding, on the other hand, would perhaps rather go along with this anonymous saying: "[t]he Patent Office is the mother-in-law of invention." But on second thought, it would perhaps be wise to follow a more nuanced approach, like the one expressed by Giles Sutherland Rich, to whom the following quote is attributed: "The good patent gives the world something it did not truly have before, whereas the bad patent has the effect of trying to take away from the world something which it effectively already had."[104]

Without taking sides here, and recognizing the generalizing nature of the statement which does not capture the complexity of the issue, it can be argued that the dividing line between those policy makers that are supporters of patent rights and those that are rather challenging their effectiveness often overlap with the one that can be observed between technology-producing countries (including those that are close to becoming technology producers) and those countries that are not – or not yet – creating significant parts of the welfare of their societies by more or less sophisticated technologies. And indeed, for a long time, and almost certainly until the conclusion of the TRIPS Agreement and perhaps even for a few years thereafter, relevant patent discussions were the hunting grounds of a limited number of technology-producing countries and regions, like Europe, Japan, the USA, and a few others. Their main

---

103 M Twain, *A Connecticut Yankee in King Arthur's Court* (1889).

104 GS Rich (1978) 60 JPOS 271, 288.

objective was obviously to provide incentives to further invent and innovate, but also to offer inventors and creators the best possible conditions for obtaining protection abroad, since due to globalization, more and more foreign markets were becoming available for the absorption of technology, both in terms of consumption and of production. At the same time, the different conditions applicable in the various countries to obtain protection would render the task increasingly complex and costly for those seeking international patent protection.

It was thus simply a question of common sense for those countries to start working towards international harmonization of patent laws at the normative level with a twofold objective: (i) to allow applicants to be able to count on uniform conditions in as many countries as possible in order to facilitate protection internationally, and (ii) to create patent-related norms that would be sufficiently uniform so as to allow at least some form of work-sharing among patent offices. Incidentally, these countries also started realizing that some form of harmonization might lead to improvements in the quality of patents, an argument that became stronger as the number of patented inventions throughout the world was increasing. For them, the current international norms, as described in Part III above, are not sufficient to meet their objectives.

(1) Some Challenges

After the conclusion of the PLT in 2000, a number of WIPO Member States expressed the wish to move to the consideration of issues related to the harmonization of substantive requirements of patent law. And indeed, discussions started in the WIPO Standing Committee on the Law of Patents (SCP) in 2001, with a view to harmonizing certain substantive patentability requirements in a so-called draft Substantive Patent Law Treaty (SPLT),[105] with a view to facilitating cooperation among patent offices in respect of search and examination results in order to reduce the workload they were increasingly facing. However, in the meantime, that is, in 1995, the TRIPS Agreement had been concluded as a part of the Agreement Establishing the World Trade Organization (WTO). In the eyes of many, in particular, in developing countries, this agreement fundamentally changed the face of the international intellectual property regime. Beyond the fact that not all developing countries were in a position to benefit from, or even to perceive the benefits of, the TRIPS Agreement, the treaty was perceived to be to a large extent responsible

[105] Documents SCP/4/2 and, among others, SCP/10/4 and 5.

for two of the challenges that we are facing today, that is: (i) an increased criticism on the effects of the intellectual property system on social, economic, and cultural development; coupled with (ii) an increasing regionalization and globalization and the imposing of "one-size-fits-all" IP standards, raising the fear in a number of developing countries that this may be only the beginning of further harmonization of IP laws and, in turn, of a reduction of the available national policy space. In addition, one factor that was undoubtedly underestimated in the multilateral discussions on the harmonization of substantive patent laws was the diverging interests at stake: while developing countries wanted to address issues relating to development, including avoiding perceived obstacles to development and technology transfer, industrialized countries were struggling with workload, quality, and the need to improve mutual cooperation. Against this backdrop, normative harmonization became practically unmanageable in the broader multilateral context.

However, despite these questions and reservations, the number of patent applications filed internationally has been increasing over the past years, and statistics show that the increase is occurring not only in the biggest patent offices, such as the EPO, the Japan Patent Office (JPO), the United States Patent and Trademark Office (USPTO), and the State Intellectual Property Office of China (SIPO),[106] but also in patent offices of other countries such as Brazil, South Africa, and India, to name just a few. As a consequence, a number of patent offices have to cope with an increasing workload coupled with limited financial and human resources, and this has led to a growing number of cooperation models throughout the world, both among industrialized and developing countries. But of course, not all offices are equally affected by that growth, as it affects mainly high- and middle-income countries, thus leading to different and sometimes opposing views by countries on how to address the issue.

(2) The Search for Solutions

The natural impulse of governments in addressing the issue was to look at how better use could be made of work undertaken by other offices, an undertaking that had initially seemed to be achievable through further harmonization of patent laws. This would have allowed the creation of

---

[106] The number of patent applications filed in Japan, Europe, the United States of America, China, and the Republic of Korea increased by over 40 percent over the 2001–2011 period (*see* WIPO statistics website <http://www.wipo.int/ipstats/en/>.

common conditions of patentability, which would in turn have led to closer cooperation among offices in examining patent applications.

In parallel, countries have constantly attempted to improve the PCT framework. Obviously, the PCT continues to be a fantastic tool for achieving work-sharing, as it aims to simplify the procedures for obtaining patent protection in many countries, making them more efficient and economical both for users of the patent system and for patent offices, who can use the PCT work products prepared by other offices. In particular, work-sharing tools are found in the central formality checking, the central international publication, the International Search Report (ISR), and the International Preliminary Reports on Patentability (preliminary, non-binding opinion on novelty, inventive step (non-obviousness), and industrial applicability). While the PCT has proven to be very successful as an international filing device,[107] it has possibly achieved less success as a work-sharing tool in practice for addressing the quality of the national examination as well as backlogs, although it does allow offices to re-use earlier work (e.g., international reports), thereby improving quality and potentially reducing the amount of work needed to achieve such quality. Each office concerned is of course free to determine the extent to which this is done, and the decision will depend on various factors, including mutual trust among offices. From the WIPO angle, one attempt to open a dialogue on those issues was the "PCT Roadmap",[108] together with the measures that followed its publication and discussion among Member States.

Considering the unsatisfactory results generated by the normative efforts at the multilateral level, the growing pressure on some offices in terms of backlogs and quality, and the difficulty to move forward with a comprehensive norm-setting program to improve the situation globally, a number of countries and non-governmental bodies have started searching for other ways to achieve results. One part of those efforts relates to initiatives in respect of geographically limited harmonization among certain like-minded countries. The other aspect covers a number of more practice-oriented measures. Below are some non-exhaustive examples of the two types of measures.

---

[107] PCT filings increased from 149,000 in 2006 to over 194,000 in 2012, and exceeded 200,000 in 2013.

[108] *See* document PCT/WG/2/3.

VII. SEEKING GEOGRAPHICALLY LIMITED HARMONIZATION

(1) Group B+

After it became clear that substantive harmonization of patent laws would not happen in WIPO, industrialized countries created, following a kick-off meeting of the Trilateral Working Group on Patent Law Harmonization in Alexandria, US, 24–27 February 2004, the so-called Group B, consisting of industrialized countries, plus the EU and the EPO. This Group started working on the basis of the WIPO documents developed for the draft SPLT in the SCP, but decided to limit the scope of those efforts, at least initially, to some prior art related issues, namely prior art, novelty, inventive step, and grace period, with the goal to achieve harmonization among industrialized countries on those issues. Quite some progress has been made in the last few years, although it seems that a few issues still remain to be discussed, such as the duration of the grace period and prior user rights.

(2) Tegernsee Group

Another attempt at harmonization was initiated by the President of the European Patent Office, who invited, in July 2011, a group of countries to a place near Munich in Germany called Tegernsee with the same objective as Group B+, namely to make headway for substantive patent law harmonization. In addition to the EPO, the countries participating in this so-called Tegernsee Group are the US, the UK, Japan, France, Germany, and Denmark. The offices reviewed recent developments in all three regions, including US Patent Reform legislation, the revision of the Japanese patent law, the European Unitary patent protection, and the results of the latest IP5 meeting. Participants agreed that, in particular, the following issues were of fundamental importance: first-to-file, grace period, prior user rights, scope of prior art, definition of novelty and non-obviousness/inventive step, and 18-month publication. All participants recognized the importance of making progress and agreed to take the process forward by means of fact finding and information gathering through a group of technical and legal experts to provide a contribution to a wider discussion involving all relevant parties and consulting stakeholders as appropriate. The Tegernsee Group met again in 2012 and 2013 to discuss four technical, fact-finding studies on the topics of the grace period, 18-month publication, the treatment of conflicting applications, and prior user rights.[109] These studies have been subject to

---

109 The four studies are available at <http://www.epo.org/news-issues/news/2012/20121108a.html>.

broad stakeholder consultations in the various regions, involving hearings and written responses to questionnaires.[110] Reports on those consultations have been prepared and should be discussed in the course of 2013 at the next meeting of the Tegernsee Heads, which was supposed to take place in late spring 2013, but which to the knowledge of the authors has not yet taken place (as at 1 September 2013).

The foregoing depicts some activities which, although limited in scope and in territorial effect, are further normative attempts to bring legal systems closer together. They also show, however, that a shift has taken place from a fully multilateral dialogue, encompassing all countries and positions in an inclusive exercise, to more restricted approaches which, ultimately, may be easier to achieve, but which will exclude those who today do not want to participate in a common endeavor.

VIII. PRACTICAL ARRANGEMENTS AMONG PATENT OFFICES

The search for improvements to the patent regime internationally and the dissatisfaction over the continuing absence of success in the area of multilateral normative cooperation, as well as the gloomy prospects in respect of achieving results in that area, have led some industrialized countries as well as intergovernmental and non-governmental organizations to explore progress that would not, or not necessarily, involve normative changes, but would generate results at a more practical level. Examples of such endeavors can be found in the work of the Trilateral Offices and the so-called IP5, and also in projects such as the Patent Prosecution Highway (PPH) and the Global Dossier proposed in the context of the PCT, as described below.

(1) The Trilateral Cooperation

The Trilateral Offices (that is, the EPO, the JPO, and the USPTO),[111] have started a number of common projects going back as far as 1983, among which are projects relating to enhancing work-sharing, developing the PCT, classification, linguistic tools, biotechnology, patent information, e-learning, examiner exchange, information technology, and a number of comparative studies. Many of these projects have given – and continue to give – ample prominence to work-sharing targets; for example, the projects relating to quality, timeliness, and the accessibility

---

[110] A summary of the Tegernsee process can be found on the EPO website: <http://www.epo.org/news-issues/news/2012/20121108a.html>.

[111] *See* the Trilateral cooperation website at <http://www.trilateral.net/index.html;jsessionid=91cp5qa58nje>.

of patent systems. They also support work-sharing based on first filings followed by a second filing in another Trilateral Office, as well as work on quality metrics with a view to achieving, in the future, common quality standards (although part of that work has been shifting to the IP5 (see below)).

(2) The IP5

The group of offices called the IP5 comprises, in addition to the EPO, JPO, and USPTO, the Korean Intellectual Property Office (KIPO) and SIPO.[112] Together, these five offices account for about 90 percent of all patent applications filed worldwide and for 93 percent of all work carried out under the PCT. They started meeting as early as 2008 when they agreed on a common vision, which reads as follows: "The elimination of unnecessary duplication of work among the offices, enhancement of patent examination efficiency and quality, and guarantee of the stability of patent right." The IP5 constitute, in terms of membership and of work program, both an extension and a deepening of the Trilateral Offices' work, in that they carry on with activities already begun by the Trilateral Offices, but also address additional new issues. As an important step for multilateral cooperation, the IP5 also agreed that the PCT played a significant role as an international framework for work-sharing, and that its use as a platform for work-sharing purposes should be strengthened by the five offices.

They further agreed on a number of what they called foundation projects for their future work, including projects on the following subjects: Common Hybrid Classification; Common Documentation; Common Application Format; Common Access to Search and Examination Results; Common Training Policy; Mutual Machine Translation; Common Examination Practice Rules and Quality Management; Common Statistical Parameter System for Examination; Common Search and Examination Support Tools; and Common Approach to Sharing and Documenting Search Strategies.

The IP5 have organized their work program into three working groups, namely WG1 "Classification", WG2 "IT-supported Business Processes", and WG3 "Harmonization", which report to more high-level fora, namely the IP5 Deputy Heads Meeting and the IP5 Heads Meeting. The five offices, shortly after the start of their own work, started cooperation with a number of private sector representatives, including the American

112 *See* the IP5 website at <http://www.fiveipoffices.org/index.html;jsessionid =ug9qgtx2jy5r>.

Intellectual Property Law Association (AIPLA), BUSINESSEUROPE, the Intellectual Property Owners Association (IPO), the Japan Intellectual Property Association (JIPA), the Korea Intellectual Property Association (KINPA), and the Patent Protection Association of China (PPAC), who are calling themselves "IP5 Industry" and meet in parallel with the IP5 meetings.

One initiative of particular relevance in the context of the IP5 is the so-called Global Dossier. In order to further improve the PCT system, the UK and the US submitted a joint proposal entitled "PCT 20/20", containing 12 proposals for further improvement of the PCT system.[113] One of them is the development and implementation of the Global Dossier and incorporation of the said system into the PCT. The Global Dossier is a concept developed within the IP5 as an all-stakeholder-inclusive electronic environment. Some of the ideas proposed by that initiative are the one-portal management of cross-filed applications, the elimination of the need to file duplicate documents in multiple offices (e.g., priority documents and prior art citations), and cost savings through the use of modern machine translation tools. Among IP offices, it should provide further work-sharing opportunities (e.g., through information exchange and examiner collaboration). The Global Dossier initiative is meant to bring consistency to the different measures (existing or planned). Under the proposed system, applicants would file a single application regardless of the number of national patents ultimately sought, and thereafter, the movement and duplication of documents would be minimized or even eliminated by the creation of a "one-stop" portal for all stakeholders in the merits of a particular invention. For example, an applicant may program the system in such a way that corresponding national, regional, or PCT applications will be automatically filed with the selected offices just before the expiration of the 12-month priority period. The required fees will be charged and disseminated, and a PCT application will be forwarded to the pre-selected ISA. The one portal would eliminate the need to file duplicated copies of documents, such as priority documents or prior art citations, in multiple offices, and would offer modern machine translation tools. By sharing the information contained in the Global Dossier (for example, search and examination reports prepared by various offices on the same invention), it would facilitate work-sharing and collaboration among examiners of different offices.

---

[113] The latest revised proposal is contained in document PCT/MIA/20/10.

In a nutshell, the Global Dossier is a highly integrated international virtual dossier, combining various supporting tools for the prosecution of patent applications and maintenance of patents. As it is still in its early stages of development, it is not feasible to analyze its impact. Nevertheless, one may assume that, if realized, such a system would lower the level of national boundaries as far as the prosecution of patent applications and maintenance of patents are concerned.

The initiative was further developed together with the JPO for introduction to the IP5 offices in the spring of 2013. At an IP5 Heads-of-Offices meeting hosted by the EPO in June 2013, continuation of the work was decided, and it is expected that this will bring new opportunities to improve the international patent system.

(3) The Patent Prosecution Highway

A particularly important development for the international patent system was the launch of the Patent Prosecution Highway (PPH).[114] In the early 2000s, at the initiative of the JPO, some patent offices started signing bilateral agreements with other patent offices to enable patent applicants to request a fast-track examination procedure where patent examiners could make use of the work products from the other office. Beyond the fact that the PPH shortens the time for processing patent applications with participating offices and potentially improves the quality of examination, two aspects deserve particular attention: first, participating offices have started including PCT work products as a basis for PPH requests, such as the written opinion of the International Searching Authority, the written opinion of the International Preliminary Examining Authority, and the international preliminary examination report.[115] The second aspect, which is still ongoing, relates to the fact that the PPH is a bundle of bilateral agreements, each one between two offices, which by growing in number become more and more onerous both to manage and to sustain in similar conditions. Again at the initiative of the JPO, participating offices started discussing the benefits of a single structure with the potential to mature into one single multilateral PPH system. Two of the main characteristics of such a system may be: (i) basing PPH eligibility on work available from any participating office, regardless of its status as office of first filing or office of second filing, so long as the applications in question are part of the same patent family and the disclosures support

---

[114] *See*, e.g., <http://www.jpo.go.jp/ppph-portal/>.

[115] More information concerning how participating offices apply the PPH can be found at <http://www.wipo.int/pct/en/filing/pct_pph.html>.

the claimed subject matter; and (ii) accepting any substantive search and examination product (i.e., those including a written opinion if other than an initial notice to grant) done by another office under any filing scenario (e.g., as a National Office under the Paris Convention or as an ISA/IPEA under the PCT). Several offices are, at this point in time, participating in a pilot project testing a multilateral PPH and in September 2013, the IP5 offices agreed to launch a comprehensive IP5 PPH pilot program starting in January 2014. The program will utilize both PCT and national work products. The PPH arrangements currently applied among the IP5 offices will be integrated in this holistic model.

IX. PRACTICAL MEASURES AT WIPO AND CONTRIBUTION OF INFORMATION TECHNOLOGY TOOLS TO THE DEVELOPMENT OF INTERNATIONAL PATENT LAW

While respecting the fact that the multilateral framework needs to be balanced and leave flexibility for national policy choices, there are nevertheless issues that need to be – and can be – addressed within the multilateral framework without limiting the flexibility of governments. WIPO has been very active in searching for and finding solutions to such issues through practical measures, and the following paragraphs will describe some of those endeavors.

In the daily operation of obtaining, maintaining, and enforcing intellectual property rights, information technology and, in particular, the continuously expanding possibility of storing, retrieving, manipulating, and communicating information, have influenced our working behaviors.

Recognizing the importance of information technology facilities and tools and the coordination and development of global IP infrastructure are included in the nine strategic goals of WIPO. The underlying idea is that developing global IP infrastructure such as tools, services, platforms, standards, etc. would enable IP institutions to work more efficiently, to collaborate more effectively, and to provide better services of high quality to their stakeholders and users. For example, equipping patent offices to digitize patent information and disseminate it online significantly improves accessibility to the patent information from every corner of the world. In the past, resource limitation prevented the publication of full patent applications (which can be quite voluminous) in the Official Gazette on paper. With online publication, such impediments no longer exist. In addition to providing state-of-the-art services, WIPO also increasingly counts on IT means to ensure data security, business continuity, and the most cost-effective delivery of its IP services. While the full analysis of the intersection between the development of information technology and that of patent laws goes beyond the scope of this article, concrete cases that demonstrate the important role of information technology in the international patent system will be described below, as the examples of the practical measures taken at WIPO.

(1) The PCT roadmap

The PCT was originally conceived to be an instrument for work-sharing and has since its initial stages made important efforts to work towards this objective. These efforts have even intensified with the changes in the international landscape in recent years and, in particular, with the increased demand for patent protection. One important milestone was a document informally called the PCT Roadmap[116] that was submitted by the WIPO Secretariat to WIPO Member States for consideration in 2009 and which outlines several steps that could be envisaged to bring the PCT closer to its original purpose. These steps include achieving a higher quality of PCT products, inclusion of PCT products as a basis for requesting PPH; and more uniformity in the application of the PCT due to the removal of incompatibilities with national law (so-called reservations), further improving databases and, in particular, PATENTSCOPE and WIPO CASE, and collaborative international search and examination, among others.

In the WIPO PCT Working Group, these issues are discussed, improved and prepared for their submission to the PCT Assembly. For example, at the latest (6th) session of the PCT Working Group held in May 2013, Member States further discussed the following issues, in particular: the formal Integration of the PPH into the PCT; the question of mandatory top-up searches (i.e. additional searches to uncover any relevant prior art documents not available at the time of the international search); improving the timeliness to issue and publish international search reports; the availability of the written opinion by the international searching authority as of the date of international publication; the supplementary international search; a status report on the collaborative search; and an examination pilot project among EPO, KIPO, and USPTO and the third-party observations' system. In addition to these more practical measures to improve the PCT system, the Working Group also addressed the issue of the coordination of the technical assistance

---

116 *See* document PCT/WG/2/3.

under the PCT. For further details on those discussions, see the website of the PCT Working Group.[117]

(2) PCT IT Framework

Further, the PCT IT framework is constantly being improved: beyond further developments of existing systems like PCT-SAFE (Secure Application Filing Electronically) or PCT-ROAD (Receiving Office Administration, a demo of which was deployed in April 2012[118]), the International Bureau (IB) has continued to develop and deploy the ePCT system. The system, at this point, now allows over 6,000 registered users from over 100 different countries to use secure file inspection to access pre-publication international applications, to inspect their files online, and to perform certain operations relating to those applications. The system has also been opened to International Authorities who can now access the service for limited functionality in their roles as RO, ISA, and IPEA. Finally, preparations are underway to introduce a fully web-based filing system for PCT applications.

(3) ePCT

ePCT is the name of a number of measures aimed at the automation of various processes in the context of the filing and processing of international applications. On the one hand, national and regional offices without automation of their own will be provided with a web browser interface for communication with the International Bureau of WIPO. On the other hand, applicants will obtain the electronic means to interact with all relevant instances under the PCT (ROs, ISAs, IPEAs, etc.), so that they will be able to file international applications with a web-based application (this is already possible with applications filed directly with the RO/IB at WIPO), but also interact with the above authorities. The system aims to simplify filing by reducing formalities defects, automating various processes, and relying more on data input by offices and applicants.

(4) Priority Document Exchange Service

In order to further facilitate cooperation among intellectual property offices, WIPO has set up the WIPO Digital Access Service (DAS), which

---

117 *See* <http://www.wipo.int/meetings/en/topic.jsp?group_id=238>.

118 The demo system is available at <https://pctroad-demo.wipo.int/PCT_ROAD/indexA.do>.

is an electronic system allowing priority documents and similar documents to be securely exchanged between participating offices. The system enables applicants and offices to meet the requirements of the Paris Convention for certification in an electronic environment. Traditionally, applicants have been obliged to request certified paper copies of documents from one office and then submit those documents to other offices. The DAS allows applicants to simply request the first office (known as the depositing office or office of first filing) to make priority documents available to the system and then to request other offices (known as the accessing offices or offices of second filing) to retrieve those documents via the service.[119] The exchange of documents then takes place electronically between the offices. Such exchange by a digital library had been initiated by the PLT, which urged WIPO in its Agreed Statements adopted by the Diplomatic Conference to expedite the creation of a digital library system for priority documents.[120] As of 1 August 2013, ten National Offices, as well as the International Bureau of WIPO as a PCT Receiving Office, participate in DAS.[121]

(5) Office modernization/databases

WIPO is conducting a program on infrastructure modernization, which is intended to develop and strengthen the capacity of national and regional IP offices through the provision of various services, covering implementation of the international classifications, improving access to databases, and digitizing paper collections, in order to develop tools for facilitating the exchange and diffusion of IP information on global infrastructure. Further, the WIPO Global Information Services aims to provide services on IP information search and retrieval from databases created within the global IP infrastructure and supporting services to IP

---

[119] As of 1 July 2012, a new procedure has been introduced for accessing offices to retrieve priority documents from the service by using access codes. Applicants can provide the access code directly to the office of second filing, instead of giving that office access authorization to retrieve a priority document via the applicant portal.

[120] *See* <http://www.wipo.int/das/en/>.

[121] *See* <http://www.wipo.int/das/en/participating_offices.html>. The Framework Provisions for the Digital Access Service, which provide a legal framework for the Service, cover priority documents under Article 4 of the Paris Convention, i.e., the service is not limited to patents, but also utility models, industrial designs, and trademarks. However, at present, the service is operational for patent documents only. Documents relating to other IP rights such as industrial designs and trademarks will be exchanged through the system once the participating offices have made the necessary operational and technical changes.

offices and the public. The related activities include Access to Specialized Patent Databases; the Technology and Innovation Support Centers ("TISCs") project; Patent Landscaping project; and the digitization of national IP documents for dissemination through IP databases.

(6) WIPO CASE

WIPO CASE (Centralized Access to Search and Examination) was developed by WIPO as a technical platform to allow patent offices which so wish to securely share search and examination documentation relating to patent applications among themselves for the purposes of work-sharing with a view to increasing both efficiency and the quality of their work.[122] The development was triggered by a request from the Vancouver Group Offices (the IP offices of Australia, Canada, and the UK). The first version started in March 2011 and offered basic functions, such as application bibliographic data and document upload or simple searching by application number or publication number. Today, the examiners of the three participating offices can also exchange documents. Other offices have in the meantime expressed interest in using WIPO CASE.

Since March 2013, any patent office may join the system by notifying the International Bureau that it is willing to participate according to the Framework Provisions of the system. The office will choose whether it wishes to be a depositing office or only an accessing office and technical choices need to be made for the exchange of documents between the office and the system. For example, as of 1 August 2013, in addition to the above three offices of Vancouver Group, which participate in the system as both the accessing offices and depositing offices, the patent office of New Zealand also participates in the system, under a bilateral agreement with WIPO, as an accessing office.

---

122 *See* <http://www.wipo.int/case/en/>.

3. The non-multilateral approach to international intellectual property normsetting

Peter K. Yu[*]

INTRODUCTION

The Agreement on Trade-Related Aspects of Intellectual Property Rights (TRIPS Agreement) of the World Trade Organization (WTO) entered into force on 1 January 1995. Although developed countries obtained most of their preferred terms during the Uruguay Round of Multilateral Trade Negotiations (Uruguay Round), negotiators from less developed countries – which, in WTO parlance, include both developing and least developed countries – managed to inject ambiguities, flexibilities, limitations and exceptions into the TRIPS Agreement. As a result, the Agreement is now filled with vague, broad, undefined and result-oriented terms such as '"effective", "reasonable", "undue", "unwarranted", "fair and equitable", and "not … unnecessarily complicated or costly"'.[1] As reflected in *China – Measures Affecting the Protection and Enforcement of Intellectual Property Rights*, Part III of the TRIPS Agreement is notoriously ineffective.[2]

Immediately after the adoption of the TRIPS Agreement, commentators were quick to extol the benefits of marrying intellectual property to trade. As Michael Ryan noted, such a marriage has allowed member

---

* This chapter draws on research from the author's earlier articles in the *Drake Law Review Discourse*, *UC Davis Law Review* and *The WIPO Journal*. The author is grateful to Kyle Mendenhall for excellent research and editorial assistance.

[1] UNCTAD–ICTSD Project on Intellectual Property Rights and Sustainable Development, *Resource Book on TRIPS and Development* (CUP 2005) 576.

[2] Peter K Yu, 'TRIPS and Its Achilles' Heel' (2011) 18 *J Intellectual Property L* 479, 483–504. On this dispute, see WTO, *China – Measures Affecting the Protection and Enforcement of Intellectual Property Rights – Report of the Panel* (26 January 2009) WT/DS362/R; Peter K Yu, 'TRIPS Enforcement and Developing Countries' (2011) 26 *American U Intl L Rev* 727; Peter K Yu, 'The TRIPS Enforcement Dispute' (2011) 89 *Nebraska L Rev* 1046.

states to 'achieve treaties in diplomatically and politically difficult areas in which agreement would otherwise be elusive'.[3] Commentators have also considered the establishment of the mandatory dispute settlement process as a crowning achievement of the Uruguay Round.[4] In an interview, Jacques Gorlin even proudly declared that the Intellectual Property Committee – an ad hoc coalition of major US corporations he led that successfully lobbied for the TRIPS Agreement – obtained 95 percent of what it wanted.[5]

As developing countries approached the end of their TRIPS transition period, which was set to expire on 1 January 2000, developed countries and their rights holders began to realize the 5 percent that they failed to secure in the TRIPS negotiations would eventually haunt them. With rapid economic and technological growth in the so-called BRICS countries (Brazil, Russia, China, India and South Africa), the failure of the TRIPS Agreement to induce less developed countries to offer effective protection and enforcement of intellectual property rights has become costly and highly troublesome.

Since the early 2000s, the European Union (EU) and the United States (US) have pushed aggressively for the development of bilateral and regional trade agreements. Termed economic partnership agreements (EPAs) or free trade agreements (FTAs) by the EU and FTAs by the US, these international instruments seek to transplant intellectual property standards from the more powerful signatories to the less powerful ones. Because the intellectual property provisions in these so-called 'TRIPS-plus agreements' often mandate protections in excess of the levels required by the TRIPS Agreement and other international intellectual property agreements, they threaten to ignore the local needs, national interests, technological capabilities, institutional capacities and public health conditions of many less developed countries.

---

[3] Michael P Ryan, *Knowledge Diplomacy: Global Competition and the Politics of Intellectual Property* (Brookings Institution Press 1998) 12.

[4] For example, see Rachel Brewster, 'Shadow Unilateralism: Enforcing International Trade Law at the WTO' (2009) 30 *U Pennsylvania J Intl L* 1133, 1134; William J Davey, 'The WTO Dispute Settlement System: The First Ten Years' (2005) 8 *J Intl Economic L* 17, 32; Rochelle Cooper Dreyfuss and Andreas F Lowenfeld, 'Two Achievements of the Uruguay Round: Putting TRIPS and Dispute Settlement Together' (1997) 37 *Virginia J Intl L* 275, 275; Ruth Okediji, 'Toward an International Fair Use Doctrine' (2000) 39 *Columbia J Transnational L* 75, 149–50.

[5] Susan K Sell, *Private Power, Public Law: The Globalization of Intellectual Property Rights* (CUP 2003) 115.

In recent years, developed countries have gone even further to establish plurilateral trade, investment and intellectual property agreements that bring together developed and like-minded countries. Using an ill-advised 'country club' approach to international intellectual property normsetting, these countries have negotiated agreements ranging from the Anti-Counterfeiting Trade Agreement (ACTA) to the Trans-Pacific Partnership (TPP) Agreement to the Transatlantic Trade and Investment Partnership (TTIP) Agreement. While ACTA focuses primarily on intellectual property issues, the TPP and the TTIP cover trade and trade-related issues, including both the trade- and investment-related aspects of intellectual property rights.

To help us take stock of the many recent developments concerning bilateral, plurilateral and regional trade, investment and intellectual property agreements, this chapter examines the international intellectual property normsetting process following the expiration of the TRIPS transition period for developing countries. The chapter focuses specifically on three distinct types of non-multilateral agreements: (1) bilateral and regional trade agreements; (2) plurilateral intellectual property agreements (as illustrated by ACTA); and (3) plurilateral trade and investment agreements (as illustrated by the TPP). Using these three types of agreements as case studies, this chapter explores the strengths and weaknesses of the non-multilateral approach to international intellectual property normsetting. The chapter also explores the ramifications of an increase in non-multilateral normsetting activities in the intellectual property field.

BILATERAL AND REGIONAL TRADE AGREEMENTS

Since the turn of this millennium, the EU and the US have begun using bilateral and regional trade agreements to enhance their bargaining positions and to avoid deadlocks in international intellectual property negotiations. The need for such agreements was apparent following the collapse of the Millennium Round of Trade Negotiations in Seattle and the premature end of the Fifth WTO Ministerial Meeting in Cancún. As a result of these debacles, developed countries began searching for what Fred Bergsten described as 'competitive liberalization'.[6] Such liberalization calls for the development of preferential arrangements to liberalize

---

[6] Fred C Bergsten, 'Competitive Liberalization and Global Free Trade: A Vision for the Early 21st Century' (1996) Peterson Institute for International

trade by promoting competition among countries, especially those in small regional markets.[7]

Today, the US is a party to the North American Free Trade Agreement (NAFTA) with Canada and Mexico (concluded in 1992) and the Central America–Dominican Republic Free Trade Agreement with Costa Rica, the Dominican Republic, El Salvador, Guatemala, Honduras and Nicaragua (concluded in 2004). The US also has standalone FTAs with Australia, Bahrain, Chile, Colombia, Israel, Jordan, Morocco, Oman, Panama, Peru, Singapore and South Korea. Similarly, the EU has established EPAs or FTAs with Chile, Colombia, Mexico, Peru, South Africa, South Korea and members of the Caribbean Forum (CARIFORUM). The EU is also currently negotiating EPAs or FTAs with Canada, India, Malaysia, Singapore, Ukraine and members of both the Association of Southeast Asian Nations (ASEAN) and the Gulf Cooperation Council. Although EPAs generally provide broader coverage than FTAs, their goals are rather similar for the purposes of this chapter.[8]

In the intellectual property arena, EPAs and FTAs generally include intellectual property standards that go beyond what is required by the TRIPS Agreement or other international agreements administered by the World Intellectual Property Organization (WIPO). To illustrate the high TRIPS-plus standards found in EPAs and FTAs, consider the Australia–United States Free Trade Agreement. Adopted on 18 May 2004, this pioneering US FTA includes in Chapter 17 distinct provisions on copyrights, trademarks, patents and other forms of intellectual property rights. For example, these provisions require the contracting parties to ratify or accede to the WIPO Copyright Treaty, the WIPO Performances and Phonograms Treaty, the Patent Cooperation Treaty (PCT), the Protocol Relating to the Madrid Agreement Concerning the International Registration of Marks and the 1991 Act of the International Union for the Protection of New Varieties of Plants (UPOV), among others. They also

---

Economics Working Paper No 96-15 <http://www.iie.com/publications/wp/wp.cfm?ResearchID=171> accessed 20 January 2014.

[7] Ibid; Albert Fishlow, 'Brazil: FTA or FTAA or WTO?' in Jeffrey J Schott (ed.), *Free Trade Agreements: US Strategies and Priorities* (Institute for International Economics 2004) 277; J Clark Leith and John Whalley, 'Competitive Liberalization and a US-SACU FTA' in Schott, *Free Trade Agreements* 331; Renato Ruggiero, 'Comment' in Schott, *Free Trade Agreements* 28.

[8] For example, EPAs cover non-trade issues such as competition policy, investment, improvement of business environment, cooperation in vocational education and training, labor and product standards, environmental protection, tourism, illegal migration and the resolution of other non-economic cross-border problems.

require the parties to extend the term of copyright protection beyond the international minimum standard and to provide detailed intellectual property enforcement provisions. Article 17.4.7(a) specifically requires each party to 'provide for criminal procedures and penalties to be applied where any person is found to have engaged wilfully and for the purposes of commercial advantage or financial gain in any of the above activities'. Finally, the Agreement threatens the success and vitality of Australia's Pharmaceutical Benefits Scheme.[9] Article 17.9.4, in particular, bans the parallel importation of cheap generic drugs.

Although the EU and the US were primarily responsible for the recent push for EPAs and FTAs, large developing countries, such as China and India, have also been quite active in negotiating their own versions.[10] Consider China, for example. Since the mid 2000s, China has negotiated bilateral agreements with Chile, Pakistan, New Zealand, Singapore, Peru, Costa Rica, Iceland and Switzerland. With the ten ASEAN members, China also established a set of regional agreements, culminating in the formation of the ASEAN–China Free Trade Area.[11]

While China's FTAs are quite important to regional trade liberalization, especially in the Asia-Pacific region, they do not include many intellectual property provisions. Nor do they introduce new standards of protection or enforcement. The only exception is China's FTA with Switzerland, a country that was heavily involved in the ACTA negotiations. Even though this recently concluded agreement includes more detailed intellectual property provisions, most of them correspond to the protection levels already required by the TRIPS Agreement. Thus, from

---

[9] Cynthia M Ho, *Access to Medicine in the Global Economy: International Agreements on Patents and Related Rights* (OUP 2011) 246–7.

[10] Henry Gao, 'The RTA Strategy of China: A Critical Visit' in Ross Buckley, Vai Io Lo and Laurence Boulle (eds), *Challenges to Multilateral Trade: The Impact of Bilateral, Preferential and Regional Agreements* (Kluwer Law International 2008) 53–64; Marc Lanteigne, 'Northern Exposure: Cross-Regionalism and the China–Iceland Preferential Trade Negotiations' (2010) 202 *China Q* 362; Wang Jiangyu, 'The Role of China and India in Asian Regionalism' in Muthucumaraswamy Sornarajah and Wang Jiangyu (eds), *China, India and the International Economic Order* (CUP 2010) 333–86; Peter K Yu, 'Sinic Trade Agreements' (2011) 44 *UC Davis L Rev* 953.

[11] Wang Jiangyu, 'Association of Southeast Asian Nations–China Free Trade Agreement' in Simon Lester and Bryan Mercurio (eds), *Bilateral and Regional Trade Agreements: Case Studies* (CUP 2009) 192–225; Yu, 'Sinic Trade Agreements' (n 10) 1007–9. The ten ASEAN members are Brunei Darussalam, Cambodia, Indonesia, Laos, Malaysia, Myanmar, the Philippines, Singapore, Thailand and Vietnam.

the standpoint of international intellectual property normsetting, these agreements do not have as significant an impact as those negotiated by the EU and the US.

Strengths

The negotiation of bilateral and regional trade agreements is beneficial for six reasons. First, these agreements can drive reforms in two areas. Through the introduction of 'multilateral-plus' provisions – provisions that exceed those required by multilateral agreements, such as the TRIPS Agreement – bilateral and regional agreements can increase the scope and extent of commitments made under their multilateral counterparts. Because the latter are generally designed as 'minimum standards' agreements, countries are free to increase their commitments, provided that those additional commitments do not interfere with the agreements' most-favoured-nation (MFN) clauses or other countervailing obligations. Even better for the *demandeur* countries, by shifting the negotiations away from multilateral fora, they do not need to worry about altering positions or reopening negotiations at the WTO and WIPO.[12] By reducing the number of negotiating parties, countries can also provide side payments that they otherwise would be unable to offer in a multilateral forum.

In addition to multilateral-plus provisions, bilateral and regional trade agreements can introduce 'multilateral-extra' provisions that cover reforms that fall squarely outside the existing multilateral agreements or that have not been fully covered by those agreements.[13] In the TRIPS context, examples of multilateral-extra provisions are those calling for the establishment of a data-exclusivity regime to protect clinical trial data submitted during the regulatory approval process, the linkage of the registration of pharmaceutical products to their patent status, and the requirement that patents be granted for 'new uses', or second indications, of known compounds. Although TRIPS-plus and TRIPS-extra provisions look quite similar, their distinction is important. Because the WTO only requires the use of its mandatory process to settle disputes arising under its agreements, TRIPS-extra provisions are technically outside the WTO rules and can therefore be subjected to unilateral trade sanctions or alternative dispute resolution mechanisms.

---

[12] Jayashree Watal, *Intellectual Property Rights in the WTO and Developing Countries* (Kluwer Law International 2001) 5.

[13] Bernard M Hoekman and Petros C Mavroidis, *The World Trade Organization: Law, Economics, and Politics* (Routledge 2007) 59; Peter K Yu, 'The International Enclosure Movement' (2007) 82 *Indiana LJ* 827, 867–70.

Second, as a matter of trade strategy, bilateral and regional trade agreements can provide important entry points into regional or plurilateral networks.[14] In so doing, they allow developed countries to explore interstate relationships with a smaller number of countries. Such an arrangement helps reduce the cost and complexity of negotiating with a large number of parties or a regional body. The negotiation of regional agreements also helps countries test the feasibility of applying specific models to a particular region.

Once a web of agreements has been built, the constituent agreements can help establish norms that will eventually be consolidated through the multilateral process. As Ruth Okediji pointed out, countries may seek to 'consolidate and (perhaps improve) [sic] the gains from bilateralism' once they have developed a network of bilateral agreements that is sufficiently dense for that purpose.[15] Cho Sungjoon concurred: '[R]egionalism may contribute to multilateralism under certain circumstances through a "laboratory effect". After experiencing trial and error as well as learning-by-doing in the regional level, countries may feel confident in ratcheting these regional initiatives up to the multilateral forum.'[16] In fact, the negotiations of many key international agreements began with mini-negotiations among a small group of key, and often like-minded, players before the negotiations were finally extended to other members of the international community – the TRIPS Agreement being a very good example.

Third, bilateral and regional trade agreements enable the participating countries to speak with a louder voice. By fostering unity, the agreements increase their leverage in multilateral and regional negotiations.[17]

---

[14] Peter Drahos, 'BITs and BIPs: Bilateralism in Intellectual Property' (2001) 4 *J World Intellectual Property* 791, 794; Jason Kearns, 'United States–Morocco Free Trade Agreement' in Lester and Mercurio, *Bilateral and Regional Trade Agreements* (n 11) 146; Sidney Weintraub, 'Lessons from the Chile and Singapore Free Trade Agreements' in Schott, *Free Trade Agreements* (n 7) 79.

[15] Ruth L Okediji, 'Back to Bilateralism? Pendulum Swings in International Intellectual Property Protection' (2004) 1 *U Ottawa L & Technology J* 125, 143.

[16] Cho Sungjoon, 'A Bridge Too Far: The Fall of the Fifth WTO Ministerial Conference in Cancún and the Future of Trade Constitution' (2004) 7 *J Intl Economic L* 219, 238.

[17] Chad Damro, 'The Political Economy of Regional Trade Agreements' in Lorand Bartels and Federico Ortino (eds), *Regional Trade Agreements and the WTO Legal System* (OUP 2006) 34; Rafael Leal-Arcas, 'The European Union and New Leading Powers: Towards Partnership in Strategic Trade Policy Areas' (2009) 32 *Fordham Intl LJ* 345, 375; Peter K Yu, 'Access to Medicines, BRICS Alliances, and Collective Action' (2008) 34 *American J L & Medicine* 345, 370.

Although less developed countries are in greater need of coalitions than are developed countries, bilateral and regional trade agreements have succeeded in increasing the leverage of the latter group. For instance, Japan pushed for the development of regional preferential arrangements to 'increase [its] leverage within the WTO'.[18] The negotiation of the Treaty of Rome, which established the European Economic Community (the precursor to the EU), was 'in part motivated by European countries' desires to increase their leverage against the United States' in negotiations under the General Agreement on Tariffs and Trade (GATT).[19]

Fourth, if the negotiating parties have equal bargaining strength, bilateral and regional trade agreements can benefit these countries by harmonizing their intellectual property standards, thereby fostering common policy positions.[20] Because multilateral agreements are usually filled with compromises and diluted standards, bilateral and regional agreements can be more effective in addressing the individual concerns and circumstances of each party.[21] For example, the latter can be carefully tailored to specific local needs, interests, conditions or priorities.[22] Such tailoring will enable the agreements to 'offer a stronger "lock-in" mechanism for policy reform than the WTO, insofar as the partners involved have stronger incentives to enforce agreements'.[23] Bilateral and regional agreements can also target practices that are problematic for each party and provide expeditious solutions.[24] In addition, the negotiations of these agreements can be completed more

---

18 John Ravenhill, *Global Political Economy* (OUP 2005) 123.

19 Ibid.

20 Jeffrey J Schott, 'Free Trade Agreements: Boon or Bane of the World Trading System' in Schott, *Free Trade Agreements* (n 7) 13.

21 Anthony D'Amato and Doris Estelle Long, *International Intellectual Property Law* (Kluwer Law International 1997) 223; Tara Kalagher Giunta and Lily H Shang, 'Ownership of Information in a Global Economy' (1993) 27 *George Washington J Intl L & Economics* 327, 339; Paul Goldstein, *International Intellectual Property Law: Cases and Materials* (Foundation Press 2001) 139; Peter K Yu, 'Currents and Crosscurrents in the International Intellectual Property Regime' (2004) 38 *Loyola Los Angeles L Rev* 323, 394.

22 Giunta and Shang (n 21) 329.

23 Hoekman and Mavroidis (n 13) 59.

24 Giunta and Shang (n 21) 340; Marshall A Leaffer, 'Protecting United States Intellectual Property Abroad: Toward a New Multilateralism' (1991) 76 *Iowa L Rev* 273, 295; Ashoka Mody, 'New International Environment for Intellectual Property Rights' in Francis W Rushing and Carole Ganz Brown (eds), *Intellectual Property Rights in Science, Technology, and Economic Performance: International Comparisons* (Westview Press 1990) 225.

quickly. Such negotiations also incur lower political costs than do multilateral negotiations.[25]

Fifth, if the negotiating parties do not have equal bargaining strength, such as in North-South agreements involving both developed and less developed countries, bilateral and regional trade agreements can benefit the more powerful parties by providing them with the 'carrots and sticks' needed to induce their less powerful counterparts to change laws, policies and standards. Oftentimes, the agreements will lead to transplants from developed countries, which result in the adoption of standards preferred by the more powerful parties. If reforms based on the transplanted standards already have some support within the recipient countries or are already under consideration, the international obligations created by bilateral and regional agreements will help overcome the domestic political resistance within those countries – whether from factions in the leadership[26] or from strong industry lobbies.[27]

Sixth, bilateral and regional trade agreements allow the more powerful parties to practice a 'divide and conquer' approach to international negotiations. By enhancing the already strong bargaining positions of these parties, bilateral and regional agreements enable them to avoid the deadlocks found in multilateral negotiations without making costly compromises.[28] For instance, the EU and the US were able to use EPAs and FTAs to reward those WTO members willing to work with them while at the same time undermining the efforts by Brazil, India and other G-20 members to establish a united negotiating front for less developed

---

[25] Andrew Christie, Sophie Waller and Kimberlee Weatherall, 'Exporting the DMCA through Free Trade Agreements' in Christopher Heath and Anselm Kamperman Sanders (eds), *Intellectual Property and Free Trade Agreements* (Hart Publishing 2007) 220; Damro (n 17) 37.

[26] Michael E DeGolyer, 'Western Exposure, China Orientation: The Effects of Foreign Ties and Experience on Hong Kong' in Peter Koehn and Joseph YS Cheng (eds), *The Outlook for U.S.-China Relations Following the 1997–1998 Summits: Chinese and American Perspectives on Security, Trade and Cultural Exchange* (Chinese UP 1999) 300; Mark A Groombridge and Claude E Barfield, *Tiger by the Tail: China and the World Trade Organization* (AEI Press 1999) 41; Yu, 'The TRIPS Enforcement Dispute' (n 2) 1107.

[27] Helen Milner, 'Regional Economic Co-operation, Global Markets and Domestic Politics: A Comparison of NAFTA and the Maastricht Treaty' in William D Coleman and Geoffrey RD Underhill (eds), *Regionalism and Global Economic Integration: Europe, Asia and the Americas* (Routledge 1998) 29; Schott, 'Free Trade Agreements' (n 20) 13.

[28] Yu, 'Currents and Crosscurrents in the International Intellectual Property Regime' (n 21) 393.

countries. As former US Trade Representative (USTR) Robert Zoellick wrote in the *Financial Times*, the US would separate the 'can-do' countries from the 'won't-do', and it would 'move towards free trade with [only] can-do countries'.[29]

Weaknesses

Although bilateral and regional trade agreements can help drive the development of new intellectual property norms that will eventually be consolidated in a multilateral forum, they also raise four major concerns. The first concern relates to their potential for undermining the existing multilateral system. Instead of providing the 'building blocks' needed to strengthen or expand the system, bilateral and regional agreements can serve as 'stumbling blocks' that make it difficult for multilateral organizations to achieve their liberalization or harmonization goals.[30] For example, they can make the multilateral system less appealing and thereby undermine its stability and growth. They can also alienate a country's multilateral partners, resulting in distractions, or even disengagements, that impede the progress of multilateral discussions.[31] The lack of such progress would be a loss to the international community. Multilateral agreements are generally more stable than their bilateral and regional counterparts. These agreements are also more likely to persist in their own right even when the interests of some signatory countries have changed.[32]

Moreover, bilateral and regional trade agreements can compete directly with the multilateral system by taking away the much-needed time, resources and energies countries can devote to multilateral negotiations.[33] While both multilateral and bilateral processes could work in tandem to maximize their strengths and effectiveness, countries – especially those in the less developed world – have limited resources.[34] As a result, they may

---

[29] Robert B Zoellick, 'America Will Not Wait for the Won't-Do Countries' *Financial Times* (London, 22 September 2003) 23.

[30] Damro (n 17) 39–41; Meredith Kolsky Lewis, 'The Prisoners' Dilemma and FTAs: Applying Game Theory to Trade Liberalization Strategy' in Buckley, Lo and Boulle (n 10) 23.

[31] Peter K Yu, 'Six Secret (and Now Open) Fears of ACTA' (2011) 64 *Southern Methodist U L Rev* 975, 1078.

[32] Arthur A Stein, 'Coordination and Collaboration: Regimes in an Anarchic World' in Stephen D Krasner (ed.), *International Regimes* (Cornell UP 1983) 138.

[33] Ruggiero (n 7) 27.

[34] Damro (n 17) 38; Schott, 'Free Trade Agreements' (n 20) 15–16.

not have the ability to dedicate efforts to normsetting in a multitude of competing fora.

Even worse, because of the power asymmetry inherent in the international trading system, bilateral and regional trade agreements could create perverse incentives for the more powerful parties to 'advance self-interested agendas because they have failed to get them accepted in the WTO'.[35] Such agendas tend to impede progress made in multilateral negotiations because they seek to create agreements or structures that eventually 'become an alternative to the multilateral system and not an exception subject to some conditionality under the rules of the WTO'.[36]

The second concern involves the growing fragmentation of the international regulatory system. As Jagdish Bhagwati warned us in the mid 1990s, when the new wave of preferential trade agreements began, the push for EPAs and FTAs could lead to the creation of a 'spaghetti bowl'[37] – or, in the Asian context, a 'noodle bowl'[38] – which is filled with 'a mish-mash of overlapping, supporting, and possibly conflicting, obligations'.[39] Although fragmentation has its benefits, commentators tend to agree that it would hurt less developed countries more than it would help them. Eyal Benvenisti and George Downs, for instance, described a number of ways in which the growing proliferation of international regulatory institutions with overlapping jurisdictions and ambiguous boundaries has helped powerful states to preserve their dominance.[40]

Bilateral and regional trade agreements could also lead to what Kal Raustiala described as 'strategic inconsistencies', which 'occur … when actors deliberately seek to create inconsistency via a new rule crafted in

---

[35] Guy de Jonquières, 'Comment' in Schott, *Free Trade Agreements* (n 7) 32.

[36] Ruggiero (n 7) 27.

[37] Jagdish Bhagwati, 'U.S. Trade Policy: The Infatuation with Free Trade Areas' in Jagdish Bhagwati and Anne O Krueger, *The Dangerous Drift to Preferential Trade Agreements* (AEI Press 1995) 2–3.

[38] Richard Baldwin, 'Managing the Noodle Bowl: The Fragility of East Asian Regionalism' (2008) 53 *Singapore Economic Rev* 449; Wang, 'Association of Southeast Asian Nations–China Free Trade Agreement' (n 11) 224.

[39] Simon Lester and Bryan Mercurio, 'Introduction' in Lester and Mercurio, *Bilateral and Regional Trade Agreements* (n 11) 2.

[40] Eyal Benvenisti and George W Downs, 'The Empire's New Clothes: Political Economy and the Fragmentation of International Law' (2007) 60 *Stanford L Rev* 595, 597–8.

another forum in an effort to alter or put pressure on an earlier rule'.[41] The more bilateral and regional agreements there are, the more opportunities there will be for powerful and geopolitically savvy countries to develop such inconsistencies. Indeed, a web of bilateral and regional trade agreements could create conflicting obligations within many less developed countries. It is bad enough to be forced to sign a bilateral or regional trade agreement that does not meet local conditions. It is even worse to be put in a position where they have to juggle two or more conflicting, or at least potentially conflicting, agreements that equally ignore local conditions.

The third concern is a direct result of the power asymmetry found in the existing international trading system. Because of such asymmetry, bilateral and regional trade agreements are likely to perpetuate, or even exacerbate, the already highly vulnerable position of less developed countries.[42] By taking away these countries' ability to form coalitions,[43] these agreements and their 'divide and conquer' approach have made less developed countries even more vulnerable than they would be in a multilateral setting.[44] Without the support of other coalition members, many less developed countries simply do not have the leverage needed to negotiate agreements that are appropriate for their needs, interests, conditions and priorities.

As mentioned earlier, when the negotiating parties do not have equal bargaining strength, bilateral and regional trade agreements tend to result in the transplant of intellectual property standards from developed to less developed countries. These transplants are harmful for many reasons.[45] For example, they tend to ignore the local needs, national interests, technological capabilities, institutional capacities and public health conditions of less developed countries. They may also stifle local development, especially when the development paths of the recipient countries do not align with those of the source countries. Without taking full

---

[41] Kal Raustiala, 'Density and Conflict in International Intellectual Property Law' (2007) 40 *UC Davis L Rev* 1021, 1027–8.

[42] Yu, 'The International Enclosure Movement' (n 13) 886–92.

[43] Yu, 'Access to Medicines, BRICS Alliances, and Collective Action' (n 17) 370–87; Peter K Yu, 'Building Intellectual Property Coalitions for Development' in Jeremy de Beer (ed.), *Implementing the World Intellectual Property Organization's Development Agenda* (Wilfred Laurier UP 2009) 79–99.

[44] William Davey, 'Dispute Settlement in the WTO and RTAs: A Comment' in Bartels and Ortino (n 17) 356; Lewis, 'The Prisoners' Dilemma and FTAs' (n 30) 26; Schott, 'Free Trade Agreements' (n 20) 16.

[45] Yu, 'The International Enclosure Movement' (n 13) 889–91.

account of the internal problems, potential conflicts and lack of correction mechanisms in the recipient countries, bilateral and regional agreements may even transplant problems from abroad, thus exacerbating the problems they sought to address. Given their many weaknesses, transplant-inducing agreements are likely to form bad precedents for future multilateral efforts and thereby harm both the recipient countries and the international trading system.[46]

More problematic, North-South agreements often force less developed countries to discard many hard-earned bargains they won through the multilateral negotiation process.[47] For instance, less developed countries may have to give up procedural and substantive safeguards and flexibilities that were built into the multilateral system to provide balance and promote the public interest.[48] In the WTO context, the omission of these important safeguards and flexibilities can be compared, to some extent, to a revision of the TRIPS Agreement without going through its carefully designed amendment process. Such revision, in effect, allows the more powerful countries to pick and choose the desirable parts of the multilateral arrangement while abandoning those they reluctantly adopted out of compromise.

Even worse, because developed countries often sold bilateral and regional trade agreements as preferential agreements, they put considerable pressure on those who failed to join the network of agreements. Given the asymmetry in the international trading system, few less developed countries would be able to reject an offer to enter into an agreement with their more powerful trading partners.[49] Many, in fact, fear that they will be left out, creating what Chad Damro described as the 'marginalization syndrome'.[50] As former WTO Director-General Mike Moore observed: 'Despite all I've written about the perils of unilateralism and bilateralism, I'd be doing it if I were in government. There's a terrible cost to being left out.'[51]

The final concern is that those powerful countries that succumb to pressure from domestic trade groups may introduce provisions that are

---

46 Schott, 'Free Trade Agreements' (n 20) 16.

47 Okediji, 'Back to Bilateralism?' (n 15) 129.

48 Yu, 'Six Secret (and Now Open) Fears of ACTA' (n 31) 1059–66.

49 Robin Gross, *IP Justice White Paper on the Proposed Anti-Counterfeiting Trade Agreement (ACTA)* (IP Justice 2008) 2.

50 Damro (n 17) 30.

51 Mike Moore, 'Preferential, Not Free Trade Deals' *Gulf News* (23 April 2007) <http://gulfnews.com/opinions/columnists/preferential-not-free-trade-deals-1.173593> accessed 20 January 2014.

considered highly unpopular at home, due in large part to the failure of the international trading system to provide the same type of safeguard and accountability as is normally found in a domestic process.[52] In fact, depending on the political structure, politicians may pursue bilateralism and regionalism 'to increase their chances of being re-elected'.[53] Short-term domestic political payoffs may therefore create perverse incentives that ultimately undermine the integrity and health of the existing multilateral system.

Although multilateralism can create the same perverse effects, bilateral and regional trade agreements greatly increase these effects and the associated risks. Because of reduced complexity, a more narrow focus and the self-selected nature of the negotiating process, it is usually easier to communicate the benefits of an EPA or FTA to domestic constituents than it would be to communicate the identical or equivalent benefits of a multilateral agreement.[54] As a result, politicians may prefer to 'pursue regional liberalization at the expense of multilateral liberalization'.[55] They may also 'try to preempt the "erosion" of their margins of preference by dragging their feet on WTO reforms'.[56]

Even worse, the lack of accountability and the political payoffs of a successful international agreement may tempt politicians to engage in what I have called 'backdoor lawmaking' – 'a process of outsourcing the legislative process to an international forum of unelected representatives in an effort to create laws that the domestic legislature would not have otherwise enacted'.[57] Through this backdoor process, the administration can present to the legislature a *fait accompli* in an attempt to make an end run around the domestic deliberative process. The new-found international obligation will greatly increase the likelihood of having the laws enacted, even though those laws would not have been enacted based on evaluation of local needs alone. After all, when the country's international reputation is on the line, the stakes in not adopting laws to implement the agreement are much higher.

---

[52] Peter K Yu, 'The Political Economy of Data Protection' (2010) 84 *Chicago-Kent L Rev* 777, 788–91.

[53] Damro (n 17) 37.

[54] Ibid.

[55] Ibid., 24.

[56] Schott, 'Free Trade Agreements' (n 20) 14.

[57] Peter K Yu, 'Anticircumvention and Anti-Anticircumvention' (2006) 84 *Denver U L Rev* 13, 54–5. On policy laundering, see Yu, 'The Political Economy of Data Protection' (n 52) 788–91.

In sum, bilateral and regional trade agreements have both strengths and weaknesses. Whether they will be beneficial ultimately depends on 'how the [agreements] are crafted and the volume of trade covered, who participates, and whether significant progress on multilateral reforms proceeds in tandem in the WTO' or other multilateral regimes.[58]

PLURILATERAL INTELLECTUAL PROPERTY AGREEMENTS

While the EU and the US have been actively negotiating EPAs or FTAs, they have also worked closely with other developed and like-minded countries to develop a new plurilateral intellectual property agreement known as ACTA. The intent to negotiate this highly controversial agreement was announced in October 2007, two weeks after WIPO adopted its recommendations for the Development Agenda.[59] As the USTR formally declared in the press release:

> [T]he goal [of the new agreement] is to set a new, higher benchmark for enforcement that countries can join on a voluntary basis. … The envisioned ACTA will include commitments in three areas: (1) strengthening international cooperation, (2) improving enforcement practices, and (3) providing a strong legal framework for [intellectual property] enforcement.[60]

Following the announcement, 11 rounds of negotiations were held over a span of close to three years, and 39 (and later 37) countries participated in the negotiations.[61] While countries were initially worried about ACTA's inconsistencies with their existing laws and international treaty obligations, the Agreement was adopted on 15 April 2011. A few months

[58] Schott, 'Free Trade Agreements' (n 20) 4–5.

[59] On the WIPO Development Agenda, see Peter K Yu, 'A Tale of Two Development Agendas' (2009) 35 *Ohio Northern U L Rev 465*, 515–22.

[60] Office of the United States Trade Representative, 'Ambassador Schwab Announces U.S. Will Seek New Trade Agreement to Fight Fakes' <http://www.ustr.gov/ambassador-schwab-announces-us-will-seek-new-trade-agreement-fight-fakes> accessed 20 January 2014.

[61] In addition to Japan, the US and the EU – the usual trilateral alliance for strengthening intellectual property protection – the negotiating parties included Australia, Canada, Mexico, Morocco, New Zealand, Singapore, South Korea and Switzerland. Although Jordan and the United Arab Emirates also participated in the first round of the negotiations, they did not continue afterwards. 'EU ACTA Negotiator Confirms EU Wants Patent Provisions in ACTA' *Inside US Trade* (8 May 2009) 11.

later, eight countries – Australia, Canada, Japan, Morocco, New Zealand, Singapore, South Korea and the US – signed the Agreement at a ceremony in Japan. In preparation to join the TPP negotiations, Mexico also signed the Agreement in July 2012.

In its final form, ACTA contains six different chapters: (1) initial provisions and definitions; (2) legal framework for enforcement of intellectual property rights; (3) enforcement practices; (4) international cooperation; (5) institutional arrangements; and (6) final provisions. Chapter II, which is the longest of all six chapters, is subdivided into five different sections: (a) general obligations; (b) civil enforcement; (c) border measures; (d) criminal enforcement; and (e) enforcement of intellectual property rights in the digital environment. The last section on digital intellectual property enforcement has been especially controversial.

As of this writing, Switzerland and five EU members (Cyprus, Estonia, Germany, the Netherlands and Slovakia) have refrained from signing the Agreement. In June 2012, the European Parliament further rejected ACTA, marking the first time its Committee on International Trade struck down a trade agreement.[62] Because Article 40.1 states that ACTA will not enter into force until six countries have deposited their instruments of ratification, it remains unclear if and when this Agreement will enter into force. Thus far, Japan is the only country to have ratified ACTA.

Strengths

Commentators, including this volume's editor and I, have described ACTA as a 'country club agreement'.[63] As Daniel Gervais elaborated: 'I refer to this approach as "Country Club" because, like a country club, the membership rules are negotiated by a number of like-minded founders. Others are then invited to join, but changes to the membership rules are

---

62 Monika Ermert, 'Unprecedented Vote: EU Parliament Trade Committee Rejects ACTA' (*Intellectual Property Watch*, 21 June 2012) <http://www.ip-watch.org/2012/06/21/unprecedented-vote-eu-parliament-trade-committee-rejects-acta/> accessed 20 January 2014.

63 Daniel Gervais, 'Country Clubs, Empiricism, Blogs and Innovation: The Future of International Intellectual Property Norm Making in the Wake of ACTA' in Mira Burri and Thomas Cottier (eds), *Trade Governance in the Digital Age* (CUP 2012) 324; Peter K Yu, 'The ACTA/TPP Country Clubs' in Dana Beldiman (ed.), *Access to Information and Knowledge: 21st Century Challenges in Intellectual Property and Knowledge Governance* (Edward Elgar Publishing 2014) 258–83.

difficult to achieve.'[64] Under the current club rules, the agreement will be administered and managed by an organizational structure known as the ACTA Committee.[65] Article 36 grants the committee broad powers to establish ad hoc committees or working groups. Article 42 delineates the procedure for amending the agreement. And Article 43 specifies the time the agreement will be open for signature and how countries can accede to it after the expiration of the specified period.

Although policymakers and commentators have widely criticized the country club approach used by the ACTA negotiating parties, the use of clubs to coordinate international regulatory standards is neither unprecedented nor without merit. Less developed countries, for example, have frequently used coalitions to shape their negotiating agenda, articulate more coherent positions and establish a united negotiating front.[66] Through the use of these coalitions, less developed countries are able to achieve leverage that otherwise would not have existed for each country on its own.

Even for developed countries, the use of club arrangements, while rare in view of their considerable geopolitical and economic strengths, is not unheard of. In *All Politics Is Global*, Daniel Drezner advanced a typology of regulatory coordination based on the variations between the costs of adjusting national regulatory standards confronting 'great powers' and those confronting the rest of the world.[67] This typology identifies four types of international regulatory standards: (1) harmonized standards; (2) sham standards; (3) rival standards; and (4) club standards (see Table 3.1).[68]

---

[64] Gervais, 'Country Clubs, Empiricism, Blogs and Innovation' (n 63) 324.

[65] Peter K Yu, 'The ACTA Committee' in Pedro Roffe and Xavier Seuba (eds), *ACTA and the Plurilateral Enforcement Agenda: Genesis and Aftermath* (CUP 2014) (forthcoming).

[66] Yu, 'Access to Medicines, BRICS Alliances, and Collective Action' (n 17) 370; Yu, 'Building Intellectual Property Coalitions for Development' (n 43) 81.

[67] Daniel W Drezner, *All Politics Is Global: Explaining International Regulatory Regimes* (Princeton UP 2008) 119–48. Drezner defines 'great powers' as those having 'a combination of internal market size and reduced vulnerability to external disruptions': ibid., 35. Only the EU and the US fit his criteria at the moment: ibid., 36.

[68] Ibid., 71–85.

Table 3.1 A typology of regulatory coordination

	High adjustment costs (The rest)	Low adjustment costs (The rest)
High adjustment costs (Great powers)	Sham standards	Rival standards
Low adjustment costs (Great powers)	Club standards	Harmonized standards

Source: Daniel W Drezner, *All Politics Is Global: Explaining International Regulatory Regimes* (Princeton UP 2008) 72.

According to Professor Drezner, club standards tend to emerge when adjustment costs are low for great powers but high for the rest of the world. As he explained:

> [a] great power concert will generate enough market power to lock in the concert's preferred set of regulatory standards. The combined market size of a great power concert will induce most recalcitrant states into shifting their standards. However, states with severe adjustment costs will still resist, and the Prisoner's Dilemma aspect of enforcement can tempt some governments into noncompliance; under this constellation of interests, the enforcement of standards becomes an issue. The crucial step for coordination to take place is a coalition of the willing among the greater powers.[69]

Although less developed countries and their supportive commentators have widely criticized the arbitrariness and exclusiveness of club standards, those standards have been used in other fields of international law. In 1989, the Group of Seven (G-7) established the Financial Action Task Force in the Paris Summit to combat money laundering (and later terrorist financing).[70] In the early 1990s, this task force was extended to countries in the Organisation for Economic Cooperation and Development (OECD) as well as to a select group of non-OECD economies, such as Hong Kong and Singapore, and to regional organizations, such as the Gulf Cooperation Council.[71]

---

69 Ibid., 75.

70 Heba M Shams, '"Club Multilateralism" and Global Supranationalism: The Case of FATF' in JB Attanasio and JJ Norton (eds), *Multilateralism v Unilateralism: Policy Choices in a Global Society* (British Institute of International and Comparative Law 2004) 461.

71 Ibid., 464.

While club standards have not been widely used in the intellectual property arena, one could arguably trace the development of the TRIPS Agreement back to a two-stage process involving these standards. The first stage took place when the US, the European Communities and Japan banded together to develop 'highest common denominator' standards for the protection and enforcement of intellectual property rights.[72] After these standards had been accepted, the second stage kicked in when these trading powers sought to multilateralize the standards by extending them to other members of the GATT, and later the WTO.

While many have considered the developed countries' use of club standards undemocratic and inequitable, the standards' more effective outcomes can justify such use.[73] As Moisés Naím, the former editor in chief of *Foreign Policy*, noted: 'a smart multilateral approach to illicit trade has to be selective.'[74] In the context of this chapter, the illicit trade he referred to is the illicit trade in pirated and counterfeit goods. Club standards can also help to avoid gridlocked situations where developed and less developed countries fail to achieve progress in multilateral negotiations – the notorious stalemate over the revision of the Paris Convention being a good example.[75]

Finally, the club arrangement found in ACTA may simply reflect the geopolitical reality behind international intellectual property negotiations. Regardless of which forum is ultimately used, countries – especially the weaker ones – rarely participate equally in the development of multilateral standards, due in part to their lack of resources, capacity and bargaining power. Even during the TRIPS negotiations, the discussions were dominated by developed countries and a small group of hardliner developing countries such as Argentina, Brazil, Cuba, Egypt, India, Nicaragua, Nigeria, Peru, Tanzania and Yugoslavia.[76] Participation by less developed countries remained rather limited. Thus, when criticizing ACTA for its country club approach, we need to keep in mind the present conditions of international intellectual property negotiations.

---

72 Daniel J Gervais, 'The TRIPS Agreement and the Doha Round: History and Impact on Economic Development' in Peter K Yu (ed.), *Intellectual Property and Information Wealth: Issues and Practices in the Digital Age*, vol 4 (Praeger Publishers 2007) 43.

73 Drezner (n 67) 75; Yu, 'Access to Medicines, BRICS Alliances, and Collective Action' (n 17) 384.

74 Moisés Naím, *Illicit: How Smugglers, Traffickers, and Copycats Are Hijacking the Global Economy* (Anchor Books 2005) 255.

75 Yu, 'A Tale of Two Development Agendas' (n 59) 508–11.

76 Watal (n 12) 19, fn 17.

Weaknesses

Although club standards can be beneficial from the international-normsetting standpoint, ACTA does not provide any major benefits to the multilateral intellectual property regime. As I noted in earlier works, the agreement is flawed not because it is a country club agreement, but also because it is a bad country club agreement.[77] Specifically, it failed to include in the negotiation process those countries that have a significant impact on the issue area. It also offers neither carrots nor sticks – the standard means to induce compliance in a regulatory environment that has no super-governmental enforcement arm.

Even worse, ACTA has been widely criticized for a lack of legitimacy, transparency, accountability and inclusiveness, and for its potential harm to consumers, small and mid-sized businesses, and the multilateral intellectual property regime.[78] It has also been criticized for the multiple threats it has posed to access to information and knowledge and the protection of free speech, free press, privacy, due process and other civil liberties. In addition, as China and India noted at the June 2010 meeting of the WTO Council for Trade-Related Aspects of Intellectual Property Rights, ACTA has raised a wide variety of systemic problems within the international trading system.[79] While its heightened enforcement standards will upset the delicate balance struck during the TRIPS negotiations, the agreement itself will increase the incoherence and unpredictability of the international regulatory framework.

In discussing club standards, commentators have widely noted the need to include in the negotiation process those countries that have a significant impact on the issue area. Consider, for instance, the standards for international financial regulation established by the G-7 and the OECD. Because all the important players in the field belong to one of the two organizations, club standards are strategically chosen to enable powerful developed countries to establish high standards without the worry of dilution by marginal players. Once these standards have been established, an important goal is to expand the club to outside players.[80]

---

77 Yu, 'ACTA and Its Complex Politics' (2011) 3 *WIPO J* 2; Yu 'Six Secret (and Now Open) Fears of ACTA' (n 31) 1074–83.

78 Peter K Yu, 'The Alphabet Soup of Transborder Intellectual Property Enforcement' (2012) 60 *Drake L Rev Discourse* 16, 20–3.

79 Council for Trade-Related Aspects of Intellectual Property Rights (2010), 'Minutes of Meeting: Held in the Centre William Rappard on 8–9 June 2010' (4 October 2011) IP/C/M/63 [248]–[273].

80 Drezner (n 67) 75–6.

Over the years, clubs have adjusted their membership to accommodate changing geopolitical and economic circumstances. For example, in the wake of the recent global economic crisis and in response to the rise of the BRICS countries, developed countries smartly redesigned their normsetting approach. By initiating discussions in the so-called G-20, which includes emerging countries such as Argentina, Brazil, China, India, Indonesia, Mexico, Russia, Saudi Arabia and South Africa, the G-7 countries successfully expanded the 'club' in the area of international financial regulation to cover new players that have increasingly significant impacts in the field. Such an expansion is unsurprising. After all, it is hard to imagine how the club could effectively respond to the sovereign debt crisis without the cooperation of powerful emerging economies.

To some extent, the transformation of the GATT to the WTO reveals a similar need to adapt to changing circumstances. In the beginning, the GATT, like the G-7, 'was perceived of as a "rich nations' club," focusing on the needs of the developed nations, though some of the more prominent developing nations such as Brazil and India played a role'.[81] Most other less developed countries merely received special and differential treatment. Today, however, the WTO consists of 159 members, including three different groups of countries (developed, developing and least developed). Although the TRIPS Agreement includes transition periods for both developing and least developed countries, these two groups still take on key obligations concerning the protection and enforcement of intellectual property rights, similar to those assumed by developed countries.

Notwithstanding the insights and lessons provided by these helpful precedents, ACTA fails to follow the formula for success for developing club standards. While the agreement was ambitiously designed to include high standards, similar to those international financial regulatory standards established by the G-7 or the OECD, the agreement does not include all the important players in the field of intellectual property enforcement. Notably excluded from the ACTA negotiations were Brazil, China and Russia – key players whose cooperation is badly needed to reduce cross-border piracy and counterfeiting.

Even worse, unlike the other club standards discussed in this chapter, ACTA has a very limited ability to induce other countries to join the club

[81] John H Barton, Judith L Goldstein, Timothy E Josling and Richard H Steinberg, *The Evolution of the Trade Regime: Politics, Law, and Economics of the GATT and the WTO* (Princeton UP 2006) 153.

after its formation. A case in point is China. The negotiating parties made a conscious and determined choice to exclude China from the negotiations from the very beginning. Such exclusion makes sense from the standpoint of these parties. After all, the massive piracy and counterfeiting problems in China provided one of the main reasons for developing new TRIPS-plus international intellectual property enforcement norms. Nevertheless, if China had been branded as unwelcome to this exclusive club, it is unclear how the ACTA members could now entice China to join this new club.

While the exclusion of China is problematic, though understandable, the exclusion of all other BRICS countries was disastrous. Like China, Brazil and India were excluded from the negotiations from the very beginning. As of this writing, neither country has shown an urgent desire to join the agreement. Nor have they found the ACTA club membership attractive. As Anand Sharma, the Indian commerce and industry minister, emphatically declared: 'If [the TRIPS Agreement] has to be revisited in any stage in [the] future, it will be only in multilateral forum – the WTO, it cannot be done outside.'[82] Likewise, Brazilian officials refused to 'recognize the legitimacy of the treaty'.[83]

The reactions of Brazil, China and India are not surprising. In today's age, these increasingly powerful developing countries are unlikely to buy into a system they did not help to shape. With their now considerably increased economic power and geopolitical leverage, those days where a system could be created in the developed world and then shoved down their throats are long gone. If 'enhanced international cooperation and more effective international enforcement' are some of ACTA's key goals, as the agreement states in its preamble, it is simply ill-advised to ignore these crucial partners in the negotiations. It is also short-sighted to consider countries 'unclubbable' by virtue of their lack of like-mindedness.

Compared to Brazil, China and India, small developing or least developed countries do not have the same bargaining leverage vis-à-vis the EU or the US. Nevertheless, it is still unclear how effective ACTA will actually be in inducing these countries to adopt higher intellectual property enforcement standards. After all, those countries that are overly

---

[82] 'India Will Not Accept Any Intellectual Property Talks Outside WTO: Anand Sharma' *Economic Times* (9 April 2011) <http://articles.economictimes.indiatimes.com/2011-04-09/news/29400634_1_intellectual-property-trips-agreement-anand-sharma> accessed 20 January 2014.

[83] Michael Geist, 'Brazil, India Speak out against ACTA' (12 October 2010) <http://www.michaelgeist.ca/content/view/5362/196/> accessed 20 January 2014.

eager to obtain trade benefits from the EU or the US are likely to agree to ACTA-like standards in non-multilateral agreements regardless of whether ACTA is adopted. By contrast, those countries that remain on the fence and that have enough power to resist pressure from the EU or the US are unlikely to find ACTA attractive. The reason is simple: ACTA offers neither carrots nor sticks.

The two 'carrots' that developed countries typically dangle in front of less developed countries to entice them to offer stronger protection and enforcement of intellectual property rights are: (1) increased foreign direct investment (FDI); and (2) accelerated transfer of technology. After more than 15 years of disillusionment in the TRIPS Agreement, many less developed countries have begun to realize that the oft-presented 'carrots' may be illusory. For instance, economists have widely questioned the link between intellectual property protection and FDI.[84] As noted economist Keith Maskus reminded us, if stronger intellectual property protection always led to more FDI, 'recent FDI flows to developing economies would have gone largely to sub-Saharan Africa and Eastern Europe … [rather than] China, Brazil, and other high-growth, large-market developing economies with weak [intellectual property rights]'.[85] Less developed countries are also keenly aware of the developed countries' long-standing failure to respect technology transfer obligations in international intellectual property agreements. Although the Doha Ministerial Decision of 14 November 2001 reaffirmed the mandatory nature of obligations explicitly stated in Article 66.2 of the TRIPS Agreement, developed countries have yet to take these obligations seriously. Thus, whether in the form of FDI or technology transfer, ACTA does not offer any attractive carrot.

The 'stick' that developed countries typically use in response to low intellectual property standards involves unilateral sanctions. However, in *United States – Sections 301–310 of the Trade Act of 1974*, the WTO dispute-settlement panel made it clear that members are not allowed to use sanctions to resolve TRIPS-related disputes until they have exhausted

---

[84] Peter K Yu, 'Intellectual Property, Economic Development, and the China Puzzle' in Daniel J Gervais (ed.), *Intellectual Property, Trade and Development: Strategies to Optimize Economic Development in a TRIPS Plus Era* (OUP 2007) 176–80.

[85] Keith E Maskus, 'The Role of Intellectual Property Rights in Encouraging Foreign Direct Investment and Technology Transfer' (1998) 9 *Duke J Comparative & Intl L* 109, 129.

all the remedies permissible under WTO rules.[86] Because ACTA is designed as a TRIPS-plus agreement and covers rights falling largely within the scope of the TRIPS Agreement, unilateral sanctions are unlikely to constitute a permissible 'stick'. To be certain, the US could still rely on the monitoring mechanism in section 301 of the Trade Act of 1974 to punish those countries that have failed to abide by ACTA standards. Nevertheless, without the teeth provided by unilateral sanctions, the section 301 process is at best a shaming device.[87]

In sum, by leaving out the key parties needed for cooperation and by providing neither carrots nor sticks to induce non-members to subsequently join the agreement, ACTA has failed dismally even as a country club agreement. Policymakers, commentators and the public at large criticized ACTA not only because of its non-transparent and undemocratic negotiation process, but also because of its inherent design flaws.[88] Given these many well-documented weaknesses and other negative side-effects, one cannot help but wonder why countries negotiated ACTA in the first place.

PLURILATERAL TRADE AND INVESTMENT AGREEMENTS

While the US was actively completing the ACTA negotiations, it also began negotiating the TPP with other countries in the Asia-Pacific region. This Agreement began as a quadrilateral agreement between Brunei Darussalam, Chile, New Zealand and Singapore, known as the Trans-Pacific Strategic Economic Partnership Agreement or more commonly as the 'P4' or 'Pacific 4'.[89] In March 2010, shortly before the eighth round of the ACTA negotiations in Wellington, New Zealand, the TPP negotiations began among Australia, Peru, Vietnam, the United States and the existing members for an expanded agreement. Since then, Malaysia, Mexico, Canada and Japan joined the negotiations.

---

[86] WTO, *United States: Sections 301–310 of the Trade Act of 1974 – Report of the Panel* (22 December 1999) WT/DS152/R.

[87] Yu, 'Sinic Trade Agreements' (n 10) 970.

[88] Peter K Yu, 'Enforcement, Enforcement, What Enforcement?' (2012) 52 *IDEA* 239, 256–61.

[89] Meredith Kolsky Lewis (2009), 'Expanding the P-4 Trade Agreement into a Broader Trans-Pacific Partnership: Implications, Risks and Opportunities' (2009) 4 *Asian J WTO & Intl Health L & Policy* 401, 403–4.

It is anticipated that the TPP will include an intellectual property chapter, similar to those intellectual property chapters found in existing US FTAs. As the USTR stated in its update on the TPP negotiations in November 2011:

> TPP countries have agreed to reinforce and develop existing [TRIPS] rights and obligations to ensure an effective and balanced approach to intellectual property rights among the TPP countries. Proposals are under discussion on many forms of intellectual property, including trademarks, geographical indications, copyright and related rights, patents, trade secrets, data required for the approval of certain regulated products, as well as intellectual property enforcement and genetic resources and traditional knowledge. TPP countries have agreed to reflect in the text a shared commitment to the Doha Declaration on TRIPS and Public Health.[90]

As of this writing, the draft text of the TPP intellectual property chapter has yet to be disclosed except through *WikiLeaks*. Although it remains unclear what intellectual property standards will ultimately be included in the TPP intellectual property chapter, the provisions in this new plurilateral agreement are likely to be more restrictive than those found in ACTA.[91] It is also worth noting that the TPP will include an investment chapter. Because intellectual property can be considered an investment, the TPP will likely provide coverage that is similar to what is found in bilateral and regional trade agreements with investment chapters.

Strengths

Compared with ACTA, the TPP is a much better country club agreement. Like its predecessor, the TPP involves only a very small number of countries. That number is actually smaller than the 39 countries involved in the ACTA negotiations, due in large part to the lack of participation of the 28-country-strong EU. Unlike ACTA, however, the TPP is more inclusive. Before Canada, Mexico and Japan joined the negotiations, more than half of the negotiating parties were outside the OECD. Based on the 2011 World Bank indicators, the GDPs per capita of Malaysia, Peru and Vietnam were $9,656, $6,009 and $1,411, respectively. Even the

---

[90] Office of the United States Trade Representative, 'Outlines of the Trans-Pacific Partnership Agreement' <http://www.ustr.gov/about-us/press-office/fact-sheets/2011/november/outlines-trans-pacific-partnership-agreement> accessed 20 January 2014.

[91] Yu, 'The Alphabet Soup of Transborder Intellectual Property Enforcement' (n 78) 27.

figures for Chile and Mexico, two OECD members, were only $14,394 and $10,064, respectively. The TPP would therefore strike a better balance between developed and less developed countries, even though the negotiations continue to exclude major developing countries such as Brazil, China and India.[92]

The TPP is also more successful than ACTA in providing the 'carrots' needed to facilitate constructive bargaining among the negotiating parties. While the former focuses narrowly on intellectual property protection and enforcement, the latter is trade-based and has a much broader scope. Because the negotiations involve more cross-cutting issues, US negotiators will be able to offer 'carrots' that they could not provide during the ACTA negotiations. For example, New Zealand may find it beneficial to make greater concessions in the intellectual property area if the US is willing to allow for more exports in dairy, lamb, wool and other sheep products. The same can be said of Vietnam and, to a lesser extent, Malaysia in regard to US concessions in textiles. In sum, because countries have a stronger ability to bargain in both directions, the TPP may ultimately end up being a better and fairer arrangement than ACTA, even for those countries with limited negotiation resources and bargaining chips.

Weaknesses

Notwithstanding these improvements over ACTA, the TPP is problematic in three different ways. First, the TPP is likely to be more dangerous than ACTA from the standpoint of protecting free speech, free press, privacy, due process and other civil liberties. Because of the different values that negotiating parties place on trade and trade-related items, some parties may be willing to concede more on intellectual property protection and enforcement in exchange for greater benefits in other trade or trade-related areas. The final TPP text could therefore end up with intellectual property standards going beyond those aspired to by the ACTA negotiators – standards some commentators have described as 'ACTA-plus'.[93]

---

[92] If these large developing countries were eventually allowed to join the negotiations, TPP would strike an even better balance between developed and developing countries.

[93] For example, see Susan K Sell, 'TRIPS Was Never Enough: Vertical Forum Shifting, FTAs, ACTA, and TPP' (2011) 18 *J Intellectual Property L* 447, 464; Yu, 'Six Secret (and Now Open) Fears of ACTA' (n 31) 1039–44.

Having such high standards in the TPP is especially likely considering the greater political and economic leverage the US has over the TPP negotiating partners than the partners in the ACTA negotiations.[94] Although ACTA brought together two major intellectual property powers – the EU and the US – the continuous disagreements between these two powers resulted in the adoption of a rather moderate agreement. For example, the US wanted to have stronger mandates concerning digital intellectual property enforcement; yet the EU was not ready to agree to provisions that the Union had not yet harmonized, such as those concerning the introduction of a graduated response system or safe harbours for online service providers.[95] Similarly, although the EU pushed hard for the inclusion of criminal liability for infringement for all forms of intellectual property (including, most notably, geographical indications), the US was reluctant to provide such a broad coverage.[96]

Thus, the dynamics of the TPP negotiations have been rather different from those involving ACTA. Without the EU at the negotiation table, the US is able to rely more on its sheer economic and geopolitical strengths to push for provisions that are in the interest of its intellectual property industries. From increased enforcement in the digital environment to greater protection of pharmaceutical products, the TPP is likely to track more closely to the high US standards than to the compromised standards developed in ACTA. In fact, if the US needs to strike compromises in the TPP negotiations, those compromises are likely to be found in other trade-related areas, not in the intellectual property area.

In an earlier article, I identified a number of additional factors that could make the TPP more dangerous from a public-interest standpoint than is ACTA.[97] For instance, the TPP will likely include newer and more draconian provisions that have already been rejected by ACTA negotiators or that have not yet been proposed. The TPP may also garner very limited attention from the mainstream media and the public at large, due in large part to the highly technical nature of its trade-based negotiations. Thus, even though the TPP is a better country club agreement, it is also a

---

94 Such leverage has diminished considerably following the entry of Canada and Japan into the negotiations.

95 Yu, 'Six Secret (and Now Open) Fears of ACTA' (n 31) 1055–7.

96 Monika Ermert, 'European Commission on ACTA: TRIPS Is Floor Not Ceiling' (*Intellectual Property Watch*, 22 April 2009) <http://www.ip-watch.org/2009/04/22/european-commission-on-acta-trips-is-floor-not-ceiling/> accessed 20 January 2014.

97 Yu, 'The Alphabet Soup of Transborder Intellectual Property Enforcement' (n 78) 24–8.

more dangerous plurilateral agreement. To some extent, its strength in not having the negotiations dominated by a number of developed countries is also its major weakness.

The second concern in regard to the TPP is that the instrument includes not only an intellectual property chapter but also an investment chapter (similar to bilateral and regional trade agreements discussed above). As a result, the TPP can cover the investment-related aspects of intellectual property rights that are not found in ACTA or the intellectual property chapter in an EPA, an FTA or even the TPP.

Because complaints involving the intellectual property provisions in bilateral and regional investment agreements have only surfaced recently, the scope of intellectual property rights covered by these agreements remains unclear.[98] Nevertheless, a plain-meaning approach to treaty interpretation is generally supported by the fact that intellectual property rights are listed as an example of a covered investment, as in the case of the TPP. Even if those rights are not explicitly listed as an example, the term 'investment' is usually broadly defined to cover both registered and unregistered intellectual property rights as well as the licensing, and perhaps even applications, of those rights.[99] The leaked draft of the TPP investment chapter, for example, defines 'investment' to cover 'every asset that an investor owns or controls, directly or indirectly, that has the characteristics of an investment, including such characteristics as the commitment of capital or other resources, the expectation of gain or profit, or the assumption of risk'. Identical or similar formulations have been used in US FTAs.

More importantly, investment agreements differ from trade agreements in a key respect: unlike trade agreements, investment agreements or investment chapters in those agreements often introduce an investor–state dispute resolution mechanism that allows private rights holders to file complaints directly against the host state over measures impairing the protections of their covered investments. In the TPP, for instance, the provisions concerning the development of such a mechanism make up close to half of the entire investment chapter.[100]

---

[98] Bryan Mercurio, 'Awakening the Sleeping Giant: Intellectual Property Rights in International Investment Agreements' (2012) 15 *J Intl Economic L* 871, 874–6.

[99] Carlos M Correa, 'Investment Protection in Bilateral and Free Trade Agreements: Implications for the Granting of Compulsory Licenses' (2004) 26 *Michigan J Intl L* 331, 335; Drahos, 'BITs and BIPs' (n 14) 794–5.

[100] On this mechanism, see Daniel Kalderimis, 'Exploring the Differences between WTO and Investment Treaty Dispute Resolution' in Susy Frankel and

Until February 2010, private rights holders have not used the investor–state dispute resolution mechanisms to resolve intellectual property disputes. This landscape, however, changed dramatically when tobacco manufacturer Philip Morris challenged restrictions on the packaging of cigarette products in Uruguay under the bilateral investment treaty between Uruguay and Switzerland. A year later, Philip Morris also challenged the Australian plain-packaging legislation under the bilateral investment treaty between Australia and Hong Kong. Most recently, Eli Lily filed a $500 million complaint against Canada under Chapter 11 of the North American Free Trade Agreement (NAFTA) following the Canadian courts' invalidation of its drug patents.[101]

To some extent, the recent developments concerning the use of bilateral and regional investment agreements to protect intellectual property rights have shown how the international intellectual property regime has now expanded beyond trade to cover investments. These developments also hint at a growing 'incentive–investment divide' in both the domestic and international intellectual property systems.[102] While intellectual property rights are generally created to promote creativity and innovation – or, in utilitarian terms, to generate incentives for such activities – intellectual property rights holders increasingly see intellectual property assets as mere investments. As a result, intellectual property rights are increasingly protected as an end in itself, rather than as a means to an appropriate end.

Even before the recent push for greater use of trade and investment agreements to protect intellectual property rights, right holders had already begun viewing intellectual property as investment assets. As Frederick Abbott reminded us:

> A patent is essentially a financial instrument that entitles its bearer to achieve greater than competitive market rates of return on investment. The Pharma companies are market-oriented enterprises that seek to maximize shareholder returns on investment. Pharma treats potential intrusion on the security of the

Meredith Kolsky Lewis (eds), *Trade Agreements at the Crossroads* (Routledge 2014) 46–65; Leon E. Trakman, 'Investor–State Dispute Settlement under the Trans-Pacific Partnership Agreement' in Tania Voon (ed.), *Trade Liberalisation and International Co-operation: A Legal Analysis of the Trans-Pacific Partnership Agreement* (Edward Elgar Publishing 2004) 179–206.

[101] Kazi Stastna, 'Eli Lilly Files $500M NAFTA Suit against Canada over Drug Patents' (*CBC News*, 13 September 2013) <http://www.cbc.ca/news/business/eli-lilly-files-500m-nafta-suit-against-canada-over-drug-patents-1.1829854> accessed 1 March 2014.

[102] Yu, 'The International Enclosure Movement' (n 13) 892–901.

> patent and regulated regulatory support as a threat to return on investment. Pharma justifies its rent seeking as necessary to the funding of research and development for new medicines. … The Pharma companies demand rules and enforcement that will protect their income streams, justifying a high return on investment as necessary to drug development.[103]

This shift of attention from incentives to investments is dangerous from a public-interest standpoint. When policymakers and trade negotiators focus on the protection of intellectual property investments by their own nationals, they will likely be less interested in evaluating the economic efficiency of the intellectual property system and the welfare gains that system produces. Instead, they will push for the development of a system that protects foreign investors (often at the expense of the public interest), the local innovative environment and the country's social-economic conditions.

The final concern regarding the TPP pertains to the potential inclusion of a provision concerning the choice of dispute resolution forum. Such a provision would largely undermine the vitality and operation of the existing WTO dispute-settlement process. Mandatory by nature, this process is not only a crowning achievement of the Uruguay Round, but also a hard-earned bargain less developed countries won through the TRIPS negotiations. At the time of those negotiations, many less developed countries reluctantly signed on to the TRIPS Agreement in part to obtain protection against the unilateral sanctions imposed by the US and other developed countries.[104] By allowing treaty parties to file a complaint in a forum other than the WTO Dispute Settlement Body, having a choice-of-forum provision in the TPP would significantly undercut this major bargain.[105]

To be certain, the US – or, for that matter, other powerful developed-country parties in a plurilateral trade agreement – will still have to defend a WTO complaint using the mandatory dispute-settlement process, unless it can persuade or compel other member states to file the complaint in an

---

[103] Frederick M Abbott, 'The Cycle of Action and Reaction: Developments and Trends in Intellectual Property and Health' in Pedro Roffe, Geoff Tansey and David Vivas-Eugui (eds), *Negotiating Health: Intellectual Property and Access to Medicines* (Earthscan 2006) 36.

[104] David Hartridge and Arvind Subramanian, 'Intellectual Property Rights: The Issues in GATT' (1989) 22 *Vanderbilt J Transnational L* 893, 909.

[105] Peter Drahos, 'The Bilateral Web of Trade Dispute Settlement' (*Third World Network*, 2005) <http://www.twnside.org.sg/title2/FTAs/DisputeResolution/TheBilateralWebOfTradeDisputeSettlementPeterDrahos.doc> accessed 20 January 2014.

alternative forum. Nevertheless, when the US serves as the complainant, it will have a choice of forum and may thereby use the alternative forum in the shadow of the WTO dispute-settlement process. Even more problematic for less developed countries, the bilateral forum may not offer the similar pro-development safeguards that the WTO Dispute Settlement Body has recognized. There is also a possibility that the treaty provisions will be interpreted differently from the decisions handed down thus far by WTO panels and the Appellate Body.

Even worse, due to the bilateral or plurilateral nature of the alternative dispute-settlement process, the process's outcome will be limited to the parties involved. Such a process may therefore threaten to undermine the WTO and the international trading system. As Peter Drahos observed in the bilateral context:

> These choice-of-forum provisions to be found in US bilaterals do not sit very comfortably with the goal of strengthening the multilateral trading system. WTO members are meant to have recourse to the DSU [Dispute Settlement Understanding] when they decide to pursue a remedy for a breach of a WTO agreement. ... There are good reasons in principle to encourage parties to use the DSU. When parties resolve a trade dispute that requires a determination of obligation in one or more of the covered agreements of the WTO they deliver a public good for other members, assuming that the dispute results in a greater certainty of the interpretation of the rules. Where an infringing state brings a measure into conformity with an obligation it has under a covered agreement it will be of benefit to all other members by virtue of the MFN principle. In short, the third party benefits of two states obtaining a ruling to a dispute under a multilateralized dispute resolution mechanism may be considerable. The same cannot be said of bilateral dispute resolution proceedings. By their nature they prop up preferential trading arrangements that operate outside of scope of the MFN principle.[106]

Although Professor Drahos's observation focuses on bilateral agreements, his insights are likely to be equally applicable to plurilateral and regional arrangements that involve only a limited number of countries, such as the TPP. The displacement effects created by an alternative dispute-settlement process in these agreements should therefore not be overlooked.

---

106 Ibid., 12–3.

RAMIFICATIONS AND THE FUTURE

Although the US has yet to complete the TPP negotiations with its trading partners in the Pacific Rim, it has already begun negotiating a new plurilateral trade and investment agreement with the EU. Known as the TTIP, these negotiations were launched on 17 June 2003, with the first round of negotiations held in Washington, DC, a month later. As the USTR declared on its website:

> The U.S. and EU economies are two of the most modern, most developed, and most committed to high standards of consumer protection in the world. T-TIP aims to bolster that already strong relationship in a way that will help boost economic growth and add to the more than 13 million American and EU jobs already supported by transatlantic trade and investment. T-TIP will be a cutting edge agreement aimed at providing greater compatibility and transparency in trade and investment regulation, while maintaining high levels of health, safety, and environmental protection. T-TIP presents an extraordinary opportunity to strengthen the bond between vital strategic and economic partners.[107]

Although the TTIP negotiations have only begun and information about the negotiations remains largely deficient, leaked position papers suggest that intellectual property issues, such as those concerning the chemical and pharmaceutical sectors and the coordination of intellectual property enforcement efforts, will receive some coverage. The Agreement's electronic commerce chapter may also include provisions on internet service providers, even though issues concerning the audiovisual sector are not being negotiated at the moment.[108]

While the US, the EU and other developed and like-minded countries are actively negotiating the TPP and the TTIP, China, India, members of ASEAN and other key Asia-Pacific neighbours launched the negotiation of the Regional Comprehensive Economic Partnership (RCEP). Building on past trade and non-trade discussions under the framework of ASEAN Plus Six (Australia, China, India, Japan, New Zealand and South Korea),

---

[107] Office of the United States Trade Representative, 'Transatlantic Trade and Investment Partnership (T-TIP)' <http://www.ustr.gov/ttip> accessed 20 January 2014.

[108] Monika Ermert, 'Controversial Debate on TTIP Mandate in EU Council of Ministers' (*Intellectual Property Watch*, 14 June 2013) <http://www.ip-watch.org/2013/06/14/audiovisual-sector-out-of-eu-mandate-for-ttip/> accessed 1 March 2014.

this new regional partnership will cover not only the two most economically powerful BRICS countries (China and India), but also major Asian economies (Japan and South Korea) as well as parties involved in the TPP negotiations (Australia, Brunei Darussalam, Japan, Malaysia, New Zealand, Singapore and Vietnam).

Given the proliferation of non-multilateral trade and investment agreements, one may rightly question whether we are now heading into a non-multilateral era – and, if so, what the ramifications of this era will be for the existing international intellectual property regime, the participating developed and less developed countries, or intellectual property rights holders? Will the present non-multilateral activities provide the much-needed transition to greater and deeper multilateral normsetting activities in the future? Or will they spark an irreversible trend that undermines these activities? If so, will this trend stay or will it be a mere passing phase?

A Non-multilateral Era?

At first glance, it is hard to tell whether this non-multilateral era, if it indeed exists, will strengthen or undermine the current international intellectual property regime. Whether it will be beneficial or harmful will depend on how long this era will last and what will happen at the end of the era. If the many diverse, and at times conflicting, normsetting activities that take place in the non-multilateral era eventually lead to norm consolidation through the multilateral process, such as the development of TRIPS II, non-multilateral activities will benefit the international intellectual property regime. By contrast, if those activities further fragment the existing international intellectual property regime or polarize the global community, those activities will greatly undermine the regime.

Most recently, WIPO adopted two new substantive intellectual property treaties – namely, the Beijing Treaty on Audiovisual Performances (Beijing Treaty) and the Marrakesh Treaty to Facilitate Access to Published Works for Persons Who Are Blind, Visually Impaired, or Otherwise Print Disabled (Marrakesh Treaty). Against the background of these treaties, commentators may point out that multilateral activities remain the rule, with non-multilateral activities serving only as temporary exceptions. As optimistic as this assessment is, history has shown that non-multilateral normsetting activities could continue for quite a long period of time before countries finally return to multilateral fora.

In an article examining the development of bilateral trade and investment agreements established by the US since the turn of this millennium,

Ruth Okediji traced the agreements back to those bilateral agreements the country has signed since its founding. As she explained:

> The so-called new bilateralism is actually more consistent with historical uses of the foreign relations/treaty power of the United States, as well as the general framework of international law, in its dealings with developing countries since the independence era. Consequently, it is probably the TRIPS Agreement that is the aberration in international intellectual property law, and not the recent spates of bilateral and regional agreements.[109]

Based on Professor Okediji's insightful observation, the TRIPS Agreement should not be considered the endpoint in the development of the international intellectual property regime.[110] Nor will the establishment of such plurilateral agreements as ACTA, the TPP, the TTIP or the RCEP be drastic deviations from the traditional path of regime development. Instead, all of these agreements merely represent the ups and downs of such development.

Battle of FTAs?

As far as bilateral and regional trade agreements are concerned, the extant literature focuses primarily on the EPAs and FTAs established by the EU and the US. However, as noted above, China, India and other large developing countries have been busy negotiating their own FTAs. This development is important because the international intellectual property norms these emerging countries want may be quite different from those that the current developed countries prefer. Because of large populations and highly uneven economic and technological developments, these latecomer countries could question the appropriateness of the super-size-fits-all norms enshrined in the TRIPS Agreement. They may also prefer norms that 'build … upon their historical traditions and cultural backgrounds and that take … account of their drastically different socio-economic conditions'.[111] If these countries indeed have

---

[109] Okediji, 'Back to Bilateralism?' (n 15) 130.

[110] Similar observations have been made in Carolyn Deere, *The Implementation Game: The TRIPS Agreement and the Global Politics of Intellectual Property Reform in Developing Countries* (OUP 2009) 304; Sell, *Private Power, Public Law* (n 5) 121.

[111] Peter K Yu, 'The Global Intellectual Property Order and Its Undetermined Future' (2009) 1 *WIPO J* 1, 13.

different preferences, the non-multilateral agreements they negotiate could easily precipitate a battle of FTAs.[112]

In an earlier article, I explored how the non-multilateral trade agreements China established are significantly different from the EPAs and FTAs negotiated by the EU and the US.[113] The differences are especially apparent in the intellectual property area – an area that China's FTAs have only covered in a cursory manner.[114] Nevertheless, China's position in the intellectual property field has been changing rapidly and drastically. In 2011, the total number of applications for and grants of patents for domestic inventions in the country already exceeded the corresponding figures in the US.[115] China is now among the top five countries filing PCT patent applications, holding the fourth spot, behind only the US, Japan and Germany.[116] If this trend continues, it will be no surprise if China becomes more active in pushing for their preferred intellectual property standards via its FTAs.

If China does so, what standards will its FTAs include? Will China push for standards that are already included in the EPAs and FTAs negotiated by the EU and the US, thereby leading to more international harmonization? Or will China push for its own version of the patent system, which calls for the introduction of three different types of patents (invention patents, design patents and utility model patents)? Such a push could be quite problematic, considering the significant differences between the Chinese and US patent systems. Although invention patents remain dominant in the US (in the form of utility patents), design patents receive only limited attention there, while utility model patents do not exist at all.

In addition, will China push for greater protection of genetic resources, traditional knowledge and traditional cultural expressions? With a wide variety of minority cultures, including the Zhuang, Hui, Uygur, Yi, Tibetan, Miao, Manchu, Mongol and Buyei, the protection of indigenous

---

112 Yu, 'Sinic Trade Agreements' (n 10) 1018–27.

113 Ibid., 961–1018.

114 Peter K Yu, 'Sinic Trade Agreements and China's Global Intellectual Property Strategy' in Christoph Antons and Reto M Hilty (eds), *Intellectual Property and Free Trade Agreements in the Asia-Pacific Region* (Springer 2015) (forthcoming).

115 Peter K Yu, 'Five Oft-Repeated Questions about China's Recent Rise as a Patent Power' (2013) *Cardozo L Rev De Novo* 78, 84–5.

116 WIPO, 'Strong Growth in Demand for Intellectual Property Rights in 2012' (19 March 2013) PR/2013/732.

materials is likely to be of great importance to China.[117] It is therefore no surprise that China was one of the co-sponsors of the proposal concerning Article 29*bis* of the TRIPS Agreement, which would require the disclosure of the source of origin of biological resources and traditional knowledge in patent applications.[118] China has also introduced the disclosure requirement in Article 26 of its patent law. Given the continuous opposition of the US, Japan and South Korea,[119] the inclusion of the disclosure requirement in China's FTAs would likely create complications, if not incompatibilities, with US FTAs.

Finally, China could include provisions concerning the interface between patents and standards in its FTAs. Although China has been somewhat reluctant to proactively assert its position in WTO committees, it did submit a paper to the WTO Committee on Technical Barriers to Trade, proposing that 'international standard setting bodies, as well as [WTO] Members, provide the Committee with relevant information regarding practices and experience on their [intellectual property] policies in standardization for Members' understanding and reference'.[120] Given China's continuous concern about the overlap between patent protection and the development of standards, it is not unforeseeable that China will push for FTA provisions that help alleviate this concern.

Peaceful Co-existence?

Despite the proliferation of bilateral, plurilateral and regional trade, intellectual property and investment agreements, countries continue to work together to establish multilateral agreements. In the past two years, for example, WIPO successfully adopted two substantive international intellectual property treaties after not having been able to do so since the adoption of the WIPO Copyright Treaty and the WIPO Performances and Phonograms Treaty in December 1996. On 26 June 2012, close to 50 WIPO members signed the Beijing Treaty, which offers protection to audiovisual performers under the existing international copyright system.

---

117 Peter K Yu, 'Intellectual Property and Asian Values' (2012) 16 *Marquette Intellectual Property L Rev* 329, 346–7, 380–2.

118 Peter K Yu, 'Cultural Relics, Intellectual Property, and Intangible Heritage' (2008) 81 *Temple L Rev* 433, 438.

119 Emanuela Arezzo, 'Struggling around the "Natural" Divide: The Protection of Tangible and Intangible Indigenous Property' (2007) 25 *Cardozo Arts & Entertainment LJ* 367, 387–8.

120 WTO Committee on Technical Barriers to Trade, 'Intellectual Property Right (IPR) Issues in Standardization' (2006) G/TBT/W/251/Add.1 [21].

A little more than a year later, WIPO also adopted the Marrakesh Treaty, which, upon ratification, will provide easy or ready access to copyrighted publications to hundreds of millions of individuals with print disabilities.

While these recent treaty-making activities could suggest the eagerness of both developed and less developed countries to return to the multilateral normsetting process, they more likely reflect a conscious choice by these countries – especially developed and large developing countries – to embrace a rather complex international intellectual property normsetting strategy that includes both multilateral and non-multilateral activities.[121] Just because these countries have actively pushed for the establishment of non-multilateral agreements such as ACTA, the TPP, the TTIP and the RCEP does not mean that they cannot actively undertake multilateral negotiations at the WTO, WIPO and other international fora at the same time. While small developing and least developed countries may not always have adequate resources to participate in both multilateral and non-multilateral normsetting fora, developed and large developing countries could easily manage to negotiate on multiple fronts.

Indeed, the recent successful negotiation of both the Beijing and Marrakesh Treaties seem to suggest that developed and large developing countries have not yet abandoned the multilateral process to set international intellectual property norms. To a large extent, the simultaneous existence of both multilateral and non-multilateral normsetting activities highlights the possibility that multilateralism and non-multilateralism could occur not only at the same time but also at the same pace.

To a large extent, the present developments also remind us that WIPO has always reinvented itself to ensure that it remains at the forefront of the international intellectual property debate.[122] Such reinvention took place in the 1960s and 1970s following the decolonization movement and the subsequent emergence of newly independent countries.[123] WIPO reinvented itself again in the mid 1990s following the establishment of the TRIPS Agreement.[124] Only a few years ago, Francis Gurry, the organization's director-general, lamented that the ACTA negotiating parties had 'tak[en] matters into their own hands to seek solutions outside of the multilateral system to the detriment of inclusiveness of the present

---

121 Schott, 'Free Trade Agreements' (n 20) 17.

122 Peter K Yu, 'Déjà Vu in the International Intellectual Property Regime' in Matthew David and Debora Halbert (eds), *The SAGE Handbook of Intellectual Property* (Sage Publications 2014) (forthcoming).

123 Yu, 'A Tale of Two Development Agendas' (n 59) 484–93.

124 Yu, 'Currents and Crosscurrents in the International Intellectual Property Regime' (n 21) 367–9.

system'.[125] Two years later, however, WIPO successfully negotiated two substantive international intellectual property treaties. As Gurry declared at the conclusion of the Marrakesh Treaty, '[t]his treaty is a victory for the blind, visually impaired and print disabled, but also for the multilateral system.'[126]

CONCLUSION

Since the expiry of the TRIPS transition period for developing countries on 1 January 2000, the EU and the US have pushed aggressively for the development of bilateral, plurilateral and regional trade, investment and intellectual property agreements. The negotiation of ACTA, the TPP and the TTIP, in particular, has sparked controversy among academic commentators, civil libertarians, consumer advocates and user communities. Interestingly, powerful developed countries do not have a monopoly over the non-multilateral approach to international intellectual property normsetting. China, India and other large developing countries have also begun establishing their own bilateral, plurilateral and regional agreements. If this trend continues, it will be interesting to see whether the non-multilateral normsetting activities will benefit or harm the existing multilateral intellectual property regime. Regardless of their impact, the growing non-multilateral activities from both developed and less developed countries will make the regime more complex than it is today. They will also create greater uncertainty over how international intellectual property norms will be set in the future.

[125] Catherine Saez, 'ACTA a Sign of Weakness in Multilateral System, WIPO Head Says' (*Intellectual Property Watch*, 30 June 2010) <http://www.ip-watch.org/2010/06/30/acta-a-sign-of-weakness-in-multilateral-system-wipo-head-says/> accessed 1 March 2014.

[126] WIPO, 'Historic Treaty Adopted, Boosts Access to Books for Visually Impaired Persons Worldwide' (27 June 2013) PR/2013/741.

4. An international *acquis*: Integrating regimes and restoring balance

Graeme B. Dinwoodie and Rochelle C. Dreyfuss[*]

The TRIPS Agreement is hardly the last word in international intellectual property lawmaking. Bilateral, plurilateral, and regional agreements, along with a multiplicity of training tools, guides, and resource books have followed in its wake. Intellectual property is a high-stakes commodity in the Knowledge Economy. Accordingly, this ferment in norm formation is unlikely to abate. Nations in the North with an interest in commodifying their knowledge-based output will continue to shop for (or create new) institutions that will endorse or develop higher standards of intellectual property protection, while those countries at the opposite end of the development spectrum will not abandon the search for fora more solicitous to user interests, distributive justice, health, and development. We have elsewhere proposed procedural and institutional mechanisms for integrating all of these activities into the TRIPS Agreement, including new approaches to interpretation of the Agreement.[1] However, interpretive approaches can go only so far. They are essentially backward-looking solutions; they do not preclude legal fragmentation and thus can only resolve the problems fragmentation produces. Yet coherence is essential to robust innovation: creativity cannot flourish without a greater degree of certainty than the current regime permits. Of course, absolute certainty is not realistic and, moreover, is less than ideal if national experimentation and cross-border trade are both valued. We believe, however, that it is possible to do better.

In this chapter, we suggest that the time has come to crystallize the learning accumulated in the century and a half since the multinational system was born. We tease out and make explicit the elements of what

* This chapter is adapted from Chapter 7 of our recent book, *A Neofederalist Vision of TRIPS: The Resilience of the International Intellectual Property Regime* (Oxford University Press 2012). Thanks to Oxford University Press for permission to adapt Chapter 7 and publish it in this volume.

[1] *See* GB Dinwoodie and RC Dreyfuss, *A Neofederalist Vision of TRIPS: The Resilience of the International Intellectual Property Regime* (Oxford University Press 2012) 143–74 [hereinafter *A Neofederalist Vision*].

we term an international intellectual property "*acquis*" – a set of basic principles that form the background norms animating the intellectual property system. The concept of an *acquis* is relatively new to international law. The World Trade Organization (WTO) borrowed it from European Union (EU) law, where the phrase "acquis communautaire" has in recent years been used to describe the body of existing legal principles and commitments to which new members of the EU must ascribe.[2] In this sense, it is easy to see why it made sense for the Dispute Settlement Body (DSB) to adopt the term; like the EU, the WTO involves a "single undertaking," and new members must sign up to the entire range of principles that govern the membership. However, the term also has a functional dimension. The Appellate Body referred to the concept of an *acquis* in *Japan – Taxes on Alcoholic Beverages* to explain that panel reports should be relevant in adjudicating future disputes because this practice would protect legitimate expectations.[3] And later scholarly treatment of the concept suggests that it reflects efforts not only to protect legitimate expectations, but also to fill gaps, and to create certainty and predictability.[4] Moreover, the *US–110(5)* panel, which issued the first TRIPS report to refer to an *acquis* (the Berne *acquis*), appeared to add another dimension to the concept, regarding the *acquis* as a body of principles reflected in a treaty regime, even if not always expressed.[5]

The concept of an *acquis* is therefore fluid. We adopt it here as much for its functional characteristics as for its (relatively new) international application. While an *acquis* is typically associated with a particular instrument or institution, the goals of an *acquis* are equally relevant to the international intellectual property system as a whole. Recognizing elements as cross-cutting features underlying all instruments constituting the system would facilitate the resolution of international disputes and

---

[2] *See* RM Gadbaw, "Systemic Regulation of Global Trade and Finance: A Tale of Two Systems" (2010) 13 *J Int'l Econ L* 551, 567.

[3] Appellate Body Report, *Japan – Taxes on Alcoholic Beverages*, WT/DS8/AB/R, WT/DS10/AB/R, WT/DS11/AB/R (4 October 1996) 14.

[4] *See* PC Mavroidis, "No Outsourcing of Law? WTO Law as Practiced by WTO Courts" (2008) 102 *Am. J. Int'l L.* 421, 465; Appellate Body Report, *United States – Final Anti-Dumping Measures on Stainless Steel from Mexico*, WT/DS344/AB/R (30 April2008) 160: emphasizing "security and predictability"; M Wabwile, "Re-examining States' External Obligations to Implement Economic and Social Rights of Children" (2009) 22 *Can JL & Juris* 407, 433: noting gap-filling role.

[5] Panel Report, *United States – Section 110(5) of the US Copyright Act*, WT/DS/160/R (15 June 2000) [hereinafter *US–110(5)*].

rectify the problems in decision making that flow from having to take account of the diverse dimensions to intellectual property law.[6] In TRIPS, it would clarify the normative underpinnings of intellectual property law, flesh out the principles and objectives found in Articles 7 and 8 of the TRIPS Agreement, and enable the DSB to situate particular challenges in the broader context of knowledge governance. Moreover, the *acquis* would complement devices of integration that we have previously discussed as a means of bringing coherence to the international intellectual property system.[7]

Prospectively, the *acquis* would create a legal framework to structure future international lawmaking and thus reduce the incidence of fragmentation. It would furnish a useful guide to international negotiators, especially those who are unfamiliar with intellectual property law and lore. As it develops in response to new challenges, the *acquis* would harness the expertise of the diverse array of institutions now operating in this arena. By establishing the norms to which all participants in the intellectual property system can be regarded as having subscribed, the *acquis* would focus debate and reduce the transaction costs of mediating among multiple conflicting initiatives. For developing countries, broad acceptance of the principles in the *acquis* would provide bargaining leverage, help address the challenges of political economy, and ameliorate the problems of capacity that TRIPS compliance has brought into relief.[8]

We draw the content of the *acquis* from national and international intellectual property law, along with associated jurisprudence and scholarship. An examination of these sources reveals that certain principles have a historical pedigree that elevates them to the status of an agreed norm. The minor exceptions doctrine, which was recognized as part of the Berne *acquis* in the *US–110(5)* report, furnishes an example. Other fundamental norms can be gleaned from the frequency with which they appear across a variety of instruments. Some elements derive from the features we see as at the heart of the international intellectual property system: diversity, balance, and historical contingency.[9] Other components emanate from the purposes that first instigated the move to international law, namely, the interdependence of nations in the production of knowledge and trade in knowledge-intensive goods. Experience with TRIPS shows that intellectual property cannot be isolated from

6 *See A Neofederalist Vision*, at 49–114.
7 Ibid. at 143–74.
8 *See* ibid. at 132–49.
9 *See* ibid. at 9–14.

broader public policy concerns, such as a commitment to expressive values or access to essential medicines. Thus, in establishing the *acquis*, we do not confine our examination to purely intellectual property instruments.

We begin this chapter with an explanation of why we believe the time to be ripe for articulating these transcendent principles. We next initiate the process of identifying the elements of the *acquis*, including principles we regard as emerging. We start with those that protect access because many of these are latent in international intellectual property instruments, and one important goal of constructing an *acquis* is to make them explicit. We then proceed to principles that protect proprietary interests and national autonomy, and reflect the interdependence of nations. We conclude with a discussion of the ways in which the *acquis* might shape the future progress of the international intellectual property system, including how it might be used to supplement Articles 7 and 8 of TRIPS, and applied and enforced in a variety of settings.

I. THE NEED FOR AN *ACQUIS*

Recent developments in international intellectual property law have produced substantial fragmentation.[10] However, those developments suggest a broader point: the pressures on the international intellectual property system are mounting. International instruments follow one another in rapid succession, promulgating rules, standards, and norms on an array of overlapping issues. Thoughtful interpretation can lessen some of the pressures, but it cannot deal with all of them as the rules, standards, and norms often cut in opposite directions and are of differing legal stature. While instruments raising the level of protection are often hard law, those that further access and other public-regarding interests tend to be softer.[11] In this climate, a new paradigm is necessary.

TRIPS can be viewed as the catalyst: its adoption produced a fundamental change in the political landscape of intellectual property law. The Paris and Berne Conventions essentially protected foreign nationals against blatant copying. This required relatively basic rights for authors, traders, and inventors. Although the standards were raised over time, they remained relatively unintrusive. Enforcement (almost exclusively through political pressure) was lax; nations retained a great deal of latitude to

---

[10] *See* ibid. at 147–56.

[11] *See generally* ME Footer, "The (Re)turn to 'Soft Law' in Reconciling Antinomies in WTO Law" (2010) 11 *Melbourne J Int'l L* 241.

pursue policies tailored to their own political objectives and consistent with their own culture and priorities.[12] The TRIPS Agreement imposed higher standards of international protection, particularly for technological innovations. It also introduced a compliance mechanism backed up by trade sanctions. Thus, it constrained states' flexibility.

More recent events introduced further constraints. The unrelenting advocacy of a "code view" of TRIPS has led developed nations to expand protection for right holders far beyond the requirements of TRIPS.[13] For developing countries, the dynamic is different, but the results are often similar. Many of these nations considered their acceptance of TRIPS as capping their international intellectual property obligations. However, they soon found themselves subject to further unilateral and bilateral trade pressures, which exacerbated rather than ameliorated political and capacity asymmetries and led to TRIPS-plus standards and fragmentation.[14] In addition, TRIPS was adopted on the cusp of important changes in science and technology without expressly addressing the legal reforms that these advances would require. Although many of these emergent issues were put on the agenda of the Council for TRIPS, negotiations in the WTO stalled, prompting further fragmentation rather than consolidation of intellectual property lawmaking in a single institution. For example, the World Intellectual Property Organization (WIPO) adopted treaties on copyright and performers' rights in the digital environment; a group consisting largely of developed countries successfully advanced (at least to the point of nominal adoption) the Anti-Counterfeiting Trade Agreement (ACTA) to raise enforcement standards beyond TRIPS; and higher levels of intellectual property protection are a part of the Trans-Pacific Partnership (TPP) Agreement currently being negotiated by the nations of the Asia-Pacific region.[15]

---

12 *See A Neofederalist Vision*, at 22–9.

13 For a discussion and critique of the view of TRIPS as a supranational code, *see* ibid. at 5–8, 14–16.

14 *See* P Drahos, 'BITs and BIPs – Bilateralism in Intellectual Property' (2001) 4 *J World Intell Prop* 791.

15 WIPO Copyright Treaty 20 December 20 1996, 2186 UNTS 121, 36 ILM 65 [hereinafter WCT]; WIPO Performances and Phonograms Treaty, 20 December 1996, 2186 UNTS 203, 36 ILM 76; Anti-Counterfeiting Trade Agreement, 31 March 2011 Text <http://trade.ec.europa.eu/doclib/docs/2011/may/tradoc_147937.pdf> [hereinafter ACTA]; Congressional Research Service, The Trans-Pacific Partnership Agreement (25 June 25 2010), <http://fpc.state.gov/documents/organization/145583.pdf>; *see also* Intellectual Property Chapter (Consolidated Text) (30 August 2013)<http://keionline.org/sites/default/files/Wikileaks-secret-TPP-treaty-IP-chapter.pdf>; T Faunce and R Townsend, "Public Health

A backlash soon followed. Many perceived TRIPS and its progeny as lacking sufficient protection for users and as leaving little room for states to further their own cultural policies, tailor the law to local economic needs and capacities, and adapt to new technological challenges. Thwarted in their efforts to ensure access to essential medicines in the midst of an epidemic, developing countries resisted TRIPS, ultimately achieving an amendment of the Agreement at Doha.[16] Emboldened by that success, user groups and developing countries brought other multilateral efforts to commodify knowledge to a halt: the proposal for a database treaty was suspended and then shelved;[17] the 2000 Diplomatic Conference on an audiovisual performers' treaty collapsed without agreement, and took another 12 years to conclude;[18] the discussion of a broadcasting treaty disintegrated amid acrimonious debate;[19] and, most recently, the formal agreement of an enforcement treaty – ACTA – by a so-called "coalition of the willing" has not ensured its ultimate entry into force in the face of protests that spilled on to the streets.[20] Simultaneously, developing countries initiated the production of counternorms by

---

and Medicines Policies" in J Kelsey (ed.), *No Ordinary Deal: Unmasking the Trans-Pacific Partnership Free Trade Agreement* 149 (Allen & Unwin 2010).

[16] *See* TRIPS, art 31*bis*. *See also* World Trade Organization, Ministerial Declaration of 20 November 2001, ¶¶ 17 & 19, WT/MIN(01)/DEC/1, 41 I.L.M. 746 (2002) [hereinafter Doha Ministerial Declaration]; World Trade Organization, Declaration on the TRIPS Agreement and Public Health, ¶¶ 4, 5(a), WT/MIN(01)/DEC/2, 20 November 2001, 41 I.L.M. 755 (2002) [hereinafter Declaration on Public Health].

[17] *See* DJ Gervais, "The Protection of Databases" (2007) 82 *Chi-Kent L Rev* 1109, 1119: noting that the draft Database Treaty was "in limbo" 11 years after it was withdrawn from the Geneva Diplomatic Conference.

[18] *See WIPO Members Fail to Agree on Performers' Rights for Audiovisual Treaty*, (2001) 61 *Pat. Trade. & Cop. J* (BNA) 231; *see also* World Intellectual Property Organization, Beijing Treaty On Audiovisual Performances, adopted by the Diplomatic Conference on 24 June 2012, WIPO Doc. AVP/DC/20 <www.wipo.int/treaties/en/ip/beijing/beijing_treaty.html>.

[19] *See* International Centre for Trade and Sustainable Development, *WIPO Broadcast Treaty Talks Collapse*, 20 June 2007 <http://ictsd.org/i/ip/39618//>; *see also* S-K Balganesh, "The Social Costs of Property Rights in Broadcast (and Cable) Signals" (2007) 22 *Berkeley Tech L J* 1303, 1314.

[20] Although ACTA was signed in October 2011, its ratification and implementation remains uncertain. In particular, the treaty provoked protests throughout Europe, both in the streets and in parliaments. *See* E Lee, "The Fight for the Future: How People Defeated Hollywood and Saved the Internet – For Now," <http://thefightforthefuture.com/wp-content/uploads/2013/07/The-Fight-for-the-Future-How-P-Lee-Edward.pdf>. In July 2012, the European Parliament

introducing the Development Agenda within WIPO (while also seeking protection for their own intellectual resources, such as folklore).[21] And international organizations, such as the UN Conference on Trade and Development (UNCTAD), the World Health Organization (WHO), and the World Blind Union (WBU) began to pay attention to intellectual property matters and to act as magnets for the increasing numbers of interested NGOs.[22]

This crescendo of activity has worried scholars, leading to several suggestions for reform. Keith Maskus and Jerry Reichman proposed a moratorium; until more is known about the impact of high standards of protection, they suggest "a time out" on international lawmaking.[23] Others analyzed the TRIPS Agreement as a contract of adhesion and

---

effectively killed European adoption of that agreement when it refused to consent to EU ratification: (using for the first time the power that had been given to it by the Lisbon Treaty). Five months later, the European Commission formally signalled the end of EU efforts to ratify ACTA with the withdrawal of its request to the Court of Justice to consider the compatibility of the Agreement with the fundamental rights provisions of EU law. The reception has been no less frosty in the US, with questions being raised not only on the substantive merits but also as regarding the ability of the Obama Administration to sign the treaty as an Executive agreement. *See* OA Hathaway and A Kapczynski, "Going It Alone: The Anti-Counterfeiting Trade Agreement as a Sole Executive Agreement" ASIL Insights (24 August 2011) <http://www.asil.org/insights/volume/15/issue/23/going-it-alone-anti-counterfeiting-trade-agreement-sole-executive>.

[21] Documents on the Development Agenda are available at <http://www.wipo.int/ipdevelopment/en/agenda/>; World Intellectual Property Organization, Program Activities, Traditional Knowledge, Genetic Resources and Traditional Cultural Expressions/Folklore<http://www.wipo.int/tk/en/>; SM Candelaria et al., *The Road to Empowerment: Strengthening the Indigenous Peoples Rights Act* (vol I, International Labor Organization 2007)<http://www.ilo.org/wcmsp5/groups/public/–asia/–ro-bangkok/–ilo-manila/documents/publication/wcms_124767.pdf>.

[22] *See,* e.g., M Chon, "A Rough Guide to Global Intellectual Property Pluralism" in R Dreyfuss, H First and D Zimmerman (eds), *Working Within the Boundaries of Intellectual Property* (Oxford University Press 2010) 445; A Kapczynski, "The Access to Knowledge Mobilization and the New Politics of Intellectual Property" (2008) 117 *Yale L J* 804; *see also infra* text accompanying note 159 (discussing treaty for the blind and visually impaired).

[23] *See* KE Maskus and JH Reichman, "The Globalization of Private Knowledge Goods and the Privatization of Global Public Goods" in KE Maskus and JH Reichman (eds), *International Public Goods and Transfer of Technology Under a Globalized Intellectual Property Regime* (Cambridge University Press 2005) 3, 37.

argued that it might be open to rescission.[24] More proactively, Bernt Hugenholtz and Ruth Okediji proposed a soft law instrument delineating exceptions and limitations on the rights of copyright owners.[25] And a conference of scholars in Washington issued a declaration spelling out the public interest components of intellectual property policy.[26] Working within the WTO framework, Annette Kur and her collaborators developed a formal proposal for amending the TRIPS Agreement and transforming it into a more balanced instrument.[27] We do not disavow those efforts; indeed, their goals are largely at one with our arguments.[28] And they could achieve important ends. However, we think proposals to abrogate or modify TRIPS are unrealistic in the present climate and that it would be dangerous to take multilateral negotiations off the international table when so much commodification is occurring under the table, through secret negotiations over new plurilateral and bilateral agreements.[29] Furthermore, new initiatives to create freestanding instruments would exacerbate fragmentation, even if they redress some of the substantive concerns about excessive protection.

In our view, any comprehensive solution to the turmoil in international intellectual property lawmaking must tackle three essential issues. First, it must grapple with the inevitability of regime shifting. Since the WTO is not institutionally suited to assume exclusive responsibility for responding to the dynamism of the creative environment, there will always be other institutions involved in intellectual property lawmaking. Their efforts will, however, be interrelated: any change made by one instrument or institution will necessarily affect others. Accordingly, the solution must apply across the entire intellectual property system – to all international intellectual property lawmaking and in all institutional

---

[24] *See* DP Harris, "Carrying a Good Joke Too Far: TRIPS and Treaties of Adhesion" (2006) 27 *U Pa J Int'l Econ L* 681; DP Harris, "TRIPS and Treaties of Adhesion Part II: Back to the Past or a Small Step Forward?" (2007) *Mich St L Rev* 185.

[25] PB Hugenholtz and RL Okediji, *Conceiving an International Instrument on Limitations and Exceptions to Copyright* (2008)<www.ivir.nl/publicaties/hugenholtz/ finalreport2008.pdf>.

[26] The Washington Declaration on Intellectual Property and the Public Interest (August 2011)<http://infojustice.org/washington-declaration>.

[27] A Kur (ed.), *Intellectual Property in a Fair World Trade System: Proposals for Reforming the TRIPS Agreement* (Edward Elgar 2011) [hereinafter *Proposals for Reforming the TRIPS Agreement*].

[28] *See,* e.g., Hugenholtz and Okediji, *supra* note 25, at 4.

[29] *See A Neofederalist Vision*, at 143–56.

settings. Otherwise, it will not fully address fragmentation or reduce uncertainty.

Admittedly, a set of meta-norms, such as we contemplate for the *acquis*, is rare in international law. But it is not unknown. For example, Benedict Kingsbury, Nico Krisch, and Richard Stewart have proposed the development of global administrative law – procedural principles that would similarly cut across institutions.[30] We believe, however, that meta-norms will not operate effectively if they are limited to the procedural realm. One reason for the ferment in intellectual property is that the stripped-down approach of conventions such as Paris and Berne, which mainly articulate minimum rights for authors and producers, is inappropriate to instruments that impose more stringent constraints on member state autonomy. Thus, the second goal of a comprehensive solution is to ensure that new international intellectual property instruments are substantively balanced. The rights of users, which were largely implicit in the older instruments and were primarily effectuated through the exercise of national flexibilities, must now be articulated in equivalent detail to those of authors and producers.

Third, experience suggests that the political economy of intellectual property tends to narrow policy options for many states. Because the DSB has decided so few TRIPS disputes, there are many aspects of the Agreement that have yet to receive an authoritative interpretation. As a result, advocates for strong protection can use the Agreement rhetorically, to block domestic legislation even when it is TRIPS-compliant. In developing countries, this problem is particularly severe: there are even fewer DSB reports dealing with the flexibilities of unique interest to these countries. Moreover, many of these states are still suffering from capacity deficits. To compound matters, they must also grapple with the linkage of intellectual property and trade, which gives developed countries with large markets exceptional leverage to impose TRIPS-plus standards. An international *acquis* would validate the range of policy choices that are available to national lawmakers. By legitimating these options as a part of the background rules animating effective intellectual property law, the *acquis* would reduce the political leverage of powerful states and impede their efforts to compel the adoption of high standards that ignore local interests.

To achieve these goals, we offer principles that we see as at the core of the *acquis*. We do not, however, intend to exhaustively articulate the

---

[30] B Kingsbury, N Krisch and RB Stewart, "The Emergence of Global Administrative Law" (2005) 68 *Law & Contemp Probs* 15.

acquis; our hope is that other scholars and policy makers will take up the challenge and augment our efforts. Moreover, we expect that the *acquis* will grow as new lawmaking occurs and new technological challenges are confronted. The capacity of the *acquis* to evolve dynamically is essential if it is to retain an ongoing legitimacy, without which countries might be tempted to withdraw from the international system.

II. THE CONTENT OF THE *ACQUIS*

We draw the content of the *acquis* from national and international sources along with associated jurisprudence and scholarship. International intellectual property treaties (including the WIPO instruments and TRIPS) represent a clear starting point, but they are not the end point of analysis. If the *acquis* is to realize the goal of bringing coherence to international lawmaking, it must reflect the work of certain nonintellectual property institutions as well. For example, human rights principles are increasingly part of intellectual property lawmaking and adjudication at national,[31] regional,[32] and international[33] levels. They comport in many instances with fundamental constitutional values at the national level. Their integration within intellectual property has become the subject of

---

[31] *See,* e.g., C Geiger, "Trade Marks and Freedom of Expression: The Proportionality of Criticism" (2007) 38 IIC 317; *Boehringer Ingelheim Ltd v VetPlus Ltd* [2007] ETMR 67 (UK); *Ashdown v Telegraph Group Ltd* [2002] QB 546.

[32] *See,* e.g., Case C-324/09, *L'Oreal SA v eBay Int'l* [2011] ETMR 52 (CJEU) at ¶ AG49 (Opinion of Advocate-General): "It should not be forgotten that the listings uploaded by users to eBay's marketplace are communications protected by the fundamental rights of freedom of expression and information provided by Article 11 of Charter of Fundamental Rights of the EU and Article 10 of the European Convention on Human Rights."; Directive 2000/31/EC of the European Parliament and of the Council of 8 June 2000 on Certain Legal Aspects of Information Society Services, in Particular Electronic Commerce, in the Internal Market, recital 9, 2000 O.J. (L 178) 1:

> The free movement of information society services can in many cases be a specific reflection in Community law of a more general principle, namely freedom of expression as enshrined in Article 10(1) of the Convention for the Protection of Human Rights and Fundamental Freedoms, which has been ratified by all the Member States. … [T]his directive is not intended to affect national fundamental rules and principles relating to freedom of expression.

[33] *See Anheuser-Busch Inc v Portugal*, App. No. 73049/01, 45 EHRR 36 [830] (Grand Chamber ECHR 2007).

substantial scholarly attention.[34] And even WTO adjudicators have not been wholly resistant to referring to such external (even soft) sources of law, as in the Shrimp-Turtle dispute.[35]

In identifying the international *acquis*, we would also have regard to national principles. Historically, treaties merely established the boundaries within which national political processes created the substantive balances that are appropriate to the circumstances of each different domestic order. Because so much of the balance in intellectual property law has been achieved in the spaces left open by international law, looking simply at the bare text of international agreements would skew the *acquis* toward over-commodification. The *acquis* must therefore take account of principles well established at the national level in both developed and developing countries. Reference to state practices to inform international law is commonplace and was approved by the panel in the *US–110(5)* case to determine the content of the Berne *acquis*.[36] The panel's decision in that case also illustrates that the principles of the *acquis* do not require verbatim replication in numerous national instruments to suggest an international consensus. Instead, we are searching for normative equivalence.

Having established the sources of the *acquis*, we would identify the content of the *acquis* by focusing primarily on three constellations of factors. First, we consider the pedigree of the principle, especially its iteration in multiple instruments, across a variety of institutions. Tomer Broude and Yuval Shany describe these as multisourced equivalent norms.[37] Repetition suggests a consensus about the validity of the principle, a consensus that should not require renegotiation each time that international lawmakers get to work. Second, we look at issues that we put at the heart of the intellectual property system: the cumulative nature of intellectual property, which demands balance among the interests of

---

34 *See* e.g., LR Helfer and GW Austin, *Human Rights and Intellectual Property: Mapping the Global Interface* (Cambridge University Press 2011).

35 Appellate Body Report, *United States – Import Prohibition of Certain Shrimp and Shrimp Products*, ¶¶ 127–131, WT/DS58/AB/R, DSR 1998:VII (6 November 1998).

36 *US–110(5)*, at ¶ 6.55.

37 *See* T Broude and Y Shany, "The International Law and Policy of Multi-sourced Equivalent Norms" in T Broude and Y Shany (eds), *Multi-sourced Equivalent Norms in International Law*, (Hart Publishing 2011) 1; *cf.* LR Helfer, "Adjudicating Copyright Claims under the TRIPS Agreement: A Case for a European Human Rights Analogy" (1998) 39 *Harv Int'l L J* 357, 431: arguing that any analysis of state practice should consciously look to the laws of states at every stage of development.

generations of producers and concern for those who build upon and use their work; the contingent nature of technology, which requires opportunities for experimentation and an openness to new creative paradigms; and a commitment to diversity.[38] Third, we include in the *acquis*, principles that are directed at solving problems of interdependence, that is, dealing with phenomena so global in effect that no state has the regulatory power to resolve them on its own. We consider the *acquis* as it applies to the interests of users, producers, nations, and the international regime as a whole.

A. Access-regarding Principles

We begin with the portion of the *acquis* that deals with access interests because these have received short shrift in most international intellectual property lawmaking. This omission is understandable in that the early instruments were genuinely minimum standards regimes – as Reichman describes it, islands of protection in a sea of public accessibility.[39] But the political economy of intellectual property tends to favor the enlargement of the islands, with the result that the important contributions made by the sea – the domain of accessible knowledge – needs to be more explicitly established and protected.[40] These principles have a number of functions. They protect the wellsprings of creativity (ideas, fundamental principles of nature, generic expressions), ensure that the frontiers of knowledge can be continually moved forward, invigorate a competitive marketplace for ideas and products, and guarantee that individuals and nations enjoy the capacity to grow, learn, and interact.[41] Because they circumscribe the control of authors, traders, and inventors, the access-regarding provisions create the balance that is essential to intellectual property lawmaking.

Such provisions can take a number of forms, consisting of subject-matter exclusions, including minimum thresholds for protection; limits on scope, such as exceptions and limitations that guarantee the rights of

---

38 *See A Neofederalist Vision*, at 9–14.

39 *See* JH Reichman, "Saving the Patent Law from Itself: Informal Remarks Concerning the Systemic Problems Afflicting Developed Intellectual Property Regimes" in FS Kieff (ed.), *Perspectives on the Properties of the Human Genome Project* (Elsevier/ Academic Press 2003) 289.

40 *See,* e.g., J Litman, "The Public Domain" (1990) 39 *Emory L J* 965.

41 *See,* e.g., A Sen, *Development as Freedom* (Oxford University Press 1999); M Chon, "Intellectual Property and the Development Divide" (2006) 27 *Cardozo L Rev* 2821.

users, competitors, and follow-on innovators; and provisions that curb abuse of intellectual property rights. These concepts have a solid pedigree and widespread recognition at both the national and international level.

1. Subject-matter exclusions

All areas of intellectual property law contain thresholds and other exclusions from protection. These are reflected in both international and national law. In copyright law, the Berne Convention mandates that "the protection of this Convention shall not apply to news of the day or to miscellaneous facts having the character of mere items of press information."[42] In addition to incorporating the quotation right, TRIPS provides that "[c]opyright protection shall extend to expressions and not to ideas, procedures, methods of operation or mathematical concepts as such," a bar which is reiterated in the WIPO Copyright Treaty (WCT).[43] And both TRIPS and the WCT preclude the grant of copyright in data, notwithstanding any compilation copyright that might exist.[44]

The Paris Convention and the TRIPS Agreement take a similar approach to trademark law. The Paris Convention precludes the grant of registrations for marks consisting of flags or state emblems,[45] and gives states flexibility to reject marks whose registration would be contrary to public order.[46] TRIPS requires states to accord trademark protection to signs "capable of distinguishing the goods or services of one undertaking

---

[42] Berne Convention for the Protection of Literary and Artistic Works, 24 July 1971, art 2.8, 1161 UNTS 3 [hereinafter Berne Convention]. *See also* S Ricketson and JC Ginsburg, 1 *International Copyright and Neighbouring Rights: The Berne Convention and Beyond*, ¶ 6.111 (2d edn, Oxford University Press 2005) 331.

[43] TRIPS, art 9.2; WCT, art 2.

[44] *See* WCT, art 5: noting that the protection afforded by copyright to compilations of data or other material "does not extend to the data or the material itself"; TRIPS, art 10.2.

[45] Paris Convention for the Protection of Industrial Property, 14 July 1967, art 6*ter*, 21 UST 1583, 828 UNTS 305 [hereinafter Paris Convention]. There are also a number of provisions that limit protection, but do so primarily to protect other interests, such as Article 6*bis* of the Paris Convention's protection for well-known marks, which includes an obligation to deny registration of certain conflicting marks; Article 5*ter* of Paris permits unlawful use of patented devices on vehicles in transit; and Article 37.1 of TRIPS, which protects the innocent incorporation of unlawfully produced circuit designs. *See also* Nairobi Treaty on the Protection of the Olympic Symbol, adopted 26 September 1981, art 1, 1863 UNTS 367 (requiring states to deny registration to marks that unlawfully incorporate Olympic marks).

[46] *See* Paris Convention, art 6*quinquies*B.

from those of other undertakings." This language suggests that words and symbols used generically should be in the public domain.[47] Furthermore, TRIPS permits states to condition registrability on use of the mark, thereby preserving unexploited signals for public use.[48]

International patent law is somewhat less explicit. The Paris Convention did not take any position on the subject matter of patents. TRIPS, however, defines patentable inventions that are "new, involve an inventive step and are capable of industrial application," implying that laws and principles of nature are excluded from protection.[49] In addition, TRIPS permits states to exclude diagnostic, surgical, and therapeutic methods; plants (so long as they are subject to sui generis protection); animals; and any invention necessary to protect public order, life, health, or prevent serious prejudice to the environment.[50]

While these exclusions may appear sparse, an examination of national legislation, judicial opinions, and commentary provides considerably more information on their breadth and content. Although none have been the subject of international dispute resolution, there are a few cases where these international provisions have been expressly interpreted by national courts. For example, a UK court has affirmed that the prohibition of protection for ideas in TRIPS imposes a ceiling on permissible protection.[51] Indeed, Mr Justice Arnold went further in that case and held that Article 2 of the WCT excludes protection for programming languages because they are methods of operation.[52] Likewise, the Canadian Supreme Court has suggested that Berne imposes an originality prerequisite for copyright protection; the Court was essentially deriving an implicit threshold from the text of the international instruments it was interpreting.[53] As Daniel Gervais explained, the notion of "work" in the

---

[47] TRIPS, art 15.1.

[48] Ibid., art 15.3.

[49] Ibid., art 27.1.

[50] Ibid., arts 27.2–27.3.

[51] *SAS Institute Inc v World Programming Ltd* [2010] EWHC 1829 (Ch), ¶ 204; *see also* TRIPS, art 9.2: "Copyright protection shall extend to expressions and not to ideas, procedures, methods of operation or mathematical concepts as such."

[52] Ibid.

[53] *CCH Canadian v Law Society of Upper Canada* [2004] 1 SCR 339, ¶ 19 (McLachlan CJ) (Can S Ct): "the idea of intellectual creation was implicit … in the Berne Convention."

Berne Convention may support a requirement of originality, in the sense of intellectual creation, to the exclusion of other criteria.[54]

In addition, national laws demonstrate the fundamental character of these exclusions and thresholds. Virtually all copyright systems exclude ideas and facts from protection. Almost without exception, national trademark laws preclude protection for functional product features and generic terms.[55] Patent laws exclude protection for laws and principles of nature and require that inventions be new and inventive. As the US Supreme Court put it in *Bilski v Kappos*: "The concepts covered by these exceptions are 'part of the storehouse of knowledge of all men … free to all men and reserved exclusively to none.'"[56]

In addition to these ubiquitous exclusions from protection, there are a series of other exclusions that are pervasive enough to establish their pedigree. In copyright, many countries deny protection to methods of operation and functional works.[57] Most countries limit trademark protection to marks that remain in use.[58] Patent statutes typically exclude mathematical methods, aesthetic creations, inventions related to plants and animals, diagnostic methods, and inventions necessary to safeguard the public order.[59] Some developing countries have raised the inventive

---

54 DJ Gervais, "*Feist* Goes Global: A Comparative Analysis of the Notion of Originality in Copyright Law" (2002) 49 *J Copyright Soc'y* 949, 971–3; S Ricketson, *The Berne Convention for the Protection of Literary and Artistic Works: 1886–1986* (Oxford University Press 1987) 900–1: suggesting that common law countries that adopt a sweat of the brow standard for originality depart from "the spirit if not the letter" of the Berne Convention. *But see* Ricketson and Ginsburg, *supra* note 42, ¶ 8.05 at 405–6: noting that countries are "allowed to adopt differing interpretations of the minimum of 'intellectual creation' that is required" to be a work within Article 2.1 of the Berne Convention.

55 *TrafFix Devices, Inc. v Marketing Displays, Inc.*, 532 US 23, 29 (2001); *Philips Electronics NV v Remington Consumer Products Ltd* [1998] RPC 283, [2002] ECR-I-5475 (ECJ).

56 *Bilski v Kappos*, 130 S.Ct. 3218, 3225 (2010) (citations omitted).

57 *See,* e.g., 17 USC § 102(b); *Lotus Development Corp v Borland Int'l Inc.*, 49 F 3d 807 (1st Cir 1995).

58 *See,* e.g., Council Regulation (EC) No. 207/2009 of 26 February 2009, on the Community Trade Mark (codified version), art 15.1, 2009 O.J. (L 78) 1, requiring mark owner to make genuine use of a mark within the European Union within five years of registration; ibid., art 51.1(a), listing non-use as ground for revocation.

59 European Patent Convention, 5 October 5 1973, arts 52 & 53, 1065 UNTS 199 (as amended December 13, 2007), <http://www.epo.org/law-practice/

step to exclude protection for second uses of previously patented materials.[60]

Finally, regard to national law shows that as these principles evolve, they become more deeply embedded into the background norms of the intellectual property regime. For example, although EU legislation has thus far resisted adopting a general standard for the originality of all works throughout Europe, the requirement that a work be "the author's own intellectual creation" in order to be protected has now been repeated in harmonization instruments pertaining to such diverse works as software, databases, and photographs.[61] Over time, this standard may arguably become a general test of originality, precluding the grant of copyright protection to sweat-of-the-brow-based works that fail to meet it.[62]

At a minimum, then, our survey of international and national sources suggests that the international *acquis* includes a set of access-regarding principles that can act as ceilings on protection. The building blocks of creativity and the basic components of expression must be in the public domain. Accordingly, laws of nature cannot be patented, ideas and facts cannot be the subject of copyright protection, and generic terms and functional features cannot be registered as trademarks. Nor, if these principles are to be respected, can they be commodified by other legal

---

legaltexts/epc.html>; L Bently et al., *Exclusions from Patentability and Exceptions and Limitations to Patentees' Rights*, Standing Committee on Patents, WIPO Doc. SCP/15/3, Annex 1 (October 2010).

[60] *See A Neofederalist Vision*, at 51–8 (discussing Indian legislation).

[61] *See* Directive 2009/24/EC of the European Parliament and of the Council of 23 April 23 2009, on the Legal Protection of Computer Programs (codified version), art 1.3, 2009 OJ (L 111) 16; Directive 96/9/EC of the European Parliament and of the Council of 11 March 1996, on the Legal Protection of Databases, art 3.1, 1996 OJ (L 77) 20; Directive 2006/116/EC of the European Parliament and of the Council of 12 December 2006, on the Term of Protection of Copyright and Certain Related Rights (codified version), art 6, 2006 OJ (L 372) 12.

[62] *See* Wittem Group, European Copyright Code, art 1.1(1)<http://www.copyrightcode.eu/>. *Cf.* JC Ginsburg, "International Copyright Law: From a 'Bundle' of National Copyright Laws to a Supranational Code" 47 *J Copyright Soc'y* 265, 273–4 (2000), making such a prediction, though not with reference to whether by further legislation or a process of interpretation. Of course, at least in the near term, a strict textual approach to interpretation by national courts might confine the evolving common standard to the works explicitly covered, allowing lower standards of originality to be applied to other works. *Cf. Newspaper Licensing Agency v Meltwater*, [2011] EWCA Civ 890; *Football Dataco Ltd v Brittens Pools Ltd*, [2010] EWCA Civ 1380.

regimes. Furthermore, the *acquis* recognizes a consensus that nations can enact other exclusions to maintain competition, reduce transaction costs, protect the social order, and ensure that authors and inventors need "to deposit more than a penny in the box" in order to make the intellectual property "turnstile revolve."[63]

2. Scope of protection

Each intellectual property regime also includes a series of scope limitations. Some are highly specific. At the international level, the Berne Convention includes a mandatory quotation right.[64] It also contains measures permitting states to enact a series of specific exceptions aimed at validating uses of copyrighted materials for teaching and reporting, as well as compulsory licenses for various broadcasting purposes.[65] For developing nations, these provisions are supplemented by the flexibilities available in the Berne Appendix.[66] Furthermore, Berne permits states to set a temporal limit on protection (so long as it exceeds a set period, for most works, 50 years after the author's death).[67] For trademark law, the TRIPS Agreement permits states to revoke trademarks after three years of nonuse or if the mark has lost distinctiveness, such as through uncontrolled licensing.[68] The geographical indications, industrial design, and topography provisions include a set of targeted limitations.[69] In patents, TRIPS gives states the right, under defined conditions, to issue compulsory licenses to meet local needs.[70] Furthermore, it permits states to limit patents to 20 years after filing.[71] For all intellectual property rights, TRIPS leaves states with substantial discretion on the remedies available when third parties are found to infringe protected works, and gives broad

---

[63] B Kaplan, *An Unhurried View of Copyright* (Columbia University Press 1967) 46.

[64] Berne Convention, art 10.1. *See also* Ricketson and Ginsburg, *supra* note 42, ¶ 13.95 at 847: "Under Article 9(1) [of TRIPS] it will be obligatory for members to provide for exceptions for quotations under article 10(1) [of Berne], this being the one mandatory exception under Berne."

[65] Berne Convention, arts 10(2) and 10*bis*. For a fuller listing, *see* Hugenholtz and Okediji, *supra* note 25, Appendix A.

[66] *See* Ricketson and Ginsburg, *supra* note 42, ¶ 14.49–14.106.

[67] Berne Convention, art 7.

[68] TRIPS, arts 19 and 21.

[69] Ibid., arts 24.4–24.9, 25.1, 37.

[70] Ibid., arts 31 and 31*bis*.

[71] Ibid., art 33.

scope for national provisions authorizing government use without the permission of the right holder.[72]

In addition to these specific exceptions and limits on scope, international instruments include provisions setting out general tests for other exceptions that states may wish to create. The origin of all these tests is Article 9.2 of the Berne Convention, which applied only to exceptions to the reproduction right. However, TRIPS negotiators adapted that provision to create exceptions tests that apply to all uses of copyrighted works and, with some modifications, to the use of patents, trademarks, and designs.[73] Later, the WCT adopted a test similar to the copyright formulation found in the TRIPS Agreement.[74]

Once again, national laws enrich our perspective and help us understand the underlying norms. Virtually all legal systems impose temporal limits on protection for copyright and patent; such limits are mandated by the US Constitution.[75] All have first sale or local exhaustion doctrines.[76] In addition, states have enacted a diverse range of exceptions. For example, the EU Copyright Directive lists 20 specific limitations that EU states may impose on the rights of copyright holders, including copying for private use; using material for the purpose of caricature, parody, or pastiche; or using a work for teaching or scientific research.[77] In addition, EU directives mandate the availability of certain exceptions in all member states. Thus, the Copyright Directive requires an exception for ephemeral copies;[78] the Software Directive ensures that users can reverse engineer computer programs to obtain interoperability information; that Directive also permits users to make backup copies, a right that cannot be overridden by contract.[79] By the same token, trademark laws permit descriptive fair uses of protected marks as well as uses in news reporting

---

72 *See, e.g.,* Panel Report, *China – Measures Affecting the Protection and Enforcement of Intellectual Property Rights*, WT/DS362/R (26 January 2009) [hereinafter *China–Enforcement*]; *see also* TRIPS, arts 31(b) and 44.2.

73 TRIPS, arts 13, 17, 26, and 30.

74 WCT, art 10.

75 US Constitution, art 1 §8 cl 8; *cf. Eldred v Ashcroft*, 537 US 186 (2003).

76 *See,* e.g., 17 USC s 109(a); Trade Marks Act 1994, s 11 (UK); *Prestonettes, Inc v Coty*, 264 U.S. 359 (1924); *Adams v Burke*, 84 U.S. 453 (1873). Some also recognize international exhaustion. *See,* e.g., *Kirtsaeng v John Wiley & Sons*, 132 S.Ct. 1905 (2012).

77 *See* Directive 2001/29/EC on the Harmonisation of Certain Aspects of Copyright and Related Rights in the Information Society, arts 5.2–5.3, 2001 O.J. (L 167) 10 [hereinafter Copyright Directive].

78 *See* ibid., art 5.1.

79 *See* Software Directive, arts 6 and 5.2; *see also* 17 USC § 117.

and parody.[80] Patent laws similarly contain various exceptions: for experimental purposes,[81] engaging in testing for premarket clearance purposes,[82] reseeding crops,[83] and noncommercial use.[84] Finally, states have begun to realize that modulating remedies can ensure that intellectual property rights are not used to hold innovation ransom.[85]

Some countries also use the strategy of an open-ended, general exceptions provision to permit use of protected works by third parties. An increasing number have transposed versions of the exceptions tests as they are laid out in the TRIPS Agreement.[86] Two panels of the DSB have interpreted these provisions narrowly. However, these decisions were heavily criticized by scholars,[87] and at least one national court has read the transposed version of the TRIPS copyright provision in ways far

---

80 *See* LP Ramsey, "Free Speech and International Obligations to Protect Trademarks" (2010) 35 *Yale J Int'l* 405. *See,* e.g., *Laugh It Off Promotions v South African Breweries Int'l* (Finance) BV, 2006 (1) SA 144 (Const Ct) (South Africa) (2005); Economic Partnership Agreement between the CARIFORUM states, of the one part, and the European Community and its member states, of the other part, 15 October 2008, art 144.F, 2008 OJ (L289) 3:

> The EC Party and the Signatory CARIFORUM States shall provide for the fair use of descriptive terms, including geographical indications, as a limited exception to the rights conferred by a trademark. Such limited exception shall take account of the legitimate interests of the owner of the trademark and of third parties.

81 *See,* e.g., Patents Act 1977, s 60(5)(b) (UK).

82 *See* Panel Report, *Canada – Patent Protection of Pharmaceutical Products*, WT/DS114/R (17 March 2000) [hereinafter *Canada–Pharmaceuticals*].

83 Patents Act 1977, s 60(5)(g) (UK).

84 Ibid., s 60(5)(a).

85 *See,* e.g., *eBay Inc v MercExchange, L.L.C.*, 547 U.S. 388 (2006).

86 *See* Copyright Directive, art 5.5; J Griffiths, "The 'Three-Step Test' in European Copyright Law – Problems and Solutions" [2009] *Intell Prop Q* 428.

87 *See Canada–Pharmaceuticals*; *US–110(5)*; *see also A Neofederalist Vision*, at 59-71; Max Planck Institute for Intellectual Property, Competition and Tax Law, *Declaration: A Balanced Interpretation of the "Three-Step Test" in Copyright Law* (April 2010)<http://www.ip.mpg.de/ww/ en/pub/news/declaration_on_the_three_step_/declaration.cfm>; JC Ginsburg, "Toward Supranational Copyright Law? The WTO Panel Decision and the 'Three Step Test' for Copyright Exemptions" (2001) 187 *Revue Internationale du Droit D'Auteur* 3, 17; Griffiths, *supra* note 76; R Howse, "The Canadian Generic Medicines Panel – A Dangerous Precedent in Dangerous Times" (2000) 5 *J World Intell Prop* 493, 494, criticizing the panel in *Canada–Pharmaceuticals* for failing to do "justice to the delicate balance of social and economic interests reflected in the stated purposes of [the TRIPS] Agreement."

more respectful of access interests.[88] The fair use provision of US copyright law illustrates how extensive this latitude for diverse third-party uses can be.[89] Unlike the interpretation of the TRIPS provisions, it articulates a nonexhaustive and noncumulative list of factors, whose collective weight determines when the social use of a copyrighted work trumps the benefits of authorial control. In the words of Justice Brennan, limiting the copyright holder's control:

> is not some unforeseen byproduct of a statutory scheme intended primarily to ensure a return for works of the imagination … This distinction is at the essence of copyright. The copyright laws serve as the "engine of free expression," only when the statutory monopoly does not choke off multifarious indirect uses and consequent broad dissemination of information and ideas. To ensure the progress of arts and sciences and the integrity of First Amendment values, ideas and information must not be freighted with claims of proprietary right.[90]

The UK Copyright Act likewise permits fair dealing with copyrighted works, albeit for the particular purposes of research, private study, criticism, review, and news reporting.[91]

As the Brennan quotation suggests, when states implement the flexibilities provided by the international agreements, they also pay attention to access interests safeguarded by commitments outside intellectual property. Some of these are based in other international agreements. Thus, Lionel Bently and Brad Sherman have noted that, "the European Convention on Human Rights, and the jurisprudence of the Strasbourg Court, appears to offer an important backdrop for the interpretation for a number of the [statutory copyright] defences."[92] Indeed, the UK Court of Appeals has recognized that human rights commitments should not only

---

[88] *See* A Kur, "Of Oceans, Islands and Inland Water – How Much Room for Exceptions and Limitations under the Three-Step Test?" (2008–2009) 8 *Rich J Global L & Bus* 287, 331, discussing decision of the Barcelona Court of Appeals in *Google – Caching*, Audiencia Provincial de Barcelona, AC\2008\1773, 17 September 2008; *see also* Griffiths, *supra* note 86 (discussing same decision, *available* in Spanish at <http://www.irpi.ccip.fr/upload/ pdf/private/decisions/ 080917_Audencia_Barcelona_GoogleSpain.pdf>).

[89] 17 USC s 107.

[90] *Harper & Row Publishers, Inc v Nation Enters*, 471 US 539, 589–90 (1985).

[91] Copyright, Designs and Patents Act 1988, ss 29–30 (UK); *see also Ashdown v Telegraph Group Ltd* [2001] 3 WLR 1368.

[92] LA Bently and B Sherman, *Intellectual Property Law* (3rd edn, Oxford University Press 2009) 2002.

inform the interpretation of existing exceptions in the UK statute, but would also, if necessary, provide the basis to develop a public interest defense that would validate uses even beyond those permitted by the fair dealing defense.[93]

While these measures are diverse, an analysis of their collective underpinnings reveals broader principles. Even when works are protected, there are important social uses (both commercial and noncommercial) that should not be within the control of the right holder. Many of these measures are designed to grow the knowledge base (for example, measures that permit teaching and experimenting); others recognize the cumulative nature of knowledge production and free material for current development and for the enjoyment of future generations (quotation and reverse engineering defenses). Other defenses permit each user to adapt works, tinker with them, and individuate them in ways that satisfy the user's own creative inclinations (exhaustion, parody, descriptive, and personal use defenses). These provisions also further free speech values and facilitate robust competition. And they promote the interest in diversity because they allow states to pursue local objectives, including public health, nutrition, and morality. An examination of the methodology of these provisions reveals another important objective: while some are specific, states also employ open exceptions to enable intellectual property law to respond effectively to changing social conditions.

3. Curbing abuse

The international system has long understood that intellectual property rights can be abused despite the limits discussed previously. Historically, this concern was at its zenith in connection with patent rights, which provide the strongest level of control. Thus, the Paris Convention allows states to issue compulsory patent licenses to check abuse (including failure to work).[94] TRIPS similarly permits compulsory patent licenses.[95] In addition, it recognizes that other intellectual property rights can be misused, and it permits states to regulate anticompetitive practices in all forms of intellectual property through cognate bodies of law.[96]

States have similarly acted to protect the competitive environment. They treat intellectual property law and competition law as two sides of a coin and achieve balance through exceptions to intellectual property,

93 *See Ashdown v Telegraph Group Ltd.*

94 Paris Convention, art 5.

95 TRIPS, art 31.

96 Ibid., arts 8 and 40.

competition law, or a combination of the two.[97] For example, when the European Commission was drafting the Database Directive, it recognized the dangers of granting exclusive rights to data that were available from a single source. During the deliberative process, the European Court of Justice handed down its Magill decision,[98] indicating a willingness to use competition law to intervene and constrain excessive assertions of intellectual property rights. As a result, the Commission decided that competition law might serve as a functional substitute for the sole source compulsory license, and the Directive was adopted on that basis.[99] Competition law mechanisms are thus part of the intellectual property toolbox.[100] Indeed, a combination of both strategies is vital to protect the creative environment. The public-regarding aspects of intellectual property law are typically asserted defensively and therefore primarily benefit individual defendants, while competition violations can be policed by the state and provide systemic protection of the creative environment. Intellectual property law defenses are easily established without substantial factual development; competition law cases are resource- and expertise-intensive, but may provide generous damages awards to encourage private attorneys general. Intellectual property law focuses on the allegedly infringing use, while competition law analysis looks at the conduct of the right holder and takes into account its market power in determining the impact of its actions.

4. Emerging elements

The Knowledge Economy is not static. Accordingly, intellectual property law must constantly adapt to new technological settings. Indeed, this

---

[97] T Dreier, "Balancing Proprietary and Public Domain Interests: Inside or Outside of Proprietary Rights?" in R Dreyfuss, DL Zimmerman and H First (eds), *Expanding the Boundaries of Intellectual Intellectual Property: Innovation Policy for the Knowledge Society* (Oxford University Press 2001) 316.

[98] Joined Cases C-241/91P and C-242/91P, *Telefis Eireann and Independent Television Publications Ltd v Commission of the European Communities* (*Magill*) (1995) ECR I-743 (ECJ), constraining exercise of copyright.

[99] *See* JH Reichman and P Samuelson, "Intellectual Property Rights in Data?" (1997) 50 *Vand L Rev* 51, 87 n.153.

[100] *See,* e.g., 15 USC ss 1–7 & 12–27; Consolidated Version of the Treaty on the Functioning of the European Union, 5 September 2008, arts 101–102, 2008 OJ (C 115) 47; *cf. F. Hoffman-LaRoche Ltd v Empagran S.A.*, 542 US 155 (2004), attempting to utilize US antitrust law extraterritorially to compensate for lack of local law. *See also Federal Trade Comm'n v Actavis*, 133 S Ct 1630 (2013), limiting the power of right holders to pay for delayed market entry to the detriment of the public interest.

principle was explicitly affirmed at the WCT Diplomatic Conference in 1996.[101] Likewise, the *US–110(5)* panel rejected the argument that permissible exceptions had been "frozen in time" and was receptive to the notion that evolving markets and consumer preferences would change the interpretation of the copyright Exceptions provision.[102]

National and regional legislatures have been equally responsive to this concern. For example, while the WCT requires states to guarantee the integrity of technological protection measures used to safeguard intellectual property rights in the digital environment, the EU Copyright Directive requires member states to ensure that these measures do not override certain public-regarding exceptions.[103] And numerous national laws have created exceptions specifically for particular technologies, such as the right to back up computer software, to make ephemeral copies while browsing the internet, and to limit the liability of internet intermediaries (for example, for using trademarks to trigger keyword advertising).[104] Similarly, the Biotechnology Directive, along with national implementing legislation and associated case law, has adapted patent principles to the challenges posed by genomic science.[105]

In light of the importance of adaptation, we see value in articulating a fuller range of exceptions (or the freedom to create exceptions) that should be regarded as part of the *acquis*. We would not want the

---

[101] WCT, Agreed Statement Concerning Article 10:

> It is understood that the provisions of Article 10 permit Contracting Parties to carry forward and appropriately extend into the digital environment limitations and exceptions in their national laws which have been considered acceptable under the Berne Convention. Similarly, these provisions should be understood to permit Contracting Parties to devise new exceptions and limitations that are appropriate in the digital network environment.

[102] TRIPS, art 13; *US–110(5)*, at ¶¶ 6.59 and 6.187.

[103] WCT, art 11; Copyright Directive, art 6.4.

[104] *See, e.g.*, 17 USC s 117; Software Directive, art 5.2; Copyright Directive, art 5.1; Joined Cases C-236/08-C238/08, *Google France v Louis Vuitton Malletier, Centre National de Recherché en Relations Humaines, and Viaticum* [2011] All ER (EC) 411 (CJEU) (holding out the possibility that Google may benefit from safe harbors in the E-Commerce Directive with respect to alleged liability for keyword advertising using marks of plaintiffs); *L'Oreal SA v eBay International AG* [2009] EWHC 1094 (Ch) (UK), Case C-324/09, [2011] ETMR 52 (CJEU) (same possibility with respect to provision of online auction services).

[105] Directive 98/44/EC of the European Parliament and of the Council of 6 July 1998, on the Legal Protection of Biotechnological Inventions, 1998 OJ (L 213) 13; *Monsanto Technology LLC v Cefetra BV*, Case C-428/08, [2010] All ER (D) 65 (Jul) (CJEU 2010).

international community to adopt a measure prematurely. However, we would expressly include optional principles in the *acquis* in order to ensure that states can experiment and tailor law to their needs with the confidence that they will not be subject to a WTO complaint or trade pressure. We take the point that optional lists of exceptions can be interpreted as exhaustive.[106] However, the very purpose of including options in the *acquis* is to encourage the development of new access provisions, and to provide a mechanism for those with expertise in emerging areas to contribute to global policy development. To the extent these measures transcend borders and implicate common challenges, the incorporation of specialized knowledge could help alleviate capacity problems. Examples of such commitments to future law development might include provisions to deal with private ordering,[107] open innovation (peer production), and private copying.[108] As discussed further later, the *acquis* should also include a commitment to deal with the mounting cost of defending the identical activity in sequential litigation in a series of national courts.[109] We illustrate how the adaptation issue should be approached in the next section.

---

[106] *See,* e.g., B Hugenholtz, "Why the Copyright Directive Is Unimportant, and Possibly Invalid" (2000) 22 *Eur Intell Prop Rev* 501.

[107] *See,* e.g., GB Dinwoodie, "Private Ordering and the Creation of International Copyright Norms: The Role of Public Structuring" (2004) 160 *J Inst and Theoretical Econ* 161.

[108] *See,* e.g., DJ Gervais, "Towards a New Core International Copyright Norm: The Reverse Three-Step Test" (2005) 9 *Marq Intell Prop L Rev* 1, 8;

> The fact that private use is not expressly mentioned as an exception in a number of national laws or the Berne Convention is not surprising: it was of little interest to copyright holders until the invention of the VCR and double-deck cassette players, which only became popular in the 1970s.

[109] *See,* e.g., *Metro-Goldwyn-Mayer Studios Inc v Grokster, Ltd.*, 545 US 913 (2005) which involved facts that were also litigated in the Netherlands; *Computer Associates, Inc v Altai, Inc.*, 126 F 3d 365 (2d Cir 1997), where the same case was litigated in France; Case C-593/03, *Roche Nederland BV v Primus* [2007] FSR 5, which envisions successive infringement litigation against related defendants throughout Europe. *See also* International Association for the Protection of Intellectual Property, Resolution, Question Q174 – *Jurisdiction and Applicable Law in the Case of Cross-Border Infringement of Intellectual Property Rights* (25–28 October 2003) <http://www.aippi.org/reports/resolutions/Q174_E.pdf>.

B. Rights of Authors, Traders, and Inventors

Historically, international intellectual property law has been driven by the agendas of authors, traders, and inventors. For example, the Berne Convention originated in meetings presided over by the author Victor Hugo, who was the president of what became the Association Littéraire et Artistique Internationale.[110] Similarly, inventors, desiring to exhibit their inventions at the Vienna Exposition of 1873, wanted assurance that their works would not be copied. The Paris Convention was the result of their efforts.[111] This etiology is reflected in the content of these instruments, which largely articulate the rights of authors and producers. Thus, by reason of pedigree, iteration, relationship to the creative process, and global interdependence, the *acquis* clearly includes the right to control reproduction of copyrighted works; the right to prevent confusing uses of a mark; the right to exclude others from (among other things) making, selling, or using patented products; and mechanisms to facilitate multinational acquisition of rights. For all regimes, the *acquis* also includes a commitment to provide effective enforcement. There is no need for us to retread this ground.

The challenge of the Knowledge Economy is therefore not in identifying the basic rights; it lies instead in addressing the emerging elements of the *acquis*, the adaptation of the core rights to reflect the impact of new technologies and the vast expansion of global trade. Consider, for example, the problem of widespread infringement through digital distribution of protected works. Right holders have experienced difficulties in effectively enforcing their interests because defendants are dispersed across the globe and can be difficult to find. Furthermore, much of the activity spans multiple jurisdictions, yet the regulatory power of each state is confined to its own territory and judicial system.

To overcome these hurdles, right holders look for a choke point. In several recent cases, they have pursued intermediaries on a variety of legal theories, often revolving around the concept of secondary liability. Examples include cases that attempt to impose liability on manufacturers of copying technologies for infringements caused by those who use their equipment; on purveyors of peer-to-peer file-sharing software for the activities of those who download material without right holders' permission; on internet service providers for subscribers' infringing postings; and on other intermediaries, such as auction sites on which counterfeit

---

[110] Ricketson and Ginsburg, *supra* note 42, ¶¶ 2.07–2.09.

[111] SP Ladas, *Patents, Trademarks, and Related Rights: National and International Protection* (Harvard University Press 1975) s 44, 59.

products are allegedly sold.[112] But despite much litigation, the problems of global distribution have yet to be resolved.[113] Case law is inconsistent across jurisdictions.[114] The resulting uncertainty for right holders, intermediaries, and the public could interfere with the development of global business models and full exploitation of the potential of the internet.

The development of e-commerce thus highlights the increasing interdependence of nations and the need for a global solution to new technological challenges. Given the leverage that right holders continue to enjoy, they have been actively pursuing an international approach – principally ACTA – to deal with this issue. But ACTA negotiations on this point largely failed.[115] The failure demonstrates that there is a corollary to the principle of balance that we have repeatedly endorsed: what might be called a "preservation of balance" principle which requires that the balance within the intellectual property regime must be comparable before and after technological change.[116] ACTA was negotiated in

---

[112] *See* e.g., *Metro-Goldwyn Mayer Studios, Inc v Grokster, Ltd.*, 545 US 913 (2005) (claim against purveyors of peer-to-peer software); *Sony Corp v Universal City Studios*, 464 US 417 (1984) (claim against manufacturers of videocassette recorders); *A&M Records, Inc v Napster, Inc.*, 239 F 3d 1004, 1010–1011 (9th Cir 2001) (claims against distributors of peer-to-peer software); *Tiffany (NJ) Inc v eBay, Inc.*, 600 F 3d 93 (2d Cir 2010) (rejecting Tiffany's attempt to hold auction site liable for sale of counterfeit items on its website); *LVMH v eBay* [2010] ETMR 10 (Tribunal de commerce, Paris 2008); *Cartoon Network LP v CSC Holdings, Inc.*, 536 F 3d 121, 123 (2d Cir 2008) (considering whether defendant cable company's digital video recorder system, allowing home recording of cable broadcasts, infringed plaintiff's copyrights); *L'Oreal SA v eBay International AG* [2009] EWHC 1094 (Ch) (UK), Case C-324/09, [2011] ETMR 52 (CJEU); *Twentieth Century Fox Film Corp v Newzbin Ltd* [2010] EWHC 608 (Ch), (2010) ECC 13 (UK); *Roadshow Films Pty Ltd v iiNet Ltd* [2010] FCA 24, (2010) 83 IPR 430, *on appeal*, *Road-show Films Pty Ltd v iiNet Ltd* [2011] FCAFC 23 (Australia).

[113] *See,* e.g., R Giblin, *Code Wars: 10 Years of P2P Software Litigation* (Edward Elgar 2011).

[114] *See* JC Ginsburg and S Ricketson, "Inducers and Authorisers: A Comparison of the US Supreme Court's Grokster Decision and the Australian Federal Court's Kazaa Ruling" (2006) 11 *Media & Arts L Rev* 1; cases cited *supra* note 112.

[115] *See* PK Yu, "Six Secret (and Now Open) Fears of ACTA" (2011) 64 *SMU L Rev* 975.

[116] *See,* e.g., Copyright Directive, art 6.4; Nat'l Comm'n on New Technological Uses of Copyrighted Works, Final Report (1978) (recommending what became 17 USC s 117); CJ Craig, "Digital Locks and the Fate of Fair Dealing in Canada: In Pursuit of 'Prescriptive Parallelism,'" (2010) *13 J World Intell Prop* 503; JH Reichman, GB Dinwoodie and P Samuelson, "Reverse Notice and

secret. However, leaked documents suggested both that early drafts were unbalanced and that the drafters sought to use accommodation to the internet as an opportunity to shift the line between permissible and impermissible uses in favor of right holders. The early version sought to impose an obligation on countries to install a system of graduated response, which would require service providers to disable the internet connections of their customers after receiving repeated notices of claimed infringement – without any judicial finding that the allegations of infringement were valid.[117] Moreover, it failed to provide safeguards for the interests of users that mirrored those found in the brick and mortar world.[118] According to the French Conseil D'Etat, procedures of this type violate the fundamental human rights of internet users.[119]

The pedigree and iterative nature of this problem of delocalized infringement suggest that the *acquis* must be understood to include a commitment to effective enforcement in the digital environment. However, any instrument that effectuates this goal must also include provisions that safeguard legitimate uses. Thus, while we would endorse a secondary liability regime, we would incorporate limits that permit the development of platform technologies and accompanying business models. In an article with Annette Kur, we drew on the adjacent body of tort law to construct a balanced rule.[120] We suggested a right of action for inducing counterfeiting or for failure to expeditiously respond to manifest infringement. In our view, this formulation is sufficiently robust to catch

Takedown Regime to Enable Public Interest Uses of Technically Protected Copyrighted Works" (2007) 22 *Berkeley Tech L J* 981, 1042, discussing the concept of prescriptive parallelism.

117 *See* A Bridy, "ACTA and the Specter of Graduated Response" (2011) 26 *Am Univ Int'l L Rev* 559; M Geist, *The ACTA Guide, Part One: The Talks To-Date* (25 January 25 2010)<http://www.michaelgeist.ca/content/view/4725/125/>.

118 *See* ACTA Communique, Washington University Conference on ACTA, 24 June 2010http://www.wcl.american.edu/pijip/go/acta-communique: "ACTA would distort fundamental balances between the rights and interests of proprietors and users, including by … introducing highly specific rights and remedies for rights holders without detailing correlative exceptions, limitations, and procedural safeguards for users."

119 CC Decision No. 2009-580DC, 10 July 2009, J.O. 9675 <http://www.conseilconstitutionnel.fr/decision.42666.html>.

120 GB Dinwoodie, RC Dreyfuss, and A Kur, "The Law Applicable to Secondary Liability in Intellectual Property Cases" (2009) 42 *NYU J Int'l Law & Pol* 201, 227.

egregious infringements. However, it would leave room for the development of new distribution technologies and businesses. Others have also proposed solutions to the digital distribution dilemma, and we are confident that further experimentation will refine these proposals.[121] Ultimately, we would hope that a rule delineating the scope of secondary liability would be adopted as an international mandatory standard. The *acquis* should recognize the need to develop such a solution.

In-transit seizure cases, where right holders require authorities to stop goods in transit (potentially) between countries where the goods do not infringe rights, are likewise a symptom of the problem of easy distribution across borders in a time of freer trade.[122] As the WTO complaint filed by India against the EU to protest the seizure of generic medicines suggested, however, these actions may interfere with rights guaranteed by the GATT and TRIPS Article 31*bis*.[123] Furthermore, they are effective partly because they are abusive in that they require shippers to engage in costly litigation far from their bases of operations. While the *acquis* clearly requires measures to facilitate right holders' ability to protect their markets, it should also include a commitment to prevent sharp practice. Once again, considerable experimentation may be required to identify solutions appropriate to local conditions. For example, it may well be better to mandate export controls at the point where the allegedly infringing goods are put into the stream of commerce (that is, at a location convenient to the shipper). TRIPS already permits states to

---

[121] *See,* e.g., European Max-Planck-Group on Conflict of Laws in Intellectual Property (CLIP), Conflict of Laws in Intellectual Property: The CLIP Principles and Commentary, art s 3–604 (Oxford Univ. Press. 2013); *see also* FW Mostert and MB Schwimmer, "Notice and Takedown for Trademarks" (2011) 101 *Trademark Rep* 249, seeking to establish a "ius gentium" on trademark law applicable to trademark infringement online. The WIPO Standing Committee on Trademarks decided it was premature to consider developing a global standard for intermediary liability for online trademark infringement. *See* Report of the Standing Committee on the Law of Trademarks, *Industrial Designs and Geographical Indications*, SCT/27/11 at ¶¶ 211–213 (27th Sess. Geneva 18–21 September 2012).

[122] *See* Joined Cases C-446/09 and C-495/09, *Koninklijke Philips Electronics NV v Lucheng Meijing Industrial Company Ltd* and *Nokia v Her Majesty's Comm'rs of Revenue and Customs* [2012] ETMR 13 (CJEU 2011).

[123] Request for Consultations by India, European Union and a Member State – Seizure of Generic Drugs, WT/DS408/1 (19 May 2010) 1; *EU, India Drop Generics Dispute to Focus on FTA Talks*, FDAnews, 24 January 2011, <http://fdanews.com/newsletter/article?issueI d=14404&articleId=133690>.

control export;[124] ACTA makes it a requirement.[125] However, these measures do not fully grapple with the ramifications of such actions: jurisdiction, choice of law, and logistical concerns regarding proof of infringement – that is, doctrines that protect due process, competition, and national autonomy and that assure prompt access to lawfully shipped products. The *acquis* should be understood to include a commitment to find solutions to both sides of the export problem.

Of course, in a free trade environment characterized by widespread online and off-line distribution, choke points will not always be available or fully effective. Attempts at developing regional and multinational agreements on a transborder litigation system for all intellectual property disputes are under way, but none has reached fruition.[126] However, a more focused response has been available for some time. Thus, the Internet Corporation for Assigned Names and Numbers has adopted the Uniform Domain Name Dispute Resolution Policy (UDRP) to resolve a certain class of trademark-domain name disputes without the need to locate and assert personal jurisdiction over the infringing registrants.[127] Formally, the UDRP is soft law, but it is made effective by a mix of contract and technology, and policed through "appeals" to national courts.[128] Experience with the UDRP suggests that the *acquis* should include a commitment to develop procedural innovations to ensure efficient adjudication of transnational disputes to protect the interests of producers (and users as well).[129]

---

124 TRIPS, art 51.

125 ACTA, art 16.1

126 American Law Institute, *Intellectual Property: Principles Governing Jurisdiction, Choice of Law, and Judgments in Transnational Disputes* (2008): CLIP, *supra* note 121. *See also* Regulation (EU) No 1257/2012 of the European Parliament and of the Council of 17 December 2012 implementing enhanced cooperation in the area of the creation of unitary patent protection, OJ L 361/1 (31 December 2012); Agreement on a Unified Patent Court, Council Document 16351/12 of 11 January 2013 <http://documents.epo.org/projects/babylon/eponet.nsf/0/A1080B83447CB9DDC1257B36005AAAB8/$File/upc_agreement_en.pdf>.

127 *See* Internet Corporation for Assigned Names and Numbers, Uniform Domain Name Dispute Resolution Policy, ¶ 4 (24 October 1999) <http://www.icann.org/en/udrp/udrp-policy-24oct99.htm>.

128 *See Barcelona.com v Excelentisimo Ayuntamiento De Barcelona*, 330 F 3d 617 (4th Cir 2003).

129 *See* LR Helfer and GB Dinwoodie, "Designing Non-National Systems: The Case of the Uniform Domain Name Dispute Resolution Policy" (2001) 43 *Wm & Mary L Rev* 141.

C. National Autonomy

As should be apparent from the discussions of both access-regarding principles and proprietary rights, states retain considerable flexibility to fulfill the objectives of intellectual property law in ways that are tailored to their individual conditions. The emphasis on flexibility suggests the *acquis* also includes a norm of national autonomy, a principle with an unimpeachable pedigree. An early attempt to establish a multinational intellectual property regime advanced a model based on universality. But that model was firmly rejected.[130] Instead, the premise of the Paris and Berne Conventions was respect for sovereignty. Subject to narrow exceptions, nations were free to determine their own innovation policies as long as they did not discriminate against foreigners.

As international law began to impose more requirements on national law, it began to explicitly endorse the national autonomy principle. Thus, the Preamble to TRIPS recognizes "the underlying public policy objectives of national systems for the protection of intellectual property, including developmental and technological objectives." Moreover, Article 1.1 includes two more specific guarantees. First, states may "determine the appropriate method of implementing the provisions of this Agreement within their own legal system and practice." Second, Article 1.1 allows states to enact more extensive protection than TRIPS requires (so long as it does not contravene the provisions of the Agreement). In addition, TRIPS gives states considerable flexibilities regarding enforcement. Article 41.5 of TRIPS confirms that there is no "obligation to put in place a judicial system for the enforcement of intellectual property rights distinct from that for the enforcement of law in general." The *China–Enforcement* panel interpreted the remedies provisions to give China a large margin of appreciation on how it structures relief.[131] Even ACTA, which attempts to reduce the states' room to maneuver, nonetheless acknowledges that its enforcement requirements must take into account "differences in [states'] respective legal systems and practices."[132]

These provisions, which instantiate the principle of national autonomy, respect differences in legal culture (hence, the flexibilities on enforcement), as well as differences in local creative environments (hence, the rights retained to enact more extensive protection). Thus, they bear an intimate relationship to the nature of knowledge production and they facilitate adaptation and experimentation. National autonomy is, in short,

---

[130] *See A Neofederalist Vision*, at 23–4.
[131] *See* ibid., at 73–6.
[132] ACTA, recital 4.

a pillar of the international *acquis*. The commitment accommodates the diverse demands of countries across a wide economic and social spectrum and recognizes that countries must have room to respond to the distributive consequences of intellectual property rights.

We recognize that there are tensions between autonomy interests and both the floors (minimum standards) and ceilings (access-regarding provisions) imposed by the *acquis*. For example, the proposal we advanced for an international standard delineating the circumstances in which an intermediary might be secondarily liable for infringing acts of others limits state autonomy at both ends. But the interdependence of nations in the distribution of knowledge sometimes requires that autonomy be effectuated in paradoxical ways. In this example, a uniform rule would actually further state autonomy. It would prevent a state with excessively broad protection from shutting down internet services legitimately operating in other countries. By the same token, it would bar information havens from undermining appropriate protection for intellectual property rights by failing to provide right holders with an effective and convenient mechanism for protecting their property.

D. Interdependence: National Treatment

Unlike national autonomy and the obligation to balance the interests of producers against access interests, national treatment has been expressly articulated in virtually every international instrument for a century and a half. It is the paradigmatic recognition of interdependence. The origins of the Paris Convention reflect the fact that the inability of foreign nationals to secure protection abroad impeded the flow of knowledge through exhibition at international expositions.[133] Likewise, Berne arose from frustration with the ease with which cheap editions of English books could be imported into England from Ireland or with which French works could be taken from Belgium to France.[134]

Because of its provenance in producer-centric agreements such as the Paris and Berne Conventions, national treatment is traditionally considered a benefit for authors, traders, and inventors. And the details of many international agreements reflect that linkage. For example, Berne ties its

---

[133] *See A Neofederalist Vision*, at 23.

[134] *See* Ricketson and Ginsburg, *supra* note 42, ¶ 1.21, at 20.

coverage to the nationality of the author or the place of first publication.[135] Similarly, the Paris Convention specifically mentions "remedies against infringement" in its articulation of national treatment.[136] But as public-regarding interests have come to the fore in recent years, the national treatment commitment must be viewed as applying more generally, to all the elements of the *acquis*, including the interests of the public. In fact, TRIPS suggests this evolution. Its national treatment provides that members shall accord "no less favorable" treatment to foreign nationals with respect to "protection" of intellectual property, which it defines for these purposes as including "matters affecting the availability, acquisition, scope, maintenance and enforcement of intellectual property rights as well as those matters affecting the use of intellectual property rights specifically addressed in this Agreement."[137] The references to scope and use recognize that foreign users have as strong an interest in enjoyment of the provisions cabining intellectual property rights as foreign authors, traders, and inventors have in securing their rights.

Digitization and internet distribution illustrate the need to enlarge the beneficiaries of the national treatment guarantee. Just as right holders require new protection in this environment, so do follow-on innovators, users, competitors, and intermediaries.[138] For example, news aggregators take full advantage of the internet. They incorporate works from around the globe and distribute them worldwide. The quotation right of Berne Article 10.1 is meaningless if it permits states to limit the enjoyment of that right to local users. Similarly, software is distributed internationally; Article 6.1 of the Software Directive, which permits reverse engineering to achieve interoperability, would distort trade if it permitted only EU nationals to distribute programs produced through reverse engineering. If secondary liability became the norm in line with our proposal, national treatment would require both that the cause of action be made available to all right holders and that the limits be equally extended to intermediaries, irrespective of nationality. National treatment must thus be

---

[135] Berne Convention, arts 3 and 5. *See also* Rome Convention for the Protection of Performers, Producers of Phonograms and Broadcasting Organisations, 26 October 1961, arts 2, 4–6, 496 UNTS 43.

[136] Paris Convention, art 2.1.

[137] TRIPS, art 3.1 and n 3 (emphasis added).

[138] *See,* e.g., V Franz, "Back to Balance: Limitations and Exceptions to Copyright" in G Krikorian and A Kapczynski (eds), *Access to Knowledge in the Age of Intellectual Property* (Zone Books 2010) 517, giving the example of exceptions permitting reproduction for the visually impaired.

considered both part of the *acquis* and equally protective of user and producer interests.

III. APPLYING THE *ACQUIS*

In conceptualizing an international *acquis*, we identified principles that constitute the backdrop to all international and national intellectual property lawmaking. The international intellectual property system has been 150 years in the making; comprehensively fleshing out its underlying principles will also take time and will require the efforts of numerous scholars and policy makers. However, the benefits are potentially vast. As the *acquis* grows, so too will its significance. Retrospectively, it can be used interpretively, to bring coherence to the international system, and to fill gaps. Prospectively, it would create a template for crafting new intellectual property instruments, and serve as a counterweight to political pressures that induce TRIPS-plus agreements. More ambitiously, the *acquis* could promote a reconceptualization of international intellectual property law as explicitly recognizing the interests of users as on a par with the interests of producers.

A. Treaty Interpretation

The most obvious application of the *acquis* is in connection with interpreting the TRIPS Agreement. There are several difficulties with the DSB's current approach to TRIPS. For instance, the DSB is unwilling to make normative judgments on such issues as what counts as a "legitimate interest" or "normal exploitation" in the exceptions tests for copyright and patent, and it refuses to give substantial weight to Articles 7 and 8, which set out the objectives and principles of the Agreement. Furthermore, the DSB will not, in effect, pass judgment on the rationale underlying national legislation. The Berne *acquis* was somewhat helpful in shedding light on the copyright exceptions provision in the *US–110(5)* case. However, the Berne *acquis* relates only to copyright. The principles it encompasses are all explicit provisions of the laws of developed countries. An international *acquis* would go much further. It would reach across disciplines and identify the commonalities among the silos of "copyright," "patent," "trademark," and related bodies of law. While we focused mainly on the laws we know (those of the US and the EU), an examination of the laws of other – more diverse – states is sure to reveal other background norms, statutory provisions, and practices that will further enrich and deepen our understanding of how the system should work. As we have illustrated in this initial attempt, there are such overarching principles, and the *acquis* would enable the DSB to take them into account.

Consider, for example, how states might deal with the access problems posed by gene patents.[139] The *acquis* demonstrates that in a large range of existing instruments, the international community is committed to releasing the building blocks of knowledge into the public domain.[140] With that insight, the DSB would be better placed to determine which types of regulation are compatible with TRIPS. Similarly, recognition of the relationship between competition and intellectual property law, and the importance of state autonomy in tailoring the law to local needs, would deepen the DSB's appreciation for the justifications states might assert for imposing a local working requirement under TRIPS.

An *acquis* would also shed light on methodological issues. The DSB has been heavily criticized for treating the three steps of the exceptions tests in copyright and patents as cumulative. That analysis, which can stop as soon as a panel finds that a particular exception is not "limited" (the first factor in all of the exceptions tests),[141] means that societal interests may never be taken into account. Under that approach, even the exception for laws of nature might be rejected as not "limited." The *acquis* exposes the fallacy in the cumulative approach. It demonstrates the strong commitment to balance inherent in all intellectual property regimes. In some cases, this is expressed explicitly. But it is often implicit – by what the system decides not to commodify. An examination of the *acquis* demonstrates how critical these considerations, which are accounted for in the latter two steps of the exceptions tests, are to any analysis of a state exception. When there are broad public interests at stake, the concept of "limited" must give way to the broader exceptions that the other steps justify.

Constructing the *acquis* would also emphasize the structural significance of Articles 7 and 8. Although explicit reference to the broader objectives and principles underlying intellectual property law was new to international law, the ideas expressed in these provisions are fully

---

139 *See A Neofederalist Vision,* at 16–19.

140 *See Ass'n for Molecular Pathology v Myriad Genetics, Inc.*, 133 S Ct 2107 (2013).

141 The first step of the copyright provision – Article 13 – speaks of exceptions being confined to "certain, special cases," but the *US–110(5)* panel interpreted this phrase as requiring in part that the challenged measure be "limited in its field of application or exceptional in its scope." *US–110(5)*, at ¶¶ 6.107–6.110.

consistent with the ethos of intellectual property law since Berne and Paris. Moreover, they have always been central to national laws.[142] And their recognition as fundamental principles of the *acquis* is reinforced by developments since TRIPS. Balance (reflected in Article 7) has become a dominant framing device in international lawmaking, including in the WIPO Development Agenda,[143] as well as in the WCT, where it shaped the entire negotiation process and was ultimately included in the Preamble.[144] Article 8 highlights policy values that have been endorsed by the Ministerial Council Declarations at Doha[145] – and even by the countries involved in ACTA.[146] Relying on these norms would not, as the *Canada–Pharmaceuticals* panel feared, constitute a renegotiation of the Agreement. Rather, according greater significance to Articles 7 and 8 would effectuate long-standing intellectual property commitments.

As the *acquis* crystallizes the principles that animate intellectual property, it should become easier to integrate the many strands of norm making that now occur. While we focus here on sketching only the basic contours of the *acquis*, the multiple institutions developing these norms could use their particular expertise to fill in the details. By recognizing that the contributions of these institutions are part of the fabric of intellectual property, the DSB, the Council for TRIPS, and other actors could more easily draw on these efforts. For example, a properly negotiated agreement on secondary liability might become part of the *acquis*. If the DSB were called upon to entertain a case on peer-to-peer file sharing, it could then use the *acquis* to determine whether the respondent was properly implementing its obligation to protect against unlawful reproduction. Thus, while we are skeptical about a full-throated

---

142 *See* Ricketson and Ginsburg, *supra* note 42, ¶ 13.02, at 756; "'Public interest' … is a shifting concept that requires a careful balancing of competing claims … . This balancing process occurs in all national copyright systems, even in those which proclaim the rights of authors most absolutely, and … the same has been true of the Berne Convention."

143 *See* World Intellectual Property Organization, The 45 Adopted Recommendations under the WIPO Development Agenda, ¶ 45<http://www.wipo.int/export/sites/www/ip-development/en/agenda/recommendations.pdf>.

144 WCT, Preamble, noting the "balance between the rights of authors and the larger public interest, particularly education, research, and access to information."

145 Doha Ministerial Declaration, ¶¶ 17 and 19; Declaration on Public Health, ¶¶ 4, 5(a).

146 ACTA, recital 6: "Desiring to address the problem of infringement of intellectual property rights … in a manner that balances the rights and interests of the relevant right holders, service providers, and users."

endorsement of the integration approach proposed by the Study Group of the International Law Commission,[147] the development of an international *acquis* would accomplish many of the same goals. The *acquis* would be guided by substance rather than by the formal canons on which the International Law Commission relied. Thus, it would bring coherence to an increasingly fragmented system by revealing consensus rather than by resolving conflict.

Finally, a fully realized *acquis* would facilitate gap filling, both in TRIPS and in other instruments. Some scholars have conceptualized TRIPS as an incomplete contract, with missing terms to be supplied by the DSB.[148] We consider that approach inconsistent with the Dispute Settlement Understanding, which appears to prohibit bare judicial activism.[149] More fundamentally, we believe that the dispute-settlement process is, in terms of representational legitimacy, far removed and insulated from appropriate democratic pressures. As a state-initiated and intentionally trade-centered process, it is likely to produce skewed results. In contrast, if the DSB were to draw upon the *acquis* as we envision it, its deliberations would be inclusive of varied national and international experience and informed by the normative underpinnings of the laws at issue. The results reached would be based on something of a consensus among nations.

Outside TRIPS, the power of the *acquis* to fill gaps would be even more valuable. For example, many of the recent bilaterals focus on providing additional detail to existing producer rights. They often lack provisions dealing with limits on these rights, which might prompt the conclusion that measures safeguarding user and broader societal interests are inapplicable. But viewed against the background rules of the *acquis*, it should be clear that these limits have not been jettisoned by silence. For example, in many bilateral investment treaties (BITs), each party agrees that it will not expropriate or nationalize the investments made by

---

147 *See* International Law Commission, *Fragmentation of International Law: Difficulties Arising from the Diversification and Expansion of International Law: Report of the Study Group on the Fragmentation of International Law*, Finalized by M Koskenniemi, UN Doc. A/ CN.4/L.682 (13 April 2006).

148 *See,* e.g., K Saggi and JP Trachtman, *Incomplete Harmonization Contracts in International Economic Law: Report of the Panel*, China – Measures Affecting Protection and Enforcement of Intellectual Property Rights, *WT/DS362/R,* adopted 20 March 2009, (2010) 10 WTR 1–2, 23–24.

149 Understanding on Rules and Procedures Governing the Settlement of Disputes, 15 April 1994, art. 3.2, Marrakesh Agreement Establishing the World Trade Organization, Annex 2, Legal Instruments – Results of the Uruguay Round (1994) vol. 31, 1869 UNTS 401, 33 ILM 1226.

investors of the other party.[150] Because these agreements define investments to include intellectual property,[151] taken literally, the expropriation provisions would suggest that these agreements override the right to issue compulsory licenses for government use under Articles 31 and 44.2 of TRIPS.[152] Recognizing the importance of compulsory licensing options would clarify to BITs arbitrators that the investment treaties are silent only because they were negotiated against a backdrop that includes these commitments.

B. Lawmaking Templates

Treaty interpretation could be improved in many different ways; what sets the *acquis* apart is its capacity to operate prospectively. Negotiators of new instruments would start with a framework within which to deliberate. ACTA, for example, might look substantially different if the *acquis* had been in place to serve as a checklist during negotiations. Had the *acquis* been available to the drafters, they might have realized the importance of including provisions protective of all the interests implicated by their enforcement agenda. This might not of itself have ensured that the debate was any more transparent. However, the *acquis* would have compensated for the absence of advocates of these broader interests. The result might have been somewhat less one-sided; at the very least, the decision to ignore these interests would have been exposed as a conscious choice with possible political ramifications. Much the same can be said for the ongoing effort to negotiate the TPP Agreement. As with ACTA, negotiations have occurred in secret and those working on the intellectual property aspects of the agreement receive advice only from a coterie of industry representatives. Once again, leaked texts reveal a lopsided regime, inattentive to free expression, health, and other access interests.[153]

---

150 United Nations Conference on Trade and Development, Bilateral Investment Treaties 1995–2006: Trends in Investment Rulemaking (United Nations 2007) 44–51<http://www.unctad.org/en/docs/iteiia20065_en.pdf>.

151 Ibid. at 8.

152 *See* HG Ruse-Khan, "Protecting Intellectual Property Under BITS, FTAs, and TRIPS: Conflicting Regimes or Mutual Coherence?" in K Miles and C Brown (eds), *Evolution in Investment Treaty Law and Arbitration* (Cambridge University Press 2011).

153 *See* H Farrell, "Five Key Questions – and Answers – About the Leaked TPP Text" *Washington Post* (15 November 2013) <http://www.washingtonpost.com/blogs/monkey-cage/wp/2013/11/15/five-key-questions-and-answers-about-the-leaked-tpp-text/>.

The *acquis* would also reduce asymmetries in capacity. Armed with the *acquis*, all participants would share a basic command of the components of an effective intellectual property system. For those developing countries that are still struggling to come up to speed with the issues involved in international intellectual property lawmaking, an *acquis* would be particularly helpful. The developed countries wrote the first draft of TRIPS, thus framing the entire debate on their terms. Developing countries therefore started at a substantial disadvantage and were unable to secure specific textual commitments that reflected their interests. The *acquis* would have reset the default to a position more appropriate both historically and substantively; with it, the final Agreement might have encapsulated a more complete understanding of the parties' commitments. While it is too late to fully revise TRIPS, there are many ongoing negotiations where an *acquis* might diminish the political leverage of the demandeurs. It would be harder to pressure a weaker party to sacrifice interests that the *acquis* recognizes as legitimate. For example, it might be more difficult to require a country to relinquish the right of farmers to save seeds if the *acquis* clarified the strength of the international commitment to nutrition.

At the national level, an *acquis* would also be of substantial use. Developing countries are now bombarded with advice – some well intentioned, some strategic – on how best to implement their obligations. Sifting through the "guidance" provided by technical assistants sent by developed countries, WIPO, WHO, UNCTAD, and assorted NGOs is time-consuming and costly. The *acquis* essentially curates this input.[154] Developed countries could also benefit from the broader perspective on intellectual property that the *acquis* would provide. For example, negotiators of the EU Database Directive extended the database right on a reciprocity basis rather than national treatment because they saw protection for investment in databases as unrelated to existing forms of intellectual property law. The *acquis* would have illuminated the depth of the international community's commitment to addressing interdependence problems by affording national treatment. Furthermore, the *acquis* would have alerted the negotiators to the character of the Directive as a regulation of unfair competition, and therefore subject to the national treatment obligations of the Paris Convention.[155]

---

[154] *See* RL Okediji, "The Regulation of Creativity Under the Internet Treaties" (2009) 77 *Fordham L Rev* 2379, 2404–8, discussing the institutional capacity of developing countries to exercise effective design choices at the national level.

[155] *See A Neofederalist Vision*, at 97–9.

C. Reorienting the Intellectual Property System: User Rights

It is often asserted that international intellectual property law (most notably, Berne, Paris, and TRIPS) constitutes only a minimum standards regime setting baseline levels of protection for authors, traders, and inventors. History suggests that this view is too simplistic. A number of provisions in the principal international instruments establish maximum levels of protection. For example, under the Berne Convention, states are prohibited from interfering with the right of the public to quote from copyrighted works. Our analysis of the broader implications of these instruments, along with national laws, demonstrates that other non-proprietary interests are similarly guaranteed. In fact, a close reading of Article 1.1 of TRIPS supports this notion. While the measure permits member states to "implement in their law more extensive protection than is required by this Agreement," it also contains an important proviso. States may not do so in ways that "contravene the provisions of the Agreement,"[156] suggesting that the Agreement must also be read to include some maxima – what might be called "user rights" or, as Jessica Litman terms them, "liberties."[157]

Indeed, immediately after the TRIPS Agreement was concluded, states began to advance proposals built around the idea of user rights. At the WCT Diplomatic Conference, a variety of countries, including Australia, South Africa, and Tanzania, suggested that the Conference consider adopting "mandatory exceptions" to the rights of copyright owners.[158] Those proposals were not pursued at that time, but the discussion has intensified in recent years. In 2009, a consortium of South American countries introduced a proposed treaty to recognize access rights for the visually impaired based on recommendations from the World Blind Union, an effort that bore fruit in the summer of 2013.[159] Scholars and NGOs have also promoted this agenda. The soft law instrument on exceptions and limitations in copyright law proposed by Hugenholtz and Okediji includes rights to private study, teaching, and research; reverse

---

[156] TRIPS, art 1.1.

[157] J Litman, "Readers' Copyright" (2011) 58 *J Copyright Soc'y* 325, 345.

[158] *See* GB Dinwoodie, "The WIPO Copyright Treaty: A Transition to the Future of International Copyright Lawmaking?" (2007) 57 *Case Western Res L Rev* 751, 760.

[159] World Intellectual Property Organization, Marrakesh Treaty To Facilitate Access To Published Works For Persons Who Are Blind, Visually Impaired, or Otherwise Print-Disabled, WIPO Doc. VIP/DC/8 (27 June 2013).

engineering; and time, space, and format shifting.[160] Annette Kur and Henning Grosse Ruse-Khan have similarly advanced the view that certain access-regarding principles require mandatory recognition.[161] Among other things, the Kur group's amendment to TRIPS would add rights to reverse engineer and parody copyrighted works; to make strictly noncommercial use of trademarks and to use them in comparative advertising; and to make noncommercial use, educational use, and experimental use of patented inventions.[162] Most comprehensive is the draft Treaty on Access to Knowledge, which was promulgated by a group of NGOs led by the Consumer Project on Technology (now Knowledge Ecology International).[163]

In some quarters, the question whether these maximum levels of protection create "rights" for users is contentious.[164] However, once the intellectual property regime is conceived holistically, it is clear that the rights view is correct; as per Justice Brennan, limits on intellectual property protection are "not some unforeseen byproduct" of the international scheme. To fully operationalize those limits that are fundamental to the system, "exclusions" and "exceptions" must be conceived affirmatively, as the rights of consumers, competitors, intermediaries, and follow-on innovators. The *acquis* would buttress this reorientation of intellectual property law by identifying principles that repeat across international regimes regulating all forms of intellectual property, that are considered mandatory at the international or regional level (requiring implementation in all member states), that are duplicated in virtually all national laws, and that are aligned with other instruments where the same interests are denominated as rights.

---

[160] Hugenholtz and Okediji, *supra* note 25.

[161] A Kur and HG Ruse-Khan, "Enough Is Enough: The Notion of Binding Ceilings in International Intellectual Property Protection" in *Proposals for Reforming the TRIPS Agreement*, *supra* note 27, at 359.

[162] Proposals for Reforming the TRIPS Agreement, *supra* note 27, arts 13.1(b) and 13.1(c)(v); 17.1(a) and 17.1(b)(iii); 30.1(a)–(d); *see also* RC Dreyfuss, "TRIPS – Round II: Should Users Strike Back?" (2004) 71 *U Chi L Rev* 21; GB Dinwoodie, "The International Intellectual Property Law System: New Actors, New Institutions, New Sources" (2004) 98 *Am Soc'y Int'l L Proc* 213. *Cf.* LR Patterson and SW Lindberg, *The Nature of Copyright: A Law of Users Rights* (University of Georgia Press 1991).

[163] Proposed Treaty on Access to Knowledge (10 May 2005) <http://keionline.org/content/view/235/1>.

[164] *See,* e.g., JC Ginsburg, "Authors and Users in Copyright" (1997) 45 *J Copyright Soc'y* 1, 6–9; J Hughes, "Recoding Intellectual Property and Overlooked Audience Interests" (1999) 77 *Tex L Rev* 923, 924–8.

Classifying public-regarding provisions as grants of rights is a philosophically fraught task; fully articulating the entire scope of these user rights is an ongoing project. However, our work on the *acquis* clarifies a few propositions. First, national treatment is best understood as applying to user rights as well as to the rights of authors, inventors, and traders. Second, access-regarding measures that are less explicit in international law can, when corroborated by iteration in national law, be regarded as so essential to the system that they amount to guaranteed rights. These would include a right of access to the fundamental principles of nature and to material that has become a part of the public domain. Third, free speech protections in national constitutions and international human rights instruments confirm that access interests in ideas, facts, and generic expressions must be carried over to intellectual property law as user rights.

Reorienting the system to recognize user rights raises a number of questions. First, if user rights are added to the *acquis*, then the scope of national autonomy, which we believe crucial, shrinks, for states will be squeezed between floors (minimum standards) and ceilings (created by user rights). However, theoretical autonomy is one thing; real autonomy requires the political ability to resist pressure. The growth of user rights provides countries interested in safeguarding access with new tools and with the international affirmation necessary to insist that their interests are recognized.

Second, is the question whether characterizing certain interests as rights would make a real difference in lawmaking. We think it would. Rights talk is important rhetorically. It would counter the view of TRIPS as a code of proprietary guarantees and stimulate efforts to put proprietary and user rights on a par with one another. Thus, David Vaver would impose a "reverse three-step test," akin to the exceptions provisions in TRIPS, which would permit the recognition of new proprietary rights under national law only if the nation in question could show a demonstrated need for them.[165] But even without imposing yet another multipart

---

[165] *See* D Vaver, "Copyright and the Internet: From Owner Rights and User Duties to User Rights and Owner Duties?" (2007) 57 *Case W Res L Rev* 731:

> If user rights were truly to be balanced against owner rights, one would expect to find a provision that owner rights should be enacted or enforced only in (1) certain special cases that (2) demonstrably encourage the production of the work, and that (3) do not unreasonably prejudice the legitimate interests of users. That feature of balance does not yet appear on any WIPO or TRIPS agenda. It should.

See also Gervais, *supra* note 108.

filter, reorienting the intellectual property system to recognize the equivalence of user and proprietary interests would have significant impacts both nationally and internationally. It would reaffirm the commitment to balance and bring user-centric provisions into focus as essential elements.[166] Furthermore, within some national systems, exceptions are narrowly construed; the use of rights terminology will tend to broaden the reach of these provisions and expand the scope of access interests.

Some have also questioned whether user rights would be enforceable as a matter of international law (in particular, within TRIPS). Among other things, critics argue that no state will have an incentive to challenge a failure by another country to protect users because the users whose interests are most directly jeopardized will likely be locals of that country. We believe that the agency problem is overstated. The interdependence of the global intellectual property economy means that the beneficiaries of access-regarding measures operate across borders and therefore have an interest in the enforcement of user rights in foreign markets. For example, a company as formidable as Google, faced with a French law that did not permit it to utilize the Berne quotation right, could presumably persuade the US to bring a complaint against France to vindicate its interests. In fact, India's challenge to in-transit seizures under EU law is an example of the enforcement of user interests. The complaint was an attempt to protect the ability of generic competitors to produce pharmaceuticals under the compulsory license plan approved by the Doha Declaration and to safeguard patients' access to these medicines. Had the case been resolved in India's favor, these user interests would have been vindicated.

IV. CONCLUSION

The Paris and Berne Conventions were vital steps in encouraging knowledge production. These instruments, built on principles of national autonomy and national treatment, established a global market for information goods and dramatically increased the incentive to invest in innovation. As cross-border trade blossomed, it produced a vibrant creative environment, for the ingenuity and inventiveness of each nation could flourish, and nations could both teach and learn from each other. Opportunities for international exchange have increased since Paris and Berne. Free trade regimes have matured, and digital communication

---

[166] *Cf.* Litman, *supra* note 157, at 6.

technologies facilitate collaboration across borders, improve information flows, and enhance access to knowledge-intensive products from distant markets.

The TRIPS Agreement updated the historical commitments in Paris and Berne, recognized the importance of intellectual property as the subject of trade, and provided an effective means for states to resolve disputes. We are only now beginning to appreciate the impact of that development. Decisions in the DSB reveal a reluctance to consider the conceptual structure of intellectual property law or its links to human rights and other societal interests. In part, this is a function of the text of the Agreement; its failure to include benchmarks and examples to guide decision makers, as well as its ill-considered transpositions from trade law. But whatever the cause, TRIPS has had unfortunate consequences at both the national and the international level. Proprietary rights continually expand, both legally and rhetorically, skewing the political process in developed countries and confounding the capacities of developing nations.

Of course, the international intellectual property system transcends TRIPS. TRIPS represented a departure from the concentration of international policy making in WIPO. Now that WIPO's exclusive domain has been breached, regime shifting has become endemic. Those dissatisfied with the view of TRIPS as imposing high levels of protection seek to establish counternorms in other institutions; those who wish to see TRIPS standards augmented have flexed their power in new lawmaking venues, including through bilateral and regional agreements. The resulting cacophony has fragmented international law, increased uncertainty, undermined incentives to invest in innovation, and exacerbated political economy problems.

We therefore believe ourselves to be in what might be called an "international constitutional moment," when the time is ripe for a new paradigm.[167] Integrating diverse regimes through interpretation helps reduce the costs of fragmentation, but it cannot solve all the problems. Thus, as a complementary device, we turn to the notion of an international *acquis*, which would crystallize the international commitment to

---

[167] *Cf.* BJ Ackerman, *Reconstructing American Law* (Harvard University Press 1984). Others have adopted this device in international law. *See,* e.g., A-M Slaughter and W Burke-White, "An International Constitutional Moment" (2002) 43 *Harv Int'l L J* 1, 2; *see also* MP Scharf, "Seizing the 'Grotian Moment': Accelerated Formation of Customary International Law in Times of Fundamental Change" (2010) 43 *Cornell Int'l L J* 439, 445, suggesting the alternative term of "Grotian moment" for such moves in international law.

intellectual property protection. It would include both express and latent components of the international regime, put access-regarding guarantees on a par with proprietary interests, and enshrine the fundamental importance of national autonomy and national treatment. Although it is unlikely that the intellectual property system will ever be centrally administered in the manner of a true federal system, the *acquis* would facilitate what might be called a neofederalist vision, in that it would coordinate international lawmaking while giving due regard to the role of nation-states in that process. We hope that in this moment of fluidity, our proposal for an *acquis* will begin a conversation about the shape of the future of international intellectual property law.

PART II

COPYRIGHT ISSUES

5. Understanding the "three-step test"

Christophe Geiger, Daniel J. Gervais and Martin Senftleben

In the current debate on flexibility in the area of exceptions and limitations (E&Ls) to intellectual property, the three-step test embodied in the Berne Convention, the TRIPS Agreement and several other more recent instruments have taken centre stage. In this chapter, we explain the history, purpose and interpretation of the test. In Part I, we consider the drafting history of the international three-step test. In Part II, we unpack the criteria of the three-step test and offer guidance on their interpretation. In Part III, we suggest that national legislation can, and in many cases probably should, preserve flexibility by allowing the courts to identify *ex post* new use privileges on the basis of the test's criteria.

I. EMERGENCE OF THE THREE-STEP TEST

A. The Three-step Test in the Berne Convention

The first version of the three-step test in international copyright law emerged as article 9(2) of the Berne Convention. It served as a counterweight to the formal recognition of a general right of reproduction at the 1967 Stockholm Berne Convention Revision Conference. It is not entirely accurate to say that the right of reproduction was added to the Berne Convention only at the Stockholm Conference. It was already there in various forms.[1] However, it is true that a general right of reproduction was recognized at the 1967 Stockholm Conference, and with it, the need for a general clause regulating exceptions and limitations. Countries agreed on the three-step test as the compromise solution instead of a finite list of specific, named exceptions as are found today in the laws of

[1] The Berlin Act of the Convention (1908) contained several "reproduction rights" or, more precisely perhaps, versions of a more general right of reproduction subsumed under those special mentions. See WIPO, Berne Convention Centenary (Geneva: WIPO, 1986), at 229.

countries like France, Germany and the Netherlands. The wording of the test was also discussed. Whereas the initial version read "in certain *particular* cases where the reproduction *is not contrary to* the legitimate interests of the author," this was later replaced by "in certain *special* cases where the reproduction *does not unreasonably prejudice* the legitimate interests of the authors."

In accordance with article 32 of the *Vienna Convention on the Law of Treaties* (VCLT) the interpretation of the test should be informed by, but cannot be entirely deduced from, its drafting history. That history is often understood to be limited to the following passage in the conference records, in which the steps were considered sequentially:

> The Committee also adopted a proposal by the Drafting Committee that the second condition should be placed before the first, as this would afford a more logical order for the interpretation of the rule. If it is considered that reproduction conflicts with the normal exploitation of the work, reproduction is not permitted at all. If it is considered that reproduction does not conflict with the normal exploitation of the work, the next step would be to consider whether it does not unreasonably prejudice the legitimate interests of the author. Only if such is not the case would it be possible in certain special cases to introduce a compulsory license, or to provide for use without payment.[2]

A more thorough analysis suggests, however, that a distinction can be drawn between the *analytical process* suggested by this paragraph and the *normative context*. Let us explain this distinction against the backdrop of article 31 VCLT which refers to the ordinary meaning of terms used, in context, in light of their object and purpose. A domestic E&L is valid under the test if it meets a series of conditions. The *sequential* nature of the conditions does not mean that they are entirely *separate*, however. In other words, the test can be seen as a single analytical whole, even though, according to the preparatory works of the Berne Convention,[3] the steps should be considered sequentially. Presumably, one or more of the steps will apply more directly depending on the E&L at hand. For example, the prima facie unreasonableness of prejudice to

---

[2] See WIPO, *Records of the Intellectual Property Conference of Stockholm June 11 to July 14, 1967*, Geneva: WIPO 1971, Report on the Work of Main Committee I, pp. 1145–6.

[3] Even if the drafting history of Berne may support sequential steps, such a reading of the test would be mandatory only in the context of the Berne three-step test and not in the context of any of the subsequent versions in other Agreements which follow other rationales and have other histories (see below).

right holders can be negated by compensation in appropriate cases, a matter to which this chapter returns below. Hence, while all criteria or steps of the test must be applied sequentially, such an application does *not* mean that the third step should automatically be cast aside if the second step is not met.

An important feature of the test as it emerged in 1967 was that it was meant as a guide to national legislators. This issue, namely the *locus* of the test, is essential to its interpretation. One example should suffice. The notion of "special case," if considered as a directive to national legislators, means that a domestic E&L rule must be "special," which one may define, as we will see later, as limited in scope, or as having a special purpose.[4] The test is thus meant to judge the exception *as a rule*, not its application in a specific case to a given author, work and user. Once the language of the test itself is transposed into national law, however (as was done, e.g., in Australia[5] and certain continental-European countries[6]), the inclusion of the test gives rise to a different set of questions. Depending on the method of implementation, the test can become a filter for the application of an exception not as a rule but rather on a case-by-case basis.[7] Transposing the three-step test in national law (that is, changing its status from international law to domestic law rule) thus radically transforms its purpose and meaning.

Before considering other instantiations of the test, we should note that the Berne test *qua* Berne still applies because most of the substantive provisions of the Berne Convention, including its article 9(2), were

---

4 See S. Ricketson and J.C. Ginsburg, *International Copyright and Neighbouring Rights: The Berne Convention and Beyond* (Oxford: Oxford University Press, 2006), vol. 1 at p. 764.

5 *Copyright Act* (Australia), art. 200AB, added by the *Act to amend the Copyright Act 1968, and for related purposes* No. 158, 2006, art. 10.

6 The basis for this development is the three-step test in art. 5(5) of the EU Information Society Directive 2001/29.

7 For a closer analysis of this development in the EU, see M.R.F. Senftleben, "Fair Use in the Netherlands – a Renaissance?", *Tijdschrift voor auteurs-, media- en informatierecht* 2009, p. 1, available at http://ssrn.com/abstract=1563986; J. Griffiths, "The 'Three-Step Test' in European Copyright Law – Problems and Solutions", *Intellectual Property Quarterly* (2009), p. 489 (495); C. Geiger, "The Three-Step Test, A Threat to a Balanced Copyright Law?", *International Review of Intellectual Property and Competition Law* 37 (2006), p. 683; "From Berne to National Law, via the Copyright Directive: The Dangerous Mutations of the Three-Step Test", *European Intellectual Property Review* (2007), p. 486.

incorporated into TRIPS. This also means that an exception permitted by another provision of Berne need not pass the test as an additional condition. For example, E&Ls (e.g., compulsory licensing) in the field of cable distribution (Berne article 11*bis*(2)) and sound recordings (Berne article 13(1)) are self-contained. This would be true of exceptions as well, such as the exception for reporting of current events (Berne article 10(2)), which is subject to its own internal test, namely "to the extent justified by the informatory purpose." Put differently, the TRIPS version of the test applies to "new" rights (e.g., the rental right in TRIPS articles 11 and 14.4) and to E&Ls not provided specifically in Berne, such as the so-called small exceptions discussed by the WTO panel dealing with section 110(5) of the US Copyright Act.[8]

B. The Test in Other International Instruments

The test is present in four provisions of the TRIPS Agreement (articles 9, 13, 26.2 and 30) and inspired the drafters of article 17. It has also been incorporated in articles 10(1) and (2) of the WIPO Copyright Treaty (20 December 1996); article 16(2) of the WIPO Performances and Phonograms Treaty (20 December 1996); article 13(2) of the Beijing Treaty on Audiovisual Performances (24 June 2012); and article 11 of the Marrakesh Treaty to Facilitate Access to Published Works for Persons who are Blind, Visually Impaired or Otherwise Print Disabled (27 June 2013).

A significant concern follows from the fact that the language of the test changes, sometimes quite significantly, each time it appears somewhere new. In TRIPS articles 26.2 and 30, "special" was replaced by "limited," and in article 13, "author" was replaced by "right holder" (assuming, it seems, that media companies exploiting works of authors always had coextensive interests with those of authors). In two instantiations of the test in TRIPS (26.2 and 30), the legitimate interests *of third parties* (not right holders) were added to the third step, a significant change to be sure. As noted in WTO dispute-settlement panel reports dealing with the three-step test,[9] this seems to change the normative equation of the third step because users' interests may not be of the same nature as those of

---

[8] *United States – Section 110(5) of the US Copyright Act*, WTO document WT/DS160/R. See D. Gervais, *The TRIPS Agreement; Drafting History and Analysis* (4th edn, London: Sweet & Maxwell, 2012), pp. 286–92.

[9] For an overview of related WTO Dispute Settlement cases, see Gervais, *The TRIPS Agreement*: ibid., pp. 282–92 and 474–5; C.M. Correa, *Trade-Related Aspects of Intellectual Property Rights: A Commentary on the TRIPS Agreement*

"right holders." It also begs the question of what happens in copyright (articles 13 of TRIPS and 9(2) of Berne as incorporated into TRIPS) where those interests are not mentioned. Of course, the exception was established for the benefit of users in the first place. Still, the essentially unexplained drafting changes (variations on the original, 1967 version are rarely well explained or documented) are something that policy makers, dispute-settlement entities and legislators must bear in mind.

The function of the three-step test as a flexible framework for the adoption of E&Ls at the national level emerges quite clearly in the 1996 WIPO "Internet treaties",[10] and specifically in the Agreed Statement concerning article 10 WCT, which allows member States to "carry forward and appropriately extend into the digital environment" copyright limitations and exceptions in their national laws.

The minutes of the WCT and WPPT negotiations mirror the determination to shelter a number of key use privileges.[11] The US delegation, for example, sought to safeguard the fair use doctrine. Denmark feared that the new rules under discussion could become "a 'straight jacket' for existing exceptions in areas that were essential for society."[12] Many delegations opposed a version of article 10(2) WCT that would have subjected extant E&Ls under the Berne Convention to the three-step test potentially in a new way.[13] Korea unequivocally suggested the deletion of

(Oxford: Oxford University Press 2007); M.R.F. Senftleben, "Towards a Horizontal Standard for Limiting Intellectual Property Rights? – WTO Panel Reports Shed Light on the Three-Step Test in Copyright Law and Related Tests in Patent and Trademark Law", *International Review of Intellectual Property and Competition Law* 37 (2006), p. 407; M. Ficsor, "How Much of What? The Three-Step Test and Its Application in Two Recent WTO Dispute Settlement Cases", *RIDA* 192 (2002), p. 111; D.J. Brennan, "The Three-Step Test Frenzy: Why the TRIPS Panel Decision might be considered Per Incuriam", *Intellectual Property Quarterly* 2002, p. 213; J.C. Ginsburg, "Toward Supranational Copyright Law? The WTO Panel Decision and the 'Three-Step Test' for Copyright Exceptions", *RIDA* 2001, p. 13; C. Geiger, "The Role of the Three-Step Test in the Adaptation of Copyright Law to the Information Society", *e-Copyright Bulletin* January–March 2007.

[10] The WIPO Copyright Treaty (WCT) and the WIPO Performances and Phonograms Treaty (WPPT),

[11] See WIPO Doc. CRNR/DC/102, § 488.

[12] See ibid., § 489.

[13] See, for instance, the statements made by the delegations of Denmark, WIPO Doc. CRNR/DC/102, § 489, New Zealand, ibid., § 495, and Sweden, ibid., § 497. See for the text of the draft provision the end of the previous subsection.

paragraph 2[14] – a proposal that was approved by a number of other delegations.[15]

Hence, the Agreed Statement concerning article 10 can be viewed as confirming the desirability of maintaining an appropriate balance in copyright law and as a guideline for the extension of existing E&Ls in the digital environment ([article 10] "should be understood to permit Contracting Parties to devise new exceptions and limitations that are appropriate in the digital network environment"). The Agreed Statement also maintains the legality of Berne-compatible E&Ls without changing the role of the test in that context ([article 10] allows Contracting Parties "to carry forward and appropriately extend into the digital environment limitations and exceptions in their national laws *which have been considered acceptable under the Berne Convention*"). The preamble of the WCT supports this analysis. It stresses the necessity, "to maintain a balance between the rights of authors and the larger public interest, particularly education, research and access to information, as reflected in the Berne Convention."[16]

Finally, the Marrakesh Treaty to Facilitate Access to Published Works for Persons Who Are Blind, Visually Impaired, or Otherwise Print Disabled (VIP Treaty) signed on 27 June, 2013, is also important because it explicitly refers to the different versions of the "three-step test" in international copyright law. Article 11 of the Treaty makes it clear that there are many versions and that an E&L must comply with all versions by which a country is bound under the Berne Convention, the TRIPS Agreement and the WIPO Copyright Treaty, including their interpretative agreements. This arguably supports interpretations of the test(s) in TRIPS, for example, that differ from earlier interpretations under Berne even though it is to be taken into account that the WIPO Copyright Treaty, according to its article 1(1), is a special agreement within the meaning of article 20 of Berne, and that WTO panels may rely on the

---

14 See WIPO Doc. CRNR/DC/102, § 491.

15 See, for instance, the statements made by the delegations of Hungary, WIPO Doc. CRNR/DC/102, § 493, and China, ibid., § 500.

16 See the preamble of the WCT. The WPPT contains a similar formulation in its preamble. The issue had already been addressed in the basic proposal for the later WCT. See WIPO Doc. CRNR/DC/4, § 12.09. Moreover, it was raised in the course of the deliberations of Main Committee I. See WIPO Doc. CRNR/DC/102, 72 and 74. Cf. as to the reference to the Berne Convention ("as reflected in the Berne Convention"), S. Ricketson, "The Boundaries of Copyright: Its Proper E&Ls: International Conventions and Treaties", *Intellectual Property Quarterly* (1999), p. 56 (61).

Berne *acquis* when it comes to the interpretation of the three-step test in article 13 TRIPS.[17]

II. THE INTERPRETATION OF THE THREE-STEP TEST

The open-ended wording of the three-step test allowed negotiators to settle the sensitive question of E&Ls at the multilateral level in a way that countries of both the civil law and the common law tradition could accept. For quite some time after the inclusion in various international treaties, the three-step test did not receive much attention, however. Its full impact on national legislation thus remained mostly speculative.

That changed on 15 June 2000,[18] when a WTO dispute-settlement panel found that the US had violated its TRIPS obligations by adopting a copyright exception in violation of article 13 TRIPS. It became clear then that the three-step test had to be taken seriously and that further work was required on limits to national legislators' freedom to implement copyright E&Ls. Suddenly, due to this interpretation of the panel (and the enforceability of WTO dispute-settlement panel reports once adopted by the WTO Dispute-Settlement Body), the three-step test became one of the main, if not *the main* issue, when trying to find a fair balance of interest in copyright law and policy. The WTO panel stated that section 110(5)(b) of the US Copyright Act, which exonerates certain commercial establishments such as bars or restaurants that broadcast non-dramatic musical works from copyright royalty payments,[19] violated *all three steps* of article 13 TRIPS.[20] For the first time, an international dispute-settlement panel also offered a formal and detailed definition of the conditions set by the test in the field of copyright law.

---

[17] This approach has been taken by the WTO panel dealing with Section 110(5) of the US Copyright Act. In its Report of the Panel, WTO Document WT/DS160/R, available at www.wto.org, para. 6.62, the panel explicitly held that the inclusion of Berne provisions by virtue of article 9.1 TRIPS included the Berne *acquis*: "If that incorporation should have covered only the text of Articles 1–21 of the Berne Convention (1971), but not the entire Berne *acquis* relating to these articles, Article 9.1 of the TRIPS Agreement would have explicitly so provided."

[18] Panel Rep. of 15 June 2000, *United States–Article 110 (5) of the US Copyright Act*, WT/DS160/R.

[19] 17 U.S.C. § 100 (5), as modified by an Act of 1998 (*Fairness in Music Licensing Act*).

[20] Concerning this decision, see e.g., Senftleben, "Towards a Horizontal Standard for Limiting Intellectual Property Rights?" (note 9 above).

A. The WTO Panel in the 110(5) Case

According to the WTO dispute-settlement panel, the first condition of the test (namely the requirement of a "certain special case", implies that "an exception or limitation in national legislation must be clearly defined" (which corresponds to the requirement of a "certain" case) and then that it has "an individual or limited application or purpose" (which corresponds to the requirement of a "special" case). The WTO panel drew a distinction between the words "certain" and "special." It interpreted the term "certain" to mean that an E&L had to be clearly defined, though there was no need "to identify explicitly each and every possible situation to which the exception could apply, provided that the scope of the exception was known and particularised."[21] On its merits, the panel thus regarded the word "certain" as requiring a sufficient degree of legal certainty.[22]

From the term "special", the panel derived the additional requirement that an E&L should be *narrow in a quantitative as well as a qualitative sense*.[23] It summarized this twofold requirement as narrowness in "scope and reach."[24] Its application to the business exemption and the homestyle exemption of section 110(5) shows that, pursuant to the panel's conception, it is particularly the number of potential beneficiaries that must be sufficiently limited in order to comply with the quantitative aspect of speciality.[25] As to the qualitative aspect, the panel eschewed an inquiry into the legitimacy of the public policy purpose underlying the adoption of the E&L at hand.[26] In the panel's view, the qualitative aspect of speciality did not mean that an E&L must necessarily serve a special purpose to be qualified as a special case under article 13 TRIPS.[27] Instead, the panel raised conceptual qualitative issues, such as the

---

[21] See Report of the Panel, 15 June 2000, WTO Document WT/DS160/R, online available at www.wto.org, para. 6.108.

[22] The panel held, for instance, that the term "homestyle equipment" was sufficiently clear and that detailed technical specifications were not necessary. See WTO Panel, ibid., para. 6.145.

[23] See ibid., para. 6.109.

[24] See ibid., para. 6.112.

[25] See ibid., para. 6.127 and 6.143.

[26] See ibid., para. 6.111.

[27] See WTO Panel, ibid., para. 6.112. Cf. J.C. Ginsburg, "Toward Supranational Copyright Law?" (note 9 above); S. Ricketson, "The Three-step Test, Deemed Quantities, Libraries and Closed Exceptions" (Centre for Copyright Studies, Strawberry Hills NSW, 2002), p. 31.

categories of works affected by an E&L and the circumstances under which it may be invoked.

The second step has the potential to restrict the freedom of national legislation to enact new E&Ls considerably more. That step is the prohibition of a conflict with a "normal exploitation" of the work. How is the phrase "normal exploitation" to be interpreted? In the panel's report in the section 110(5) case, the criterion of normal exploitation was deemed to involve consideration of the forms of exploitation that *currently generate income* for the right holder as well as those which, in all probability, *are likely to be of considerable importance* in the future.[28] While this interpretation is understandable, it implies certain risks. On the one hand, it could impose a status quo and prevent any extension of E&Ls to new situations unforeseen by the letter of the text, but which could be derived from its spirit. On the other hand, reference to future forms of exploitation runs the risk of restricting policy space for exceptions every time a technical evolution allows control of previously uncontrollable uses and thus creates new possibilities for exploitation.[29] Bearing in mind the new possibilities for right holders to control the uses of their works through technical measures, in the long run, this could even significantly restrict E&Ls in the digital environment.[30]

This takes us to the third step of the test, which seems to require an examination of the *justification* that underlies the E&L at issue. Under the third step, copyright E&Ls must be prevented from causing an *unreasonable* prejudice. An interesting linguistic twist must be noted at this juncture. The official text of the Berne Convention, in case of discrepancy between linguistic versions, is the French version.[31] In French, the third step reads in part as follows: "*ne cause pas un préjudice injustifié,*" which changes the meaning at least slightly because it seems

---

[28] WTO Panel, note 21 above, para. 6.180.

[29] In this sense also M. Buydens and S. Dusollier, "Les exceptions au droit d'auteur: évolutions dangereuses", *Comm. com. électr.* Sept. 2001, at 13; J.C. Ginsburg, "Toward Supranational Copyright Law?" (note 9 above) at p. 48, underlining the risk that "the traditionally free uses, such as for training purposes or parody, be considered as normal exploitations, supposing that right holders manage to implement a profitable collecting system."

[30] See C. Geiger, J. Griffiths and R.M. Hilty, "Towards a Balanced Interpretation of the 'Three-step test' in Copyright Law", *European Intellectual Property Review* (2008) 489, stating that under the interpretation of the WTO Panel, "the second step of the 'test' becomes a form of 'show-stopper', precluding law-makers from taking into account any interests other than the private economic interests of right-holders."

[31] Berne Convention (1971), art. 37(1)(c).

to affirm that some degree of prejudice is *justified*. Put differently, the English (original) version imposes a test of *reasonableness* while the French translation (which guides the interpretation in case of discrepancy) imposes a test of *justification*.

This language indicates that the right holder is not intended to have the power to control *all* uses of her works. It also suggests that some interests may not be legitimate in this context,[32] and that a certain amount of prejudice is acceptable.[33] The formulation of the third step thus allows WTO Members to use *a proportionality test*,[34] as is often done to settle conflicts between rights.[35] A legislature or judge must consider the justification behind the E&L and come to a differentiated analysis in light of the many interests at stake.

B. Possible Alternative Approaches

The predominantly economic interpretation chosen by the WTO dispute-settlement panel can be criticized for not taking sufficiently into account the diverse social, economic and cultural policy objectives of WTO Members.[36] Hence, a more normative reading especially of the second step has been proposed by a number of scholars and commentators.[37] In

---

[32] WTO Panel, note 21 above, para. 6.222. Reasoning on the basis of conflicting fundamental rights, the German Constitutional Court specified this very clearly in its "School Book" decisions of 7 July 1971, *GRUR* 1972, 481.

[33] In this sense also WTO Panel, note 21 above, para. 6.229, noting that "a certain amount of 'prejudice' has to be presumed justified as 'not unreasonable'."

[34] M.R.F. Senftleben, *Copyright, Limitations and the Three-Step Test: An Analysis of the Three-Step Test in International and EC Copyright Law* (The Hague/London/New York: Kluwer Law International 2004), p. 226; S. Dusollier, *Droit d'auteur et protection des œuvres dans l'univers numérique* (Larcier: Bruxelles 2005), p. 221. See also Geiger, "The Three-Step Test" (note 7 above), p. 696.

[35] C. Geiger, "The Role of the Three-Step Test in the Adaptation of Copyright Law to the Information Society" (note 9 above), p. 18; "Fundamental Rights, a Safeguard for the Coherence of Intellectual Property Law?", *International Review of Intellectual Property and Competition Law* 35 (2004), p. 277.

[36] For a normative approach of the second step, see also Ginsburg, "Toward Supranational Copyright Law?" (note 9 above) p. 23; Ricketson and Ginsburg, "*International Copyright and Neighbouring Rights*" (note 4 above) § 13.21, stating that the second step requires to take into account "non-economic as well as economic normative considerations."

[37] See for further references C. Geiger, "Exploring the Flexibilities of the TRIPS Agreement Provisions on Limitations and Exceptions", in: A. Kur and V. Mizaras (eds), *The Structure of Intellectual Property Law – Can One Size Fit All?*

the specific context of the TRIPS Agreement, such a normative interpretation may rely on the objectives and principles laid down in the Agreement's preamble and in articles 7 and 8.[38] In the context of public international law, this approach is fully consistent with article 31(1) VCLT, stating that "a treaty shall be interpreted in good faith in accordance with the ordinary meaning to be given to the terms of the treaty in their context and in the light of its *object and purpose*" (emphasis added).[39]

Article 7 of TRIPS lays down a principle of balance between rights and obligations and emphasizes that the Agreement has the goal of fostering not only economic development, but also social welfare. This means that while interpreting the provisions of TRIPS, a pure economic perspective should not be followed to the exclusion of other values and objectives.[40] Article 8 of TRIPS goes in the same direction, as it allows Members to adopt measures for the promotion of "the public interest in sectors of vital importance to their socio-economic and technological development." Then, the preamble to the TRIPS Agreement refers not

---

(Cheltenham, UK/Northampton, MA: Edward Elgar, 2011), at pp. 287 seq; C. Geiger, "The Social Function of Intellectual Property Rights, Or How Ethics can Influence the Shape and Use of IP law", in: G.B. Dinwoodie (ed.), *Intellectual Property Law: Methods and Perspectives,* 153 (Cheltenham, UK/Northampton, MA, Edward Elgar, 2014).

[38] H. Grosse Ruse-Khan, "Proportionality and Balancing within the Objectives for Intellectual Property Protection", in: P. Torremans (ed.), "*Intellectual Property and Human Rights*" (Austin/Boston/Chicago/New York/ The Netherlands, Kluwer Law International, 2008), p. 162; and Geiger, in A. Kur and V. Mizaras, note 37 above.

[39] See detail on this issue S. Frankel, "WTO Application of 'the Customary Rules of Interpretation of Public International Law' to Intellectual Property", *Virginia Journal of International Law* 46 (2006), p. 365. See also the Doha Declaration on the TRIPS Agreement and Public Health adopted by the Ministerial conference (WT/Min (01)/DEC/2, 20 November 2001), where it is explicitly stated that "in applying the customary rules of interpretation of international law, each provision of the TRIPS Agreement shall be read in the light of the object and purpose of the Agreement as expressed, in particular, in its objectives and principles" (art. 5 a).

[40] See more detailed: H. Grosse Ruse-Khan, "A Comparative Analysis of Policy Space in WTO Law" (November 26, 2008), Max Planck Institute for Intellectual Property, Competition & Tax Law Research Paper Series No. 08-02 (published under the title "Assessing the Needs for a Public Interest Exception in the TRIPS Agreement", in: A. Kur and M. Levin (eds.), *Intellectual Property in a Fair World Trade System – Proposals for Reforming TRIPS,* 167 (Cheltenham, UK/Northampton, MA: Edward Elgar, 2011).

only to the objective of promoting adequate protection mechanisms. It also recognizes the "underlying public policy objectives of national systems" and, with regard to least-developed countries, the needs "in respect of maximum flexibility in the domestic implementation."[41]

Henning Grosse Ruse-Khan has argued that there is a principle of proportionality in international trade law that has to be respected while interpreting TRIPS.[42] "Proportionality" is a notion mostly used in the context of issues of fundamental rights, especially as a method to solve conflicts between different values at stake.[43] Indeed, one may find support for this approach in the field of patent law. A different WTO panel dealing with the protection of pharmaceutical products in Canada noted in its report that "both the goals and the limitations stated in articles 7 and 8.1 must obviously be borne in mind when (examining the wording of the provision) as well as those of other provisions in the TRIPS Agreement which indicate its object and purposes."[44]

In the *Canada-Pharmaceuticals* case, the WTO panel seemed to adhere to a more normative approach in interpreting article 30 TRIPS – the three-step test version applicable to exceptions to patent rights.[45] According to the report, "exploitation" should be considered "normal" when it is "essential to the achievement of the goals of patent policy."[46] That formulation remains somewhat vague, but it may provide the

---

[41] More detailed on the preamble and its impact on the interpretation of the Agreement, see Gervais, *The TRIPS Agreement* (note 8 above), pp. 159–64.

[42] Grosse Ruse-Khan in: Torremans (note 38 above), p. 161.

[43] C. Geiger, "'Constitutionalizing' Intellectual Property Law, The Influence of Fundamental Rights on Intellectual Property in Europe", *International Review of Intellectual Property and Competition Law* 37 (2006), p. 371; "Copyright's Fundamental Rights Dimension at EU Level", in: E. Derclaye (ed.), "Research Handbook on the Future of EU Copyright", 27 (Cheltenham, UK/Northampton, MA: Edward Elgar, 2009); C. Geiger and E. Izyumenko "Copyright on the Human Rights Trial: Redefining the Boundaries of Exclusivity through Freedom of Expression", *International Review of Intellectual Property and Competition Law* 45 (2014), p. 316.

[44] WTO Panel Report of March 17, 2000, *Canada – Patent Protection of Pharmaceutical Products*, WT/DS114/R, §7.26.

[45] Article 30 TRIPS: "Members may provide limited exceptions to the exclusive rights conferred by a patent, provided that such exceptions do not unreasonably conflict with a normal exploitation of the patent and do not unreasonably prejudice the legitimate interests of the patent owner, taking account of the legitimate interests of third parties."

[46] WTO Panel Report of 17 March 2000, *supra*, § 7.58. On this report, see Senftleben, "Towards a Horizontal Standard for Limiting Intellectual Property Rights?" (note 9 above).

possibility for the legislature more easily to take normative (not strictly economic) elements into account.[47]

Admittedly, the wording of the second step (in TRIPS article 30) is different from the copyright provision in article 13 of TRIPS. It seems to imply that a conflict with normal exploitation can be justified under a more normative approach. Under article 30, "exceptions must not *unreasonably* conflict with a normal exploitation of the patent." Similarly, according to article 26.2 TRIPS, "members may provide limited exceptions to the protection of industrial designs, provided that such exceptions do not *unreasonably* conflict with the normal exploitation of protected industrial designs" (emphasis added). The explicit reference to a notion such as the "reasonableness" of the restriction to the exclusive right allows taking into account other interests than those of the right holder.[48] Articles 26.2 and 30 of TRIPS thus seem to allow a more flexible application of the test. However, there is no stated reason in TRIPS to explain why restrictions to the rights of patent owner or industrial design should be treated differently from those of the owner of authors' rights/copyright.[49]

Future WTO panels dealing with article 13 TRIPS are not formally bound by the approach taken in the report on section 110(5) of the US Copyright Act, for there is no principle of *stare decisis* in WTO law.[50] That said, a "WTO jurisprudence" may be said to exist because dispute-settlement panels understandably strive to maintain consistency with

---

47 More generally, for an analysis of exclusions to patent law provisions in TRIPS from an international Human Rights perspective, see H.M. Haugen, "Human Rights and TRIPS Exclusion and Exception Provisions", *Journal of World Intellectual Property* 5/6 (2009), p. 345.

48 See Part I: Emergence of the three-step test.

49 As A. Kur, "Of Oceans, Islands, and Inland Water – How much Room for Exceptions and Limitations under the Three-step Test?", *Richmond Journal of Global Law and Business* 8 (2009), p. 287, interestingly points out, the drafting history of the TRIPS agreement also does not offer an explanation as to why these differences in wording occurred and whether they were intended to have a special meaning.

50 See in general I. Brownlie, *Principles of Public International Law* (Oxford: Clarendon Press 1998), at pp. 19–22. Cf. J.H. Jackson, *The Jurisprudence of GATT and the WTO – Insights on Treaty Law and Economic Relations* (Cambridge: Cambridge University Press 2000), at p. 127; P.E. Geller, "Geistiges Eigentum auf dem Weltmarkt: Welche Bedeutung hat die Streitbeilegung nach TRIPS?", *Gewerblicher Rechtsschutz und Urheberrecht Internationaler Teil* 1995, 935 (943).

previous reports and frequently refer to findings of prior panels.[51] Yet, as pointed out by John H. Jackson, there are "several specific instances in the GATT jurisprudence, where panels have consciously decided to depart from the results of a prior panel."[52] Therefore, it cannot be assumed that the panel report on section 110(5) poses an insurmountable hurdle for future panels seeking to recalibrate the test as interpreted in the 110(5) case. Future panel reports may wish to identify which features of the interpretation by that panel are lasting and which may not be. Due to its heightened position in the WTO hierarchy the Appellate Body could proceed afresh on the issue.

Should they wish to refine the approach developed in the report on section 110(5) of the US Copyright Act, a future panel or the Appellate Body could rely on alternative approaches suggested since 2000. Indeed, a more flexible, normative approach to the three-step test might even be mandated by international obligations resulting from treaties protecting human rights and fundamental rights.[53] Obligations and/or applicable principles can be found, for example, from the Universal Declaration of Human Rights (UDHR) of 1948 and the International Covenant on Economic, Social and Cultural Rights (ICESCR) of 1966. Both may be seen as providing guidelines for the interpretation of the TRIPS Agreement, and therefore also of the test. An interpretation of TRIPS in the light of international fundamental rights could result from the General Rule of interpretation of treaties found in article 31 of the Vienna Convention.[54] According to article 31(3)(c), for the interpretation of a

---

[51] Panel reports might refer to so-called "dispute settlement practice." See for instance WTO Panel – Copyright 2000, §§ 6.13, 6.111, 6.162, 6.185, 6.231.

[52] See Jackson (note 50 above) at p. 127.

[53] Geiger, in: Kur and Mizaras (note 37 above) at pp. 297 seq. On the interaction between IP and international human rights provisions see L.R. Helfer and G. Austin, *Human Rights and Intellectual Property, Mapping the Global interface* (Cambridge, CUP, 2011); L.R. Helfer, "Three Approaches for Reconciling Human Rights and Intellectual Property Rights", in: ALADDA (ed.), *Copyright and Freedom of Expression, ALAI Study Days 2006* (ALADDA, Barcelona, 2008), at p. 116; C. Geiger, "Fundamental Rights as Common Principles of European (and International) Intellectual Property Law", in: A. Ohly (ed.), *Common Principles of European Intellectual Property Law*, 223 (Mohr Siebeck, Tübingen, 2012); C. Geiger (ed.), *Research Handbook on Human Rights and Intellectual Property* (Cheltenham, UK / Northampton, MA: Edward Elgar, forthcoming 2014).

[54] United Nations, Treaty Series, Vol. 1155, 331. However, it is true that some important WTO members such as the US have not ratified the Vienna Convention.

treaty, "any relevant rules of international law applicable in the relations between the parties" should be taken into account.[55] Given the ethical questions involved, it is hard to completely exclude the relevance of the human rights instruments.

Those who support a reading of the test that departs from the 110(5) panel report often point to the fact that national courts have started to interpret the test more liberally than the WTO panel.[56] Doctrinal proposals to "rethink" the test more holistically have been put forward. It was proposed, for example, to examine it in reverse, that is, to start with the third step, the second step being examined afterwards as a corrective measure to eliminate abusive conflicts with the exploitation of the work.[57] It has also been argued that the comparison of the wording of article 13 TRIPS with other TRIPS provisions modeled on the three-step test suggests that the "third step" could be considered as the most important one. Article 17 (trademarks) for example provides for only one main criterion, namely to "take account of the legitimate interests of the owner of the trademark and of third parties."[58] The "psychological" effect of a reverse reading of the steps of the test is not negligible: after having

---

[55] See Frankel, "WTO Application of 'the Customary Rules of Interpretation of Public International Law' to Intellectual Property" (note 39 above), at p. 420.

[56] See e.g., the decision of the Swiss Supreme Court, 1st Civil Division, 26 June 2007, *International Review of Intellectual Property and Competition Law* 39 (2008), p. 990. For a comment see C. Geiger, "Rethinking Copyright Limitations in the Information Society: The Swiss Supreme Court Leads the Way", *International Review of Intellectual Property and Competition Law* 39 (2008), p. 943; Court of Appeal of Barcelona (SAP), 17 September 2008. For a discussion of the three-step test as a basis for flexible fair use legislation, see M.R.F. Senftleben, "The International Three-Step Test: A Model Provision for EC Fair Use Legislation", *Journal of Intellectual Property, Information Technology and E-Commerce Law* 1 (2010), p. 67, available at http://ssrn.com/abstract=1723867.

[57] See C. Geiger, "Right to Copy v. Three-Step Test, The Future of the Private Copy Exception in the Digital Environment", *Computer Law Review international* (CRi) (2005) 12; "The Three-Step Test, a Threat to a Balanced Copyright Law?" (note 7 above) p. 696; "The Role of the Three-Step Test in the Adaptation of Copyright Law to the Information Society" (note 9 above).

[58] The full wording of article 17 TRIPS is: "Members may provide limited exceptions to the rights conferred by a trademark, such as fair use of descriptive terms, provided that such exceptions take account of the legitimate interests of the owner of the trademark and of third parties." The first "step" is therefore still present through the reference to the need of providing only "limited" exceptions. Anyhow, it has to be noted that no reference to the normal exploitation can be found.

balanced the different interests involved, a court or tribunal may be less inclined to prohibit the exception or E&L in question by adopting a purely economic approach.

Another interpretation that has been proposed is to read the test as stating a number of factors that need to be considered by the judge, based on the model of the American fair use doctrine.[59] Those who support this approach draw a parallel with the fourth factor contained in article 107 of the US Copyright Act, which codified the fair use doctrine as elaborated by US courts since the nineteenth century. According to this fourth factor, the *effect of the use on the potential market* for or value of the copyrighted work must be taken into account in determining whether a particular use is fair. Similarly, one could say that the second step (impact on normal exploitation of the work) is *one of the criteria* to take into account during the analysis of the application of an exception or E&L, but not the only one. Under this type of approach, the three-step test could be renamed the "three-factor test."

Whatever path is chosen to interpret the test, most observers agree that, normatively, a just balance of the different interests involved should be achieved.[60] This is especially true because, today, the test affects all debates concerning the future of E&Ls to copyright.[61] In this vein, the *Declaration on a Balanced Interpretation of the Three-Step Test,* elaborated jointly by a group of copyright scholars from several different

---

[59] K.J. Koelman, "Fixing the Three-Step Test", *European Intellectual Property Review* 2006, p. 407; M.R.F. Senftleben, "L'application du triple test: vers un système de fair use européen", 2007 *Propr. Intell.* 453, and from the same author: "Fair Use in the Netherlands – A Renaissance?", 2009 *Tijdschrift voor auteurs-, media- en informatierecht* 1.

[60] C. Geiger, "From Berne to National Law, via the Copyright Directive: The Dangerous Mutations of the Three-Step Test", *European Intellectual Property Review* (2007), p. 486; "The Role of the Three-Step Test in the Adaptation of Copyright Law to the Information Society" (note 9 above); Senftleben, *Copyright, Limitations and the Three-Step Test: An Analysis of the Three-Step Test in International and EC Copyright Law* (note 34 above), p. 226; Dusollier, *Droit d'auteur et protection des œuvres dans l'univers numérique*, (note 34 above), p. 221.

[61] See the Green Paper "Copyright in the Knowledge Economy" of the Commission of the European Communities, COM(2008) 466/3, p. 5, stating that the three-step test "has become a benchmark for all copyright limitations." See further, in the EU context, C. Geiger and F. Schönherr, "Defining the Scope of Protection of Copyright in the EU: The Need to Reconsider the *Acquis* regarding Limitations and Exceptions", in: T.-E. Synodinou (ed.), *Codification of European Copyright Law, Challenges and Perspectives* (Alphen aan den Rijn (NL), Kluwer Law International, 2012), p. 133.

jurisdictions, considers the different tests as an indivisible entirety requiring a comprehensive overall assessment.[62] The payment of equitable remuneration is regarded as a universal balancing tool that also impacts the decision on a conflict with a normal exploitation.[63]

III. THE ENABLING FUNCTION OF THE THREE-STEP TEST

There can be little doubt that the three-step test does not *only* serve the purpose of restricting national E&Ls. As explicated above, the first version of the three-step test was devised as a flexible framework at the 1967 Stockholm Conference on the Revision of the Berne Convention, within which national legislators would enjoy the freedom of safeguarding national E&Ls and satisfying domestic social, cultural, and economic needs.[64] The provision was intended to serve as a basis of national E&Ls to the reproduction right.

Many use privileges that have become widespread at the national level are directly based on the international three-step test. A provision that permits the introduction of national exemptions for private copying, for instance, is not expressly provided in international copyright law. It is the

---

[62] See C. Geiger, J. Griffiths and R.M. Hilty, "Declaration on a Balanced Interpretation of the 'Three-Step Test' in Copyright Law", 39 *Int'l Rev Intell Prop & Competition L* 707 (2008), Article 1. The aim of this declaration was "to restore the 'three-step test' to its original role as a relatively flexible standard precluding clearly unreasonable encroachments upon an author's rights without interfering unduly with the ability of legislatures and courts to respond to the challenges presented by shifting commercial and technological contexts in a fair and balanced manner" (C. Geiger, J. Griffiths and R.M. Hilty "Towards a Balanced Interpretation of the 'Three-step test' in Copyright Law" (note 30 above). See also R.M. Hilty, "Declaration on the Three-Step Test – Where do we go from here?," 1 *J Intell Prop, Info Tech & E-Com L* 83 (2010).

[63] See ibid.

[64] See WIPO, *Records of the Intellectual Property Conference of Stockholm June 11 to July 14, 1967*, Geneva: WIPO 1971, Doc. S/1, p. 81. For a discussion of the breathing space offered by the three-step test, Kur, "Of Oceans, Islands, and Inland Water – How Much Room for Exceptions and Limitations Under the Three-Step Test?" (note 49 above), p. 287; M.R.F. Senftleben, "Grundprobleme des urheberrechtlichen Dreistufentests", *Gewerblicher Rechtsschutz und Urheberrecht International* 2004, p. 200 (206–7). For a proposal to use the three-step test as an instrument to delineate the exclusive rights of copyright owners, see D. Gervais, "Toward a New Core International Copyright Norm: The Reverse Three-Step Test", *Marquette Intellectual Property Law Review* 9 (2005), p. 1.

international three-step test that creates space for the adoption of this type of E&L at the national level. Many other examples of national E&Ls resting on the international three-step test can easily be found in the copyright laws of parties to the Berne Convention, for example reproduction for research or teaching purposes; the privilege of libraries, archives and museums to make copies to preserve cultural material; and the exemption of reproduction required for administrative, parliamentary or judicial proceedings.

Confirming the test's role in creating room for social, cultural and economic interests that have to be balanced against the rationales of copyright protection,[65] the test has been used in this enabling sense in a number of court decisions. For instance, the German Federal Court of Justice underlined the public interest in unhindered access to information in a 1999 decision concerning the Technical Information Library Hannover. It offered support for the library's practice of copying and dispatching scientific articles on request by single persons and industrial undertakings.[66] The legal basis of this practice was the statutory E&L for personal use in § 53 of the German Copyright Act. Under this provision, the authorized user need not necessarily produce the copy herself but is free to ask a third party to make the reproduction on her behalf. The Court admitted that the dispatch of copies came close to a publisher's activity.[67] Nonetheless, it refrained from putting an end to the library's practice as conflicting with a work's normal exploitation. Instead, the Court deduced an obligation to pay equitable remuneration from the three-step test as compensation to copyright holders, and enabled the continuation of the information service in this way.[68]

---

[65] See further in this sense, with a special emphasis on the role of the three-step test in adapting copyright limitations to the opportunities created by the digital environment, C. Geiger and F. Schönherr, "Limitations to Copyright in the Digital Age", in: A. Savin and J. Trzaskowski (eds.), "Research Handbook on EU Internet Law", 110 seq. (Cheltenham, UK / Northampton, MA, Edward Elgar, 2014).

[66] See Bundesgerichtshof, February 25, 1999, case I ZR 118/96, *Juristenzeitung* 1999, p. 1000, with case comment by H. Schack. For an English description of the case, see M.R.F. Senftleben, *Copyright, Limitations and the Three-Step Test:* (note 34 above), pp. 206–8.

[67] See Bundesgerichtshof, February 25, 1999, ibid., p. 1004.

[68] See ibid., pp. 1005–7. Cf. P. Baronikians, "Kopienversand durch Bibliotheken – rechtliche Beurteilung und Vorschläge zur Regelung", *Zeitschrift für Urheber- und Medienrecht* 1999, p. 126. In the course of subsequent amendments to the Copyright Act, the German legislator modeled a new copyright E&L

In a 2002 decision concerning the scanning and storing of press articles for internal e-mail communication within a private company, the German Federal Court of Justice held that digital press reviews had to be deemed permissible under § 49(1) of the German Copyright Act just like their analog counterparts if the digital version – in terms of its functioning and potential for use – essentially corresponded to traditional analog products. To overcome the problem of an outdated wording of § 49(1) that seemed to indicate the E&L's confinement to press reviews on paper, the Court stated that, in view of new technical developments, a copyright E&L could be interpreted more liberally. This extension of the analog press review exception to the digital environment, the Court maintained, was in line with the three-step test.

Similarly, in a decision dated 26 June 2007, the Swiss Supreme Court used the three-step test to propose an extensive and liberal interpretation of the private use exception included in article 19(1)c of the Swiss Copyright Act,[69] in order to legitimize the use of press articles by specialized commercial services providing electronic press reviews upon demand to enterprises.[70] The court held that in order to guarantee the diversity of opinion needed for democracy to function and flourish and to permit the development of a true "information society," there was a clear public interest in facilitating the making and offering of press reviews by commercial services without having to obtain the authorization of each publisher. The judges then went on to consider that even if the text of the law had been drafted with analog reproduction in mind, its application had to be extended to the digital world in order to achieve its objectives. The court then examined in detail the solution adopted in the light of the three-step test. After having recalled the content of the different steps, the Supreme Court held that the third step of the test was worded differently in the different international documents and it was not obvious what interests were to be taken into account in this step. While in the Berne Convention and the WIPO Treaty the exceptions and limits must not

---

on the Court's decision. § 53a of the German Copyright Act goes beyond the court decision by including the dispatch of digital copies in graphical format.

[69] According to art. 19(1)c, private use is understood to mean the reproduction of copies of works within enterprises, public administrations, institutions, commissions and similar organizations for internal information or documentation purposes.

[70] Swiss Supreme Court, 1st Civil Division, 26 June 2007, *International Review of Intellectual Property and Competition Law* 39 (2008), p. 990. For a comment see C. Geiger, "Rethinking Copyright Limitations in the Information Society: The Swiss Supreme Court Leads the Way" (note 56 above), p. 943.

cause "an unjustified prejudice to the legitimate interest of the author," the TRIPS Agreement addresses "the legitimate interests of the right-holder." As the interests of the authors and those of the other right holders are not always identical, it follows, according to the court, that the three-step test serves to protect the author's interests at least as much as those of the exploiters. Consequently, the test must not be interpreted solely in the light of the latter's interests. The Swiss court, therefore, made a very interesting and crucial distinction, unfortunately often overlooked in the debates around the application of the three-step test: the interests of authors do not have to be identical to those of the publishers, in certain situations they can even clash. The court was of the opinion that this was the case, since the Swiss Act foresees a right to remuneration for the authors as a compensation for the private use of their work.

In Spain, the Supreme Court, in an attempt to safeguard search engine and caching services, resorted to general principles of the law, such as the social function of property, the exercise of rights in good faith and the prohibition of abuse of rights in its interpretation and application of the three-step test. In *Megakini.com v. Google Spain*, Google had been sued for copyright infringement on the grounds that its search service involved the reproduction and display of fragments of copyrighted website content, and the accompanying cache service led to the reproduction and making available of entire web pages.[71] The Court found that the three-step test in the Spanish Copyright Act did not only have a "negative" meaning (in the sense of setting forth the limits of permissible exceptions), but also a "positive" meaning in the sense of reflecting the need to set aside copyright protection in certain cases.[72]

National legislation using the three-step test as a basis for fair use legislation can go beyond the court decisions just described. It may allow

---

[71] Spanish Supreme Court, 3 April 2012, judgment 172/2012 (*Megakini.com v. Google Spain*), part 5, para. 5. For a short description and discussion of the judgment in English, see R. Xalabarder, "Spanish Supreme Court rules in favour of Google search engine", *Kluwer Copyright Blog*, 15 June 2012, online available at http://kluwercopyrightblog.com/2012/06/15/spanish-supreme-court-rules-in-favor-of-google-search-engine/. On the Spanish case law in relation to the three-step test, see also R. Xalabarder, "Fair Use in Spain. The EUCD Aftermath", in: G. Ghidini and L.M. Genovesi (eds), *Intellectual Property and Market Power* (Buenos Aires, EUDEBA, 2008), p. 811; "Google News and Copyright", in: A. Lopez-Tarruella (ed.), *Google and the Law* (T.M.C. Asser Press, The Hague, 2012), p. 164.

[72] Spanish Supreme Court, 3 April 2012, judgment 172/2012 (*Megakini.com v. Google Spain*), part 5, para. 5.

the courts, especially but not exclusively in common law jurisdictions, to create new E&Ls by interpretation while respecting the test's abstract criteria. Fair use and fair dealing legislation provide good examples of this type of flexible lawmaking. Besides the well-known fair use doctrine codified in US legislation in 1976,[73] other open-ended, flexible copyright E&Ls have been adopted in several countries.[74] In the framework of a 2006 amendment, Singapore adopted an open fair dealing provision that allows the identification of privileged uses on the basis of a catalogue of abstract factors.[75] The 2007 Copyright Act of Israel permits fair use for purposes such as private study, research, criticism, review, journalistic reporting, quotation, or instruction and examination by an educational institution.[76] A 2012 amendment to the Copyright Act of Malaysia resulted in a fair dealing provision for purposes including research, private study, criticism, review or the reporting of news or current events.[77] The 2013 Copyright Act of Korea exempts fair use, among other things, for reporting, criticism, education, and research.[78] In consultations on new copyright legislation, open-ended copyright E&Ls have also been proposed in Australia, Ireland and the UK.[79] An opening clause in the catalogue of use privileges in current EU legislation has been recommended in the European Copyright Code, which is the result of the

---

[73] The codification was not intended to change the open-ended character of the fair use doctrine. See Senate and House Committee Reports, as quoted by L.E. Seltzer, *Exemptions and Fair Use in Copyright – The Exclusive Rights Tensions in the 1976 Copyright Act* (Cambridge (Massachusetts)/London: Harvard University Press 1978), pp. 19–20.

[74] See J. Band and J. Gerafi, "The Fair Use/Fair Dealing Handbook", policy bandwidth March 2013, available at http://infojustice.org/wp-content/uploads/2013/03/band-and-gerafi-2013.pdf.

[75] Sections 35 and 36 of the Copyright Act of Singapore.

[76] Article 19 of the Copyright Act of Israel. For a discussion, see O. Fischman Afori, "An Open Standard 'Fair Use' Doctrine: A Welcome Israeli Initiative", *European Intellectual Property Review* (2008), p. 85; G. Pessach, "The New Israeli Copyright Act: A Case-Study in Reverse Comparative Law", *International Review of Intellectual Property and Competition Law* 41 (2010), p. 187 (189–93).

[77] Section 13(2)(a) of the Copyright Act of Malaysia.

[78] Article 35-3 of the Copyright Act of the Republic of Korea.

[79] I. Hargreaves, *Digital Opportunity. A Review of Intellectual Property and Growth*, May 2011, p. 5, available at http://www.ipo.gov.uk/ipreview-finalreport.pdf; Copyright Review Committee, *Copyright and Innovation – A Consultation Paper* (Dublin: Department of Jobs, Enterprise and Innovation 2012), pp. 111–23; Australian Law Reform Commission, *Copyright and the Digital Economy*, Discussion Paper 79, Sydney: ALRC 2013, pp. 59–98.

Wittem Project established in 2002 as a collaboration between copyright scholars across the EU concerned with the future development of EU copyright law.[80]

We cannot leave this topic without noting that the US was not obliged to amend its fair use doctrine when adhering to the Berne Convention in 1989 or to the TRIPS Agreement (via its ratification of the WTO Agreement) in 1995. Was it understood that the doctrine complies with the three-step test laid down in Berne article 9(2)?[81] One can perhaps find an answer at the 1996 Diplomatic Conference which adopted the WIPO "Internet" treaties, at which the US delegation underscored that, "[I]t was essential that the [WIPO 'Internet' treaties] permit the application of the evolving doctrine of 'fair use', which was recognized in the laws of the United States of America, and which was also applicable in the digital environment."[82]

The delegation went on to stress that the three-step test "should be understood to permit Contracting Parties to carry forward, and appropriately extend into the digital environment, limitations and exceptions in their national laws which were considered acceptable under the Berne Convention."[83] We found no objection in the Conference's record. In fact, as explained in Part I, this language finally made its way into the Agreed Statement which accompanies the three-step tests of article 10 WCT.

---

[80] The proposed European Copyright Code of the Wittem Project is available at www.copyrightcode.eu. See article 5.5. On the Code and its provision on E&Ls, see T. Dreier, "The Wittem Project of a European Copyright Code", in: C. Geiger (ed.), *Constructing European Intellectual Property: Achievements and New Perspectives* (Cheltenham, UK/Northampton, MA, Edward Elgar, 2013), p. 292. As to the need for flexible fair use solutions in the EU, see P.B. Hugenholtz and M.R.F. Senftleben, *Fair Use in Europe. In Search of Flexibilities* (Amsterdam: Institute for Information Law/VU Centre for Law and Governance 2011), pp. 17–18, available at http://ssrn.com/abstract=1959554; M.R.F. Senftleben, "Bridging the Differences between Copyright's Legal Traditions – The Emerging EC Fair Use Doctrine", *Journal of the Copyright Society of the U.S.A.* 57 (2010), p. 521.

[81] Cf. P. Samuelson, "Challenges for the World Intellectual Property Organization and the Trade-related Aspects of Intellectual Property Rights Council in Regulating Intellectual Property Rights in the Information Age", *European Intellectual Property Review* (1999), 578 (582–3).

[82] See Minutes of Main Committee I, WIPO Doc. CRNR/DC/102, 70.

[83] Ibid.

CONCLUSION

The three-step test in international copyright law constitutes a flexible balancing tool that offers national policy makers breathing space for the creation of an appropriate system of copyright E&Ls at the national level. At the 1967 Stockholm Conference for the Revision of the Berne Convention, the first three-step test in international copyright law was devised as a flexible framework, within which national legislators would enjoy the freedom of adopting national E&Ls to satisfy domestic social, cultural and economic needs. With the inclusion of the test in the TRIPS Agreement, the WIPO "Internet" treaties and the VIP Treaty, it has not lost this function of enabling tailor-made solutions at the national level. The WIPO "Internet" treaties confirmed that the three-step test allows the extension of traditional copyright E&Ls into the digital environment and the development of appropriate new E&Ls.

The abstract criteria of the three-step test offer room for different interpretations. The approach taken by a WTO panel in the case concerning section 110(5) of the US Copyright Act need not be seen as the final word on the test's interpretation. Various alternative approaches have been developed in literature and applied by national courts, including an understanding of the three-step test as a refined proportionality test, the use of its abstract criteria as factors to be weighed in a global balancing exercise and a reverse reading of the test starting with the last, most flexible criterion. In light of the need to balance copyright against competing interests, in particular freedom of expression and information, these flexible interpretations may prevail in the future.

6. Orphan works: A comparative and international perspective

Katharina de la Durantaye

In the last decade, orphan works have entered the spotlight of global copyright debate. The issue behind orphan works, though, is not new. From the early days of modern copyright law, rights holders of some protected works were unknown; others were impossible to find. Their works, left without an owner to negotiate with (and thus orphaned), could not be lawfully exploited if the use required permission of the copyright owner.[1]

The reasons for orphan works' current "fame" are partially legal and partially technological: over the past decades, copyright protection has expanded both in scope and in duration. Today, more works are protected, and for a longer period of time, than ever before. Since, as a rule, the older (and less valuable) a work, the harder it is to find its rights holder(s), chances are that more works will become orphans.

Simultaneously, a number of countries – most notably the U.S. – which previously requested the fulfillment of formalities as a precondition for copyright protection have abolished such requirements.[2] While admittedly problematic in some respects,[3] formalities such as notice and

---

[1] According to the U.S. Copyright Office, "orphan work" is a "term used to describe the situation where the owner of a copyrighted work cannot be identified and located by someone who wishes to make use of the work in a manner that requires permission of the copyright owner." *Cf.* U.S. Copyright Office, *Report on Orphan Works: A Report of the Register of Copyrights* (2006) 1 [hereinafter *Report on Orphan Works*] <http://www.copyright.gov/orphan/orphan-report-full.pdf>. The definition is one of many; for a close scrutiny of several orphan works definitions, *cf.* DR Hansen, "Orphan Works: Definitional Issues" *Berkeley Digital Library Copyright Project, White Paper* No. 1 (2011) <http://papers.ssrn.com/sol3/papers.cfm?abstract_id=1974614>.

[2] The U.S. did so in order to align its copyright law with art 5(2) Berne Convention.

[3] For an account of the possible advantages and disadvantages of formalities, *cf.* JC Ginsburg, "The US Experience with Formalities: A Love/Hate Relationship" (2010) 33 *Col. J. L. & Arts* 311.

registration requirements publicly document the ownership status of copyrighted works and thus function as safeguards against orphanage.

Meanwhile, digital technologies not only make it easier to separate information about rights holders from copyrighted works; they also enable users, be they public libraries, commercial enterprises, or private individuals, to exploit copyrighted works on a massive scale. In the past, the status of a work as orphaned mainly prevented individual uses of copyrighted works. Today, it proves, among other things, an obstacle to the creation of digital libraries.[4]

It was in this context that orphan works achieved their present notoriety: In fall 2004, Google launched its Google Books project, vouching to create a comprehensive digital library. The following year, a group of publishers as well as the Authors Guild brought a class action against Google. After several years of negotiations, the parties proposed an initial settlement agreement the scope of which was much broader than the legal issue at trial and which would have allowed Google the use of orphan books.[5] Because of treaty obligations, the proposed settlement agreement would have covered works by rights holders from all Berne Convention member states.[6] Not surprisingly, both support of and

---

[4] There is no lack in anecdotal evidence about the prevalence of the problem but very little hard data. The European Commission estimates that 13 percent of in-copyright books, 90 percent of photographs and 95 percent of newspapers from before 1912 are orphaned. *Cf.* A Vuopala, "Assessment of the Orphan Works Issue and Rights Clearance" in *European Commission, DG Information Society and Media Unit E4: Access to Information* (2010) 5 <http://ec.europa.eu/information_society/activities/digital_libraries/doc/reports_orphan/anna_report.pdf>. The British Library estimates that 40 percent of its holdings could consist of orphan works, *cf.* British Library, "Response to HM Government – Consultation on Copyright" 6 <http://pressandpolicy.bl.uk/imagelibrary/downloadMedia.ashx?MediaDetailsID=1423>. A study conducted by the British Library and ARROW (Accessible Registries of Rights Information and Orphan Works towards Europeana) came to similar findings (43 percent of the potentially copyrighted works in the sample used were orphans). *Cf.* B Stratton, *Seeking New Landscapes* (2011) 5 <http://www.arrow-net.eu/sites/default/files/Seeking%20New%20Landscapes.pdf>. The Strategic Content Alliance gives a more conservative estimate for the U.K., assuming that 5–10 percent of in-copyright works are orphans. *Cf.* JISC, *In from the Cold* (2009) 18.

[5] Settlement Agreement, *The Authors Guild, Inc. v. Google, Inc.*, No. 05 CV 8136 (S.D.N.Y. 28 October 2008), art IV.3(b)(i)(1). *Cf. The Authors Guild, Inc. v. Google, Inc.*, 770 F. Supp. 2d 666, 672, 678–679 (S.D.N.Y. 2011).

[6] *Cf.* DJ Gervais, "The Google Books Settlement and the TRIPs Agreement" (2011) 1 *Stan. Tech. L. Rev.* 1–10.

opposition to the proposal were virtually global. After intense public debate and additional negotiations among the parties, the District Court for the Southern District of New York struck down an amended version of the proposed settlement agreement[7] in 2011.[8] In November 2013, the court of first instance held that Google's actions constitute fair use.[9] As of this writing, the plaintiffs have appealed to the U.S. Court of Appeals for the Second Circuit.[10]

The proposed Google Books Settlements, as they are commonly called, had different effects in different parts of the world. In the U.S., the Copyright Office issued a Report on Orphan Works while the case was pending.[11] Based on that report, two sets of orphan works bills were introduced into Congress;[12] neither of them passed.[13] After the parties to the Google Books case had presented their first settlement proposal, Congress stalled further actions. Now that the amended settlement proposal is rejected and the case does not touch upon the issue of orphan works anymore, the Copyright Office is preparing for a new attempt to enact orphan works legislation.[14]

---

[7] Amended Settlement Agreement, *The Authors Guild, Inc. v. Google, Inc.*, No. 05 CV 8136 (S.D.N.Y. 9 November 2009).

[8] *The Authors Guild, Inc. v. Google, Inc.*, 770 F. Supp. 2d 666 (S.D.N.Y. 2011). In October 2012, the five publishers who had been part of the lawsuit reached a (confidential) settlement agreement with Google; since their suit was not a class action, it did not need court approval. *Cf.* <http://www.publishers.org/press/85/>.

[9] *The Authors Guild, Inc. v. Google, Inc.*, No. 05 CV 8136 (S.D.N.Y. 14 November 2013). In July 2013, the U.S. Court of Appeals for the Second Circuit had vacated the class certification and had remanded the case for consideration of fair use. *Cf. The Authors Guild, Inc. v. Google, Inc.*, No. 12-3200-cv (2nd Cir. 1 July 2013).

[10] Notice of Appeal, *The Authors Guild, Inc. v. Google, Inc.*, No. 05 CV 8136 (S.D.N.Y. 23 December 2013).

[11] *Report on Orphan Works.*

[12] Orphan Works Act of 2006, H.R. 5439, 109th Cong. (2006) (later that year, this bill was embedded in The Copyright Modernization Act of 2006, H.R. 6052, 109th Cong. (2006)); Orphan Works Act of 2008, H.R. 5889, 110th Cong. (2008); Shawn Bentley Orphan Works Act, S. 2913, 110th Cong. (2008).

[13] Shawn Bentley Orphan Works Act, S. 2913, 110th Cong. (2008) passed Senate on 26 September 2008, but did not pass the House before the 110th term of Congress ended.

[14] For all relevant documents, *see* <http://www.copyright.gov/orphan/>.

Elsewhere, the settlement proposals spurred rather than delayed legislative action. The European Commission had for a long time, and mostly unsuccessfully, pleaded EU member states to address the orphan works problem.[15] The Google Books case vividly proved that the problem was real and that Google Books might get a valuable head start if the EU did not enable its own digitization projects to use orphan works. Consequently, the EU enacted a directive on the matter.[16]

On the international stage, negotiations have started as well. At WIPO, the issue is being considered as one possible topic for a Treaty on Exceptions and Limitations for Libraries and Archives.[17] To this end, WIPO conducted a survey designed, among other things, to find out which of its member states already allow for the use of orphan works, and if so, how and under what conditions.[18]

Since the orphan works problem did not come into existence with the Google Books case, a few countries already provided mechanisms for the use of orphan works when the case was filed. None of them were designed to deal with mass digitization projects. Consequently, and partially due to the Google Books case's publicity, (additional) changes in legislation were discussed and/or enacted.[19]

Orphan works legislation commonly falls into one of four groups: compulsory licensing, statutory exceptions or limitations to copyright's exclusive rights, limitations on remedies, and designation to the public

---

[15] A notable exception is Hungary. *Cf.* Hungarian Copyright Act, art 57/A <http://www.hipo.gov.hu/English/jogforras/hungarian_copyright_act.pdf>.

[16] Directive 2012/28/EU on certain permitted uses of orphan works [2012], OJ L299/5.

[17] For the meeting documents of the Standing Committee on Copyright and Related Rights, *see* <http://www.wipo.int/meetings/en/topic.jsp?group_id=62>.

[18] WIPO Second Survey on Voluntary Registration and Deposit Systems (questions no. 21 ss.) <http://www.wipo.int/export/sites/www/copyright/en/pdf/registration_and_documentation.pdf>. For the 80 responses, *see* <http://www.wipo.int/copyright/en/registration/replies_survey_copyright_registration.html>.

[19] Both the U.S. and the EU commissioned reports on orphan works before entering the formal legislative process. *Cf. Report on Orphan Works*; IViR, *Recasting of Copyright and Related Rights for the Knowledge Economy* (2006) <http://www.ivir.nl/publications/other/IViR_Recast_Final_Report_2006.pdf>; IViR, *Study on the Implementation and Effect in Member States' Laws of Directive 2001/29/EC on the Harmonisation of Certain Aspects of Copyright and Related Rights in the Information Society* (2007) <http://www.ivir.nl/publications/guibault/Infosoc_report_2007.pdf>.

domain.[20] The following sections examine all of them in turn, explain their respective benefits and downsides, as well as possible measures which legislatures might take to prevent works from losing their parents, and ways to work around the orphan works problem currently considered in some countries around the world.

I. LICENSE SOLUTIONS

Most countries that had dealt with the issue of orphan works before mass digitization became a technical possibility precondition the right to use orphan works on the grant of a license. Such license solutions come in different forms.

A. (Compulsory) License Granted by a Public Body

Countries may provide that a potential user of an orphan work has to apply for a license from a public body, such as a government agency. Such a system exists, in various levels of breadth, in Canada,[21] France,[22] Hungary,[23] India,[24]

---

[20] For an older treatment of similar issues by the author, *cf.* K de la Durantaye, "How to Build an Orphanage, and Why" (2011) 2 (3) *JIPITEC* 226–34 <http://www.jipitec.eu/issues/jipitec-2-3-2011/3177>.

[21] Canadian Copyright Act, s 77.

[22] French Intellectual Property Act, art L. 122-9 and L. 211-2, allow the court of first instance (*tribunal de grande instance*) to take appropriate measures so that the Ministry of Culture as well as individuals with a justified interest may use orphan works. The law is, however, limited to cases where either the author has died and his/her heir is unknown, or where the author does not have any heirs.

[23] According to Hungarian Copyright Act, art 57/A, the Hungarian Patent Office has the power to grant non-exclusive licenses for a term of five years for works whose rights holders cannot be found. This provision, which entered into force in 2009, is designed to complement the already existing system of extended collective licenses in Hungary. *See* below at I.C.

[24] Indian Copyright Act, art 31A(1), used to allow the Indian Copyright Board to grant licenses for the publication of previously unpublished Indian works if "the author is dead or unknown or cannot be traced, or the owner of the copyright in such work cannot be found". *See* <http://www.wipo.int/wipolex/en/text.jsp?file_id=128098>. Now, the article is amended so that where a published or unpublished work is "withheld from the public in India, the author is dead or unknown or cannot be traced, or the owner of the copyright in such work cannot be found, any person may apply to the Copyright Board for a license to publish or communicate to the public such work or a translation thereof in any

Japan,[25] South Korea,[26] and the U.K.[27] The issuance of a license is usually conditional upon the user's diligent search for the work's rights holder.[28] The public body charged with granting licenses may issue guidelines establishing the sources that have to be consulted in order for a search to be deemed diligent. In most countries, the user has to document his or her search and present the documentation to the public body. After establishing that the user has met his or her search obligations, the public body may issue a license.

Experience has shown that relatively few licenses are applied for. The Hungarian Patent Office granted 42 licenses to use (sometimes multiple) orphan works since the introduction of its orphan works statute in 2009.[29] The Japanese Commissioner of the Agency for Cultural Affairs granted 82 licenses between 1972 and 2010, covering a total of 158,601 works.[30] In Canada, users have applied for 441 licenses between 1990 and 2010,

---

language". *Cf.* Amendment No. 17, The Copyright (Amendment) Act, 2012, No. 27 of 2012 <http://www.wipo.int/edocs/lexdocs/laws/en/in/in066en.pdf>. As for the licensing procedure, *cf.* Ministry of Human Resource Development, Notification, March 14, 2013, Chapter V, <http://copyright.gov.in/Documents/CopyRight-Rules-2013.pdf>

[25] According to Japanese Copyright Act, art 67 (1), the Commissioner of the Agency for Cultural Affairs may issue a compulsory license for the use of published works whose rights holders remain, despite a diligent search, unknown or cannot be found. According to art 67*bis*, which came into force on 1 January 2010, users may start using orphan works while their application for a license is pending. For an English language version of the Copyright Act, *see* <http://www.cric.or.jp/english/clj/cl2.html>.

[26] The minister of culture, sports, and tourism may issue a license for the use of a published work if, "despite considerable efforts", a rights holder cannot be found. *Cf.* South Korean Copyright Act, art 50 (1); for an English language version, *see* <http://www.wipo.int/wipolex/en/details.jsp?id=7182>.

[27] The Copyright Tribunal may allow a user to "make a copy of a recording of a performance … where the identity or whereabouts of the person entitled to the reproduction right cannot be ascertained by reasonable inquiry." *Cf.* Copyright, Designs and Patents Act of 1988, s 190.

[28] For an overview of the various search requirements, *cf.* DR Hansen, G Hinze, and J Urban, "What Constitutes a Diligent Search Under Present and Proposed Orphan Work Regimes?" (2013) *Berkeley Digital Library Copyright Project, White Paper* # 5 <http://papers.ssrn.com/sol3/papers.cfm?abstract_id=2229021>.

[29] For the register of licenses, *see* <http://sztnh.gov.hu/szerzoijog/arva/ARVA-muvek-nyilvantartas_teljes.pdf>.

[30] M Favale et al., *Copyright, and the Regulation of Orphan Works* (2013) IPO 45 <http://www.ipo.gov.uk/ipresearch-orphan-201307.pdf>.

for a total of roughly 12,640 works.[31] Until today, the Canadian Copyright Board granted 281 licenses, eleven of which in 2013[32] Eight applications were denied.[33]

According to the Canadian Copyright Board, users have only rarely sought orphan works licenses because of the high administrative burdens they have to meet.[34] In Canada, a person who wishes to use an orphan work must search the Internet, contact collective management organizations (CMOs), publishing houses, libraries, universities, museums, and provincial departments of education, and, if the author is dead, try to determine who inherited the copyright or who administers the estate.[35]

Elsewhere, requirements are considerable as well. Users in India must, after having conducted an unsuccessful search for the rights holder, file notice in the national daily English and Hindi newspapers, or, if the work is written in a regional language, in a respective regional language newspaper, and give a time limit during which the rights holder may object to the use.[36] In Hungary, potential users of orphan works must, in addition to looking for the

---

31 J de Beer and M Bouchard, "Canada's 'Orphan Works' Regime: Unlocatable Copyright Owners and the Copyright Board" (2010) 10.2. *Oxford Univ. Commonwealth L. J.* 215, 242.

32 For the register of licenses, *see* <http://www.cb-cda.gc.ca/unlocatable-introuvables/licences-e.html>.

33 For the register of rejections, *see* <http://www.cb-cda.gc.ca/unlocatable-introuvables/denied-refusees-e.html>.

34 The French orphan works' commission of the conseil supérieur de la propriété littéraire et artistique came to the same conclusion for the French provision ("*ce mécanisme, prévu pour l'exploitation ponctuelle d'œuvres, paraît peu praticable dans le cas d'une demande massive*"). *Cf.* Conseil supérieur de la propriété littéraire et artistique, commission sur les œuvres orphelines, [2008] *Rapport* 15 <http://www.ladocumentationfrancaise.fr/var/storage/rapports-publics/094000049/0000.pdf>. According to members of the Canadian Board, one problem is that the Board only has jurisdiction to issue a license if it is established that the work in question was published with the author's consent, and that the work is still protected under copyright law. *Cf.* J de Beer and M Bouchard, "Canada's 'Orphan Works' Regime: Unlocatable Copyright Owners and the Copyright Board" (note 31 above), 221–2; M Bouchard, "Le régime canadien des titulaires de droits d'auteur introuvables" (2010) 22 *Les Cahiers de prop. intell.* 483, 489–90, 499; WJ Vancise (Chairman of the Copyright Board of Canada), *Speech at a Seminar jointly sponsored by the Intellectual Property Institute of Canada and McGill University in Montreal*, Quebec (15 August 2007) 4–5 <www.cb-cda.gc.ca/about-apropos/speeches-discours/20070815.pdf>.

35 *Cf.* <http://www.cb-cda.gc.ca/unlocatable-introuvables/brochure1-e.html>.

36 WIPO, Standing Committee on Copyright and Related Rights, Working Document Containing Comments on and Textual Suggestions Towards an Appropriate International Legal Instrument (in Whatever Form) on Exceptions

rights holder in various databases and information resources, advertise their intentions in national newspapers.[37] In Japan, users may choose between a newspaper advertisement and an advertisement on the website of Japan's Copyright Research and Information Center.[38]

Even after all these requirements have been fulfilled, the licensing process is often slow and burdensome – in many countries, the government body has to double-check each individual search,[39] and users must pay some form of remuneration before being allowed to use the work.[40]

Thus, such a licensing system is not well equipped to deal with mass digitization of copyrighted works. The licensing process creates high administrative costs and makes the use dependent on the payment of a fee which, if the work is truly orphaned, may never be claimed. It comes as no surprise, then, that Canada and other countries are considering an overhaul of their orphan works schemes.[41] In its impact assessment for the 2012 EU directive on certain permitted uses of orphan

---

and Limitations for Libraries and Archives, (2012) SCCR/23/8, 40 <http://www.wipo.int/edocs/mdocs/copyright/en/sccr_23/sccr_23_8.pdf>.

[37] Government Decree 100/2009, art 3 (1) (c). (V.8) Korm. of the Government on detailed rules relating to the licensing of certain uses of orphan works <http://www.hipo.gov.hu/English/jogforras/100_2009.pdf>. This, however, may not be needed in every single case. According to Decree, art 2 (2), a user must have "taken the appropriate measures in a matter that are deemed reasonable under the given circumstances and with regard to the concerned type of work and mode of use." *Cf. also* Hungarian Copyright Act, art 57A (1) (a user has to take "measures that can generally be expected under the given circumstances").

[38] Agency for Cultural Affairs, *Handbook of Exploitation of Works* 11 (in Japanese), quoted after M Favale et al., *Copyright, and the Regulation of Orphan Works* (note 30 above).

[39] For India, *cf.* WIPO, SCCR/23/8, 40 (2012); Canadian Copyright Act, s 77 (1).

[40] Such rules are in place, for example, in India and Japan. *Cf.* WIPO, SCCR/23/8, 40, 43 (2012). In Canada, the Board has, when the use was "benign", sometimes ordered that royalties only be paid if the rights holder claims his or her rights. *Cf.* WJ Vancise, (note 34 above), 7. According to M Bouchard, "Le régime canadien des titulaires de droits d'auteur introuvables" (note 34 above), 500, "benign" cases are those where the user is a public institution, the use has a public purpose, a license might be unnecessary and other rights holders who could be found have granted their rights free of charge.

[41] *Cf.*, e.g., the U.K.'s Intellectual Property Office, *Orphan Works Impact Assessment*, BIS1063 (15 June 2012) <http://www.ipo.gov.uk>; Intellectual Property Office, *Government Response to the Technical Consultation on Orphan Works*, DPS/E200-05/14 (30 May 2014), <https://www.gov.uk/government/consultations/copyright-uk-orphan-works-licensing-scheme>.

works [hereinafter: orphan works directive], the European Commission also strongly cautions against government licenses:

> The government licence covering orphan works … constitutes a public certification of the diligent search and thus grants a high level of legal certainty to the digital library. But this certainty comes at a price: individual licenses would have to be obtained for the "making available" of each orphan work. The administrative burden inherent in such a system becomes obvious. This is why earlier incarnations of this system have had limited impact and are not used in relation to large-scale digital library projects.[42]

B. (Compulsory) License Granted by a Private Authority

An alternative to furnishing public authorities with the right to grant orphan works licenses would be to give that same right to CMOs, institutions which are active in many parts of the world, including and above all in Europe.[43] For example, in 2013, the U.K. – whose copyright law had allowed for the issuance of licenses by a public body (the Copyright Tribunal) for the creation of copies of a recorded performance – enacted legislation which allows the Secretary of State to provide for the grant of non-exclusive licenses in respect of orphan works (by U.K. authors and for uses in the U.K. alone) by an "independent authorizing body" and in return for a license fee.[44] In Switzerland, CMOs may grant licenses for the use of orphaned sound or video recordings which are contained in publicly accessible archives or in archives of broadcasting institutions and which were published or distributed in Switzerland at least ten years previously.[45]

In theory, licenses issued by a private authority should have similar advantages and drawbacks for users as ones granted by a public authority. In particular, private authorities should be similarly poorly equipped to deal

---

[42] European Commission, *Proposal for a Directive of the European Parliament and of the Council on Certain Permitted Uses of Orphan Works*, COM (2011) 289 final (24 May 2011) 3.

[43] For an overview of CMOs that administer reproduction rights, *cf.* <www.ifrro.org>. For a list of CMOs in other fields, *cf.* <www.cisac.org>.

[44] The Enterprise and Regulatory Reform Act (ERRA) 2013, s 77 (which provides for the creation of a new art 116A for the Copyright, Designs and Patents Act 1988). *Cf. also* Intellectual Property Office, *FACTSHEET – Orphan Works Licensing Scheme and Extended Collective Licensing* (June 2013) 1 <http://webarchive.nationalarchives.gov.uk/20140603093549/http://www.ipo.gov.uk/orphanworks-licensing.pdf>.

[45] Swiss Copyright Act (SR 231.1), art 22b.

with massive uses of copyrighted works such as required by mass digitization projects. The administrative burden of double-checking whether a reasonable search has been conducted would simply shift from a public to a private entity. One would thus assume that CMOs were not very keen on being dragged into the issue of orphan works.

In fact, though, CMOs in Europe have repeatedly suggested that they be involved in a pan-European orphan works system. Even the European Commission was more favorably disposed towards that idea than towards government licenses. In its impact assessment, the Commission did not mention any burdens which CMOs would have to carry.[46]

The Commission may be right: CMOs in Europe, which lobbied for their involvement in the issue of orphan works, did not provide any obligation to control the diligence of users' searches. Even if such an obligation to double-check the diligence of searches existed, CMOs would have strong incentives not to take it too seriously but to instead grant as many licenses as possible, and in return for a fee. They would be the ones to receive the remuneration which users would have to pay. They would administer the money and distribute it to rights holders; should any of it go unclaimed, they would keep it, such as in the U.K.,[47] or distribute it among their members and/or to the general public. *De facto*, then, a system relying on CMOs would provide users with less certainty than one in which a license is granted by a government agency while, at the same time, being more costly.

C. Extended Collective Licenses

For quite some time now, the laws of the Nordic countries (Denmark, Finland, Iceland, Sweden, and Norway) have provided for extended collective licenses (ECLs);[48] so do those of the Czech Republic[49] and

---

46 COM (2011) 289 final, Impact Assessment, at 3.

47 *Cf.* Intellectual Property Office, *FACTSHEET – Orphan Works Licensing Scheme and Extended Collective Licensing* (June 2013) 1.

48 *Cf.* Danish Consolidated Act on Copyright 2010, ch 2 <http://www.wipo.int/wipolex/en/text.jsp?file_id=191420>; Finnish Copyright Act, ch 2 <http://www.wipo.int/wipolex/en/text.jsp?file_id=208099>; Icelandic Copyright Act, art 15a, 23, 23a, 25, 32 <http://www.wipo.int/wipolex/en/text.jsp?file_id=190313>; Swedish Act on Copyright in Literary and Artistic Works, ch 3a <http://www.wipo.int/wipolex/en/text.jsp?file_id=290912>; Norwegian Act relating to Copyright in Literary, Scientific and Artistic Works, ch 2 <http://www.wipo.int/wipolex/en/text.jsp?file_id=244824>.

49 Czech Copyright Act, art 101 (9) (with exceptions regarding audiovisual works) <http://www.wipo.int/wipolex/en/text.jsp?file_id=186403>.

Hungary.[50] Under a system based on ECLs, a CMO representing a "substantial" number of rights holders of a specific category of copyrighted works may also grant licenses for works of that category which are owned by non-members.

ECLs were not created in order to deal with orphan works. In fact, although their scope has continuously been expanded over the past few decades, none of the CMOs can grant licenses for all or even most possible uses of orphan works.[51] And yet, the system's advantages for possible users of orphan works, especially for those who wish to use multiple works, are apparent – the saving of search costs. Instead of having to look for individual rights holders, users have a one-stop-shop with which to negotiate.

CMOs like the system for two reasons: it creates incentives for non-members to join, and it provides CMOs with additional funds to administer and, eventually, distribute. Non-members, so the rationale goes, benefit as well, since their works are being licensed for the same conditions as those of members. Had they bargained on their own, they would in all likelihood not have been able to obtain better conditions.[52]

Because of their benefits, ECLs have become a point of interest for lawmakers in several countries. Canada is debating the introduction of such licenses.[53] In 2013, the U.K. enacted a statute allowing the Secretary of State to enable CMOs to apply for voluntary schemes of

---

[50] Hungarian Copyright Act, art 57/A (7), 85–93.

[51] It should be noted, however, that, since Statute Nr. 587 entered into force on 20 June 2008, s 50(2) of the Danish Copyright Act allows the grant of extended collective licenses for "other uses" than the named ones.

[52] T Koskinen-Olsson, "Collective Management in the Nordic Countries" in DJ Gervais (ed.), *Collective Management of Copyright and Related Rights* (2nd edn, Kluwer Law International, 2010), 283, 291, 292; H Olsson, *The Extended Collective License as Applied in the Nordic Countries*, Speech at Kopinor 25th anniversary international symposium (20 May 2005) 5 <http://www.kopinor.no/en/copyright/extended-collective-license/documents/the-extended-collective-license-as-applied-in-the-nordic-countries>.

[53] *Cf.* M Bouchard, *Speech at Facilitating Access to Culture in the Digital Age – WIPO Global Meeting on Emerging Copyright Licensing Modalities, Theme V: Making Orphan Works Available* (4 November 2010) <www.wipo.int/multimedia-video/en/meetings/wipo_cr_lic_ge_10/bouchard_05112010.mp3>; DJ Gervais, *Application of an Extended Collective Licensing Regime in Canada, Study Prepared for the Department of Canadian Heritage* (2003) <http://aix1.uottawa.ca/~dgervais/publications/extended_licensing.pdf>; Rights Holders Initial Proposal, Collective Licensing: Liability Limits for Collectives and Users <http://www.ic.gc.ca/eic/site/crp-prda.nsf/eng/rp01129.html>.

ECLs.[54] According to the Intellectual Property Office (IPO), these licenses are meant to simplify rights clearance in situations where individual negotiations with rights holders "are not feasible."[55]

However, the IPO states that CMOs should not grant ECLs for mass-uses of orphan works: "ECL [extended collective licensing] cannot be used for the mass licensing of orphan works because, until a diligent search has been conducted, it will not be known whether the works were orphan."[56]

The IPO does not explain why rights holders of orphan works should be treated differently than non-members of CMOs which are known and can be found. The following rationale might be at stake: the EU's orphan works directive provides that a "work or phonogram which is considered an orphan work… in a Member State shall be considered an orphan work in all Member States."[57] ECLs prove inherently problematic for such cross-border recognition of a work's status as an orphan. Each member state has its own CMOs, and none of them represent a significant number of rights holders from all member states. If a user could obtain an ECL from a British CMO, without having to search for the work's rights holder, and if such ECL were valid across the EU, the interests of rights holders would be significantly impaired.[58] Consequently, ECLs are usually only valid in the country in which they are granted.

In addition, ECLs are only an option when and where rights are already administered collectively; only then does a CMO represent a high enough number of rights holders to justify an extension of its portfolio. Even in Nordic countries and in the U.K., users can obtain ECLs only for certain categories of works. For example, music, movie, and software producers in the Nordic countries and photographers in the U.K. traditionally license their rights directly.[59]

---

54 ERRA, 2013, s 77 (providing for the creation of a new art 116B for the Copyright, Designs and Patents Act 1988).

55 Intellectual Property Office, *FACTSHEET – Orphan Works Licensing Scheme and Extended Collective Licensing* (June 2013) 4.

56 Ibid. at 5.

57 Directive 2012/28/EU, art 4.

58 The European Commission mentions these problems in its proposal for an orphan works directive. *Cf.* COM (2011) 289 final, Impact Assessment, at 3. The directive, however, does not offer any solution. Extended collective licenses are only mentioned in recital 24. It states that the "Directive is without prejudice to the arrangements in the Member States concerning the management of rights such as extended collective licences."

59 T Riis and J Schovsbo, "Extended Collective Licenses and the Nordic Experience" (2010) 33 *Colum. J.L. & Arts* 471, 491; Intellectual Property Office,

Despite their rising popularity, ECLs thus do have their downsides. They go beyond the more practical problems already mentioned. ECLs replace the market with a forced collective administration of rights at a time when, due to technological advances (think about search engines, databases, etc.), it is theoretically easier than ever for copyright holders and users to find each other (although transaction costs remain an issue for individual licenses). What is more, ECLs touch the very heart of copyright law. Traditionally, copyright owners are granted rights of exclusion. In a system based on ECLs, these rights are turned into rights of remuneration;[60] in most Nordic countries, copyright owners may not opt-out of ECLs.[61] Even where ECLs provide for an opt-out,[62] they change copyright's default rule: Usually, rights holders must opt-in if they want to be covered by a license agreement, not opt-out should they not wish to license their rights.

II. STATUTORY EXCEPTIONS OR LIMITATIONS

A possible alternative to licensing solutions are statutory exceptions or limitations on some or all of rights holders' exclusive rights, with or without a right to compensation for (re)appearing rights holders. The EU took this path in its orphan works directive.[63] There, it requires its

---

FACTSHEET – Orphan Works Licensing Scheme and Extended Collective Licensing (June 2013) 1, 4.

[60] The same is true for other kinds of collective rights management. *Cf.* DJ Gervais and A Maurushat, "Fragmented Copyright, Fragmented Management: Proposals to Defrag Copyright Management" (2003) 2 *Can. J. L. & Tech.* 15, 25–6.

[61] *Cf.* G Karnell, "Extended Collective License Clauses and Agreements in Nordic Copyright Law" (1985) 10 *Colum.-VLA J.L. & Arts* 73, 76; T Riis and J Schovsbo, "Extended Collective Licenses and the Nordic Experience" (note 59 above), 476; V Verronen, "Extended Collective License in Finland: A Legal Instrument for Balancing the Rights of the Author with the Interests of the User" (2002) 49 *J. Copy. Soc'y* 1143, 1150–1.

[62] *Cf.* Swedish Copyright Act, art 42b–e; Danish Copyright Act, ss 24a, 30, 30a, 50(2); Copyright, Designs and Patents Act 1988, art 116B (3).

[63] Notably, some European (non-EU) copyright laws go even further; they not only grant limitations on rights holders' rights but presume ownership for the first user of orphan works. Albanian Copyright Act, art 5.3, provides that if an anonymous or pseudonymous work whose author is unknown is made available to the public, the person/entity which has made the work first available is allowed to exercise the copyright until the author is found or reveals his or her identity. *Cf.* Albania's Response to question 21 of WIPO's Second Survey on

member states to provide for a limitation or exception to the right of reproduction and the right of making available to the public.[64]

For policy reasons, the range of beneficiaries, covered works, and allowed uses is fairly restricted.[65] The directive's framers clearly wanted to allow the use of orphan works in a specific scenario which they described in recital 1:

> Publicly accessible libraries, educational establishments and museums, as well as archives, film or audio heritage institutions and public-service broadcasting organizations, established in the Member States, are engaged in large-scale digitization of their collections or archives in order to create European Digital Libraries. They contribute to the preservation and dissemination of European cultural heritage, which is also important for the creation of European Digital Libraries, such as Europeana. Technologies for mass digitization of print materials and for search and indexing enhance the research value of the libraries' collections. Creating large online libraries facilitates electronic search and discovery tools which open up new sources of discovery for researchers and academics who would otherwise have to content themselves with more traditional and analogue search methods.[66]

The directive's aim is thus to foster "the preservation and dissemination of European cultural heritage" by certain public institutions through "large-scale digitization of their collections or archives." While orphan works statutes in other parts of the world are designed for individual uses of individual copyrighted works, the EU directive wants to provide for "mass digitization of print materials."

Even though neither Google nor the Google Books Settlement is explicitly mentioned, the directive is very much a reaction to both. The European Commission, the driving force behind the directive, had for a long time urged member states to spur the digitization of copyrighted

---

Voluntary Registration and Deposit Systems <http://www.wipo.int/export/sites/www/copyright/en/registration/replies/pdf/albania.pdf>. Liechtenstein's copyright law has a similar provision in art 8 (2) of its Copyright Act. *Cf.* Liechtenstein's Response to question 21 of WIPO's Second Survey on Voluntary Registration and Deposit Systems <http://www.wipo.int/export/sites/www/copyright/en/registration/replies/pdf/liechtenstein.pdf>.

[64] Directive 2012/28/EU, art 6 (1). The deadline for transposition of the directive ended on October 29, 2014, *see* art 9 (1). For an overview of national implementing measures, *see* <http://eur-lex.europa.eu/collection/n-law/mne.html>.

[65] Interestingly, the directive does not mention any concerns regarding compliance with international law.

[66] Directive 2012/28/EU, r 1.

works by allowing for orphan works to be used – with little success.[67] When the Google Books Settlement was published and public outcry in Europe was at its highest, the then-Commissioner for Information Society and Media, Viviane Reding, started referring to Europe's cultural heritage in order to induce member states to enact orphan works legislation: "Europe, with its rich cultural heritage, has most to offer and most to win from books digitization. If we act swiftly, pro-competitive European solutions on books digitisation may well be sooner operational than the solutions presently envisaged under the Google Books Settlement in the United States."[68] The term cultural heritage, no stranger to EU law,[69] seems to have stuck.

The directive's attempt to allow for the preservation of Europe's cultural heritage by way of mass digitization might simultaneously be its strength and one of its greatest weaknesses: individual (or mass-) uses by private individuals and companies are not privileged, irrespective of whether they are conducted for commercial or non-commercial purposes. Only "publicly accessible libraries, educational establishments and museums, as well as ... archives, film or audio heritage institutions and public-service broadcasting organizations, established in the Member States" may use orphan works.[70]

On its face, the directive covers works published in the form of books, journals, newspapers, magazines, or other writings, as well as cinematographic or audiovisual works and phonograms contained in the collections of a beneficiary,[71] including "works and other protected subject-matter that are embedded or incorporated in, or constitute an integral part of, the works or phonograms."[72] Even works and phonograms which have never been published or broadcast but which have been made publicly

---

[67] For a detailed description of the Commission's efforts, *cf.* K de la Durantaye, "Finding a Home for Orpahns: Google Book Search and Orphan Works Law in the United States and Europe" (2011) 21 *Fordham Intell. Prop. Media & Ent. L.J.* 229, 251–6, 282–6.

[68] Press Release, *European Commission put challenges of books digitisation for authors, libraries and consumers on EU's agenda*, IP/09/1544 (19 October 2009).

[69] *Cf.* Treaty on the Functioning of the EU, art 167.

[70] Directive 2012/28/EU, art 1 (1).

[71] Ibid., art 2 (1). A search is deemed diligent if the conditions mentioned in art 3 are fulfilled, including consultation of a list of sources which can be found in the directive's annex.

[72] Ibid., art 1 (4).

accessible by a beneficiary are included, "provided that it is reasonable to assume that the rightholders would not oppose the uses."[73]

In practice, though, the directive is useful for (analogue) print matter only. Beneficiaries have to reasonably search for each and every rights holder of a work or phonogram before they may use it.[74] If a work has more than one rights holder, as movies and other audiovisual works usually do, the costs for searching for all these rights holders will, in all likelihood, prove prohibitively expensive. Even the digitization of an illustrated book may create considerable problems; theoretically, a beneficiary would have to search for the rights holder of each individual embedded illustration before it could reproduce the work.

Beneficiaries may only reproduce works and make them available to the public.[75] They may not distribute, perform, or publicly display them. Within Europe, then, a film archive can restore a movie and show it on its website but it may not show said movie in its own movie theater, even though the movie was, in all likelihood, made in order to be shown in a cinema, not on the Internet. This distinction is without rational basis; it can only be explained by the EU's focus on (publicly funded) digital libraries.

The establishment of digital libraries requires significant financial investments. The EU is trying to ease that burden for public institutions in two ways. Despite their obligation to use orphan works "only in order to achieve aims related to their public-interest missions, in particular the preservation of, the restoration of, and the provision of cultural and educational access to, works and phonograms contained in their collection,"[76] beneficiaries may condition access to orphan works on the payment of a fee designed to cover their costs of digitization and online availability.[77] In addition, beneficiaries may enter into partnerships with private companies.[78] However, they should not grant their commercial partners any rights to use or control the use of orphan works.[79] Time will tell how many commercial partners will be willing to fund digitization

---

73 Ibid., art 1 (3).
74 Ibid., art 2 (1), (2).
75 Ibid., art 6 (1).
76 Ibid., art 6 (2) sentence 1.
77 Ibid., art 6 (2) sentence 2.
78 Ibid., art 6 (4).
79 Ibid., r 22 sentence 3.

projects if they, in return, do not obtain any rights to use the digitized works.[80]

III. LIMITATION ON REMEDIES

Unlike a limitation or an exception to copyright's exclusive rights, a limitation on remedies would enable orphan works' rights holders to keep their rights under copyright law; what would be limited would be their ability to claim compensation from and/or to obtain an injunction against users who have fulfilled certain conditions.

Limitations on remedies are especially attractive in legal systems that provide for statutory damages, i.e., damages which are fixed by statute and not (exclusively) measured by actual losses; often, these damages are calculated. One such country is the U.S. – there, a rights holder may claim between US$750 and US$30,000 per work for copyright violations;[81] if the infringement was willful, the award may be increased to a maximum of US$150,000 per work.[82] It comes as no surprise, then, that limitations on remedies ranked highly when the U.S. legislature discussed possible national solutions for the orphan works problem. In its Report on Orphan Works, the Copyright Office suggested the introduction of such limitations for infringers of copyrighted works who, in vain, have conducted a "reasonably diligent search" (a term which the report does not define) for the work's right(s) holder(s) and who, where possible, have granted attribution to author and rights holder.[83]

The three orphan works bills which have since been introduced into Congress (one in 2006, two in 2008) all followed the Copyright Office's suggestions.[84] The scope of the law would thus have been much broader than the EU directive on the topic: the bills would have covered all categories of published and unpublished works. All users, be they individuals, private or public entities, commercial ones or those who

---

[80] Very sceptical in this regard, Intellectual Property Office, *Government response to the technical consultation on orphan works* (May 30, 2014) 27, *see* https://www.gov.uk/government/uploads/system/uploads/attachment_data/file/315078/Orphan_Works_Government_Response.pdf

[81] U.S.C. Title 17, s 504(c)(1).

[82] Ibid., s 504(c)(2).

[83] *Report on Orphan Works*, at 8–10.

[84] Orphan Works Act of 2006, H.R. 5439, 119th Cong. (2006) (later that year, the bill was embedded in The Copyright Modernization Act of 2006, H.R. 6052, 109th Cong. (2006)); Orphan Works Act of 2008, H.R. 5889, 110th Cong. (2008); Shawn Bentley Orphan Works Act of 2008, S. 2913, 110th Cong. (2008).

work not-for-profit, would have qualified, provided that they had "reasonably diligently searched" for the rights holder, and had granted attribution. Individual as well as mass-uses of orphan works would have been made possible. If a rights holder came forward and sued an infringer who had fulfilled its obligations under the statute, he or she could ask for monetary damages only in the form of a "reasonable compensation." Injunctive relief would remain available except in cases where the infringer had created a derivative work of the orphan work.

None of the three bills passed Congress, and as of now, no orphan works legislation has been enacted in the U.S. Still, the proposal for a limitation on remedies is not moot. In 2012, the Copyright Office renewed its efforts to find a legislative solution for orphan works. It issued a notice of inquiry on orphan works and mass digitization.[85] Comments suggest that many users would want Congress to pass a bill modeled on the ones of 2006 and 2008.[86]

At the same time, a growing number of stakeholders and academics in the U.S. are of the opinion that no such piece of legislation is necessary. According to them, the use of orphan works is defensible under existing U.S. copyright law's fair use defense.[87] Along the same lines, the U.S. Court of Appeals for the Second Circuit decertified the class action in the Google Books case and held that Google's actions may be covered under fair use.[88] Similarly, the U.S. District Court for the Southern District of New York ruled that the actions of Google Books' partner libraries, including their contribution of digitized works to the HathiTrust Digital Library, was protected under fair use.[89] The U.S. Court of Appeals for the Second Circuit affirmed that judgment.[90]

---

85 Orphan Works and Mass Digitization, Notice of Inquiry, 77 FR 64555 (22 October 2012) <http://www.copyright.gov/fedreg/2012/77fr64555.pdf>.

86 For the initial comments, *see* <http://www.copyright.gov/orphan/comments/noi_10222012>. For the reply comments, *see* <http://www.copyright.gov/orphan/comments/noi_11302012/>.

87 *Cf.* J Urban, "How Fair Use Can Solve the Orphan Works Problem" (2012) 27 *Berkeley Tech. L. J.* 1379.

88 *Authors Guild, Inc. v. Google, Inc.*, No. 12-3200-cv (2nd Cir. 1 July 2013).

89 *Authors Guild, Inc. v. HathiTrust*, 902 F.Supp.2d 445, 104 (S.D.N.Y. 2012).

90 *Authors Guild v. HathiTrust*, No. 12-4547-cv (2d. Cir. June 10, 2014).

IV. PUBLIC DOMAIN SOLUTION

Compulsory licenses, limitations and exceptions to copyright's exclusive rights, and limited liability for users of orphan works all curtail a rights holder's legal position. The most extreme way of doing so would be to determine that a work that has become an orphan would fall into the public domain. Rights holders would thus lose all rights; even if they later reappeared, they could not claim compensation or stop other peoples' uses by way of an injunction.

Doing so would go against general principles of (international) copyright law; authors and other rights holders are under no obligation to make themselves known and findable in order to obtain or keep their rights. And yet, some Latin American countries do have laws which create a situation similar to the one just described. These laws are not designed to deal with all kinds of orphan works. They do, however, apply to works whose authors are unknown.

Some of them were obviously created in order to prevent monopolization of cultural traditions – a concept related to that of "cultural heritage" used in EU law.[91] The Chilean Intellectual Property Act, for example, provides that works whose authors are unknown (*desconocido*), including songs, legends, dances, and expressions of folkloric heritage, belong to the "common cultural heritage" (*patrimonio cultural común*); they may be used by anybody without permission and free of charge.[92] However, attribution (*paternidad*) has to be granted, and integrity has to be respected.[93]

The classification as common cultural heritage, however, is not irreversible:[94] if a work of an unknown author is published, and the author later comes forward, the publisher has to pay the author 10 percent of the revenue he generates, starting at the moment at which the author has

---

[91] This might be the reason why they are held to pass the three-step test. *Cf.* the ongoing discussions at WIPO about the protection of traditional knowledge and traditional cultural expressions <http://www.wipo.int/tk/en/>; African Regional Intellectual Property Organization, *Swakopmund Protocol on the Protection of Traditional Knowledge and Expressions of Folklore* (2010) <http://www.cbd.int/doc/measures/abs/msr-abs-aripo-en.pdf>.

[92] Chilean Intellectual Property Act, art 11 b) <http://www.wipo.int/wipolex/en/text.jsp?file_id=270205>.

[93] Ibid., sentence 2.

[94] In this respect, Chilean law differs from that of Colombia, Brazil, and Mexico.

made him- or herself known.[95] In addition, the author has a first right to purchase any copies which the publisher has in stock.[96] Works whose authors are known but whose rights holders are unknown or cannot be found, however, remain protected, and can, under current Chilean law, not be used by anybody in a manner that requires the rights holder's permission.

Similarly but more narrowly, folkloristic and traditional works of unknown authors (*obras folclóricas y tradicionales de autores desconocidos*) form part of the public domain (*dominio público*) in Colombia.[97] Again, the works' integrity has to be respected; the Colombian Culture Institute is entrusted with supervising that this obligation is not violated.[98]

Other countries do not limit the application of their respective statutes to traditional cultural or folkloristic works. One such example is Brazil. There, a work whose author is unknown (*desconhecido*) is in the public domain (*domínio público*) – everybody may, notwithstanding legal protection of ethnic and traditional knowledge, use it without compensation.[99] Currently, Brazil is considering a copyright reform which would, among other things, allow for the use of works by rights holders who are unknown or cannot be found.[100]

The situation in Mexico is similar to the one in Brazil. The use of works whose authors cannot be identified by name, signature, or sign (*obras anónimas*)[101] does not require the rights holder's permission until the author makes him- or herself known, or until a rights holder is identified.[102]

---

95 Chilean Intellectual Property Act, art 53 I.

96 Ibid., art 53 II.

97 Colombian Copyright Act, art 187 no. 2 <http://www.wipo.int/wipolex/en/text.jsp?file_id=126023>.

98 Ibid., art 30 III. Similar provisions can be found in Brazilian Copyright Act, art 24 s 2 <http://www.wipo.int/wipolex/en/text.jsp?file_id=125393>; Mexican Federal Copyright Act, art 20 II <http://www.wipo.int/wipolex/es/text.jsp?file_id=254993>.

99 Brazilian Copyright Act, art 45 II. The definition of an anonymous work (*obra anônima*) can be found in art 5 VIII b) of that statute. They fall into one of two categories: works whose authors willfully choose non-attribution (*sua vontade*), and those whose authors are not known (*desconhecido*).

100 *Cf.* <http://www.ip-watch.org/2011/12/12/brazils-leaked-copyright-reform-draft-bill-shows-latest-thinking/>.

101 Mexican Federal Copyright Act, art 4 A II.

102 Ibid, art 153

V. PREVENTATIVE MEASURES

The most elegant way of dealing with the orphan works problem, at least prospectively, would be to prevent orphanage and the market failure associated with it. The orphan works problem is mainly an information problem.[103] It comes in three forms: a work may have never contained any ownership information, ownership information may have gotten lost, or the information may be outdated, either because the author has died or because ownership has changed for other reasons.

Preventing orphanage thus requires a better system of ownership information than the one we currently have. As mentioned above, two legal developments have, over the past decades, led to the present situation. Both of them are at least partially based on international copyright obligations; neither one is therefore easily reversed.

As to options for shortening the copyright term, article 7 (1) Berne Convention requires its member states to protect (most) copyrighted works for life of the author plus 50 years.[104] Most countries thus cannot go below that level and provide for a shorter term of protection. Over the past decade and a half, though, both the U.S. and EU member states have extended their default copyright term to the author's life plus 70 years.[105] Some countries even go beyond that: in Mexico, exploitation rights (*derechos patrimoniales*) expire 100 years after the author's death.[106] Here, shortening the copyright term would, even though not very likely, be possible without running afoul of Berne requirements.

With regard to the introduction of formalities, the Berne Convention again sets strict limits. According to its article 5 (2), enjoyment and exercise of copyrights may not be made dependent on formalities. Berne member states thus may only induce copyright owners to provide notice, to embed rights management information into (digital) copies of their works, to voluntarily register them and, in doing so, make themselves findable, but they may not require these actions as a precondition for copyright protection.

---

[103] *Cf. also* S van Gompel and PB Hugenholtz, "The Orphan Works Problem: The Copyright Conundrum of Digitizing Large-Scale Audiovisual Archives, and How to Solve It" (2010) 8.1 *Popular Communication* 61, 64.

[104] Several exceptions are mentioned in Berne Convention, art 7 (2)–(4).

[105] *Cf.* Sonny Bono Copyright Term Extension Act, s 102 (b), Pub.L. 105-298 (105th Cong., 2008); Directive 2006/116/EC; Directive 2011/77/EU.

[106] *Cf.* Mexican Federal Copyright Act, art 29. Moral rights (*derechos morales*) do not expire. They are non-transferable and can only be claimed by authors and their heirs.

The U.S. already creates such incentives by requiring rights holders of U.S. works to register prior to filing suit,[107] and by limiting the ability to claim statutory damages to rights holders who have registered their work.[108] Currently, scholars are debating the feasibility of introducing further recordation requirements that would be compatible with the country's obligations under the Berne Convention.[109] One such option would be to request registration for works the authors of which have been dead for more than 50 years.[110] Another one would be the obligation to record changes in ownership status.[111]

Other countries achieve a similar result in areas in which collective rights management is prevalent: CMOs do have the contact information of their members. Their registries, therefore, are a – if not the – prime source for copyright ownership information.

The EU has gone a step further. It has created open, pan-European databases for ownership information and orphan works. The European Commission has funded ARROW, the Accessible Registries of Rights Information and Orphan Works.[112] ARROW integrates multiple national databases and is one of the sources which potential users of orphan works will have to consult before they may begin their use.[113]

In addition, the EU established a "single publicly accessible online database" for orphan works, administered by the Office for Harmonization in the Internal Market, located in Alicante, Spain.[114] Member states must designate a national authority – such as a Patent and Trademark Office – which will collect information they will receive by

---

107 17 U.S.C s 411 (a).

108 17 U.S.C s 412.

109 *Cf., e.g.*, Berkeley Tech. L. J.'s Symposium edition on Reform(aliz)ing Copyright for the Digital Age (18 – 19 April 2013); JC Ginsburg, "'With Untired Spirits and Formal Constancy': Berne-Compatibility of Formal Declaratory Measures to Enhance Title-Searching" Columbia Public Law Research Paper No. 13-346 (6 May 2013) <http://papers.ssrn.com/sol3/papers.cfm?abstract_id=2262924>; S van Gompel, *Formalities in Copyright Law: An Analysis of Their History, Rationales and Possible Future* (Kluwer Law International, 2011); MA Pallante, *Statement Made in Front of the Subcommittee on Courts, Intellectual Property and the Internet, Committee on the Judiciary* (20 March 2013) <http://www.copyright.gov/regstat/2013/regstat03202013.html>; C Sprigman, "Reform(aliz)ing Copyright" (2004) 57 *SLR* 485.

110 Ginsburg, ibid., 18–20; Pallante, ibid., 2.

111 Ginsburg ibid., 26–35.

112 <www.arrow-net.eu>.

113 2012/28/EU, annex (1)(e).

114 Ibid., art 3 (6).

the beneficiaries of the orphan works directive on the results of their diligent searches, the uses they wish to make, the relevant contact information of the beneficiary, and, most importantly, any changes in the orphan works status of a work or phonogram used.[115]

Fairly soon, then, the EU will have one list of orphan works in use in the EU, thereby allowing rights holders to make themselves (and, possibly, their license conditions) known towards a single organization. In addition, the database will allow for crowd sourcing; since it is publicly accessible, anyone interested may start looking for and finding rights holders of registered orphan works.[116]

VI. THE BIGGER PICTURE: OUT-OF-COMMERCE WORKS

One of the aims of digital library projects is the making available of works which cannot be obtained through regular channels of commerce. So far, most of these projects focus on print matter; they want to grant access to writings that are out-of-print, including but not limited to orphan works. Consequently, they regard orphan works as just one group of works that no one considered commercially valuable enough to put out/keep on the market, and for which they are, at considerable cost, struggling to clear rights.

It is for this reason that the Google Books Settlement would have allowed Google not only the use of orphan works but the use of out-of-print works more generally (virtually all orphan works are out-of-print but not all out-of-print works are orphaned).[117] And it is for the same reason that the EU urged its member states to make licensing of out-of-commerce works more easy. In 2011, and based on an initiative by the European Commission, libraries, publishers, author associations, and CMOs signed a "Memorandum of Understanding – Key Principles on the Digitisation and Making Available of Out-of-Commerce Works."[118] The memorandum of understanding applies to books and journals that are to be digitized and made publicly available by publicly accessible cultural

---

115 Ibid., art 3 (5).

116 Some member states already have orphan works databases. *Cf., e.g.*, German Copyright Act, s 61a IV.

117 Google Books Settlement, art. 3.2(d)(ii); Amended Settlement Agreement, art 3.2(d)(ii).

118 <http://ec.europa.eu/internal_market/copyright/docs/copyright-infso/20110920-mou_en.pdf>.

institutions.[119] It contains three principles: the signatories oblige themselves to enter into voluntary agreements to make out-of-commerce works available to the public, and to negotiate the required steps; licenses are to be granted by CMOs, may include ECLs, and should include a right for rights holders to opt-out. Finally, if an agreement allows for cross-border access to out-of-commerce works, its scope may be limited to rights holders which the CMO represents; other rights holders should, where possible, be notified.

Following that memorandum of understanding and simultaneously with its transposition of the orphan works directive, Germany, in 2013, enacted a law regarding out-of-print works.[120] It provides for a system of ECLs for out-of-print works that were published before 1 January 1966.[121] The group of beneficiaries is limited to those institutions which may use orphan works according to the orphan works directive.[122]

Meanwhile, the French Parliament passed a law which allows for the exploitation of out-of-print works.[123] Any such work has to be listed in a special database administered by the *Bibliothèque nationale de France*.[124] If no objection has been filed within six months after registration, a specially designated CMO may grant a non-exclusive, renewable license for the book's reproduction and digital exploitation for a period of five years.[125]

It is likely that we will see more of these laws in the years to come. Like ECLs which may be used for orphan works but whose scope goes beyond that, they have one significant benefit over specific orphan works legislation: users do not have to search for rights holders before they may use the works in question; consequently, it is likely that the German exception for the use of orphan works,[126] which was simultaneously enacted, will only rarely be used.

---

119 Memorandum of Understanding – Key Principles on the Digitisation and Making Available of Out-of-Commerce Works, recital 1.

120 German Act on Collective Rights Management, s 13d-e.

121 Ibid., s 13d I.

122 See above at II.

123 French Intellectual Property Act, art L.134-1.

124 Ibid., art L.134-2.

125 Ibid., art L.134-3.

126 German Copyright Act, s 61–61c.

VII. CONCLUSION

None of the options to solve the orphan works problem are without drawbacks. Some, such as the various licensing solutions (licenses granted by a public body, licenses granted by a private body, and ECLs) require users to negotiate and, in most cases, pay license fees before they take up their uses. The associated transaction costs may be considerable while the fees will, for works which are truly orphaned, not be claimed. ECLs have the additional drawback of replacing the market with a forced collective administration of rights. If the license in question is not an extended collective one, users will, however, have to incur significant search costs.

Search costs will also accrue under an exception or limitation on exclusive rights or on remedies, as well as under a public domain designation. Unlike license schemes, though, these solutions require users to negotiate (and pay) for their uses only if and once a rights holder has come forward and claimed his or her rights. In many cases, users will thus be able to use a work without having to pay for doing so. At the same time, users will have less certainty that their actions are legal than they do if they obtain a license before they start their use; no one will have checked and validated that they have fulfilled the necessary requirements for using an orphan work.

Since the orphan works problem is first and foremost an information problem, one, if not the most important, element of any orphan works solution is the establishment of publicly accessible, interlinked online databases for rights information. These databases should not be limited to ones for orphan works specifically. Ideally, they should contain as much information as possible about authors and known rights holders as well, thereby preventing works from losing their parents in the first place.

PART III

PATENTS AND INNOVATION ISSUES

7. Traditional knowledge and innovation as a global concern

Susy Frankel

1. INTRODUCTION

Worldwide, many countries and indigenous peoples have raised concerns over how creators and inventors make use of, frequently without consent, their traditional knowledge and then obtain intellectual property rights relating to those uses. The problem is that those whose knowledge and cultural objects are used most often are not properly acknowledged and derive no economic benefit from such uses.[1] This situation is justified on the basis that the knowledge and cultural products (where they exist) are in the so-called public domain. In other words, the knowledge and its manifestations are free from legal constraints over their use. The fact that there is no definitive agreement over the contours, or indeed the cultural norms, behind the public domain[2] appears not to be a deterrent to those who assert that much traditional knowledge is or should be in the public domain. As the public domain is the arena from which the difficulties of not protecting traditional knowledge arise, consequently a discussion of the public domain is both where this chapter begins and also where it will end.

A common theme that those who seek protection of traditional knowledge articulate is their relationship with the knowledge and its uses. This includes their role as holders, and sometimes users, of the

[1] For a detailed overview of the intellectual property issues, *see* P Drahos and S Frankel, "Indigenous Peoples' Innovation and Intellectual Property: The Issues", in P Drahos and S Frankel (eds), *Indigenous Peoples Innovation: Intellectual Property Pathways to Development* (ANU epress 2012).

[2] For a discussion of various conceptions of the public domain, *see* L Guibault and PB Hugenholtz (eds), *The Future of the Public Domain – Identifying the Commons in Information Law* (Information Law Series Kluwer Law International 2006).

knowledge on behalf of others. This might be described as a guardianship role.[3] Accordingly this chapter uses the phrase "knowledge guardians".

Knowledge guardians' opposition to the unchecked use of traditional knowledge relates to its use in works of culture including arts and craft, books and other publications, films, and performances. The concerns of knowledge guardians are also about inappropriate use of biological and genetic resources, and related traditional knowledge, particularly where the knowledge guardians have an ongoing coexistence and relationship with those resources. In this chapter, traditional knowledge and the human-made objects and biological and genetic resources to which that knowledge relates are collectively referred to as "knowledge assets".

From a legal perspective, "assets" incorporates both tangible and intangible assets. Traditional knowledge guardians do not separate the two but consider the overlaps and links to be important features of the knowledge. Knowledge is not an isolated commodity but rather is part of a holistic system of relationships.[4] Knowledge about a plant, for example, is not very useful unless the plant is accessible. For many knowledge guardians, their knowledge assets have become endangered and they face difficulties developing their knowledge in the modern world. This situation has arisen because of a lack of access to tangible knowledge assets as a result of many knowledge guardians having been divested of their lands. A lack of financial resources may also be a barrier to development of the knowledge in modern economies. This chapter does not intend to sever the linkage between the tangible and intangible knowledge assets, however; its focus is the intangible knowledge assets and their relationship to intellectual property law and policy.

A central concern of many knowledge guardians is not only that their knowledge assets are used without permission, but that others derive commercial benefit from that knowledge without any acknowledgement of, or recompense to, the source of the knowledge. This arises in part because the framework of intellectual property law does not require such

---

[3] Others may choose a different word. I adopt guardianship from the recognized translation of being a kaitiaki (guardian) of mātauranga Māori, *see* Waitangi Tribunal, *Ko Aotearoa Tēnei: A Report into Claims Concerning New Zealand Law and Policy Affecting Māori Culture and Identity* (2011) <http://www.waitangi-tribunal.govt.nz/news/media/wai262.asp> accessed 22 November 2013 ("*Ko Aotearoa Tēnei*"). Translated, *Ko Aotearoa Tēnei* means "This is Aotearoa/New Zealand." Aotearoa is the Māori name for New Zealand.

[4] See *Ko Aotearoa Tēnei,* note 3 above, at 12–18 and 33–8. This may also be described as a cosmological view, *see* Drahos and Frankel, note 1 above, at 13–17.

acknowledgement or recompense. The problem is exacerbated where the knowledge guardians, in addition to not gaining any commercial benefit from use of the knowledge assets, are also prevented from fulfilling their role as knowledge guardians. Admittedly, factors other than intellectual property contribute to this, but some aspects of intellectual property law make a significant contribution to the problem.

The expansion of global trade and the discussion of the role of intellectual property internationally have fuelled the discussion of the protection of traditional knowledge.[5] In particular, developing countries have had to protect intellectual property originating from elsewhere more than ever before[6] and, therefore, have become acutely aware that a key form of their intellectual property (i.e., traditional knowledge assets) is often not protected sufficiently at home or at all elsewhere. This tension over what sort of intellectual property is protected and what is not is also a concern for indigenous populations of both developing and developed countries, and particularly minority populations in developed countries with high levels of intellectual property protection. These developed countries are New Zealand, Australia, the United States (US), and Canada.[7]

In international negotiations about protecting traditional knowledge, the key potential beneficiaries of proposed protection are both developing countries and indigenous peoples. The interests of developing countries (particularly large countries such as India and Brazil) and indigenous peoples who are minority populations may sometimes coincide, but in other instances are quite different. Additionally, developed countries are somewhat divided on some of the issues. The US is largely opposed to any international obligations for the protection for traditional knowledge.[8] The positions of New Zealand, Australia, and Canada sometimes

---

[5] *See* A Taubman, "Preface: Indigenous Innovation: New Dialogues, New Pathways", in Drahos and Frankel, note 1 above, at xv.

[6] It is widely recognized that for many countries significant changes were required to bring their laws into compliance with the minimum standards of the Agreement on Trade-Related Aspects of Intellectual Property Rights, Marrakesh Agreement Establishing the World Trade Organization, Annex 1C, 1869 UNTS 299; 33 ILM 1197 (adopted on 15 April 1994, entered into force 1 January 1995) ("TRIPS Agreement").

[7] For a discussion of perspectives from each of these countries, *see* C Graber, K Kuprecht and J Lai (eds), *International Trade in Indigenous Cultural Heritage: Legal and Policy Issues* (Edward Elgar 2012).

[8] *See, e.g.*, Intergovernmental Committee on Intellectual Property and Genetic Resources, Traditional Knowledge and Folklore Eighteenth Session, Geneva, 9–13 May 2011, "The Protection of Traditional Knowledge: Revised

coincide and also vary from each other depending on the issue.[9] The European Union (EU) has at times indicated support for the protection of traditional knowledge, particularly in exchange for developing country support for its expansion of geographical indications.[10]

A key tension is the scope of protection of knowledge assets. One difficulty, which those who oppose protection often exploit, is that strict definition is not easy. Part 2 discusses what traditional knowledge and related terms mean. Part 3 analyzes the role of the public domain as it relates to traditional knowledge assets. Part 4 explains the intersection of the protection of traditional knowledge assets and intellectual property. The international institutions and negotiations for the protection of traditional knowledge assets is analyzed in Part 5. Part 6 focuses on implementing protection at a national level. It first discusses compliance with the TRIPS Agreement[11] and then analyzes the New Zealand situation as an example of how a national regime might be implemented. The chapter concludes with a discussion of calibrating traditional knowledge protection and consequently the contours of the public domain to local needs.

2. DEFINITIONS AND THE SCOPE OF TRADITIONAL KNOWLEDGE

Definitions are like "quicksand".[12] To the extent that definitions attempt to capture how cultures form and develop their knowledge, such definitions are bound to run into some difficulties. Consequently, definitions

---

Objectives and Principles", Annex at p 8. For a discussion of these objections, *see* S Frankel, "'Ka Mate Ka Mate' and the Protection of Traditional Knowledge", in R Dreyfuss and J Ginsburg (eds), *Intellectual Property at the Edge* (Cambridge University Press 2013).

[9] These countries were relatively slow to join United Nations Declaration on the Rights of Indigenous Peoples (UNDRIP), in part because of views about its effects, *see generally* discussion in C Charters and R Stavenhagen (eds), *Making the Declaration Work: The United Nations Declaration on the Rights of Indigenous Peoples* (International Work Group for Indigenous Affairs Copenhagen 2009).

[10] For positions on the debate, *see* TRIPS Review: Article 27:3(b) and Related Issues, Background and the Current Situation, <http://www.wto.org/english/tratop_e/trips_e/art27_3b_background_e.htm> accessed 22 November 2013.

[11] TRIPS Agreement, note 6 above.

[12] *See* Drahos and Frankel, note 1 above, at 9–13.

should not be used in a legalistically formalistic way, but definitions which are guiding may be useful rather than determinative of what falls in and what is out of the scope of traditional knowledge assets.

One difficulty is that the phrase traditional knowledge is in many ways a misnomer. It suggests that the knowledge is only traditional in the sense of old. Much traditional knowledge may be old, but that is not all that it is. The knowledge is traditionally passed from generation to generation, but one of the key purposes of passing on knowledge is to develop that knowledge for current needs, as well as guarding the knowledge for future generations. Some types of knowledge may be more traditionally preserved rather than used for developmental purposes (this is true of all knowledge). An obvious example is where the knowledge is sacred or religious in some way.[13] The word traditional, however, should not be viewed as confining the knowledge to its past; rather, knowledge guardians and others use traditional knowledge innovatively.[14] This is because knowledge holders have actively developed knowledge through the ages. Also, if knowledge assets lacked innovative capacity, others would not seek to use them in order to innovate.

The difficulty is that not all innovative contributions are the same and the existing intellectual property system chooses to recognize innovations in the field of patents that manifest as useful inventions[15] and in copyright as original works.[16] As far as copyright is concerned, the embodiment of some knowledge assets may not qualify as original works if the art of exact replica is involved. Even where such uses of traditional knowledge do create something which qualifies as a copyright work, copyright does not protect the embodied knowledge from subsequent inappropriate use. As far as patents are concerned, indigenous peoples'

---

[13] The Lego Company in its bionicle toy range made use of Māori words which had sacred meaning; after discussion with Māori other words were used. This incident is reported in the television documentary "New Zealand Up For Grabs", directed by T Mill and M Maniapoto. It is also discussed in *Ko Aotearoa Tēnei*, note 3 above. *See also* DJ Gervais. "Spiritual but not Intellectual? The Protection of Sacred Intangible Traditional Knowledge", (2003) 11 *Cardozo J. of International & Comparative L* 467.

[14] Examples include the use of Australian Aboriginal fire control techniques and Māori management of New Zealand waterways, *see* Drahos and Frankel, note 1 above, at 18–19.

[15] TRIPS Agreement, note 6 above, at art 27 requires that patents are available in all field of technology provided they are new, involve an inventive step (non-obvious), and capable of industrial application (useful).

[16] *See* Berne Convention, art 2, incorporated into the TRIPS Agreement, note 6 above, at art 9:1.

innovation often takes a different form. Peter Drahos and I have discussed this innovative nature of traditional knowledge. Among other things we have found that:[17]

> [I]ndigenous innovation is often place-based innovation that is cosmologically linked to land and an indigenous group's relationship with that place, rather than to laboratories. Supporting indigenous innovation requires an integrated model of IP rights, real property, and traditional law and customs. That poses a challenge for Western legal traditions that have over a long period parsed property into finely grained taxonomies of real and personal property rights.

In order to provide some guidance about the scope of traditional knowledge assets, it is perhaps useful to consider the following broad definition of traditional knowledge that the World Intellectual Property Organization (WIPO) uses. According to WIPO, traditional knowledge is:[18]

> … [I]ntellectual activity in a traditional context, and includes the know-how, skills, innovations, practices and learning that form part of traditional knowledge systems, and knowledge embodying traditional lifestyles of indigenous and local communities, or contained in codified knowledge systems passed between generations and continuously developed following any changes in the environment, geographical conditions and other factors. It is not limited to any specific technical field, and may include agricultural, environmental and medicinal knowledge, and any traditional knowledge associated with cultural expressions and genetic resources.

Unsurprisingly and understandably, the WIPO definition has an intellectual property focus. In other international bodies the focus may be on something else, such as the rights of traditional knowledge guardians. The United Nations Declaration on the Rights of Indigenous Peoples (UNDRIP) provides an example.[19]

> Indigenous peoples have the right to maintain, control, protect and develop their cultural heritage, traditional knowledge and traditional cultural expressions, as well as the manifestations of their sciences, technologies and cultures, including human and genetic resources, seeds, medicines, knowledge of the properties of fauna and flora, oral traditions, literatures, designs, sports

---

[17] Drahos and Frankel note 1 above, at 13.

[18] The Protection of Traditional Knowledge: Revised Objectives and Principles, WIPO Document WIPO/GRTKF/IC/18/5 (10 January 2011), annex 18.

[19] United Nations Declaration on the Rights of Indigenous Peoples, adopted by General Assembly Resolution 61/295 on 13 September 2007, art 31. *See also* discussion in Charters and Stavenhagen, note 9 above.

and traditional games and visual and performing arts. They also have the right to maintain, control, protect and develop their intellectual property over such cultural heritage, traditional knowledge, and traditional cultural expressions.

Appropriately, neither the WIPO nor UNDRIP definitions draw a line between what is and what is not in the public domain. Both definitions capture, at a high level, traditional knowledge, whether it is in or out of the so-called public domain.

3. THE PUBLIC DOMAIN

From an intellectual property law perspective, the public domain is the place where intellectual property rights either do not exist (because they never arose or have expired[20]) or they give way to other interests (such as exceptions to copyright like fair use,[21] experimental use in patents,[22] or descriptive uses in trademarks[23]). Much of the contest over the public domain is about the scope of those exceptions or flexibilities relating to intellectual property rights. The protection of traditional knowledge largely fits the first defining characteristic of this intellectual property related perspective on the public domain: that the rights do not exist. There are exceptions, as some traditional knowledge is protected in some countries,[24] but those places are usually not where those who "borrow" from this public domain reside.

From this public domain perspective, the core objection to the protection of traditional knowledge is that creativity and innovation depend on

---

[20] Trademarks can be perpetual if renewed and fees are paid. Copyright and patents are exclusive rights for a limited term. The international minimum term for copyright is life of the author plus 50 years or 50 years from the making of the copyright work, *see* TRIPS Agreement, note 6 above, at art 12, and for patents 20 years from grant, *see* TRIPS Agreement, note 6 above, at art 33.

[21] Depending on the jurisdiction, exceptions to copyright are known as fair use, fair dealing, or permitted acts. Under the TRIPS Agreement, note 6 above, such exceptions must comply with art 13, which is also known as the three-step test.

[22] Experimental use exceptions are for the most part narrow and ineffective, *see generally* KJ Strandburg, "What Does the Public Get?: Experimental Use and the Patent Bargain" (2004) 1 *Wisconsin L Rev*. 81. Such exceptions must comply with TRIPS Agreement, note 6 above, at art 30.

[23] Descriptive uses may not amount to trademark infringement in some jurisdictions. If they do amount to infringement, any exception must comply with TRIPS Agreement, note 6 above, at art 17.

[24] Examples include China and Peru.

the ability to utilize and develop what is publicly known and available. Put differently, the ability to use the knowledge and works of others is integral to the development of the outputs associated with innovation and creativity. The ability to utilize knowledge in pursuit of further knowledge creation and innovation is one of several justifications for why and how intellectual property grants rights.[25] Indeed, the parameters for much intellectual property law are premised on the value of the ability of others to extract information or inspiration from existing works[26] or inventions and giving time-limited exclusive rights in exchange for a creation or invention eventually entering the so-called public domain.[27] However, the key to development may be getting "off the path" of always being on the giving end of extraction. As one commentator has noted:[28]

> [I]t is also a time of opportunity for … indigenous people. … [T]he symbolic recognition of the value of their knowledge has never been greater. They have also regained some or most of the incidences of ownership over more of their land than at any other time in the history of colonization. If they can overcome the danger of symbolic regulation that follows symbolic recognition they may yet be able to find a better future for themselves.

Those who seek greater protection for their traditional knowledge assets do not, for the most part, accept that this intellectual property driven construction of the public domain is legitimate.[29] Indigenous systems of knowledge governance and how it is used in innovation do not recognize

---

[25] Copyright is primarily justified on the basis that the giving of exclusive rights encourages creative works. The exclusive right is "tolerated" because the works will, after copyright expires, be available for others to copy. During copyright they may be used for inspiration, knowledge, and entertainment, but not infringe the exclusive right.

[26] A core feature of copyright, for example, is the idea/expression dichotomy and the notion that ideas are free to use but the particular expression of ideas is protected. For a discussion of the extractive nature of intellectual property, *see* P Drahos, *Intellectual Property, Indigenous People and Their Knowledge* (Cambridge University Press 2014).

[27] For a general discussion of the public domain and intellectual property law, *see* P Samuelson, "Enriching Discourse on Public Domain" (2006) 55 *Duke L J* 783.

[28] See Drahos, note 26 above, at 1.

[29] *See* S Frankel and M Richardson, "Cultural Property and 'the Public Domain' Case Studies from New Zealand and Australia", in C Antons (ed.), *Traditional Knowledge, Traditional Cultural Expressions and Intellectual Property Law in the Asia-Pacific Region* (Kluwer Law International 2009).

the concept of unrestricted public domain rights that has become a key concept in some intellectual property systems.[30] The nuances of how to conceptualize the public domain will vary from culture to culture. These variations are likely to arise from factors such as the position in society of the claimants in the country where they seek protection and often whether or not they were colonized.[31] These histories are important, but full coverage is beyond the scope of this chapter. Thus, examples are used, particularly from New Zealand, where the extent of the debate is well developed, even though the extent of protection is still wanting.[32] Māori, for example, do not necessarily view their knowledge assets as being in the public domain.[33] That does not necessarily mean that Māori keep all of their knowledge secret, but they do expect it to be treated in accordance with kaitiakitanga (Māori values and relationships).[34] The full picture shows that also there have been many instances in which Māori have shared knowledge with Europeans and made their knowledge and culture (mātauranga Māori)[35] available. Many Europeans have worked closely with Māori in order to document mātauranga Māori. An example

---

30 *See* K Bowery, "Indigenous Culture, Knowledge and Intellectual Property: The Need for a New Category of Rights?", in K Bowery, M Handler, and D Nicol (eds), *Emerging Challenges in Intellectual Property* (Oxford University Press 2011) 47.

31 *See*, e.g., Drahos's discussion of trust in Australia, note 26 above, and *compare with* claims to traditional knowledge in India, "Protecting India's Traditional Knowledge" <http://www.wipo.int/wipo_magazine/en/2011/03/article_0002.html> accessed 22 November 2013.

32 As discussed below, the issues in New Zealand have been full analyzed by the Waitangi Tribunal. That Tribunal makes recommendations to government, which at the time of writing have not been fully adopted.

33 *See* Frankel and Richardson note 29 above.

34 *Ko Aotearoa Tēnei*, note 3 above, at 17, stating "… Kaitiakitanga is the obligation, arising from the kin relationship, to nurture or care for a person or thing".

35 Mātauranga Māori includes traditional knowledge, although one is not the translation of the other. The National Library of New Zealand describes mātauranga Māori as follows:

> Mātauranga Māori in a traditional context means the knowledge, comprehension or understanding of everything visible or invisible that exists across the universe. Mātauranga Māori takes many forms, including language (te reo), traditional environmental knowledge (tāonga tuku iho, mātauranga o te taiao), traditional knowledge of cultural practice, such as healing and medicines (rongoā), fishing (kai moana) and cultivation (mahinga kai).

See <www.natlib.govt.nz>. *See also* the discussion of mātauranga Māori in, *Ko Aotearoa Tēnei*, note 3 above, at 32–8.

is the work of Elsdon Best, an anthropologist working in New Zealand in the early twentieth century.[36] Another more modern example is Murdoch Riley's very detailed book about traditional healing.[37] Māori also publish their own cultural works which embodies their knowledge. *Ngā Mōteatea*, a compendium of waiata (songs and chants), is such an example.[38] In addition to these published examples of laying open of mātauranga Māori, there are many less formal examples where mātauranga Māori is shared. Several Māori have said that sharing knowledge and how much you can give away is important, but they did not and do not expect their knowledge assets to be used and treated in ways which do not respect the culture from which the knowledge comes. Māori do not expect their knowledge to be used offensively or in ways that defeat the ability of Māori to use their own knowledge.[39]

4. THE TRADITIONAL KNOWLEDGE AND INTELLECTUAL PROPERTY OVERLAP AND DISJUNCTURE

The leading international intellectual property agreements – the TRIPS Agreement[40] and its incorporated agreements, the Berne Convention,[41]

---

[36] E Best, *Spiritual and Mental Concepts of the Māori* (Wellington, Dominion Museum Monograph No 2, GP 1922).

[37] M Riley, *Māori Healing and Herbal* (Viking Sevenseas 1994).

[38] *Ngā Mōteatea*, collected and translated by A Ngata and PTH Jones (Auckland University Press 2004).

[39] I make these comments based on my role as consulting counsel and report drafter on intellectual property law for the Waitangi Tribunal. I attended many hearings and heard much of the evidence first hand, *Ko Aotearoa Tenei* note 3 above. These observations are of course my own, not the views of the Tribunal.

[40] See note 6 above.

[41] Berne Convention for the Protection of Literary and Artistic Works, 1161 UNTS 30 (adopted on 9 September 1886), as revised at Paris (24 July 1971), art 15(4), which is incorporated into the TRIPS Agreement, note 6 above, art 9(1), provides:

> (a) In the case of unpublished works where the identity of the author is unknown, but where there is every ground to presume that he is a national of a country of the Union, it shall be a matter for legislation in that country to designate the competent authority which shall represent the author and shall be entitled to protect and enforce his rights in the countries of the Union …

This was incorporated into the Berne Convention primarily to protect so-called folklore as copyright, which might not otherwise be protected under Berne and the Paris Convention[42] – do not protect traditional knowledge assets as described above. As noted above, these agreements and their implementation in national legal systems do, however, have an impact on traditional knowledge assets and their uses. While it is recognized that intellectual property and traditional knowledge are different, there are also overlaps.

4.1 Trademarks and Geographical Indications

There are examples of trademarks being used as a second-best option to protect traditional knowledge assets. In the *Ko Aotearoa Tēnei*, Māori attempts to protect the longest place name as a trademark are described.[43] The witness who gave this evidence explains he used the trademark system because he had little choice, but it was not effective to protect mātauranga Māori associated with the place name.[44] Trademark laws protect marks as they are used in commerce. If applied to traditional knowledge assets, those assets must first be represented by a trademark and, second, be used in commerce. For some traditional knowledge assets, being trademarked may not be desirable and where it is desirable, the trademark may only provide partial protection for the knowledge asset in any event. Also, the requirement in most jurisdictions for a named owner on the trademark register may well be incompatible with traditional knowledge guardians' customary rules that do not name one owner of the knowledge assets; rather, there are several guardians of the knowledge.[45]

---

because of the requirements of identified authors. See discussion of this provision in S Ricketson and JC Ginsburg, *International Copyright and Neighbouring Rights: The Berne Convention and Beyond* (2nd edn, Oxford University Press 2006) paras 8.117–8.118. This is not however sufficient protection for traditional knowledge.

[42] Paris Convention for the Protection of Industrial Property, 828 UNTS 303 (adopted on 20 March 1883, entered into force 16 April 1970), as revised at Stockholm (14 July 1967).

[43] *Ko Aotearoa Tēnei*, note 3 above, at 65–6.

[44] Ibid., at 38–9.

[45] For a discussion of the overlap of trademark and traditional knowledge, *see* S Frankel, "Trademarks and Traditional Knowledge and Cultural Intellectual Property Rights", in GB Dinwoodie and MD Janis (eds), *Trademark Law and Theory* (Edward Elgar 2008).

The prospect, however, of perpetual intellectual property rights such as trademarks or geographical indications (GIs)[46] and collective ownership suggests some compatible aspects between these intellectual property rights and the protection of traditional knowledge assets.[47] The misfit between GI protection and the aims of protecting traditional knowledge assets is similar to the trademark issues discussed above. GIs are also primarily directed at commodities. Some of the rationales behind some GIs, such as wines reflecting the *terroir* where the grapes are grown and traditional methods used to make the wine, often are explained in a narrative that resembles how traditional knowledge holders explain their relationship with the land and uses of plants.[48] That similarity only goes so far. The GI related narrative supports the identification for a commodity relating to the knowledge, rather than protection of the knowledge, regardless of whether it is commoditized or not.[49] As Gervais notes, innovation connected to traditional knowledge "may often be situated at the intersection of 'culture' and technology. By contrast, GIs are generally situated at the intersection of culture and commerce".[50] Another difference is that GIs are frequently static in nature, as they require users of the GI to adhere to certain specific rules about how a product is made and its related quality;[51] conversely, traditional knowledge can be utilized for innovative purposes. The more practical hurdle is that GIs often involve significant costs to establish and enforce. At most they can be tools to support development, but they are not

---

46 GIs here is used broadly as in TRIPS Agreement, note 6 above, at art 22:1, which provides "Geographical indications are, for the purposes of this Agreement, indications which identify a good as originating in the territory of a Member, or a region or locality in that territory, where a given quality, reputation or other characteristic of the good is essentially attributable to its geographical origin."

47 D Gervais, "Traditional Innovation and the Ongoing Debate on the Protection of Geographical Indications", in Drahos and Frankel, note 1 above.

48 *See* A Taubman, "Saving the Village: Conserving Jurisprudential Diversity in the International Protection of Traditional Knowledge", in JH Reichman and KE Maskus (eds), *International Public Goods and Transfer of Technology Under a Globalized Intellectual Property Regime* (Cambridge University Press 2005) 521. *See also* T Josling, "The War on Terroir: Geographical Indications as a Transatlantic Trade Conflict" (2006) 57 (3) *J Agricultural Economics* 337; E Barham, "Translating terroir: the global challenge of French AOC labeling" (2003) 19 *J Rural Studies JRS* 127.

49 *See* S Frankel, "The Mismatch of Geographical Indications and Innovative Traditional Knowledge" (2011) 29(3) *Prometheus* 253.

50 Gervais, note 47 above, at 134.

51 There is opposition to this from those who wish that a broader notion of *terroir* is incorporated into the EU system.

the path to development. Consequently, for those short on development funds and whose plan for development of knowledge is not primarily commodification in products, is likely to be a waste of scarce resources.[52]

4.2 Copyright and Patents

Some aspects of traditional knowledge that qualify as copyright works, for example, will be protected, but copyright protects the particular expression of works[53] (collectively, literary and artistic works[54]). There are also examples of traditional knowledge holders using patents to protect their contribution to some inventions. An example is where some indigenous innovators, together with scientists, built what they described as a common network in order to join their different approaches of testing and observation to create new developments.[55] David Claudie, Chairman of the Chuulangun Aboriginal Corporation, and his co-researchers describe the goal of their research process as involving indigenous peoples to a degree that is more than benefit-sharing so that they are able to have their "own planning for sustainable natural resources management and economic development. Furthermore, indigenous peoples need to have the rights and legal mechanisms to protect their own cultural and intellectual property".[56] This sort of arrangement is relatively rare and relies on good relationships. What has been more common is the extraction of knowledge and the patentee using that knowledge and owning the patents independently of the source and holders of the knowledge.[57]

---

52 This may vary as some advocate the use of GIs for western rural development, *see* D Giovannucci, E Barham and R Pirog, "Defining and Marketing Local Foods: Geographical Indications for U.S. Products" (2010) 13 *J World Intellectual Property* 94.

53 The TRIPS Agreement, note 6 above, at art 9:2, provides that "copyright protection shall extend to expressions and not to ideas, procedures, methods of operation or mathematical concepts as such".

54 Berne Convention, note 41 above, at art 2.

55 DJ Claudie, SJ Semple, NM Smith, and BS Simpson, "Ancient but New: Developing Locally Driven Enterprises Based on Traditional Medicines in Kuuku I'yu Northern Kaanju Homelands, Cape York, Queensland, Australia", in Drahos and Frankel, note 1 above.

56 Ibid., at 35–6.

57 D Fabricant and N Farnsworth, "The Value of Plants used in Traditional Medicine for Drug Discovery" (2001) 109 *Environmental Health Perspectives* 69; *see* discussion in Claudie et al, note 55 above.

The difference between approaches to ownership of intellectual property and traditional knowledge assets are well documented and so are other differences, such as the time limits on copyright and patents, the scope of the protection and so on.[58] While patents and copyright expire, the notion of developing knowledge assets for future generations is not limited. In fact, the very purpose of using knowledge for the benefit of present and future generations, while honouring the tradition of the knowledge assets, suggests no time limit. As noted above, this is one of the reasons that traditional knowledge is thought by some to best fit the framework of potentially perpetual rights, such as trademarks and GIs. Fundamentally, however, copyright and patent laws provide protection for applied knowledge, which is commoditized in the form of creative and inventive products.[59] As discussed above, sometimes these goals can coincide with the goals of protecting traditional knowledge assets, but they are fundamentally different and thus there is a disjuncture between the two.

4.3 The Disjuncture and *Sui Generis* Rules

Traditional knowledge assets which do not fit the developmentally innovative or creative framework (the sacred and the secret)[60] may be worthy of a different kind of protection. This might be something analogous to the protection of flags and emblems, which is recognized internationally.[61] Trade secrets[62] and breach of confidence[63] doctrines do not provide a solution to breach of any secrecy where it relates to traditional knowledge. The existence of these doctrines shows, however,

---

58 *See* S Frankel, *Intellectual Property in New Zealand* (LexisNexis 2013) 132–51.

59 Patents can also protect processes.

60 *See* Gervais, note 13 above.

61 *See* Frankel, note 58 above, at 135. *See also* B Beebe, "Intellectual Property Law and the Sumptuary Code" (2010) 123 *Harv L Rev* 809, discussing how traditional cultural expressions (terminology used in WIPO negotiations, discussed below) are sumptuary uses of intellectual property. Flags and emblems protection may also fit this category where regulations control their use and customs around them.

62 *See generally* RC Dreyfuss and KJ Strandburg, *The Law And Theory Of Trade Secrecy. A Handbook of Contemporary Research* (Edward Elgar 2006).

63 *See generally* T Aplin, L Bently, P Johnson and S Malynicz, *Gurry on Breach of Confidence. The Protection of Confidential Information* (2nd edn, Oxford University Press 2012).

that intellectual property law is not foreign to the notion of secrecy. Secret traditional knowledge assets are not unimportant but are analytically distinct from the core difficulty facing the protection of many traditional knowledge assets, which is that they are in the public domain and the norms that traditional knowledge holders consider should govern them are not respected. Those sorts of traditional knowledge assets often involve innovation and creativity.

Intellectual property law was not designed to protect traditional knowledge assets, and many traditional knowledge holders do not want their assets slotted into intellectual property norms. Some of the misfit relates to how innovation is conceived and reflected in the law (in different ways, this is arguably a problem with which intellectual property law in general struggles) and whether it is seen as a product-based paradigm of applied innovation, or whether there is more of a focus on the system of innovation. Taking a systems' oriented view of innovation includes the institution's role in innovative performance, "as well as the distinctive linkages and interactions amongst institutional actors that characterise an innovation system".[64] The problem for many indigenous peoples is that their social structure and rules are not legally recognized and are not part of the institutional structure that the existing intellectual property system supports. Institutional linkages that the broader intellectual property context recognizes in modern economies include firms, industrial research laboratories, universities, government laboratories, and their financing arrangements. The institutional linkages in indigenous peoples' innovation systems are predominantly relationship based and include kinship systems and connections with the environment (cosmological and sacred institutions).[65]

The solution, which is therefore emerging, is not to try and fit traditional knowledge protection into the intellectual property system, but to find protection for it in what is called a *sui generis* system.[66] *Sui generis* rules avoid the problem of having to make general rule changes to intellectual property law, which could have deleterious consequences beyond traditional knowledge (such as giving indefinite protection to all rights), or exceptions within intellectual property law based on non-intellectual property norms. *Sui generis* regimes may differ from each other. Some may involve pluralistic elements where the customary laws

---

64 Drahos and Frankel, note 1 above, at 4.

65 In some societies, indigenous peoples' institutions may have some legal recognition. In modern day New Zealand, for example, the iwi (tribal grouping) is a legally recognized institution for some purposes.

66 *Sui generis* means a standalone system.

of the traditional knowledge holders are incorporated into the system, such as in the *Ko Aotearoa Tēnei* recommendations, discussed below, where the kaitiaki relationship is central to the regime proposed.[67]

Sui generis systems are not without difficulty because they do not necessarily attract global support and are ineffective if they are isolated systems. Additionally, *sui generis* protection needs to work effectively with intellectual property law so that one does not defeat the other. In other words, the systems need to effectively interface. New Zealand has provided a partial interface in both trademark and patent law where the statutes require that there be Māori advisory committees to provide the Commissioners of Trade Marks and Patents respectively with advice on conflicts with Māori culture.[68] In the trademark context, a conflict with Māori values which amounts to offensiveness means that the trademark must not be registered.[69] In the patent context, which is a comparatively newer interface, a clash with Māori values may or may not prevent registration.[70] A patent disclosure requirement (discussed further below) would also provide an interface between traditional knowledge assets and the patent system. The effects of disclosure systems vary and that variation may make the interface more or less direct.[71]

In sum, the overlap between intellectual property law and the existing, developing, and aspirational protection of traditional knowledge assets and the use of that knowledge for creativity and innovation is vast. The overlap is both practical and legal. As a legal matter, there are few jurisdictions in which traditional knowledge is formally protected. At the international level, there are several ongoing negotiations about how traditional knowledge might be protected and what the overlap with intellectual property law is and might become.

---

[67] *Ko Aotearoa Tēnei*, note 3, above. *See also* M Forsyth, "Do You Want it Gift Wrapped?: Protecting Traditional Knowledge in the Pacific Island Countries", in Drahos and Frankel, note 1, above.

[68] Discussed in S Frankel, "A New Zealand Perspective on the Protection Traditional Knowledge", in *International Trade in Indigenous Cultural Heritage: Legal and Policy Issues*, note 7, above, at 439.

[69] Trade Marks Act 2002, s 17(1).

[70] Patents Act 2013, ss 225–228. *Ko Aotearoa Tēnei*, note 3 above, at 212, recommends expansion of this interface and also recommends the development of a *sui generis* regime. To contribute towards achieving this, the Tribunal recommended that the committee should have powers greater than merely being advisory and that the Commissioner should be "required to take formal advice from it, and work in partnership with a member of the Māori committee when making patent decisions that affect the kaitiaki relationship".

[71] *See* discussion, below.

5. INTERNATIONAL BODIES AND TRADITIONAL KNOWLEDGE

The international dialogue about intellectual property has grown immensely. There are a variety of international bodies that have considered intellectual property rights and traditional knowledge holders' rights to their knowledge assets. Many of those seeking protection of traditional knowledge assets also express concern about the effect of modern practices on the environment. Internationally, this has led to a discussion of intellectual property in the Convention on Biological Diversity (CBD).[72] This part discusses the international negotiations relevant to the protection of traditional knowledge at the CBD, the World Intellectual Property Organization (WIPO), and the World Trade Organization (WTO) in connection with the TRIPS Agreement.

5.1 The Convention on Biological Diversity and the Nagoya Protocol

The CBD has the primary goal of sustaining "the diversity of life on Earth". Very broadly, the Convention recognizes state ownership and control over biological and genetic resources found in a state's territory.[73] This has given rise to questions about the rights of indigenous peoples within those territories in relation to both the biological and genetic resources and the traditional knowledge associated with it. Article 8(j) of the CBD is directly relevant to traditional knowledge assets. It states:

> Each contracting Party shall, as far as possible and as appropriate: Subject to national legislation, respect, preserve and maintain knowledge, innovations and practices of indigenous and local communities embodying traditional lifestyles relevant for the conservation and sustainable use of biological diversity and promote their wider application with the approval and involvement of the holders of such knowledge, innovations and practices and

---

[72] Rio Convention on Biological Diversity 1760 UNTS 79; 31 ILM 818 (opened for signature 5 June 1992, entered into force 29 December 1993) <www.cbd.int/> accessed 22 November 2013 (CBD). Article 2 defines biological resources as including "genetic resources, organisms or parts thereof, populations or any other biotic component of ecosystems with actual or potential use or value for humanity". Genetic resources are defined as "genetic material of actual or potential value", and genetic material is defined as "any material of plant, animal, microbial or other origin containing functional units of heredity".

[73] *See* CBD, note 72 above.

encourage the equitable sharing of the benefits arising from the utilization of such knowledge innovations and practices.

There has been much discussion in the working group of the CBD about how Article 8(j) might work to give protection to traditional knowledge assets.[74] This discussion has resulted in the Nagoya Protocol,[75] which recognizes rights of indigenous peoples to genetic resources. Perhaps the greatest limitation of the Nagoya Protocol is that its framework is entirely dependent on the state recognizing rights of indigenous peoples to their traditional knowledge in the first instance.[76] In other words, the Protocol only expands the rights of those who have them. It does not give traditional knowledge rights to those who do not have them independent of the Protocol. There are two key mechanisms that the Protocol adopts from the CBD. The first is the requirement of prior approval from knowledge holders before some biological and genetic resources and associated traditional knowledge is used, known as prior and informed consent (PIC). The second is the equitable sharing of benefits from the use of the resources and the knowledge.[77]

5.2 WIPO and Traditional Knowledge

WIPO acknowledges that its work is designed to complement the work of the CBD.[78] The members of WIPO meet as an intergovernmental committee (WIPO-IGC) to discuss the protection of traditional knowledge. The WIPO-IGC has an extensive negotiation process underway for treaties to protect traditional knowledge,[79] both as it relates to biological

---

[74] *See* "The Nagoya Protocol on Access and Benefit-sharing" Convention on Biological Diversity <http://www.cbd.int/abs/> accessed 22 November 2013.

[75] The Nagoya Protocol is a supplementary agreement to the CBD; Nagoya Protocol on Access to Genetic Resources and the Fair and Equitable Sharing of Benefits Arising from their Utilization to the Convention on Biological Diversity (UN Doc. UNEP/CBD/COP/DEC/X/1, adopted on 29 October 2010). According to the CBD website, "[i]ts objective is the fair and equitable sharing of benefits arising from the utilization of genetic resources, thereby contributing to the conservation and sustainable use of biodiversity".

[76] Nagoya Protocol, note 74 above, at arts 5 and 6.

[77] CBD, note 72 above, at art 15.

[78] WIPO also states that its work complements the International Treaty on Plant Genetic Resources for Food and Agriculture of the United Nations Food and Agriculture Organization, *see* <http://www.wipo.int/tk/en/genetic/>.

[79] Prior to this, WIPO also provides a model set of provisions for protection of expressions of folklore Model Provisions for National Laws on the Protection

and genetic resources and to traditional cultural expressions (TCEs).[80] WIPO describes TCEs as follows:[81]

> TCEs are integral to the cultural and social identities of indigenous and local communities, they embody know-how and skills, and they transmit core values and beliefs. Their protection is related to the promotion of creativity, enhanced cultural diversity and the preservation of cultural heritage.

Before its members authorized the negotiation of a treaty, WIPO undertook fact-finding missions on issues surrounding traditional knowledge with the particular aim of identifying and documenting traditional knowledge-related needs.[82] One recommendation of the report, resulting from those fact-finding missions, was the need to improve awareness about both traditional knowledge holders' concerns and the reality of intellectual property law. The report recommended a series of actions to develop this awareness, including preventing unauthorized acquisition of traditional knowledge; investigating options for collective acquisition, management and enforcement of intellectual property rights by traditional knowledge holders; development of new intellectual property related mechanisms to protect and enforce the protection of traditional knowledge; and the development and testing, with the close involvement of indigenous peoples and local communities, of "best contractual practices", guidelines and model clauses for contracts, as well as the provision of information on and protection against "unfair contract terms".[83]

WIPO's work on traditional knowledge and genetic resources has covered three main areas. The first is improved search tools and

---

of Expressions of Folklore Against Illicit Exploitation and Other Prejudicial Actions (WIPO/UNESCO 1985).

80 For WIPO's work, *see generally* <www.wipo.int> 22 November 2013. Prior to its current phase of treaty negotiations, WIPO undertook a fact finding mission, *see* WIPO Intellectual Property Needs and Expectations of Traditional Knowledge Holders: WIPO Report on Fact-finding Missions on Intellectual Property and Traditional Knowledge (1998–1999) (WIPO, Geneva, 2001) 26.

81 *See* "Traditional Cultural Expressions" at <http://www.wipo.int/tk/en/folklore/> 22 November 2013.

82 WIPO, "Intellectual Property Needs and Expectations of Traditional Knowledge Holders: WIPO Report on Fact-finding Missions on Intellectual Property and Traditional Knowledge (1998–1999)" (WIPO, Geneva, 2001). The report of that exercise is several hundred pages long. It contains lengthy details of the fact-finding missions and a number of conclusions, which the report accepted could not all be addressed by WIPO.

83 Ibid.

classification systems of traditional knowledge (in some countries, registers are emerging[84]) so that patent examination does not result in patents over not new and obvious genetic resources or uses thereof. The second was a technical study on disclosure requirements,[85] and the third is developing objectives and principles.[86] In the WIPO-IGC negotiations, these evolving objectives and principles have become the basis of draft treaties in the areas of both TCEs and genetic resources.[87] With regard to traditional knowledge and TCEs, a key objective includes providing beneficiaries with appropriate legal measures and practical means to prevent the misappropriation and misuse/offensive and derogatory use of their TCEs and to give them greater control over uses of their traditional knowledge.[88] The text relating to this has many square bracketed options. The square brackets indicate the wording that is not yet agreed. The complexity of the negotiations and division over wording of the treaties is also present in relation to traditional knowledge and genetic resources. The square bracket problem is starkly illustrated by the negotiating text of a key objective. It provides:[89]

> Ensure [applications for [intellectual property rights] [patents] [utilizing] genetic resources [their derivatives] and [associated traditional knowledge] [traditional knowledge associated with genetic resources]] [those accessing [and/or using]] genetic resources [,their derivatives] and [associated traditional knowledge] [traditional knowledge associated with genetic resources] comply with [international rights and national legislations] [national law and relevant conditions] for [requirements of the country providing for prior informed

---

[84] *See* "Online Databases and Registries of Traditional Knowledge and Genetic Resources" <http://www.wipo.int/tk/en/resources/db_registry.html> 22 November 2013.

[85] WIPO, "Technical Study on Disclosure Requirements Related to Genetic Resources and Traditional Knowledge" Doc 786, <http://www.wipo.int/export/sites/www/freepublications/en/tk/786/wipo_pub_786.pdf> accessed 22 November 2013.

[86] WIPO, Intergovernmental Committee on Intellectual Property and Genetic Resources, Traditional Knowledge and Folklore "Consolidated Document Relating to Intellectual Property and Genetic Resources", Document prepared by the Secretariat, WIPO/GRTKF/IC/25/5, 30 May 2013.

[87] The latest versions can be found at <http://www.wipo.int/tk/en/igc/> 22 November 2013.

[88] WIPO, Intergovernmental Committee on Intellectual Property and Genetic Resources, Traditional Knowledge and Folklore "The Protection of Traditional Cultural Expressions: Draft Articles", Document prepared by the Secretariat, WIPO/GRTKF/IC/25/7, 19 July 2013, Annex, page 2, para 1.

[89] *See* note 86 above, annex, p 6.

> consent, mutually agreed terms, fair and equitable] [access and benefit-sharing] [and disclosure of origin].

Whether WIPO members will be able to agree on the principles and objectives, which will form the basis of any traditional knowledge treaty, remains to be seen. In the meantime, the principles and objectives serve as useful guidance to domestic lawmakers who might want to protect traditional knowledge at a national level ahead of any international agreement to do so.

5.3 The TRIPS Agreement

Because of the correlation between, on the one hand, global protection of intellectual property and increased global trade and, on the other hand, an increase in uses of traditional knowledge assets, the TRIPS Agreement is important in this sphere. As discussed above, TRIPS does not cover the protection of traditional knowledge. The Doha Round of multilateral trade negotiations included a discussion, in the TRIPS Council, on the protection of traditional knowledge as part of a review of Article 27:3(b) of the TRIPS Agreement. That also included a discussion about the relationship between the TRIPS Agreement and the CBD.[90] There is little agreement between members of the WTO on this relationship. An added complexity is that the discussions have been tied to equally controversial discussions over the protection of geographical indications, over which the EU and the US do not agree. This negotiation is unlikely to proceed, both because negotiations in all areas of the WTO are stalled and also because the US has contested the mandate of the TRIPS Council to discuss traditional knowledge.[91]

Prior to the discussion stalling, its focus became whether the TRIPS Agreement should be amended to include a requirement that patent applicants must disclose, in the relevant patent application, the source of any biological or genetic material and/or the use of traditional knowledge used in the invention. This is known as a disclosure requirement. There are many variables about what such a requirement might require be

---

90 *See generally* the "Article 27.3b, traditional knowledge, biodiversity" at <http://www.wto.org/english/tratop_e/trips_e/art27_3b_e.htm> accessed 22 November 2013. *See also* DJ Gervais, *TRIPS Agreement Drafting History and Analysis* (Sweet & Maxwell 2012), paras 1.79–1.94.

91 *See* M Blakeney, "The Pacific Solution: The European Union's Intellectual Property Rights Activism in Australia's and New Zealand's Sphere of Influence", in Drahos and Frankel note 1, above, at 178–83.

disclosed in the patent application.[92] At one extreme would be disclosure of the genetic or biological resource if it was integral to the invention. This presumably should be disclosed in any event.[93] Often it could be said that the knowledge asset at issue provided inspiration for or pointed towards a field of research which led to the invention, but the knowledge asset was not integral to the invention. If, for example, the invention is a synthesized version of the isolated active ingredient of a plant, the knowledge that the plant had therapeutic properties, which led to the isolation of the active ingredient and invention of the synthesized product, would not necessarily be integral to the invention. At the other extreme of potential disclosure requirements is that use of a biological or genetic resource in any way related to the research that led to the invention must be disclosed.[94] In addition to what the scope of the disclosure requirement is, another factor is whether failure to disclosure should have any consequences.[95] One possibility is no consequence and at the other extreme is that a failure to disclose could lead to revocation of the patent. Several possibilities exist in between these two extremes, such as re-examination of the patent application in light of the disclosure or a penalty of some kind.[96]

Many developed countries are opposed to any form of compulsory disclosure requirement in patent law. The US, for example, is of the view that there is not a conflict between the CBD (it has not ratified the CBD) and the TRIPS Agreement. The US has suggested that any issue of access to genetic resources and benefit-sharing can and should be resolved through contracts.[97] As mentioned above, the EU is supportive of

---

[92] See note 84 above.

[93] TRIPS Agreement, note 6 above, art 29 requires that an applicant for a patent shall disclose the invention "in a manner sufficiently clear and complete for the invention to be carried out by a person skilled in the art and may require the applicant to indicate the best mode for carrying out the invention known to the inventor at the filing date".

[94] This is recommended in *Ko Aotearoa Tēnei,* note 3 above.

[95] *See* note 84 above.

[96] Ibid. *See also* C Guneratne "Disclosure of origin of genetic resources and traditional knowledge", in *Genetic Resources, Equity and International Law* (Edward Elgar 2012).

[97] Council for Trade-Related Aspects of Intellectual Property Rights, "Communication from the United States: Article 27:3 (b), Relationship Between the Convention on Biological Diversity and the TRIPS Agreement", IP/C/W/257, 13 June 2001. *See also* J Carr, "Agreements that Divide: TRIPS vs. CBD and

mandatory disclosure, but not of patent revocation being a consequence of non-disclosure.[98]

5.4 Other Trade Agreements

Many free trade agreements refer in one way or another to the protection of traditional knowledge. For the most part, these agreements do not provide substantive norms on the protection of knowledge.[99] This seems to be the situation even where the two countries may each have protections for traditional knowledge. The failure to use free trade agreements to achieve some norms may be because those parties who seek protection for traditional knowledge assets have not used trade agreements to drive norms more generally in the intellectual property field. It may also be because it is difficult to finalize standards.[100] If the multilateral negotiations to protect traditional knowledge assets do not progress, norms may very well develop in other trade agreements. Some parties to the Trans-Pacific Partnership Agreement, for example, appear to be considering such norms.[101]

6. IMPLEMENTING PROTECTION AT NATIONAL LEVEL

6.1 The Compatibility of Traditional Knowledge Protection with the TRIPS Agreement

While the international negotiations do not progress, many countries are considering implementing traditional knowledge protection. A fundamental question which policy makers and lawmakers must consider is whether potential domestic measures are compatible with international agreements and, in particular, the TRIPS Agreement. The answer is that

---

Proposals for Mandatory Disclosure of Source and Origin of Genetic Resources' in Patent Applications" (2008) 18 *Journal of Transnational Law and Policy* 131, 144–8.

[98] *See also* Carr, note 97 above, at 149–52.

[99] *See* S Frankel, "Attempts to Protect Indigenous Culture through Free Trade Agreements", in *International Trade in Indigenous Cultural Heritage: Legal and Policy Issues,* note 7 above.

[100] For discussion of these points, *see* ibid.

[101] The leaked negotiating text of the Trans-Pacific Partnership negotiations, available at <http://tppinfo.org/resources/leaked-texts-country-info/> accessed 22 November 2013.

such protection can be designed to be compatible with TRIPS. First, where the protection is not covered by the TRIPS categories, the protection falls outside the scope of TRIPS[102] and consequently is not governed by the requirements of the Agreement. This is the nature of *sui generis* protection. However, where there is an overlap between a TRIPS Agreement requirement and the protection of traditional knowledge assets, the TRIPS Agreement must be complied with. The overlaps are most likely to occur when mechanisms are used to interface intellectual property with traditional knowledge holders' interests or *sui generis* systems that recognize those interests. So, for example, a disclosure requirement in patent law must also be compatible with the TRIPS Agreement.[103] Those seeking a disclosure requirement internationally wish to incorporate it into TRIPS so that the requirement is mandatory, but that does not mean countries cannot implement these rules in any event.

While the international talks are not progressing fast, national jurisdictions may take action. The next section summarizes the New Zealand recommendations as a leading example of how to achieve the balance between intellectual property and traditional knowledge interests.

6.2 Recommendations of the Waitangi Tribunal in New Zealand

In 1991, several Māori lodged a claim before the Waitangi Tribunal.[104] Six claimants brought the proceedings on behalf of their iwi (tribe) and

---

[102] The TRIPS Agreement, note 6 above, protects intellectual property as listed in Part II: Standards Concerning the Availability, Scope and Use of Intellectual Property Rights.

[103] TRIPS Agreement, note 6 above, arts 29 and 62.1 will be relevant. A full analysis of these articles and every nuance of all potential disclosure requirements are beyond the scope of this chapter.

[104] The Waitangi Tribunal is a tribunal of inquiry established by the Treaty of Waitangi Act 1975 (NZ), s. 5. The Tribunal investigates claims made under the Treaty of Waitangi (Te Tiriti O Waitangi). The Treaty is a founding document of New Zealand. For the Treaty's history, *see* C Orange, *The Treaty of Waitangi* (Bridget Williams Books 1992). The Treaty sets out the agreement between Māori and the Crown over the governance of New Zealand and is consequently of constitutional significance. The Treaty of Waitangi is in both Māori and English and both versions are official versions, as they are not direct translations of each other, *see* Treaty of Waitangi Act 1975, s 2, which defines "the Treaty" as including both the English and Māori version set out in schedule 1 to the Act.

as individual claimants,[105] alleging that successive governments had failed to allow Māori to exercise te tino rangitiratanga[106] (self-determination and control) over things Māori and, in particular, over the body of knowledge: mātauranga Māori.[107] The Waitangi Tribunal hears evidence and argument and then reports on a claim, including making recommendations to the government. The report in this matter, *Ko Aotearoa Tēnei*, was issued in 2011. "In essence the report is about Māori culture and identity; New Zealand's laws, government policies and practices that affect that culture; and whether Māori are able to live and develop (both culturally and economically) as Māori."[108]

Ko Aotearoa Tēnei breaks the intellectual property related discussion into chapters entitled "Taonga Works and Intellectual Property" and "Genetic and Biological Resources of Taonga Species". Taonga works is the phrase used to define those works which embody mātauranga Māori.[109] Both chapters begin with narratives that illuminate Māori culture and Māori concerns over the use of their knowledge assets. The claimants[110] saw the control of their knowledge assets as necessary so as to maintain and develop their guardianship (kaitiaki) relationship with taonga works, including the freedom to develop the works as kaitiaki.[111] The notion of the kaitiaki relationship frames the Tribunal's reasoning whereby the Tribunal concluded that the Treaty of Waitangi guarantees to Māori an appropriate degree of protection for the relationship. Consequently, if the relationship does not exist, there is not the need for protection.[112] In many instances where the relationship is either present

---

The Second Article, *Ko te Tuarua*, is of direct relevance to intellectual property and is the Treaty basis for *Ko Aotearoa Tēnei,* note 3 above.

105 The claimants were Haana Murray of Ngāti Kurī, Hema Nui a Tawhaki Witana of Te Rarawa, Te Witi McMath of Ngāti Wai, Tama Poata of Ngāti Porou, Kataraina Rimene of Ngāti Kahungunu and John Hippolite of Ngāti Koata

106 Te tino rangitiratanga is guaranteed to Māori under the Second Article of the Treaty of Waitangi.

107 *Ko Aotearoa Tēnei,* note 3 above.

108 Frankel, note 68 above, at 440.

109 *Ko Aotearoa Tēnei,* note 3 above,

110 Not all of the claimants made identical submissions. They are here referred to collectively for convenience.

111 *Ko Aotearoa Tēnei*, note 3 above, at 38–43.

112 Works for which there is a kaitiaki are taonga works. If there is not kaitiaki the report calls the works taonga-derived works, *Ko Aotearoa Tēnei*, note 3 above, at 84–5. The distinction between taonga-derived works and taonga works might also be seen as reflecting the reality that allowing non-Māori to use Māori culture is also a benefit for Māori, as such use contributes to the culture's

or missing, there may be competing interests, which the Waitangi Tribunal concluded should be weighed against the Māori interests in taonga works. These competing interests include the rights of existing intellectual property owners and the general public interest in the use of Māori culture.[113] The existing intellectual property regime usually results in the competing interests winning. In sum, *Ko Aotearoa Tēnei* recommends shifting that balance so that the Māori interests, in appropriate circumstances, become a key protected interest. The broad recommendations that the Tribunal made in order to achieve the protection of taonga works and mātauranga Māori are:

1. New standards of legal protection governing the use of taonga works, taonga-derived works, and mātauranga Māori …
   (a) A general objection mechanism to prohibit the derogatory or offensive public use of taonga works, taonga-derived works, or mātauranga Māori …[114]
   (b) A mechanism by which kaitiaki can prevent any commercial exploitation of taonga works or mātauranga Māori (but not taonga derived works) unless and until there has been consultation and, where found appropriate, kaitiaki consent …[115]
2. An expert commission to have wider functions in relation to taonga works, taonga-derived works, and mātauranga Māori.[116]

---

survival. It is for that reason that the Tribunal also said it did not recommend mātauranga Māori be treated as owned by Māori. The Tribunal said that "building a legal wall around mātauranga Māori would … choke it", *Ko Aotearoa Tēnei*, note 3 above, at 92.

[113] Some people with competing interests, including New Zealand artists and designers as well as other holders of intellectual property rights, gave third-party evidence at the hearings of the claim, *Ko Aotearoa Tēnei*, note 3 above, at 74–7.

[114] The Tribunal recommended that anybody should be entitled to object to the derogatory or offensive public use of taonga works, taonga-derived works, or mātauranga Māori.

[115] The Tribunal recommended that only kaitiaki should be entitled to object to any non-derogatory or non-offensive commercial use of taonga works or mātauranga Māori.

[116] In order to achieve effective calibration the Tribunal's recommendations include that the government establish a commission with multi-disciplinary expertise (encompassing mātauranga Māori, IP law, commerce, science, and stewardship of taonga works and documents at both commissioner and secretariat levels). The proposed Commission should have adjudicative, facilitative and administrative functions. *Ko Aotearoa Tēnei*, note 3 above, at 99.

This goes further than the WIPO objectives under negotiation. Some Māori do not see the Waitangi Tribunal recommendations as enough. One commentator has expressed the view that only complete ownership is appropriate.[117] *Ko Aotearoa Tēnei* could alternatively be viewed as a thorough attempt to balance competing interests in order to calibrate them appropriately for the New Zealand environment.

Intellectual property aspects of genetic and biological resources are discussed along with issues arising in other parts of the research process relating to bioprospecting and biosecurity.[118] The Tribunal concluded that the Treaty of Waitangi requires a reasonable degree of protection of the kaitiaki relationship between Māori and biological and genetic resources, described as taonga species.[119] In this context the kaitiaki relationship is described as:

> … the elements that make [Māori culture] distinctive in the world can be traced to the relationships kaitiaki built up with the land, water, flora, and fauna of [New Zealand]. In this way, the mauri, or inner well-being of land and water spaces, and the whakapapa of flora and fauna do not just serve to articulate the human relationships with these things; they are the building blocks of an entire world view and of Māori identity itself. They play a similar role to the core definers of Western culture such as the arts, democracy, the rule of law, and so forth. But while the more human-centred Western culture tends to define itself by reference to its own thought and labour, Māori culture relies on pre-existing, pre-human definers – mountains, rivers, plants, animals, and so on. Māori culture seeks to reflect rather than dominate its surroundings. That is why the relationship between humans and taonga species is a definer of Māori culture itself. It is a preoccupation of the body of distinctive Māori knowledge that today we call mātauranga Māori.[120]

The Tribunal's overall recommendation was that decision-making mechanisms, such as registering patents, need to value the Māori interest as a key factor. In relation to an application for a patent, this would include consideration of the kaitiaki interest in the criteria for patentability (for example, whether a patent is novel and involves an inventive step)[121] or

---

[117] *See* M Jackson commenting on video "Moana Jackson Considers the Waitangi Tribunal Report for Wai 262 Claim and How Well it Meets the Wishes and Desires of the Original Claimants", Wai 262. Taonga. Kaitiaki, available at <http://wai262.weebly.com/moana-jackson.html> accessed 22 November 2013.

[118] *Ko Aotearoa Tēnei*, note 3 above, at 115.

[119] Ibid., at 114–15.

[120] Ibid.

[121] The criteria for when an invention is patentable include novelty and inventive step. Both are legal concepts of some depth and difference. They both,

whether the invention should be excluded on the basis that it conflicts with the kaitiaki relationship more broadly and is therefore contrary to ordre public.[122] In order to achieve this, the Tribunal recommended the establishment of a Māori committee "to advise the Commissioner of Patents about whether mātauranga Māori or taonga species have contributed in any way to the invention, and whether the proposed use is consistent with or contrary to tikanga Māori".[123]

7. CONCLUSION: PROTECTING TRADITIONAL KNOWLEDGE AS A MEANS OF CALIBRATION

In order to overcome some of the international difficulties in protecting traditional knowledge assets, some agreed minimum standards are necessary. That is the rationale behind all international intellectual property protection. While international standards remain a topic of negotiation rather than the subject of firm agreement, many national jurisdictions might consider how to balance protection with existing intellectual property protection. The recommendations of the Waitangi Tribunal are an example of how a country can calibrate[124] its laws to meet local needs. These sorts of examples can also help show how international protection is possible.[125] Just as some countries chose to increase intellectual property protection, such as extending copyright term and limiting fair

---

however, use the prior art as the key evidence in analyzing whether there is novelty or inventive step in any particular case. The issue relevant to traditional knowledge is whether and how that knowledge forms part of the prior art. If it does, it might affect these criteria. However, even if some traditional knowledge is part of the prior art the use of the traditional knowledge may not necessarily affect the patentability criteria of novelty or inventive step.

[122] The Patents Act 2013, s 15, enacted an ordre public exception. Section 15(3) states that: "The Commissioner may, for the purpose of making a decision under this section, seek advice from the Māori advisory committee or any person that the Commissioner considers appropriate." The exception is not explicitly expressed as providing an ordre public exception to protect Māori interest to the extent that the Tribunal recommended. It could be interpreted that way, but it remains to be seen how it will be interpreted.

[123] *Ko Aotearoa Tēnei*, note 3 above, at 212.

[124] On the calibration narrative, *see* DJ Gervais, "TRIPS and Development", in DJ Gervais (ed.), *Intellectual Property, Trade and Development* (Oxford University Press 2007).

[125] *See* Frankel, note 8 above, where I discuss how some international objections at an abstract level are not sustainable when examples are used to show how protection could work.

use, other countries may choose to protect traditional knowledge. Each will have different arguments about their merits, which lawmakers and policy makers must weigh. Put differently, what a country protects, over and above the minimum standards that the TRIPS Agreement requires, is a matter of domestic policy which ought to reflect that country's preferences. The public domain in one country will not be the same as in another country, but that does not mean it is necessarily smaller or indeed bigger. It is different and calibrated appropriately for that place.

8. The limits of patents

Elizabeth F. Judge and Daniel J. Gervais

INTRODUCTION

Intellectual property rights are increasingly subject to skepticism that they indeed function as promised to generate more creativity and innovation in society. The critiques link to such larger movements, such as the access to knowledge movement and the development agenda, and have launched calls for more evidence-based inquiries as to whether society truly gains a net benefit by according these exclusive rights to creators and inventors.[1] Patents raise particularly acute public policy questions, given the potential that the limited term monopoly rights accorded by patent law could negatively impact access to, and wide dissemination of, technology and research tools. There are growing concerns that the patent bargain has been struck too favorably for patentees, and that the uneven balance is growing even more skewed. Critics assert that too many patents are being granted for "inventions" that amount to no more than common knowledge, trivial increments on existing knowledge, and old ideas. In a related concern, many argue that patent rights are expanding to restrict access to the basic building blocks required for research (such as genes and standards).[2] With the advent of the TRIPS Agreement, which links intellectual property with international trade and sets fairly high thresholds for minimum intellectual property rights, there have also been concerns about the significant

[1] *See generally*, P Drahos and J Braithwaite, *Information Feudalism: Who Owns the Knowledge Economy?* (New Press 2002); L Lessig, *The Future of Ideas: The Fate of the Commons in a Connected World* (Vintage 2002); J Boyle (special edn), "Duke Conference on the Public Domain: Collected Papers" (2003) 66 *L. & Contemporary Problems* 1–483; J Litman, "The Public Domain" (1990) 39 *Emory L. J.* 965–1009; D Lange, "Recognizing the Public Domain" (1981) 44 *L. & Contemporary Problems* 147–78.

[2] *See* J Farrell, J Hayes, C Shapiro, and T Sullivan, "Standard Setting, Patents, and Hold-Up" (2007) 74 *Antitrust L. J.* 603; MA Lemley, "Intellectual Property Rights and Standard-Setting Organizations" (2002) 90 *Cal. L. Rev.* 1889; JM Mueller, "Patent Misuse Through the Capture of Industry Standards" (2002) 17 *Berkeley Tech. L. J.* 623.

impact of patents on developing nations and indigenous populations, especially with respect to health- and agriculture-related inventions, and calls to align the international intellectual property system with the human rights regime.[3] In this brief chapter, we attempt to present a realistic picture of the value, and limits, of patents.

I. BASIC PATENT PRINCIPLES

A patent is a limited term monopoly that the government grants to an inventor of a new invention that results from an inventive step and is capable of industrial application, in exchange for the inventor disclosing the details of the invention to the public.[4] A patent allows the patentee to exclude other people from making, using, or selling the invention for up to 20 years.[5] As such, a patent comprises what are often referred to as "negative rights," that is, rights to prevent use; it neither requires the patentee to exercise the rights, nor does it grant the patentee "positive rights," that is, a right to use the invention, because additional use or marketing approvals unrelated to the patent may be required. Thus, a patentee may hold a valid patent but nevertheless be unable to begin marketing a product until regulations set out under other laws (as, for example, requirements that might be imposed by laws regulating pharmaceuticals, agriculture, or weapons) are satisfied. But the patentee is able to prevent other people from exploiting the invention for commercial advantage for the duration of the patent term.

Patents may be seen as a form of monopoly (though a patent does not always give actual market monopolistic power if there are unpatented alternatives) but no monopoly should be taken lightly. Hence, patents, like any monopoly, are normatively justified only if their net benefits in increased innovation outweigh the patent rent (or "monopoly costs"), to which one should add the systemic resource costs to administer and enforce the patent system and other transaction costs. The question for policy makers is not to assess each patent individually, but whether, in

---

3 *See* LR Helfer and GW Austin, *Human Rights and Intellectual Property: Mapping the Global Interface* (Cambridge University Press 2011).

4 According to international texts such as TRIPS and NAFTA, countries may deem the terms "inventive step" and "capable of industrial application" to be synonymous with the terms "non-obvious" and "useful," respectively. TRIPS Agreement, art 27.1 n1, and NAFTA, art 1709(1).

5 Patent Act, R.S.C. 1985, c. P-4, art 44 (20 years from the date of application for patents filed on or after 1 October 1989).

aggregate or perhaps by type or category of invention, patents fulfill their role in promoting innovation without negative impacts on access to and use of technological knowledge.[6]

Under the traditional view, the patent system is designed to benefit the public by effecting increased innovation. As the Supreme Court of Canada observed in *Apotex v. Wellcome Foundation*:

> A patent, as has been said many times, is not intended as an accolade or civic award for ingenuity. It is a method by which inventive solutions to practical problems are coaxed into the public domain by the promise of a limited monopoly for a limited time. Disclosure is the quid pro quo for valuable proprietary rights to exclusivity which are entirely the statutory creature of the Patent Act. Monopolies are associated in the public mind with higher prices. The public should not be expected to pay an elevated price in exchange for speculation, or for the statement of "any mere scientific principle or abstract theorem" (s. 27(3)), or for the "discovery" of things that already exist, or are obvious. The patent monopoly should be purchased with the hard coinage of new, ingenious, useful and unobvious disclosures.[7]

Patents are supposed to provide incentives for people to innovate (and thus to bring more new and useful inventions to the public) by according the inventor a statutory limited term monopoly of exclusive rights. To put it conversely, patents are supposed to ameliorate the disincentives that would otherwise exist under a commons system. Under a commons system, there are no property-like rights restricting the use of an invention, which, as intangibles, are inherently non-exclusive and non-rivalrous. Anyone is free to exploit someone else's invention. The traditional justification of patents is premised on a critique of the suboptimal effects that a commons system may produce.

Although it may be true that a commons system offers advantages for the public by allowing anyone access to the inventions that already exist (which could lead, for example, to cheaper versions, more improvements, and greater efficiencies), these advantages accrue only in the short term. In the long term, if there were no patent law and all inventions were in the commons, the traditional view asserts that the cost-benefit analysis shifts: inventors would be likely to reason that they would be unable to recoup their opportunity costs in such a system and choose not to invent

---

[6] Patent offices and courts do, however, assess the utility and non-obviousness/inventive step of an individual patent in enforcement proceedings, but they are not required to determine whether a particular patent contributes to innovation beyond the need to meet the patentability criteria.

[7] *Apotex Inc v. Wellcome Foundation Ltd*, 2002 SCC 77, [2002] 4 S.C.R. 153, para 37.

(which would lead to fewer inventions), or, if they did proceed to invent, they would be likely to choose legal methods, such as trade secrets, that require secrecy rather than public disclosure (which would deprive the public of information about the invention). In either of these two scenarios, the traditional view posits that the public is *worse* off under a commons system, than under the positive law statutory regime of patents, because there would be less total innovation for society.

All intellectual property rights must balance incentives for the creators and access for the public, but, of course, the difficulty is in striking an optimal balance of rights, exceptions, and defenses that provides incentives for creators without overcompensating them and permits access so that others can build on that creativity. That balance might also include appropriate limits on remedies and user-focused remedies in case of abuse of rights.[8] In order for the patent bargain to be advantageous for society, patentees should bear concomitant duties to the public in return for their exclusive rights.[9] Traditionally, the core act required of patentees before they are granted patent rights is that they must tell society about the details of the invention. Under this bargain theory, the legal protection of a patent is granted in exchange for public disclosure about a useful invention.

Again drawing from the Supreme Court of Canada in *Apotex Inc. v. Wellcome Foundations Ltd.*:

> Patent litigation is usually protracted and costly. [. . .] There is in the meantime a chilling effect on other researchers. They will tend to invest their talents in less litigious areas. Parliament considered this chilling effect to be a worthwhile price for the disclosure of a "new and useful" invention, bringing into the public domain information that might otherwise remain a trade secret, but

---

[8] Limitation of remedies, most notably injunctive relief, in the case of patents enforced by certain non-practicing entities seems to be the main balancing tool under consideration by various jurisdictions as of this writing (December 2013). *Cf.* M Dolmans and D Ilan, "European Antitrust and Patent Acquisitions: Trolls in the Patent Thickets" (2012) 8:2 *Competition L. Int'l* 7. Remedies against abuse as an issue has many subparts which this chapter cannot fully discuss. For example, while TRIPS Article 40 mentions cases of anti-competitive practices, the choice and application of the proper test for abuse may determine the outcome of a case, as in *U.S. Philips Corp. v. International Trade Commission*, 424 F.3d 1179 (Fed. Cir. 2005). Administrative steps such as maintenance fees in the later years of a patent may also be considered part of a balanced system. *Cf.* n 17, below.

[9] EF Judge, "Intellectual Property Law as an Internal Limit on Intellectual Property Rights and Autonomous Source of Liability for Intellectual Property Owners" (2007) 27:4 *Bulletin of Sci. Techn. & Soc'y* 301–13.

> there is nothing in the Act to suggest that Parliament was prepared to accept the chilling effect in exchange for nothing but speculation.[10]

A patent is merited only if there is an actual "invention" which satisfies all patentability criteria, namely, that the invention is within the scope of patentable subject matter, is novel, inventive/non-obvious, industrially applicable/useful, and whose details are fully disclosed to the public in way which enables persons versed in the art concerned to understand, test, and eventually practice the invention. Adherence to the patentability criteria is supposed to ensure that the public gets something of greater value than the disadvantages incurred by the anti-competitive effects and inefficiencies of a limited term monopoly. This is not always the case, however, as we shall now see.

II. MODERN CRITIQUES

There is growing skepticism that the patent system as it currently operates overall has the intended effect of producing more innovation relative to a commons system or to other forms of public support such as prizes or subsidies. At the very least, critics suggest that the effects of patents may be very different depending on the industry or country concerned. Against this backdrop, how can one answer the simple question whether patents support or hinder innovation?

A. Patents As the "One-Size-Fits-All" Incentive

As modern critiques point out, there is little empirical evidence to support a general link between the patent system as a whole and its purported systemic benefits of increased innovation and corollary advantages such as increased wealth, less unemployment, better health, and improved agricultural yield.[11] This lack of convincing empirical data is not surprising; given the range of subject matter encompassed by patents and the strong tendency for inventors to use the existing patent system if they meet its requirements, it is difficult to design research to address what *would* have happened in the absence of a patent system (i.e. would that same invention have been invented if there were no patent rights to

---

[10] *Apotex Inc v. Wellcome Foundation Ltd*, 2002 SCC 77, [2002] 4 S.C.R. 153, para 37.

[11] AW Torrance and B Tomlinson, "Patents and the Regress of Useful Arts" (2009) 10 *Columbia Sci. & Techn. L. Rev.* 130.

protect it). Moreover, even if patents were proven to be the preferred mechanism to encourage innovation and its spread within society, it is not clear that the relatively high thresholds for minimal protections set under international conventions are optimally calibrated to produce the greatest innovation globally, nor whether the "one-size-fits-all" approach can adequately address the divergent economic levels of development and the different social and cultural values among countries.

One specific and very obvious issue is the single term (20 years from filing) imposed by article 33 of TRIPS. While this may be suboptimal, there are no definitive answers given to questions such as whether the optimal term for a patent is 20, 16, or 24 years. It seems very plausible that, beyond a certain optimal point, patent protection may decrease innovation.[12] One could thus argue that for certain categories of invention or creation – indeed, for specific inventions or works – a certain term is optimal, while a different one is more adequate in a different context.[13] These high-level discussions can take the form of perpetual balancing acts, making it harder to get to a policy solution.[14]

Policy analyses could also try to factor in the added value of *each creation or invention* to determine an appropriate term of level of protection, which could in turn depend on measuring the exact size of the inventive step[15] and/or the degree to which this step overlaps the

---

[12] *See* F Laforgia, F Montobbio, and L Orsenigo, "IPRs and Technological Development in Pharmaceuticals: Who Is Patenting What in Brazil after TRIPS" in N Netanel (ed.), *The Development Agenda: Global Intellectual Property and Developing Countries* (Oxford Univ. Press 2009) 293, 301; NT Gallini, "Patent Policy and Costly Imitation" (1992) 23(1) *RJE* 52–63; O Cadot and S A Lippman "Barriers to Imitation and the Incentive to Innovate" (1995) 095/23/EPS <ssrn.com/abstract=7187>.

[13] One ex post sign would be whether the invention is still actively being exploited at the expiration of the patent. However, if only inventions whose value had lapsed fell into the public domain, the societal value of granting a 20-year monopoly would come into question. In the U.S., there is a long history of extending the term of specific patents by private bills. CL Stanley, "A Dangerous Step Toward the Over Protection of Intellectual Property: Rethinking *Eldred v. Ashcroft*" (2003) 26 *Hamline L. Rev.* 679, 694–5. Historically, the term of a patent was set by private bill until a standard term was introduced into federal law. *See* TB Nachbar, "Intellectual Property and Constitutional Norms" (2004) 104 *Columbia L. Rev.* 272, 338–9.

[14] R Falvey, N Foster, and D Greenaway, "Intellectual Property Rights and Economic Growth" (2004) Internationalisation of Economic Policy Research Paper No. 2004/12 <http://ssrn.com/abstract=715982> 2.

[15] In the area of pharmaceuticals, a difference is often made between pioneer drugs and so-called "me-too" drugs. The latter are variations on a molecule

predictable industrial or commercial applicability of the invention. One could add to this equation the degree of competition in the industrial or economic sector that is impacted by the invention and, correlatively, whether there are dominant players by market share.[16] Even if such proposals could pass the test of transaction costs, however, experts could at best only guess the future utility of the invention. In terms of predictability, time, and transition/protection costs, a single term of protection may thus be better, even if it may seem a theoretically less refined solution. It is certainly simpler and does not entirely exclude options such as the reasonable modulation, subject to TRIPS constraints, of maintenance fees and even remedies after a certain number of years.[17]

B. Industry-specific Impacts

Beyond the issue of the single term for all patents, there is growing, though not undisputed, evidence that, at a more fundamental level, patents are causing more harm than good in certain sectors. There is a relatively short list of industries generally considered to be highly patent-sensitive. The variegated list of industries concerned includes pharmaceuticals[18] and many types of laboratory instruments, but also organic chemicals, plastic chemicals, and steel mill products.[19] This classification goes back in part to Mansfield's studies of the field, in which he found that, while 90 percent of pharmaceutical innovations were dependent on patent protection, only about 20 percent of chemical,

---

developed by another laboratory that tends to have the same physiological/therapeutic effect, but without infringing the "pioneer's" patent. *See U.S. v. Generix Drug Corp.*, 460 U.S. 453 (1983).

[16] *See* A Hollis, "An Efficient Reward System for Pharmaceutical Innovation" (2004) <http://econ.ucalgary.ca/fac-files/ah/drugprizes.pdf>.

[17] *Cf.* BJ Love, "An Empirical Study Of Patent Litigation Timing: Could A Patent Term Reduction Decimate Trolls Without Harming Innovators?" (2013), 161 *Univ. Pennsylvania Law Rev.* 1309–59; F Cornelli and M Schankerman, "Patent Renewals and R&D Incentives" (1999) 30 *RAND J. Econ*, 197. TRIPS mandates the availability of certain remedies but does not specify the conditions pertaining to such availability in individual cases.

[18] KE Maskus, "Lessons from Studying the International Economics of Intellectual Property Rights" (2000) 53 *Vand. L. Rev.* 2219, 2232.

[19] TK Cheng, "A Developmental Approach to the Patent-Antitrust Interface" (2012) 33 *Northwestern J. Int'l L. & Business* 1, 35.

electronics, and machinery innovations were patent-dependent.[20] Beyond those limited fields, controversy concerning the role and impact of patents on innovation quickly emerges. Are the benefits to innovation within the computer software and online commerce sectors greater than the aggregate cost of obtaining, enforcing, and defending against patent infringement claims, especially those owned by non-practicing entities?[21] This question is front and center in a number of both developed and developing countries.[22] In 2013, New Zealand restricted patents on computer programs ostensibly for that very reason.[23] The European Patent Convention, which applies to 38 European countries (it is not independent from and thus not limited to the EU), states that programs for computers "shall not be regarded as inventions."[24]

The high technology sector more generally is mired in a debate on the potential negative effects of "patent assertion entities" (or the derisive term "patent trolls"), that is, non-inventing entities that purchase patents and use them to license and litigate against third parties, especially those who refuse to license.[25] Proposals to recognize differences between sectors have been made in the U.S. but not enacted; if the legislator is unwilling to separate industries by applying different standards, perhaps

---

20 E Mansfield, "Patents and Innovation: An Empirical Study" (1986) 32(2) *Management Science* 173–81; E Mansfield, M Schwartz, and S Wagner, "Imitation Costs and Patents: An Empirical Study" (1981) 91 *Econ. J.* 907–18; Cheng, note 19 above, 33.

21 Many U.S. studies have been published on this topic. *See* Exec. Office Of The President, Patent Assertion and U.S. Innovation 2 (2013) <http://www.whitehouse.gov/sites/default/files/docs/patent_report.pdf>; BH Hall and D Harhoff, "Recent Research on the Economics of Patents" (2012) 4 *Annual Rev. Econ.* 541, 546–9; AB Jaffe, "The U.S. Patent System in Transition: Policy Innovation and the Innovation Process" (2000) 29 *Research Pol'y* 531; CV Chien, "Reforming Software Patents" (2012) 50 *Houston L. Rev.* 325.

22 SK Shrestha, "Trolls or Market-Makers? An Empirical Analysis of Non-practicing Entities" (2010) 110 *Columbia L Review* 114–60.

23 New Zealand, H.R., Supp. Order Paper (14 May 2013), Patents Bill Proposed Amendments to SOP No 120. To comply with TRIPS art 27.1, which requires that patents be available for all fields, New Zealand's amendment to the pending patent bill declares that pure software (software that is not integrated with novel hardware) is not an "invention." *Cf.* TB Lee, "New Zealand just abolished software patents. Here's why we should, too" *Washington Post* (29 August 2013) <http://www.washingtonpost.com/blogs/the-switch/wp/2013/08/29/new-zealand-just-abolished-software-patents-heres-why-we-should-too>.

24 European Patent Convention, art 52(2)(c).

25 For a taste of the U.S. debate, *cf.* J Bessen and MJ Meurer, "The Direct Costs from NPE Disputes" (2014) 99 *Cornell L. Rev.* 378–424; and the reply:

courts can.[26] Compliance with TRIPS's mandated uniform term may remain a significant hurdle.

While no system is perfect, there are growing questions whether the patent system strikes an optimal balance, for either developed or developing countries. For example, the length of the patent term should be only as long as required to coax the most inventions into existence, but no longer. Is 20 years from the application date the Goldilocks solution or is it longer (or shorter) than needed? Some critics have suggested that the patent system would be improved if inventions from different fields were treated differently – for example, by shortening the term of protection for inventions from dynamic technologically intensive areas, such as software or pharmaceuticals, to avoid the potential that the patent term might outstrip the number of years that the invention was actually useful for the public. The implications of TRIPS article 27.1 for such proposals, which precludes discrimination between technologies, is discussed below.

C. Patent Quality

The core aspects of the patent bargain seem to be more often interpreted in favor of the patentees, with the effect that society is extending too much and the patentees offering too little in return – too stingy public disclosure from patentees at the same time that there is too expansive a scope for patentable subject matter and too permissive standards for novelty, utility, and non-obviousness. On public disclosure, critics argue that applicants do not disclose enough in the application to enable other people to learn from the invention during the duration of the patent term and to replicate the invention at the expiration of the patent term. With respect to software, for example, patentees can typically satisfy public disclosure without having to reveal the source code.

There are additional charges that the patent examination process is too lax and the quality control is insufficient, resulting in patents being granted for claims that fail to satisfy one or more of the statutory patentability requirements (i.e. subject matter, novelty, utility, and non-obviousness) and thus resulting in a grant of exclusive rights to the applicant even though there has not been a reciprocal true innovation to

---

DL Schwartz and JP Kesan, "Analyzing the Role of Non-Practicing Entities in the Patent System" (2014) 99 *Cornell L. Rev.* 425–456.

[26] DL Burk and MA Lemley, "The Patent Crisis and How The Courts Can Solve It" (2010) 23 *Syracuse Science & Technology L Reporter* 1–22.

benefit the public.[27] A related aspect of this is the controversy over how liberally the statutory provision on patentable subject matter should be interpreted. The definition of "invention" and the patentability criteria in many domestic and regional patent laws are broadly worded to be forward looking. This has raised the question whether higher life forms (such as genetically modified animals), constituent parts of the human body (such as genes), software (which the TRIPS Agreement already explicitly includes as a subject matter for copyright), and business methods (such as a "one-click" e-commerce checkout function) fit the subject matter definition and whether they fit the other criteria for patentability.

Metrics to measure patent quality have emerged and may help policy makers avoid the issuance of (too many) "bad patents" and a misguided policy focused exclusively on the *quantity* of patents issued.[28]

D. Patents as Rights to Exclude

Another critique relates to the fact that patentees are not required to positively exercise their rights or make the patented product or process available. Do patents support rent seeking rather than innovation *per se*? Although the patent system has incentives on the macro-level to encourage inventions and their spread within society, at the micro-level a single patentee may choose not to exercise its rights, in which case that invention effectively languishes, and, if the patentee elects not to make, use, or sell the invention but pursues third parties for possible infringement, the patent may effectively obstruct rather than facilitate innovation. That said, nonuse of a patent may be a justifiable decision – for example, if a patentee has decided to sell a different product (presumably protected under a different, probably more recent patent).

In some industries, where there is a prevalence of existing patent rights, the transaction costs associated with patents may be heightened because a complex web of cross-licensing may need to be negotiated before an invention can be brought to market.[29] Most inventions constitute improvements, and if the improvement is to a product or process that

---

27 *See* WM Cohen and SA Merrill, *Patents in the Knowledge-Based Economy* (National Research Council 2003) 17–119.

28 *See* e.g. Dan Prud'homme, *Dulling the Cutting-Edge: How Patent-Related Policies and Practices Hamper Innovation in China*, European Union Chamber of Commerce in China, August 2012.

29 I Hargreaves, *Digital Opportunity: A Review of Intellectual Property and Growth* (UK, May 2011) <http://www.ipo.gov.uk/ipreview-finalreport.pdf>.

is still protected by a patent, licensing will be required before the improvement can be made or sold. "Patent thickets" occur when a product or process comprises several overlapping patent rights, which will require that the various patentees agree on cross-licensing arrangements before the product or process can go to market. Such negotiations involve multiple patents, which may be held by a few large players in the sector or by numerous right holders if the market is segmented. The degree to which patent thickets undermine innovation and in which industries there may be anti-competitive barriers to entry is still being studied, but it is suggested that the problem is more widespread in telecommunications, software, biotechnology, nanotechnology, and pharmaceuticals.[30]

E. Patents v. Other Incentives

It seems clear that optimizing domestic innovation outcomes often requires some form of incentive.[31] Recent studies have argued that the risk (which some see as having been conclusively demonstrated) that patents will generate negative welfare impacts in certain sectors at least could be mitigated by resorting to other, non-exclusive right based forms of innovation incentives, such as innovation prizes, tax credits, and subsidies.[32]

III. THE TRIPS AGREEMENT

Article 27.1 of the TRIPS Agreement[33] requires that patents be available in all fields of technology, based on the three usual criteria, i.e. novelty, industrial applicability, and involving an inventive step. A footnote makes clear that the terms "useful" and "non-obvious" correspond to the latter

---

30 Intellectual Property Office Patent Informatics Team, *Patent Thickets: An Overview* (UK 2011) <http://www.ipo.gov.uk/informatic-thickets.pdf> 4.

31 *See* S Scotchmer, *Innovation and Incentives* (Cambridge, MA, MIT Press 2004) 1–27.

32 *See* PS Menell and S Scotchmer, "Intellectual Property Law" in AM Polinsky and S Shavell (eds), *Handbook of Law and Economics* vol. 2 (vol 2, North Holland 2007) 1530–4; DJ Hemel and LL Ouellette, "Beyond the Patents-Prizes Debate" (2013) 92 *Texas L. Rev.* (forthcoming) <http://ssrn.com/abstract=2245691>.

33 Agreement on Trade-Related Aspects of Intellectual Property Rights, 15 April 1994, Marrakesh Agreement Establishing the World Trade Organization, Annex 1C, 1869 U.N.T.S. 299, 33 I.L.M. 1197.

two. Combined with an explicit inclusion of both product and process inventions and the part of the last sentence that prohibits any distinction concerning the field of technology, one might say that a general principle of eligibility to be patented is established. Any exclusion from patentability would therefore be looked upon as an exception to that rule. Indeed, article 27.1 is "subject to" articles 65.4 (which allows members a five-year delay in extending the provisions on product patents to areas of technology that had not already been protectable in its territory) and 80.8 (which tends to confirm that it does establish a principle).

The exact scope of the principle is unclear. It seems to require that all inventions be eligible to be patented, but not that they necessarily all be treated the same. In practice, courts often seem to apply the patentability criteria (especially non-obviousness and utility) differently depending on the type or field of invention.[34]

In determining the eligibility of an invention to be patented, and the enjoyment of patent rights, article 27.1 prohibits discrimination based on whether the invention is locally produced or imported, subject to a number of exceptions in the following paragraphs. This concerns working requirements and possible compulsory licenses, which, before the TRIPS Agreement, were regulated only by the narrowly drafted article 5A of the Paris Convention (1967),[35] which prohibits forfeiture for importation without restricting other measures to control or restrict importation and left contracting states free to impose compulsory licenses for failure to work after a prescribed delay. It can be inferred from article 27.1 that importation must be accepted among the WTO member states as a legally effective working of a patent under national law.

Article 27.2 of TRIPS contains a restriction to the general principle of eligibility to be patented: inventions may be excluded from patentability based on a risk that their commercial exploitation within their territory could endanger *ordre public* or morality within the territory of the WTO member concerned. Examples given are the protection of human, animal, or plant life or health. There are a number of key conditions to be met for article 27.2 to apply. First, the exclusion must apply to certain inventions, not categories of inventions (compare with article 27.3). Second, the risk must come not from the invention as such, but from its commercial exploitation and its impact within the territory of the country concerned.

---

[34] In the U.S. context, *see* DL Burk and MA Lemley, "Is Patent Law Technology-Specific?" (2002) 17 *Berkeley Techn. L. J.* 1155, on the divergent application of patent law to biotechnology and software.

[35] Paris Convention for the Protection of Industrial Property, 20 March 1883, 21 U.S.T. 1583, 828 U.N.T.S. 305, as last revised at Stockholm in 1967.

The term *ordre public*, well known in civil law, expresses concerns about matters threatening the social structures which tie a society together. The phrase "to protect human, animal or plant life or health" is used in article 27.2 to give examples of circumstances where preventing the commercial exploitation of an invention may be necessary to protect *ordre public* or morality. The word "necessary" is usually interpreted as meaning that a measure is justified only if no alternative measure, which a WTO member could reasonably be expected to employ and not inconsistent or less inconsistent with GATT, is available.[36] Under TRIPS article 27.2, members may exclude diagnostic, therapeutic, and surgical methods for humans or animals from patentable subject matter.[37]

Article 27.3 contains more "focused" exceptions that do not need to be justified in the same way as exceptions under article 27.2. The first category applies first and foremost to biotechnological inventions. Under the text as it stands, and assuming that article 27.1 does establish a principle of eligibility to be patented (see above), these provisions should probably be interpreted restrictively. Yet, the expression "plants and animals" is semantically broader than "plant and animal varieties" used in the European Patent Convention. One may question whether the exclusion of diagnostic, therapeutic, and surgical methods for the treatment of humans or animals applies to processes involving something less than the entire human or animal body (e.g. testing or treatment of blood, stimulation of an immune response).

IV. PATENTABILITY OF SCIENCE AND RESEARCH TOOLS

The exclusion of scientific principles and abstract theorems from patentable subject matter is reasonably well accepted as a normative matter. Indeed, it is expressed as such in the patent Acts of many countries.[38] Traditionally, a distinction has been made between (noncommercial)

---

[36] *Cf. United States – Measures affecting the cross-border supply of gambling and betting services*, WTO document WT/DS/285/AB/R, 7 April 2005, paras 304–307.

[37] In Canada, therapeutic and surgical methods are excluded from patentability, but diagnostic methods may be patented. *See* Canadian Intellectual Property Office, *Manual of Patent Office Practice*, ss 12.04.02 and 17.02.03.

[38] For example, in Canada, *see* R.S.C. 1985, c. P-4, art 27(8). However, the Canadian Act adds the word "mere" to this exclusion, as if to indicate that there is a significant limitation to the exclusion.

science and (commercial/industrial) technology, also referred to as "applied science." However, the distinction is not one that can be easily wrestled to the ground, especially in legal terms. This traditional distinction may be summarized as follows. "Basic" science is mostly done in universities and public laboratories, often with government funding. That science is then used by the private sector and sometimes universities or university-based researchers to develop (applied) technologies.[39] If the distinction is used as a binary tool to delineate the domain of patents, one can posit that patents should be granted on the latter but not the former (basic science) because: (a) normatively basic science was seen as a public (common) good that should not be appropriated, and (b) it did not meet patentability criteria, in particular that a patentable invention be "useful" or industrially applicable.[40] Indeed, basic science does not produce inventions but rather knowledge in the form of discoveries, mental steps, and abstract ideas, all of which are (still) presumptively non-patentable subject matter.[41]

Science is also different because it must be validated by peers while technology is "validated" by the marketplace, whether it be industry professionals or consumers. Technology is developed with a view to making a new product or process available on a commercial or industrial basis. Its aim is not to understand the environment, but to transform it.[42] New scientific knowledge will remain there until proven untrue, that is, until history decides its fate, but a new technology might disappear because its maker is bankrupt due to mismanagement, etc. The impact is different because science gives birth to new science that is much more upstream in the tree of knowledge creation, and in a way that is much more likely to have an impact on society than even the best consumer-manufactured device like a vacuum cleaner.

A new scientific breakthrough is likely to develop into multiple scientific research projects. Those projects, in turn, will lead to potential practical applications, initially in the form of pioneer applications (first of

---

39 *Cf.* S Sterckx, "Patenting and Licensing of University Research: Promoting Innovation or Undermining Academic Values?" (2011) 17 *Sci. & Engineering Ethics* 45, 48.

40 *Cf.* DJ Triggle, "Patenting the Sun: Enclosing the Scientific Commons and Transforming the University – Ethical Concerns" (2005) 63 *Drug Development Research* 139, 141.

41 *Cf.* R Eisenberg, "Proprietary Rights and the Norms of Science" (1987) 97 *Yale L. J.* 177, 185–6.

42 *Cf.* ED Keoke and KM Porterfield, *Science and Technology* (Facts on File 2005) viii.

its kind in its field) and then improvements thereof and possible "me too" quasi-copies. Patents may affect this development. They are "negative rights," that is, in this context, rights to prevent others from using the patented invention. There is no obligation for the patentee to use or license the technology, unless perhaps it constitutes an abuse of the patent monopoly, in which case measures such as compulsory licensing may be imposed. While there are exceptions for experimental use in a number of domestic patent laws, it is often very limited in scope and not subject to an internationally recognized standard.[43] In other words, a patentee owning an area of scientific research may be able to prevent others from doing research in that area. The patentee, however, has no obligation to devote any resources to such research. Even a well-intentioned patentee will have limited resources and may have other priorities. In addition, scientific progress often happens in unexpected ways. Hence, by not doing research, those unexpected developments simply will not occur.

Licensing and "letting the market operate" is not always a realistic alternative to those concerns. True, licensing of patents is often beneficial. However, with respect to "basic science," licensing may compound, rather than solve, the problem by preventing a person other than the patentee who was working in the same field from disclosing her own research under the license.[44] If a patent is hard to invent around, is not licensed at acceptable terms, or if the basic element covered by the patent controls a large section of the design space by being abstract, broad, upstream in the flow of knowledge, and/or is crucial for establishing connections with other elements of the design space, major industry-blocking may occur.[45] Professors Rai and Eisenberg have identified a number of cases in the electrical lighting, radio, automobile, and aircraft

---

[43] In Canada, *see* Patent Act, R.S.C. 1985, c. P-4, art 55.2(6). In the U.S., the Court of Appeals of the Federal Circuit has greatly reduced the scope of the "exception." *See* A Devlin, "Restricting Experimental Use" (2009) 32 *Harvard J. L. & Pub. Policy* 599.

[44] *Cf.* R Mazzoleni and RR Nelson, "The Benefits and Costs of Strong Patent Protection: A Contribution to the Current Debate" (1998) 27 *Research Policy* 273–84.

[45] P Rouvinen and R Stankiewicz, "Are Intellectual Property Rights Hindering Technological Advance? The Need for Technological Commons" (2009) 26 *R. Policy Research* 195.

industries.[46] The negative impact seems empirically verifiable in genetic and biomedical research.[47]

One such example is provided by the BRCA1 and BRCA2 genes, two genes associated with breast cancer. A woman with one or both genes is more likely to develop the disease and her doctor may recommend that she undergo more frequent screening. Yet, the two genes as indicators of a higher risk of breast cancer are "owned" by Myriad genetics, which reportedly charges US$3,000 for each test and makes research on the genes by others (who might help develop a cure) reportedly out of reach for many.[48] What Myriad "invented" was the discovery of a link between those genes and breast cancer. The BRCA patents illustrate how exclusive rights have the potential to block an important area of research. While not altogether blocking, Myriad's licensing practices arguably hinder scientific advancement, not least because Myriad effectively dictates what is being done and how.[49] A significant part of Myriad's BRCA patent was struck down by the U.S. Supreme Court.[50]

Even in biomedical research, a science commons tends to increase overall efficiency. The justification for more patents on basic science is thus questionable. The profit motive, which may work well to develop applications (e.g. a new molecule sold as a pharmaceutical) fails to achieve the same results in basic science because efficiency is increased when many disparate firms can draw on a common pool of knowledge and data. Allowing science to be owned and granting monopoly control over its development may also prevent a major accelerator of scientific progress: the network effects that obtain by involving a variegated group of researchers in an open – if at times competitive – environment. Less centrally coordinated development encourages a greater variety and quantity of research, for example done by laboratories in different environments, with different tools, insights, cultures, and knowledge.[51]

Few universities can show a sharp increase in net royalty income when the extra expenditures of much more developed technology transfer

---

[46] AK Rai and RS Eisenberg, "Bayh–Dole reform and the progress of biomedicine" (2003) 66 *L & Contemporary Problems* 289–314.

[47] Triggle, note 40 above, at 143.

[48] Ibid.

[49] Rouvinen and Stankiewicz, note 45, above, at 206.

[50] *Cf.* JA Camacho and C Brahma, "*Myriad*: The Supreme Court Isolates DNA Discoveries From Genetic Inventions In Deciding Patent Eligibility" (2013) 25 *Intell. Prop. & Techn. L. J.* 3.

[51] *Cf.* Y Benkler, "Coase's Penguin, or Linux and the Nature of the Firm" (2002) 112 *Yale L. J.* 369.

offices and the much higher licensing costs paid to other universities to use their science and research tools are factored in. Universities and publicly funded research institutions have traditionally operated according to a "communal" model, in the sense that scientists tend to "share" and discuss with people outside their research team more than engineers developing new technologies.[52] One can legitimately ask whether the zeal that some universities have demonstrated in applying for patents is compatible with their public interest mission, in particular when they claim ownership over fundamental scientific knowledge or research tools.[53] Are centuries of history of universities being (and being perceived as) public interest actors about to be erased, for meager returns, and at a potentially huge cost including a diminution and retardation of scientific progress? The costs are high on other levels as well. "Public confidence in the objectivity of science and the role of the university as a symbol of the public good is diminished when the statements and writings of academic scientists are seen as influenced by corporate money and influence."[54]

University patenting might, for example, lead scientists to restrict communication with colleagues due to confidentiality clauses required by business partners. Therefore, here too there is a conflict between the norms of science and the norms of patent law.[55] Even the presentation of research, traditionally in a way that maximizes dissemination (to maximize returns such as notoriety, etc.) may be gradually transformed by patent imperatives.

While the above should lead policy makers to strike a note of caution in allowing patents on or close to basic science, it may also prompt them to create robust exceptions for noncommercial experimental uses. Social or industry norms may be at play here as well. Some reports tend to show that even where the law does not formally allow much in terms of

---

[52] CG Moore, "Killing the Bayh-Dole Act's Golden Goose" (2006) 8 *Tulane J. Techn. & Intell. Prop. L.* 151; D Gervais, "The Patent Target" (2013) *Federal Circuit Bar J.* (forthcoming); AK Rai, "Regulating Scientific Research: Intellectual Property Rights and the Norms of Science" (1999), 94 *Northwestern. Univ. L. Rev.* 77; MA Heller and RS Eisenberg, "Can Patents Deter Innovation? The Anticommons in Biomedical Research" (1998) 280 *Science* 698.

[53] *Cf.* R Geiger and C Sa, *Tapping the Riches of Science. Universities and the Promise of Economic Growth* (Cambridge, MA, Harvard University Press 2008) 144.

[54] Triggle, note 40 above, at 144.

[55] *Cf.* D Blumenthal, EG Campbell, MS Anderson, N Causino, and KS Louis, "Withholding research results in academic life science: Evidence from a national survey of faculty" (1997) 227 *J. Am. Medical Assoc'n* 1224–8.

experimental use, patents are not often enforced against such uses. This may explain why the empirical support for claims that patent may harm basic scientific research is real yet does not provide an overwhelmingly bleak picture. Put differently, patents may be technically infringed in university laboratories on a regular basis but the use is tolerated. Whether patent holders' restraint is by choice (not to sue) or because they are unaware of experimental uses has not been precisely measured.

A final risk worth mentioning in this category, beyond the specific category of genetic research, is that education, especially of graduate students, may also suffer, as a curiosity-led, disinterested research and teaching ethos is replaced by an entrepreneurial approach. Increased focus on patent outputs and direct financial rewards for doing so may in fact create incentives for professors to reduce their time and commitment to some of their teaching or other non-patent-producing activities. Again, the question one comes back to is what net benefits from increased university patenting and, generally, patenting of basic science can be observed in terms of net increased scientific progress, when measured against the negative impacts on the role and place of universities as key societal actors.

V. PATENTS AND HUMAN RIGHTS

In the late 1990s, public health activists launched a vigorous debate about the ethical aspects of using patents to limit access to antiretroviral therapy in the least-developed countries. Flanked by Nelson Mandela and *Médecins Sans Frontières*, they brought the issue of intellectual property, and specifically patents, to the forefront of international public debate.[56] They advocated flexibility on behalf of poorer countries and challenged the rights of patent owners to deny access to those who could not afford the therapy. The debate has since been extended to other pharmaceutical products for various tropical and other diseases.

The problem, it must be stressed, does not lie entirely with patents – far from it. In a number of African countries, for example, antiretroviral drugs are not patented. Additionally, many of those countries have until 2016 to adopt pharmaceutical patent protection under WTO rules. There are serious problems of distribution, which can be solved, though with

---

[56] *Cf.* D Gervais, "TRIPS 3.0" in NW Netanel (ed.), *The Development Agenda: Global Intellectual Property and Developing Countries* (Oxford University Press 2009) 51–75.

colossal efforts, by setting up distribution mechanisms and other measures such as local clinics. Concerns about interrupted treatments and the possible emergence of more aggressive strains of viruses must be taken seriously.

The patent-related part of the problem stemmed from the lack of funds and the inability to use compulsory licensing to produce complex pharmaceutical products. The debate was largely won by the least-developed countries. It resulted in the adoption of the only amendment to the TRIPS Agreement to date, which itself followed the adoption of a WTO *Declaration on TRIPS and Public Health* in 2001 and the adoption of a Ministerial Decision by the WTO in 2003, allowing the least-developed countries to import pharmaceuticals manufactured in third countries under a compulsory license, subject to a number of notifications.[57]

The debate left scars on research-based pharmaceutical companies and impressions on public opinion. An ethical, human rights approach to public health now dictates limits on patent rights when no market is possible. No one is forcing pharmaceutical companies to produce at or below cost. However, when the patent holder cannot reasonably hope to have a significant market in a territory for a product that has life-saving potential, an approach informed by human rights leads to the conclusion that there is then no legitimate reason to prevent access to that product if someone is willing to produce it at a cost that the country can afford. The real issue becomes one of *diversion*, for there will always be "arbitrage entrepreneurs" who will try to buy the inexpensive product produced for a least-developed country and try to resell it (often illegally) in a more affluent market, thus preventing the patent holder from making legitimate gains.

The ripple effect of the clash between patents and human rights is far from over. The World Health Organization, for example, has actively entered the field and broadened the discussion to the entire financing of pharmaceutical research, questioning the predominance of private, profit-driven enterprises.[58] There is indeed an enormous amount of publicly funded research (e.g. the National Institutes of Health in the U.S.), including in hundreds of universities worldwide.

Human rights may also have a direct impact on the WTO itself. The WTO Appellate Body found that the WTO Agreement "is not to be read

---

57 Ibid.

58 *Cf.* World Heath Organization, *Research and Development to Meet Health Needs in Developing Countries: Strengthening Global Financing and Coordination*, 5 April 2012 <http://www.who.int/phi/CEWG_Report_5_April_2012.pdf>.

in clinical isolation from public international law."[59] This principle was reflected in subsequent decisions that relied on the jurisprudence of other international tribunals, namely the International Court of Justice, the European Court of Human Rights cases, and the Inter-American Court of Human Rights, in interpreting the provisions of the WTO Agreement, but only at a high level of generality.[60] This could of course extend to TRIPS, but the extent to which, for example, patent rights might be limited by using a human rights doctrine in the context of a WTO dispute-settlement proceeding is far from clear. What is clearer, however, is that intellectual property now forms part of trade and, as such, the very causes of action under TRIPS seem linked to demonstrable losses of income, or otherwise clear incompatibility between a statute and the text of TRIPS. This means that, if a national law is facially compliant with TRIPS, and no demonstrable loss of income is caused by limiting a right or its application (e.g. remedy) in a particular case, it may be more difficult to convince a WTO dispute-settlement panel to find fault with such a decision. This is visible in the application of the so-called "three-step test" to patent and copyright cases in previous reports of dispute-settlement panels where the main focus was on whether an exception to exclusive rights caused a loss of income to the right holder.[61]

Naturally, in fields of industrial activity other than pharmaceuticals affected by patents, effects would be wholly different, though there may well be developmental impacts and more diffused calls for technology transfers, deeper disclosure of working methods, and abuse issues where no supply of the domestic market is present.

VI. PATENTS AND HUMAN AND ECONOMIC DEVELOPMENT

What role should patents play in a domestic policy-setting effort aiming to maximize innovation while minimizing negative welfare impacts? In crafting a set of policy objectives, one can and probably should use a combination of human *and* economic development factors which, in recent years, have been translated into a series of objectives amenable in

[59] *US – Standards for Reformulated and Conventional Gasoline*, WTO document WT/DS2/AB/R, 29 April 1996, para III.B.

[60] Ibid., n 36; *Japan – Taxes on Alcoholic Beverages*, WTO document WT/DS8/AB/R, 4 October 1996, part D., n 19.

[61] *See* Ch 5 in this volume by C Geiger, D Gervais, and M. Senftleben on the three-step test.

part at least to the kind of metrics that evidence-based policy-making might call for, including the United Nations Human Development Index.[62] Development is "a pseudonym for a complex network of benefits associated with economic growth and human social capital."[63] It is:

> the sum of the changes in social patterns and mentalities through which the production devices coupled with the population: the latter acquires the capacity to utilize the production device to achieve what is considered to be a satisfactory growth rate, and the production device supplies a product that serves the population instead of being "alien" to it. This dialectic of production device and population is the essence of development.[64]

Developing countries are obviously not all identical. The U.K. IPR Commission Report[65] has stressed that it is important not to consider developing countries as a homogeneous group.[66] Yet, the TRIPS Agreement treats them all on the same footing. All developing countries other than LDCs had until 1 January 2000, to implement TRIPS – with up to five more years to apply product patent protection to pharmaceuticals for those, like India, that did not provide such protection.

Professor Gibbons, for example, grouped developing countries according to three stages of development, from imitation to absorption to innovation.[67] Stage one, which may be seen as including LDCs, is characterized by foreign direct investment that is rare and limited to specialized sectors, unskilled inexpensive labor, and foreign businesses which create the necessary infrastructure and invest in human capital. In stage two, the economy is able to absorb technology, imitate it, and contribute minor improvements with a well-educated workforce, and

---

62 The United Nation's Human Development Index comes to mind. *See* <hdr.undp.org/en/media/HDR_2013_EN_TechNotes.pdf>.

63 RL Okediji, "History Lessons for the WIPO Development Agenda" in N. Netanel (ed.), *Intellectual Property and Developing Countries* (Oxford Univ. Press 2009) 137, 140.

64 F Perroux, "The pole of development's new place in a general theory of economic activity" in B Higgins and D Savoie (eds), *Regional Economic Development: Essays in Honour of François Perroux* (Boston Unwin Hyman 1988), 48–76, at 70.

65 UK Commission on Intellectual Property Rights, *Integrating Intellectual Property Rights and Development Policy* (2002) <http://www.iprcommission.org/papers/pdfs/final_report/CIPRfullfinal.pdf>.

66 Ibid., 2–3.

67 LJ Gibbons, "Do As I Say (Not As I Did): Putative Intellectual Property Lessons for Emerging Economies from the Not So Long Past of the Developed Nations" (2011) 64 *SMU L. Rev.* 923, 932–3.

domestic research focused on technology transfer. In stage three, the newly industrialized country produces its own intellectual property and is selective about which intellectual property rights it will more zealously protect and for which rights it may be less inclined to discourage (mis)appropriation This three-stage progression tracks the innovation theorists' view that innovation follows a path from imitation to adaptation to true global innovation.[68] "Stage 2" countries likely overlap with the countries mentioned previously where innovation outcomes do not (yet) outweigh the additional rent extraction made possible by the implementation of TRIPS-compatible norms. As countries build innovation-focused industries, they typically develop more sophisticated and nuanced views of their intellectual property policies.[69] The various groupings of countries all point towards a similar path of progression. Along that path, which the evolution of IP rules in developed countries would seem to confirm, countries gradually make more and better use of IP rights.[70] Simply put, over time, countries play the IP game better.

Beyond patent and other IP rules, there are two major innovation-related policy areas to consider: spillovers and clusters. The former may be described as process- or method-related; the latter is more institutional in nature.

The process by which innovation often happens has been described as *spillover*. A number of endogenous growth models have identified R&D spillovers as a central factor in innovation optimization.[71] The theory suggests that more developing countries should adopt strategies to maximize spillovers, including by allowing entrepreneurs to consult patent applications and even attend top trade shows.[72] If an increase in intellectual property protection leads to more innovation, there should be

---

68 D Gervais "TRIPS and Innovation: How Recent Developments Might Inform Canada's Foreign Technology Policy" (2013) 29(1) *Canadian Intell. Prop. Rev.* 141, 161–2.

69 *Cf.* D Gervais, "Intellectual Property and Development: The State of Play" (2005), 74 *Fordham L. Rev.* 505–35.

70 S Ragavan, *Patent and Trade Disparities in Developing Countries* (Oxford Univ. Press 2012), 12–29; KE Maskus, "The WIPO Development Agenda: A Cautionary Note" in N Netanel (ed.), *The Development Agenda: Global Intellectual Property and Developing Countries* (Oxford Univ. Press 2009) 169.

71 RM Solow, "A Contribution to the Theory of Economic Growth" (1956) 70(1) *Quarterly J. Econ,* 65–94; Cheng, note 19 above, at 12; P Romer "Endogenous Technological Change" (1990) 98 *J. Political Econ.* S71–S102.

72 RC Levin, AK Klevorick, RR Nelson, and SG Winter, "Appropriating the Returns from Industrial Research and Development" [1987] *Brookings Papers on Econ. Activity* <www.jstor.org/stablc/2534454>.

more spillover effects and, consequently, more imitation. This may sound somewhat counterintuitive (more IP leading to more imitation) but available data do bear this out.[73]

Interestingly, available data suggest that it is a "foreign firm's *perception* of the strength of an IPR regime in a given *country* – rather than the actual strength of the regime within particular industries – that is responsible for determining the level of FDI."[74] If this is true, it would suggest that countries should "promote" their IP regimes and pay attention to third-party assessments of such regimes.[75] Other variables, such as the political situation, economic freedom, natural resource allocation, technological absorptive capability, WTO accession, and regional instability, also play a key role.[76]

Foreign investment is often mentioned first as a way of increasing domestic innovation capabilities. However, it is but one of four main methods to encourage transfer of technological knowledge. Those methods are: licensed technology transfers unauthorized imitation ("piracy"); patent disclosure; and reverse engineering.[77] All except the second one are legal. The first method, which includes but is not limited to FDI transactions that contain technology transfers, is voluntary; the other three are not, although arguably patent disclosure is consented to when one applies for a patent, because publication of the application after 18 months is part of the patent bargain. A potential patentee could instead

---

[73] EL-C Lai, "International Intellectual Property Rights Protection and the Rate of Product Innovation" (1998) 55(1) *J. of Development Econ.* 133, 135.

[74] G Halydier, "A Hybrid Legal and Economic Development Model That Balances Intellectual Property Protection and Economic Growth: A Case Study of India, Brazil, Indonesia, and Vietnam" (2012) 14 *Asian-Pacific L. & Policy J.* 86, 99.

[75] Some studies tend to support the view that the perception of stronger intellectual property in LDCs and developing countries may increase the volume of FDI. *Cf.* Y Qian, "Are National Patent Laws the Blossoming Rains? Evidence fron Domestic Innovation, Technology Transfers, and International Trade Post Patent Implementations in the Period 1978–2002" in NW Netanel (ed.), *The Development Agenda: Global Intellectual Property and Developing Countries* (Oxford Univ. Press 2009).

[76] Halydier, note 74 above, at n 64. Maskus, Fink and Primo Braga's work points in a similar direction. *See* KE Maskus, "The Role of Intellectual Property Rights in Encouraging Foreign Direct Investment and Technology Transfer" (2004) 9 *Duke J. Comparative & Int'l L.* 109–61; CA Primo Braga and C Fink, "The Economic Justification for the Grant of Intellectual Property Rights: Patterns of Convergence and Conflict" (1996) 72 *Chicago-Kent L. Rev.* 439–61.

[77] Cheng, note 19 above, at 48.

choose confidential information protection, which is based on maintaining reasonable secrecy, as the form of legal protection, and avoid disclosure. Developing countries can help develop patent information systems, informing their local entrepreneurs of published patent applications or at least making it easier for them to find them. They can provide information on reverse engineering and ensure that their laws permit the practice, as, for example, do laws in Europe and the U.S.[78]

A very concrete and powerful way to develop spillovers is to foster the establishment of *clusters*. Clusters can be seen as ways of organizing and maximizing both structured research efforts and serendipitous advances, the latter being often the most important. Available data and studies suggest that clusters involving *private capital, higher education resources relevant to the area, and government support* (in various forms from subsidies to tax incentives) are a successful form of industrial policy.[79] Clusters have the advantage of being focused on one industry or area, although that technology can evolve and change over time, just as Silicon Valley has moved from computers to cloud-based services over the past three decades. Clusters can be used by domestic companies, of course, but may also be used to attract FDI with a significant R&D component by branches of multinational corporations increasingly interested in having a broader geographical R&D footprint. In an age where capital and innovation are mobile, clusters can serve to attract the best minds in both research and business. Often, however, this will also require infrastructural investments by governments (e.g. roads, transportation, stable electrical supply, and access to the internet).[80]

Clusters are also – and perhaps more importantly – meant to reflect the fact that "economic development does not spread itself evenly throughout space. … Innovation tends to be concentrated in particular enterprises,

---

[78] P Samuelson and S Scotchmer, "The Law and Economics of Reverse Engineering" (2002) 111 *Yale L. J.* 1575–663; TM Evans, "Reverse Engineering IP" [2013] *Marquette Intell. Prop. L. Rev.* 61–101.

[79] *Cf.* D Gervais, "Of Clusters and Assumptions: Innovation as Part of a Full TRIPS Implementation" (2009) 77:5 *Fordham L. Rev.* 2353–77 <http://bit.ly/15mlbgG>.

[80] A Hargadon, *How Breakthroughs Happen: The Surprising Truth about How Companies Innovate* (Harvard Business School Press 2003). JC Stratton, "Idea Work Style – A Hypothetical Web-Based Approach to Monitoring the Innovative Health of Organizations" in JT Yao and P Lingras (eds), *WSS 2003: WI/IAT 2003 Workshop on Applications, Products and Services of Web-based Support Systems* (Halifax 2003) 69, 70.

the propulsive industries … ."[81] This means that a policy designed to maximize innovation need not be "national." In fact, if the national policy focuses as it should on clusters, the objective should be to allow a region to "maximize the aggregate net product while attending the desired structure of the national economy."[82]

Finally, information-sharing, through both formal and informal processes, should be part of the "culture" of clusters, in part to help maximize productive spillovers.

CONCLUSION

It has been a central tenet of patent law that patents affect economic growth and innovation in society. This proposition is increasingly being challenged, however, as scholars, countries, and international organizations examine whether the costs associated with the limited-term patent monopoly are actually outweighed by its benefits, at least in some industries or for some categories of countries. Critics worry that the patent bargain has been unevenly struck and that the transaction costs of the patent monopoly are an inordinately high price for society to pay. For many areas of concern highlighted above, it may fairly be argued that the problem lies in an over-expansion of patent law to areas that patent theory itself would contend were unsound. Patents are intended to be for technology, not basic knowledge, and are supposed to be reserved for actual "inventions," that is, new, non-obvious/inventive, and useful/industrially applicable inventions whose details are fully disclosed to the public in a way which enables persons versed in the art concerned to understand, test, and eventually practice the invention. A more serious adherence to the requirements of the patent bargain could ameliorate many of the more serious problems associated with patents. The internationalization of patents through TRIPS and other bilateral and regional trade agreements, which has insisted on a general principle of uniform thresholds despite divergences in countries' level of development and cultural values, has caused other strains. The scientific innovations of the late twentieth and twenty-first centuries, in biotechnology, telecommunications, nanotechnology, and genetics – included genetically modified organisms and seeds, gene therapy, and personal and mobile computing –

---

[81] B Higgins, "François Perroux" in Higgins and Savoie (note 64 above), 31, 42.

[82] Perroux (note 64 above), 48, 54–5.

has especially highlighted the human rights implications of patents and their consequences for access to knowledge and global development.

9. A protocol to evaluate the impact of intellectual property on innovation outcomes

Geoffrey R. Scott

INTRODUCTION

There have been numerous recent challenges to the structure of the domestic and global regimes that define and protect interests in intellectual property (IP). These include advances in technology, changes in product configuration and market structure, perceived evolution in innovation paradigms, and shifts in the perspectives of individuals and groups with respect to access to and use of products of the mind. While the need to address the delicate balance between the demands of those who have lent their hands, minds, talents and time to the creation of new works and those who desire access to the creative products has been an inherent attribute of most systems, there does appear to be current urgency to revisit the topic. Whatever the catalyst, consideration of the issues is very dynamic, and may, at times, be pressing and dramatic.

Perhaps the forces most responsible for the debate are the overwhelming effect of technological advances and corollary changes in social norms. Technology has driven us into an era where economies often deal more with soft products (for example, information) than with tangible products. While traditional IP laws have offered some protection to expanding creative efforts, the adequacy and proper reach of global IP regimes remains at the heart of the current dialogue. As a result, it is essential to fully understand the present legal construct in order to reach a cogent decision about how, or whether, to affect any change.

To assess alternative strategies that might be employed to respond to the demands of innovation it is necessary to understand the relationships between the forms of protection for IP and the advancement of creativity. The purpose of this chapter is to propose and demonstrate four discriminate and differential factors that can be employed in developing a responsible protocol to evaluate the various approaches to the topics. While the four chosen categories are intended to precipitate a discussion of many inchoate assumptions often unconsciously overlooked or intentionally avoided by policy makers, they are not intended to be exhaustive; nor are they to be necessarily viewed as separate and discrete. Rather, the pillars are rough and interrelated approximations that may be used to identify subject areas around which legitimate concerns cluster. These differential categories are: I. Technological/Transactional, II. Cultural, III. Principled, and IV. Political and Economic.

I. TECHNOLOGICAL/TRANSACTIONAL DIFFERENTIAL

The first factor relates to a consideration of advances in the technological environment and the manner in which strategies concerning the proprietary treatment of products of the mind are crafted in order to keep pace with and respond responsibly to developing nonproprietary pressures. As a vehicle of discussion, attention will be given to the phenomenon of user-centered innovation and what has been characterized as a consequent need for the free exchange of information. While not actually new, this approach to 'open-access' innovation is often contrasted with the traditional manufacturer- and seller-based process.[1] The claimed and distinguishing characteristics of 'open-access' are that users intend to benefit directly from their creative work, tend to share their innovations rather freely with other users, and often depend upon noneconomic rewards in order to recognize their achievement.[2] In contrast, the traditional manufacturing sector is frequently viewed as inclined to provide general customer solutions, rely heavily upon principles of IP to restrict access to information and processes, and seek to benefit by selling products or knowledge. However, user innovation should not be perceived as completely independent of manufacturer or seller innovation;[3]

---

1 Steven Weber, *The Success of Open Source* (Harvard UP 2004) 138. See also Yochai Benkler, *The Wealth of Networks: How Social Production Transforms Markets and Freedom* (Yale UP 2006) 3.

2 *Jacobsen v Katzer* 535 F 3d 1373, 1379 (Fed Cir 2008). The Court recognized such advantages as increase in national and international reputation, improvement in software due to user contributions, and increased market share in other products. This phenomenon may occur, for example, when a professor licenses an article to an academic publication without charging a fee or when a smartphone company promotes the sale of hardware by advertising free 'apps'. *See also, Planetary Motion, Inc v Techsplosion, Inc* 261 F 3d 1188, 1200 (11th Cir 2001).

3 Eric von Hippel, *Democratizing Innovation* (MIT Press 2005) 126.

there are, in fact, significant interrelationships between them. First, with respect to the character of innovative activity, users and manufacturers usually develop different, and at times complementary, types of information. User-generated invention tends to respond directly to specific, identified and often immediate individual needs of a discrete creator. Furthermore, due to the cost and inconvenience of moving information from forum to forum, individual innovators tend to use information they have readily available. To the contrary, the product of interest to sellers is often more complex, mature and developed, and directed toward general solutions. Consequently, traditional manufacturers tend to develop more generic solutions that can be marketed to a broader community.[4] Thus, one obvious effect of a shift to user-centered innovation is the type of information being generated. Second, it is extraordinarily important to place innovation into the proper market context and observe how the interest and opportunities of users and sellers may blend. To the extent that user innovation is discrete, eschews monetization and is solution driven, individual innovators may be fulfilled by benefits such as the application of their creative solution to the personal task at hand or by an enhanced community reputation. As a result, users may feel at liberty to freely disclose their innovations to others and, as a corollary, purport to claim no interest in IP protection. A consequence of this point of view, however, is that the information also becomes available to the traditional manufacturing sector. If the manufacturing sector elects to economically exploit the advance, the public also receives a benefit – namely, improved and general-use products.

This latter phenomenon has led to the development of an industrial movement that applies user-created information to revolutionize the manufacturing component in the delivery of goods.[5] Inspired by groups like Threadless, an open-design t-shirt company,[6] and Local Motors, a community-powered vehicle design and manufacturing organization,[7] some innovators have moved toward producing community – or crowd-sourced – products. In this context, participant firms tap into designers who lack the financial resources necessary to develop an adequate manufacturing infrastructure to exploit their ideas and through 'build

---

[4] Eric von Hippel, '"Sticky Information" and the Locus of Problem Solving: Implications for Innovation' (1994) 40 *Management Science* 429, 429.

[5] Chris Anderson, 'In the Next Industrial Revolution, Atoms Are the New Bits' *Wired* (25 January 2010) <http://www.wired.com/magazine/2010/01/ff_newrevolution/all/> accessed 26 January 2014.

[6] Threadless <http://www.threadless.com/> accessed 26 January 2014.

[7] Local Motors <http://localmotors.com/> accessed 26 January 2014.

centers', translate community-sourced ideas into tangible products. This has come to be known as micro-manufacturing.

This community-grounded effort has not been limited to a narrow domestic market. Global design chains and intermediaries, such as Alibaba,[8] are becoming scale-free in response to a proliferation of inexpensive and powerful prototyping tools capable of use by non-professionals.[9] The major impediment that apparently existed had been a lack of manufacturing instruments capable of bringing the intangible ideas to a tangible reality. Recently, however, there has been a considerable and observable shift in available manufacturing resources, and more factories are becoming willing and able to respond to low-volume internet-based orders that present the potential for high marginal profit.

Many of these micro industries are located in China. This is likely due to Chinese businesses responding quickly to Web-centric activity and exhibiting a willingness to accept orders via email and payment by credit card or PayPal; it is also potentially fueled by the current 'deflationary spiral of commodity goods',[10] which has caused companies to look to new means by which to turn a profit. Whatever the stimulus, the change is seen and promoted by many as revolutionary.

A. Influx of Information, but at What Cost?

Advocates of open source information and community-sourced products tend to emphasize and extol the virtues and potential positive attributes of these methods to the exclusion of disclosure and critical analysis of opportunity costs. These attributes may include enhanced opportunities for non-market creativity through the elimination or reduction of market-based or industrial barriers to both information and products; the technical superiority of the products due to contributions of numerous and diverse individuals; an improvement of social welfare through

---

[8] Alibaba Group <http://www.alibaba.com/> accessed 26 January 2014; Jillian D'Onfro, 'How Jack Ma Went From Being A Poor School Teacher To Turning Alibaba Into A $160 Billion Behemoth', *Business Insider* (14 September) 2014 http://www.businessinsider.com/the-story-of-jack-ma-founder-of-alibaba-2014-9accessed 20 October 2014. Alibaba began trading on the New York Stock Exchange on 19 September 2014.

[9] TechShop, for example, is a community-sourced program that provides tools, equipment and classes, enabling members to build their dream products. TechShop, 'What We Offer' <http://www.techshop.ws> accessed 26 January 2014.

[10] Anderson (n 5).

opportunities for inter-human connectedness; and finally, a process that 'democratizes' innovation and production to the political benefit of all.

In the effort to promote the cause, however, there is often a failure to acknowledge and disclose limitations and qualifications on access and use. A responsible protocol of evaluation, however, requires a more objective approach. Consequently, it would be quite hazardous to summarily infer that the open source models described above provide cost-free and/or readily accessible benefits to all. The following are just a few of the negative externalities that one could consider when evaluating the model.

1. Costs of open source works

The use of free and open source software (FOSS),[11] commercial open-source software (COSS), and works covered by the Creative Commons[12] arrangement are not actually 'free'. Even in an open source forum, access to information and code is generally conditioned upon a user's agreement to restrictive and conditional terms of use. These limitations are usually contained within an IP license.[13] While a license may embrace a philosophy of freedom of use, it is also very important to take serious note of the imposed conditions or restrictions on exploitation, which one could consider a cost. While a particular license could simply state that a user can do anything with the code, it is rare to actually find such liberal terms.

---

[11] For a discussion of some of the differences between advocates of free versus open source access, see Richard Stallman, 'Why Open Source Misses the Point of Free Software' (GNU Operating System, 26 November 2013) <http://www.gnu.org/philosophy/open-source-misses-the-point.html> accessed 26 January 2014. For a definition of 'open source', see Open Source Initiative, 'The Open Source Definition' <http://opensource.org/docs/osd> accessed 26 January 2014.

[12] Creative Commons, 'Attribution-NonCommercial-NoDerivs 3.0 Unported' <http://creativecommons.org/licenses/by-nc-nd/3.0/legalcode> accessed 26 January 2014. See also Greg Vetter, 'Open Source Software and Information Wealth' in Peter K Yu (ed.), *1 Intellectual Property and Information Wealth: Issues and Practices in the Digital Age* (Praeger Publishers 2007) 421.

[13] A commonly used license is the GNU General Public License (GPL) offered by the Free Software Foundation. 'Licenses' (GNU Operating System, 29 July 2013) <http://www.gnu.org/licenses/> accessed 26 January 2014. Note that the preamble to the license indicates that the term 'free software' is a reference not to price but to use.

One such 'open source' license, the GPU, conditions use upon full disclosure of the source code downstream.[14] While this restriction is fully consistent with the principles of the US Copyright Act, it may seem antagonistic to an implied philosophy of free access. The Act, however, grants to an author of a covered work the ability to control not only the creation of derivative works, but also certain distributions. For example, the language of the GPU license itself makes specific note that it is grounded in principles of copyright law, and that its terms may not be modified without permission. Consequently, if a user is not compliant with the conditions of the license, she would be liable as an infringer. While it might appear strange to the lay person that a purported 'anti-intellectual property' or 'CopyLeft' initiative would rely on the Copyright Act to enforce the obligations contained within the license, it is not, in fact, unusual.[15]

2. Open source creators often have a profit motive

As suggested above, it is improper to assume that the alleged 'non-market phenomenon' of open- or community-source innovation necessarily excludes users who possess a profit motive. To create a market, one only needs to have something to sell and someone willing to purchase the product. Indeed, the tens of thousands of free 'apps' available for the iPhone provide a good examples of the 'invent it now; sell it later' approach.[16] It is not unusual for innovators to create these 'apps' and initially distribute them free of charge. After capturing an interested market and clientele, many of these innovators turn their attention to economic exploitation of their creations by either selling advertisements to generate income or marketing enhanced services for an additional fee.[17]

---

[14] See, e.g., Copyright Act (US) s 101. See also *Gardner v Nike, Inc* 279 F3d 774, 779-80 (9th Cir 2002); *Everex Systems, Inc v Cadrak Corp* 89 F 3d 673, 679 (9th Cir 1996).

[15] Heather J Meeker, 'Open Source and the Legend of Linksys' (*Linux Insider*, 28 June 2005) <http://www.linuxinsider.com/story/43996.html> accessed 26 January 2014.

[16] A corollary to the 'invent now; sell later' approach is the 'Ready, Fire, Aim' strategy in business. The latter approach focuses on shortening the planning process, actively getting the product to market, and thereafter invigorating and revising the business plan based on information gained through marketing. *See, e.g.,* Michael Masterson, *Ready, Fire, Aim: Zero to $100 Million in No Time Flat* (Wiley 2008).

[17] In this latter regard, consider the marketing strategy of such organizations as Pandora. Tom Conrad, 'Pandora One: Upgrade the Pandora Experience'

While some licenses, such as those of the Creative Commons, attempt to limit monetization downstream, others, such as the FOSS license, appear to accept, if not embrace, the traditional market concept. In fact, open source may be a wonderful vehicle for small companies to become economically competitive. By opening up communications, an entrepreneur may not only access more participating developers, but may also open markets.[18] The approach has actually worked, even for larger and established companies. For example, as a commercial alternative to FOSS that requires that source code be made freely available downstream, Microsoft has commenced The Shared Source Initiative through which it affords to qualified partners and customers expanded access to source code.[19]

In the context of micro-manufacturing in China, however, the rewards may not be as generous as those provided by domestic businesses. One possible reason for this phenomenon arises from concern about the respect that some Chinese companies have for the principles of IP ownership. A good number of these manufacturing entities are built upon platforms that had previously (and in some cases appear to continue to be) involved in unauthorized activities.[20] Thus, innovative designs submitted to such organizations are at risk of misappropriation as well as

---

(Pandora, 19 May 2009) <http://blog.pandora.com/2009/05/19/pandora_one_upg/> accessed 26 January 2014. For an article that addresses business models related to distributing television programming, see Chris Anderson, 'Tech is Too Cheap to Meter: It's Time to Manage for Abundance, Not Scarcity' *Wired* (22 June 2009) <http://www.wired.com/techbiz/it/magazine/17-07/mf_freer?currentPage=3> accessed 26 January 2014.

[18] By sponsoring design competitions, Local Motors is able to engage in direct commercial exploitation of its crowd-sourced designs. Winners of the competitions receive a monetary award but must agree to assign the rights, title and interest in the design to Local Motors, thereby enabling Local Motors to commercially exploit the design. Local Motors, 'Challenge Terms and Conditions' <https://forge.localmotors.com/static.php?p=legal> accessed 26 January 2014.

[19] Microsoft, 'Shared Source Initiative' <http://www.microsoft.com/en-us/sharedsource/default.aspx> accessed 26 January 2014.

[20] These factories are sometimes known as *Shanzhai*, a term that has been used to refer to bandits, pirates or a source of knock-off goods. See also Kathy Chu and Laurie Burkitt, 'Knockoffs Thrive on Alibaba's Taobao' *The Wall Street Journal* (28 April 2014) <http://online.wsj.com/news/articles/SB10001424052702304049904579517642158573008> accessed 20 October 2014; Sky Canaves, 'Imitation Is the Sincerest Form of Rebellion in China' *The Wall Street Journal* (22 January 2009) <http://online.wsj.com/article/SB123257138952903561.html> accessed 26 January 2014.

later independent and competitive exploitation by the Chinese partners. Will Chapman, a former 'small batch' innovator of Lego compatible accessories, noted, '[I]f your molds are in China, who knows what happens to them when you're not using them? They could be run in secret to produce parts sold in secondary markets that you would not even know existed.'[21]

For others in the FOSS (non)market, the product is not the sale of a product, but rather the marketing of a personal service in the form of 'know-how'. Innovators interested in capitalizing on products built upon an open source platform need not actually sell the code. Rather, they can sell consulting/installing services to companies who want to use the improved FOSS version and keep it up to date. Additionally, they might charge a fee to downstream users who want to incorporate the particular version, provided by the upstream innovator, into their own business software. In a more extreme case, a successor company may not only purchase the know-how of an entrepreneur, but also require a service provider to recode a program to a proprietary form so that no FOSS is included. In this manner, a successor could attempt to eliminate an 'infection' of its proprietary programs with FOSS code and would not be under any obligation to pass its additions on to competitors in accord with an antecedent FOSS arrangement.

A final possible approach to monetizing open source software is a dual licensing program. This hybrid blends the use of GPL open source methodology with a privatized approach to software development. If, for example, a distributor employs a general FOSS license with downstream users, those users are obligated to pass their innovations downstream to their successors without restriction. On the other hand, a distributor licensor may elect to license the otherwise open source software on a royalty bearing basis. The licensee can then choose to either monetize the software or employ it as open source. To the extent that the royalty side includes open source products, however, he would have to make that code information available to successors.

3. Quality of open source information

The actual value of the information made available through the medium of enhanced and open communication might be questionable to a serious researcher. One of the features of a democratic information revolution is that individuals are now able to communicate their views rather freely; however, while some of these contributions might have considerable

---

[21] Anderson (n 5).

value, such as in a mediated software creation environment, many may not. There is no assurance that the non-market information generated is thoughtful, based upon reflection, or grounded in reality.

Even in the software sector, little (if any) open source information comes with any warranties, much less one for fitness for a particular use. In fact, the typical open source license not only disclaims warranties but also fails to provide any indemnification for loss resulting from reliance upon the information. In comparison, warranties, indemnifications, obligations to defend, and performance insurance arrangements are commonplace in many proprietary IP licenses.[22] Such assurances can be of considerable importance to those who anticipate investing resources in reliance upon the information or governments that promote such use; the absence of such terms should give one pause. Unfortunately, the political lure of the appeal of open source, when coupled with reduced costs of access, may overshadow legitimate concerns of suitability. A more rational and responsible approach to use and implementation should counsel caution and a view that the information be fully vetted before one invests resources in reliance upon it.

Unfortunately, a more reserved view is often overlooked or undervalued by advocates of open source. For example, some open source advocates have observed with wonder how many contributors have joined to produce *Wikipedia*, all without compensation. In the course of extolling the virtue of this democratic approach to development, many also claim it to be a serious online alternative to more traditional hard-cover encyclopedias. Critical contributory research protocols, however, suggest that a source of information is not reliable if it is not reviewed editorially, is capable of being modified by any reader, and lacks an identified author who can be held accountable.[23] While it is certainly true that publishers of commercial research resources are in the business of selling information for profit, there is a resulting and corollary assurance that the veracity and credibility of the information has been at least minimally reviewed and confirmed.

---

[22] *See generally* Xuan-Thao N Nguyen and others, *Intellectual Property, Software, and Information Licensing: Law and Practice* (BNA Books 2006).

[23] 'Evaluating Information Found on the Internet' (Johns Hopkins University, Sheridan Libraries, 28 May 2013) <http://www.library.jhu.edu/researchhelp/general/evaluating> accessed 26 January 2014.

4. Open source information becomes fragmented in ordinary course

The fragmentation of information in the course of development presents some difficulty in its evaluation and use. As one downstream user modifies the open source, he generally does so in order to respond to a particular and often focused need. That 'specialization', while useful to the particular user, can make the product unsuitable to other users with distinct and discrete needs. This phenomenon has been a general concern in the software realm and has, in particular, presented considerable challenges to Google's competitors in the Linux-based operating system market.[24] In this context, it is not the use of the basic algorithm that has given rise to Google's distinctive success; it is its constant and particularized refinement and consequent fragmentation.

5. Open Source creates more information but removes our social interactions

While the free sharing of information may offer an expanded, rewarding and enhanced social and intellectual life for some, it can also lead to isolation or mental impairment of others. Although it is certainly convenient to have easy access to email and the ability to freely and quickly exchange information with others remote from your location, there can be considerable costs. Those in the mental health field have clinically observed that symptoms of anxiety may be heightened due to the constant bombardment by 'news' of world events.[25] Furthermore, many users have traded a social life with direct human contact for an indirect one, derived from an expanded relationship with one's computer. For example, the ease with which anyone, including children, can gain access to pornographic material has greatly expanded,[26] episodes of gender harassment have increased,[27] and serious problems of addiction to

---

[24] Agam Shah, 'Google OS Could Put Squeeze on Other Flavors of Linux' (*PCWorld*, 8 July 2009) <http://www.pcworld.com/article/168099/google_os_could_put_squeeze_on_other_flavors_of_linux.html?tk= rss_news> accessed 26 January 2014.

[25] Andrew Weil, 'Q&A Library' (*Weil*, 5 September 2008) <http://www.drweil.com/drw/ecs/ask_dr_weil/qa_ library.html> accessed 26 January 2014.

[26] *See, e.g*, Nancy Rommelmann, 'Anatomy of a Child Pornographer' *Reason* (July 2009) <http://reason.com/archives/2009/06/04/anatomy-of-a-child-pornographe> accessed 26 January 2014. See also Judith Newman, 'Porn Has Gone Interactive – and Your Kids Are at Risk: From "Sexting" to Video Chats, How to Fight Back' *Reader's Digest* (May 2009) 119.

[27] Danielle Keats Citron, 'Law's Expressive Value in Combating Cyber Gender Harassment' (2009) 108 *Michigan L Rev* 373, 373.

internet games have been reported.[28] In China, for example, numerous internet-addiction treatment centers have been established for the purpose of deprogramming.[29] In addition, intimate human relationships are being technologically mediated through a proliferation of internet dating sites.

6. Open source threatens privacy and security

Increased access to information can result in a loss of individual privacy and security. Not only has this been observed through the inconvenient receipt of spam, but the internet has also provided an avenue for destructive and criminal conduct. Numerous individuals have had their identities compromised through misappropriation and unauthorized use of personal information, viruses have been developed for the sheer joy of injuring others, spyware products have been used to steal passwords, and other valuable information has been purloined through a plethora of phishing schemes and other forms of online fraud. Increased accessibility and the ability to consolidate a myriad of legitimate public information sites have also resulted in practical compromise of one's sanctuary through disclosure and the ease of access and dissemination. Facebook and other social websites may contain considerable personal and, at times, sensitive information, while the security protocols or strategies are often inadequate or ignored by users. For example, website content may include dates when individuals plan to be away from their homes – useful information for burglars and thieves in planning their heists. In addition, law enforcement agencies routinely access the private information contained on social sites in the course of investigating and curtailing crimes of all types. At times, even legitimate use can result in a terrible inconvenience and loss to citizens through mischaracterization of their actions. The problem has been exacerbated by legal standards, currently extant in the US, in situations where courts have given considerable deference to, access to, and use of information by others. This has been observed in the context of claims of defamation insofar as the courts decline to distinguish between information about which the public is

---

[28] 'Shrinks Join World Game' mX (Melbourne), July 27, 2009, at 10. See also 'Virtually Addicted: Weaning Koreans Off Their Wired World' *CNN* (25 March 2010) <http://www.cnn.com/2010/TECH/03/25/online.gaming.addiction/index.html?iref=allsearch> accessed 26 January 2014.

[29] *See, e.g.,* Jonathan Adams, 'In an Increasingly Wired China, Rehab for Internet Addicts' *Christian Science Monitor* (6 January 2009) <http://www.csmonitor.com/World/Asia-Pacific/2009/0106/p01s03-woap.html> accessed 26 January 2014.

merely curious and information deemed to be within the legitimate interest of the public.

7. Freedom of information as a competing interest

Expanded public demand for entertainment, lauded by some as a symbol of the positive features of the non-market revolution, could be said to have led to the erosion of many competing interests. This state of affairs might be exacerbated by the growing inclination of US courts to give considerable purchase to claims of freedom of expression and their failure to distinguish between various types and uses of information. Some of these interests include the protection of victim identifications and other sensitive information, or the protection of an individual's reputation (in defamation actions).[30] This has been true even at the expense of viable proprietary IP interests, such as the right of publicity of celebrities.[31] An unfortunate byproduct of this particular indulgence shown by the courts may be, for example, a blurring of the distinction between entertainment and news, thereby providing deference to the creation of news over the reporting of actual news.

8. More information opens doors for more regulation

While there may be a reduction in the traditional market barriers to information, other groups have intervened and filled the void. Thus, internet service providers and owners of servers, such as universities and governments, have interposed themselves between users and information sources. These intervening forces have led to frustration of otherwise free access to information. It has been reported, for example, that certain governments have selectively blocked citizen access to Google, YouTube, and Twitter and have employed agents to curtail online political dissent.[32] In addition, many service providers now charge a fee for access, while others engage in subtle censorship of content.

9. The public may underappreciate the extra information yet feel entitled to it

Perhaps due to the intangible nature and attributes of products of the mind, it is distinctly possible that the public fails to possess a full

---

30 *New York Times v Sullivan* 376 US 254, 304-5 (1964). See also *Cox Broadcasting Corp v Cohn* 420 US 469, 491 (1975); *Florida Star v BJF* 491 US 524, 533 (1989).

31 J Thomas McCarthy, *The Rights of Publicity and Privacy* (2nd edn, West 2012).

32 Christopher Stewart, 'The Lost Boy' *Wired* (February 2010) 70.

appreciation for the precious character of the commodity of accurate information and, as such, undervalues it. Consequently, the public may become impatient, frustrated or even hostile when access is limited. There are several causes.

First, many confront and form their opinions about IP in a non-vocational, noncompetitive or entertainment context. In such circumstances, it is not uncommon that they perceive the providers of the IP as also functioning in an avocational mode. Since the consumer is 'having fun' operating in a non-vocational manner, the assumption may be that so, too, is the provider of the good or service. Consequently, there may be a failure to understand that many individuals, such as the software game provider, the professional artist, athlete or performer, are in business and must reap an economic benefit from their creativity if they are to thrive. This lack of appreciation may lead to a lessening of the extrinsic value placed upon innovative activities and the loss of a key distinction between amateur and professional content.

Second, since the public is not always accustomed to paying directly for access to IP, it misperceives that much information is 'free'. Whether it is the music broadcast by terrestrial providers, the applications available to iPhone users for no apparent charge, or access to information through a search engine like Google, there is no obvious tollgate barring their access. Many fail to fully appreciate the alternative means by which such activities are monetized, and thus much of the public has come to feel entitled to receive IP for no personal charge.

Third, many individuals are more experienced in dealing with tangible property than they are with intangible property, and this familiarity influences their perceptions of value and entitlement. Since IP may not be obviously exhaustible through individual consumption and because access to IP is often through possession of a tangible object such as a CD or DVD, many draw the erroneous conclusion that purchase and ownership of the medium of fixation carries with it the ownership of the intangible that is embodied in or on the tangible object. This misperception has often been exploited by others in the name of profit.[33]

Fourth, some who routinely deal with issues of IP fail to appreciate the contextual and legal significance of their activities and claim a superseding right to proceed in accord with their own view of custom. For example, film producers have been heard to claim during IP disputes that

---

[33] *Metro-Goldwyn-Mayer Studios, Inc v Grokster, Ltd* 545 US 913, 919 (2005). See also *A&M Records, Inc v Napster, Inc* 284 F 3d 1091, 1095-96 (9th Cir 2002)

they failed to adhere to mandated means of transfer of interests because '[m]oviemakers do lunch, not contracts'.[34] Several record companies recently filed suit against The Ellen DeGeneres Show claiming willful failure to pay royalties for the use of music on the show. When approached by the record company inquiring why it had not paid, the defendant purportedly replied that it 'didn't roll that way'.[35]

Fifth, in the course of pressing their cause before the public, many advocates mischaracterize principles, provide less than full and adequate information, or permit miscommunications and misunderstandings to persist in order to achieve an apparent goal. For example, the National Association of Broadcasters and affiliated stations have used broadcasts, contests and the internet, to lobby against a change in the Copyright Act that would require them to internalize a cost of their business by paying a royalty to musical performers (similar to that which they currently pay to musical composers) for use of their IP. In so doing, the broadcasters specifically trade on the public's misperception that music is 'free', draw upon the public's emotive reactions by mischaracterizing the royalty as a tax, and suggest that the imposition of the 'tax' will not only line the pockets of foreign-owned record companies, but also result in a loss of services to and jobs within the local communities served by the stations.[36]

II. A CULTURAL DIFFERENTIAL

A. Significance of Culture

Recognizing, cultivating and protecting innovation is heavily influenced by the content and the dynamics of the cultural environment in which the creative effort is initiated. Concerns and questions once catalyzed by local, national or regional organizations, such as the North Atlantic Treaty Organization and the European Union, are now being considered at a much broader level. Globalization, in large part stimulated by technological advances, including those in the communication industries,

---

34 *Effects Associates, Inc v Cohen* 908 F.2d 555, 556–57 (9th Cir 1990)

35 Travis Loller, 'Record Companies Sue "Ellen" Show over Copyrights' (*Times Free Press*, 10 September 2009) <http://www.timesfreepress.com/news/2009/sep/10/record-companies-sue-ellen-show-over-copyrights/> accessed 26 January 2014.

36 Stop the Performance Tax 'The Issue' <http://www.noperformancetax.org/issue.asp> accessed 26 January 2014.

has accentuated the need to better understand those with whom we deal and who more proximately affect our lives. This is not a new phenomenon. As observed by John Stuart Mill in 1848:

> It is hardly possible to overstate the value … of placing human beings in contact with persons dissimilar to themselves, and with modes of thought and action unlike those with which they are familiar … Such communication has always been … one of the primary sources of progress.[37]

This has, in fact, been the subject of comparative study for some time. Once conceived as a means by which to discover universal truths inchoate in human organization, recent movements have been directed at actually uncovering the differences among peoples.[38] The object of the inquiry is to stimulate new judgments through challenging individual ethnocentric perspectives. As a result, harmonization of diverse interests may be a more proper goal than an assumption of homogenization.

It may be that each country, community, and group of people develops its own way of doing things. In turn, these norms of thinking and behavior heavily influence why and how those people act in virtually every situation. Therefore, in order to effectively compare different IP regimes, it is first necessary to comprehend 'why and how' decisions are made and effected. Absent an understanding of the cultural underpinnings, the regime would be taken out of context and any proposed changes would be less likely to succeed.

Culture is influenced by both geographic boundaries and social and professional phenomena. Virtually all communities, including the scientific and academic, have individualized philosophies, pop-cultures and practices. As Edward Hall has observed:

> [a]nthropologists do agree on three characteristics of culture: it is not innate, but learned; the various facets of culture are interrelated …; it is shared and in effect defines the boundaries of different groups. … Culture is man's medium; there is not one aspect of human life that is not touched and altered by culture. This means personality, how people express themselves[,] … the way they think, how they move, how problems are solved … as well as how economic and government systems are put together and function. However,

---

37 John Stuart Mill, *Principles of Political Economy* (1871), ch XIII s 5.

38 Vivian Grosswald Curran, 'Cultural Immersion, Difference and Categories in U.S. Comparative Law' (1998) 46 *American J Comparative L* 43, 50–54.

> like the purloined letter, it is frequently the most obvious and taken-for-granted and therefore the least studied aspects of culture that influence behavior in the deepest and most subtle ways.[39]

This perspective is espoused not only by academics but also by those actively involved in the transnational media community. As Hiroshi Kukimoto observed, 'The appearance of a document or Web page is imbued with culture, custom and history conveyed through the arrangement of text and the appearance of written characters. Graphical expression must exhibit kansei, a largely untranslatable Japanese concept of "look and feel" combined with sense awareness.'[40]

B. Cultural Components

Social scientists usually examine two significant characteristics when assessing the effect of culture on operations and overt practices. They are, first, the relationship between the individual and the group within the particular system – that is, the degree of individualism as opposed to collectivism – and, second, the extent to which information is communicated in specific codes – that is, high- versus low-context transmission.

1. Individualism and collectivism

The individualist/collectivist dichotomy describes the relationship between and relative importance of individuals and groups within a given culture.[41] Societies denoted as individualistic tend to emphasize personal achievement and place a high value on independence, self-reliance, risk-taking, competitive behavior, personal pleasure, pluralism, and self-determination. Americans, for example, are generally characterized as being competitive and goal-oriented, and success is often measured in terms of personal advancement rather than by the development of strong interpersonal relationships.[42] Australia, Britain, Canada, the Netherlands and New Zealand are also often classified as individualistic. In contrast,

---

39 Edward T Hall, *Beyond Culture* (Anchor Books 1989) 16–17.

40 Raj Reddy and others, 'WTEC Panel Report on Digital Information in Japan' (International Technology Research Institute, February 1999) 133 <http://euro.ecom.cmu.edu/people/faculty/mshamos/1999DigitalJapan.pdf> accessed 26 January 2014.

41 Geert Hofstede and Gert Jan Hofstede, *Cultures and Organizations: Software of the Mind* (2nd edn, McGraw-Hill 2005) 78.

42 Geoffrey R Scott, 'A Comparative View of Copyright as Cultural Property in Japan and the United States' (2006) 20 *Temple Intl & Comparative LJ* 283, 288.

collectivist societies emphasize the interdependence of persons, cooperative behavior, social homogeneity, family bonds, and a developed system of hierarchy. Japan, China, South Korea, Peru, Venezuela and Pakistan are often classified as collectivist societies, placing a high value upon group harmony and social cohesion.[43] One can certainly observe the influence of these varying perspectives upon regimes of personal property and the degree of recognition of a propriety approach to innovation.

In Japan, for example, *shudan ishiki*, or group consciousness, is a fundamental social tenet. It is born in the structure of the household (*ie*), the smallest political unit, and its values extend to virtually all relationships. Groups establish discrete codes of behavior and understanding that are acceptable to, and shared by, members of the community (*uchi*) and are often unknown to outsiders (*soto*). Loyalty is rewarded with security, and group solidarity is often revered above all else.[44] Personal independence is rare, as reflected in the Japanese proverb, 'The nail that stands up will be pounded down (*Deru kui wa utareru*).' The difference between *uchi* and *soto* is distinct and often cited as one reason why outsiders perceive the Japanese to be uncomfortable dealing with outsiders or while in alien international environments.

2. High vs. low context

The second consideration is the high-context/low-context component of communication. 'A high-context message is one in which most of the data is either found within the physical or social context of the communication or is internalized within the recipient and employed by him in the course of understanding the meaning of the communication.'[45] In high-context situations, information is shared through simple messages that precipitate significant meaning. In contrast, a low-context communication depends upon very explicit transmissions, and it relies very little on the prior experience of the recipient or the relevance of the surrounding environment. It is characterized by detail and a highly structured organization. In low-context situations, communication between people is more explicit and impersonal.

In Japan, for example, silence (*chinmoku*) is an important communicative device and may reflect the implicit mutual understandings among

---

43 Hofstede and Hofstede (n 41) 79.

44 Xinzhong Yao, *An Introduction to Confucianism* (CUP 2000) 279.

45 Scott (n 42) 289. See also Richard D Lewis, *When Cultures Collide: Leading Across Cultures* (3rd edn, Nicholas Brealey Publishing 2006) 8.

people born of group consciousness (*uchi*).[46] Not all cultures understand, much less revere, such values, and people from other cultures may interpret the significance of non-communication in variant ways. Western and other low-context cultures that value open communication and emphasize detailed verbal expression may misinterpret silence and infer rejection, indifference, or insult as its meaning.[47]

Issues of context are often raised in IP disputes when construing ambiguous terms found in licensing agreements. In order to address the paucity of information in such low-context countries as the US, resort may be made to evidence demonstrating course of dealing, course of performance, and usage of trade within a particular industry to help explain or interpret ambiguous circumstances such as unclear language in a license. Absent a 'merger clause', resort may also be made to other forms of extrinsic evidence, such as prior negotiations through use of the parole evidence rule, in order to discern the intent of the parties to an agreement.[48]

Context is also extremely important in a contemporary technological sense – for example, in the production and use of software, the internet, and search engines. As noted above, Google's search engine is founded upon an open source algorithm. Its success, however, is due largely to the repetitive tweaking and refinement it has undergone over the years, which has made it superior to other search engines. One of the most significant advances was 'Pagerank', a system invented in 1997 by Larry Page. Pagerank rates pages hierarchically based upon the number and quality of links that point to them.[49] It is, however, the contextual clues that are found on the pages that actually permit the most relevant sites to surface. When a user inputs a query, the contextual signals determine the location of a particular page in the search results. Contextual signals provide relevance, and Google uses over 200, including the title of the

---

46 Robert M March, *The Japanese Negotiator: Subtlety and Strategy Beyond Western Logic* (Kodansha 1990) 9–10.

47 Satoshi Ishii and Tom Bruneau, 'Silence and Silences in Cross-Cultural Perspective: Japan and the United States' in Larry A Samovar and Richard E Porter (eds), *Intercultural Communication: A Reader* (Wadsworth Publishing 1994) 246–7.

48 *Kepner-Tregoe, Inc v Vroom* 186 F.3d 283, 287 (2nd Cir 1999). See also Nguyen and others (n 21) 92.

49 Phil Craven, 'Google's PageRank Explained and How to Make the Most of It' <http://www.webworkshop.net/pagerank.html> accessed 26 January 2014; Mark Horrell, 'The Google PageRank Algorithm' <http://www.webmarketingezine.com/search-engine-optimization/google-pagerank-algorithm.shtml> accessed 26 January 2014.

page, anchor text, freshness, the location and geographical coordinates of the user, and the user's personal search history. As an individual user queries individual terms, the algorithm assimilates the semantics employed and comprehends relationships between words and the context in which they are used. As a result, if an individual inputs a term such as 'hot dog', the search engine algorithm now 'understands' the context as related to a food product. It would exclude associations with such other terms as the American Kennel Club and would instead bring up only relevant results.[50]

3. A coalescence of the cultural principles and their effect on use of innovation

An example of the interrelationship between principles of culture and their effect on innovation and IP at a macro-cultural level is illustrated with the development of the printing press. As above noted, researchers have generally concluded that the US is a low-context society, while Japan and China are high-context countries. This characterization is particularly exemplified by the differing roles that the printing press played in the development of copyright, as well as artists' rights, writ large, in Asia and the West.

First, let us observe the technological backdrop. The invention of paper in AD105 by Cai Lun of China fueled the duplication of manuscripts in the East, and transcription by hand was the general method employed to produce manuscripts. Although there is evidence of mechanical reproduction in Japan as early as AD770, printing usually employed the woodblock form known as *seihanbon*. While there is some debate concerning when and where moveable type was first invented, there is consensus that moveable type existed in Asia near the end of the first millennium. Second, let us overlay the extant cultural conditions. Japanese and Chinese are essentially pictographic languages, and the various symbols take much from the context in which they are used. While various forms of printing were introduced into Japan throughout the centuries, the calligraphic and pictorial forms of written Japanese constrained the utility of the printing press. Notwithstanding the movement toward Westernization during the Meiji Period (1868–1912), printing in Japan continued to be dominated by the woodblock until approximately 1890. Likely due to the complexity of linguistic forms, the traditions in the East were

---

50 Taher H Haveliwala, 'Efficient Computation of PageRank' (Stanford University, 18 October 1999) 14 <http://ilpubs.stanford.edu:8090/386/1/1999-31.pdf> accessed 26 January 2014.

primarily oral. The Japanese people were not generally considered 'literate' until the Edo period (1603–1867), and even then only the aristocracy and merchants could read.

Protection of artists' rights in general, and copyright in particular, followed the trend of the innovation and use of printing. Due to widespread illiteracy and the inefficiency of printing pictographic language characters, there was little demand for printed text. In addition, the collective tradition of Japan tended to discourage the identification of individual authorship. For example, during the Heian period, the paternity of a written work was rarely identified. If individuals were identified as contributors to published volumes, it was not uncommon that all who participated in the publication were named, including editors, helpers, block carvers, as well as authors. It was not until 1869 that an ordinance directed at publishing was promulgated, and in 1877, an independent copyright ordinance was passed. True recognition of intellectual property rights did not occur in Japan, however, until the end of the nineteenth century. In 1899, in order that Japan might fulfill certain obligations imposed by international treaties to which it was a party, the Copyright Act, the Patent Act, the Design Act, and the Trademark Act were passed.[51]

Innovation in printing and the utility of the press in effecting social change took a different path in the West. As noted by Francis Bacon in *Novum Organum*,

> Again, we should notice the force, effect, and consequences of inventions, which are nowhere more conspicuous than in those three which were unknown to the ancients; namely, printing, gunpowder, and the compass. For these three have changed the appearance and state of the whole world: first in literature, then in warfare, and lastly in navigation; and innumerable changes have been thence derived, so that no empire, sect, or star, appears to have exercised a greater power and influence on human affairs than these mechanical discoveries.[52]

First, in contrast to the structure of language in the East, Western language is primarily phonetic, and European languages have fewer than

---

[51] For detailed information on the development of printing in Asia, see Scott (n 42) 316–26.

[52] Sir Francis Bacon, *Novum Organum, Aphorisms – Book 1: On the Interpretation of Nature and the Empire of Man* (1620) s CXXIX. See also Elizabeth L Eisenstein, 'The Emergence of Print Culture in the West: "Defining the Initial Shift"' in Keith Whitlock (ed.), *The Renaissance in Europe: A Reader* 55 (Yale UP 2000) 55.

50 letters in their alphabets. The language system is predominantly low-context, and the general peasant populous was semi-literate in the post-classical era due to their familiarity with religious manuscripts. In addition, the fabric of ancient Greek philosophy, contrary to the Eastern view of legitimate curiosity, suggested that knowledge of the human condition should be shared by and accessible to everyone and that faith to underlying information required replication of facts, duplication of a predecessor's efforts, and demonstrated respect and veneration. Thus, the foundation for recognition and acceptance of efficient means of communication existed.

Later, the Protestant Reformation of the early-sixteenth century fed the growing propriety interest in ideas and their expression. As the movement spread across Western Europe the social conflagration that ensued was facilitated by the reinvention of the printing press in the mid-fifteenth century.[53] Thus, a powerfully felt need to express one's self, a means to accomplish that end, and a semi-literate audience burning for the products of opinioned authorship serendipitously coalesced to fuel the fusion of innovation and an interest in intellectual property.

Many political states responded by attempting to control and censor authors, and in 1557, the Crown gave the Stationers Company in London right to control printing and publication. In 1695, the grant to the Stationers Company expired and what has been labeled the first modern copyright act, the Statute of Anne, was passed in 1710.

The influence of the Age of Enlightenment[54] and its emphasis upon skepticism, empiricism, scientific inquiry and the use of one's mind were significant in the West and upon the American colonies in particular. A budding republic and participatory democracy in early America was much defined by its commitment to individualism, and it was through the use of documents that embodied this spirit that the message of colonial independence was spread. An example was Joseph Addison's play Cato.[55] Initiatives for protecting IP flourished – the first US Copyright Act was passed in 1790, and the French Law of 1793 gave European authors the right to control copying, distribution, and sale of works.

---

53 Scott (n 42) 351–2.

54 Immanuel Kant, *What is Enlightenment?* (1784).

55 Joseph Addison, 'Cato' in *The Miscellaneous Works of Joseph Addison*, vol 2 (DA Talboys 1830) 41. George Washington ordered that the play be performed for his officers during the encampment at Valley Forge, and it was a line from the play that inspired Patrick Henry to utter his famous 1775 line: 'Give me liberty, or give me death.' Albert Furtwangler, 'Cato at Valley Forge' (1980) 41 *Modern Language Q* 38, 43–4.

Throughout and following the Romantic Era, with its emphasis upon artistic free expression and originality, the concept of the 'author' emerged. Handwritten text had given way to the printed word, and writing had become a profession.[56]

C. Legal Traditions

Legal regimes also possess underlying conventions or precepts that distinguish them from one another, and these characteristics can affect approaches to innovation and IP protection. As John Henry Merryman writes:

> A legal tradition… is not a set of rules of law … . Rather it is a set of deeply rooted, historically conditioned attitudes about the nature of law, about the role of law in the society and in the polity, about the proper organization and operation of a legal system, and about the way law is or should be made, applied, studied, perfected, and taught. The legal tradition relates the legal system to the culture of which it is a partial expression. It puts the legal system into cultural perspective.[57]

The effect of the deeply rooted traditions of individual countries upon the world community can be seen in the contemporary context. For example, US courts have declined to afford comity to or to enforce a French court's judgment that a photographer infringed the IP of a fashion designer by the unauthorized publication of photographs of certain fashion designs.[58] In general, fashion designs are not considered the subject of copyright protection in the US due to their useful nature. In addition, US courts and legislatures have declined to support judgments of UK legislatures and courts in the area of defamation.[59] This refusal is grounded in the US legal system's principle of freedom of expression. Finally, in a recent suit brought by the US against China for purported violations of the TRIPS Agreement, the WTO decided that China's censorship of IP, which the US claimed was impairing the rights of US

---

[56] Scott (n 42) 355.

[57] John Henry Merryman and Rogelio Pérez-Perdomo, *The Civil Law Tradition* (3rd edn, Stanford UP 2007) 2.

[58] *Sarl Louis Feraud International v Viewfinder Inc* 406 F Supp 2d 274, 279, 284 (SDNY 2005).

[59] *Telnikoff v Matusevitch* 702 A 2d 230, 248–49 (Md 1997).

copyright and trademark and thus violating the international agreement, was acceptable as an act of government.[60]

III. A PRINCIPLED DIFFERENTIAL

A. Generally, The Characteristic of IP

Perhaps the most significant distinguishing feature of a product of the mind is its intangible quality. This intangible nature influences the choice to afford protection to a particular expression as well as the effectiveness and the efficiency of the regime selected. In evaluating the qualities of such goods in this regard, modern microeconomics provides some insight. First, the traditional private market depends upon the premise that an individual's consumption of a good is contingent upon her paying the price for the good. A person who fails to pay in this context is generally presumed to be unable to use the good. The mechanism of exclusion may be grossly physical, technologically enabled, or legally enforced through recognition of principles of property. Another characteristic of the traditional private market is rivalry of consumption. This second characteristic implies that the person who pays the price possesses the prerogative of internalizing all of the benefits of his purchase and that his choice excludes others from securing a corollary benefit.[61] The private market can fail, however, if the particular good is non-rivalrous, if exclusion is not possible, or should the two conditions coalesce.

Intellectual property is particularly vulnerable to market failure due to its intangible character. It is frequently considered inexhaustible and thus, by nature, has been characterized as non-rivalrous. In addition, IP has, at times, suffered at the hands of a public that has been permitted, or perhaps even encouraged, to believe that, due to this characteristic, it is or should be a public good; consequently, there is a feeling of entitlement

---

60 Daniel Gervais, World Trade Organization panel report on China's enforcement of intellectual property rights, (2009) 103 *American J Int'l L 549*, 549–54.

61 *See,* e.g., Richard A Musgrave, *The Theory of Public Finance: A Study in Public Economy* (McGraw-Hill 1959); Richard A Musgrave and Peggy B Musgrave, *Public Finance in Theory and Practice* (2nd edn, McGraw-Hill 1976); Michael Pickhardt, 'Fifty Years After Samuelson's "The Pure Theory of Public Expenditure": What Are We Left With?' (2006) 28 *J History & Economic Thought* 439.

that leads to free riding. For many, since IP appears so freely accessible, it is viewed as less valuable than tangible property. It is, perhaps, a fear that the private market will not be able to adequately respond to these perspectives that precipitates an apprehension that a decline in the supply of creative products of the mind might result and that a consequent impoverishment of the public domain might occur. It is also, perhaps, this view that drives the utilitarian patent and copyright regimes found in the United States and the international community. As observed over a century ago by Justice Oliver Wendell Holmes:

> The notion of property starts, I suppose, from confirmed possession of a tangible object, and consists in the right to exclude others from interference with the more or less free doing with it as one wills. But in copyright property has reached a more abstract expression. The right to exclude is not directed to an object in possession or owned, but is in vacuo so to speak. … It is a prohibition of conduct remote from the persons or tangibles of the party having the right. It may be infringed a thousand miles from the owner and without his ever becoming aware of the wrong … .[62]

B. Theories of Property and the Protection of IP

It is naïve to presume that mere adjustment of the basic and expressed definitions of property that have been incorporated into the various global regimes of IP will bring about new cultural understandings and practices. In actuality, many of the varied preferences expressed are a mere gloss on what are truly significant and fundamental differences of social, cultural, and political philosophy.[63] As a result, the various regimes may be considered within the following categories:

1. A natural-law approach; 2. Utilitarian and economic theory; and 3. Property as a product of community and social relationships.

These categories not only identify certain recognized themes of property but also acknowledge certain legal or political institutions implicated in the function of property. They also are themes commonly mentioned in the literature concerning intellectual property.

---

62 *White-Smith Music Publishing Co v Apollo Co* 209 US 1, 19 (1908) (Holmes, J, concurring).

63 Nestor M Davidson, 'Property and Relative Status' (2009) 107 *Michigan L Rev* 757, 763, fn 16.

1. A natural-law approach

Generally, an IP regime that adopts a natural-law approach protects a property interest on the grounds that the person expended personal effort to create the property. There are myriad theories that could be considered endowment based; however, two seem to possess the greatest purchase: the labor-mixing and entitlement theories of John Locke and the Philosophy of Right Theory of GWF Hegel.

Locke described the endowment theory in his Second Treatise on Government as follows:

> Though the earth, and all inferior creatures, be common to all men, yet every man has a property in his own person. This no body has any right to but himself. The labour of his body, and the work of his hands, we may say, are properly his. Whatsoever then he removes out of the state that nature hath provided, and left it in, he hath mixed his labour with, and joyned to it something that is his own, and thereby makes it his property. … [T]hat excludes the common right of other men. For this labour being the unquestionable property of the labourer, no man but he can have a right to what that is once joyned to, at least where there is enough, and as good left in the common for others.[64]

Thus, a person may acquire rights over a thing that is not owned either by mixing his labor with it or through incorporation into his person (for example, by ingestion). It is through the process of labor mixing, however, that value purports to be added to the natural good, and the recognition of strong propriety rights are perceived as a reward for the expenditure of one's individual. It is through this process that entitlement is established against claims by the state or by others.

Of course, others have questioned the basis of the assumptions made by Locke. One theorist, Robert Nozick, has rhetorically asked why, when mixing one's tomato juice with the sea, one should think that he is acquiring the sea rather than losing the juice.[65] Others have pointed to the last phrases of Locke's proposition, which assert a qualification of the endowment theory that leaves room for charity or welfare.[66] In sum, however, the labor perspective recognizes the positive value of extracting of objects from the state of nature, the consequent use of things that

---

[64] John Locke, *Second Treatise of Government* (1689) ch V s 27.

[65] Robert Nozick, *Anarchy, State, and Utopia* (Basic Books 1974) 174–5.

[66] David C Snyder, 'Locke on Natural Law and Property Rights' in Thom Brooks (ed.), *Locke and Law* (Ashgate Publishing 2007) 3; Leif Wenar, 'Original Acquisition of Private Property' in Brooks ibid., 109, 117–18.

would otherwise have been wasted, and the injection of such objects into commerce.

A second natural-law perspective is that property plays an important role in human identity. Georg Wilhelm Friedrich Hegel, in the *Elements of the Philosophy of Rights*,[67] suggests that mastery over objects was a significant step through which humans became aware and first moved toward individual free will. Free will enables an individual to become part of a community of other mature beings. Margaret Radin in her article 'Property and Personhood'[68] contributes to this view by arguing that it is through control over resources that one gains one's identity.[69] No matter the theory, the natural-law premise recognizes a moral claim upon private property.

Certain discrete forms of IP purport to be grounded directly in the endowment theory. For example, in some jurisdictions in the US the recognition of a right of publicity is an acknowledgement of the substantial investment that individual celebrities make in their images.[70] In Australia, the natural-law argument finds support in some of the earliest of cases that addressed the protection of IP. For example, the court in *Millar v Taylor* concluded that natural justice would prevent an individual from reaping the economic benefits of another's work.[71] In certain civil law countries, including France, Germany and Japan, as well as other countries that are signatories to the Berne Convention, moral rights, as distinct from economic rights in expression, flow from the author's person.[72] Finally, some have argued that natural rights are embodied in an understanding of the broader concept of human rights and may in fact be found existing at the international level in Article 27(2) of the Universal Declaration of Human Rights.[73]

---

[67] SW Dyne (tr), GWF Hegel, *Philosophy of Right* (Batoche Books 2001) s 44.

[68] Margaret Jane Radin, 'Property and Personhood' (1982) 34 *Stanford L Rev* 957, 957.

[69] Charles Reich, 'The New Property' (1964) 73 *Yale L J* 733.

[70] To the contrary, the 'sweat of the brow' doctrine has been explicitly rejected as a sufficient basis for US copyright protection. *Feist Publications, Inc v Rural Telephone Service Co, Inc* 499 US 340, 353 (1991).

[71] *Millar v Taylor* (1769) 4 Burr 2303, 98 ER 218.

[72] Amy M Adler, 'Against Moral Rights' (2009) 97 *California L Rev* 263, 266.

[73] *See,* e.g., Orit Fischman Afori, 'Human Rights and Copyright: The Introduction of Natural Law Considerations into American Copyright Law' (2004) 14 *Fordham Intellectual Property Media & Entertainment LJ* 497, 507–10.

2. Utilitarian and economic theory

Pursuant to rhetoric of incentives, recognition of property within utilitarian theory is in response to a recognized scarcity in the resource. Since IP's economic nature is that of a non-rival mixed good, there is the inherent risk that those who create such products will not be able to capture the value of those contributions through traditional sale. In the absence of providing appropriate assurance to a creative individual that she can control, gain the benefit of, and exclude others from the enjoyment of the product of her effort, there would be a paucity in the production of that which is valued by society. In order to precipitate the necessary supply of products of the mind, a carrot of security must often be dangled before potential authors and inventors in order to encourage their production of original works or novel inventions.[74]

In the US and pursuant to statutes grounded upon Article I, Section 8, Clause 8 of the US Constitution, individuals may be afforded a legal monopoly for a limited period of time. Along with this legal right, authors and inventors are given the opportunity for, and security of, limited economic exploitation. While the immediate beneficiary appears to be the owner of the interest, the real party in interest is the public, and the genuine purpose behind copyright and patent laws is the enrichment of the public domain. Hence, the Supreme Court has, on many occasions, opined that the philosophy supporting some of these laws is utilitarianism.[75] The Copyright Act accommodates more immediate interests of the public's access to information by providing that ideas are not contained within the subject of copyright, that certain discrete and statutorily recognized interest are specifically accommodated, and that access can be obtained through the affirmative defense of fair use.[76] The utilitarian presumption in the US is, however, that if a work falls within the protection of the Copyright Act and without the above exceptions, the author should be entitled to compensation.

3. Property as a product of community and social relationships

A final conception posits that, in lieu of perceiving property as an object, one should instead view it as a political and social phenomenon. Rather than a thing, property is a reciprocal system through which the interests of myriad community members are considered and accommodated.

---

[74] *Harper & Row Publishers, Inc v Nation Enterprises* 471 US 539, 558 (1985).

[75] *Twentieth Century Music Corp v Aiken* 422 US 151, 156 (1975).

[76] Copyright Act (US) s 107.

Born of the work of early-twentieth century legal realists such as Morris Cohen, this approach proffers that actual property rights can only be fully appreciated in the context of restrictions and positive duties imposed by the state upon the otherwise exclusive interest of one traditionally and economically perceived as an 'owner'. Among the legitimate limits to an interest in exclusion are those deemed communally necessary to vindicate social interests in public safety, peace, health, morals, housing, education and the preservation of natural resources.[77]

Other contemporary commentators in this school have turned attention away from the role of state-enforced obligations to those that result from the consensus of a working community. The civic republican tradition, for example, posits that economic inequality is a prime threat to democracy and freedom. As a consequence, the notion of property as a commons is considered indispensable not only to fulfill individual needs and define obligations among community members, but also to facilitate participation in self-governance. Therefore, property has the capacity to define community as much as it creates boundaries among and between individuals.[78]

Another thread in the fabric is a recent intellectual movement that has come to be known as 'communitarianism'. The movement emphasizes the importance of fellowship and community over economic relations and market interactions, and it relies much less upon the institutions of government and far more on the dynamics of persons who share an interest in certain common principles. The vision statement of the organization provides:

> Communitarians believe that strong rights presume strong responsibilities and that the pendulum of contemporary society has swung too far in the direction

---

[77] Morris Cohen, 'Property and Sovereignty' in CB Macpherson (ed.), *Property: Mainstream and Critical Positions* (U Toronto Press 1978) 155, 168, 170; CB Macpherson, 'The Meaning of Property' in CB Macpherson (ed.), *Property: Mainstream and Critical Positions*, ibid., 1, 4.

[78] In 1785, Thomas Jefferson, in a letter to James Madison, wrote:

> I am conscious that an equal division of property is impracticable. But the consequences of this enormous inequality producing so much misery to the bulk of mankind, legislators cannot invent too many devices for subdividing property … . Whenever there is in any country, uncultivated lands and unemployed poor, it is clear that the laws of property have been so far extended as to violate natural right.

Letter from Thomas Jefferson to Rev James Madison (28 October 1785) *The Thomas Jefferson Papers Series* <http://hdl.loc.gov/loc.mss/mtj.mtjbib001389> accessed 26 January 2014.

> of individual autonomy at the expense of individual and social responsibility. One key to solving contemporary America's social problems is replacing our pervasive 'rights talk' with 'responsibility talk'.[79]

The thoughts of Karl Marx are also an exemplar of the critique of the liberal position. The philosophy of Marx considers economic inequalities within the context of freedom. For him, economic inequalities affect political equalities, as he writes:

> To be a capitalist, is to have not only a purely personal, but a social status in production. Capital is a collective product, and only by the united action of many members, nay, in the last resort, only by the united action of all members of society, can it be set in motion.
>
> Capital is therefore not a personal, it is a social power.
>
> When, therefore, capital is converted into a common property, into the property of all members of society, personal property is not thereby transformed into social property. It is only the social character of the property that is changed. It loses its class-character.[80]

Inequality thus exists inherently between those who own the means of economic production and those wage-laborers who are exploited in the creation of capital. Consequently, for Marx, genuine freedom would only exist in a classless society, for in that context, not only would everyone own the means of production, but they would also be productive and fulfill their nature.

Finally, one might consider the influence of Confucian Theory upon definitions of property, particularly in the East. Among the guiding principles of Confucianism relevant to our current discussion are:

a. Complementary Obligations: The stability of society is based upon unequal relationships between people. *Wu lun*: Relationships are based upon mutual and complementary obligations such as ruler–subject, father–son, older–younger brother, husband–wife, senior–junior friend;[81] and
b. The Individual is Part of a Group: The family is the prototype of all social organizations. A person is not primarily an individual; rather he or she is a member of a family. The task of everyone is to

---

79 'Civil Society' (*The Communitarian Network*) <http://communitariannetwork.org/communitarian-vision/civil-society> accessed 26 January 2014.

80 Karl Marx and Friedrich Engels, *Manifesto of the Community Party* (1848), ch II para 17–19.

81 Xinzhong Yao (n 44) 32–4, 148, 178–9.

> overcome individuality and seek harmony. Harmony is found when everybody maintains face in dignity, self-respect and prestige.[82]

Through the application of these and other apposite tenets, the notion of property is, in countries like China, infused with a considerable social character.

IV. AN ECONOMIC AND POLITICAL DIFFERENTIAL: THE PROTECTION OF IP IN THE GLOBAL TRADING ARENA

The rapidly accelerating influence of transnational trade has precipitated a growing interest in the global recognition and regulation of IP. For example, the need for international protection of IP emerged when foreign exhibitors refused to attend the International Exhibition of Inventions in Vienna in 1873. It was reported that they feared their ideas 'would be stolen and exploited commercially in other countries' without their approval. In 1884, the Paris Convention for the Protection of Industrial Property, the first major international treaty designed to address IP, entered into force with 14 members.[83] Many countries, however, offered little protection to those outside their national borders. The US, for example, had no international copyright relations until 1891.

Today, IP has a considerable observable effect on the economies of most countries around the globe. Consider the observation of the World Trade Organization:

> Ideas and knowledge are an increasingly important part of trade. Most of the value of new medicines and other high technology products lies in the amount of invention, innovation, research, design and testing involved. Films, music recordings, books, computer software and on-line services are bought and sold because of the information and creativity they contain, not usually because of the plastic, metal or paper used to make them. Many products that used to be traded as low-technology goods or commodities now contain a higher proportion of invention and design in their value – for example brandnamed [sic] clothing or new varieties of plants.[84]

---

82 Hofstede and Hofstede (n 41) 209.

83 WIPO, 'WIPO Treaties – General Information' <http://www.wipo.int/treaties/en/general> accessed 26 January 2014.

84 WTO, 'Intellectual Property: Protection and Enforcement' <http://www.wto.org/english/thewto_e/whatis_e/tif_e/agrm7_e.htm> accessed 26 January 2014.

As a consequence, there has been tremendous pragmatic pressure to facilitate trade by harmonizing the treatment of IP, and there are a large number of important bilateral, trilateral, plurilateral and multilateral international treaties and agreements that address these issues.[85] Some, such as the 1886 Berne Convention for the Protection of Literary and Artistic Works, have been in place for a considerable time and have continued to progressively attract adherents. Others of considerable note – such as the 1992 North American Free Trade Agreement between Canada, the United States and Mexico; the Australia-USA Free Trade Agreement of 2004; the 1994 Agreement on Trade-Related Aspects of Intellectual Property Rights (TRIPS), Including Trade in Counterfeit Goods, which is perhaps the most far reaching; and certain bilateral 'TRIPS-Plus' agreements – are of more recent vintage.

Let us turn our attention to just two of the treaties, – the Berne Convention and TRIPS – to help place the discussion into an institutional context.

A. The Berne Convention

The Berne Convention was originally concluded in 1886 and was revised on a number of occasions, including Paris in 1971.[86] The US acceded to Berne in November 1988, and the Convention entered into force in the US on March 1, 1989. As of August 2013, there were 166 contracting parties to the Berne Convention.[87] The treaty contains three basic premises: national treatment of works; automatic protection of works without conditional formalities; and independence of protection.

The Berne Convention is administered by the World Intellectual Property Organization (WIPO), a specialized agency of the United Nations. WIPO also administers 22 other intellectual property and global protection treaties and agreements, including the Patent Law Treaty, the Patent Cooperation Treaty, the Trademark Law Treaty, and the Madrid

---

[85] Graeme Dinwoodie and Rochelle Dreyfuss, 'Designing a Global Intellectual Property System Responsive to Change: The WTO, WIPO, and Beyond' (2010) 46 Houston L Rev 1187.

[86] Berne Convention for the Protection of Literary and Artistic Works (adopted 9 September 1886, as revised at Paris 24 July 1971) 828 UNTS 221 (Berne Convention).

[87] For a list of the parties, see WIPO, 'Contracting Parties > Berne Convention' <http://www.wipo.int/treaties/en/ShowResults.jsp?lang=en&treaty_id=15> accessed 26 January 2014.

Protocol.[88] Pursuant to pressure from the US and certain European countries to address a digital agenda, two additional treaties – the WIPO Copyright Treaty and the WIPO Performances and Phonograms Treaty – were concluded in December 1996.

Unfortunately, however, WIPO lacks adequate direct enforcement power and must generally refer matters to the International Court of Justice. The TRIPS portion of the World Trade Organization Agreement was the mechanism devised to more efficiently enforce international norms of intellectual property practice. In 1995, the World Trade Organization (WTO) was born. It is headquartered in Geneva. Of the many agreements the WTO has promulgated, TRIPS is perhaps the most important.

B. The TRIPS Agreement

TRIPS was adopted in 1994 by 107 countries that had participated in the Uruguay Round of the General Agreement on Tariffs and Trade.[89] As of March 2, 2013, the WTO had 159 members.

Among the fundamental subjects covered by TRIPS are:

(1) Basic principles of the trading system and other international intellectual property agreements to be enforced;
(2) The minimum protection to be given to intellectual property rights;
(3) Obligations of enforcement of IP rights within the territories of members;
(4) Dispute settlement between members of the WTO.[90]

The Agreement addresses myriad forms of IP, including: '[1] copyright and related rights; [2] trademarks, including service marks; [3] geographical indications; [4] industrial designs; [5] patents; [6] layout-designs (topographies) of integrated circuits; and [7] undisclosed information, including trade secrets'.[91] It also establishes minimum standards for intellectual property protection, starting with the main

---

88 WIPO <http://www.wipo.int/portal/index.html.en> accessed 26 January 2014.

89 The TRIPS Agreement is Annex 1C of the Marrakesh Agreement Establishing the World Trade Organization.

90 WTO, 'Intellectual Property: Protection and Enforcement' <http://www.wto.org/english/thewto_e/whatis_e/tif_e/agrm7_e.htm> accessed 26 January 2014.

91 Ibid.

agreements – namely, the Paris Convention and the Berne Convention – previously extant in the world community and enforced by the World Intellectual Property Organization.

1. The Doha Declaration

TRIPS attempts to strike a balance between the long-term interest of enriching the public domain and the short-term desire of users for liberal access. One of the means by which that balance is struck is through the use of compulsory licensing.[92] Although the term is not specifically employed in TRIPS, reference is made in Article 31 to 'Use Without Authorization of the Right Holder', the intent of which is to permit, in appropriate circumstances, the use of a patent not only by governments for their own purposes but also by others authorized by government.

The compulsory license and its terms under TRIPS were specifically addressed by the Doha Ministerial Conference of 2001 and in the Declaration on the TRIPS Agreement and Public Health, adopted by WTO member organizations on November 14, 2001. By means of the Doha Declaration, the group agreed that TRIPS did not and should not prevent members from taking measures to address public health issues and acknowledged that the TRIPS Agreement permitted the use of compulsory licensing and parallel importing.[93] The Conference did not, however, specify the grounds upon which a compulsory license might be issued. Rather, that was left to the prerogative of the member country in need of the pharmaceutical.

Article 31(f) of TRIPS also presented difficulty insofar as it specifically states that a use under a compulsory license shall be authorized predominantly for the supply of the domestic market of the member authorizing such use. On August 30, 2003, WTO members agreed to shared understandings on certain waivers that would make it easier for countries unable to manufacture an adequate domestic supply of needed medicines to employ compulsory licensing that would permit the importation of cheaper generics. In December 2005, an agreement was reached with respect to the direct translation of the waivers into law. The waivers

---

[92] Agreement on Trade-Related Aspects of Intellectual Property Rights (adopted 15 April 1994, entered into force 1 January 1996) 1869 UNTS 299 (TRIPS Agreement) arts 7–8; WTO, 'Philosophy: TRIPS Attempts to Strike a Balance' <http://www.wto.org/english/tratop_e/trips_e/factsheet_pharm01_e. htm> accessed 26 January 2014. Importantly, the TRIPS Agreement provides explicitly that there can be no compulsory license of a trademark. TRIPS Agreement, s 2.

[93] WTO, 'Obligations and Exceptions' <http://www.wto.org/english/tratop_e/trips_e/factsheet_pharm02_e.htm#dohadecl5b> accessed 26 January 2014.

will enter into force when they are accepted by two-thirds of the members.[94]

2. Comments on TRIPS

TRIPS is generally perceived as born of Western principles and grounded in the utilitarian philosophy of a mass-market, seller-based economy.[95] It is believed that US interests during the 1980s, and particularly the interest in enforcement of international obligations with respect to IP, led to the initial linkage of trade and innovation. It is also generally accepted that TRIPS emerged thereafter through the combined efforts of industrialized countries, such as the US, Japan and certain members of the EU, and established research-based pharmaceutical and software companies.[96] Commentators with divergent philosophical views, economists with different policy approaches, and countries, nations, groups and individual community members with numerous cultural traditions often disagree with respect to their support of TRIPS and other international norms for the protection of IP.

Numerous countries have either declined to become a treaty party or, if they have formally acceded to treaty terms, have failed to fully meet treaty obligations. Among the numerous reasons and rationalizations for this state of affairs is the fact that IP protection is, by nature, territorial, and that divergent cultural, political or economic perspectives produce different results. So, as previously observed, common law countries whose IP philosophies are predominately grounded in utilitarian theory have often emphasized the protection of pecuniary interests, while others, such as those of civil law countries that possess a more vibrant natural-law perspective, have tended to emphasize and reward moral and non-pecuniary interests. Another observable trend has been that developing countries that perceive their economic survival as dependent upon liberal access to intellectual property have found it propitious to afford less protection to intellectual property interests than have more economically developed countries, such as the US and Japan.

---

94 Amendment of the TRIPS Agreement (6 December 2005) WT/L/641, <http://docs.wto.org>. The current deadline for acceptance is 31 December 2015. See, http://www.wto.org/english/tratop_e/trips_e/amendment_e.htm

95 *See generally* Katherine J Strandburg, 'Evolving Innovation Paradigms and the Global Intellectual Property Regime' (2009) 41 *Connecticut L Rev* 861 (2009).

96 Daniel J Gervais, 'TRIPS and Development' in Daniel J Gervais (ed.), *Intellectual Property, Trade and Development* (OUP 2007) 385.

Thus, the debate continues as to whether the utilitarian incentive system and a system of strong protection of IP actually enhance the productivity of authors and inventors.[97] For some advocates, the proper focus is not upon protection of IP but rather upon global welfare. They argue that perhaps a more homogeneous communitarian arrangement that permits more liberal access to innovation would best serve the interests of everyone. For others, however, strong IP protection is indispensable, as it fosters the research and development necessary to produce improvements and innovations in areas like the pharmaceutical industry.

Still others observe that political forces in some countries are actually anti-IP because the average citizen actually considers IP to be 'Other People's IP' (OPIP); the better system would be an anti-TRIPS model that recognizes the interest of some communities in independently pursuing a non-Western model founded upon discrete and separate communal rights.[98]

Finally there are those who are directed by pragmatic political pressures. To them, the IP laws of particular jurisdictions are tested annually through the evaluation of the effectiveness of IP enforcement by the US Trade Representative's 'Special 301 Report'. This source identifies IP issues of concern, placing countries viewed as significantly lacking in IP protection on a Watch or Priority Watch List. More importantly, membership (or lack thereof) in the WTO does not dictate who is or is not on the list. In 2013, for example, Canada, Israel, Italy, the Philippines and Vietnam were on the Watch List. WTO members China, India and Thailand were on the Priority Watch List that same year. Of considerable note, the Ukraine, a member of the WTO since May 2008, gained the dubious distinction of being named a Priority Foreign Country in the 2013 Special 301 Report.[99]

---

[97] Alan Story, Colin Darch and Debora Halbert (eds), *Issues in the Economics, Politics, and Ideology of Copyright in the Global South* (The Copy/South Research Group 2006) 160.

[98] Ibid., 52. See also Edward Kelly, 'Advocating IP Protection as an Aspect of National Competitiveness' in Jessie CY Lee (ed.), *IP Client Strategies in Asia* (Aspatore 2009) 29, 48.

[99] This was the first time in seven years that a country was characterized as a Priority Foreign Country, a designation reserved for the most egregious IP violations. Office of the US Trade Representative, '2013 Special 301 Report' (May 2013) 28. <http://www.ustr.gov/sites/default/files/05012013%202013%20Special%20301%20Report.pdf> accessed 26 January 2014.

C. Conflict by Example

Is the light we see at the end of the tunnel a promise for a quick resolution of the conflicts or the headlight of an oncoming train that threatens collision and catastrophic consequences? While there is no need to be pessimistic, there is a need to realistically acknowledge that there are significant differences of opinion, many of which are based on deeply held political, philosophical and cultural beliefs. There are several examples of recent discord suggesting that continued attention is required.

First, weak patent laws in some countries have permitted those countries to become centers for the production of generic pharmaceuticals through implementation of a system of reverse engineering. India has been considered such a country. On January 1, 2005, however, India promulgated a new patent law designed to protect pharmaceutical compositions rather than merely the processes for making them. The alleged purpose of the legislation is to provide a catalyst that may enable India's 'drug-manufacturing sector to evolve from reverse engineering to innovation'.[100] The law does, however, have some significant limitations on protection. For example, if any Indian pharmaceutical firm began the manufacture of a generic drug before 2005 that is later covered by a patent, they may continue to make and sell the drug (although they may have to pay certain royalties).[101] Second, the law contains extensive provisions for compulsory licensing.[102] Third, there is an opposition provision in the law that permits public interest groups and others to challenge the issuance of a patent.[103]

India became embroiled in a lengthy and public dispute with Novartis, a Swiss pharmaceutical company, over the denial of a patent for various modalities of the drug Gleevec, the company's brand-name version of imatinib mesylate. In large part due to the opposition of advocacy groups, a patent for the drug was denied. In response, Novartis decided to reverse a prior decision to invest hundreds of millions of dollars in an Indian-based research program. It is reported to have moved considerable resources to China.[104]

---

100 Janice M Meuller, 'Taking TRIPS to India – Novartis, Patent Law and Access to Medicines' (2007) 356 *New England J Medicine* 541, 541–2.

101 Ibid.

102 Ibid.

103 Ibid.

104 Chris Morrison, 'Novartis' Herrling Talks China With PharmAsiaNews' (*In Vivo Blog*, 6 May 2008) <http://invivoblog.blogspot.com/2008/05/novartis-herrling-talks-china-with.html> accessed 26 January 2014.

Second, in April 2006, Playboy magazine, then headquartered in Jakarta, published its first Indonesian edition. Since the inhabitants of Indonesia were predominantly Muslim, the decision was made that the issue would contain neither nude photographs nor sexually oriented discussions.[105] A public interest group, the Front Pembela Islam, objected to publication of the magazine, and another group, Indonesian Society Against Piracy and Pornography, filed a criminal complaint against the editor, Erwin Arnada, and one of the models who appeared in the magazine. The company moved its headquarters to Bali, a predominately Hindu area, and published its second issue in June 2006. In April 2007, the parties were acquitted after a lengthy trial, however, the Supreme Court reinstated the conviction of Arnada upon appeal by prosecutors. Following judicial review Arnada was finally released from prison in 2011.[106] An October 2009 issue of National Geographic magazine reported that Playboy had ceased publication of its Indonesian issue.[107]

Indonesia is not alone in attempting to control access to various forms of expression. Iran, for example, has engaged in considerable policing of the internet for the purpose of censoring what it considers offensive content. There is even a proposal to impose the death penalty against pornographers.[108]

Third, Egypt purports to have an economic, legal and social environment amenable to foreign direct investment: the level of education is adequate, labor is relatively cheap, many of the people speak English, and investment laws have been liberalized. In addition, the country has taken formal steps to modernize its intellectual property laws.[109] For

---

[105] Jane Perlez, 'Playboy Tests Tolerance in Indonesia – Business – International Herald Tribune' *New York Times* (July 2006) http://www.nytimes.com/2006/07/23/business/worldbusiness/23iht-playboy.2272396.html?_r=0 > accessed 20 February 2014. See also, Erwin Arnada, 'Playboy of the Muslim World' *Playboy* (September 2007).

[106] Ali Kotarumalos, 'Erwin Arnada, Playboy Indonesia Editor, Freed From Prison After Indecency Conviction Is Overturned' *The World Post* (24 June 2011) <http://www.huffingtonpost.com/2011/06/24/erwin-arnada-playboy-indonesia-editor-freed-prison-indecency-_n_883777.html>accessed 20 February 2014.

[107] Michael Finkel, 'Facing Down the Fanatics' *National Geographic* (October 2009) 77, 92.

[108] Kenly Walker, 'Death Penalty For Porn In Iran?' *CBS News* (14 June 2007) <http://www.cbsnews.com/news/death-penalty-for-porn-in-iran/> accessed 26 January 2014.

[109] Law No 82 of 2002 (Pertaining to the Protection of Intellectual Property Rights) (Egypt). See also Sahar Aziz, 'Linking Intellectual Property Rights in Developing Countries with Research and Development, Technology Transfer, and

example, although Egypt expanded its protection of pharmaceutical products in order to comply with TRIPS, the law does, however, include a provision for compulsory licensing under Article 31. This provision would permit the use of certain patents without permission of the patent holder.[110]

Article 23(2) of Egypt's patent law permits the Minister of Health to grant a compulsory license if the quantity of available medicine fails to meet the nation's needs and (1) the failure is due to the poor quality of alternatives; (2) there is a prohibitive price for alternatives; or (3) there is a presence of incurable or endemic diseases.[111] Finally, Article 23(1)(c) allows the Egyptian government to grant a license when it is deemed necessary to support certain national efforts.[112]

In 1998, Pfizer applied for regulatory approval to enter the market for the drug Viagra, which was approved in 2002. Local drug manufacturers, however, placed pressure on the Egyptian Ministry of Health, and approximately two months after Pfizer's entry into the Egyptian market, it granted authorization to produce Viagra to all Egyptian companies who applied for the privilege.[113] The interest of the poor was cited as the justification for the issuance of compulsory license. In response, Pfizer withdrew plans to develop research and development facilities in Egypt.[114]

Fourth, Chinese piracy of US intellectual property is a serious problem. It has been estimated that the US loses more than four billion dollars annually as a result of that activity.[115] That assertion may, however, be too simplistic. Indeed, 'a crime' from the US perspective may be viewed quite differently from the Confucian-influenced and Socialist-inspired Chinese perspectives.

From a cultural Confucian perspective, copying is considered more a noble art than a moral or legal offense. The past is an embodiment of cultural and social values and, in accord with the spirit of Confucianism,

---

Foreign Direct Investment Policy: A Case Study of Egypt's Pharmaceutical Industry' (2003) 10 *Intl L Students Association J Intl & Comparative L* 1, 13.

[110] TRIPS Agreement, art 31.

[111] Law No 82 of 2002, art 23(2).

[112] Ibid., art 23(1)(c).

[113] Richard A Castellano, 'Patent Law for New Medical Uses of Known Compounds and Pfizer's Viagra Patent' (2006) 46 *IDEA* 283, 289.

[114] Ibid., 289.

[115] Agencies, 'Bollywood Piracy Fighters Take Battle to US Congress' *The Economic Times* (22 April 2008) <http://economictimes.indiatimes.com/business-of-bollywood/bollywood-piracy-fighters-take-battle-to-us-congress/articleshow/2987223.cms> accessed 26 January 2014.

such materials must be in the public domain if one is to learn about and venerate one's ancestors. Furthermore, and consistent with the tenets of Confucianism, the rights of individuals in property may well be subordinate to the collective; and in accord with philosophical communist and socialist views, property belongs to the state not to individuals. It has been said that views such as these may lead one to conclude that 'stealing an object that is owned by someone else is less corrupt than owning it outright yourself'.[116]

Additionally, China often voices the politically expeditious opinion that the East has, for far too long, been under the oppressive hand of the West, and liberal access to intellectual property is necessary to permit the East to 'catch up'.

From these principles is derived a premise: to engage in censorship of Western ideas is, in fact, to protect China's culture. This claim of a right of censorship was one of a number of subjects under review in a recent dispute before the WTO. The US filed a complaint alleging that China was in violation of certain intellectual property obligations, and questioning China's content review and censorship procedures applicable to copyrighted works. China responded: 'China, like many countries in the world, bans from publication and dissemination such works as those that consist entirely of unconstitutional or immoral content. … [The law] simply provides that such a work also shall not be protected by the Copyright Law …'[117] The Panel concluded that while China's IP laws were not in complete compliance with its obligations under TRIPS, there was no prohibition under the Agreement for a proper exercise of content review by a country.

CONCLUSION

Misunderstanding, whether through failure of inquiry, failure to truly appreciate the presumptions and perspectives of others in the dialogue, or nondisclosure of assumptions or expectations, seems to often punctuate

---

[116] Susan Tiefenbrun, 'Piracy of Intellectual Property in China and the Former Soviet Union and its Effects upon International Trade: A Comparison' (1998) 46 *Buffalo L Rev* 1, 38; Hofstede and Hofstede (n 41) 209.

[117] WTO, *China: Measures Affecting the Protection and Enforcement of Intellectual Property Rights – Report of the Panel* (26 January 2009) WT/DS362/R [7.53].

discussion and has led to considerable tension and unsatisfactory outcomes in the global IP community. One could compare this misunderstanding to neglecting to inquire about or disclose the location of a water main before excavation for a land improvement. Breach of the line can cause flooding and considerable frustration, or in some cases, total failure of the project.

The recognition of changing themes in innovation and creative products and the treatment given to IP is, today, a significant issue in the world community. Success in harmonizing differing viewpoints will likely only be achieved, however, when discussants actually discuss the same implications in the same context. As such, it is indispensable to effective decision-making that participants investigate, understand and appreciate not only the debate's political and monetary implications, but its social and cultural implications as well. It would also benefit commentators and proponents to possess a critical comprehension of such elements in their comments and to disclose the motives, philosophical and political agendas, and fundamental assumptions underlying their propositions. In any case, a cogent protocol for evaluation is necessary to catalyze positive progress, and it is proposed that features such as those described above may begin to aid analysts in achieving some consensus.

10. The Patent Cooperation Treaty

Cees A.M. Mulder

1. HISTORY

In the mid 1960s, national patent offices became worried about the rapid increase in the number of patent applications they had to digest. Backlogs in substantive examination of applications resulted in delayed decisions on the grant of patents. An additional problem was caused by the fact that, during pendency, applications were often kept secret.[1] This secrecy created uncertainty among the public – and in particular potential competitors – about potential inventions for which protection was sought. Proposals for a new system to publish the applications within a relatively short period of time were thus seen as desirable, as was having a preliminary report (even if non-binding) available on the patentability of the claimed invention.[2]

At that time only national patent laws existed. Hence, an inventor seeking protection for an invention needed to file applications in several countries more or less at the same time to avoid destroying the novelty of the invention. All national patent offices would then perform more or less the same search (of the patent literature) and examination work. There was little if any exchange or use of this work among patent offices.

It is also important to note that most patent offices require the use of a specific language for the drafting of the national application, forcing applicants seeking protection in several countries to translate their application into a number of languages.

The duplicative nature of this process work might lead one to argue that, in an optimal situation, a single procedure would result in the grant of a worldwide patent. However, this was not a realizable goal in the decades that followed the Second World War and still today it is far from realization. Individual States are simply unwilling to forego the prerogative of granting patents based on their own specific conditions.

---

[1] E.g., in the United States, patent applications filed before November 2000 were not published and remained secret until they were granted.

[2] WIPO, *The First Twenty-Five Years of the Patent Cooperation Treaty (PCT) 1970–1995* (WIPO 1995) pp. 7–9.

In 1967 the World Intellectual Property Organization (WIPO) was created in Geneva as a special agency of the United Nations, the purpose of which was 'to encourage creative activity, to promote the protection of intellectual property throughout the world'.[3] The government of the United States encouraged WIPO to take up the task of simplifying patent protection worldwide. This resulted in the adoption of the Patent Cooperation Treaty (PCT), which was signed in Washington, DC, on 19 June 1970. The PCT entered into force on 24 January 1978,[4] and the first 'international application' was received on 1 June 1978.[5]

The creators of the PCT aimed at simplifying procedures for obtaining patent protection internationally. Although the PCT did not provide a 'complete solution' in the form of a worldwide patent, it reduced the concern of repetitive searches and examination and the numerous translations required by national patent laws and regulations.

Another important aspect of the PCT is that it provides more time for an applicant to decide whether and, if so, how to continue an international application, after he or she knows more about the technical and economic value of the claimed invention and its potential patentability. This constitutes a better basis for evaluating the chances of obtaining protection.

Any State who is a member of the Paris Convention for the Protection of Industrial Property may become a party to the PCT.[6] As of 1 March 2014, the PCT was in force for 148 States of the 175 States that are members of the Paris Convention.[7]

The principal advantage for applicants wishing to protect their inventions in countries party to both the PCT and any of the various regional

---

[3] Convention Establishing the World Intellectual Property Organization (adopted 14 July 1967, entered into force 26 April 1970) 828 UNTS 3 (WIPO Convention) preamble. WIPO was the successor of the 'United International Bureaux for the Protection of Intellectual Property' (known by the French acronym BIRPI), which was established in 1893 to administer the Paris Convention for the Protection of Industrial Property (adopted 20 March 1883, as revised at Stockholm 14 July 1967) 828 UNTS 305 (Paris Convention) and the Berne Convention for the Protection of Literary and Artistic Works (adopted 9 September 1886, as revised at Paris 24 July 1971) 828 UNTS 221 (Berne Convention).

[4] Patent Cooperation Treaty (opened for signature 19 June 1970, entered into force 24 January 1978) 1160 UNTS 231 (PCT).

[5] On 1 June 1978, 18 States were party to the PCT.

[6] See PCT, art 62(1).

[7] WIPO, 'States Party to the PCT and the Paris Convention and Members of the World Trade Organization' (19 November 2013) <http://www.wipo.int/export/sites/www/pct/en/texts/pdf/pct_paris_wto.pdf> accessed 18 November 2014.

patent treaties (such as the European Patent Convention) results from the combined use of the PCT system and those regional systems.[8] Indeed, the PCT is fully compatible with such regional patent systems.[9]

Since 2000, efforts were undertaken to simplify and streamline the procedural requirements of the PCT. The conclusion of the Patent Law Treaty[10] on 1 June 2000 also influenced the PCT.[11] Amendments to the PCT included the adaptation of several requirements related to the filing of an international application – in particular, introducing the filing of missing parts of the description or missing drawings[12] and restoration of the right to priority.[13] [14] A disadvantage of these amendments is that they resulted in a comprehensive list of 'reservations' made by PCT States, that the amendment (currently) is 'not compatible with the national law' in that State.[15]

---

8 In addition to designations of PCT Contracting States for the purposes of obtaining national patents, an international application includes designations for regional patents in respect of States party to any of the following regional patent treaties: the Harare Protocol on Patents and Industrial Designs Within the Framework of the African Regional Intellectual Property Organization (ARIPO Harare Protocol), the Eurasian Patent Convention, the European Patent Convention, and the Agreement establishing the African Intellectual Property Organization (OAPI Agreement). WIPO, 'PCT Applicant's Guide – International Phase' (International Guide) para 3.004 <http://www.wipo.int/export/sites/www/pct/en/eqe/ip.pdf> accessed 18 November 2014.

9 PCT, art 45. Instead of entering the national phase in each of the individual countries party to a regional patent treaty, the applicant may choose to enter a regional phase. The concepts of PCT 'phases' are discussed below.

10 Patent Law Treaty (adopted 1 June 2000) 39 ILM 1047 (2000).

11 Cees Mulder, 'Filing Date Requirements Under the Patent Cooperation Treaty: Alignment with the Patent Law Treaty?' (2011) 2 WIPO J 173.

12 PCT, art 11; PCT Regulations, r 20.

13 PCT Regulations, r 26*bis*.3.

14 On 1 April 2007, the Regulations Under the Patent Cooperation Treaty (PCT Regulations) were amended to better align the PCT with requirements of the Patent Law Treaty. The requirements for according an international filing date could not be fully aligned with the Patent Law Treaty, however, because these requirements are 'carved in stone' in art 11(1) of the PCT. While articles of the PCT can be revised by a Revision Conference of the PCT Contracting States (art 60(1)), the fact that there are currently more than 145 PCT Contracting States will make it difficult to achieve consensus about the required revision of the articles. Furthermore, while the Regulations under the PCT may be amended by the Assembly (art 58(3)), such amendment requires unanimous consent.

15 In order to make acceptable certain amendments to the PCT Regulations, transitional reservations are frequently incorporated in the amended Regulations. A PCT Contracting State declaring that such an amendment is not compatible

BOX 10.1 ADDITIONAL INFORMATION

Up-to-date versions of the PCT and Regulations are available from the webpage 'PCT Resources' on the website of WIPO.[16] News about the PCT is available from the 'PCT Newsletter', a monthly publication.[17] In addition, various e-mail update services are available for users of the PCT system. A comprehensive guide for applicants is published comprising general information on the Patent Cooperation Treaty.[18] The complete texts of the PCT Articles and the corresponding Rules containing cross-references between the Articles and Rules giving the reader a better overview of the structure of the PCT, is published annually.[19]

A more recent development is that patent offices tend to rely on the results of international search and preliminary examination established in the international phase to assist and accelerate examination during the national phase. The concept of the Patent Prosecution Highway (PCT-PPH) is to permit examiners in one patent office to use the results of the international search and preliminary examination established by an international authority. Where claims of an international application have been found allowable in one office, another office may allow a 'fast track' for the substantive examination of a corresponding application, thereby reducing duplication of work. Many patent offices have signed

---

with the national law of the State need not apply the amended provision until such time as the position might be solved under its national law. See WIPO, 'PCT Reservations, Declarations, Notifications and Incompatibilities' (12 November 2013) (PCT Reservations) <http://www.wipo.int/pct/en/texts/reservations/res_incomp.html> accessed 18 November 2014.

[16] The webpage 'PCT Resources' on the WIPO website comprises a wealth of information related to the Patent Cooperation Treaty; the content of the webpage is regularly updated. World Intellectual Property Organization, 'PCT Resources' <http://www.wipo.int/pct/en/> accessed 18 November 2014.

[17] The PCT Newsletter publishes the current list of PCT Contracting States, reports of international meetings concerning the PCT, amendments to the PCT Regulations, changes to PCT forms, statistics relating to the filing of international applications, practical advice for PCT users, information about forthcoming PCT seminars and tables of PCT fees. WIPO, 'PCT Newsletter' <http://www.wipo.int/pct/en/newslett/> accessed 18 November 2014.

[18] WIPO, 'International Guide' (n 8); WIPO, 'PCT Applicant's Guide – National Phase' (National Guide) <http://www.wipo.int/export/sites/www/pct/en/eqe/np.pdf> accessed 18 November 2014.

[19] Cees Mulder, *The Cross-Referenced Patent Cooperation Treaty* (12th edn, Helze 2014) <www.helze.com> accessed 18 November 2014.

bilateral agreements enabling applicants to request a fast-track examination procedure. By requesting that their applications be processed under this procedure, applicants can generally obtain patents more quickly before the participating offices.[20]

2. PURPOSE OF THE PCT

According to the Preamble, the PCT aims:[21]

- To simplify and render more economical the obtaining of protection for inventions in several countries;
- To facilitate access by the public to patent information; and
- To promote economic development of developing countries by increasing the efficiency of the national patent systems and facilitating access to modern technology.

Under the PCT, an applicant files only one application (known as the 'international application') in one place, in one language and by paying one initial set of fees.[22] Importantly, the goal of the PCT – namely, the issuance of national (or regional) patents – has not changed; there is still no such thing as an international patent. However, one of the main advantages of the PCT is that the decision to start the national 'processing' of applications by individual patent offices is postponed by at least 30 months from the filing date of the initial international application or, if the international application claims priority from an earlier filed application, from the priority date, which would be the date of an earlier national patent application.[23] During this period, the applicant typically

---

[20] For further information concerning forms and administrative procedures of each participating Office, see WIPO, 'PCT-Patent Prosecution Highway Pilot (PCT-PPH)' <http://www.wipo.int/pct/en/filing/pct_pph.html> accessed 18 November 2014. The United States Patent and Trademark Office (USPTO) has PCT-PPH agreements with 13 Offices including the European Patent Office and the patent offices of Australia, Canada, Japan, Korea, and the Russian Federation. ibid.

[21] WIPO, 'International Guide' (n 8) Ch 2.

[22] Ibid. para 4.003.

[23] As explained below, an applicant can file a PCT (international) application first, or he or she may file a national application followed by a PCT application. If the latter is filed within 12 months of the initial application, the PCT application may be deemed to have been filed on the same date as the earlier national application (the so-called 'priority date').

receives valuable information that facilitates the decision whether to enter the national/regional phases. For example, the applicant normally obtains an international search report prepared by an International Searching Authority. This report contains a preliminary non-binding opinion on the patentability of the invention claimed in the international application.[24]

Eighteen months after the initial application or priority date,[25] the International Bureau (secretariat) of WIPO publishes the international application together with the international search report.[26] An important advantage of the PCT is that, if the international application is published in a language other than English, the International Bureau also prepares and publishes an English translation of the title of the invention, the abstract and the international search report.[27] To obtain additional information with respect to the patentability of the invention, the applicant can request a supplementary international search report[28] and/or an international preliminary examination report.[29] These latter two procedures are, however, infrequently used.

As already mentioned, the PCT did not eliminate the necessity of prosecuting the patent application before the national/regional patent offices. It did, however, facilitate such prosecution in important respects by virtue of the procedures carried out on all international applications during the international phase. In addition to the publication and translation features just described, the PCT increased uniformity. The form of the international application is prescribed by the PCT and this form must be accepted by all national/regional offices.[30] This limits the variation in formal requirements in the countries where protection is sought. It is important to note, however, that while the PCT increased uniformity in procedural and formal matters, nothing in the PCT limits the freedom of Contracting States to apply their own substantive conditions of patentability. In particular, when determining the patentability of an invention claimed in an international application, any PCT Contracting State is free to apply the criteria of its national law in regard to prior art and other

---

[24] See Part 4.3.

[25] For a definition of 'priority date', see PCT Article 1(xi).

[26] PCT, art 21. If the international search report is not available in time to be published together with the international application, the search report will be published separately. PCT Regulations, r 48.2(g).

[27] PCT Regulations, r 48.3; WIPO, 'International Guide' (n 8) para 9.017.

[28] See Part 4.3.

[29] WIPO, 'International Guide' (n 8) ch 4. Also see Part 4.5.

[30] PCT, art 27(1).

conditions of patentability (subject, of course, to other applicable international rules, such as those contained in the TRIPS Agreement).[31]

3. A BRIEF OVERVIEW OF PCT PROCESS AND PROCEDURES

The PCT process falls into two main phases: the 'international phase' and the 'national or regional phase'. It starts with the filing of an international application and ends (if the outcome is favorable for the applicant) with the grant of a number of national and/or regional patents granted by the national/regional offices.[32]

The international phase consists of five stages. The first three occur automatically for all international applications; the last two are optional. These steps are as follows:[33]

1) The filing of the international application by the applicant and its processing by the receiving Office;[34]
2) The establishment of the international search report and written opinion by one of the International Searching Authorities;[35]
3) The publication of the international application together with the international search report by the International Bureau of WIPO;[36]
4) The carrying out of a supplementary international search by another International Searching Authority, resulting in the establishment of a supplementary international search report;[37] and
5) The carrying out of international preliminary examination by an International Preliminary Examining Authority, resulting in the establishment of the international preliminary examination report.[38]

The third step includes communication of the published international application and the international search report and, where applicable, the supplementary international search report, as well as the international

---

31 PCT, art 27(5).

32 In this chapter, unless otherwise indicated, all references to articles refer to articles of the PCT.

33 WIPO, 'International Guide' (n 8) ch 3.

34 PCT, arts 3–14; see Parts 4.1, 4.2.

35 PCT, arts 15–18; see Part 4.3.

36 PCT, art 21; see Part 4.4.

37 PCT Regulations r 45*bis*; see Part 4.3.

38 PCT, arts 31–38; see Part 4.5.

preliminary examination report, by the International Bureau to the national/regional offices or the jurisdictions for which the applicant wishes to obtain a patent. This transmittal is effected shortly before the end of the international phase.[39]

At the end of the international phase, the applicant must act. If the applicant desires to continue with his international application, he must choose before which national/regional offices he wants to enter the national/regional phase that is, the national or regional jurisdictions in which he or she ultimately wishes to obtain a patent. The applicant must then pay national/regional fees, provide required translations of the application and, where required, appoint a representative (patent agent). Those actions must be completed within a certain time limit.[40] The national/regional offices then examine the application and grant or refuse the national/regional patent on the basis of the applicable legislation.

4. THE INTERNATIONAL PHASE

4.1 Filing an International Application

An international application must contain the following elements: a request, a description, one or more claims, one or more drawings (where required), and an abstract.[41]

The request includes a petition for the international application to be processed according to the PCT. It must also contain certain indications such as the title of the invention.[42] In addition, the request must identify the applicant (normally the inventor) and the agent, if any.[43] The request should also contain, where applicable, a priority claim,[44] an indication of the applicant's choice of competent International Searching Authority and a reference to any relevant earlier search.[45] The request must be signed.[46] The filing of the request constitutes a designation of all Contracting States bound by the PCT on the international filing date, for

---

39 PCT, arts 20, 39; see Part 5.

40 PCT, arts 22, 39; PCT Regulations, r 76; see Part 5.

41 PCT, arts 3–7; WIPO, 'International Guide' (n 8) Ch 5.

42 PCT, art 4(1)(i); PCT Regulations, r 4.1(a).

43 PCT Regulations, rr 4.1(a)(iii), 4.5–4.7.

44 PCT, art 8; PCT Regulations, rr 4.1(b)(i), 4.10.

45 PCT Regulations, rr 4.1(b), 4.11–4.14*bis*.

46 PCT Regulations, rr 4.1(d), 4.15.

the grant of every kind of protection available and for the grant of both regional and national patents.[47]

The description must disclose the invention in a manner sufficiently clear and complete for it to be carried out by a person skilled in the art.[48] [49] Where the international application contains the disclosure of a nucleotide and/or amino acid sequence, the description must also contain a listing of the sequence.[50] [51]

The claim (or claims) must define the matter for which protection is sought. Claims must be clear and concise. They must be fully supported by the description.[52]

Drawings must be contained in the international application if they are necessary to understand the invention.[53]

Finally, the abstract must consist of a summary of the disclosure as contained in the application[54] and should primarily be related to what is new in the art (field) to which the invention pertains.[55]

In addition to these elements, the international application must be filed with a prescribed 'receiving Office'.[56] Each PCT Contracting State has indicated which nationals and residents may, as applicants, file international applications at its national office.[57] Where there are several applicants who are not all nationals and/or residents of the same Contracting State, any receiving office of or acting for a Contracting State of which at least one of the applicants is a resident or national is competent to receive an international application filed by those applicants.[58] Alternatively, the international application may be filed with the International Bureau in Geneva, regardless of the Contracting State of which the applicant is a resident or national.[59] If the international

---

47 PCT, art 4(1)(ii); PCT Regulations, r 4.9.

48 PCT, art 5; PCT Regulations, r 5.

49 A functional synonym of the US notion of 'Person Having Ordinary Skill in the Art' (PHOSITA).

50 PCT Regulations, r 5.2.

51 Administrative Instructions under the Patent Cooperation Treaty (PCT Instructions) annex C <http://www.wipo.int/pct/en/texts/ai/ai_index.html> accessed 18 November 2014.

52 PCT, art 6; PCT Regulations, r 6.

53 PCT, art 7; PCT Regulations, r 7.

54 PCT, art 3(3); PCT Regulations, r 8.

55 WIPO, 'International Guide' (n 8) para 5.165.

56 PCT, art 10; PCT Regulations, r 19.1.

57 WIPO, 'International Guide' (n 8) annex C.

58 PCT Regulations, r 19.2.

59 PCT Regulations, r 19.1(a)(iii).

application is erroneously filed with a non-competent receiving office, the application will be transmitted to the International Bureau.[60]

Each receiving office prescribes the language(s) in which an applicant must file the international application.[61] If the applicant files the international application in a language other than a language of publication, or if the International Searching Authority tasked to carry out the international search does not allow the language, the applicant must provide a translation of the international application for the purposes of international search and/or international publication.[62] If the applicant files the international application in a language not prescribed by the receiving office, the application will be transmitted to the International Bureau. An international application so transmitted will be considered to have been received by the International Bureau on the date on which it was filed with the receiving office.[63] Where the International Bureau serves as the receiving office, an applicant may file an international application in any language.[64]

The international application should be drafted so that the claims relate to only one invention or to a group of inventions so linked as to form a single inventive concept.[65] The International Searching Authority is responsible for reviewing the unity of any group of inventions.[66]

The international application is subject to payment of the prescribed fees.[67] Those fees must be paid to the receiving office[68] within one month from the date on which the receiving office receives the international application.[69] These fees include:

---

[60] The international application so transmitted will be considered to have been received by the International Bureau on the date on which it was filed with the receiving office. PCT Regulations, rr 19.4(a)(i), 19.4(b).

[61] The international application must be filed in a 'prescribed' language. PCT, art 3(4)(i); PCT Regulations, r 12.1.

[62] PCT Regulations, rr 12.3, 12.4.

[63] PCT Regulations, rr 19.4(a)(ii), (b).

[64] WIPO, 'International Guide' (n 8) annex C. The international application must also comply with the prescribed physical requirements. PCT, art 3(4)(ii); PCT Regulations, r 11. These requirements include paper size, margins, line spacing, size of characters, etc.

[65] PCT, art 3(4)(iii); PCT Regulations, r 13.

[66] See Part 11.4.3.

[67] PCT, art 3(4)(iv).

[68] PCT Regulations, rr 4.1(b), 15.2, 16.1(b).

[69] PCT Regulations, rr 14.1(c), 15.3, 16.1(f).

- A transmittal fee for the work done by the receiving Office (rule 14);
- An international filing fee for performance of various tasks by the International Bureau, including the publication of the international application and the communication with the applicant, the International Authorities and the designated and elected offices (rule 15); and
- A search fee for carrying out the international search by the International Searching Authority (rule 16).

Obvious mistakes in the international application and other documents may be rectified on request of the applicant.[70] The competent authority will authorize the rectification only if it is obvious that the applicant intended something other than what appears in the application or other document and that the applicant could have intended nothing other than the proposed rectification.[71] In the case of a mistake in the description, claims or drawings, the competent authority will only take into account the contents of the description, claims and drawings.[72]

Each receiving office may apply its own national law to require applicants to be represented by an agent.[73] Any person who can act as an agent before a particular receiving office may be appointed as an agent for any international application filed with that office.[74]

The international application may contain a declaration claiming the priority of one or more earlier applications filed in or for any country that is a party to the Paris Convention for the Protection of Industrial Property.[75] The priority claim may also claim the priority of an application filed in or for any member of the World Trade Organization.[76] Because an international application has the effect of a regular national application in each designated State, it may claim priority from another application and be used as the basis for a priority claim in a later application.[77] In the international phase, the priority claim is particularly important because it establishes a priority date for the purpose of

---

70 PCT Regulations, r 91.

71 PCT Regulations, r 91.1(c).

72 PCT Regulations, r 91.1(d).

73 PCT, art 27(7); PCT Regulations, r 51*bis*.1(b); WIPO, 'International Guide' (n 8) Annex C.

74 PCT, art 49; PCT Regulations, rr 83, 90.

75 PCT, art 8(1).

76 PCT Regulations, r 4.10.

77 PCT, art 11(3), (4).

computing time limits under the PCT.[78] The validity of a priority claim is not determined during the international phase.[79]

Preferably, the priority claim should be made upon filing the international application.[80] A priority claim may also be withdrawn by the applicant;[81] where the withdrawal causes a change in the priority date, any time limit that has not already expired will be computed from the changed priority date.[82]

The PCT allows for a restoration of the right of priority if the international application is filed after expiry of the priority period but within a period of two months of that date.[83,84] Upon requesting restoration, the applicant must file information demonstrating that the failure to file the international application within the priority period occurred 'in spite of due care' or was 'unintentional'.[85] Even if the receiving office refuses the applicant's request to restore the right of priority, the PCT system continues to calculate time limits as if the priority period were valid.[86] The purpose of this provision is to allow a designated office to permit the restoration in the national phase.[87] A number of receiving and designated offices have made a reservation with respect to restoration of the right to priority.[88] Some offices allow restoration of the right or priority where that office acts as a receiving office but not where that office acts as a designated/elected office.[89]

---

78 PCT, art 2(xi).

79 WIPO, 'International Guide' (n 8) para 5.060.

80 PCT Regulations, rr 4.1(b)(i), 4.10. A priority claim may be added or corrected after filing under certain conditions. PCT Regulations, rr 26*bis*.1(a), 91.1(g)(iv).

81 PCT Regulations, r 90*bis*.3(a).

82 PCT Regulations, r 90*bis*.3(d).

83 PCT Regulations, rr 26*bis*.2, 26*bis*.3, 49*ter*.

84 The priority period is 12 months from the filing date of the earlier application. Paris Convention for the Protection of Industrial Property (adopted 20 March 1883, as revised at Stockholm 14 July 1967) 828 UNTS 305 (Paris Convention) art 4C(1). See also PCT Regulations, r 2.4.

85 PCT Regulations, r 26*bis*.3(a)(i), (ii).

86 PCT Regulations, r 26*bis*.2(c)(iii).

87 PCT Regulations, r 49*ter*.2(c)(iii).

88 PCT Regulations, rr 26*bis*.3(j), 49*ter*.1(g), 49*ter*.2(h); WIPO, 'PCT Reservations' (n 13).

89 As of 12 November 2013, the following Intellectual Property Offices have made a reservation under rules 49*ter*.1(g) and 49*ter*.2(h) but not under rule 26*bis*.3(j): Canada, China, Lithuania, Mexico, Turkey and the United States. WIPO, 'PCT Reservations' (n 13).

4.2 Processing Before the Receiving Office

The receiving office will accord the 'international filing date' to the international application if it finds at the time of receipt that:[90]

(i) The applicant does not obviously lack, for reasons of residence or nationality, the right to file an international application with the receiving office;[91]
(ii) The international application is in the prescribed language;[92] and
(iii) The international application contains at least the following elements:
    (a) an indication that it is intended as an international application,[93]
    (b) a request which constitutes the designation of a Contracting State bound by the PCT on the international filing date,[94]
    (c) the name of the applicant,[95] [96]
    (d) a part which on the face of it appears to be a description,[97] and
    (e) a part which on the face of it appears to be a claim or claims.[98]

Non-payment of fees, omission of a title, abstract or signature, or non-compliance with the physical requirements will not affect the international filing date. However, the presence of at least one claim is required for the international filing date to be accorded.[99] The PCT has

---

[90] PCT, art 11(1); PCT Regulations, r 20(1); WIPO, 'International Guide' (n 8) ch 6.

[91] PCT, art 10; PCT Regulations, r 19.

[92] PCT, art 3(4)(i); PCT Regulations, r 12.1.

[93] PCT Regulations, r 4.2.

[94] PCT Regulations, r 4.9(a).

[95] PCT Regulations, r 4.5.

[96] For the purposes of PCT art 11(a)(iii)(c), it is sufficient if the name of the applicant is indicated in a way that allows his identity to be established, even if the name is misspelled or the given names are not fully indicated or, in the case of legal entities, the indication of the name is abbreviated or incomplete. PCT Regulations, r 20.1(b).

[97] PCT, arts 3(2), 5.

[98] PCT, arts 3(2), 6.

[99] This is contrary to the Patent Law Treaty's art 5(1)(iii) provision that filing of 'a part which on the face of it appears to be a description' should be sufficient. See Mulder, 'Filing Date Requirements' (n 11), Part 5.3.

no provision for filing an international application by 'reference to a previously filed application'.[100] In other words, if the international application does not comply with the requirements of Article 11(1), an international filing date will not be accorded; instead, the receiving office will invite the applicant to file the required corrections.[101] If the applicant does not in due time file the necessary corrections, the application will not be dealt with as an international application.[102] [103]

Where the receiving office, after according the international filing date, finds that parts of the description, claims or drawings are, or appear to be, missing, it notifies the applicant accordingly and invites the applicant to correct the defect or else, where appropriate, to confirm that the missing part was 'incorporated by reference' under rule 4.18.[104] [105] Alternatively, if the applicant, by his own initiative, notices and wishes to correct the defect, this is also permitted if undertaken within two months from the date on which the receiving office first received the application.[106] If the applicant furnishes the missing parts within the two-month window, the date of their receipt becomes the international filing date.[107] If, however, the applicant is able to confirm that the missing part concerned was 'incorporated by reference' under rule 4.18, it may be possible for the applicant to retain the earlier date as the international filing date.[108] An international application with a valid international filing date has the effect of a regular national application in each designated

---

[100] Article 5(7)(a) of the Patent Law Treaty prescribes that 'a reference, made upon the filing of the application … to a previously filed application shall, for the purposes of the filing date of the application, replace the description and any drawings'. See Mulder, 'Filing Date Requirements' (n 11), Part 5.5.

[101] PCT, art 11(2)(a); PCT Regulations, r 20.3.

[102] PCT Regulations, r 20.4.

[103] National security prescriptions may also require a receiving office not to treat an international application as such. PCT, art 27(8); PCT Regulations, r 22.1; WIPO, 'International Guide' (n 8) para 6.010.

[104] PCT Regulations, r 20.6.

[105] The time limit for furnishing such missing parts is two months from the date of the invitation. PCT Regulations, r 20.7.

[106] PCT Regulations, r 20.6.

[107] Where the international filing date has been corrected, the applicant may, in a notice submitted to the receiving office within one month from the date of mailing of the notification of later submitted parts (Form PCT/RO/126), request that the missing part be disregarded in order to preserve as the international filing date the date on which papers were first received and, where applicable, to retain the priority claim. PCT Regulations, r 20.5(e).

[108] WIPO, 'International Guide' (n 8) paras 6.025–6.031.

state and will be regarded equivalent to a regular national application within the meaning of the Paris Convention.[109]

After according an international filing date, the receiving office will verify the international application to determine whether it contains any of the following defects:[110]

- Missing signature;[111]
- Missing indications (name, address, nationality or residence) concerning the applicant;[112]
- Missing title;[113]
- Missing abstract;[114]
- Non-compliance with the prescribed physical requirements.[115]

If the international application does not comply with formal requirements, the receiving office will invite the applicant to file the necessary corrections.[116] In addition, the receiving office checks whether the prescribed fees have been paid within the prescribed periods.[117] If any fee is missing, the applicant will be invited to pay the missing amount, including a late-payment fee.[118] If the required corrections are not filed in due time or if the required fees have not been duly paid, the international application will be considered withdrawn.[119]

4.3 International Search

Each international application will be the subject of an international search[120] carried out by an International Searching Authority.[121] Each receiving office (except the International Bureau[122]) has specified the competent International Searching Authority (or Authorities) tasked with

---

109 PCT, art 11(3), (4).
110 PCT, art 14(1)(a).
111 PCT Regulations, rr 4.15, 26.2*bis*.2(a), 51*bis*.1(a)(vi).
112 PCT Regulations, rr 4.4, 4.5, 26.2*bis*, 51*bis*.1(a)(vii).
113 PCT Regulations, rr 4.3, 37, 44.2.
114 PCT Regulations, rr 8, 38, 44.2.
115 PCT Regulations, rr 11, 26.3.
116 PCT, art 14(1)(b); PCT Regulations, r 26.1, 26.2.
117 PCT, art 14(3); PCT Regulations, rr 27.1, 14, 15, 16.
118 PCT Regulations, r 16*bis*.
119 PCT, art 14(1)(b); PCT Regulations, r 29.1.
120 PCT, art 15(1).
121 PCT, art 16(1); WIPO, 'International Guide' (n 8) ch 7.
122 PCT Regulations, r 35.3(c).

searching international applications filed with each receiving office.[123] If several International Searching Authorities are competent, the applicant must indicate his or her preference in the request.[124] There are several International Searching Authorities operating under the PCT, including the United States Patent and Trademark Office and the European Patent Office.[125]

The purpose of the international search is to identify relevant prior art.[126] Prior art consists of everything made available to the public anywhere in the world by means of written disclosure prior to the international filing date.[127] The prior art also includes oral disclosure and prior use or disclosure at an exhibition when a written disclosure refers to it.[128] The international search is made on the basis of the claims, with due regard to the description and the drawings (if any).[129]

The applicant can request that the International Searching Authority take into account the results of an earlier search.[130] Additionally, the International Searching Authority must, to the extent possible, take into account the results of any earlier search if the earlier search was carried out by the same office.[131] If, however, the earlier search was carried out by another International Searching Authority or national/regional office, the International Searching Authority may choose whether it takes into account the results of the earlier search.[132] To the extent that the International Searching Authority takes such earlier search results into account, the International Searching Authority is obligated to reduce the search fee to the extent and under the conditions provided for in the agreement between the International Searching Authority and the International Bureau of WIPO.[133, 134]

---

123 PCT, art 16(2); PCT Regulations, r 35; WIPO, 'International Guide' (n 8) Annex C.

124 PCT Regulations, rr 4.1(b)(iv), 4.14*bis*.

125 WIPO, 'International Guide' (n 8) Annex D.

126 PCT, art 15(2); PCT Regulations, rr 33.1, 34.

127 PCT Regulations, r 33.1(a).

128 PCT Regulations, r 33.1(b).

129 PCT, art 15(3); PCT Regulations, r 33.3.

130 PCT Regulations, r 4.12.

131 PCT Regulations, r 41.1(i).

132 PCT Regulations, r 41.1(ii).

133 PCT, art 16(3)(b); PCT Regulations, r 16.3.

134 Agreements with the International Bureau of WIPO in relation to the functioning of International Searching and International Preliminary Examining Authorities under the PCT. WIPO, 'PCT Resources' (n 15).

An International Searching Authority may decide not to search an international application in relation to subject matter such as scientific and mathematical methods, plant or animal varieties, methods of doing business, methods for treatment of the human or animal body by surgery or therapy, and diagnostic methods.[135] In addition, if an International Searching Authority determines that the description, claims and drawings fail to comply with the prescribed requirements to such an extent that no meaningful search can be carried out,[136] the International Searching Authority will make up a declaration that no international search report will be established, the so-called 'declaration referred to in Article 17(2)(a)'.

If during international search, the International Searching Authority finds that the international application does not comply with the requirement of unity of invention, it will invite the applicant to pay additional fees.[137] There is a protest procedure if the applicant does not agree with the finding of the International Searching Authority.[138] The protest will be examined by a review body constituted in the framework of the International Searching Authority.[139] Where the review body finds that the protest is entirely justified, the protest fee will be refunded.[140]

The International Searching Authority establishes the international search report.[141] The international search report or the 'declaration referred to in Article 17(2)(a)' is sent to the applicant and to the International Bureau.[142] The International Bureau will publish the international search report in the language in which the international application is published.[143] If the international application is not published in English, the International Bureau prepares and publishes an English translation of the international search report.[144] If the international search report is not available at the time of completion of the technical preparations for international publication, the international search report will be published separately (a so-called 'A3 publication').[145]

---

135 PCT, art 17(2)(a)(i), (b); PCT Regulations, r 39.1.
136 PCT, art 17(2)(a)(ii).
137 PCT, art 17(3)(a); PCT Regulations, r 40.
138 PCT Regulations, r 40.1(ii).
139 PCT Regulations, r 40.2(c).
140 PCT Regulations, r 40.2(e).
141 PCT, art 18(1); PCT Regulations, r 42.1.
142 PCT, art 18(2); PCT Regulations, r 44.1.
143 PCT, art 21(3), (4); PCT Regulations, r 48.2.
144 PCT, art 18(3); PCT Regulations, r 45.1.
145 PCT, art 18(2); PCT Regulations, rr 44.1, 48.2(g).

At the same time that the International Searching Authority establishes the international search report, it will provide a written opinion.[146] The written opinion gives a preliminary, non-binding view on whether the claimed invention appears to be novel, to involve an inventive step and to be industrially applicable.[147] [148] The international search report, viewed alongside the written opinion, normally gives the applicant a useful assessment of the patentability of the applied-for invention. By studying both documents the applicant may thus come to an informed decision whether or not to enter the national/regional phase at the end of the international phase of the PCT process.

Together with the international search report, the written opinion is sent to the applicant and the International Bureau.[149] The written opinion is not published with the international search report; instead, it is kept confidential until the expiry of 30 months from the priority date.[150]

After receiving the international search report, the applicant is given an opportunity to amend the claims contained in the international application.[151] [152] The applicant may file a brief statement explaining the amendments.[153] The amendments to the claims may not go beyond the scope of disclosure in the international application as it was originally filed.[154] The amendments must be accompanied by replacement sheets for the complete set of claims as filed originally.[155] At the same time, the applicant must file a letter indicating the differences between the claims as filed and as amended. The applicant must also indicate the basis for the amendments.[156]

---

146 PCT Regulations, r 43*bis*.1(a).

147 PCT Regulations, r 43*bis*.1(a)(i).

148 According to a footnote in Article 27.1 of the TRIPS Agreement, the latter two conditions may be deemed to be synonymous with nonobvious and useful, respectively. Agreement on Trade-Related Aspects of Intellectual Property Rights (adopted 15 April 1994, entered into force 1 January 1996) 1869 UNTS 299 (TRIPS Agreement).

149 PCT Regulations, r 44.1.

150 PCT Regulations, r 44*ter*.1(a).

151 PCT, art 19(1). The description and drawings may not be amended.

152 Amendments to the claims under PCT art 19 are not allowed where the International Searching Authority has declared, under PCT art 17(2), that no international search report will be established. WIPO, 'International Guide' (n 8) para 9.004.

153 PCT, art 19(1); PCT Regulations, r 46.4.

154 PCT, art 19(2).

155 PCT Regulations, r 46.5(a).

156 PCT Regulations, r 46.5(b).

If the applicant does not file a request for an international preliminary examination, the written opinion of the International Searching Authority will be converted by the International Bureau into an international preliminary report on patentability (Part I of the PCT).[157] After the expiry of 30 months from the priority date, the International Bureau will communicate this report to the designated offices[158] and, at the same time, make it available for public inspection.[159]

The applicant also has the option to request, in addition to the main international search,[160] one or more supplementary international searches to be carried out by an International Searching Authority who has indicated its preparedness to carry out the supplementary international search.[161]

A supplementary search request must be submitted to the International Bureau within 19 months from the priority date.[162] In the supplementary search request, the applicant must designate the International Searching Authority tasked to carry out the supplementary international search.[163] A supplementary-search handling fee and the supplementary-search fee must be paid to the International Bureau.[164]

The supplementary international search report is transmitted to the applicant and to the International Bureau.[165] Unlike the main international search, no written opinion will be established with the supplementary international search report.[166] However, the supplementary international search report may contain explanations concerning citations of documents;[167] some Authorities regard these explanations as a written opinion.[168]

---

157 PCT Regulations, r 44*bis*.1; WIPO, 'International Guide' (n 8) para 7.031.

158 PCT Regulations, r 44*bis*.2.

159 PCT Regulations, r 44*ter*.1.

160 PCT, art 15(1).

161 PCT Regulations, rr 45*bis*.1, 45*bis*.9. See WIPO, 'International Guide' (n 8) Ch 8; WIPO, 'International Guide' (n 8) annex SISA. As of 1 March 2014, only a limited number of International Searching Authorities offer the supplementary international search service: Austria, the European Patent Office, Finland, the Russian Federation, Sweden and the Nordic patent office.

162 PCT Regulations, r 45*bis*.1.

163 PCT Regulations, r 45*bis*.1(b)(ii).

164 PCT Regulations, rr 45*bis*.2, 45*bis*.3.

165 PCT Regulations, r 45*bis*.8(a).

166 WIPO, 'International Guide' (n 8) para 8.049.

167 PCT Regulations, r 45*bis*.7(e).

168 The scope of a supplementary international search by the European Patent Office is the same as the scope of the 'main' international search performed by

4.4 International Publication

The International Bureau publishes the international application promptly after the expiration of 18 months from the priority date,[169] unless the applicant requests earlier publication.[170] [171] The publication is governed by rule 48 and takes place entirely in electronic form.[172] As of 1 March 2014, languages of publication are Arabic, Chinese, English, French, German, Japanese, Korean, Portuguese, Russian or Spanish.[173] If the international application is filed in one of these languages, it will be published in the same language.[174] If the international application is published in a language other than English, English translations of the title, the abstract and the international search report (or the 'declaration referred to in Article 17(2)(a)') will be prepared under the responsibility of the International Bureau and included in the published international application.[175] There will be no international publication if the international application is withdrawn or considered withdrawn before the technical preparations for publications have been completed.[176] [177]

An interesting feature of the PCT is that, after publication of the international application, third parties may submit 'observations'. These 'observations' identify prior art that the submitting party believes to be

---

the European Patent Office. Although no separate written opinion is established, the European Patent Office provides explanations under rule 45*bis*.7(e), which are equal in value to written opinions provided by the European Patent Office as International Searching Authority. 'Notice from the European Patent Office Dated 24 March 2010 Concerning the Carrying Out of Supplementary International Searches Under the PCT' [2010] Official J EPO 316, pt 6.

169 PCT, art 21(1); WIPO, 'International Guide' (n 8) ch 9.

170 PCT, art 21(2)(a); PCT Regulations, r 48.4.

171 The International Bureau charges a fee if the applicant requests early publication where the international search report or the declaration under PCT art 17(2)(a) is not available for publication with the international application. PCT Regulations, r 48.4(a); WIPO, 'International Guide' (n 8) annex B2.

172 WIPO, 'International Guide' (n 8) paras 9.012–9.016.

173 PCT Regulations, r 48.3(a).

174 PCT Regulations, r 48.3(a).

175 Where applicable, the International Bureau also prepares French translations of the title and the abstract. WIPO, 'International Guide' (n 8) para 9.017.

176 PCT, art 21(5); PCT Regulations, r 90*bis*.1(c).

177 The technical preparations for publication are completed by the 15th day prior to the date of publication. WIPO, 'International Guide' (n 8) para 9.017. The notice of withdrawal of the international application may state that the withdrawal is to be effective only on the condition that international publication can still be prevented. WIPO, 'International Guide' (n 8) para 11.049.

relevant to the question of whether the invention claimed in the international application is novel and involves an inventive step.[178]

4.5 International Preliminary Examination

The international application may be subjected to an international preliminary examination (under Chapter II of the PCT) in order to obtain a preliminary, non-binding opinion on whether the claimed invention appears to be novel, to involve an inventive step (i.e., is nonobvious) and to be industrially applicable (i.e., useful).[179] The international preliminary examination is carried out by an International Preliminary Examining Authority upon the request – referred to in Article 31(1) of the PCT as 'demand' – of the applicant. Each receiving office has specified the International Preliminary Examining Authority or Authorities that are competent to carry out international preliminary examination.[180] The usefulness of international preliminary examination has been greatly diminished since the time limits for entry into the national/regional phase have been equalized independently of whether an applicant filed a demand for such an examination.[181] Therefore, the procedure is only very briefly described here.

The 'demand' must be filed within the later of three months from transmittal of the international search report to the applicant or 22 months from the priority date.[182]

The filing of a demand constitutes the 'election' of all PCT Contracting States designated in the international application.[183] It is subject to the payment of a handling fee and the preliminary examination fee.[184] If the

---

[178] WIPO, 'International Guide' (n 8) paras 11.109–11.117.

[179] PCT, art 33(1); WIPO, 'International Guide' (n 8) Ch 10.

[180] PCT, art 32(3); PCT Regulations, r 63; WIPO, 'International Guide' (n 8) annex E.

[181] Effective 1 April 2001, the time limit for entry into the national/regional phase before designated Offices under PCT Article 22(1) was changed from 20 months to 30 months. This time limit is therefore the same as the 30-month time-limit for entry into the national/regional phase before elected Offices under PCT Article 39(1)(a). The number of demands for international preliminary examination were: 81,091 in 2001; 64,908 in 2003; 25,861 in 2005; 19,501 in 2007; 15,258 in 2009, 13,703 in 2011 and 10,652 in 2012. WIPO, 'PCT Yearly Review' (n 64).

[182] PCT Regulations, r 54*bis*.1; WIPO, 'International Guide' (n 8) para 10.010.

[183] PCT, art 31(4); PCT Regulations, r 53.7.

[184] PCT, art 31(5); PCT Regulations, rr 67, 58.

applicant does not pay these fees, the International Preliminary Examining Authority will invite the applicant to pay the missing amount, including a late-payment fee.[185] If the applicant fails to pay the required fees in due time, the demand will be deemed not to have been submitted.[186]

The international preliminary examination is based on the international application, including any amendments filed after receiving the international search report[187] or filed concurrently with the demand.[188] In this stage of the PCT process, the applicant has the right to amend the claims as well as the description and the drawings.[189] Amendments made after the applicant files the demand are also taken into account for purposes of the international preliminary examination; they need not be taken into account, however, for purposes of the international preliminary report on patentability (Chapter II of the PCT) if they are received after the International Preliminary Examining Authority has begun to draw up that opinion or report.[190]

If, during an international preliminary examination, the International Preliminary Examining Authority finds that the international application does not comply with the requirement of unity of invention, it may invite the applicant to restrict the claims or to pay additional fees.[191] There is a protest procedure if the applicant does not agree with the finding of the International Preliminary Examining Authority.[192]

The written opinion of the International Searching Authority[193] will be regarded as the first written opinion of the International Preliminary Examining Authority.[194, 195] The International Preliminary Examining

---

185 PCT Regulations, rr 58*bis*.1(a), 58*bis*.2.

186 PCT Regulations, r 58*bis*.1(b).

187 PCT, art 19.

188 PCT, art 34(2)(b).

189 PCT Regulations, r 66.1(b), (d).

190 PCT Regulations, r 66.4*bis*.

191 PCT, art 24(3)(a); PCT Regulations, r 68.1, 68.2.

192 PCT Regulations, r 68.2(v), 68.3(e).

193 PCT Regulations, r 43*bis*.1.

194 PCT Regulations, rr 66.1*bis*, 43*bis*.1(c).

195 Only the European Patent Office as International Preliminary Examining Authority has made a reservation under rule 66.1*bis*(b) to the extent that it will accept the written opinion of the International Searching Authority as a written opinion of the International Preliminary Examining Authority only if that written opinion has been established by the EPO acting as International Searching Authority. See WIPO, 'PCT Reservations' (n 13).

Authority is not obligated to issue a written opinion of its own.[196] [197] The applicant may respond to the written opinion by filing amendments and/or arguments.[198] In addition, the applicant may communicate informally with the examiner (for example, via a personal interview over the telephone).[199]

The International Preliminary Examining Authority establishes the international preliminary examination report.[200] This report is also referred to as the 'international preliminary report on patentability (Chapter II of the PCT)'[201] and will be transmitted to the applicant and the International Bureau.[202] After the expiry of 30 months from the priority date, the International Bureau will communicate the report to the elected offices[203] and, at the same time, make it available for public inspection.[204]

5. THE NATIONAL (OR REGIONAL) PHASE

The time limit for entering the national/regional phase before a national/regional office is set by the PCT at 30 months from the priority date. It is no longer dependent on whether the applicant filed a demand for international preliminary examination (Article 22(1) in respect of designated Offices or Article 39(1)(a) in respect of elected offices).[205] The

---

196 PCT Regulations, rr 66.4, 66.2.

197 The European Patent Office acting as International Preliminary Examining Authority issues one additional written opinion. 'Notice from the European Patent Office Dated 31 August 2011 Concerning the Issuance of a Second Written Opinion in the Procedure Under Chapter II PCT' [2011] Official J EPO 532–5.

198 PCT, art 34(3)(a); PCT Regulations, rr 66.3, 66.5, 66.8.

199 PCT Regulations, rr 66.6.

200 PCT, art 35.

201 PCT Regulations, r 70.15.

202 PCT, art 36; PCT Regulations, r 71.

203 PCT, art 36(3)(a); PCT Regulations, r 73.2.

204 PCT, art 38(1); PCT Regulations, r 94; WIPO, 'International Guide' (n 8) para 10.080.

205 WIPO, 'International Guide' (n 8) paras 5.006, 10.050. A few designated States have notified the International Bureau that the current 30-month time limit under art 22(1) is incompatible with their national law. However the 31-month time limit of art 22(3) applies in respect of these designated offices. See WIPO, 'PCT Reservations' (n 13).

national law of a PCT Contracting State may fix longer time limits.[206] On the express request of the applicant, the national phase may be started earlier.[207]

Shortly before the end of the international phase, the International Bureau will communicate the international application and the international search report to each designated office.[208] Where required by the designated office, the communication will include the translation of the international search report.[209] If the applicant in the international phase did not file a demand for international preliminary examination, the International Bureau will also transmit the 'international preliminary report on patentability (Chapter I of the PCT)' to the designated offices after expiry of 30 months from the priority date.[210] Any designated office may request an English translation of the report.[211]

If the applicant in the international phase requested international preliminary examination, the International Bureau will communicate the international application and the international search report to each elected office.[212] In addition, the 'international preliminary report on patentability (Chapter II of the PCT)' will be transmitted to the elected offices 30 months after the priority date.[213]

The national phase starts only if the applicant performs certain acts in due time. The applicant should not expect a notification inviting him to perform these acts. As a reminder, the International Bureau, shortly before the end of the international phase, will inform the applicant about the designated or elected States.[214] In addition, some offices issue reminders.[215] However, failure to timely comply with the requirements for entry into the national phase in any PCT State will result in the international application no longer having the effect of a regular national application. The result will be the same as withdrawal of a national

---

206 PCT, arts 22(3), 39(1)(b); WIPO, 'International Guide' (n 8) para 5.006; WIPO, 'Time Limits for Entering National/Regional Phase under PCT Chapters I and II' (21 January 2014) <http://www.wipo.int/pct/en/texts/time_limits.html> accessed 18 November 2014.

207 PCT, arts 23(2), 40(2).

208 PCT, art 20(1)(a); PCT Regulations, r 47.1.

209 PCT, art 20(1)(b); PCT Regulations, rr 47.1(d), 45.1.

210 PCT Regulations, r 44*bis*.2; WIPO, 'International Guide' (n 8) 7.031.

211 PCT Regulations, r 44*bis*.3.

212 PCT, art 39(1)(a); PCT Regulations, r 76.5.

213 PCT, art 36(3)(a); PCT Regulations, r 73.

214 PCT Regulations, rr 47.1(c), 61.3.

215 WIPO, 'National Guide' (n 19) para 3.003.

application in that State.[216] The designated or elected office may invite the applicant to remedy the failure using any provisions available in the national law in respect of that office.[217]

Entry into the national/regional phase before a designated/elected office requires the applicant to carry out the acts prescribed in the PCT.[218] In addition, the applicant is required to fulfill additional requirements set by each designated/elected offices. Before the expiry of the period for entering the national phase, the applicant must pay the national fee to each designated/elected office.[219] The national fee is usually split into a number of fees as prescribed by the national/regional laws and regulations.[220] In addition, a designated/elected office may require that the applicant provide a translation of the international application in a language accepted by that office.[221]

At the start of the national/regional phase, each designated/elected office must give the applicant at least one opportunity to amend the description, claims and drawings.[222] The amendments may not go beyond the disclosure of the originally filed international application.[223] The amendments may, however, take a different form depending on the national/regional law.[224]

Most designated/elected offices regard the results of the international search as insufficient for starting substantive examination of the application. Therefore, they perform a supplementary national/regional search for which the applicant must pay a separate search fee.[225] The designated/elected offices use the international preliminary report on

---

216 PCT, arts 24(1)(iii), 39(2).

217 PCT, arts 24(2)), 39(3).

218 PCT, arts 22(1)), 39(1)(a).

219 PCT, arts 22(1), 39(1)(a); PCT Regulations, rr 49.1(a)(ii), 76.5.

220 WIPO, 'National Guide' (n 19) 22–1073.

221 PCT Regulations, rr 49.2, 49.5, 76.5.

222 PCT, arts 28(1), (3), 41(1), (3); PCT Regulations, rr 52.1, 78.1.

223 PCT, arts 28(2), 41(2).

224 Once processing of an international application has started in the national phase, the designated/elected office applies its national laws and regulations on matters such as the requirement that the applicant be represented by an agent before the designated/elected Office. PCT, art 27(7); PCT Regulations, r 51*bis*.1(b).

225 This does not apply to those designated or elected offices that are only registration offices and that do not have the capacity to examine the application substantially. These offices process the application based on the content of the international preliminary report on patentability established during the international phase.

patentability established during the international phase as a mere starting point for their own work. Most designated/elected offices will only start the substantive examination of the application when the applicant so requests (and pays an applicable fees).[226] Upon such request and payment of applicable fees, the national/regional offices examine the application and grant or refuse the national/regional patent on the basis of the patentability criteria in their national laws.[227]

6. CONCLUSION

The PCT offers a number of advantages to the applicant. By the single act of filing an international application under the PCT, protection is sought in more than 145 countries. Before the applicant goes to the effort and expense of having translations prepared, paying the national or regional fees and appointing agents in the various countries, he obtains the international search report accompanied by the written opinion of the International Searching Authority. Further information may be gathered by requesting the establishment of a supplementary international search report or an international preliminary report on patentability (PCT Chapter II). These documents combined with the longer time the applicant has for making decisions (at least 30 months from the priority date) allow him to estimate the chances of obtaining protection. A favorable international preliminary report on patentability under either Chapter I or II, may speed up the subsequent the granting procedure before the national and regional patent offices.

---

[226] The applicant need not pay the examination fee to the USPTO as designated/elected office where the written opinion was prepared by the USPTO as International Searching Authority or where the international preliminary report on patentability (Chapter II of the PCT) was prepared by the USPTO as International Preliminary Examining Authority. See WIPO, 'National Guide' (n 19) 985–1044. The examination fee to be paid by the applicant to the European Patent Office (EPO) as elected office is reduced by 50 percent where the international preliminary report on patentability (Chapter II of the PCT) has been established by the EPO. See WIPO, 'National Guide' (n 19) 305–40. Some designated/elected offices give the applicant a reduction in the examination fee depending on any acts performed by that office during the international phase.

[227] PCT, art 27(5).

PART IV

TRADEMARKS AND RELATED ISSUES

11. Reconciling trademark rights and free expression locally and globally

Lisa P. Ramsey[*]

I. INTRODUCTION

There is a growing consensus that domestic and international trademark laws must be revised to better protect the right to freedom of expression.[1] Trademark rights have expanded in many ways, and there is significant

* I am grateful for helpful comments from Margaret Chon, Deven Desai, Daniel Gervais, Leah Chan Grinvald, Michael Handler, Justin Hughes, Molly Land, Herbert Lazerow, Jacqueline Lipton, Mark McKenna, David Owen, Ole-Andreas Rognstad, Elizabeth Rosenblatt, Jennifer Rothman, Martin Senftleben, Rebecca Tushnet, David Welkowitz, and the participants of the Second International Intellectual Property Scholars Roundtable at the University of San Diego School of Law, the Thirteenth Intellectual Property Scholars Conference at Cardozo Law School, the faculty workshop at the University of San Diego School of Law, and the 32nd Annual Congress of the International Association for the Advancement of Teaching and Research in Intellectual Property at the University of Oxford.

[1] For example, see the discussion and sources cited in Rochelle Cooper Dreyfuss, 'Reconciling Trademark Rights and Expressive Values: How To Stop Worrying and Learn To Love Ambiguity' in Graeme B Dinwoodie and Mark D Janis (eds), *Trademark Law and Theory: A Handbook of Contemporary Research* (Edward Elgar 2008) 261–7; Annette Kur and Henning Grosse Ruse-Kahn, 'Enough Is Enough – The Notion of Binding Ceilings in International Intellectual Property Protection' in Annette Kur and Marianne Levin (eds), *Intellectual Property Rights in a Fair World Trade System: Proposals for Reform of TRIPS* (Edward Elgar Publishing 2011) 359–407; William McGeveran, 'The Trademark Fair Use Reform Act' (2010) 90 *Boston U L Rev* 2267, 2298–320; Lisa P Ramsey, 'Increasing First Amendment Scrutiny of Trademark Law' (2008) 61 *Southern Methodist U L Rev* 381, 404–57; Lisa P Ramsey and Jens Schovsbo, 'Mechanisms for Limiting Trade Mark Rights to Further Competition and Free Speech' (2013) 44 *Intl Rev Intellectual Property & Competition L* 671, 672–4, 690–6; Wolfgang Sakulin, *Trademark Protection and Freedom of Expression: An Inquiry into the Conflict Between Trademark Rights and Freedom of Expression under European Law* (Kluwer Law International 2011) 1–20, 181–351. See also the sources cited in n 24.

uncertainty regarding what types of unauthorized third-party uses of marks are allowed. The lack of clear trademark defenses or safe harbors for expression incorporating the trademarks of others can chill communicative uses of marks by critics, commentators, artists, news reporters, legitimate competitors and other third parties.[2] It can also lead to government restrictions of protected expression in trademark litigation via court injunctions that ban the use of another's trademarked language.[3] In addition, the risk of contributory trademark liability for Internet companies such as Facebook creates incentives for these private entities to prohibit certain unauthorized uses of marks on their websites, remove allegedly infringing content, and suspend or terminate the accounts of users who are accused of repeat trademark violations.[4] Expression incorporating another's mark is less likely to be stifled by judges or private parties applying trademark law if governments enact more speech-protective trademark laws and provide better guidance at the local and global level on what third-party uses of marks are permissible.

Such reforms would not violate international obligations to protect trademarks required by the Agreement on Trade-Related Aspects of Intellectual Property Rights (TRIPS) and Paris Convention for the Protection of Industrial Property (Paris Convention).[5] While these international agreements contain rules that contracting states must follow,

---

[2] Graeme B Dinwoodie, 'Lewis & Clark Law School Ninth Distinguished IP Lecture: Developing Defenses in Trademark Law' (2009) 13 *Lewis & Clark L Rev* 99, 101–2, 126–52; McGeveran (n 1) 2271, 2299–320.

[3] Mark A Lemley and Eugene Volokh, 'Freedom of Speech and Injunctions in Intellectual Property Cases' (1998) 48 *Duke LJ* 147, 216–24; Ramsey (n 1) 404–47. This chapter does not address whether the right to freedom of expression is harmed when governments refuse to register or protect certain signs as trademarks. For a discussion of this issue, see Jonathan Griffiths, 'Is There a Right to an Immoral Trade Mark' in Paul LC Torremans (ed.), *Intellectual Property and Human Rights* (Kluwer Law International 2008) 309, 322–33.

[4] Lisa P Ramsey, 'Brandjacking on Social Networks: Trademark Infringement by Impersonation of Markholders' (2010) 58 *Buffalo L Rev* 851, 857, 867–8. For scholarship about contributory trademark liability, see the sources cited in n 157.

[5] Paris Convention for the Protection of Industrial Property (adopted 20 March 1883, as revised at Stockholm 14 July 1967) 828 UNTS 305 (Paris Convention); Agreement on Trade-Related Aspects of Intellectual Property Rights (adopted 15 April 1994, entered into force 1 January 1996) 1869 UNTS 299 (TRIPS Agreement). While other international agreements also regulate trademarks – see, for example, the Anti-Counterfeiting Trade Agreement (adopted 3 December 2010) (2011) 50 ILM 243 – this chapter focuses on TRIPS and the Paris Convention because violations of obligations in these international

they are also sufficiently flexible to allow states to protect the public interest in free expression in their domestic trademark laws.[6] Unfortunately, some countries have not taken advantage of this flexibility to limit intellectual property rights to protect the public interest. Instead they have entered into bilateral or regional free trade agreements providing for more extensive protection of intellectual property than is required by TRIPS ('TRIPS-plus' protection).[7] In response, some scholars have proposed that the World Trade Organization (WTO) members amend TRIPS to add mandatory defenses and other binding ceilings on intellectual property protection, and thereby discourage the adoption of TRIPS-plus laws.[8] Despite its benefits, such an amendment to TRIPS may be politically difficult to achieve today.[9] It may be easier to limit intellectual property rights at the national or regional level due to the time it would take to amend TRIPS, and because of disagreement today about the proper scope of trademark rights and the right to freedom of expression.

This chapter argues that states and free speech advocates should currently focus their efforts on developing a global 'soft law' instrument that contains specific, speech-protective model trademark laws that clarify how states can protect expressive interests in domestic trademark

---

agreements can be enforced through the WTO Dispute Settlement System and a significant number of states are members of the WTO and parties to the Paris Convention.

[6] Lisa P Ramsey, 'Free Speech and International Obligations to Protect Trademarks' (2010) 35 *Yale J Intl L* 405, 412–44. As of this writing, there are 160 members of the WTO and 176 parties to the Paris Convention. 'Understanding the WTO: the Organization' World Trade Organization <http://www.wto.org/english/thewto_e/whatis_e/tif_e/org6_e.htm> accessed 26 June 2014; 'Paris Convention for the Protection of Industrial Property' WIPO <http://www.wipo.int/treaties/en/ShowResults.jsp?lang=en&treaty_id=2> accessed 16 October 2014.

[7] Marianne Levin, 'The Pendulum Keeps Swinging–Present Discussions On and Around the TRIPS Agreement' in Kur and Levin (n 1) 3, 18–9, 35; Peter K Yu, 'Currents and Crosscurrents in the International Intellectual Property Regime' (2004) 38 *Loyola Los Angeles L Rev* 323, 392–400.

[8] Kur and Grosse Ruse-Kahn, 'Enough Is Enough – The Notion of Binding Ceilings in International Intellectual Property Protection' (n 1) 359, 360–6, 401–2. For the proposed amended text and explanatory memorandum, see Kur and Levin, *Intellectual Property Rights in a Fair World Trade System: Proposals for Reform of TRIPS* (n 1) 455–606.

[9] Graeme B Dinwoodie and Rochelle C Dreyfuss, *A Neofederalist Vision of TRIPS: The Resilience of the International Intellectual Property Regime* (OUP 2012) 179–81; Ramsey (n 6) 460–7.

laws without violating their international obligations to protect trademarks.[10] These guidelines could be developed in the World Intellectual Property Organization (WIPO) or another forum in a manner similar to the Joint Recommendation Concerning Provisions on the Protection of Well-Known Marks. The Joint Recommendation on Well-Known Marks was the first implementation of the WIPO's policy to accelerate the development of international harmonized common principles in intellectual property law, and it attempted to clarify the international obligations relating to protection of well-known trademarks.[11] Like that Joint Recommendation, the speech-protective model trademark laws could include examples of different types of specific language that states can adopt and still comply with their obligations under TRIPS and the Paris Convention. The goal would be to encourage decision-makers to consider how the unreasonable expansion of trademark protection can harm the public interest, and provide states with the tools to reconcile trademark rights and free expression in their domestic trademark legislation, regulations, and litigation. States would have the flexibility to experiment and

---

[10] In the copyright area, Bernt Hugenholtz and Ruth Okediji have proposed that states create a global 'soft law' instrument that sets forth possible exceptions and limitations to copyright that comply with the treaty obligations of the current international copyright system. P Bernt Hugenholtz and Ruth Okediji, *Conceiving an International Instrument on Limitations and Exceptions to Copyright* (2008), available at <http://www.ivir.nl/publications/hugenholtz/limitations_exceptions_copyright.pdf>, accessed 24 June 2014.

[11] The Assembly of the Paris Union for the Protection of Industrial Property and the General Assembly of the World Intellectual Property Organization, 'Joint Recommendation Concerning Provisions on the Protection of Well-Known Marks' (29 September 1999) WIPO Doc. 833(E) (Joint Recommendation on Well-Known Marks). For more details, see the discussion in Part III.B.3. Compared to the WTO, the WIPO can be more responsive to changing circumstances because, among other things, it 'has restructured its norm development process to enable it to respond expeditiously to new issues through the adoption of soft law instruments.' Graeme B Dinwoodie and Rochelle C Dreyfuss, 'Designing a Global Intellectual Property System Responsive to Change: The WTO, WIPO, and Beyond' (2009) 46 *Hous L Rev* 1187, 1193–5, 1214–33. See also Margaret Chon, 'Global Intellectual Property Governance (Under Construction)' (2011) 12 *Theoretical Inquiries in the Law* 349, 351–3, 369–71. While the WIPO's contributions to intellectual property lawmaking have tended to promote the protection of intellectual property rights, its institutional structure 'has always forced it to strike a balance between access and proprietary interests.' The WIPO has also recently renewed its commitment to a 'Development Agenda' and considered questions about overprotection of intellectual property rights. Dinwoodie and Dreyfuss, *supra*, at 1193–5, 1229.

select which speech-friendly trademark reforms work best given their domestic law and culture. Experimentation is better than harmonization in this area until more states agree on whether and how to protect expressive interests in trademark law. Among other advantages, it would be easier to negotiate a non-binding soft law agreement with possible limits on trademark rights. Importantly, the norms created could eventually evolve into a speech-protective amendment of TRIPS or a new 'hard law' treaty.[12]

After providing some background regarding the increasing conflict between trademark rights and free expression, this chapter demonstrates how the provisions of TRIPS and the Paris Convention enable states to protect expression in their trademark laws. It also sets forth a framework for the development of speech-protective model trademark laws relating to what is protectable subject matter in trademark law, the scope of rights, defenses, remedies, and secondary trademark liability. These guidelines could provide a useful 'menu' of options for legislators, trademark offices, and courts trying to balance the various rights and interests in trademark law.

II. TRADEMARK RIGHTS AND FREE EXPRESSION ARE INCREASINGLY IN CONFLICT

Trademarks are words, names, symbols, designs and other signs that help consumers identify and distinguish goods and services. Examples include 'Sony' for computers, 'Louis Vuitton' and the 'LV' monogram for handbags, 'Felfort' for chocolate, 'Stolichnaya' for vodka, 'Air India' for airline services, and the name 'McDonald's' and the golden arches logo for restaurant services. When a third party uses another's trademark without authorization, it may violate national laws regulating trademarks.[13] In the past, courts in trademark disputes primarily focused on preventing deceit and the illegitimate diversion of trade; they banned the

---

[12] Cf Hugenholtz and Okediji (n 10) 5. To increase the chance that this 'soft law' will eventually turn into hard law or become relevant in interpretation of the TRIPS provisions, states should strive for a significant degree of transparency, diversity of input by interested stakeholders (including civil society organizations), and endorsement of the recommendations by the members of the WIPO and WTO. Dinwoodie and Dreyfuss (n 11) 1226–7. See also Chon (n 11) 370–1.

[13] For examples of national trademark laws, see 15 USC ss 1051–1141n (US); Trade Marks Act 1994 (UK); Trade Marks Act 1995 (Cth) (Australia).

misleading use of a competitor's mark to pass off the third party's commercial goods as those of the markholder.[14] These trademark injunctions generally did not conflict with the right to freedom of expression because they restricted untruthful commercial expression – false or misleading statements that may cause confusion about the source or origin of trademarked goods sold in the marketplace.[15]

Today, trademark laws in many jurisdictions have expanded to cover unauthorized uses of marks in noncommercial expression and non-misleading commercial expression, not just misleading commercial expression.[16] For example, in the United States, trademark infringement liability can now be premised on use of another's mark to cause confusion about the source of political activities, as well as third-party uses of marks that are likely to cause confusion about the third party's affiliation, connection or association with the markholder, or the markholder's sponsorship or approval of the third party's goods, services or commercial activities.[17] Thus current trademark infringement law can restrict the use of trademarked language by companies selling dissimilar goods or services, and people who are only selling artistic or literary expression. Examples include trademark claims based on use of the 'Mutual of Omaha' mark and logo for insurance and financial services by a person selling 'Mutant of Omaha' T-shirts with an anti-nuclear message,[18] a filmmaker's use of the 'Dairy Queen' mark for restaurant services in the title of the film *Dairy Queens* about beauty pageants in

---

[14] Lionel Bently, 'From Communication to Thing: Historical Aspects of the Conceptualisation of Trade Marks as Property' in Dinwoodie and Janis, *Trademark Law and Theory* (n 1) 3, 6–15; Mark P McKenna, 'The Normative Foundations of Trademark Law' (2007) 82 *Notre Dame L Rev* 1839, 1841, 1849–96.

[15] Robert C Denicola, 'Trademarks as Speech: Constitutional Implications of the Emerging Rationales for the Protection of Trade Symbols' (1982) *Wisconsin L Rev* 158, 165–6; Ramsey, 'Increasing First Amendment Scrutiny of Trademark Law' (n 1) 383–4, 414–21.

[16] For a discussion of this expansion, see the sources cited in n 1 and n 24.

[17] *United We Stand America Inc v United We Stand America New York Inc* 128 F3d 86, 92-3 (2d Cir 1997) (holding the Lanham Act's 'use in commerce' language is not limited to profit-seeking uses of another's mark); 15 USC s 1125(a)(1). For more information about the US trademark laws discussed in this chapter, see Mary LaFrance, *Understanding Trademark Law* (2nd edn, Lexis Nexis 2009); J Thomas McCarthy, *McCarthy on Trademarks and Unfair Competition* (4th edn, West 2014).

[18] *Mutual of Omaha Insurance Co v Novak* 836 F2d 397, 398–403 (8th Cir 1987).

the Midwest,[19] and a humor magazine's use of the 'Michelob Dry' marks for beer in a fake magazine ad for 'Michelob Oily' beer with a message about water pollution.[20]

In addition, United States trademark law now protects famous marks from third-party uses in commerce that are likely to cause dilution of the mark by blurring or tarnishment, even where there is no confusion, competition or actual economic injury.[21] An example is Victor and Cathy Moseley's use of 'Victor's Secret' and 'Victor's Little Secret' for an adult novelty store in Kentucky that sold sex-related products, which the court found was likely to dilute the internationally known 'Victoria's Secret' mark for lingerie by creating an association that harms the reputation of the famous mark.[22] Companies can now also obtain trademark rights in descriptive terms ('Fish Fri' for batter used in frying fish) and slogans consisting of common phrases ('Fair & Balanced' for Fox News Network's news reporting services) if the mark has become distinctive – meaning that the term now identifies a single source of the product – due to extensive advertising and sales of the product under this mark.[23] These types of expansive trademark laws may harm free expression, competition, and other public interests because they do not limit application of trademark laws to misleading uses of marks in commercial expression.[24]

---

19 *American Dairy Queen Corp v New Line Productions* 35 FSupp2d 727, 730–5 (D Minn 1998). The film was later released under the title *Drop Dead Gorgeous.*

20 *Anheuser-Busch Inc v Balducci Publications* 28 F3d 769, 773–9 (8th Cir 1994).

21 15 USC s 1125(c)(1). The European Union has a similar law that prohibits certain uses of marks that take unfair advantage of a mark with a reputation. Council Directive 2008/95/EC of 22 October 2008 to approximate the laws of the member states relating to trade marks [2008] OJ L299/25 (EU Trade Mark Directive) art 5(2); Council Regulation (EC) 207/2009 of 26 February 2009 on the Community trade mark [2009] OJ L78/1 (EU Trade Mark Regulation) art 9(1)(c).

22 *Victoria's Secret Catalogue Inc v Moseley* 605 F3d 382, 387–90 (6th Cir 2010).

23 Lisa P Ramsey, 'Descriptive Trademarks and the First Amendment' (2003) 70 *Tennessee L Rev* 1095, 1110–21; Lisa P Ramsey, 'Intellectual Property Rights in Advertising' (2006) 12 *Michigan Telecommunications & Technology L Rev* 189, 195, 206–14.

24 For a discussion of United States law, see Margreth Barrett, 'Domain Names, Trademarks, and the First Amendment: Searching for Meaningful Boundaries' (2007) 39 *Connecticut Rev* 973, 975–8; Ann Bartow, 'Likelihood of Confusion' (2004) 41 *San Diego L Rev* 721, 724–816; Michael K Cantwell,

Moreover, the predominant theories justifying trademark rights today may not adequately protect expressive interests. Many commentators use an economic perspective of trademark law and argue that trademark

---

'Confusion, Dilution, and Speech: First Amendment Limitations on the Trademark Estate' (1997) 87 *Trademark Rep* 48, 53–76; Dreyfuss (n 1) 262–7; Rochelle Cooper Dreyfuss, 'Expressive Genericity: Trademarks as Language in the Pepsi Generation' (1990) 65 *Notre Dame L Rev* 397, 400–24; Alex Kozinski, 'Trademarks Unplugged' (1993) 68 *New York University L Rev* 960, 972–8; Mary LaFrance, 'No Reason To Live: Dilution Laws as Unconstitutional Restrictions on Commercial Speech' (2007) 58 *South Carolina L Rev* 709, 709–11; Mark A Lemley, 'The Modern Lanham Act and the Death of Common Sense' (1999) 108 *Yale LJ* 1687, 1697–713; Mark A Lemley and Mark P McKenna, 'Irrelevant Confusion' (2010) 62 *Stanford L Rev* 413, 414–6; Jacqueline D Lipton, *Internet Domain Names, Trademarks and Free Speech* (Edward Elgar Publishing 2010) 92–140; Jacqueline D Lipton, 'Commerce Versus Commentary: Gripe Sites, Parody, and the First Amendment in Cyberspace' (2006) 84 *Washington U L Rev* 1327, 1330–3; Glynn Lunney Jr, 'Trademark Monopolies' (1999) 48 *Emory LJ* 367, 371–3; McGeveran (n 1) 2268–72; William McGeveran, 'Rethinking Trademark Fair Use' (2008) 94 *Iowa L Rev* 49, 51–4; William McGeveran and Mark P McKenna, 'Confusion Isn't Everything' (2013) 89 *Notre Dame L Rev* 253, 254–74 ; Ramsey (n 1) 386–90; Ramsey (n 6) 407–8; Jennifer E Rothman, 'Initial Interest Confusion: Standing at the Crossroads of Trademark Law' (2005) 27 *Cardozo L Rev* 105, 106–14, 159–78; Rebecca Tushnet, 'Gone in Sixty Milliseconds: Trademark Law and Cognitive Science' (2008) 86 *Texas L Rev* 507, 510–1, 546–58, 561; Rebecca Tushnet, 'Trademark Law as Commercial Speech Regulation' (2007) 58 *South Carolina L Rev* 737, 744–56; Rebecca Tushnet, 'Truth and Advertising: The Lanham Act and Commercial Speech Doctrine' in Dinwoodie and Janis, *Trademark Law and Theory* (n 1) 294, 312–22; Eugene Volokh, 'Freedom of Speech and Intellectual Property: Some Thoughts After *Eldred*, *44 Liquormart*, and *Bartnicki*' (2003) 40 *Houston L Rev* 697, 732–9. For a discussion of how trademark law protects expressive interests in the US, see Pierre N Leval, 'Trademark: Champion of Free Speech' (2004) 27 *Columbia J L & Arts* 187, 188–210.

For a discussion of European law, see Christophe Geiger, 'Trade Marks and Freedom of Expression – The Proportionality of Criticism' (2007) 38 *Intl Rev Intellectual Property & Competition L* 317, 317–27; Christophe Geiger, '"Constitutionalising" Intellectual Property Law? The Influence of Fundamental Rights on Intellectual Property in the European Union' (2006) 37 *Intl Rev Intellectual Property & Competition L* 371; Andreas Rahmatian, 'Trade Marks and Human Rights' in Torremans (n 3) 335, 348–51; Ramsey and Schovsbo (n 1) 675–82; Sakulin (n 1) 25–180; Martin RF Senftleben, 'Keyword Advertising in Europe– How the Internet Challenges Recent Expansions of EU Trademark Protection' (2011) 27 *Connecticut J Intl Law* 39, 41–57; Katja Weckström, 'The Lawfulness of Criticizing Big Business: Comparing Approaches to the Balancing of Societal Interests Behind Trademark Protection' (2007) 11 *Lewis & Clark L Rev* 671, 672,

doctrines will increase social welfare if they focus on reducing consumer search costs and increasing incentives to maintain quality.[25] Others believe trademarks and the brand image are akin to property that should be protected from misappropriation and free riding due to the mark-holder's investment in advertising and sales of the trademarked products.[26] They note that many brands are valuable in themselves above and beyond their source-identifying function. These theoretical justifications for trademark law often ignore or discount free speech values, which further increases the risk that trademark laws will conflict with the right to freedom of expression.

Many countries shield expression from government regulation because a marketplace of ideas leads to the discovery of truth and because free expression is essential in a democratic society.[27] Offensive and unpopular

---

682–93. For a recent proposal for reform of European trademark law, see the Max Planck Institute for Intellectual Property and Competition Law, 'Study on the Overall Functioning of the European Trade Mark System' (15 February 2011) (MPI Study), <http://www.ip.mpg.de/files/pdf2/mpi_final_report.pdf> accessed 10 July 2014, which is discussed in Annette Kur, 'Evaluation of the Functioning of the EU Trademark System: the Trademark Study' in Christophe Geiger (ed.) *Constructing European Intellectual Property – Achievements and New Perspectives* (Edward Elgar Publications 2013) 123, 123–36.

[25] Stacey L Dogan and Mark A Lemley, 'Trademarks and Consumer Search Costs on the Internet' (2004) 41 *Houston L Rev* 777, 786–99; William M Landes and Richard A Posner, *The Economic Structure of Intellectual Property Law* (Harvard 2003) 166–209; William M Landes and Richard A Posner, 'Trademark Law: An Economic Perspective' (1987) 30 *J L & Economics* 265. While search costs theory may suggest certain principles for limiting trademark rights, Stacey L Dogan and Mark A Lemley, 'A Search-Costs Theory of Limiting Doctrines in Trademark Law' (2007) 97 *Trademark Rep* 1223, this theory has its critics. Mark P McKenna, 'A Consumer Decision-Making Theory of Trademark Law' (2012) 98 *Virginia L Rev* 67, 73–111; Jeremy N Sheff, 'Marks, Morals, and Markets' (2013) 65 *Stanford L Rev* 761, 765–8.

[26] Jerre B Swann and Theodore H Davis Jr, 'Dilution, an Idea Whose Time Has Gone; Brand Equity as Protectable Property, The New/Old Paradigm' (1994) 84 *Trademark Rep* 267, 267–70, 282–99. For a discussion and critique of Lockean labor-desert, natural rights, and moral rights theories of trademark law, see Robert G Bone, 'Hunting Goodwill: A History of the Concept of Goodwill in Trademark Law' (2006) 86 *Boston U L Rev* 547, 616–8; Mark A Lemley and Mark P McKenna, 'Owning Mark(et)s' (2010) 109 *Michigan L Rev* 137, 181–4; Sheff (n 25) 763–4, 768–87. For a discussion of how trademark law has failed to adapt to the rise of brands as true information resources, see Deven R Desai, 'From Trademarks to Brands' (2012) 64 *Florida L Rev* 981.

[27] For a detailed discussion, see Larry Alexander, *Is There a Right of Freedom of Expression?* (CUP 2005); Eric Barendt, *Freedom of Speech* (2nd edn,

speech, and even certain types of false speech, may be protected to give breathing space to truthful expression and create an environment that encourages the free flow of information and ideas.[28] Freedom of expression is considered a fundamental right in the constitutions of some countries, including Canada, Germany, Ireland, Japan, South Africa and the United States.[29] In Australia, New Zealand and the United Kingdom, there is no explicit constitutional right to freedom of expression, but free expression is still protected to varying degrees in judicial decisions and legislation.[30]

Some national courts invoke the constitutional right to freedom of expression when ruling in favor of defendants who used trademarks without authorization to criticize or parody the markholder. For example, a French court allowed a Greenpeace parody of Esso's logo on a website criticizing the oil company, and a German court held an anti-smoking organization could use the Marlboro marks in a parody of a Marlboro advertisement.[31] Other courts narrowly construe their domestic trademark laws to protect free expression, such as the South African court that declined to find trademark liability when a T-shirt manufacturer used the Carling Black Label marks for beer in a parody Black Labour beer label displayed on T-shirts.[32] In addition, some United States courts have required proof of commercial use of the mark for infringement liability

---

OUP 2007); Ronald J Krotoszynski, Jr, *The First Amendment in Cross-Cultural Perspective: A Comparative Legal Analysis of the Freedom of Speech* (NYU Press 2006); Sakulin (n 1) 130–48.

[28] *Snyder v Phelps* 131 S Ct 1207, 1219 (2011); *New York Times Co v Sullivan* 376 US 254, 270–3, 280 (1964).

[29] Constitution Act, 1982, pt. I (Canadian Charter of Rights and Freedoms), s 2(b); The Basic Law for the Federal Republic of Germany, art 5; Constitution of Ireland, art 40(6)(1); Constitution of Japan, art 21 para 1; The Constitution of South Africa, s 16; Constitution of the United States, amendment I. See also Krotoszynski (n 27) 1, 12, 26–51, 93–104, 139–45.

[30] *Lange v Australian Broadcasting Corp* (1997) 189 CLR 520; New Zealand Bill of Rights Act 1990, s 14; Human Rights Act (UK) 1998, s 12; ibid Sch 1, pt 1, art 10. See also Krotoszynski (n 27) 183–213.

[31] *Esso plc v Greenpeace France*, Cour d'Appel de Paris, Fourth Chamber, 16 November 2005, case 04/12417 [2006] ETMR 53; *Re the Parodying of Cigarette Advertising*, German Federal Supreme Court, 17 April 1984, VI ZR 246/82 [1986] ECC 1, 4–7.

[32] *Laugh It Off Promotions CC v South African Breweries International (Finance) BV t/a Sabmark International and the Freedom of Expression Institute* 2006 (1) SA 144 (CC).

because of concerns regarding the constitutionality of applying trademark law to noncommercial speech.[33]

At the international and regional level, human rights treaties require protection of the right to freedom of expression. One example is the International Covenant on Civil and Political Rights (ICCPR), which provides in Article 19(2) that 'the right to freedom of expression … shall include the freedom to seek, receive and impart information and ideas of all kinds, regardless of frontiers, either orally, in writing or in print, in the form of art, or through any other media of his choice'.[34] In Europe, the Convention for the Protection of Human Rights and Fundamental Freedoms (also known as the European Convention on Human Rights) states in Article 10(1) that: 'Everyone has the right to freedom of expression. This right shall include freedom to hold opinions and to receive and impart information and ideas without interference by public authority and regardless of frontiers'.[35] Similar language appears in Article 11 of the Charter of Fundamental Rights of the European Union,[36] and the American Convention on Human Rights.[37]

Importantly, invoking the right to freedom of expression in a trademark case does not automatically resolve the dispute, as the free speech right is not absolute. Some restrictions of expression are allowed if justified under applicable legal standards. For example, speech regulations are generally constitutional in the United States if the expression is categorically unprotected by the First Amendment (such as misleading commercial speech) or the regulation satisfies intermediate or strict scrutiny

---

33 *Utah Lighthouse Ministry v Foundation for Apologetic Information and Research* 527 F3d 1045, 1051–3 (10th Cir 2008); *Bosley Medical Institute Inc v Kremer* 403 F3d 672, 676–7 (9th Cir 2005); *Taubman Co v Webfeats* 319 F3d 770, 775, 778 (6th Cir 2003).

34 International Covenant on Civil and Political Rights (adopted 16 December 1966, entered into force 23 March 1976) 999 UNTS 171 (ICCPR) art 19(2). This treaty has 168 parties. 'United Nations Treaty Collection: International Covenant on Civil and Political Rights' <https://treaties.un.org/pages/ViewDetails.aspx?src=TREATY&mtdsg_no=IV-4&chapter=4&lang=en> accessed 10 July 2014.

35 Convention for the Protection of Human Rights and Fundamental Freedoms (opened for signature 4 November 1950, entered into force 3 September 1953) 213 UNTS 221 (ECHR) art 10(1).

36 Charter of Fundamental Rights of the European Union [2000] OJ C364/1 (Charter of Fundamental Rights) art 11.

37 American Convention on Human Rights (22 November 1969, entered into force 18 July 1978) OASTS No. 36, 1144 UNTS 123, art 13.

analysis.[38] In addition, Article 19(3) of the ICCPR states that the right to freedom of expression may 'be subject to certain restrictions ... [f]or respect of the rights or reputations of others' as long as the restrictions 'are provided by law and are necessary.' Similarly, Article 10(2) of the European Convention on Human Rights provides that the government may restrict speech 'for the protection of the reputation or rights of others' where that restriction is 'prescribed by law' and 'necessary in a democratic society.' According to the European Court of Human Rights, trademark rights are among the 'rights' covered by Article 10(2) and are property rights protected under Article 1 of the first protocol of the European Convention on Human Rights.[39] Yet, like the free speech right, intellectual property rights are not absolute rights.[40] States are therefore required to balance their constitutional, international and regional obligations to protect trademark rights against the right to freedom of expression.[41]

While constitutional laws and human rights treaties provide courts with an external mechanism for limiting trademark rights to further expressive interests, legislators can also internalize free speech principles within domestic and regional trademark laws.[42] Trademark statutes may enable courts to protect the right to freedom of expression on a case-by-case basis (the traditional approach in the United States), or set forth specific categorical limits on trademark rights that permit certain expressive uses

---

38 For more information on constitutional analysis in the US, see Ramsey (n 1) 412–47.

39 *Anheuser-Busch Inc v Portugal* App no 73049/01 (EctHR, 11 January 2007) paras 72–8. See also Laurence R Helfer, 'The New Innovation Frontier? Intellectual Property and the European Court of Human Rights' in Torremans (n 3) 25, 27–8, 43–5; Rahmatian (n 24) 335, 346–7.

40 Case C-70/10 *Scarlet Extended SA v Société Belge des auteurs, compositeurs et éditeurs SCRL* (SABAM) [2011] ECR I-nyr, para 43.

41 Ibid paras 44–45; Case C-275/06 *Productores de Música de España (Promusicae) v Telefónica de España SAU* [2008] ECR I-271, paras 65, 68. For a general discussion of normative and systemic adjustments needed to strike a more appropriate balance between intellectual property and human rights systems, see Peter K Yu, 'Intellectual Property and Human Rights in the Nonmultilateral Era' (2012) 64 *Florida L Rev* 1045, 1091–9.

42 Dreyfuss (n 1) 267–88; McGeveran (n 1) 2298–320; Ramsey (n 1) 447–53. For an argument against invoking the right to freedom of expression to constrain trademark rights, see Robert Burrell and Dev Gangjee, 'Trade Marks and Freedom of Expression: A Call for Caution' (2010) 41 *Intl Rev Intellectual Property & Competition L* 544.

of marks by third parties (the European Union's traditional approach).[43] Scholars have suggested various statutory and judicial reforms of trademark doctrine to better protect freedom of expression, competition and other public interests, including exclusions of certain subject matter from protection, limits on the scope of trademark rights, defenses, speech-protective trademark remedies, and revisions to secondary trademark liability provisions.[44]

This chapter proposes that we facilitate such reforms of trademark law across the globe by developing a set of specific, speech-protective model trademark laws that could be used by legislators, trademark offices, and courts interested in doing a better job of reconciling trademark rights and free expression. States could choose from this 'menu' of trademark laws that protect expressive uses of marks and determine what doctrines and specific statutory language work best for that country or region. Even though most countries protect the right to freedom of expression, the scope of this right varies. There is no global consensus on whether and how the government can regulate political speech, commercial speech, entertainment, erotica and other types of expression.[45] Until there is more agreement on the proper scope of trademark and free speech rights, it may be easier to achieve speech-protective reforms of trademark law at the domestic or regional level than to amend TRIPS to add global mandatory limits on trademark rights.

III. A FRAMEWORK FOR CREATING SPEECH-PROTECTIVE MODEL TRADEMARK LAWS THAT COMPLY WITH INTERNATIONAL OBLIGATIONS TO PROTECT TRADEMARKS

The TRIPS Agreement and Paris Convention contain minimum standards of protection for trademarks and other types of intellectual property.[46]

---

43 Ramsey and Schovsbo (n 1) 674–88.

44 See, for example, the sources cited in n 1 and 24.

45 Krotoszynski (n 27) 5, 214–22. See also Sakulin (n 1) 109–19, 149–75.

46 For detailed information about these international agreements, see GHC Bodenhausen, *Guide to Application of the Paris Convention for the Protection of Intellectual Property* (BIRPI 1968); Carlos M Correa, *Trade Related Aspects of Intellectual Property Rights* (OUP 2007); Carlos M Correa and Abdulqawi A Yusuf (eds), *Intellectual Property and International Trade: The TRIPS Agreement* (2nd edn, Kluwer Law International 2008); Daniel Gervais, *The TRIPS Agreement: Drafting History and Analysis* (4th edn, Sweet & Maxwell 2012); Stephen

The obligations in the agreements must be construed in a manner that considers the right to freedom of expression. The Vienna Convention on the Law of Treaties – which contains the customary rules of treaty interpretation used to clarify the meaning of the TRIPS and Paris Convention provisions – provides that 'any relevant rules of international law applicable in the relations between the parties' must be taken into account when interpreting the treaty language.[47] As trademark laws regulate expression, the relevant rules of international law include treaties protecting the right to freedom of expression.[48]

When interpreting the provisions of TRIPS and the Paris Convention, it is also important to note that TRIPS Articles 1.1, 7 and 8 reinforce the ability of WTO members to protect expressive interests in their trademark laws.[49] TRIPS Article 1.1 provides that WTO members may 'determine the appropriate method of implementing the provisions of this Agreement within their own legal system and practice.'[50] Daniel Gervais explains that this provision recognizes 'the flexibility of countries implementing TRIPS vis-à-vis their legal systems and practices,' and notes that states may 'develop their own law and policies within the framework established by the Agreement.'[51] Article 7 contains the 'Objectives' of TRIPS. Among other things, it provides that member states 'should' consider 'social and economic welfare' when protecting intellectual property rights and 'balance' these 'rights and obligations' against other relevant rights and obligations,[52] which would include the right to freedom of expression protected in human rights treaties. Protection of free speech values in trademark law can be conducive to 'social and economic

---

P Ladas, *Patents, Trademarks and Related Rights: National and International Protection* (Harvard UP 1975) 59–278, 965–1322.

47 Vienna Convention on the Law of Treaties (adopted 22 May 1969, opened for signature 23 May 1969) 1155 UNTS 331 (Vienna Convention) art 31(3)(c); Understanding on Rules and Procedures Governing the Settlement of Disputes (adopted 15 April 1994, entered into force 1 January 1995) 1869 UNTS 401 (Dispute Settlement Understanding) art 3(2). For information about the Dispute Settlement Understanding, see Dinwoodie and Dreyfuss (n 9) 49–82, 158–68.

48 Ramsey (n 6) 447–52. See also Neil W Netanel, 'The Next Round: The Impact of the WIPO Copyright Treaty on TRIPS Dispute Settlement' (1997) 37 *Virginia J Intl L* 441, 475–90.

49 Ramsey (n 6) 445–7. See also Dinwoodie and Dreyfuss (n 9) 75, 89–90, 110–2 (discussing these provisions); Peter Yu, 'The Objectives and Principles of the TRIPS Agreement' (2009) 46 *Hous L Rev* 979, 1000–18.

50 TRIPS Agreement, art 1.1.

51 Gervais (n 46) 174–6.

52 TRIPS Agreement, art 7.

welfare' when it promotes the free flow of ideas and truthful information while still protecting the ability of trademarks to identify and distinguish goods and services.[53]

Protection of the public interest is also allowed under Article 8, which contains the 'Principles' of TRIPS. Article 8 provides that members may 'adopt measures necessary … to promote the public interest in sectors of vital importance to their socio-economic and technological development' and 'prevent the abuse of intellectual property rights by right holders or the resort to practices which unreasonably restrain trade' as long as those measures are consistent with TRIPS.[54] While Article 8 does not allow states to ignore explicit provisions of the agreements, such as the prohibition on compulsory licensing of trademarks in TRIPS Article 21, states do have discretion to implement laws that promote free expression, fair competition and other public interests when the trademark obligations are narrow or the provisions contain language that is ambiguous or which explicitly permits consideration of the interests of third parties.[55] In 2001, the WTO members agreed in the WTO Declaration on the TRIPS Agreement and Public Health (also known as the 'Doha Declaration') that Articles 7 and 8 are relevant to interpretation of the TRIPS provisions. The Doha Declaration states that the substantive provisions of the TRIPS Agreement 'shall be read in the light of the object and purpose of the Agreement as expressed, in particular, in its objectives and principles.'[56]

If a WTO member fails to comply with its international obligations under TRIPS or Articles 1–12 and 19 of the Paris Convention (which are incorporated into TRIPS by TRIPS Article 2.1) the WTO's Dispute Settlement Understanding contains mechanisms for allowing a complaint to be filed against that member.[57] As of this writing, the state-to-state trademark disputes resolved by the WTO have not focused on a conflict between trademark rights and the right to freedom of expression.[58] States

---

[53] Ramsey (n 6) 446.

[54] TRIPS Agreement, art 8.

[55] Ramsey (n 6) 446–7.

[56] World Trade Organization, 'Declaration on the TRIPS Agreement and Public Health' (14 November 2001) WT/MIN(01)/DEC/2 [5(a)]. See also Dinwoodie and Dreyfuss (n 9) 38–9, 56, 81, 89, 110–2, 196.

[57] TRIPS Agreement, art 64; Dispute Settlement Understanding, arts 16(4), 17(14). See also Dinwoodie and Dreyfuss (n 9) 49–82; Joel P Trachtman, 'The Domain of WTO Dispute Resolution' (1999) 40 *Harvard Intl LJ* 333, 336–45.

[58] WTO Panel Report, *China: Measures Affecting the Protection and Enforcement of Intellectual Property Rights* (26 January 2009) WT/DS362/R

may therefore wonder whether and how they can amend their trademark laws to protect free speech rights without violating their obligations under TRIPS and the Paris Convention. As explained below, the language in the TRIPS and Paris Convention provisions is sufficiently flexible to give WTO members discretion to find the proper balance between trademark rights and free expression when complying with their international obligations to protect trademarks.[59]

In addition to highlighting the flexibilities in TRIPS and the Paris Convention, this section of the chapter also attempts to provide a framework for the development of speech-protective model trademark laws that would comply with TRIPS and the Paris Convention. When crafting this instrument (and the domestic trademark laws themselves), it is important to remember that the different choices made on the design of the trademark law will affect who has the burden of proof and could alter the balance of protection for trademarks and free speech.[60] In addition to considering whether limits on trademark rights should be implemented as rules or standards, countries must determine where in the structure of

(*China-Enforcement*); WTO Panel Report, *European Communities: Protection of Trademarks and Geographical Indications for Agricultural Products and Foodstuffs* (15 March 2005) WT/DS174/R (*European Communities-GI*) (complaint by the US); WTO Appellate Body Report, *United States: Section 211 Omnibus Appropriations Act of 1998* (2 January 2002) WT/DS176/AB/R (*United States-Section 211*).

[59] For a more detailed discussion, see Ramsey (n 6) 412–44. See also Dinwoodie and Dreyfuss (n 9) 24–6, 111, 192–3 (discussing the flexibility countries have when satisfying their obligations). Professors Dinwoodie and Dreyfuss reject the argument that TRIPS is a supranational code and conclude that 'member states retain significant discretion under TRIPS, but agree to operate within an international framework.' Dinwoodie and Dreyfuss (n 9) 5. But cf Gerald J Mossinghoff, 'National Obligations Under Intellectual Property Treaties: The Beginning of a True International Regime' (2000) 9 *Federal Circuit B J* 591, 603 (stating that TRIPS tells all countries '*what* they must do and *when* and *how* they must do it'); Yu (n 7) 442 (referring to TRIPS as a 'supranational code').

[60] McGeveran (n 1) 2268, 2291–7. In addition to categorical defenses and safe harbors for certain expressive uses of marks, McGeveran proposes that the US Congress enact a statutory provision that requires courts to apply a rebuttable 'presumption that uses of a mark are not likely to cause actionable confusion of consumers under this act if they primarily support communication of information, ideas or expression beyond merely proposing a commercial transaction,' including but not limited to nominative uses of marks and uses of marks in comparative advertising, for commentary, and to promote a communicative work. Ibid at 2319–20, Appendix, § 3(b).

trademark law to place these limitations. The party claiming trademark rights generally must prove it has a valid and protectable trademark and establish all of the elements of a trademark cause of action. The party accused of trademark violations usually has the burden to prove that an affirmative defense applies.

Professor Graeme Dinwoodie argues that states should conceive of trademark limits as affirmative defenses in order to ensure that courts consider the benefits of socially desirable third-party uses of marks, and not focus solely on confusion-avoidance or the harm caused by a particular third party's unauthorized use of the mark.[61] Yet if evidence is difficult to obtain on a particular issue, the party with the burden of proof may have a difficult time persuading the court or jury that it should prevail. Free speech values are generally better served if the burden of proof can reasonably be placed on the party seeking to restrict expression.[62] Given their international and constitutional obligations to protect the right to freedom of expression, states should consider adopting speech-protective trademark laws that place the burden of proof on the markholder. They could do this by excluding certain subject matter from trademark registration and protection, and conceptualizing some third-party uses of trademarks as outside the scope of trademark rights rather than as affirmative defenses. For example, states may refuse to register or protect trademark rights in descriptive terms, or require commercial use of the mark by the accused infringer as an element of an infringement claim.

The rest of this chapter sets forth the various ways that states can protect free expression and other public interests in trademark law. Among other things, states can (A) carve out exceptions to the subject matter that can be registered and protected as a trademark; (B) limit the scope of rights conferred by a trademark; (C) create more affirmative defenses and other exceptions to trademark rights; (D) give courts discretion to award speech-protective remedies in disputes involving expressive uses of marks, and provide remedies for innocent parties falsely accused of trademark violations; and (E) craft secondary trademark liability rules that discourage the private suppression of expression incorporating the trademarks of others without a fair hearing on the merits of the trademark dispute.

---

[61] Dinwoodie (n 2) 108–12.

[62] Ramsey (n 1) 425; Ramsey (n 6) 435–6.

A. Subject Matter That Can Be Registered and Protected as a Trademark

The TRIPS Agreement and Paris Convention give states significant discretion in how to administer their trademark systems. These agreements also allow states to promote the public interest by imposing limits on what qualifies as subject matter that can be registered and protected as a trademark.

The parties to the Paris Convention agreed in Article 6(1) of the Paris Convention that '[t]he conditions for the filing and registration of trademarks shall be determined in each country of the Union by its domestic legislation.' Paris Convention Article 6*quinquies*(A)(1) requires states to accept for filing and protect any trademark registered in the country of origin 'as it is', but this requirement is subject to the rules in Article 6*quinquies*. Among other things, Article 6*quinquies*(B) provides that countries 'may' deny registration of trademarks for signs that: (1) are 'devoid of any distinctive character' (non-distinctive signs such as a simple rectangle shape for a computer); (2) 'consist exclusively of signs or indications which may serve, in trade, to designate the kind, quality, quantity, intended purpose, value, place of origin, of the goods, or the time of production' (descriptive words such as 'speedy' for a computer); or (3) are 'customary in the current language or in the bona fide and established practices of the trade of the country where protection is claimed' (generic words such as 'computer' for a computer).[63] Importantly, these last two provisions expressly allow states to refuse to recognize trademark rights in descriptive and generic signs regardless of whether the words have acquired distinctiveness.[64]

---

[63] Paris Convention, art 6*quinquies*(B)(2). See also Bodenhausen (n 46) 114–6 (discussing these provisions). Countries may also deny registration where the mark would infringe rights previously acquired by third parties, or be contrary to morality or public order or be of such a nature as to deceive the public. Paris Convention, art 6*quinquies*(B)(1), (3). If states determine that certain subject matter cannot be registered as a trademark, Article 6*quinquies*(B) provides that they are still bound to provide protection against unfair competition by Article 10*bis* of the Paris Convention (which will be discussed later). Parties to the Paris Convention must also refuse registration and prohibit the unauthorized use of marks consisting of armorial bearings, flags, and other emblems of the contracting states and certain international intergovernmental organizations. Paris Convention, art 6*ter*.

[64] Ramsey (n 6) 416–20. Despite Article 6*quinquies*(C) of the Paris Convention – which provides: 'In determining whether a mark is eligible for protection, all the factual circumstances must be taken into consideration, particularly the

TRIPS incorporates these Paris Convention provisions,[65] and also contains additional rules regarding what can qualify as a trademark. Per TRIPS Article 15.1,

> Any sign, or any combination of signs, capable of distinguishing the goods or services of one undertaking from those of other undertakings, shall be capable of constituting a trademark. Such signs, in particular words including personal names, letters, numerals, figurative elements and combinations of colours as well as any combination of such signs, shall be eligible for registration as trademarks. Where signs are not inherently capable of distinguishing the relevant goods or services, Members may make registrability depend on distinctiveness acquired through use. Members may require, as a condition of registration, that signs be visually perceptible.

Thus TRIPS gives states the flexibility to register and protect trademark rights in signs that have acquired distinctiveness rather than inherent distinctiveness (such as descriptive words or product configurations), or in signs that are not visually perceptible (such as scents and sounds), but it does not require states to register or protect such marks.

Per TRIPS Article 15.2, member states may also refuse to register trademarks for reasons not set forth in Article 15.1 as long as the 'other grounds' for denial of trademark rights 'do not derogate from the provisions of the Paris Convention.' The 'other grounds' for refusal must be consistent with the Paris Convention, but note that WTO members are not limited to the grounds for rejection expressly set forth in the Paris Convention.[66] There is no indication that the contracting parties of the Paris Convention consented to be bound to register or protect as a trademark *anything* capable of carrying source-identifying meaning, such

---

length of time the mark has been in use' – states can categorically deny trademark protection to the types of signs listed in 6*quinquies*(B)(2) in trademark statutes and regulations, although trademark examiners must consider the trademark on its individual merits when refusing or invalidating the registration on the ground that it is devoid of distinctive character or is descriptive or generic in the country where protection is claimed. Bodenhausen (n 46) 115–6; Gervais (n 46) 320.

[65] TRIPS Agreement, art 2.1.

[66] *United States-Section 211* (n 58) para 155–9, 174–8 (discussing TRIPS Agreement, art 15.2). See also *European Communities-GI* (n 58) para 7.600; Correa (n 46) 177–80; Gervais (n 46) 320–1, 324; Ramsey (n 6) 416–20. But cf Bodenhausen (n 46) 114 (Article 6*quinques*(B)'s introductory language indicates the grounds for refusal 'are *limitative*' so states 'are therefore not free to apply *other* grounds for refusal or invalidation of the registration of *trademarks covered by the Article*.') (emphasis in original).

as culturally significant artistic and literary works in the public domain, informational language, functional three-dimensional product configurations, and other inherently valuable non-traditional trademarks used in connection with goods and services. States could argue it is therefore consistent with the Paris Convention to categorically deny trademark registration and protection to these types of subject matter to protect the public interest in free expression and fair competition, regardless of whether the sign is registered in other member states or has acquired distinctiveness.

It is clear that states have some discretion in how they implement their trademark obligations under Article 6(1) and Article 6*quinquies* of the Paris Convention and Article 15 of the TRIPS Agreement. Thus, speech-protective model trademark laws should acknowledge these flexibilities and clarify how states can protect expressive values by limiting what can qualify as protectable subject matter under trademark law.

1. Signs that are not distinctive, generic signs, and descriptive signs

Due to the language in Paris Convention Article 6*quinquies*(B)(2) and TRIPS Article 15.2,[67] speech-protective model trademark laws can give states the option to categorically refuse to register or protect trademark rights in signs that are devoid of any distinctive character, and in generic terms or descriptive terms regardless of whether they have become distinctive. Currently some jurisdictions (including the United States) refuse trademark rights in non-distinctive signs and generic terms, but allow registration and protection of descriptive terms as trademarks if they have acquired distinctiveness.[68]

---

[67] *United States-Section 211* (n 58) paras 165–78; Correa (n 46) 178–80; Gervais (n 46) 320-1; Ramsey (n 6) 416–20.

[68] For a discussion of the laws of various countries relating to refusals to register non-distinctive, generic, and descriptive signs, see WIPO's Committee on Development and Intellectual Property, 'Study on Misappropriation of Signs,' CDIP/9/INF/5 (14 March 2012), <http://www.wipo.int/edocs/mdocs/mdocs/en/cdip_9/cdip_9_inf_5.pdf> accessed 26 June 2014, which was prepared by Martin Senftleben and includes reports by intellectual property scholars from around the world. For US law, see 15 USC ss 1052(e)(1), (f), 1064(3); Ramsey, 'Descriptive Trademarks and the First Amendment' (n 23) 1097, 1110–24. In the European Union, states may refuse registration of marks that are devoid of distinctive character, descriptive, or customary, but these three grounds for refusal may be set aside if it can be shown that the sign has acquired a distinctive character. EU Trade Mark Directive, arts 2, 3; EU Trade Mark Regulation, arts 4, 7; Sakulin (n 1) 30–2.

If WTO members conclude (as I have) that granting and enforcing exclusive trademark rights in descriptive language can suppress the free flow of commercial information and harm competition,[69] they should refuse to register and protect trademark rights in descriptive signs regardless of whether they have acquired distinctiveness. This is the approach that is the most speech protective and pro-competitive, as it will allow all traders to use descriptive words to advertise and sell their products, including as part of their brand name, slogan, domain name, or username. It will also make it more difficult for established companies to bully new entrants in the marketplace, as no one company would be able to acquire trademark rights in descriptive language regardless of the extent of its advertising and sales. An alternative, moderately speech-protective trademark law would allow registration and protection of trademark rights in descriptive signs, but require strong proof that the mark has acquired distinctiveness. This would prevent companies from acquiring exclusive rights in descriptive language on a first-come, first-served basis. If this approach is used, states should also consider narrowing the scope of trademark protection for descriptive signs, and adopt defenses that allow good faith uses of trademarked terms in a descriptive manner regardless of whether some people are confused, such as the defense for descriptive fair use in the United States.[70]

2. Inherently valuable subject matter

In addition, speech-protective model trademark laws should give states the option to create additional limitations on protectable subject matter to promote free expression, fair competition and other public interests as long as these subject matter exclusions 'do not derogate from the provisions of the Paris Convention,' as permitted by TRIPS Article 15.2.[71] Even if 'almost anything at all that is capable of carrying meaning' could serve as a trademark,[72] WTO members may decide to exclude certain subject matter from trademark registration and protection

[69] Ramsey, 'Descriptive Trademarks and the First Amendment' (n 23) 1099–101, 1146–74.

[70] 15 USC s 1115(b)(4) (US); *KP Permanent Make-Up Inc v Lasting Impression I Inc*, 543 US 111, 117, 123 (2004).

[71] TRIPS Agreement, art 15.2; *United States-Section 211* (n 58) paras 155–9, 174–8. See also Correa (n 46) 178–80; Graeme B Dinwoodie, William O Hennessey, Shira Perlmutter, and Graeme W Austin, *International Intellectual Property Law and Policy* (2nd edn, Lexis Nexis 2008) 224; Gervais (n 46) 320–21, 324; Ramsey (n 6) 416–20.

[72] *Qualitex Co v Jacobson Prods Co*, 514 US 159, 162 (1995).

for important normative reasons. As explained below, some trademark advocates want to expand trademark law to allow registration and protection of certain types of subject matter that is inherently valuable before it is adopted as a trademark. Examples include artistic and literary works formerly protected by copyright law but now in the public domain, and words, names, symbols, designs, and other signs that are significant to our cultural heritage or that intrinsically convey information.

A state may conclude that no one should be able to obtain trademark rights in inherently valuable artistic or literary expression that is part of our cultural heritage, such as paintings (the *Mona Lisa*), photographs (a portrait photograph of the actress Marlene Dietrich) and songs (*Für Elise*).[73] Some scholars have questioned whether states should allow the acquisition of trademark rights in artistic and literary works currently or formerly protected under copyright law. Irene Calboli has argued that copyright owners should not be allowed to use trademark law to extend their rights to copyrighted works once the work enters the public domain.[74] To prevent 'cultural heritage grabbing' and preserve the public domain, Martin Senftleben has proposed that states categorically deny trademark protection to culturally significant artistic and literary works in the public domain.[75] While states could deny protection on a case-by-case basis on the ground that this particular image or sound is not distinctive for the goods or services, relying on a non-distinctiveness rejection in each trademark dispute does not adequately protect the public domain. A company may be able to eventually establish distinctiveness through extensive use of the painting, photograph, song, or other artistic or literary work in connection with the advertising and sales of its goods or services. States should have the option to refuse to grant and enforce trademark rights in this inherently valuable subject matter regardless of whether it has acquired distinctiveness.

---

[73] Martin RF Senftleben, 'Public Domain Preservation in EU Trademark Law–A Model for Other Regions?' (2013) 103 *Trademark Rep* 775, 799–800, 803–4 (discussing these examples).

[74] Irene Calboli, 'Overlapping Rights: Using Trademark Law to Enforce "Copyright"?' in Susy Frankel and Daniel Gervais (eds), *The Evolution and Equilibrium of Copyright in the Digital Age* (Cambridge University Press 2014). See also Viva R Moffat, 'Mutant Copyrights and Backdoor Patents: The Problem of Overlapping Intellectual Property Protection' (2004) 19 *Berkeley Technology Law J* 1473, 1475, 1521–3; *Dastar Corp v Twentieth Century Fox Film Corp* 539 US 23, 33-34 (2003).

[75] Senftleben (n 73) 812–17.

States may also decide that trademark rights should not be granted in common phrases or symbols that were culturally, historically, politically, religiously, or socially significant ('culturally significant expression') before they were adopted as trademarks for films, television shows, T-shirts, toys, mugs and similar expressive goods and services.[76] Examples in the United States include 'Dia de los Muertos' or Day of the Dead (a traditional holiday celebrated in Mexico and Latin America to honor the lives of lost family members and friends), and 'Seal Team 6' (the informal name of the US Navy Seal team that killed Osama Bin Laden), which were both the subject of trademark applications filed by Disney Enterprises for various expressive goods and services.[77] Enterprising individuals have also applied to register the phrase 'Let's Roll,' which was yelled by Todd Beamer when he and other airline passengers tried to stop hijackers from crashing their airplane on September 11, 2001 (9/11),[78] and the slogans 'Occupy Wall Street' and 'We are the 99%' relating to the Occupy Wall Street protests in New York in 2011, for T-shirts and similar goods.[79]

Government agencies in the United States have also claimed the exclusive right to display certain ideas and informational language on

---

[76] It is important to note that this subject matter is different than trademarks that have become culturally significant *after* they were adopted as trademarks, such as the 'Barbie' mark for dolls. For a proposal that would allow the use of trademarks that now have expressive significance under an 'expressive genericity' defense, see Dreyfuss (n 24) 399, 418–24.

[77] Cindy Y Rodriguez, 'Day of the Dead Trademark Request Draws Backlash for Disney' *CNN* (11 May 2013), <http://www.cnn.com/2013/05/10/us/disney-trademark-day-dead> accessed 24 June 2014; Adolfo Flores, 'Disney Withdraws Trademark Filing for "Dia de los Muertos"' *LA Times* (8 May 2013), <http://www.latimes.com/entertainment/envelope/cotown/la-et-ct-disney-dia-de-los-muertos-20130507,0,5334483.story> accessed 24 June 2014.

[78] Iman Abdallah, 'LETS ROLL' (US Trademark Serial No 76316210, filed 22 September 2001); Marja Mills, '"Let's Roll" United a Nation, Now It's a Trademark Target' *Chicago Tribune* (4 April 2002), <http://articles.chicagotribune.com/2002-04-04/features/0204040009_1_todd-m-beamer-foundation-lisa-beamer-phrase> accessed 24 June 2014.

[79] Occupy Wall Street AKA Friends of Liberty Park, 'OCCUPY WALL STREET' (US Trademark Serial No 85454550, filed 24 October 2011); Ian McLaughlin, 'WE ARE THE 99%' (US Trademark Serial No 85441931, filed 7 October 2011); Paul Elias, 'Occupy Wall Street Protesters Inspire Trademark Bid, T-Shirts' *Huffington Post* (6 November 2011), <http://www.huffingtonpost.com/2011/11/06/occupy-wall-street-protests-trademark-bid_n_1078521.html> accessed 24 June 2014.

expressive merchandise. For example, the Texas Department of Transportation owns a registered trademark in the slogan 'Don't Mess With Texas' for brochures, signs, bumper stickers, T-shirts, mugs and key chains used to discourage drivers in Texas from littering on public highways. The agency has enforced its trademark rights against the University of Texas when it sold T-shirts displaying this phrase, and an abortion rights group that sold 'Don't Mess With Texas Women' T-shirts.[80] In 2011, the agency sued author Christie Craig, her publisher and a bookstore when Craig used 'Don't Mess With Texas' as the title of a romance novel.[81] While the court denied the agency's request for a temporary restraining order to ban sales of the book while the lawsuit was pending,[82] Craig's website currently indicates that she changed the title of her book to 'Only in Texas' and rereleased it with the new title in August 2011.[83]

Another example involves the Metropolitan Transportation Authority (MTA) in New York, which has a registered trademark in the phrase 'If You See Something, Say Something' for '[p]romoting public awareness of public safety and security issues.'[84] The MTA first used this phrase on posters in subway cars, buses and trains after 9/11 to encourage the public to report suspicious activity, and it has licensed the mark to

---

[80] Associated Press, '"Don't mess" with this Texas Slogan: State Agency Might Sue Over Use of its Catchphrase' *NBCNews.com* (6 June 2004), <http://www.nbcnews.com/id/5151681/ns/business/t/dont-mess-texas-slogan/#.TlPFHagS6uI> accessed 23 February 2014; Lianne Hart, 'No Messing Around With Texas' Slogan' *L.A. Times* (6 July 2004), <http://articles.latimes.com/2004/jul/06/nation/na-texas6> accessed 24 June 2014.

[81] Complaint, *Texas Department of Transportation v Christie Craig, Hachette Book Group USA, Grand Central Publishing, and Barnes & Nobel Inc*, No 1:11-cv-00726 (filed in WD Tex 19 August 2011).

[82] Order, *Texas Department of Transportation v Christie Craig*, No 1:11-cv-00726 (filed in WD Tex 23 August 2011); Christopher Calnan, 'Judge: Author can "mess with Texas" all she wants' *Austin Business Journal* (24 August 2011), <http://www.bizjournals.com/austin/news/2011/08/24/judge-author-can-mess-with-texas.html> accessed 23 February 2014.

[83] Christie Craig, *Only in Texas* <http://www.christie-craig.com/onlyintexas.html> accessed 24 June 2014. As of 24 June 2014, the home page of Christie Craig's website, <http://www.christie-craig.com/>, notes that her book *Only in Texas* was '*[o]rignally published by Hachette Book Group as Don't Mess with Texas*.' (emphasis in original).

[84] Metropolitan Transportation Authority, 'IF YOU SEE SOMETHING, SAY SOMETHING' (US Trademark Registration No 3217091, filed 19 August 2005).

government transportation agencies around the world.[85] The MTA has enforced its trademark rights against people who sell T-shirts displaying the phrase, as well as the Harvard University police, who wanted to use the slogan to promote a student-safety campaign on campus. Per the MTA spokesperson, 'The slogan is not allowed for use in communications other than the intended anti-terrorism message.'[86]

Regardless of whether a popular slogan or informational phrase has acquired distinctiveness, it is troublesome from a free speech perspective if trademark law is so expansive that the government believes it has the right to decide when and how people use the phrase 'Don't Mess With Texas' or 'If You See Something, Say Something' in book titles or displayed on T-shirts or other expressive products. Yet the United States trademark office allows registration of words, names, symbols, or designs that convey information or that are otherwise intrinsically attention-grabbing or decorative when the subject matter 'functions as a trademark' or 'serves primarily as a source indicator' for those goods or services.[87] Since such marks can become distinctive through use on brochures, posters, T-shirts, and other expressive merchandise, the government, companies, and individuals can argue they have distinctive trademarks that entitle them to control or profit from any third-party use of the trademarked language in connection with similar expressive goods or services. States should therefore consider whether the benefits of protecting such language as a trademark outweigh the burdens this trademark law imposes on the free flow of ideas and information.

States can justify their refusal to register and protect trademark rights in such inherently valuable subject matter by citing concerns about free

---

[85] Manny Fernandez, 'A Phrase for Safety After 9/11 Goes Global' *The New York Times* (10 May 2010), <http://www.nytimes.com/2010/05/11/nyregion/11slogan.html?_r=0> accessed 24 June 2014.

[86] Annie Karni, 'MTA sees something – says stop!' *New York Post* (4 September 4 2011), <http://www.nypost.com/p/news/local/mta_sees_something_says_stop_B5W9Moodq0Vl8d6NbvW5RO> accessed 24 June 2014.

[87] Per section 1202.04 of United States Patent and Trademark Office's *Trademark Manual of Examining Procedure* (2014), slogans and other terms that are merely informational are generally not registrable, but informational matter can be registered if it 'functions as a trademark' (as 'perceived by the relevant public') and is 'not merely descriptive and/or merely informational.' Section 1202.03 of the *Trademark Manual of Examining Procedure* provides that examiners can refuse registration when the mark is merely a 'decorative feature' or 'ornamentation' of the goods, but can register subject matter 'that serves primarily as a source indicator, either inherently or as a result of acquired distinctiveness, and that is only incidentally ornamental or decorative.'

expression and preservation of the public domain and our cultural heritage, among other public interests.[88] Article 6*quinques*(B)(2) of the Paris Convention explicitly allows states to deny registration where a mark is 'devoid of any distinctive character,' and TRIPS Article 15.1 says that trademarks must be 'capable of distinguishing' goods and services to be 'capable of constituting a trademark.' Thus courts and trademark offices can reject specific claims of trademark rights in inherently valuable subject matter on the ground of lack of distinctiveness. One important question, however, is whether states must evaluate distinctiveness on a case-by-case basis, or whether state legislatures or courts can categorically conclude that certain types of inherently valuable subject matter can never be sufficiently distinctive for trademark registration or protection, just like generic words in the United States. While TRIPS Article 15.1 says that distinctive signs shall be 'capable of constituting a trademark' and 'eligible for registration' as a trademark, unlike 'personal names, letters, numerals, figurative elements and combinations of colours,' there is no evidence the WTO members intended to require the registration and protection of trademark rights in culturally significant expression or informational language that has intrinsic value before it is adopted as a trademark. As the WTO members did not explicitly consent to be bound to register and protect such trademarks, it is reasonable to conclude that states may decline to protect this subject matter as a trademark to promote the public interest, as permitted by TRIPS Articles 1.1, 7, 8, 15.1 and 15.2 and Paris Convention Article 6*quinques*(B)(2).

Thus, speech-protective model trademark laws can and should include an optional provision that allows states to deny registration and protection for subject matter that is inherently valuable before it was adopted as a trademark, including but not limited to artistic and literary expression in the public domain, and words, names, symbols, designs, and other signs that are culturally significant or that intrinsically convey information.[89] While it will be difficult to define this category of excluded

[88] For a discussion of how various countries limit trademark rights to protect the public domain, see WIPO's Committee on Development and Intellectual Property, 'Study on Misappropriation of Signs' (n 68).

[89] Importantly, excluding this subject matter from trademark registration and protection does not mean that there will be no intellectual property protection for it. Artistic or literary works may be protected by copyright or design law. In addition, certain words, names, symbols, and designs associated with indigenous groups may be protected by laws recognizing rights in traditional cultural expression. Yet free speech interests should also be considered when the government restricts third party uses of this type of intellectual property.

subject matter, legislatures and courts should still attempt to draw the line here to protect expressive values and preserve the public domain. If trademark registration and protection is possible for inherently valuable subject matter, it will be easier for trademark bullies to threaten individuals and small businesses with a frivolous cease and desist letter or complaint that claims the mark is distinctive and infringed. If it is clear this subject matter can never become a valid trademark, it will be easier for accused infringers to challenge such allegations and avoid costly litigation. Regardless of whether such marks can become distinctive, some states may conclude that this link in the minds of consumers to a single source of goods or services is not sufficient to justify the restriction on free expression that will be imposed once the government grants trademark rights in this subject matter that has inherent communicative value.

An alternative, moderately speech-protective model law would allow states to require strong proof of acquired distinctiveness before registering or protecting inherently valuable subject matter. This approach would still protect speech interests to a certain degree by requiring evidence of secondary meaning in the mark, and may be more acceptable to states that currently protect trademark rights in this subject matter. It may also be preferred if states believe one person, organization, company, government entity, or group should have control over use of this trademarked subject matter with certain goods and services to ensure the consistency of the message, prevent overuse, or reduce consumer confusion about the source of expression. Such model laws could also give states the option to limit who can own trademark rights in inherently valuable subject matter. For example, states may decide to grant trademark rights in artistic and literary works currently or formerly protected by copyright, but only to authors or their heirs or assignees. States could also prohibit for-profit companies from obtaining trademark rights in culturally significant expression or informational language, but protect trademark rights when an indigenous group claims certain words, names, symbols, or designs are part of their traditional cultural expressions, or a nonprofit organization or government entity is the first to use an informational phrase in connection with the provision of particular goods or services that benefit the public. Such rules will enable only a limited number of markholders to control and profit from certain uses of trademarked language that are deemed to violate trademark laws, and thus may not be as harmful to expressive values as laws which allow anyone to trademark inherently valuable subject matter. Yet such rules may still harm speech interests if the markholder aggressively enforces its rights against expressive use of the mark by third parties.

If states elect to protect inherently valuable subject matter as a trademark once it becomes distinctive, they should also consider narrowing the scope of trademark rights. As discussed in more detail below, states could impose threshold requirements for trademark liability, such as a requirement of commercial use of the mark, trademark use of the mark, or use of the mark for identical or related goods or services. They could also require proof of a likelihood of confusion about the source of the third party's goods, services, or expression, and not deem confusion about affiliation or sponsorship sufficient for liability. Another option is to limit the trademark right to use of the mark with non-expressive goods or services, and permit third-party use of the trademarked language when it is displayed on T-shirts, posters, or other types of expressive merchandise or used in connection with films, television shows, and other entertainment services. Moreover, the model trademark laws could permit specific defenses, such as for noncommercial use or nontrademark use of the mark, ornamental or decorative display of the mark on expressive merchandise, or use of the mark in political speech, news reporting, or the content or titles of artistic or literary expression. States could also limit the remedies available in trademark disputes involving this subject matter, such as by requiring use of a disclaimer rather than enjoining use of the trademarked language. Limiting trademark rights in these various ways would protect free speech interests. It could also increase competition, and thereby lower prices and increase choices for those consumers who want products that communicate a certain message.

B. The Scope of Rights Conferred by a Trademark

The TRIPS Agreement and Paris Convention also contain minimum obligations on the scope of rights conferred by a trademark. Like the rules relating to protectable subject matter, these obligations are limited in certain ways that give states discretion to balance trademark rights and other public interests such as free speech and fair competition.

1. Protection against unfair competition

Article 10*bis*(1) of the Paris Convention requires states to provide 'effective protection against unfair competition.'[90] Specifically, Article

---

[90] For more information about Paris Convention Article 10*bis*, see, e.g., Marcus Höpperger and Martin Senftleben, 'Protection Against Unfair Competition at the International Level – The Paris Convention, the 1996 Model Provisions and the Current Work of the World Intellectual Property Organisation', in Reto M Hilty and Frauke Henning-Bodewig (eds), *Law Against*

10*bis*(3)(1) requires states to prohibit 'all acts of such a nature as to create confusion by any means whatever with the establishment, the goods, or the industrial or commercial activities, of a competitor.' (Article 10*bis* does not use the word 'trademark' but this provision has been interpreted to apply in the trademark context.) Article 10*bis*(3)(1) is therefore limited in two ways that enable states to balance trademark rights and free speech interests: States only need to prohibit use of another's mark where (1) that use creates confusion and (2) the use is by a competitor.[91] As Article 10*bis*(3)(1)'s obligation to protect against unfair competition in the trademark context only arises if both conditions are satisfied, speech-protective model trademark laws would not violate this provision if they allowed (1) non-confusing use of another's mark by anyone, including competitors (such as in legitimate comparative advertising); or (2) use of a mark by third parties who are not competitors (such as consumers) regardless of whether the use is confusing in some way.

2. Prevention of third party uses of marks likely to result in confusion

TRIPS Article 16 contains additional obligations to protect trademarks that are limited in ways that enable states to protect free expression. Article 16.1 provides in relevant part that:

> The owner of a registered trademark shall have the exclusive right to prevent all third parties not having his consent from using in the course of trade identical or similar signs for goods or services which are identical or similar to those in respect of which the trademark is registered where such use would result in a likelihood of confusion. In case of the use of an identical sign for identical goods or services, a likelihood of confusion shall be presumed. The

---

Unfair Competition – Towards a New Paradigm in Europe? (Springer 2007) 61–76. The International Bureau of WIPO created the 1996 Model Provisions on Protection Against Unfair Competition to implement the obligations under Article 10bis of the Paris Convention and Article 2 of TRIPS. This document is not a treaty or soft law instrument, as it was not formally adopted by WIPO, but it was 'intended to serve as a model for law-making activities and a reference point for court decisions.' Ibid at 73. Free speech advocates and other interested stakeholders could create a similar document with a focus on speech-protective model provisions for trademark law that comply with the Paris Convention and TRIPS.

[91] Ramsey (n 6) 421.

> rights described above shall not prejudice any existing prior rights, nor shall they affect the possibility of Members making rights available on the basis of use.[92]

Article 16.1 therefore only requires members to protect against unauthorized use of (a) registered trademarks, (b) used in the course of trade, (c) where the signs and goods/services are identical or similar to those of the markholder, and (d) this use of the mark causes a likelihood of confusion.[93] Each of these limitations on the scope of trademark rights is similar to the elements of a trademark infringement claim and must be established for Article 16.1 to apply. Thus even where unauthorized use of mark is likely to cause confusion, there is no obligation under Article 16.1 to protect against infringement where the mark is not registered or used in the course of trade, or where the signs, goods, or services are dissimilar.

(a) Registered trademarks Although member states can opt to provide infringement protection to unregistered marks, Article 16.1 only requires such protection when a mark is 'registered.'[94] WTO members can therefore include registration of the mark as an element of a trademark infringement claim unless the mark is well known (as discussed below). A threshold registration requirement would make it easier for potential users of trademarked language to learn about a claim of trademark rights in certain words, names, symbols, or designs. It would also limit the ability of trademark bullies to chill expression based on frivolous claims of trademark rights, as the mark would need to be deemed valid and protectable by a trademark office for registration. Speech-protective model trademark laws could include a registration requirement for trademark infringement, and permit regulation of unauthorized uses of unregistered marks under unfair competition law or laws offering special protection for well-known marks.

(b) Use of the mark in the course of trade A second limitation on the obligations in Article 16.1 is that member states need only protect trademarks against infringement when the third party is 'using' the mark 'in the course of trade.' Carlos Correa explains that this refers to use of the mark 'in commercial activities,' and would 'not control the use of

---

92 TRIPS Agreement, art 16.1.

93 *European Communities-GI* (n 58) para 7.601.

94 Ibid para 7.600; *United States-Section 211* (n 58) para 186; Correa (n 46) 185; Gervais (n 46) 330; Ramsey (n 6) 422.

trademarks, for instance, in writings not intended to promote the sales of the trademarked products and services … .'[95] Article 16.1 therefore applies to use of another's mark in commercial expression, which in the United States is defined as speech that does no more than propose a commercial transaction.[96] An example is an advertisement for a television. It is less clear whether use 'in the course of trade' also applies to use of another's mark in any type of expression that is sold for profit (such as songs, books, films, or expressive merchandise such as T-shirts or posters) or supported by advertising revenues (such as news reporting or commentary on blogs). The 'using in the course of trade' language could also refer to use of a mark 'as a trademark' or 'designation of the source' of the third party's goods or services, also known as a 'trademark use' of the mark. As the phrase 'using in the course of trade' is arguably ambiguous, the best approach under TRIPS Article 1.1, 7 and 8 would be to defer to member states in their interpretation of this language and allow them to limit the scope of trademark rights to commercial and/or trademark uses of marks to comply with constitutional or international obligations to protect the right to freedom of expression.[97] Narrowly interpreting 'using in the course of trade' in this way would promote the free flow of ideas and information, as it would mean trademark law does not ban the use of trademarked language in noncommercial expression (such as political speech) or the nontrademark use of another's mark in commercial expression (such as in legitimate comparative advertising).

Speech-protective model trademark laws should give states the option to include use of the mark 'in the course of trade' or 'commercial use' of the mark as a threshold requirement for infringement liability to clarify that political expression and other noncommercial uses of marks are outside the scope of trademark rights.[98] To safeguard legitimate comparative advertising and other nontrademark uses of marks from allegations of trademark violations, states could also require proof of the third

---

[95] Correa (n 46) 186. In Case C-206/01, *Arsenal Football Club Plc v Reed* [2002] ECR I-10273, para 40, the Court of Justice of the European Union held that 'use in the course of trade' in EU Trade Mark Directive art 5 means use of another's marks that 'takes place in the context of commercial activity with a view to economic advantage and not as a private matter.'

[96] *Board of Trustees of the State University of New York v Fox* 492 US 469, 473–4, 482 (1989); *Nissan Motor Co v Nissan Computer Corp* 378 F3d 1002, 1017 (9th Cir 2004).

[97] Ramsey (n 6) 423–7.

[98] As discussed previously in n 33, some US courts have required commercial use of a mark for infringement liability.

party's 'trademark use' of the mark, or use of the mark 'as a trademark' or 'designation of the source' of the third party's goods or services.[99] The markholder would have the burden of establishing that these elements of its infringement claim are satisfied, which is the most speech-protective rule. Alternatively, states could frame the rule as an affirmative defense, and allow the accused infringer to escape trademark liability with proof that it did not use the mark in the course of trade, or only used the mark in a noncommercial or nontrademark way. A more limited defense would allow nontrademark use of the mark in noncommercial expression, and still permit states to regulate confusing use of another's mark to falsely indicate the markholder is the source of the third party's noncommercial goods, services, or expression.[100] These last two options protect expressive interests, but are arguably less speech protective since the burden of proof is on the defendant.

States should be encouraged to define 'using in the course of trade,' 'commercial use,' 'trademark use,' and any other terms used as elements of an infringement claim or an affirmative defense. Among other things, legislatures and courts should clarify whether infringement law applies to noncommercial expression sold for profit or supported by advertising revenues; to use of another's mark in the content or titles of artistic or literary works; to decorative use on T-shirts, posters, and other expressive merchandise; or to use of another's trademarked language in slogans, domain names, or usernames in a descriptive or informative manner. It will sometimes be difficult to draw the line between commercial and noncommercial expression, and to clearly identify all the circumstances where a third-party use of a mark qualifies as a trademark use. Still, such a categorical approach will increase clarity and predictability in trademark disputes involving expression that is clearly noncommercial or that clearly incorporates nontrademark uses of marks, and may discourage

---

[99] Australia has a statutory requirement of use 'as a trade mark' for infringement liability. Trade Marks Act 1995 (Australia) s 120(1) ('A person infringes a registered trade mark if the person uses as a trade mark …'); Robert Burrell and Michael Handler, *Australian Trade Mark Law* (OUP 2010) 321–32. While some scholars believe trademark laws should include a threshold requirement of trademark use for liability, for example, Mark A Lemley and Stacey L Dogan, 'Grounding Trademark Law Through Trademark Use' (2007) 92 *Iowa L Rev* 1669, 1675–98, others disagree, Graeme B Dinwoodie and Mark D Janis, 'Confusion Over Use: Contextualism in Trademark Law' (2007) 92 *Iowa L Rev* 1597, 1622-67; Graeme B Dinwoodie and Mark D Janis, 'Lessons from the Trademark Use Debate' (2007) 92 *Iowa L Rev* 1703, 1704, 1714–21.

[100] Ramsey (n 1) 455–6; Ramsey, 'Brandjacking on Social Networks' (n 4) 925; Ramsey (n 6) 425.

frivolous claims of trademark violations. Adding threshold requirements of use in the course of trade, commercial use, or trademark use to an infringement claim could also make it easier for judges to dispose of speech-harmful trademark suits early in the litigation. Article 16.1 allows states to do this, just as it allows states to impose rules relating to the similarity of the parties' signs, goods, and services, as discussed next.

(c) Similarity of the parties' signs and goods/services TRIPS Article 16.1 only obligates states to protect trademarks against infringement where the parties' signs are 'identical or similar' and the third party uses that sign 'for goods or services' that are 'identical or similar to those in respect of which the trademark is registered.' Members therefore need not offer infringement protection in circumstances where a third party is causing confusion while using a dissimilar mark, or is using a mark identical or similar to the protected mark but not for goods or services (such as use by a critic or consumer in a review of the product). Confusing use of the mark by a company to advertise or sell dissimilar goods or services is also not covered by Article 16.1, although TRIPS Article 16.3 may apply if the mark is well known (as discussed below).[101] Speech-protective model trademark laws could therefore require the parties' signs and goods/services to be identical or similar for infringement liability without violating Article 16.1.

In addition, Article 16.1 contains a double identity rule which requires states to presume a likelihood of confusion where the third party uses 'an identical sign for identical goods or services.' This rule clearly applies to counterfeit merchandise. It is less clear whether the presumption applies to legitimate comparative advertising. For example, a competitor may use the leading brand's exact mark to inform consumers that its competing goods or services sold under a different brand name are less expensive, or of higher quality, than the markholder's products. Requiring a presumption of infringement in these circumstances could harm commercial expression and effective competition, as the markholder could prevail without providing evidence of any likelihood of confusion caused by this use of the mark. States have the flexibility under Articles 1.1, 7 and 8 to interpret the double identity rule narrowly to protect the free flow of expression, promote competition, and otherwise further the public interest. Speech-protective model trademark laws should urge states to clarify

---

[101] Ramsey (n 6) 427–8.

the circumstances where the double identity rule is relevant. The presumption of likelihood of confusion should apply to counterfeit merchandise, but it can harm commercial speech interests and competition if applied in trademark disputes involving legitimate comparative advertising.

(d) Likelihood of confusion TRIPS Article 16.1 only requires states to protect against unauthorized uses of marks that result in 'a likelihood of confusion.' TRIPS does not define this phrase. According to Correa, '[t]he meaning of "confusion" should be understood in the light of Article 15.1; that is, in relation to the capacity of a trademark to distinguish identical or similar goods or services of one undertaking from those of another.'[102] A speech-protective interpretation of Article 16.1 would only require infringement laws to cover unauthorized use of a mark that results in a likelihood of confusion about the source or origin of the third party's goods or services. Trademark advocates may argue that 'likelihood of confusion' covers not just confusion about source or origin but also confusion about affiliation, connection, association, sponsorship, or approval. Although some states, including the United States, currently protect markholders against these types of confusion,[103] a broad interpretation of 'likelihood of confusion' in Article 16.1 is not required. This phrase is ambiguous, and therefore Articles 1.1, 7 and 8 of TRIPS give WTO members discretion to determine what types of confusion are relevant for infringement claims and consider free speech concerns and other public interests when making that determination.[104] Unless there is clear evidence that the WTO members consented to a broad reading of Article 16.1, a narrow and speech-protective interpretation of Article 16.1 would give states the option to only prevent uses of marks that cause a likelihood of confusion about the source or origin of the third party's goods or services.

Prohibiting unauthorized uses of trademarks that cause only a likelihood of confusion about consent or other immaterial types of confusion can harm competition and stifle the free flow of information and ideas.[105] Certain expressive uses of marks may benefit society overall even if they create confusion in the minds of some consumers about whether the

---

102 Correa (n 46) 186.

103 15 USC s 1125(a).

104 Ramsey (n 6) 428–9.

105 Lemley and McKenna (n 24) 427–44; Ramsey (n 1) 395–404; Rothman (n 24) 130–9, 150–9; Jeremy N Sheff, 'Veblen Brands' (2012) 96 *Minnesota L Rev* 769, 816–26.

markholder approved of this use of its mark. One example is use of another's mark to refer to the markholder's goods or services in legitimate comparative advertising by competitors, and other truthful commercial expression by resellers or companies who sell accessories, repair services, or other goods or services related to the trademarked product. Other examples include the non-misleading use of another's trademarked language in Internet domain names, Facebook usernames, Twitter hashtags, Google keywords, the titles or content of artistic and literary works, and the headlines or content of news reporting and commentary. Expressive values are protected in trademark law if companies and people can use the marks of others to truthfully describe or indicate the purpose of the goods, services, or expression of the third party; to criticize, parody, or otherwise comment on the markholder or its goods or services; or to communicate about the world in general. Unless an expressive third-party use of another's mark is likely to cause confusion about the source or origin of goods, services, or expression, enforcing trademark rights in this context may be inconsistent with states' constitutional and international obligations to protect the right to freedom of expression.[106]

3. Special trademark rights for well-known marks

When a trademark is well known (such as Coca-Cola for beverages), it is entitled to a distinct type of protection under the Paris Convention and TRIPS Agreement. Article 6*bis*(1) of the Paris Convention provides:

> The countries of the Union undertake, ex officio if their legislation so permits, or at the request of an interested party, to refuse or to cancel the registration, and to prohibit the use, of a trademark which constitutes a reproduction, an imitation, or a translation, liable to create confusion, of a mark considered by the competent authority of the country of registration or use to be well-known in that country as being already the mark of a person entitled to the benefits of this Convention and used for identical or similar goods. These provisions shall also apply when the essential part of the mark constitutes a reproduction of any such well-known mark or an imitation liable to create confusion therewith.

This doctrine protects trademarks not registered in a member country but still widely known in that country's marketplace against third parties who

[106] Ramsey (n 6) 428–9.

attempt to register or use the well-known mark in a confusing manner.[107] The TRIPS Agreement incorporates Paris Convention Article 6*bis*,[108] and TRIPS Article 16.2 extends Article 6*bis*'s protection for well-known marks to services, as Paris Convention Article 6*bis* only applies to goods.

TRIPS Article 16.2 also clarifies that advertising and other promotion of a mark in a foreign state is relevant in 'determining whether a trademark is well known' in that state; it says 'Members shall take account of the knowledge of the trademark in the relevant sector of the public, including knowledge in the Member concerned which has been obtained as a result of the promotion of the trademark.'[109] The 'relevant sector of the public' could include customers and potential customers of both the markholder and the third party accused of trademark violations.[110] For example, if the McDonald's mark for restaurant services is well known to potential customers in Botswana, the well-known mark doctrine would protect that mark against third-party registration or use of the mark for similar services even before McDonald's registered its mark or expanded its hamburger franchise into that country.[111]

These obligations to protect well-known marks in Paris Convention Article 6*bis* and TRIPS Article 16.2 are limited in certain ways that enable member states to protect free speech interests. Trademark protection for well-known marks is only required where: (1) the mark is well-known in the country where protection is sought; (2) the third party's mark is 'a reproduction, an imitation, or a translation' of the well-known mark; (3) the third party's mark is 'liable to create confusion' with the well-known mark; (4) the third party is using the mark for goods or services; and (5) the goods or services of the parties are identical or similar. If any of these elements are not satisfied, Paris Convention Article 6*bis* and TRIPS Article 16.2 do not apply.[112]

---

[107] Frederick W Mostert (ed.), *Famous and Well-Known Marks: An International Analysis* (2nd edn, International Trademark Association 2004 and 2007 Supp.) 26, 1:33–35. See also Correa (n 46) 188–93; Gervais (n 46) 331–4.

[108] TRIPS Agreement, art 2.1.

[109] TRIPS Agreement, art 16.2. See also Correa (n 46) 188–93; Gervais (n 46) 331–4.

[110] Mostert (n 107) 1:11, 1:36–44.

[111] Cf *McDonald's Corp v Joburgers Drive-Inn Rest Pty Ltd* 1997 (1) SA 1 (A) (South Africa).

[112] Ramsey (n 6) 429–31.

If the parties' goods or services are dissimilar (as in the case of 'Kodak' bicycles),[113] protection is available under TRIPS Article 16.3 if the third party's use of the well-known mark suggests a 'connection' with the markholder and is likely to damage the markholder's interests. TRIPS Article 16.3 provides that the protection in Paris Convention Article 6*bis* for well-known marks now applies

> to goods or services which are not similar to those in respect of which a trademark is registered, provided that use of that trademark in relation to those goods or services would indicate a connection between those goods or services and the owner of the registered trademark and provided that the interests of the owner of the registered trademark are likely to be damaged by such use.[114]

Thus, member states need only protect trademark rights in well-known marks used in connection with dissimilar goods or services if, in addition to the first four limitations listed in the preceding paragraph, the following elements are satisfied: (5) this use of the mark 'would indicate a connection' between the third party's goods or services and the markholder; (6) the interests of the markholder are 'likely to be damaged' by this third-party use; and (7) the markholder has 'registered' the well-known mark in at least one WTO member country.[115]

There is disagreement over whether TRIPS Article 16.3 requires WTO members to protect well-known marks against dilution or otherwise prohibit free riding on the investment in a well-known mark where the third party's use of the mark is not likely to cause confusion.[116] A narrow interpretation of the Article 16.3 obligations would permit states to adopt infringement laws that apply to third-party uses of marks for dissimilar goods or services that are likely to create confusion about whether the markholder has a connection to the third party. For example, Australia protects well-known marks under infringement laws that cover use of another's mark with 'unrelated' goods or services in a manner that indicates a connection with the registered owner of the mark and is likely

---

113 *Eastman Photographic Materials Co Ltd v John Griffiths Cycle Corp Ltd and Kodak Cycle Co Ltd* (1898) 15 RPC 105, 110 (High Ct. of Justice). See also Frank I Schecter, 'The Rational Basis of Trademark Protection' (1927) 40 *Harv L Rev* 813, 825.

114 TRIPS Agreement, art 16.3.

115 Correa (n 46) 192–3; Mostert (n 107) 1:75–127; Ramsey (n 6) 431–2.

116 Ramsey (n 6) 432–5.

to adversely affect its interests.[117] Other countries, such as the United States, protect well-known marks against blurring or tarnishment in dilution statutes and do not require proof of any likelihood of confusion for this type of trademark liability.[118] Commentators in the United States disagree about whether trademark dilution laws benefit the public, and some argue such laws may stifle non-misleading commercial expression more than necessary in violation of the constitutional right to freedom of expression.[119]

A few years after TRIPS was enacted, the WIPO members met in an attempt to clarify their international obligations relating to trademark protection of well-known marks and to establish international harmonized common principles on this issue. As discussed in the introduction to this chapter, in 1999, the General Assembly of the WIPO and the Members of the Assembly of the Paris Union for Industrial Property adopted the Joint Recommendation Concerning Provisions on the Protection of Well-Known Marks.[120] This Joint Recommendation provides that members 'shall protect a well-known mark against conflicting marks.'[121] It also says a 'mark shall be deemed to be in conflict with a well-known mark' when used on any goods or services 'where at least one of the following conditions is filled': (i) 'the use of that mark would indicate a connection between the goods and/or services for which the mark is used, is the subject of an application for registration, or is registered, and the owner of the well-known mark, and would be likely to damage his interests'; (ii) 'the use of that mark is likely to impair or dilute in an

---

[117] Trade Marks Act 1995 (Australia) s 120(3); Burrell and Handler (n 99) 349–55; Michael Handler, 'Trade Mark Dilution in Australia?' (2007) 29 *European Intellectual Property Review* 307. Some scholars argue that s 120(3) can be read as an anti-dilution provision, see for example, Maurice Gonsalves and Patrick Flynn, 'Dilution Down Under: The Protection of Well-Known Trade Marks in Australia' (2006) *European Intellectual Property Review* 174, 174–6; Megan Richardson, 'Trade Marks and Language' (2004) 26 *Sydney Law Review* 193, 218 n 172.

[118] 15 USC s 1125(c)(1)–(2) (US). The European Union has a similar law. EU Trade Mark Directive, arts 5(2), 5(5). See also Martin Senftleben, 'The Trademark Tower of Babel – Dilution Concepts in International, US and EC Trademark Law' (2009) 40 *Intl Rev Intellectual Property & Competition L* 45.

[119] For example, compare Dogan and Lemley 'Trademarks and Consumer Search Costs on the Internet' (n 25) 788–91, 826–7 with Tushnet, 'Gone in Sixty Milliseconds" (n 24) 519–22, 527–45. See also LaFrance (n 24) 709–11; Ramsey (n 1) 426, n 269.

[120] Joint Recommendation on Well-Known Marks (n 11).

[121] Ibid art 3(1).

unfair manner the distinctive character of the well-known mark'; or (iii) 'the use of that mark would take unfair advantage of the distinctive character of the well-known mark.'[122] States have discretion to decide exactly how to protect well-known marks in their trademark laws.[123] While 'the Joint Recommendation explicitly requires anti-dilution protection for well-known marks,' this 'soft law' document is not a treaty and thus does not create any binding legal obligation on the members of the WIPO or the WTO to protect a well-known mark against dilution.[124] This Joint Recommendation has subsequently become binding on the United States and other countries that have entered into free trade agreements that incorporate it,[125] but these obligations are not enforceable through the WTO Dispute Settlement Body.

As Article 16.3 does not explicitly require anti-dilution protection for well-known marks (or at least is ambiguous on this point), TRIPS Articles 1.1, 7 and 8 dictate that WTO members have flexibility in how they implement their obligations under Article 16.3 and can limit the scope of trademark rights to protect free expression.[126] Speech-protective model trademark laws would give states the option to protect well-known marks against third-party registration or use with dissimilar goods or services using infringement law (like Australia) or dilution law (like the United States), and include the threshold requirements in Paris Convention Article 6*bis* and TRIPS Article 16 discussed above. If a state decides to protect well-known marks against dilution, it should then protect free speech interests by requiring commercial use or trademark use of the mark for dilution liability and adopt defenses for certain expressive uses of marks.[127]

C. Defenses and Other Exceptions to Trademark Rights

TRIPS Article 17 provides WTO members with additional flexibility to protect speech interests in domestic trademark laws. Article 17 says:

---

[122] Ibid art 4(1)(b)(i)–(iii).

[123] Senftleben (n 118) 50–3.

[124] Dinwoodie and others (n 71) 210–11. See also Correa (n 46) 190–2.

[125] For example, see the United States-Singapore Free Trade Agreement (adopted 6 May 2003, entered into force 1 January 2004) art 16.1(2)(b)(i), which requires both countries to give effect to arts 1– 6 of the Joint Recommendation.

[126] Ramsey (n 6) 435.

[127] For an example of defenses, see 15 USC § 1125(c)(3) (US). For the argument that states should protect against dilution but include a free speech defense, see Richardson, 'Trade Marks and Language' (n 117) 217–20.

'Members may provide limited exceptions to the rights conferred by a trademark, such as fair use of descriptive terms, provided that such exceptions take account of the legitimate interests of the owner of the trademark and of third parties.' Compared to the provisions in TRIPS allowing exceptions to copyright (Article 13) and patent rights (Article 30), WTO members have significantly more discretion to create exceptions to trademark rights under Article 17.[128] Moreover, as noted by the WTO panel that interpreted this provision in *European Communities-GI*, Article 17 'presupposes that a certain degree of likelihood of confusion can be permitted' when states adopt affirmative defenses and other limitations on trademark rights.[129]

A WTO member that creates an exception to trademark rights has the burden under Article 17 to prove that the exception (1) is limited and (2) takes into account the legitimate interests of both the markholder and third parties.[130] An exception is 'limited' when it is narrow and permits only a small diminution of the rights conferred by a trademark.[131] The markholder should still generally have the right to prevent third-party uses of its mark that are likely to cause confusion.[132] The phrase 'legitimate interests' refers to 'a normative claim calling for protection of interests that are "justifiable" in the sense that they are supported by relevant public policies or other social norms.'[133] In the *European Communities-GI* dispute, the WTO panel found that the EU's geographical indication regulations – which allowed the use of trademarks that contained a protected geographical indication – complied with Article 17, as the markholders still had an exclusive right against other third parties and the rule took into account the legitimate interests of everyone affected by the regulations.[134]

---

[128] *European Communities-GI* (n 58) para 7.649, 7.671; Gervais (n 46) 337–40; Ramsey (n 6) 436–7. For a detailed discussion about Article 17, see Ramsey (n 6) 436-43; Katja Weckström, 'When Two Giants Collide: Article 17 and the Scope of Trademark Protection Afforded Under the TRIPS Agreement' (2007) 29 *Loyola Los Angeles Intl & Comparative L Rev* 167, 183–8.

[129] *European Communities-GI* (n 58) para 7.670. See also Correa (n 46) 193–5; Gervais (n 46) 336–40; cf *KP Permanent Make-Up Inc v Lasting Impression I Inc*, 543 US 111 (2004).

[130] *European Communities-GI* (n 58) paras 7.645, 7.648.

[131] Ibid paras 7.650–7.654.

[132] Ibid paras 7.653–7.654, 7.659.

[133] Ibid paras 7.663–7.664. Gervais believes 'This would include interests in the economic value in the goodwill associated with the mark.' Gervais (n 46) 337.

[134] Ibid paras 7.655–7.666, 7.670.

Importantly, Article 17 requires consideration of the legitimate interests of the markholder *and* third parties, which could include trademark licensees, competitors, other traders, the accused infringer, customers or potential customers, and the rest of the general public.[135] As noted by the WTO panel in *European Communities-GI*, '[c]onsumers have a legitimate interest in being able to distinguish the goods and services of one undertaking from those of another, and to avoid confusion.'[136] At the same time, everyone has a legitimate interest in freedom of expression.[137] As long as states continue to generally protect trademark rights against infringement, Article 17 allows WTO members to enact a variety of limited exceptions to trademark rights to ensure that trademarked language is available for legitimate use by others. As 'nothing in the text of Article 17 indicates that a case-by-case analysis is a requirement under the TRIPS Agreement,'[138] implementing speech-protective categorical defenses for certain types of uses of marks is consistent with the WTO members' obligations under Article 17. TRIPS Articles 1.1, 7 and 8 further support WTO members' ability to use defenses and other exceptions to trademark rights to protect the public interest in free expression in their trademark laws.[139]

Speech-protective model trademark laws could include a variety of potential affirmative defenses, such as a categorical defense for noncommercial use of a mark,[140] nontrademark use of a mark, or for nontrademark use of a mark in noncommercial expression. Other more specific options include a defense for use of another's mark in political commentary, social commentary, news reporting, artistic and literary works, informational websites, parody, satire, and criticism regardless of whether the expression is sold for profit or supported by advertising revenues. States could also permit descriptive fair use of a mark to describe the qualities or characteristics of products, and allow nominative or referential use of a mark to refer to the markholder or its goods or services.[141] They could also allow use of another's mark in legitimate

135 Ramsey (n 6) 439–43.

136 *European Communities-GI* (n 58) para 7.676.

137 Ramsey (n 6) 441; cf Daniel J Gervais, *Intellectual Property and Human Rights: Learning To Live Together*, in Torremans (n 3) 3, 18; Netanel (n 48) 475.

138 *European Communities-GI* (n 58) para 7.672.

139 Ramsey (n 6) 445–59.

140 15 USC s 1125(c)(3)(C) (US) (exclusion from federal dilution liability).

141 15 USC s 1115(b)(4) (US) (descriptive fair use); *Toyota Motor Sales USA Inc v Tabari*, 610 F3d 1171, 1175-80 (9th Cir 2010) (nominative fair use); MPI Study (n 24) 121-23 (honest referential use in Europe). See also Correa (n 46)

comparative advertising and promotion, and other truthful commercial expression.[142] If states adopt one or more of these categorical defenses, the legislature or courts should define the categories – which may be difficult for some rules – to make it easier for courts and parties to decide whether a particular third-party use of a mark fits within the category. While case-by-case balancing of trademark rights and free expression may result in more fair and just decisions in individual cases, the definitional balancing that occurs with categorical defenses may be more fair and just overall because it increases predictability and clarity in trademark disputes and enables courts to resolve meritless trademark disputes early in litigation.[143] Legislators should include these defenses in the trademark statute, and also indicate that courts have discretion to further limit trademark rights to protect free expression, fair competition and other public interests.[144]

Article 17 would also permit the creation of other exceptions to trademark rights that protect free expression. For example, in the United States, some courts apply the *Rogers'* balancing test for infringement in trademark cases involving artistic and literary works (such as the song *Barbie Girl*), which requires courts to construe trademark law to apply 'only where the public interest in avoiding consumer confusion outweighs the public interest in free expression.'[145] In such cases, '[a]n artistic work's use of a trademark that otherwise would violate the Lanham Act is not actionable unless the use of the mark has no artistic relevance to the underlying work whatsoever, or, if it has some artistic relevance, unless it explicitly misleads as to the source or the content of

---

195 (noting examples of fair use of descriptive terms allowed under Article 17 include 'the use of the trademark in news, magazines, commentaries, and other writings' as well as the 'good faith use of one person's name, address, or pseudonym' or 'the use of a name that indicates the purpose of a product').

[142] Trade Marks Act 1995 (Australia) s 122(1)(d) (defense for use 'for the purposes of comparative advertising'). See also Burrell and Handler (n 99) 365–6; Correa (n 46) 195.

[143] William McGeveran, 'Four Free Speech Goals for Trademark Law' (2008) 18 *Fordham Intellectual Property Media & Entertainment LJ* 1205, 1214–19; McGeveran (n 1) 2279–91; Ramsey (n 1) 447–57.

[144] Ramsey and Schovsbo (n 1) 674, 690–8. See also Correa (n 46) 195 (noting exceptions 'may also be grounded on public interest considerations' such as public health).

[145] *Rogers v Grimaldi*, 875 F2d 994, 999 (2d Cir 1989). See also *University of Alabama Bd of Trustees v New Life Art Inc*, 683 F.3d 1266, 1276-8 (11th Cir 2012); *Mattel Inc v MCA Records Inc* 296 F3d 894, 901–2 (9th Cir 2002).

the work.'[146] In addition, the Court of Justice of the European Union has recently focused on how third-party use of a mark affects the 'functions of the trade mark' when determining the scope and limits of trademark protection, and has said that trademark rights 'must be reserved to cases in which a third party's use of the sign affects or is liable to affect the functions of the trade mark.'[147] This doctrine could be used to limit trademark rights in cases involving expressive uses of marks that do not harm the origin function of the mark, or the other functions of 'guaranteeing the quality of the goods or services in question and those of communication, investment, or advertising.'[148]

These various categorical defenses and exceptions to trademark rights could be included in speech-protective model trademark laws, as they comply with the two requirements in TRIPS Article 17. First, the exceptions only apply in limited circumstances involving certain expressive uses of trademarks. Markholders would still be able to enforce their marks against third-party infringers selling goods or services that do not convey information or ideas. Second, the exceptions to trademark rights take into account the legitimate interests of everyone involved in a trademark dispute, including trademark and free speech interests.

D. Remedies

Member states also have the flexibility to tailor remedies for trademark violations in ways that protect speech interests under TRIPS' enforcement provisions (Article 41–61). Per TRIPS Article 41.1, members must implement enforcement procedures that 'permit effective action against any act of infringement of intellectual property rights covered by this Agreement, including expeditious remedies to prevent infringements and remedies which constitute a deterrent to further infringements.' Among other things, TRIPS provides that 'judicial authorities shall have the authority' to issue injunctions (Article 44), award compensatory damages and expenses, including attorney's fees (Article 45), award other remedies such as the disposal of infringing goods (Article 46), and 'order prompt and effective provisional measures' (Article 50).

Importantly, these provisions in TRIPS do not require judges to issue an injunction or award damages in every case where the markholder prevails on its trademark claims – the judge only has to have 'authority'

146 *ESS Entertainment 2000 Inc v Rock Star Videos Inc*, 547 F3d 1095, 1099–1100 (9th Cir 2008) (internal brackets and quotes omitted).

147 Case C-487/07 *L'Oréal SA v Bellure NV* [2009] ECR I-05185, para 58.

148 Ibid. See also Ramsey and Schovsbo (n 1) 673, 677–80.

to provide these remedies.[149] In cases involving expressive uses of marks where a trademark violation is found, such as a confusing parody of the markholder, states could allow courts to protect free speech interests by limiting remedies to an injunction requiring use of a disclaimer when the third party uses the trademark. Alternatively, courts could have the option to award damages in lieu of an injunction, although the possibility of a large damage award could still chill expressive uses of marks.[150] As a temporary restraining order or preliminary injunction banning expressive use of a trademark is a prior restraint on speech (which is generally discouraged in the United States),[151] states may also protect expressive values by allowing judges to refuse to enjoin use of the mark before a full hearing on the merits of the dispute. Model speech-protective trademark laws should include enforcement provisions authorizing judicial authorities to award injunctions, damages, attorney's fees, expenses and other remedies, yet they should also give judges discretion to limit remedies to a disclaimer, damages and/or a permanent injunction in certain cases to protect speech interests and comply with constitutional and international obligations to protect the right to freedom of expression.

While TRIPS contains rules relating to trademark remedies and enforcement of intellectual property rights, it does not require WTO members to provide (or prohibit them from providing) remedies to innocent third parties who are falsely accused of trademark violations. TRIPS and the Paris Convention are silent on this issue. Thus WTO members can decide whether and how to provide remedies to accused infringers when markholders file frivolous trademark lawsuits, send groundless cease and desist letters, or otherwise act like 'trademark bullies' to discourage legitimate uses of language, symbols, colors, or

---

[149] Dinwoodie and Dreyfuss (n 9) 71-82; *China-Enforcement* (n 58) para 7.236 ('The obligation is to "have" authority, [it is] not an obligation to "exercise" authority.'). See also *United States-Section 211* (n 58) para 215 ('Making [civil judicial enforcement] available means making it "obtainable", putting it "within one's reach" and "at one's disposal" in a way that has sufficient force or efficacy'); TRIPS Agreement, art 1.1.

[150] For a proposal to limit the use of injunctions in trademark disputes involving dilution claims, see LaFrance (n 24) 723. See also Michael Spence, 'Intellectual Property and the Problem of Parody' (1998) 114 *L Q Rev* 594, 617–9.

[151] Lemley and Volokh (n 3) 169–81.

product designs claimed as a trademark.[152] TRIPS Article 8.1 permits states to adopt certain measures to prevent the abuse of intellectual property rights as long as those laws are consistent with TRIPS. States could therefore prohibit or discourage abusive behavior by trademark holders who make unfounded claims that their trademark rights are violated.

Among other things, a country's trademark statute or rules of civil procedure could permit courts to punish a trademark owner who engages in abusive litigation tactics in trademark disputes. For example, in the United States, innocent third parties wrongfully accused of trademark violations can get an award of reasonable attorney's fees in 'exceptional cases' under the trademark statute.[153] Federal courts in the United States can also impose sanctions on the markholder where a frivolous complaint violates Federal Rule of Civil Procedure 11. In some US jurisdictions, a defendant can obtain quick dismissal of a meritless complaint that is deemed to be a 'strategic lawsuit against public participation' intended to silence critics of the plaintiff by burdening them with litigation costs.[154] Another remedy that can be used against trademark bullies is the 'groundless threats' action in Australia and the United Kingdom. This law provides a cause of action where the markholder falsely claims that a legitimate business is engaging in infringement of a registered trademark, which may scare off customers or other traders, and chill expressive uses of the mark. If the threat is groundless, the aggrieved party can secure a judgment of non-infringement, an injunction restraining the markholder from continuing to make the threat, and damages for any loss sustained as a result of the groundless threat.[155] These remedies for innocent parties who are the targets of trademark bullies should be included in speech-protective model trademark laws along with any other proposed laws that prohibit or discourage baseless claims of trademark violations.

---

152 Leah Chan Grinvald, 'Shaming Trademark Bullies' (2011) *Wisconsin L Rev* 625, 632–52; Irina D Manta, 'Bearing Down on Trademark Bullies' (2012) 22 *Fordham Intellectual Property Media & Entertainment LJ* 853, 854–65.

153 15 U.S.C. § 1117(a).

154 California has such an 'Anti-SLAPP' law, Cal. Civ. Proc. Code s 425.16(a), and accused infringers have invoked it in trademark disputes, for example *Bosley Medical Institute Inc v Kremer*, 403 F3d 672, 682 (9th Cir 2005).

155 Trade Marks Act 1995 (Australia) s 129; Trade Marks Act 1994 (UK) s 21. See also Burrell and Handler (n 99) 516–21.

E. Secondary Trademark Liability

A trademark holder may sue a company or organization for contributing to trademark violations when they provide a place for third parties to use the trademarks of others without authorization in connection with the advertising, sale, distribution, or display of goods, services, or expression. Facebook, Google, eBay, website hosting services, operators of swap meets, art galleries, and other entities may be liable for contributory trademark infringement if they actively induce a third party to infringe a trademark, or continue to provide goods or services to a party they know or have reason to know is using those goods or services to engage in trademark violations.[156] The TRIPS Agreement and Paris Convention do not create any international obligations on states to protect markholders against contributory trademark infringement or other types of secondary trademark violations, such as vicarious trademark infringement. Thus states have discretion on how to regulate this area of trademark law.[157]

Speech-protective model trademark laws should include claims for secondary trademark liability to protect trademark interests, but these rules should also protect free speech interests by reducing the incentive for private companies to censor third-party uses of trademarks in expression without a fair hearing on the merits by that private entity or a court. Today there are many Internet companies, swap meet operators,

---

[156] *Inwood Lab Inc v Ives Lab Inc*, 456 US 844, 854 (1982); *Rosetta Stone Ltd v Google Inc* 676 F3d 144, 163 (4th Cir 2012); *Tiffany Inc v eBay Inc*, 600 F3d 93, 104–10 (2d Cir 2010).

[157] A full discussion of secondary trademark liability is beyond the scope of this chapter, but for more details see, for example, Mark Bartholomew, 'Copyright, Trademark, and Secondary Liability after Grokster' (2009) 32 *Columbia J L & Arts* 445, 454–60; Mark Bartholomew and John Tehranian, 'The Secret Life of Legal Doctrine: The Divergent Evolution of Secondary Liability in Trademark and Copyright Law' (2006) 21 *Berkeley Technology L J* 1363, 1378–417; David H Bernstein and Michael R Potenza, 'Why the Reasonable Anticipation Standard is the Reasonable Way to Assess Contributory Trademark Liability in the Online Marketplace' (2011) *Stanford Technology L Rev* 9; John T Cross, 'Contributory Infringement and Related Theories of Secondary Liability for Trademark Infringement' (1994) 80 *Iowa Law Rev* 101; John T Cross, 'Contributory and Vicarious Liability for Trademark Dilution' (2001) 80 *Oregon Law Review* 625; McCarthy (n 17) ss 25:17–25; Yvette Joy Liebesman and Benjamin Wilson, 'The Mark of a Resold Good' (2012) 20 *George Mason L Rev* 157; Mark McKenna, 'Probabilistic Knowledge of Third Party Trademark Infringement' (2011) *Stanford Technology L Rev* 10; Katja Weckström, 'Liability for Trademark Infringement for Internet Service Providers' (2012) 16 *Marquette Intellectual Property L Rev* 1.

and other entities that provide virtual and physical spaces for the public to buy and sell goods and services and communicate with each other. Due to the risk of secondary trademark liability and the lack of clarity in trademark laws on what types of expressive uses of marks are lawful, these private entities will have an incentive to overprotect trademark rights, ban unauthorized uses of marks in their terms and conditions (to which users must agree), and stop any use of another's mark by third parties when a markholder complains. The risk-averse choice today is to favor trademark rights over free speech interests when the two conflict.

To protect free expression in private trademark disputes, governments should strive to increase clarity and predictability in their trademark laws so that private entities can better determine whether a particular use of another's mark violates trademark law. Categorical rules will likely achieve this goal better than standards. States should therefore consider enacting more requirements for trademark liability (such as commercial use or trademark use), and safe harbors and affirmative defenses for certain uses of trademarks, and not rely on the likelihood of confusion or dilution analysis to provide guidance on trademark liability. States should also enact secondary trademark liability statutes that encourage private entities resolving trademark disputes to consider free speech interests and provide a fair hearing on the merits of a trademark dispute, or require a court hearing, before prohibiting or suppressing expressive uses of marks by third parties.

IV. CONCLUSION

States and free speech advocates should collaborate in WIPO or another forum to develop a global soft law instrument that contains specific, speech-protective model trademark laws that comply with international obligations to protect trademarks in TRIPS and the Paris Convention. These model-rules could be useful to decision-makers who are attempting to reconcile trademark rights and free expression locally and globally, including legislators, trademark offices, and courts. This flexible approach will allow experimentation by states on what speech-protective trademark laws work best, and does not require an amendment to the TRIPS Agreement. When there is more global consensus on the best way to balance trademark rights and free expression, perhaps mandatory limitations on trademark rights can be included in a new multilateral treaty, trade agreement, or amendment to TRIPS. Until then, free speech advocates should work state-by-state to increase protection for free expression in trademark legislation, trademark office determinations, and court decisions.

12. Reconciling international obligations to protect health and trademarks: A defense of trademarks as property

Sam F. Halabi[*]

I. INTRODUCTION

This chapter explores the increasing confrontations between states' obligations to protect trademarks under international agreements and states' duties to protect their citizens' health under international human rights law. Trademark holders have asserted international protections for their logos, images, symbols and words to thwart regulatory efforts to use graphic warnings to inform consumers about the risks of alcohol and tobacco consumption, fight child malnutrition through promotion of breastfeeding and protect consumers from packaging and labeling tactics which hide health risks. In response, governments have invoked their responsibility to respect, protect and fulfill the right to health, including the duty to protect citizens from threats posed by third parties.[1] Scholars exploring these confrontations have tended to include trademark holders' challenges as another variety of the problems caused by 'propertization' of trademarks. According to their critique, lawmakers in industrialized states have over recent decades expanded the circumstances under which trademark holders may assert their rights to prohibit unauthorized uses of their marks (even for political commentary or truthful comparative advertising), enjoin actions by third parties that might diminish the value of a mark (even if it is not an unauthorized use nor in the course of

[*] Portions of this chapter originally appeared in Sam Foster Halabi, 'International Trademark Protection and Global Public Health: A Just Compensation Regime for Expropriations and Regulatory Takings' (2012) 61 Catholic U L Rev 325.

[1] International Covenant on Economic, Social and Cultural Rights (opened for signature 16 December 1966, entered into force 3 January 1976) 993 UNTS 3 (ICESCR) art 12(1); United Nations Economic and Social Council (ECOSOC), 'Substantive Issues Arising in the Implementation of the ICESCR – General Comment No 14' (11 August 2000) UN Doc E/C.12/2000/4, para 48.

trade), and demand compensation where regulatory measures result in direct or indirect expropriations of marks.

Critics of trademark propertization assert that before this process unfolded, trademark law focused on the effect a mark or tradename had on consumers, providing an inexpensive source of product information that the law reasonably protected from imitators. This protection benefited both firms and consumers.[2] Now, however, trademark law focuses on the investments made by the trademark holder and the corresponding (though speculative) goodwill generated by those investments, including acts by third parties with attenuated and difficult-to-prove effects on the value of a mark.[3]

Industrialized states have sought to export stronger trademark protection through bilateral, regional and multilateral investment and trade treaties. The World Trade Organization's (WTO) Agreement on Trade-Related Aspects of Intellectual Property (TRIPS), for example, requires participating governments to define minimum criteria for trademark registrability and resulting rights of use; limits the exceptions governments may impose; and establishes an enforcement regime that orients judicial authorities in particular towards robust protection of trademarks and other intellectual property.[4] Regional integration instruments like NAFTA and EU Council Directives have similarly broadened the protections trademark proprietors enjoy from both commercial competitors and regulatory obstacles.[5] Bilateral investment and trade treaties have further ratcheted up these protections by equating trademarks with more secure forms of property and enabling foreign trademark holders to (1) demand

---

[2] Eugene C Lim, 'Dilution, the Section 22 Debacle, and the Protection of Business Goodwill in Canada: Some Insights from U.S. Trademark Law and Policy' (2011) 101 Trademark Rep 1232, 1268.

[3] Jeremy Sheff, 'Marks, Morals, and Markets' (2013) 65 STANFORD L REV 761; Ruth Okediji, 'The International Intellectual Property Roots of Geographical Indicators' (2008) 82 Chicago-Kent L Rev 1329, 1332.

[4] Agreement on Trade-Related Aspects of Intellectual Property Rights (adopted 15 April 1994, entered into force 1 January 1996) 1869 UNTS 299 (TRIPS Agreement) art 16.

[5] North American Free Trade Agreement (US–Canada–Mexico) (adopted 17 December 1992, entered into force 1 January 1994) (1993) 32 ILM 289 (NAFTA) art 1708; Council Directive 2004/48/EC of 29 April 2004 on the enforcement of intellectual property rights [2004] OJ L157/45, 61.

that governments justify to international arbitrators any regulatory measures and (2) demand compensation for direct and indirect expropriations resulting from regulatory action.[6]

With respect to states' duty to protect citizens' health from threats posed by third parties, this chapter challenges the property critique of expanding trademark protection with two arguments.[7] First, while the critical commentary focuses on the 'propertization' driven by international trademark law, it neglects trademarks' increasing 'expressification,' that is, executive, legislative and judicial measures equating trademarks and other distinguishing symbols with generally more protected forms of social and political expression. The expressification of trademarks poses a more significant challenge for states' obligations to protect the right to health. Instead of trademark law focusing on the informational content of a mark so far as it affects consumers' health-related decisions, it focuses on the right of a trademark proprietor to speak and impart information about its product or its corporate self. Second, the health objectives embodied in trademark restrictions are more likely to be achieved the more trademarks are evaluated as a form of property, not expression. The trend toward 'propertization' should therefore be viewed as relatively preferable to a world where commercial speech is treated as artistic, political and/or social speech and protected accordingly by strong domestic and international human rights law. Regulators enjoy far more flexibility in defining and limiting property rights than speech rights, which often impose a comprehensive bar to regulatory action.

Strong trademark protections carry substantial implications for international obligations to respect, protect and fulfill the right to health. In product sectors like alcohol, breastmilk substitutes, food, non-alcoholic beverages, and tobacco, trademarks and tradenames can subtly convey dubious health information. They may also obscure (and thus undermine) warnings intended to achieve better informed health decisions. These effects are often intended. For example, where it is still permitted, cigarette manufacturers use the words 'light' and 'mild' and associated color spectra in their brands to suggest those cigarettes are less risky than 'full flavor' cigarettes.[8] Similarly, combinations of pictograms, colors and

[6] Agreement on the Reciprocal Promotion and Protection of Investments (Switzerland–Uruguay) (adopted 17 October 1988, entered into force 22 April 1991) 1976 UNTS 389, art 5(1).

[7] ICESCR, art 12(1).

[8] *United States v Philip Morris USA, Inc.*, 449 F. Supp. 2d 1, 26–27 (D.D.C. 2006).

descriptors shape consumers' perception of the nutritional value of packaged food and the safety of consuming alcohol.[9]

Focusing on the duty of states to protect individual and public health sheds light on the normative hierarchy taking shape in the treaties and agreements that form international trademark law. Those agreements, both in the hands of drafters and their judicial and arbitral interpreters, are dismantling trademarks as an independent field of law where optimal balancing of public and private interests is likely. Rather, shaped by international agreements, trademark law worldwide is now the subject of a subtle but critical confrontation between expression and property analogies.[10] It therefore does little good to call for a return of trademark law to its golden age of consumer protection; rather, the focus must be on which of these analogies better accommodates the flexibility that judges, legislators and regulators must enjoy in order to reconcile competing international obligations.

II. THE GLOBAL EXPANSION OF TRADEMARK PROTECTIONS

The basic purpose of trademark law has been remarkably consistent over the course of history.[11] Within limits, trademark protection provides an incentive for firms to invest in the quality of goods and services and, relatedly, to reduce the costs to consumers of identifying products with desirable quality and price.[12] Without laws prohibiting trademark infringement or misappropriation, imitators are enabled to free-ride on those investments and dupe consumers.[13] Where the product supplied is not only inferior but hazardous – for example, as may be true of foods

---

[9] Gill Cowburn and Lynn Stockley, 'Consumer Understanding and Use of Nutrition Labelling: A Systematic Review' (2005) 8 Public Health Nutrition 21, 21–22; David Jernigan and James O'Hara, 'Alcohol Advertising and Promotion' in Richard J Bonnie and Mary Ellen O'Connell (eds), *Reducing Underage Drinking: A Collective Responsibility* (National Academies Press 2004) 625.

[10] Sonia Katyal, 'Trademark Intersectionality' (2010) 57 UCLA L Rev 1601, 1605.

[11] Benjamin G. Paster, 'Trademarks – Their Early History' (1969) 59 Trademark Rep. 551, 552.

[12] William M Landes and Richard A Posner, 'Trademark Law: An Economic Perspective' (1987) 30 J L & Economics 265, 275–80.

[13] Robert G Bone, 'Hunting Goodwill: A History of the Concept of Goodwill in Trademark Law' (2006) 86 Boston U L Rev 547, 555–6.

and medicines – the concern about quality is magnified. Trademark protection thus promises a mutual benefit to firms and consumers.

In recent decades trademark protections have expanded from a relatively narrow focus on protecting consumers' expectations to protecting firms' investments in the creation, advertising and marketing of goods or services. This expansion ranges from the incremental and procedural to the substantive and sweeping.[14] In the United States, the Lanham Act has historically provided injunctive and monetary relief for firms able to prove that a competitor's mark created a 'likelihood of confusion' as to the source of goods or services.[15] In 1995 and 2006, Congress strengthened protections for well-known marks, enabling trademark holders to enjoin activities that affected marks even absent a 'likelihood of confusion.'[16] Rudolph Rayle has traced the progress of German trademark law from relatively modest protections based on consumer expectations in brands to a 1979 German Federal Constitutional Court judgment determining that trademarks constituted 'property' under the Constitution of Germany.[17] Because trademarks are an 'expression of an entrepreneur's achievement motivation',[18] German law protects as trademark holders artists, holding companies and advertising firms.[19] Rayle views this progress as largely consistent with relevant EU Council Directives, 'i.e., de-emphasizing the traditional source identifying function and emphasizing the trademark owner's rights'.[20] Under French law, trademarks have the same protections as copyrights and patents, and 'the [trademark] proprietor must be entitled to enjoin any kind of unauthorized use, no matter for which purpose.'[21]

---

14 Graeme W Austin, 'Trademarks and the Burdened Imagination' (2004) 69 Brooklyn L Rev 827, 829–31.

15 Lanham Act 1946 (US) ss 32, 43.

16 Federal Trademark Dilution Act of 1995 (US); Trademark Dilution Revision Act of 2006 (US).

17 Rudolf Rayle, 'The Trend Towards Enhancing Trademark Owners' Rights – A Comparative Study of U.S. and German Trademark Law' (2000) 7 J Intellectual Property L 227, 235–6, fn 40.

18 Ibid 236.

19 Ibid 270.

20 Ibid.

21 Annette Kur, 'Fundamental Concerns in the Harmonization of (European) Trademark Law' in Graeme B Dinwoodie and Mark D Janis (eds), *Trademark Law and Theory: A Handbook of Contemporary Research* (Edward Elgar Publishing 2008) 151; Jeremy Phillips, *Trade Marks at the Limit* (Edward Elgar Publishing 2006) 163–4.

These non-confusion based protections have been exported through investment and trade agreements. [22] Developed states introduced at the 1986 Uruguay Round of negotiations for the WTO a set of uniform protections for trademarks (TRIPS).[23] TRIPS grants trademark holders rights to prevent confusing uses of an identical or similar mark on identical or similar goods and limits conditions states may impose on trademark rights.[24] In addition to substantive provisions, TRIPS also outlines minimal enforcement obligations.[25] Many WTO member states have passed trademark laws exceeding the minimum requirements set by TRIPS.[26] Some bilateral and regional investment and trade treaties define trademarks as covered investments without the normal public interest exceptions domestic law or TRIPS allows; others require governments to justify regulatory measures and, even then, mandate compensation for direct or indirect expropriations.[27]

For many areas of consumer products, expanding the property protections of trademarks generates benign or welfare-enhancing effects for consumers.[28] Consumers who know that a particular brand of product

---

[22] Burton Ong, 'The Trademark Law Provisions of Bilateral Free Trade Agreements' in Dinwoodie and Janis (n 21) 229–30.

[23] .JH Reichman, 'Universal Minimum Standards of Intellectual Property Protection Under the TRIPS Component of the WTO Agreement' (1995) 29 INTL LAWYER 345, 385.

[24] .TRIPS Agreement, art 16(1). Owners of well-known marks receive additional protection against uses of their marks on dissimilar goods: arts 16(2)–(3). Article 20 limits the encumbrances that can be placed on trademarks. According to Nuno Pires de Carvalho, art 20 did not contemplate restrictions on health, food, or security measures; rather, restrictions specifically related to a course of trade required, for example, that a foreign trademark be associated with a domestic licensee. Nuno Pires de Carvalho, *The TRIPS Regime of Trademarks and Designs* (Aspen Publishers 2006) 331. According to Daniel Gervais and Susy Frankel, health measures are also subect to review under art 20 but the public health nature of the measure may be used as a justification under that article. Daniel Gervais and Susy Frankel, 'Plain Packaging and the Interpretation of the TRIPS Agreement' (2013) VAND. J. TRAN'L. L.

[25] TRIPS Agreement, art 21.

[26] Carsten Fink and Beata K Smarzynska, 'Trademarks, Geographical Indications, and Developing Countries' in Bernard Hoekman, Aaditya Mattoo and Philip English (eds) *Development, Trade and the WTO: A Handbook* (World Bank Publications 2002) 403, 410.

[27] United Nations Conference on Trade and Development, *Intellectual Property Provisions in International Investment Arrangements* (United Nations 2007) 5.

[28] Jeremy Sheff, 'Biasing Brands' (2011) 32 CARDOZO L REV 1245, 1250.

offers them the right balance of quality and price spend less time comparing prices or searching for third-party evaluations. Trademark law justifiably acts to protect from encroachment by competitors the expectations that consumers build into those brands. Internationally, ensuring stronger trademark protection lowers the costs for manufacturers to do business across national boundaries because their well-known brands facilitate entry into new markets.[29]

However, it is in the economic sectors most likely to affect health that the welfare-enhancing benefits of trademark protection give way to efforts to suggest false product attributes and hide health risks. A 1999 study, for example, concluded that the 'three most valuable brand names were Marlboro, Coca-Cola and Budweiser, in that order.'[30] The extraordinarily competitive environment of consumer products guarantees that firms will use trademarks to increase consumer demand in ways other than quality improvement.[31] Common tactics include minimizing or obfuscating mandatory health warnings, using descriptors likely to lead to false impressions, and shaping packaging and labeling to appeal to target populations.[32] Trademark holders can communicate certain product qualities by way of design suggestion and implication, circumventing prohibitions against explicitly deceptive representations.[33]

Tobacco firms, for example, accompanied 'light', 'mild' descriptors in cigarette brands with corresponding color schemes such that even after governments slowly adopted bans on those marks, the 'light' and 'mild' message remained effectively communicated:

> Even after the [EU] ban, Benson & Hedges Lights will be recognizable by their silver color, contrasting with the gold of the regular packs. White-and-gold Marlboro Lights will still suggest 'lightness' just by the stark contrast to

---

[29] Keith E Maskus, 'Intellectual Property Challenges for Developing Countries: An Economic Perspective' 2001 U Illinois L Rev 457, 461.

[30] Kevin R Casey, 'Problem Trademarks of the Descriptive-Misdescriptive-Deceptive Types' [Summer 2012] Pennsylvania Bar Association Intellectual Property L Newsletter 7, 7.

[31] Jon D Hanson and Douglas A Kysar, 'Taking Behavioralism Seriously: Some Evidence of Market Manipulation' (1999) 112 Harvard L Rev 1420, 1466.

[32] American Heart Association and others, 'Deadly in Pink: Big Tobacco Steps Up its Targeting of Women and Girls' (18 February 2009) 1 <http://www.lung.org/assets/documents/publications/other-reports/deadly-in-pink.pdf> accessed 22 January 2014; WHO, *Gender, Women, and the Tobacco Epidemic* (WHO 2010) 106.

[33] Rebecca Tushnet, 'Running the Gamut From A to B: Federal Trademark and False Advertising Law' (2011) 159 U Pennsylvania L Rev 1305, 1318–19.

> the red, full-strength Marlboros. The powder-blue Camel Lights with their pastel camel will still look milder than the ornery desert-ocher animalon the regular 'Filters' pack.[34]

This strategic marketing is not limited to cigarettes. The symbols and color schemes on alcoholic beverage containers effectively obscure government-mandated warnings,[35] and the image of a healthy, smiling baby or cartoon characters held in breastfeeding positions on an infant formula container may lead consumers to misunderstand the nutritional inferiority and risks inherent in food alternatives for infants.[36] In states in which illiteracy rates are high and symbols are a principal means to both warn and sell, trademark protections pose greater barriers to the promotion of individual and public health.[37]

As governments across the globe enhance trademark protections, they are undertaking an unprecedented effort toward fulfilling obligations to secure their citizens' right to the highest attainable standard of health.[38] Governments have both aspirational and pragmatic reasons for doing so. The right to health has been a principle of international human rights law since the Universal Declaration on Human Rights. Article 12 of the International Covenant on Economic, Social and Cultural Rights (ICESCR) ensures 'the right of everyone to the enjoyment of the highest attainable standard of physical and mental health.'[39] Moreover, 'the right to health, like all human rights, imposes three types or levels of obligations on States parties: the obligations to *respect, protect and fulfil* … . The obligation to *protect* requires States to take measures that prevent third parties from interfering with article 12 guarantees.'[40] Even

---

34 Geoff Winestock, '"Light" Tobacco Ads Found Deceptive, EU Says' *The Wall Street Journal* (*Legacy Tobacco Documents Library*, 8 November 2000) <http://legacy.library.ucsf.edu/tid/tze92c00/ pdf> accessed 22 January 2014.

35 Center for Science in the Public Interest, 'Alcohol Warning Labels Go Unnoticed, Poll Finds' (17 August 2001) <http://www.cspinet.org/booze/batf_labels2001_press.htm> accessed 22 January 2014.

36 Hubert Barennes and others, 'Misperceptions and Misuse of Bear Brand Coffee Creamer as Infant Food: National Cross Sectional Survey of Consumers and Paediatricians in Laos' (2008) 337 BRITISH MEDICAL J 379.

37 Surendra J Patel, 'Trademarks and the Third World' (1979) 7 WORLD DEVELOPMENT 653, 653.

38 David Fidler, 'After the Revolution: Global Health Politics in a Time of Economic Crisis and Threatening Future Trends' (Fall 2008/Spring 2009) 2(2) GLOBAL HEALTH GOVERNANCE 1.

39 ICESCR, art 12(1).

40 ECOSOC, 'Substantive Issues Arising in the Implementation of the ICESCR – General Comment No. 14' (11 August 2000) UN Doc E/C.12/2000/4

in states that are not parties to the ICESCR, the state's responsibility to safeguard individual and public health is either constitutionally codified or a generally understood obligation.[41]

The increasing costs of an unhealthy population encourage policies aimed at controlling sources of communicable and noncommunicable disease. There is a close relationship between this latter public health burden – cancer, diabetes, heart disease, obesity – and the products associated with some of the most valuable and well-known trademarks. Tobacco consumption, which annually kills approximately five million people worldwide, represents the principal preventable threat to individual and public health in both developed and developing countries.[42] Alcohol consumption not only results in greater harm to third parties relative to other drugs like cocaine and heroin,[43] but also increases risks of cancer and heart disease in users.[44]

Interventions to address these health threats conflict with trademark protections in at least two ways. First, prohibiting or restricting certain word or stylistic trademarks conflicts generally with trademarks' purpose of source identification. Second, large or graphic warnings, especially if required on packaging and labeling, may distort trademarks' appearance.[45] Prohibitions on tobacco trademarks that create false impressions are now common as are graphic warnings. Governments are now exploring 'traffic light' systems to inform consumers about the nutritional content of packaged food.[46] In 2010, Thailand proposed legislation requiring that graphic warning labels cover 30 percent of the surface of

---

(General Comment 14) [33] (emphasis added). General Comment 14 further states that 'violations of the right to health can occur through the direct action of States or other entities insufficiently regulated by States.' ibid, para 48.

41 Valentina S Vadi, 'Trade Mark Protection, Public Health and International Investment Law: Strains and Paradoxes' (2009) 20 European J Intl L 773, 802.

42 Theodore H Tulchinsky and Elena A Varavikova, *The New Global Public Health* (2d edn, Academic Press 2008) 23.

43 David J Nutt and others, 'Drug Harms in the UK: A Multicriteria Decision Analysis' (2010) 376 The Lancet 1558, 1560–1. Alcohol consumption and its corresponding negative effects are increasing worldwide.

44 WHO, *Alcohol and Injuries: Emergency Department Studies in an International Perspective* (WHO 2009) iv.

45 '*IP in the Media*' (Complete IP News, September–October 2010) 1–2 <http://www. completeip.com.au/attachments/File/Issue___22.pdf> accessed 22 January 2014.

46 Carolyn L Engelhard, Arthur Garson, Jr and Stan Dorn, *Reducing Obesity: Policy Strategies from the Tobacco Wars* (Urban Institute 2009) 34–5.

beer, wine, and spirits containers.[47] Regulators are likely to push for trademark restrictions on products that impose direct costs on governments.

Critics of trademark 'propertization' contest the social worth of expanding trademark protections based on their conflict with a number of public interests, including health. In a well-known critique of judicial and legislative expansion of grounds for infringement claims in the U.S., Mark Lemley concluded that

> [P]ropertizing trademarks comes at a rather significant cost to society ... Important political and social commentary and works of art may be suppressed entirely ... . And perhaps most important, trademark licensing is expensive. The more we propertize, the more transaction costs we impose on everyone.[48]

Kal Raustiala echoes this criticism in the context of the global expansion of IP rights, noting that trademarks often impose strong protections 'upon developing countries that neither need nor desire' them, and concluding that 'propertization will serve to wall off still more from the public domain, further draining an already reduced global commons.'[49] Valentina Vadi has broadly criticized the propertization of trademark protections in the context of international investment law and public health, drawing examples from Canada, the EU, Guatemala and Nicaragua.[50]

III. THE EXPANSION OF SPEECH-BASED PROTECTIONS FOR TRADEMARKS

Analogizing the expansion of trademark holders' rights to stronger property protections is understandable. The basic motivation of trademark law is to give the trademark proprietor the right to exclude others and control use. Generally, trademarks may be freely bought, sold, or licensed. Trademarks are regularly assigned a monetary value. The

---

47 WTO, '*Tobacco and Alcohol Technical Barriers Among Members' Trade Concerns*' (24–25 March 2010) <http://www.wto.org/english/news_e/news10_e/tbt_24mar10_e.htm> accessed 22 January 2014.

48 Mark A. Lemley, 'The Modern Lanham Act and the Death of Common Sense' (1999) 108 Yale L.J. 1687, 1696.

49 Kal Raustiala, 'International Rights Approaches to Intellectual Property' (2007) 40 UC Davis L Rev 1021, 1032–3.

50 Vadi (n 41) 802.

'propertization' of trademark law is, in essence, the expanding circumstances under which a trademark right holder is empowered to invoke the power of the state to ensure these rights to exclusion, alienation and compensation, mostly against other private parties.

The trademark holder's ability to exclude and control, of course, is largely exercised over specific forms of aural and visual communication.[51] Trademark protection is therefore fundamentally tied to expression and speech. This relationship presents a dilemma for judges and legislators who are forced to draw lines between a trademark proprietor seeking to assert a lawful claim to protect the integrity and value of a mark and a private party seeking to parody or criticize the party with whom the mark is associated. For example, the environmental advocacy group Greenpeace adapted the logo of the French firm Esso as part of a campaign criticizing the company's industrial activities.[52] Esso sued Greenpeace, and the trial court awarded Esso an injunction, along with potential fines of €5,000 per day.[53] The French civil supreme court (*Cour de cassation*) ultimately vindicated Greenpeace's position, finding the parody within the scope of free expression implicit in French trademark law. It is exactly this situation that TRIPS Article 17 contemplates, creating the flexibility for a state to adopt a conforming trademark law that nevertheless allows the use of a trademark for artistic, political or social commentary.[54]

Relative to property, however, free expression enjoys substantially wider protection under international human rights law. Article 19 of the International Covenant on Civil and Political Rights provides that:

> everyone shall have the right to freedom of expression; this right shall include freedom to seek, receive and impart information and ideas of all kinds, regardless of frontiers, either orally, in writing or in print, in the form of art, or through any other media of his choice.[55]

---

[51] Landes and Posner (n 12) 275–80.

[52] Greenpeace, 'Greenpeace Shuts Down Esso' (25 October 2002) <http://www.greenpeace.org/international/en/news/features/greenpeace-shuts-down-esso/> accessed 22 January 2014.

[53] Tribunal de Grande Instance de Paris, 30/01/2004, Esso c/ Greenpeace France et SA Internet FRCCE 10/04/04 n° 4 p. 24 juris data n 2005.

[54] Lisa P Ramsey, 'Free Speech and International Obligations to Protect Trademarks' (2010) 35 Yale J Intl L 405, 407.

[55] International Covenant on Civil and Political Rights (adopted 16 December 1966, entered into force 23 March 1976) 999 UNTS 171 (ICCPR) art 19.

International human rights law protects persons' rights to seek, receive and impart information as part of this crucial democratic right.[56] Exceptions are permitted for, inter alia, 'public health' but measures limiting rights to speech and information must be 'necessary,' a frequently fatal requirement if less speech restrictive means are available.[57] The European Convention on Human Rights, The American Convention on Human Rights, and the Canadian Charter of Freedoms broadly track ICCPR Article 19's structure and content. The European Court of Human Rights has emphasized that freedom of expression is necessary for 'each individual's fulfillment.'[58]

Trademark holders have successfully tied the source identification function of trademarks with the human right to impart information and the right to define the self. In a recent case adjudicating South Africa's restrictions on the display of tobacco trademarks, the South Africa Supreme Court of Appeal concluded that:

> It is clear that under s 16(1)*(b)* of the Constitution that [British American Tobacco] is entitled to the right to freedom of expression, which includes the 'freedom to receive or impart information or ideas', in this case, to consenting adult consumers of its tobacco products ... The right to freedom of expression guarantees the intrinsic right of persons to communicate information and ideas. It is an indispensable element of a democratic society.[59]

In short, the self-distinction identified as a core part of freedom of expression overlaps considerably with the justifications proffered for strong trademark protections. Relatedly, in some industry sectors a trademark's value may comprise the majority of a company's worth

---

56 ICCPR, art 19; Convention for the Protection of Human Rights and Fundamental Freedoms (European Convention on Human Rights, as amended) (opened for signature 4 November 1950, entered into force 3 September 1953) 213 UNTS 221 (ECHR) art 10; American Convention on Human Rights (opened for signature 22 November 1969, entered into force 18 July 1978) 1144 UNTS 123 (ACHR) art 13; African Charter on Human and Peoples' Rights (adopted 27 June 1981, entered into force 21 October 1986) (1982) 21 ILM 58 (Banjul Charter).

57 A similar analysis obtains for trade-restrictive public health measures in the WTO system. However, other trademark-specific flexibilities allow substantial space for public health regulation.

58 *Ceylan v Turkey* (1999) 30 EHRR 73, para. 32.

59 *British American Tobacco South Africa (Pty) Ltd v Minister of Health* (463/2011) [2012] ZASCA 107, [2012] 3 All SA 593 (SCA) (20 June 2012) [13].

precisely because of indivisibility of advertising, promotion, and marketing costs from consumer preference for the trademark.[60] As the CEO of a major brewer noted, 'A beer is a beer is a beer … so therefore it is all about brands … We are not selling beer, we are selling image.'[61] Firms express themselves, indeed *make themselves distinct*, through their trademarks. Wally Olins phrased the concept this way:

> Identity is expressed in the names, symbols, logos, colours and rites of passage which the organization uses to distinguish itself, its brands and its constituent companies. At one level, these serve the same purpose as religious symbolism, chivalric heraldry or national flags and symbols … At another level, they represent consistent standards of quality and therefore encourage consumer loyalty.[62]

Yet corporate identity does not play the role conventionally associated with the public opinion shaping importance of freedom of expression. The purpose of the expression is *always* to sell a product.

The more fiercely firms compete to distinguish themselves and their products through distinctive emblems, logos, and other protected symbols, the more that expression looks like the self-actualizing activity strong international human rights law is intended to protect. Rebecca Tushnet has explored this phenomenon in the U.S. context where she anticipates that trademark law's ability to regulate commercial expression will collapse as the U.S. Supreme Court abandons distinctions between commercial, political and social speech.[63] Even when a substantial public interest justifying a speech restriction is asserted, it is balanced against the full force of free expression and its constituent human rights norms.[64] Market pressures ensure that this expression will not aim *only* to distinguish, but will also aim to increase consumption, especially by appealing to young consumers. Alcohol, food and tobacco industries have

---

[60] Shawn K Baldwin, '"To Promote the Progress of Science and Useful Arts": A Role for Federal Regulation of Intellectual Property as Collateral' (1995) 143 U PENNSYLVANIA L REV 1701, 1704.

[61] Jernigan and O'Hara (n 9).

[62] Wally Olins, *Corporate Identity: Making Business Strategy Visible Through Design* (Thames & Hudson 1990) 9.

[63] Rebecca Tushnet, 'Trademark Law as Commercial Speech Regulation' (2007) 58 South Carolina L Rev 737, 741.

[64] *RJR-MacDonald v Canada (A-G)* [1995] 3 SCR 199, 209.

all used trademarks like cartoon characters and color schemes to appeal to children and adolescents.[65]

IV. PROPERTY, SPEECH AND THE DUTY TO PROTECT HEALTH IN INTERNATIONAL TRADEMARK LAW

Trademarks as a 'form of expression the speaker is entitled to issue' or a 'form of property with narrow rights to exclude and alienate' are analogies which will influence the ability of lawmakers to safeguard individual and public health. Given the strength accorded to free expression under international human rights law and many national constitutions, the property paradigm for trademark law offers greater flexibility for judges, legislators and regulators confronted with situations in which trademarks create false impressions or where a product warning regime interferes with trademark expectations.

A property-based approach to trademarks allows regulators to tailor their protective scope to their commercial function. Indeed, one of the possibilities Lisa Ramsey explores for reconciling private parties' use of trademarks under TRIPS for artistic, political and social commentary is Article 16's specification that trademark holders be empowered to prevent third parties' use of identical, similar or confusing marks 'in the course of trade.'[66] This limitation may be similarly read to exempt regulatory measures which prohibit certain trademarks (like misleading descriptors) or affect trademarks by requiring large warnings on packaging and labeling or other point of sale restrictions. The plain language of TRIPS, after all, confers no positive right to use a trademark.[67] In other words, as a form of property the existence of which is the result of state largesse, the state can similarly confine its use against competitors and their ilk.

---

[65] Aron M Levin and Irwin P Levin, 'Packaging of Healthy and Unhealthy Food Products for Children and Parents: The Relative Influence of Licensed Characters and Brand Names' (2010) 9 J Consumer Behaviour 393, 393–94; Jernigan and O'Hara (n 9); Centers for Disease Control, 'Changes in the Cigarette Brand Preference of Adolescent Smokers – United States, 1989–1993' (1994) 43 Morbidity & Mortality Weekly Rep 577.

[66] Ramsey (n 54), 407.

[67] Allyn Taylor, Prabhat Jha, Emmanuel Guindon and Michaelyn Corbett, 'The Impact of Trade Liberalization on Tobacco Consumption' in Prabhat Jha and Frank J Chaloupka (eds), *Tobacco Control in Developing Countries* (OUP 2000) 343–64.

But TRIPS flexibilities do little in the context of bilateral investment treaties, which include some of the strongest trademark protections. For example, the Switzerland-Uruguay bilateral investment treaty, under which Philip Morris International is pursuing a trademark-based investment claim against Uruguay's cigarette packaging regulations, categorically defines trademarks as 'investments,' imposes a requirement that measures affecting investments be adopted for 'reasons of the public interest, as defined by the law and on the condition that such measures are not discriminatory' and, even then, requires compensation for measures having the direct or indirect effect of expropriation.[68]

Expropriation is fundamentally a question of property rights, so both the extent of those rights and their derivative financial worth may be shaped by the state. National authorities and international arbitrators enjoy sufficient flexibility to craft an expropriation proceeding that balances the state's duty to protect individual and public health with the trademark holder's legitimate interest in the distinguishing characteristics of its mark.[69] For example, lawmakers and adjudicators may place an evidentiary obligation on the trademark holder to show that a state-imposed trademark restriction *actually* causes consumers to switch to competing goods, effectively aligning the economic structure of trademark ownership and use with the interests trademark protections are intended to promote.

As a preliminary matter, many states sensibly require trademark holders to police the use of their trademarks. Because trademarks grant the holder control over the use of a particular form of communication, trademark holders abandon the right to that monopoly when the trademark becomes synonymous with the underlying product.[70] Trademark holders are also obligated to police their marks to show that consumers may be confused by similar marks and to prove damages like lost sales.[71] Indeed, many

---

[68] Indeed, NAFTA and many other trade and investment agreements include this as an explicit requirement. NAFTA, art 1110. *See also* Agreement Between the Swiss Confederation and the Oriental Republic of Uruguay On the Reciprocal Promotion and Protection of Investments (Switzerland–Uruguay) (adopted 7 October 1988, entered into force 22 April 1991) 1976 UNTS 413 (Switzerland–Uruguay BIT) art 3.

[69] Sam Foster Halabi, 'International Trademark Protection and Global Public Health: A Just Compensation Regime for Expioprations and Regulatory Takings' (2012) 61 CATH. U. L. REV. 325.

[70] Landes and Posner (n 12) 291.

[71] Michael S Mireles, Jr, 'Towards Recognizing and Reconciling the Multiplicity of Values and Interests in Trademark Law' (2011) 44 *Indiana L Rev* 427, 451–2, 470–2.

trademark holders maintain elaborate trademark policing systems to guard against infringement as well as counterfeiting.[72] Tobacco firms, for example, long ago adopted worldwide trademark registration, policing, and exploitation programs.[73] Similar infrastructure exists for alcohol and packaged-food brands.[74] Manufacturers and their trademark developers excel in gathering information as to what causes consumers to prefer one brand, image, or logo over another.[75] Trademark holders are served by global consultancies that report the (admittedly subjective) value of trademarks as a function of competitors' market share.[76]

Requiring trademark proprietors to show that consumers are switching to competitors' goods or services furthers the presumptive goal of trademark restrictions: better informed consumers. Government-mandated warnings and trademark restrictions are, after all, aimed at influencing consumption through better information. For example, when the U.S. banned the descriptors 'light' and 'low' from cigarette brands, it recognized that the elimination might lead some consumers to quit smoking and prevent others from starting to smoke.[77] In the product

---

[72] Philip Morris Management Corp, Memorandum from Robert J Eck on September Trademark Activities (*Legacy Tobacco Documents Library*, 11 October 1999) <http://legacy.library.ucsf.edu/tid/rhm62c00/pdf> accessed 22 January 2014.

[73] British American Tobacco, 'Strategic Management of Trade Marks and Other Intellectual Property' (*Legacy Tobacco Documents Library*, undated) PINCITE <http://legacy.library.ucsf.edu/tid/riq34a99/pdf> accessed 22 January 2014; British American Tobacco, 'Effective Trade Mark Management' (*Legacy Tobacco Documents Library*, 2 February 1998) <http://legacy.library.ucsf.edu/tid/rcn93a99/pdf> accessed 22 January 2014.

[74] Kraft General Foods International, 'Kraft General Foods International: 1992–1996 Five Year Plan' (*Legacy Tobacco Documents Library*, 4 March 1992) 1–4 <http://legacy.library.ucsf.edu/tid/dsm42e00/pdf> accessed 22 January 2014; Miller Brewing Company, 'Miller Brewing Company Five-Year Plan 1992–1996' (*Legacy Tobacco Documents Library*, 1992) 1–6 <http://legacy.library.ucsf.edu/tid/psm42e00/pdf> accessed 22 January 2014.

[75] Ross D Petty, 'The Codevelopment of Trademark Law and the Concept of Brand Marketing in the United States Before 1946' (2011) 31 J MACROMARKETING 87, 90, 93–99.

[76] Alexandra Ourusoff, 'What's in a Name? (Brand Name Valuation)' Financial World Partners (Legacy Tobacco Documents Library, 1 September 1992) 1–4 <http://legacy.library.ucsf.edu/tid/xkd42d00/pdf> accessed 22 January 2014.

[77] CG Husten and LR Deyton, 'Understanding the Tobacco Control Act: Efforts by the US Food and Drug Administration to Make Tobacco-Related Morbidity and Mortality Part of the USA's Past, not Its Future' (2013) THE LANCET 381.

sectors most closely tied to health, requiring that trademark holders prove consumer switching is consistent with their asserted reasons for wanting strong trademark protections: firm and product distinction. By definition, trademarks are protected only to the extent that they effectively distinguish the producer's products.[78] Trademark holders have no general right to a given level of consumption and certainly no right to attract young persons, which is often an ulterior objective of certain trademarks. As such, the trademark holder is not entitled to recoup its investments in trademark quality or advertisements; rather, it may recoup only its narrow interest in distinguishing its product from products of others.

A property-based paradigm, of course, would not always require compensation. As Professor GC Christie argues, if a prohibition concerning the use of property 'can be justified as being reasonably necessary to the performance by a State of its recognized obligations to protect the public health, safety, morals or welfare, then it would normally seem that there has been no "taking" of property.'[79] When the state encumbers or 'takes' a trademark by partially or totally prohibiting its use or by requiring additional product information (including warnings),[80] the state has in effect concluded that some or all of the mark *as it appears to consumers* must be taken for a public purpose.[81]

Critics of expanding trademark protections are correct that the dominant paradigm in international trademark law now is the 'propertization' trend. So why worry about trademarks as expression? The first reason is the expanding protections given to commercial speech worldwide. Tamara Piety and Rebecca Tushnet have noted not only the expanding reach of First Amendment protection for commercial speech in the U.S., but the evident willingness of a majority of U.S. Supreme Court justices to dispense with the commercial speech doctrine entirely. The latter has specifically anticipated the problems that dispensation will cause for

---

78 TRIPS Agreement, art 15(1) (emphasis added).

79 David Schneiderman, 'NAFTA's Takings Rule: American Constitutionalism Comes to Canada' (1996) 46 U Toronto LJ 499, 530, fn 168.

80 *Commonwealth Brands, Inc v United States* 678 F Supp 2d 512, 531 (WD Ky 2010); Joseph J Lewczak and Angela M Bozzuti, *Will Federal Food Ad "Guidelines" Tread on Brand Trademarks?* (Washington Legal Foundation, 2011) 1–2 <http://www.wlf.org/Upload/legalstudies/legalopinionletter/10-21-11 LewczakBozzutti_LegalOpinionLetter.pdf> accessed 22 January 2014.

81 Roseann B Termini, 'The Family Smoking Prevention and Tobacco Control Act and Public Health' (2010) 81 Pennsylvania Business Association Q 147, 149.

trademark regulation.[82] Roger Shiner has documented the expansion of free speech protections to commercial advertising in Canada, the U.S. and in both the constitutional courts of Europe as well as the European Court of Justice and the European Court of Human Rights.[83] While there is no right to free expression, per se, protected in international trade law, the WTO Appellate Body has also made relatively strong statements as to the expressive nature of trademarks:

> Every trademark owner has a legitimate interest in preserving the distinctiveness, or capacity to distinguish, of its trademark so that it can perform that function … Taking account of that interest will also take account of the trademark owner's interest in the economic value of its mark arising from the reputation that it enjoys and the quality that it denotes.[84]

V. CONCLUSION

The growing burden of cancer, diabetes, and heart disease and the relationship of that burden to the practices of global alcohol, food and tobacco industries will force more confrontations between international trademark protections and the right to the highest attainable standard of health. The 'propertization' critics of modern trademark law are correct as to its deleterious effects on the public domain and the costs of consumer products. Yet the expressification of trademarks engenders even more significant threats to regulatory action. Giving trademarks the legal status of artistic, political or social expression presents a powerful tool to prevent sensible public health interventions in favor of far less effective ones like governmental education campaigns. Through large pictorial warnings and aggressive restriction of implied health messages, regulators attempt to bring information about long-term health effects as close to the time of purchase or consumption as possible. As a form of property, trademarks present less of an obstacle to accomplishment of individual and public health objectives than as expression, where their clearly persuasive influence is imagined to be just one of many voices in the market.

---

[82] Tamara R Piety, *Brandishing the First Amendment* (U Michigan Press 2012); Tushnet (n 63).

[83] Roger Shiner, *Freedom of Commercial Expression* (OUP 2003).

[84] WTO, *European Communities: Protection of Trademarks and Geographical Indications for Agricultural Products and Foodstuffs – Report of the Panel* (15 March 2005) WT/DS174R [7.664].

13. Anti-dilution protection of luxury brands in the global economy

*Haochen Sun**

I. INTRODUCTION

In June 2008, the Paris Commercial Court held eBay secondarily liable for offering online venues to sell counterfeit Louis Vuitton products. In particular, the court ruled that eBay had harmed the reputation of Louis Vuitton's trademarks.[1] On the other side of the Atlantic, eBay was sued in the United States (US) by another luxury company, Tiffany, for facilitating the sale of counterfeit Tiffany products on the eBay website. In this case, the Southern District Court of New York ruled in favor of eBay, holding that eBay did not harm the reputation of the Tiffany trademark.[2]

Why did these two factually similar trademark dilution cases yield judicial decisions that were at odds with each other? This chapter aims to explore the policy responsible for this rift. It reveals that the rift is actually the tip of the iceberg in the global anti-dilution protection of luxury brands. In fact, luxury companies face two major challenges in securing adequate anti-dilution protection. At the international level, the major intellectual property treaties do not afford clear-cut minimum standards for anti-dilution protection of well-known trademarks. At the domestic level, divergences in anti-dilution protections in the world's three main luxury markets – the European Union (EU), the US, and China – have rendered it more difficult for luxury companies to prevent dilution of their brands. Based on the analysis of these two challenges, the chapter will offer thoughts about how policy makers should improve

* I am grateful to Professor Daniel Gervais for the kind invitation to contribute a chapter and for his very helpful comments on an earlier draft. I also benefited a lot from the conversations with Irene Calboli, Rochelle Dreyfuss, Susan Scafidi and Peter Yu. As always, any errors or oversights are mine alone.

1 *SA Louis Vuitton Malletier v eBay*, [2010] Inc., Tribunal de grande instance [TGI] [ordinary court of original jurisdiction] Paris, June 30, 2008, 10 E.T.M.R. 10.2010, 177.

2 *Tiffany Inc v eBay, Inc* 600 F 3d 93, 111-12 (2nd Cir 2010).

anti-dilution protection for luxury brands while meeting their duties to adequately protect the public interest.

II. ANTI-DILUTION PROTECTION AS THE LIFEBLOOD OF LUXURY BRANDS

A. The Rise of the Luxury Industry in the Global Economy

During the past two decades, the luxury industry rapidly developed and expanded its presence in many major cities around the world. In 2011, global luxury goods sales reached approximately $250 billion.[3] Europe, the US, and China are the three major luxury markets in the world.[4] Europe stands alone, however, as the global hub for designing, producing, and merchandizing luxury goods. Most luxury brands have originated from Europe. The major luxury conglomerates, such as Kering, Louis Vuitton Moët Hennessy (LVMH), and Compagnie Financière Richemont SA (Richemont), are headquartered in Europe. Moreover, three of the four fashion capitals (London, Milan, New York, and Paris) are located in Europe. Sales volume is very high. Research shows that Europe accounted for 37 and 35 percent of global luxury goods sales in 2011 and 2012, respectively.[5] Despite the economic slowdown in Europe, tourists who come from around the world help the European luxury market grow steadily. Indeed, tourist luxury shopping counts for a big portion of luxury sales in Europe.[6] For example, Gucci reportedly sells

---

[3] Bain & Company, 'Luxury Goods Wordwide Market Study, 2011' (20 January 2012) 3 <http://www.slideshare.net/Ikusmer/luxury-goods-worldwide-market-study> accessed 25 January 2014.

[4] Japan was the second largest luxury market in the world. However, due to the recent years' economic downturn, the Japanese luxury market has been shrinking. A recent study shows that Chinese, European and American consumers purchased the largest number of luxury handbags. 'Luxury Goods in China: Beyond Bling' *The Economist* (8 June 2013) <www.economist.com/news/business/21579015-life-getting-harder-purveyors-luxury-china-growth-prospects-are-still> accessed 25 January 2014.

[5] Bain & Company, 'Worldwide Luxury Markets Monitor, Spring 2013 Update' (16 May 2013) 4 <www.fccihk.com/files/dpt_image/5_committees/library/LibraryLuxury/2013BainLuxuryStudySpringUpdate.pdf> accessed 25 January 2014.

[6] Adam Greaves, 'How China's Anticorruption Drive is Hitting Sales of European Luxury Brands' (*Bribery Library*, 10 June 2013) <www.briberylibrary.

more than 50 percent of its products to tourists in Europe,[7] and Chinese tourists alone account for around 30 percent of Burberry's total London sales.[8]

The US market has also been vibrant. For example, it was reported that 52 percent of Christian Louboutin shoes were sold in the US, while this French luxury shoemaker sold 30 percent of its footwear in Europe, the Middle East and Russia combined.[9] And while the US market was hit hard during the 2008 financial crisis, the US remains one of the important luxury markets in the world. As the US economy continues to improve, sales of luxury goods are recovering.[10] It was estimated that major luxury brands had seen 10–20 percent sales growth by August 2011.[11]

China has become the world's largest luxury market based on country-specific calculations.[12] Wealthy Chinese consumers have been eager to shop for luxury goods and services to upgrade their lifestyles. It is estimated that China accounted for 25 percent of the global luxury spending in 2012 – 5 percent higher than the US.[13] Research also shows that Chinese consumers make half of the luxury purchases in Asia and one-third of those in Europe.[14] Responding to the exploding demand

---

com/gifts-hospitality/how-chinas-anticorruption-drive-is-hitting-sales-of-european-luxury-brands/> accessed 25 January 2014.

[7] Kathy Gordon, 'Chinese Tourists Boost Europe Luxury Sales' *The Wall Street Journal* (2 December 2010) <online.wsj.com/article/SB1000142405274870459480457564848259841828.html> accessed 25 January 2014.

[8] Ibid.

[9] Miles Socha, 'Getting a Handle on Louboutin' (*Women's Wear Daily*, 4 February 2008) <www.wwd.com/accessories-news/handbags/getting-a-handle-on-louboutin-467853> accessed 25 January 2014.

[10] Stephanie Clifford, 'Even Marked Up, Luxury Goods Fly Off Shelves' *The New York Times* (3 August 2011) <www.nytimes.com/2011/08/04/business/sales-of-luxury-goods-are-recovering-strongly.html?_r=0> accessed 25 January 2014.

[11] Ibid.

[12] The World Luxury Association predicted that China will replace Japan as the world's largest luxury market by 2012 because of China's growing demand and Japan's declining consumption. See 'China to Pass Japan as Top Luxury Market in 2012' *China Daily* (10 June 2011) <http://www.chinadaily.com.cn/bizchina/2011-06/10/content_12670694.htm> accessed 25 January 2014.

[13] Bain & Company, 'Chinese Shoppers World's Top Luxury Goods Spenders, While China Luxury Market Cools to Seven Percent Growth in 2012' (12 December 2012) <www.bain.com/about/press/press-releases/bains-china-luxury-market-study-2012.aspx> accessed 25 January 2014.

[14] Ibid.

from Chinese customers, luxury companies have opened up stores in major cities there and have highlighted the role of the Chinese market in their long-term development strategies.[15] By setting prices higher in China than in Europe and the US, luxury companies are said to earn more profits there.[16] Meanwhile, fueled by talented Chinese fashion designers and a combination of Eastern and Western design inspirations, China's domestic luxury brands have been growing rapidly, garnering domestic and international fame.[17]

B. Luxury Brands and Anti-Dilution Protection

As a form of enhanced trademark protection, the anti-dilution right entitles the owner of a well-known trademark to prevent and stop acts that would either blur the distinctiveness or tarnish the reputation of the trademark, even absent consumer confusion.[18] Hence, the rise of the anti-dilution right has advanced trademark protection from preventing consumer confusion to granting a strong property right[19] in the 'uniqueness' of a well-known mark.[20]

Anti-dilution protection preserves the strong exclusivity of global brands, which is particularly crucial for luxury companies. The key function of luxury products is their ability to signal social distinction. There are two related types of social goals underlying consumer attitudes toward luxury brands: consumption of luxury goods to gain social status, and consumption of luxury goods to reflect personal choices (a more

---

15 Rachel Sanderson, 'Luxury Goods Sales Slow as China Clamps Down on Gift Giving' *Financial Times* (16 May 2013) <www.ft.com/intl/cms/s/0/d530e34e-be02-11e2-bb35-00144feab7de.html#axzz2a3noyHqU> accessed 25 January 2014.

16 Wei Gu, 'Luxury-Goods Firms' Little China Secret' *The Wall Street Journal* (25 April 2013) <online.wsj.com/article/SB10001424127887324474004578444090260265834.html> accessed 25 January 2014.

17 Uche Okonkwo, *Luxury Fashion Branding: Trends, Tactics, Techniques* (Palgrave Macmillan 2008) 74 ('China has a host of upcoming designers that will likely to play influential roles in the world of fashion.'); Laurie Burkitt, 'As Luxury Tastes Evolve, Hermès Banks on China' *The Wall Street Journal* (8 October 2012) <blogs.wsj.com/scene/2012/10/08/as-luxury-tastes-evolve-hermes-banks-on-china/> accessed 25 January 2014.

18 Lanham Act (US) s 43(c).

19 Mary LaFrance, *Understanding Trademark Law* (2nd edn, LEXISNEXIS 2009) 204.

20 Frank I Schechter, 'The Rational Basis of Trademark Protection' (1927) 40 *Harvard L Rev* 813, 831.

self-centered expressive function). Luxury companies cater to the combination of these two needs by maintaining the exclusivity of their products and services. Commentators have pointed out that luxury companies, like magicians, seek to 'perform an illusion where actual scarcity is replaced by a perceived rarity.'[21] For a brand to function as a distinctive sign of luxury, it 'must be desired by all but consumed only by the happy few.'[22] Luxury companies have strived to appeal to the general public, but meanwhile make their products or services available only to the few who can afford them. For that exclusivity purpose, they have adopted production and price policies to use high-quality designs and materials in order to keep the prices of their products very high. They have also limited production (or given that impression) and innovated means of delivering products and services perceived to be highly distinctive.[23] In parallel, luxury companies have adopted distribution policies to either sell products only in their own company stores or to authorize selected dealers to sell on their behalf, often with strict licensing terms. Last but not least, luxury companies have actively carried out communication policies designed to enhance brand exclusivity. They routinely utilize celebrity images to associate their products or services with upper-class people and elite lifestyles.[24]

Anti-dilution protection plays three important roles in protecting and enhancing the exclusivity of luxury brands. First, it prevents or stops a third party from using a luxury brand in classes of goods or services that are not desirable to the luxury company, even absent any likelihood of confusion. The anti-blurring doctrine, for example, prohibits association arising from the similarity between a mark or trade name and a famous mark that impairs the distinctiveness of the famous mark.[25] Thereby, it functions to prevent the prestigious images of luxury brands from being diluted as brands accessible to the mass public or on products perceived as such – an effect that would gradually whittle away the prestigious

---

[21] Bernard Catry, 'The Great Pretenders: The Magic of Luxury Goods' (2003) 14 *Business Strategy Rev* 10, 11.

[22] Jean-Noel Kapferer, *Strategic Brand Management: New Approaches to Creating and Evaluating Brand Equity* (Kogan Page Ltd 1997) 82.

[23] Andrew Roberts, 'Building Luxury Brand Loyalty via Exclusive Experiences' *Bloomberg Businessweek* (31 January 2013) <www.businessweek.com/articles/2013-01-31/building-luxury-brand-loyalty-via-exclusive-experiences> accessed 25 January 2014.

[24] Klaus Heine, *The Concept of Luxury Brands* (2nd edn, Technische Universität Berlin 2012) 86–87.

[25] Lanham Act (US) s 43(c)(2)(C).

images of luxury brands. Typical examples of blurring the prestigious images of luxury brands include using the Rolls Royce mark to identify restaurants, cafeterias, pants, candies, or hot chocolate. If such uses of the mark were allowed, then the mark would no longer conjure up in the minds of the public a prestigious brand associated with cars made for the super-rich. Instead, the mark would stand for goods or services available to 'the masses.' Luxury companies would therefore face the grave risk of losing the brands' 'selling power'[26] and attractiveness to many of their consumers.

In his seminal paper that laid the foundation of modern anti-dilution doctrine, Frank Schechter highlighted the importance of the anti-blurring function in protecting the commercial interests associated with luxury brands.[27] In 1932, the New York Supreme Court enjoined a motion picture producer from using the Tiffany mark in connection with his business. It held that such use would dilute the distinctiveness of Tiffany as a mark for jewelry. The court so ruled in order to protect the interest of the Tiffany Company, which was already a famous jewelry maker by that time.[28] Today, judges still use examples concerning luxury brands to examine the policy justifications for the anti-blurring doctrine.[29]

The second type of dilutive act is concerned with the use of luxury brands in the products or advertising of non-luxury brands. These acts are different from the first type of dilutive acts, which involve use of luxury brands to identify the junior user as the provider of goods or services. Under the second type of dilutive acts, luxury brands are used for the purpose of adding luxury elements to the products or services offered by the non-luxury user of the mark. Courts have ruled that a non-luxury brand causes harm to a luxury brand when it associates itself with that luxury brand. Indeed, a recent dispute between Louis Vuitton and Hyundai concerned exactly this type of dilutive use. In this dispute, Hyundai's commercial for its Sonata car model contained a scene of an inner-city basketball game featuring the use of a modified version of the Louis Vuitton monogram. According to Hyundai, the purpose of the

---

[26] Schechter (n 20) 832.

[27] Ibid., 825.

[28] *Tiffany & Co v Tiffany Productions, Inc* 264 NY Supp 459, 461 (1932), affd 237 App Div 801, 260 NY Supp 821 (1932), affd 262 NY 482, 188 NE 30 (1933).

[29] *Ty Inc v Perryman* 306 F 3d 509, 511–12 (7th Cir 2002) (using hypotheticals about Tiffany & Co. as an example to raise three policy concerns about dilution: raising consumer search costs; brand tarnishment; and eliminating free riding in advertising).

commercial was to 'redefine the concept of luxury by communicating to consumers that [its] Sonata offered "luxury for all."'[30] The US court ruled that Hyundai had diluted the distinctiveness of the Louis Vuitton trademark. This case shows that the unauthorized use of a luxury brand in a non-luxurious setting may cause trademark dilution.

The third type of dilutive acts occur when luxury goods are sold through unauthorized distribution channels (those not controlled by the luxury company). In the European case *Copad SA v Christian Dior Couture SA*, there was a licensing agreement between the plaintiff, Christian Dior, and the defendant, Copad. To maintain 'the repute and prestige of'[31] the Dior mark, the agreement prohibited the sale of Dior products in discount stores that were not authorized by Dior. The defendant, however, did just that, selling Dior products in its discount stores after Dior refused to give permission. Recognizing that 'luxury goods are high-class goods,'[32] the European Court of Justice ruled that the Copad had 'damage[d] the allure and prestigious image which bestows on [the Dior products] an aura of luxury.'[33]

Apart from preserving the exclusiveness of luxury brands, anti-dilution protection guards against dilutive acts that would cause harm to the luxury brands' reputation for quality. Some might think that the fame of luxury goods and services is determined by the high quality of those goods and services. Indeed, the perceived (and sometimes empirically verified) premium craftsmanship that luxury companies have endeavored to instill into their products, coupled with after-sale services, is key to convincing consumers to make purchases.[34] Premium service standards are also the cornerstone of luxury service providers, such as luxury hotels and exclusive clubs. Therefore, some scholars have suggested that the perceived quality of goods and services is the foremost factor in defining the concept of luxury.[35] According to this view, as luxury goods are pricey, luxury consumers routinely deem the high prices as the direct indicator of high quality that luxury companies endeavor to offer.

Tarnishment of a brand's reputation for quality would affect the overall demand for the luxury goods. The anti-tarnishment doctrine thus guards

---

30 *Louis Vuitton Malletier, SA v Hyundai Motor America* 2012 WL 1022247, 2 (SDNY, 22 March 2012).

31 Case C-59/08 *Copad SA v Christian Dior Couture SA and others* [2009] ECR I-03421 [8].

32 Ibid., [25].

33 Ibid., [37].

34 Catry (n 21) 10.

35 Ibid.

against dilutive use of a luxury brand in a way that would harm this reputation. Tarnishment may occur when a trademark is linked to 'products of shoddy quality, or is portrayed in an unwholesome or unsavory context.'[36] The harm caused by dilutive use in this context is 'that the public will associate the lack of quality or lack of prestige in the defendant's goods with the plaintiff's unrelated goods.'[37] Tarnished reputation would affect the overall demand for the luxury goods, whether the consumers use the luxury products for self-presentation or self-expression.

Before the US Congress passed a law to provide national anti-dilution protection, the US courts had examined the unique role of anti-tarnishment doctrine in protecting the quality reputation of luxury brands. In *Rolex Watch USA v Canner*,[38] the US District Court for the Southern District of Florida admitted that a rational purchaser would not be misled to believe that a $25 counterfeit Rolex watch available at a flea market was a real one. But the court noted that trademark law must weed out counterfeits in this context by relying on the policy concern that today justifies anti-tarnishment protection. The court noted that the availability of counterfeit watches would deter Rolex consumers from purchasing its watches after learning of the poor quality of counterfeit watches. If poor-quality counterfeit watches became readily available (legally), the prestige image of Rolex and its goodwill would be diluted. That would discourage consumers from buying real Rolex watches.[39]

This conclusion has now been confirmed by more recent judicial decisions on luxury brands. In the *Dior* case discussed above, the European Court of Justice asserted that 'an impairment to the aura of luxury is likely to affect the actual quality of those goods.' In a later US case, *Fendi Adele SRL v Filene's Basement*,[40] Filene's sold counterfeit merchandise bearing one or more of the Fendi marks. The case record reflected that the marks on the counterfeit items were virtually identical to, or exact replicas of, one or more of the Fendi marks. The US court held that 'Filene's use of the Fendi Marks dilutes the quality of the

---

[36] *Deere & Co v MTD Products, Inc* 41 F 3d 39, 43 (2nd Cir 1994).

[37] Ibid.

[38] *Rolex Watch USA, Inc v Canner* 645 F Supp 484, 492 (SD Fla 1986).

[39] Ibid., 495. See also *Ferrari SPA v Roberts* 944 F 2d 1235, 1244 (6th Cir 1991).

[40] *Fendi Adele SRL v Filene's Basement, Inc* 696 F Supp 2d 368, 391 (SDNY 2010).

Marks by diminishing their capacity to identify and distinguish the Fendi Products.'[41]

III. ANTI-DILUTION PROTECTION IN INTERNATIONAL TRADEMARK LAW

The preceding Part discussed the paramount importance of anti-dilution law in protecting luxury brands. Given that global marketing is key to luxury companies, this Part will examine whether international trademark treaties have provided minimum standards that member states must adopt in their domestic trademark systems. It will show that the Paris Convention for the Protection of Industrial Property (the Paris Convention)[42] and the Agreement on the Trade-Related Aspects of Intellectual Property Rights (the TRIPS Agreement)[43] have not made clear that member states should provide full anti-dilution protection.

A. The Paris Convention

Article 6*bis* of the Paris Convention is a specific provision dealing with the protection of well-known trademarks. Article 6*bis*(1) mandates protection of well-known trademarks against registrations or uses of any junior marks that are likely to cause confusion concerning source of goods.[44] It follows that member states should refuse or cancel registrations of, and prohibit use of, those junior marks in identical or similar goods. Article 10*bis* further provides that member states should prohibit '[a]ny act of competition contrary to honest practices in industrial or commercial matters that constitutes an act of unfair competition.'[45] The wording of this provision seems to guard against dilutive registrations or uses of marks that may cause unfair competition. However, this provision is construed to encompass only unfair competition acts that would be

---

[41] Ibid., 390.

[42] Paris Convention for the Protection of Industrial Property (adopted 20 March 1883, as revised at Stockholm 14 July 1967) 828 UNTS 305 (Paris Convention).

[43] Agreement on Trade-Related Aspects of Intellectual Property Rights (adopted 15 April 1994, entered into force 1 January 1996) 1869 UNTS 299 (TRIPS Agreement).

[44] Paris Convention, art 6*bis* (1).

[45] Ibid., art 10*bis* (2).

likely to cause confusion.[46] The types of prohibited acts that the provision highlights are those that 'create confusion', constitute 'false allegations' or would tend to 'mislead the public.'[47] Therefore, with respect to protection of well-known trademarks, the Paris Convention only requires adequate protection against acts that would cause consumer confusion regarding sources of goods in the marketplace. It does not require member states to afford anti-dilution protection.

B. The TRIPS Agreement

The TRIPS Agreement expands the scope of anti-confusion protection of well-known trademarks under the Paris Convention. Article 16.2 of the TRIPS Agreement extends protection to cover services[48] and clarifies how to determine whether a mark is well known. Furthermore, Article 16.3 extends protection of well-known trademarks to dissimilar classes of goods and services as follows:

> Article 6*bis* of the Paris Convention (1967) shall apply, *mutatis mutandis*, to goods or services which are not similar to those in respect of which a trademark is registered, provided that use of that trademark in relation to those goods or services would indicate a connection between those goods or services and the owner of the registered trademark and provided that the interests of the owner of the registered trademark are likely to be damaged by such use.[49]

The language of this provision arguably shows that the TRIPS Agreement mandates anti-dilution protection of well-known trademarks. For example, the word 'connection' may refer to the mental association caused by dilutive acts that blur the distinctiveness of a senior mark. Additionally, the wording about damaging the interests of the owner of a senior trademark may be broad enough to encompass dilutive acts that tarnish the reputation of the senior mark. This literal reading of the Article may lead to the conclusion that the TRIPS Agreement requires member states to prohibit dilutive uses of well-known trademarks.

---

46 David S Welkowitz, *Trademark Dilution: Federal, State, and International Law* (2nd edn, BNA Books 2012) 647.

47 Paris Convention, art 10*bis* (3).

48 TRIPS Agreement, art 16.2.

49 TRIPS Agreement, art 16.3.

However, there is significant disagreement on whether the TRIPS Agreement requires full anti-dilution protection.[50] On one side of the debate, Professor Daniel Gervais, a leading authority on the TRIPS Agreement, argues that Article 16 of the Agreement requires two types of trademark protection: Article 16.2 requires anti-confusion protection, and Article 16.3 requires something akin to anti-dilution protection (though not necessarily as it exists in current US law).[51] Several other leading experts – namely, Professors Jerome Reichman[52] and Carlos Correa[53] – hold the same position.

Yet, there is still ample room for interpreting Article 16.3 restrictively by arguing that it merely covers more types of anti-confusion protection and thereby serves only to supplement Article 16.1. For example, one may argue that Article 16.3 allows the owner of a registered well-known mark to sue a competitor on the basis of unfair competition that has led to false indications of a connection between these two parties and may damage the interest of the owner of the well-known mark. These causes of action can be found under Article 10*bis* of the Paris Convention, which prohibits unfair competition acts such as the misappropriation of goodwill associated with a mark and a false allegation that discredits the reputation of a mark. For example, reverse passing off illustrates the expanded protection under Article 16.3 but is not covered by Article 16.1.

Moreover, the Joint Recommendation Concerning Provisions on the Protection of Well-Known Marks (the WIPO Recommendation)[54] adds further complication in interpreting Article 16.3 of the TRIPS Agreement. The WIPO Recommendation was adopted by the WIPO in 1999, five years after the inception of the TRIPS Agreement. Although the WIPO Recommendation is merely an international soft law creating no legal

---

[50] Lisa P Ramsey, 'Free Speech and International Obligations to Protect Trademarks' (2010) 35 *Yale J Intl L* 405, 432.

[51] Daniel Gervais, *The TRIPS Agreement: Drafting History and Analysis* (4th edn, Sweet & Maxwell 2012) 333.

[52] *See* JH Reichman, 'Universal Minimum Standards of Intellectual Property Protection Under the TRIPS Component of the WTO Agreement' (1995) 29 *Intl Lawyer* 345, 361.

[53] Carlos Correa, *Trade Related Aspects of Intellectual Property Rights: A Commentary on the TRIPS Agreement* (OUP 2007) 192.

[54] The Assembly of the Paris Union for the Protection of Industrial Property and the General Assembly of the World Intellectual Property Organization (WIPO), 'Joint Recommendation Concerning Provisions on the Protection of Well-Known Marks' (29 September 1999) 833(E).

obligations,[55] it is still an important international instrument for harmonizing global trademark protection. Under Article 4(1) of the WIPO Recommendation, a junior mark used for dissimilar goods or services is deemed to be in conflict with the well-known trademark if the junior mark constitutes a reproduction, an imitation, a translation, or a transliteration of the well-known mark *and* if one of the following conditions is satisfied:

(i) the use of that mark would indicate a connection between the goods and/or services for which the mark is used, is the subject of an application for registration, or is registered, and the owner of the well-known mark, and would be likely to damage his interests;
(ii) the use of that mark is likely to impair or dilute in an unfair manner the distinctive character of the well-known mark;
(iii) the use of that mark would take unfair advantage of the distinctive character of the well-known mark.[56]

With this provision, the WIPO Recommendation shed light on whether Article 16.3 of the TRIPS Agreement has embraced full anti-dilution protection as a minimum standard for global trademark protection. As shown above, Article 4(1)(b) of the WIPO Recommendation has three parts. The first part contains language that is identical to that of Article 16.3 of the TRIPS Agreement. The second and third parts expressly require member states to provide full anti-dilution protection to the owners of well-known trademarks.[57] Additionally, the language of Article 4(1)(b) of the WIPO Recommendation – specifically, 'impair or dilute … the distinctive character' of the well-known mark – accords with the typical anti-dilution terminologies used in US and EU anti-dilution law.

It therefore seems that this provision of the WIPO Recommendation would be redundant if Article 16.3 of the TRIPS Agreement were interpreted as requiring full anti-dilution protection. However, the Explanatory Notes attached to the WIPO Recommendation make it clear that the first part of Article 4(1)(b) of the WIPO Recommendation deals only with likelihood of confusion stemming from false association or sponsorship:

---

[55] MRF Senftleben, 'The Trademark Tower of Babel – Dilution Concepts in International, US and EC Law' (2009) 40 *Intl Rev Intellectual Property & Competition L* 45, 51.

[56] WIPO Recommendation, art 4(1).

[57] Senftleben (n 55) 53.

> Under this item, a connection between a well-known mark and a third party's goods or services may be indicated, for example, if the impression is created that the owner of the well-known mark is involved in the production of those goods, or the offering of those services, or that such production or offering was licensed or sponsored by him. The interests of the owner of the well-known mark could be damaged if the goods and/or services with which the connection is established have a down-market image, thereby reflecting negatively on the goodwill of the well-known mark.

This note shows that both Article 4(1)(b) of the WIPO Recommendation and Article 16.3 of the TRIPS Agreement are intended to extend anti-confusion protection of well-known trademarks from confusion regarding sources of goods to confusion regarding false association and/or sponsorship. Both types of confusion may cause harm to the legitimate interests of trademark owners. Based on this consideration, Article 4(1)(b) of the WIPO Recommendation further separates two more provisions requiring anti-dilution protection. It reaffirms that the protection of well-known trademarks can take two forms: anti-confusion and anti-dilution protection. Each type protects the interests of trademark owners in different ways. Anti-dilution protection is afforded in the absence of a likelihood of confusion. Therefore, there is a need to have separate provisions setting forth each type of protection. If this arrangement of the WIPO Recommendation were inappropriate, representatives from member states of the TRIPS Agreement would not have supported the passage of this document at the WIPO's meetings of the assemblies.

IV. DIVERGENCES IN DOMESTIC ANTI-DILUTION LAWS

The preceding Part showed that the major international treaties do not set forth clear-cut minimum standards in the context of full anti-dilution. The absence of such standards makes it more difficult for luxury companies to enforce their rights and to rely on international law requirements in convincing national governments to provide adequate anti-dilution protection. This Part will further show that the lack of minimum standards concerning full anti-dilution protection in international trademark treaties has led to the second major challenge that the luxury industry faces. The new challenge stems from the wide divergences in anti-dilution protection established at domestic levels. This Part will analyze divergences between the US, the EU and China – the three largest luxury markets in the world. Then it will examine whether these divergences have created hurdles that the luxury industry must overcome in order to protect their brands against dilutive uses.

A. Divergences in the US and EU

The US Federal Trademark Dilution Act, adopted in 1995 and revised by the Trademark Dilution Revision Act (TDRA) in 2006, provides federal anti dilution protection of famous marks. On the other side of the Atlantic, the Trademark Harmonization Directive, adopted by the European Council in 1988, provides EU-wide anti-dilution protection. While both of these laws were designed to prohibit trademark dilution, there are wide discrepancies in the standards of anti-dilution protection. This section will discuss these major discrepancies.

1. Requisite level and proof of fame/reputation

Anti-dilution protection is afforded only to well-known trademarks. To prove the fame/reputation characteristic of well-known trademarks, there is a substantial overlap of factors considered by the courts in the US and EU.[58] Both jurisdictions consider sales or turnover, though a lower level of sales will suffice to reach the threshold in the EU.[59] Other common factors include usage in terms of duration and extent, advertising effort, and third-party recognition of status (for example, professional rankings).[60]

There is a major difference in protection of marks that have reached the requisite level of recognition among customers. In the US, the TDRA mandates that only marks that enjoy nation-wide fame will qualify for anti-dilution protection. Nation-wide fame is defined as being 'widely recognized by the general consuming public of the US as a designation of source of goods or services of the mark's owner.'[61] In contrast, marks that enjoy only niche fame in the marketplace will still be protected under the EU anti-dilution law, as long as a mark has a reputation in a substantial part of the relevant sector of an industry.[62] As such, the level of fame required in the US is arguably higher than that required in the EU.

---

[58] Ilanah S Fhima, *Trade Mark Dilution In Europe And The United States* (OUP 2011) para 2.86.

[59] Ibid., para 2.96.

[60] Ibid., para 2.46–2.83, 2.88–2.123.

[61] Lanham Act (US) s 43(c)(2)(A).

[62] *General Motors Corp v Yplon SA* [1999] ETMR 122 [21]; *DataCard Corp v Eagle Technologies Ltd* [2011] RPC 17 [291].

In the US, the reference to the general public eliminates any possibility that a brand owner can claim anti-dilution protection by relying on the brand's niche fame in a limited geographic area or a specialized market.[63] The stakes in alleging dilution and proving fame are high. If a plaintiff fails to provide sufficient evidence of fame as defined in Lanham Act § 43(c)(2)(A), then its dilution claim fails. The Federal Circuit's recent decision in *Coach Services, Inc v Triumph Learning LLC* demonstrates significant evidentiary pitfalls that even the owner of a very familiar brand may face in proving the fame required for anti-dilution protection. In this case, plaintiff Coach opposed the registration of the defendant's mark (also Coach) for educational materials used to prepare students for standardized tests. Plaintiff Coach asserted that the defendant's trademark registration would blur the distinctiveness of its own Coach mark for luxury goods. Plaintiff Coach successfully proved the famous mark status of Coach for its anti-confusion claim. But plaintiff Coach failed to prove that the fame of Coach was high enough to deserve anti-dilution protection.[64] In this respect, the court ruled that although Coach handbags are extremely well-known and highly regarded by many consumers in the US, Coach had failed to submit sufficient evidence to prove that its mark had become a household name, and thus was not famous for anti-dilution protection.

As *Coach Services* demonstrates, luxury brands may encounter difficulty in proving nation wide fame for anti-dilution protection. Not all luxury brands been recognized as well-known trademarks. Of course, US courts have recognized some luxury brands as famous marks entitled to anti-dilution protection. They include Audi, Rolex, Louis Vuitton, Victoria's Secret, and Tiffany. Luxury brands that have adopted lower-profile marketing strategies,[65] however, may face grave challenges in proving national recognition of their marks. For example, Bottega Veneta is known for not using logos on the surfaces of their products for the

---

63 *Top Tobacco, LP v North Atlantic Operating Co* 509 F 3d 380, 384 (7th Cir 2007).

64 *Coach Services, Inc v Triumph Learning LLC* 668 F 3d 1356, 1376 (Fed Cir 2012). See also J Thomas McCarthy, *McCarthy on Trademarks and Unfair Competition* (4th edn, West 2011) s 24:104.

65 There is also a belief that '[a] true luxury brand doesn't have to advertise'. Tim Hill, 'How Experiences Are Redefining Luxury' (*The Guardian*, 30 October 2013) <www.guardian.co.uk/media-network/partner-zone-brand-union/luxury-experiences> accessed 25 January 2014.

purpose of increasing brand exclusivity.[66] Hermès has been marketing their products without much promotion.[67] Because the fame of a mark is essentially measured by advertising and marketing efforts made by the owner of the mark, such low-profile marketing strategies could make it difficult for the relevant luxury companies to prove the well-known status of their trademarks.

2. Requisite degree and proof of association

Under US and EU anti-dilution law, the senior mark owner must prove that there is an association between the senior and junior marks that would likely cause dilution.[68] The EU and US take different approaches in establishing association of junior and senior marks in the public's mind. Association is a separate stage of the dilution analysis in EU law stipulated in *Intel v CPM*. This decision ruled that factors such as similarity of marks, similarity of goods/services, strength of reputation of the senior mark, distinctiveness of the senior mark, and likelihood of confusion to the public have to be examined.[69] By comparison, US law focuses less on assessing the presence of association; accordingly, similarity of marks plays a greater role than do other factors.

To assess the similarity of marks, EU courts require a lower standard than do their US counterparts; although US courts use a 'near identity' standard,[70] this test focuses primarily on the dominant elements of the marks and largely ignores differences in less dominant elements.[71] The US standard is exemplified in the *Jada Toys v Mattel* case,[72] in which the court found Hot Wheels and Hot Rigz to be nearly identical – while the second word in each mark was different, both marks were accompanied by a flame of similar color. Nevertheless, there remains a stark contrast because in the EU, the junior mark will be regarded as a similar

---

66 *See* Kate Betts, 'Fashion: The Height of Luxury' *TIME* (23 April 2006) <http://www.time.com/time/magazine/article/0,9171,1186563,00.html> accessed 25 January 2014.

67 *See* Jing Jing, 'Fashion Forward' *China Daily* (2 July 2007) <www.chinadaily.com.cn/bw/2007-07/02/content_907229.htm> accessed 25 January 2014.

68 *See* Fhima (n 58) para 3.01–.02.

69 Case C-252/07 *Intel Corp Inc v CPM United Kingdom Ltd* [2008] ECR I-8823, para 42.

70 *Perfumebay.com Inc v eBay, Inc* 506 F 3d 1165, 1180–81 (9th Cir 2007).

71 *Jada Toys, Inc v Mattel, Inc* 518 F 3d 628, 635 (9th Cir 2008).

72 Ibid.

one to the senior mark, once it brings the senior mark to the mind of the consuming public.[73]

3. Blurring/detriment to distinctive character

In the US, dilution by blurring is defined as the association arising from the similarity between a junior mark and a senior mark, the effect of which impairs the distinctiveness of the famous mark.[74] While in the EU, it is noted that detriment to a mark's distinctive character is also referred to as dilution or whittling away or blurring.[75]

US anti-dilution law lists six non-exhaustive factors for consideration in cases of dilution by blurring: the degree of similarity between parties' marks; the degree of inherent or acquired distinctiveness of the famous mark; the extent to which the senior user is engaging in substantially exclusive use of the senior mark; the degree of recognition of the senior mark; whether the user of the mark or trade name intended to create an association with the famous mark; and any actual association between the parties' marks.[76] In relative agreement, *Intel v CPM* suggests that EU anti-dilution law examines five factors in determining detriment to distinctive character: the existence of a link between parties' marks; the strength of distinctiveness of the senior mark; the reputation of the senior mark; the degree of uniqueness of the senior mark; and any change in the economic behavior of customers.[77]

Both the US and EU tests for blurring focus on the strength of the senior mark and the likelihood of association, without paying any regard to circumstantial evidence of harm. The existence of association only shows that the conditions for blurring are there for the junior mark to harm the distinctiveness of the senior mark, rather than showing that harms did take place.

The major difference between these two tests is that the EU test requires proof of change in the economic behavior of customers. In practical terms, this means that senior users are required to show that damage has been caused or that there is a strong likelihood that damages will result.[78] This heightened requirement makes the EU test more restrictive than its US counterpart; accordingly, it will be more difficult

---

73 *Intel* (n 69) para 44.
74 Lanham Act (US) s 43(c)(2)(B).
75 *Intel* (n 69) para 29.
76 Lanham Act (US) ss 43(c)(2)(B)(i)–(vi).
77 *Intel* (n 69) para 42.
78 Ibid., para 77.

for owners of luxury-brand trademarks to prove that their marks have been blurred in the EU.

4. Taking unfair advantage of distinctive character or repute

Another major difference in anti-dilution law between the US and the EU is that the US law does not contain a provision prohibiting free-riding acts. US law only prohibits dilution by blurring and tarnishing. EU law not only guards against these two types of dilution, but also penalizes any dilutive act that takes unfair advantage of the distinctive character or repute of a well-known mark. In simple terms, to determine whether an act takes unfair advantage of a well-known mark (described as 'riding on the coat-tails of the senior mark'), the EU court undertakes a global assessment by considering the strength of the mark's reputation, the degree of the mark's distinctiveness, the degree of similarity between the marks at issue, and the nature and degree of proximity of the goods/ services concerned.[79]

5. Defenses

Defenses against dilution claims are intended to promote the protection of freedom of expression and prevent anti-dilution from unduly constraining legitimate market competition. In general, there are three statutory defenses against dilution claims in the US: fair use, news reporting, and non-commercial use. In the EU, however, there are no such defenses expressly provided in the Trademark Directive. Instead, defendants have to rely on general defenses to trademark infringement that have been interpreted narrowly and subject to greater restraint. As a result, US anti-dilution law is believed to provide stronger protection of freedom of expression.

The category of fair use in the US includes nominative fair use, descriptive fair use, comparative advertising, and parodic use. Nominative fair use exempts a user from liability when he uses the senior mark to identify the senior user. Descriptive fair use applies where a junior user uses the senior mark to describe its own goods.[80] In the EU, the nominative use defense is not available. However, the descriptive fair use defense is available following *Adam Opel AG v Autec AG*, given that such junior use is 'in accordance with honest practice in industrial and commercial matters.'[81] Otherwise, junior users may have to rely on the general defense of use with due cause, which is limited in effect (for

[79] Case NVC-487/07 *L'Oréal SA v Bellure* [2009] ECR I-5185, para 44.
[80] Lanham Act (US) s 33(b)(4).
[81] Case C-48/05 *Adam Opel AG v Autec AG* [2007] ECR I-1017, para 43.

example, the claim that the senior mark is particularly suitable for identifying the junior goods is insufficient) and uncertain in scope.[82]

In the US, the comparative advertising defense that contains fair advertisement or promotion legally permits consumers to compare goods/services.[83] There is no such defense in EU trademark law. Rather, comparative advertising is regulated under the Misleading and Comparative Advertising Directive.[84] Nevertheless, the additional requirements, namely that junior users must not have discredited the senior marks and cannot take unfair advantage of the reputation of the senior mark, appear to render this defense toothless in the EU.[85]

US anti-dilution law also provides for parodic use. It is a blanket exception for all parodies of trademarks regardless of whether or not there is a commercial context, provided that such parodic use is fair and is not as a designation of source for the junior user's goods/services. However, there is no such an equivalent defense in the EU.

In addition, the news-reporting defense under US anti-dilution law covers newspapers, television news, and news commentary that make use of trademarks.[86] Again, there is no such equivalent defense in the EU. The defense of non-commercial use in the US has a role to play because the parodic use defense does not apply where the junior use involves designation of source. In the EU, although there is no such equivalent defense, dilution action is limited to use in the context of commercial activity with a view to economic advantage and therefore will be upheld by courts for covering non-commercial uses.[87] Despite this, the parodic use defense is limited in effect in the EU because it will not shelter the junior user who used the mark in question for commercial purposes even where he did so for the public interest.

6. Summary

This section summarized the major differences between US and EU anti-dilution law. However, these are not the only differences. For example, the proprietors of senior marks (whether the mark is registered

---

[82] Fhima (n 58) para 7.75.

[83] Lanham Act (US) s 43(c)(4)(A).

[84] Council Directive 2006/114/EC of 12 December 2006 concerning misleading and comparative advertising [2006] OJ L367/21, art 4.

[85] Fhima (n 58) para 7.36.

[86] The defense covers all forms of news reporting. *BidZick LLC v Smith* 2007 WL 3119445, *5–*7 (DSC 2007).

[87] Case C-206/01 *Arsenal Football Club plc v Matthew Reed* [2002] ETMR I-10273, para 40.

or not) can institute dilution infringement claims against any junior user in the US, but only proprietors of registered senior marks can bring such claims in the EU.[88] Furthermore, an injunction is the general remedy available in the US; other remedies are available only upon meeting certain criteria specified in § 43(c)(5) of the Lanham Act. In the EU, however, monetary remedies are normally available.[89]

More luxury brands will be likely to receive anti-dilution protection in the EU because of the recognition of niche fame, which enlarges the scope of marks that are entitled to anti dilution protection. However, as a result of *Intel*, it is more difficult for owners of luxury brands to prove dilution by blurring in the EU than in the US. As the section showed, the public interest has been better protected in US anti-dilution law, as evidenced by the existence of more defenses against dilution claims. This means that the dilution claims made by luxury brand owners may face strong statutory defenses (like parody) in the US, while in the EU they would face weaker defenses.

B. China

As noted in Part I, China has become the world's largest luxury market. But compared with the US and the EU, counterfeiting is still highly rampant in China. Against this backdrop, China's anti-dilution law is critically important for luxury companies to protect their brands in China.

1. Statutory sources of anti-dilution protection

The Chinese Trademark Law is the major statute containing the principles, standards and rules for trademark protection in China. Although there are no specific provisions in the Chinese Trademark Law that provide explicit recognition of the anti-dilution doctrine,[90] the Chinese Trademark Law does contain one article that deals specifically with the protection of well-known trademarks. Article 13(i) of the Chinese Trademark Law provides:

---

88 Ng-Loy Wee Loon, 'The Sense and Sensibility in the Anti-Dilution Right' (2012) 24 *Singapore Academy LJ* 927, 941.

89 Ibid.

90 Melaine Zhu and Cecilia Zhou, 'Anti Dilution: A Powerful Tool for Well Known Mark Protection in China' *China Law & Practice* (March 2011) <http://www.chinalawandpractice.com/Article/2781459/Channel/7576/Anti-Dilution-a-powerful-tool-for-well-known-mark-protection-in-China.html> accessed 25 January 2014.

> A trademark shall not be registered and its use shall be prohibited where the trademark constitutes a reproduction, an imitation, or a translation, of a well-known trademark of another person not registered in China and is likely to create confusion, if the trademark is the subject of an application for registration in respect of goods which are identical or similar to the goods to which the well-known trademark applies.

This provision protects registered well-known trademarks against unauthorized uses that would cause a likelihood of confusion. Protection extends to all classes of goods and services, as required by the TRIPS Agreement. Article 13(ii) of the Chinese Trademark Law further provides protection of unregistered well-known trademarks, although it limits protection to identical or similar classes of goods and services. Thus, the language of Article 13 of the Chinese Trademark Law suggests that it provides only anti-confusion protection of well-known trademarks; anti-dilution protection is not explicitly covered. Nonetheless, whether anti-dilution protection is implicitly covered is open to debate.[91]

The Judicial Interpretation Concerning the Trial of Civil Cases of Protection of Well-known Marks was issued by the Supreme People's Court on 1 May 2009 (the 2009 Supreme Court Interpretation).[92] It clarifies Article 13 of the Chinese Trademark Law by defining 'likelihood to create confusion' as misleading the public as to the sources of the goods of the well-known mark and the junior mark or as to the relationship between the well-known mark and the junior mark:

> '[M]isleads the public, and the interests of the registrant of the well-known mark are likely to be damaged by such use' can be defined as use of the accused mark is sufficient for the relative public to believe that there are associations to some extent between the accused mark and the well-known mark, so as to weaken the distinctive characteristics of the well-known mark and tarnish the reputation of well-known mark in the market, or the accused parties can take free ride on the reputation of well-known mark by improper means, as provided by the Article 13(ii) if the Trademark Law.[93]

---

[91] Liu Guizeng, 'Protection against Dilution of a Trademark' (International Association for the Protection of Intellectual Property, 6 April 2010) 2 <https://www.aippi.org/download/commitees/214/GR214china.pdf> accessed 25 January 2014.

[92] Supreme People's Court's Interpretation of Several Issues Relating to Application of Law to Trial of Cases of Civil Disputes Involving Protection of Well-Known Marks (China) (adopted 22 April 2009, entered into force 1 May 2009).

[93] Ibid., art 9.

This provision is said to form the legal basis of the anti-dilution doctrine in China.[94] According to this provision, if a mark can be recognized as a well-known mark, then it is entitled to anti-dilution protection against blurring or tarnishment.

2. Recognition of well-known marks

Under the 2009 Supreme Court Interpretation, only a well-known mark, equivalent to one that is famous in the US or having a reputation in the EU, qualifies for anti-dilution protection.[95] According to Article 2 of the Provisions on the Determination and Protection of Well-Known Marks, another interpretation issued by the Chinese Supreme Court, a well-known mark is defined as one that is widely known to the relevant sector of the public, which includes consumers, competitors and other relevant people in the channels of distribution.

It thus appears that the wording of the law is subject to wider and more flexible interpretation than the stricter US requirement of 'general consuming public.' The 2009 Supreme Court Interpretation suggests that in China, proving either a national reputation from a geographical perspective[96] or a niche fame from an industrial point of view[97] could be sufficient for the purpose of showing that a mark is well known. As a result, 3180 trademarks were, by 2011, recognized as well-known marks. This figure supports the estimation that China is the country that protects the largest number of well-known trademarks in the world.[98]

Article 14 of the Chinese Trademark Law provides that the following factors must be considered in determining whether a mark is well known: (1) knowledge of the mark in the relevant public sector; (2) duration of use of the mark, and duration, degree, and geographical scope of any publicity for the mark; and (3) history of protection of the mark as a well-known trademark.[99] To prove these elements, Article 5 of the 2009

---

[94] Liu (n 91) 2.

[95] Liu (n 91) 3.

[96] Yangyue Chen, 'Should China Protect Trademarks against Dilution? A Critical Look at the Experience of the United States and the Prospects for Application in China' (Munich Intellectual Property Law Center, 23 March 2013) 29 <papers.ssrn.com/sol3/papers.cfm?abstract_id=1683082> accessed 25 January 2014.

[97] Ibid.

[98] Linda Chang and Elliot Papageorgiou, 'Three Ways to Rescue the Trademark Law' *China Law & Practice* (April 2012) <http://www.chinalawandpractice.com/Article/3002552/Three-ways-to-rescue-the-Trademark-Law.html> accessed 25 January 2014.

[99] Trademark Law of the People's Republic of China, art 14.

Supreme Court Interpretation provides that the following evidence must be submitted: the market share, geographical area of sales, interests and taxes of the goods bearing the mark; the duration of use; the manner, duration of time, degree, monetary investment, and geographical range of any publicity or sales promotion of the mark; any record of the mark being protected as a well-known mark; and goodwill and reputation of the mark.[100]

Compared with the factors considered by the EU and US courts in determining fame and reputation, perhaps the most striking feature of Chinese anti-dilution law is that Chinese courts also consider the history of protection of the mark as a well-known trademark. This means that if other jurisdictions have recognized the mark as a well-known mark, the Chinese court may simply adopt the reasoning and conclusion of these other jurisdictions, unless it is convinced that there has been a change of circumstances since the last determination.[101]

3. Prohibited dilutive acts

In the US and EU, there is a separate requirement of showing a mental association between a junior and senior mark. In China, the law does not explicitly contain such a requirement. But Chinese courts in practice often require proof that such an association between the two marks exists, which typically suggests detriment to the distinctiveness or tarnishment of reputation.[102]

The acts prohibited by trademark dilution law are broader in the US and the EU than in China. In China, while proof of the 'public being misled' is enough for proving the dilution of a registered well-known mark, 'public's confusion as to the origin of the goods' has to be further proven for unregistered well-known marks. While China provides limited protection to a larger number of well-known marks than does the US (owing to its more flexible threshold to recognize well-known marks), the US affords a wider scope of protection to a much smaller number of well-known marks.[103]

As for proof of degree of dilution, a likelihood of dilution is sufficient in China.[104] This contrasts with the EU, where actual damage – namely, a change of economic behavior of customers – is required. Therefore,

---

[100] Judicial Interpretation (n 92) art 5.
[101] Chen (n 96) 30.
[102] Liu (n 91) 10.
[103] Ibid.
[104] Ibid 11.

owners of well-known luxury brands bear a lighter burden of proof in proving dilution in China.

4. Dilution doctrine in action

Despite the lack of formal recognition of the anti-dilution doctrine in the Chinese Trademark Law, a survey reviewing the 100 latest trademark decisions in China (as of 2009) showed that 31 of them referred specifically to 'dilution.'[105] The decision in *Kodak v Keda*[106] demonstrates how the court recognized Kodak as a well-known mark and ruled in favor of Kodak by holding that Keda's usage of the word 'Kodak' would erode the distinctiveness and be detrimental to the Kodak mark. Some practitioners believe that this decision implies that the court is more inclined to apply the anti-dilution doctrine when foreign marks are involved.[107] Others believe that, in spite of this decision, foreign companies still encounter difficulty in obtaining well-known status for their marks, largely due to the fact that their marks require to be registered in Chinese.[108] In any event, in the absence of an independent doctrine for anti-dilution protection, companies should rely on the confusion doctrine as their main cause of action to convince the court to find for infringement; a dilution claim may add weight, but will not stand alone as a cause.[109] For example, when Ferrari litigated against a Chinese clothing company's attempt to register the prancing horse logo on its clothing products, Ferrari relied on the confusion doctrine, arguing that the registration may cause a likelihood of confusion and that the registration was therefore invalidated. Ferrari did assert that the prancing horse logo it uses on cars should be recognized as a well-known trademark, but Ferrari did not claim that the registration of the prancing horse logo by the Chinese company for clothes would cause dilution of its logo.[110]

The large number of well-known marks recognized in China has created problems beyond those relating to adequately proving confusion.

---

[105] Luckie Hong, 'China's Dilution of the Dilution Doctrine' [April/May 2009] *World Trademark Rev* 24, 27.

[106] *Eastman Kodak Corp. v Suzhou Keda Hydraulic Elevators Co., Ltd.*, Jiangsu Province Suzhou City Intermediate People's Court's Civil Judgment, No. Suzhongminsanchuzi 0213/2005 (2006).

[107] Hong (n 105) 28.

[108] Patricia Marquez, 'Trademark: A. Comparative Look at China and the United States' (2011) 14 *Touro Intl L Rev* 334, 351.

[109] Ibid.

[110] Jing 'Brad' Luo and Shubha Ghosh, 'Protection and Enforcement of Well-Known Mark Rights in China: History, Theory and Future' (2009) 7 *Northwestern J Technology & Intellectual Property* 119, 141–3.

An informal poll conducted by an author suggested that some well-known marks recognized through the administrative process are not really well known in the marketplace.[111] For instance, 'Wu-Mu', 'Unique' and 'Qingsen' are marks on clothing sold at the retail level but not yet familiar to many local Chinese citizens.[112] On the judicial side, it is alarming that courts in less-developed areas recognized more marks as well known than do courts in big cities like Beijing and Shanghai.[113] This contrast casts doubts on whether the well-known trademark status was properly designated by courts in less-developed areas.[114] Moreover, officials are motivated to recognize more well-known marks due to the political environment in China. As the performance of many local governments partially is evaluated on the basis of how successfully they assisted the enterprises to develop their trademarks,[115] it is no surprise that they employ a lax standard even when such marks are not qualified.

The third problem is associated with the Chinese brand names that luxury companies use for their brands when they merchandize in China. When foreign companies enter the Chinese market, they usually come up with Chinese names for their brands. For marketing purposes, coming up with these Chinese names is essential – if the foreign companies did not, Chinese consumers would come up with their own. Recently, Hermès, an ultra-luxury product maker, encountered a big problem with their brand protection in China. A Chinese court ruled that the Chinese name for Hermès was not a well-known trademark in China on the grounds that Hermès lacked promotional activities to increase its fame in China.[116]

---

111 Chen (n 96) 39.

112 Ibid.

113 Ibid.

114 Tao Xinliang, 'Woguo Chimin Shangbiao Rending Yu Baohu De Xianzhuang Fenxi Jiqi Falv Guizhi (Analysis of Existing Situations and Legal Regulation on China's Well-known Mark Recognitin and Protection)' <http://article.chinalawinfo.com/Article_Detail.asp?ArticleID=68740> accessed 25 January 2014.

115 Guowuyuan Guanyu Yinfa Zhishichanquan Zhanlve Gangyao De Tongzhi [Circular of the State Council on Issuing the Outline of National Intellectual Property Strategy] (promulgated by the State Council, June 5, 2008, effective June 5, 2008). Issued by the State Council, it is a general guideline on China's further development of intellectual property right.

116 'France's Hermes Loses China Trademark Fight' (*Reuters*, 26 February 2012) <www.reuters.com/article/2012/02/27/hermes-china-idUSL4E8DR01820120227> accessed 25 January 2014.

V. CONCLUSION

The challenges that luxury companies face in the global protection of their brands, as discussed in this chapter, will also loom large for other industries when they market their products or services globally. High-profile dilution cases in the US and EU have been litigated by companies from other industries, including financial service providers, coffee makers, and computer chip makers.

Therefore, it is high time to consider how anti-dilution protection should be developed globally.[117] There are different approaches that we may consider. The first path might be to amend the TRIPS Agreement to include an explicit requirement about anti-dilution protection. In this respect, the WIPO Recommendation's provision could be a template upon which the amendment could be constructed. Second, if decision makers do not decide to amend the TRIPS Agreement, we can rely on an expansive application of the national standard to link the fragmented domestic anti-dilution laws together. Under the expansive application of the national standard, if the US provides high anti-dilution protection for its domestic brands, it must also provide the same protection to foreign brands. Third, decision makers must consider the limitations that should be carved out in anti-dilution protection. Overzealous trademark protection may jeopardize freedom of expression and impede healthy market competition. Last but not least, further research is needed to ascertain the appropriate level of anti-dilution law in protecting brands. Commentators have pointed out that contemporary anti-dilution protection in the EU and US may have become too stringent in ways that have stifled freedom of expression and legitimate market competition.

Indeed, global anti-dilution protection involves a host of complicated issues. In a market-oriented economy, branding-based strategies are crucial for companies to fare well in the marketplace. Globalization has made global branding strategies as well as global brand protection critically important for multinational companies. From this perspective, reforming the global anti-dilution system will have far-reaching impact on the economic and cultural vibrancy of different industries.

---

[117] Tara D Rose, 'The High Price of Fame Deserves a Discount: A Call for Uniform Dilution Law in North America for the Protection of Well Known Trademarks' (2007) 14 *Southwestern J L & Trade Americas* 195, 197.

14. Of markets, culture, and *terroir*: The unique economic and culture-related benefits of geographical indications of origin

*Irene Calboli**

I. INTRODUCTION

The protection of geographical indications of origin (GIs)[1] has historically been the subject of heated debate and controversy among members of the international community. Defenders of GIs – mostly, although not exclusively, European countries and other "old world" countries – have generally advocated that GIs should be protected because they identify products that embody unique qualities and characteristics, which are

* I thank Daniel Gervais for the invitation to contribute to this volume and his insightful comments. I am also indebted to many colleagues for comments and conversation on this topic. In particular, I thank Jim Chen, Maggie Chon, Christine Haight Farley, Susy Frankel, Shubha Ghosh, Christophe Geiger, Koh Kheng Lian, Marshall Leaffer, Doris Long, Jerry Reichman, Srividhya Ragavan, Lisa Ramsey, Marketa Trimble, Jacques de Werra, and Peter Yu. I also thank Aakanasha Kumar for excellent research assistance and the Centre for Asian Legal Studies, Faculty of Law, National University of Singapore, for research support.

1 The term "geographical indications of origin" [hereinafter GIs] is used in the sense of the definition of Article 22 of Agreement on Trade-Related Aspects of Intellectual Property Rights. *See* Agreement on Trade-Related Aspects of Intellectual Property Rights, 15 April, 1994, Marrakesh Agreement Establishing the World Trade Organization, Annex 1C, LEGAL INSTRUMENTS – RESULT OF THE URUGUAY ROUNDS [1994] vol. 31, 33 I.L.M. 81, <http://www.wto.org/english/docs_e/legal_e/27-trips.pdf> [hereinafter TRIPs]. For a brief review of the additional definitions used for signs indicating the geographical origin of products see infra Part III. *See also* R.J. Coombe and N. Aylwin, "Bordering Diversity and Desire: Using Intellectual Property to a Mark Place-Based Products" (2011) 43 *Environment & Planning* 2027, 2027–9 (coining the definition "marks indicating conditions of origin," which encompasses GIs, appellations and denomination of origin, as well as collective and certification marks indicating products' geographical origin).

directly linked to the *terroir* – a deep traditional connection to the land – where the products are grown, processed, or manufactured. In contrast, the United States (US), Australia, and a number of other "new world" countries have rejected calls for a stronger protection for GIs. These countries have argued against the *terroir* argument by highlighting that most products can be replicated almost anywhere today thanks to modern agricultural and manufacturing techniques. In addition, these countries have underscored that several GIs are generic terms on their soil – Champagne, Chablis, and Feta are some contested examples – and that a shift toward preventing the public from using these terms would damage businesses, which could no longer describe products using those terms. In turn, this might create confusion amongst consumers who have come to identify those terms as generic product names in these countries. In some countries, names similar or identical to foreign GIs are also registered and used as trademarks by entities that have no relationship with the original GI-denominated locality. In these instances, countries have quarreled over the possible cancellation of these marks and whether the registrations were made in good faith – the ongoing multinational legal war between Anheuser-Busch and Budějovický Budvar over the use of the name "Budweiser" to identify their respective beer products is one of the most famous examples in this respect.[2]

Despite the controversy surrounding GIs, the final text of the Agreement on Trade Related Aspects on Intellectual Property Rights (TRIPs) succeeded, however, in establishing a minimum standard for GI protection – an important milestone in advancing GI protection at the international level due to the high number of TRIPs signatories. Notably, all Members of TRIPs had to implement protection against confusing and misleading uses of GIs, even though TRIPs left Members free to choose how to implement such protection – whether by creating a *sui generis* type of protection or through existing protection, commonly with trademarks.[3] TRIPs additionally required enhanced GI protection – protection beyond consumer confusion and against GI usurpation per se – for GIs identifying wines and spirits.[4] Against these pro-GIs provisions, TRIPs nonetheless safeguarded the use of terms that are deemed generic in

---

[2] For a detailed analysis of the litigation between Anheuser-Busch and Budějovický Budvar, *see* C. Heath, "The Budweiser Case: A Brewing Conflict" in C. Heath and A. Kamperman Sanders (eds) *Landmark Intellectual Property Cases and Their Legacy* (Kluwer Law International, 2011) 181.

[3] TRIPs, *supra* note 1, art 22.

[4] Ibid., art 23.

individual countries – like Champagne or Parmesan in the US.[5] TRIPs also "grandfathered" pre-existing national trademark rights based upon the principle of territoriality.[6] Still, supporters of GI protection were able to bind all TRIPs Members into participating in future negotiations considering the expansion of GI protection – namely to enhance the protection granted to GIs identifying wines and spirits by creating an ad hoc registry (whose proposal was later extended to all GIs) and heighten protection for all GIs following the anti-usurpation model of protection granted to GIs for wines and spirits.[7] Almost two decades after the adoption of TRIPs, however, these negotiations have stalled,[8] and the discussion about GI protection has shifted from the World Trade Organization (WTO) forum to bilateral and pluri-lateral free trade agreements (FTAs),[9] where countries belonging to different camps – for or against enhanced GI protection – try to influence other signatories to join their position. In parallel, the World Intellectual Property Organization (WIPO) is working to update its GI registry (created under the Lisbon Agreement) to address some of the concerns expressed by GI critics, including the US.[10]

Hence, no matter how controversial the discussion on GI protection may be, the current international gridlock with respect to the GI protection agenda at the multilateral WTO level is not a positive development. In this chapter, I argue against this gridlock and consider whether expanding GI protection beyond the current international standards could be desirable for WTO/TRIPs Members. In particular, I evaluate both the economic and cultural benefits that derive from GI protection, benefits that could likely be enhanced by the expansion of GI

---

5 Ibid., art 24.

6 Ibid.

7 Ibid.

8 *See* G.E. Evans and M.M. Blakeney, "The Protection of Geographical Indications after Doha: Quo Vadis?" (2006) 9 *J. Int'l Econ. L* 575, 581. *See also* F.G. Zacher, "Pass the Parmesan: Geographic Indications in the United States and the European Union – Can There Be Compromise?" (2005) 19 *Emory L. Rev.* 427, 431.

9 *See, e.g.*, Trans-Pacific Partnership, arts QQ.D.1-14, Intellectual Property [Rights] Chapter, Consolidated Text (August 2013) <https://wikileaks.org/tpp/static/pdf/Wikileaks-secret-TPP-treaty-IP-chapter.pdf>. The TPP is currently being negotiated between Australia, Brunei Darussalam, Canada, Chile, Japan, Malaysia, Mexico, New Zealand, Peru, Singapore, Vietnam, and the US.

10 *See* D.J. Gervais, "Reinventing Lisbon: The Case for a Protocol to the Lisbon Agreement" (2010) 11 *Chicago J. Int'l L.* 67, 126 [hereinafter Gervais, "Reinventing Lisbon"].

protection to the anti-usurpation level. Due to the limited scope of this chapter, however, my analysis is not exhaustive and aims primarily at highlighting the positive aspects and unique benefits of GI protection when compared to other intellectual property rights on a general, theoretical level.[11] Accordingly, I do not elaborate on the controversy surrounding the creation of a GI registry for wine and spirits as indicated in TRIPs, as well as for other GIs as highlighted in the Doha Development Round of the WTO.[12] Likewise, I do not address the impact of GI protection on sustainable development, which is an increasingly important part of the GI debate, especially in the developing world.[13] Generally, my analysis focuses on the GI debate at the international level and not on the protection granted by individual countries or groups of countries, for instance the EU, whose system of GI protection is one of the most developed among WTO Members.[14] Finally, my observations refer

---

[11] For an exhaustive analysis of the debate on GIs, *see* D. Gangjee, *Relocating the Law of Geographical Indications* (Cambridge University Press, 2012) 1[hereinafter Gangjee, *Relocating GIs*].

[12] *See* Ministerial Declaration, WTO document WT/MIN(01)/DEC/1 (14 November 2011) adopted at Doha, Quatar [hereinafter Doha Declaration]. For a detailed analysis of the Doha Declaration, *see* <http://www.wto.org/ english/ tratop_e/trips_e/gi_background_e.htm>. Some authors suggest the establishment of a multilateral register for GIs – *see* consolidated statement by C. Geiger, D.J. Gervais, N. Olzak, and V. Ruzek, "Towards a Flexible International Framework for the Protection of Geographical Indications" (2010) 1 *WIPO J.* 147, 157–8. *See also* Gervais, "Reinventing Lisbon" *supra* note 10, at 123–5.

[13] In this respect, see D. Zografos, "Geographical Indications and Socio-economic Development" (December 2008) IQSensato, Working Paper 3, 11-12 , <http://papers.ssrn.com/sol3/papers.cfm?abstract_id=1628534>; *see also* D. Rangnekar, "The International Protection of Geographical Indications: The Asian Experience" (November 2004) 1, 19, UNCTAD/ICTSD Regional Dialogue in collaboration with IDRC, University of Hong Kong, Hong Kong <http:// www.iprsonline.org/unctadictsd/dialogue/docs/Rangnekar_2004-11-08.pdf>.

[14] For a detailed review of the protection of GIs in the European Union, *see* A. Kur and S. Cocks, "Nothing But a GI Thing: Geographical Indications Under EU Law" (2007) 17 *Fordham Intell. Prop. Media & Ent. L.* 999.

> Since 1992, the EU has effected protection of geographical indications … for foodstuffs and agricultural products via a special GI Regulation … establishing a unitary regulatory regime for GIs binding upon all the member nations of the European Union. The EU has also established separate protection schemes for GIs relating to wines, spirits, and mineral waters.

Ibid. (citations omitted). In particular, *see* Council Regulation 2081/92, on the protection of geographical indications and designations of origin for agricultural products and foodstuffs, 1992 O.J. (L 208) 1 (EC), *superseded by* Council

primarily to GIs that identify products that originate entirely from the territory in question either because these products are grown in, or are made with ingredients coming from the territory, or because they are manufactured therein. In this respect, I note that TRIPs accepts that GIs can identify products that are only "essentially," and not necessarily "exclusively," grown or made in the GI-denominated *terroir*.[15] Yet, in this chapter, I advocate for interpreting the wording "essentially" strictly, namely as "exclusively," as the use of GIs on products with a looser territorial linkage raises serious doubts, in my opinion, as to the legitimacy of GI protection.

Based upon this premise, the remainder of this chapter is structured as follows. In Part II, I review the definition of GIs, and highlight the theoretical challenges that the protection of GIs creates for the traditional intellectual property system, at least based on the current law and economic framework that dominates the Anglo-American interpretation of the scope of intellectual property protection. In Part III, I recount the protection granted to GIs before the adoption of TRIPs, the main traits of the protection granted under TRIPs, and the post-TRIPs controversy that has characterized the Doha Development Round of WTO negotiations. In Part IV, I review and evaluate the economic justifications for intellectual property protection and consider the unique benefits that GI protection and perhaps an enhanced protection against usurpation could provide for the groups operating in the GI-denominated regions, as well as for the marketplace in general. In Part V, I consider an additional, more recent, argument to justify GI protection, particularly the ability of GIs to protect cultural heritage and cultural knowledge and thus promote cultural diversity. In Part VI, I address some of the arguments against GI protection, both under an economic approach and a cultural analysis approach, and I offer possible counterarguments in favor of moving the international agenda for GI protection forward. Ultimately, I conclude the chapter by highlighting that both under a traditional economic approach as well as under a cultural analysis approach, granting GIs protection, including enhanced anti-usurpation protection, may produce benefits that can outweigh the costs of such protection.

Regulation 510/2006, on the protection of geographical indications and designations of origin for agricultural products and foodstuffs, 2006 O.J. (L 93) 12 (EC). The Regulation was amended as a result of the complaint that the UnS and Australia brought in front of the WTO. *See* Panel Report, *European Communities – Protection of Trademarks and Geographical Indications for Agricultural Products and Foodstuffs* (15 March 2005) ¶ 7.106, WT/DS174/R.

[15] *See* TRIPS, *supra* note 1, art 22. *See also* discussion *infra* Part VI.

II. A BRIEF PRIMER OF GEOGRAPHICAL INDICATIONS OF ORIGIN: DEFINITION, TERRITORIAL LINKAGE, AND THEORETICAL CHALLENGES FOR PROTECTION

As I highlighted in a previous work,[16] the first challenge for TRIPs negotiators in discussing GI protection was the lack of a widely accepted existing definition of what constituted a GI. The only definition available pre-TRIPs was provided by the Lisbon Agreement[17] with respect to "appellations of origin," which were defined as "geographical name[s] of a country, region, or locality, which serve to designate a product originating therein, the quality and characteristics of which are due exclusively or essentially to the geographical environment, including natural and human factors."[18] Since only a limited number of countries were part of the Lisbon Agreement, a more widely accepted definition of GIs was needed to identify the subject matter protected under TRIPs. After considerable controversy, TRIPs negotiators agreed on the definition of Article 22, which states that GIs are "indications which identify a good as originating in the territory … or a region or locality in that territory, where a given quality, reputation or other characteristic of the good is essentially attributable to its geographical origin."[19] Similar to the definition of the Lisbon Agreement, Article 22 did not only include in the definition of GIs agricultural products, but extended it to all the products whose "quality, reputation or other characteristics" can be attributable to a specific geographical region. This includes locally made handicrafts as well as traditional local products, such as "Bohemia" crystal, "Sheffield" sterling, "Swiss" watches, "Banarasi" silk, and

---

[16] I. Calboli, "Expanding the Protection of Geographical Indications of Origin Under TRIPs' 'Old' Debate or 'New' Opportunity?" (2006) 10 *Marq. Intell. Prop. L. Rev.* 181, 184.

[17] Lisbon Agreement for the Protection of Appellations of Origin and their International Registration, 31 October 1958, 923 U.N.T.S. 205 <http://www.wipo.int/clea/docs/en/wo/wo012en.htm> [hereinafter Lisbon Agreement].

[18] Ibid., art 2(1).

[19] TRIPs, *supra* note 1, art 22(1). Similarly, the World Intellectual Property Organization [hereinafter WIPO] defines GIs as "sign[s] used on goods that have a specific geographical origin and possess qualities, reputation or characteristics that are essentially attributable to that origin." WIPO, "Overview of Geographical Indications" <http://www.wipo.int/geo_indications/en/>.

"Chanderi" saris.[20] As I highlight in Part V, the acceptance of this extended definition confirmed the growing importance of the human factor as a possible additional component of the unique quality, characteristics, and thus reputation, of GI-denominated products.

At its core, the language of Article 22 of TRIPs continues to emphasize the linkage between the GI-denominated territory and the specific characteristics, or the reputation, of the GI-denominated products. This territorial linkage remains the *sine qua non*, the "essential" component, for the international protection of GI under TRIPs,[21] even though TRIPs slightly deviates from the Lisbon Agreement, which states that the products' quality and characteristics have to be "exclusively or essentially" linked to the GI-denominated territory,[22] whereas TRIPs only adopts the wording "essentially." Hence, as GI opponents have pointed out, it is precisely the focus on this territorial linkage – the relationship with the *terroir* – that makes it particularly complex to reconcile GI protection with the traditional justification for intellectual property rights, namely property rights and incentive-based theories.[23] More specifically, GI opponents have pointed out that, because GIs are collective rights, they cannot be owned by just one or a few individuals and cannot be registered to a named individual, group of individuals, or entity. In particular, due to their impersonal nature, GIs cannot be commercialized like other intellectual property rights, that is, GIs cannot be assigned or licensed because their use strictly depends on the tie that the users establish with the geographical place that is identified by the GI. To the contrary, GIs can be used by anyone creating a product that satisfies the conditions established by a given GI in the GI-denominated territory.[24] Besides being difficult to categorize from a property standpoint, GI opponents have also underscored that GIs do not encourage and reward innovation, as other intellectual property rights (are supposed to) do.

---

20 "[GIs] may also highlight qualities of a product which are due to human factors associated with the place of origin of the products, such as specific manufacturing skills and traditions." WIPO, "*About Geographical Indications*", <http://www.wipo.int/geo_indications/en/about.html>. *See also* D. Gangjee, "*Geographical Indications and Cultural Heritage*", (2012) 4 *WIPO J.* 92, 98 [hereinafter Gangjee, "GIs and Cultural Heritage"].

21 TRIPs, *supra* note 1, art 22(1).

22 Lisbon Agreement, *supra* note 17, art 2(1).

23 *See generally* D. Gangjee, "Quibbling Siblings: Conflicts Between Trademarks and Geographic Indications" (2007) 82 *Chicago-Kent L. Rev.* 1253, 1256-9 [hereinafter Gangjee, "Quibbling Siblings"] (offering a very detailed overview of the scholarly discussion over the possibility to protect GIs under trademark law).

24 Ibid., at 1259.

Instead, GIs follow a different path and primarily reward product conformity within a very specific geographical region and, as such, promote the sustainability, transmission, and continued development of tradition rather than individual creativity and innovation.[25]

Still, against these arguments contrary to the territorial linkage between the territory and products identified by GIs, supporters of GIs have defended the importance of this linkage by highlighting the economic benefits that can derive from GIs precisely because of it. In particular, GI supporters have highlighted the unique communicative function that GIs exert, specifically regarding the geographical origin of the products to which they are affixed. Likewise, GIs play a fundamental role as promoters and guarantees of the quality of these products, again because of the specific characteristics of the territory where the products are grown or manufactured. In this respect, GI supporters have also expressed skepticism over the position that indications of geographical origin could be easily protected under a national trademark system rather than with a *sui generis* system of GI protection – such a position has been adopted in the US, for instance, and is generally supported by the opponents of GI protection.[26] By contrast, GI supporters have argued that trademarks are intrinsically different from GIs, specifically because trademarks are not linked to a territory, can be assigned, licensed, and so on, and ultimately can be exploited beyond the geographical boundaries of the GI-denominated territory, whereas GIs are invariably attached to such territory. In general, GI supporters have better received the argument that certification and collective marks could represent alternative forms of protection for indicators of geographical origin, due to the stricter requirements that are usually built into the granting, and the more communal nature, of these marks. In particular, certification marks can be used by all entities adopting certain production standards, and the

---

25 *See, e.g.*, K. Raustiala and S.R. Munzer, "The Global Struggle Over Geographic Indications" (2007) 18 *EJIL* 337, 359–60. *Cf.* D. Rangnekar, "The Socio-Economics of Geographical Indications: A Review of Empirical Evidence from Europe" (May 2004) UNCTAD-ICTSD Project on IPRs and Sustainable Development 15<http://ictsd.org/i/publications/12218/?view=document>.

26 *See generally* L. Beresford, "Geographical Indications: the Current Landscape" (2007) 17 *Fordham Intell. Prop. Media & Ent. L. J.* 981–5, 994–7 (arguing that protection through trademark law is the appropriate method of protection for signs indicating geographical origin).

territorial linkage can be built into the requirements to obtain a certification mark.[27]

As I elaborate in Part VI, despite the different views of opponents and supporters of GIs, the *terroir* argument must nonetheless remain front and center to support a shift towards a system of enhanced GI protection for all GIs. The relevance of this argument reaches well beyond the traditional debate of the economic benefits of GIs. Notably, the relevance of the linkage between the GI-denominated territory and the GI-denominated products has become increasingly relevant with respect to another aspect of GI protection: the rising argument that GIs play a fundamental role in identifying and protecting culture-related interests. Notably, since GIs identify regional products, the argument has been made that GIs represent a portion of local knowledge – in other words, that GIs embody and, in turn, promote parts of the cultural identity of the locality that they identify.[28] As I stress in Part V, this function of protecting and promoting culture-related interests has become an important component of the GI debate, due in part to the increasing importance of the human factor as a fundamental element of a growing number of GI-denominated products, especially non-agricultural products. By being recognized as potential expressions of local culture and local tradition, GIs have thus become a source for local, regional, and even national pride, in addition to representing the source of potential economic revenues for the same localities and regions. Yet, this rising role of GIs as promoters of culture-related interests has added fuel to the existing controversy between supporters and opponents of GIs. Disputes in this respect have even reached national governments while negotiating for

---

[27] On how certification marks can serve to protect consumers and guarantee products' characteristics, *see* M. Chon, "Marks of Rectitude" (2009) 77 *Fordham L. Rev.* 2311. *See generally* Gangjee, "GIs and Cultural Heritage" *supra* note 20, at 95 (highlighting the two "main contenders" among the forms of protection for indicators of origin: "collective and certification marks within national or regional trademark registration systems" and "sui generis GI protection."); D.J. Gervais, "A Cognac After a Spanish Champagne? Geographical Indications as Certification Marks" in J.C. Ginsburg and R.C. Dreyfuss (eds), *Intellectual Property at the Edge* (Cambridge University Press, 2014) 130.

[28] *See* discussion *infra* Part V. Among the pioneers of these arguments, *see* R.J. Coombe, "Legal Claims to Culture in and against the Market: Neoliberalism and the Global Proliferation of Meaningful Difference" (2005) 1 *L., Culture & Humanities* 32. *See also* D. Zographos, "Can Geographical Indications Be a Viable Alternative for the Protection of Traditional Cultural Expressions?" in F. Macmillan and K. Bowrey (eds), *New Direction in Copyright Law* (Edward Elgar Publishing, 2006) 37, 38.

particular GIs – France for "Champagne," India for "Basmati," etc. This further reflects the political, national, and often personal nature of GIs, and the clashes of the visions between supporters and opponents of GI protection, both at the national and international level.

III. THE EXISTING INTERNATIONAL FRAMEWORK OF PROTECTION AND THE GRIDLOCKED DEVELOPMENT AGENDA

Prior to TRIPs, the most relevant sources for international protection of GIs were found in three separate international agreements: the Paris Convention for the Protection of Industrial Property (Paris Convention);[29] the Madrid Agreement for the Repression of False and Deceptive Indications of Source on Goods (Madrid Agreement);[30] and the Lisbon Agreement for the Protection of Appellations of Origin and their International Registration (Lisbon Agreement).[31] Notably, the original 1883 version of the Paris Convention provided, in Article 10, protection for "indications of source and appellations of origin" with respect to certain protective measures at the border and for false or misleading uses of GIs – that is, for "false, fictitious, or deceptive trade names."[32] In 1967, the introduction of Article 10*bis* into the Paris Convention reinforced this protection. Article 10*bis* states that indications that were "liable to mislead the public as to the nature, the manufacturing process, the characteristics, the suitability for their purpose, or the quantity, of the goods"[33] ought to be forbidden as acts of unfair competition. Similarly, the 1891 Madrid Agreement offered protection against misleading and confusing uses of indications of source. The Madrid Agreement introduced additional protection for indications related to wines – a feature that was later re-introduced in TRIPs.[34] Lastly, in 1958, the Lisbon Agreement created the most comprehensive system of protection for

---

[29] Paris Convention for the Protection of Industrial Property, 20 March 1883, 21 U.S.T. 1583, 828 U.N.T.S. 305 <http://www.wipo.int/clea/docs/en/wo/wo020en.htm> [hereinafter Paris Convention].

[30] Madrid Agreement for the Repression of False and Deceptive Indications of Source, 14 April 1891, 828 U.N.T.S. 168 <http://www.wipo.int/clea/docs/en/wo/wo032en.htm> [hereinafter Madrid Agreement].

[31] Lisbon Agreement, *supra* note 17.

[32] Paris Convention, *supra* note 29, art 10(1).

[33] Ibid., art 10*bis*(3).

[34] Madrid Agreement, *supra* note 30, art 4.

indications of origin both against confusing and misleading uses, as well as against "imitation or usurpation," including their unauthorized use accompanied by terms such as "like, type, or style."[35] As I highlighted in Part II, the Lisbon Agreement also offered a specific definition of "appellations of origin" based upon the territory from which the products originate.[36] Finally, the Lisbon Agreement created a system of international registration for indications of origin.[37] Still, both the Madrid and Lisbon Agreements had few signatories, primarily because of their strict level of protection.[38]

The adoption of TRIPs in 1994 marked a milestone in advancing the GI protection agenda on a worldwide scale. In particular, in Article 22, TRIPs established that Members ought to provide the "legal means" for interested parties to prevent the use of GIs that mislead "the public as to the geographical origin of the goods," or that "constitute an act of unfair competition within the meaning of Article 10*bis* of the Paris Convention."[39] To facilitate acceptance of GI protection, TRIPs did not mandate, however, any specific means to achieve these objectives, leaving TRIPs Members free to adopt the means that best suited their respective legal systems. Still, Article 22 requires that Members "refuse or invalidate the registration of a trademark which contains or consists of a geographical indication with respect to goods not originating in the territory indicated" when the use of the GI "is of such a nature as to mislead the public as to the true place of origin."[40] Besides mandating protection against misappropriation for all GIs, TRIPs established a system of higher protection for GIs relating to wines and spirits, requiring Members to protect those GIs against "usurpation," regardless of consumer confusion or unfair competition.[41] The fact that TRIPs Members from both the "old world" and "new world" camps had, and have, considerable interests in the wine and spirits business undoubtedly contributed to the double standard

---

35 Lisbon Agreement, *supra* note 17, art 3.

36 Ibid., art 2(1). For a detailed discussion on the definition of "appellation of origin" and issues related thereto, *see* D.J. Gervais, "The Lisbon Agreement's Misunderstood Potential" (2009) 1 *WIPO J.* 87, 88–94.

37 Lisbon Agreement, *supra* note 17, art 5.

38 As of June 2013, only thirty-six States are signatories of the Madrid Agreement. *See* <http://www.wipo.int/treaties/en/ShowResults.jsp?lang=en& treaty _id=3>. Similarly, only twenty-eight States are signatories to the Lisbon Agreement. *See* <http://www.wipo.int/treaties/en/ShowResults.jsp?lang=en&treaty_ id=10>.

39 TRIPs, *supra* note 1, art 22(2).

40 Ibid., art 22(3).

41 Ibid., art 23(1).

created between general GIs and GIs related to wines and spirits. Article 23 encapsulates this higher protection by prohibiting the use of terms similar or identical to GIs related to wines and spirits when products do not "originat[e] in the place indicated by the geographical indication," including when "the true origin of the goods is indicated or the [GI] is used in translation or accompanied by expression such as 'kind', 'type', 'style', 'imitation', or the like."[42] Article 23 also provides that Members may refuse or invalidate trademark registrations containing or consisting of GIs identifying wines or spirits.[43]

Besides these provisions, TRIPs nonetheless carved out relevant limitations to GI protection. Notably, Article 24 grandfathers existing rights for trademarks that were in use or had been registered in good faith before the date of the implementation of TRIPs in the Member country where the mark was registered, or before the GI was protected in its country of origin.[44] In addition, because of existing similar names of regions of the world, Article 24 exempts Member countries from having to "prevent continued and similar use of a particular [GI] of another Member identifying wines or spirits in connection with goods and services" where the GI has been used "in a continued manner with the same or related goods or services" in the territory of that Member for at least ten years prior to 15 April 1994 (the date on which TRIPs was formally concluded), or where this continuous use has been in good faith.[45] Furthermore, according to Article 24, terms that have entered the lexicon as the generic names of a type of product in a Member of TRIPs can also continue to be used as such in the territory of that Member.[46] The ongoing disputes over the use of words like Champagne, Parmesan, or Feta between Europe and North American countries are relevant examples of the impact of this exception and likely the reason behind the adoption of this provision.

Still, TRIPs requested that Members agree to engage in further negotiations to consider enhancing GI protection. Article 23 specifically provides for future negotiations in order to establish a multilateral system of notification and registration of GIs for wines and spirits that would facilitate their enforcement and prevent their illegal use.[47] Article 24 also

---

42 Ibid.

43 Ibid., art 23(2).

44 TRIPs, *supra* note 1, art 24(5).

45 Ibid., art 24(4).

46 Ibid., art 24(6).

47 Ibid., art 23(4). *See also* J.M. Waggoner, "Acquiring A European Taste for Geographical Indications" (2008) 33 *Brooklyn J. Int'l L.* 569, 578.

recites that "Members agree to enter into negotiations aimed at increasing the protection of individual geographical indications under Article 23."[48] In an attempt to promote future negotiations on GIs, the Doha Ministerial Declaration of 2001 directly placed the protection of GIs on the agenda of the Doha "Development" Round of WTO negotiations.[49] The Doha mandate included primarily the discussion of two major issues: (a) creating a multilateral register for wines and spirits (and possibly for all GIs); and (b) extending the higher level of protection provided by Article 23 beyond wines and spirits.[50] According to the Declaration, both issues were to be debated by the end of 2003. Yet when WTO Members met in Cancun, Mexico,[51] in October of 2003 to discuss GI protection, the controversies between supporters and opponents of GI protection caused the negotiations to collapse. In particular, opposite camps could not agree on the extension of GI protection. Countries also bickered about specific procedural aspects of the Doha mandate, namely to what extent they could proceed on "outstanding implementation issues."[52] More recently, in a 2011 report, the Director General of the WTO again confirmed that WTO Members' positions on GIs continue to diverge sharply[53] and no solution to the controversy seems currently in sight.

---

48 TRIPs, *supra* note 1, art 24(1).

49 *See* Doha Declaration, *supra* note 12, para 18.

50 Ibid.

51 Details about the WTO negotiations in Cancun are available at <http://www.wto.org/english/ tratop_e/trips_e/gi_background_e.htm>.

52 Doha Declaration, *supra* note 12, para 12(b). "[T]he other *outstanding implementation issues* shall be addressed as a matter of priority by the relevant WTO bodies, which shall report to the Trade Negotiations Committee [TNC], established under paragraph 46 below, by the end of 2002 for appropriate action." Ibid. (emphasis added). Argentina supported that additional consensus was required to negotiate "outstanding implementation issues," in particular with respect to a registry for all GIs. Several other countries, from Europe, India, Kenya, Mauritius, Nigeria, Pakistan, Sri Lanka, and Thailand argued, instead, that negotiations on those issues could proceed immediately.

53 *See* WTO, Document No. TN/C/W/61, 21 April 2011, <http://www.wto.org/english/tratop_e/trips_e/ art27_3b_e.htm>.

> *Status of Play* – Delegations continued to voice the divergent views that have characterized this debate, with no convergence evident on the specific question of extension of Article 23 coverage: some Members continued to argue for extension of Article 23 protection to all products; others maintained that this was undesirable and created unreasonable burdens.

Ibid., at 4.

Notably, with respect to the possibility of expanding GI protection to the anti-usurpation level to all GIs, supporters of such expansion continue to repeat that intellectual property protection emphasizes the natural rights of creators and producers and, as such, should protect GIs from usurpation.[54] In contrast, opponents of enhanced GI protection continue to argue that the overarching purpose of intellectual property rights is to incentivize innovation on a termed basis, which in turn cannot justify *ex post facto* and perpetual rewards for creation. In this respect, opponents of enhanced protection advocate that protection against consumer confusion is sufficient to provide sufficient market incentives to GI-denominated products and GI-denominated regions – protection against GI usurpation would unnecessarily restrict market competition, they say, and would ultimately become a subsidy and a tool for local markets' protectionism.[55] In the remainder of this chapter, I will specifically address these points and consider the benefits and possible disadvantages of enhanced GI protection. Ultimately, I will note that GI protection does not seem to represent a subsidy for GI-denominated products and regions any more than copyright protection may constitute a subsidy for the entertainment industry, or patent protection may constitute a subsidy for other industries (for example, the pharmaceutical or biotechnology industry). Thus, I will conclude that, when it is carefully weighted and monitored, GI protection, including at the anti-usurpation level, could contribute to the promotion of investments in local production, niche-markets, and product quality, which in turn can benefit sustainable development, the environment, localized and high-skilled labor, and also public health and human rights.

---

[54] For an overview of these arguments, see F. Addor and A. Grazioli, "Geographical Indications Beyond Wines and Spirits – A Roadmap for a Better Protection for Geographical Indications in the WTO TRIPS Agreement", (2002) 5 *JWIP* 865, 867. *But see* S.A. Bowers, "Location, Location, Location: The Case Against Extending Geographical Indication Protection Under the TRIPS Agreement", (2003) 31 *AIPLAQJ* 129, 140.

[55] *See* Raustiala and Munzer, *supra* note 25, at 351. *Cf.* M. Ricolfi, "Geographical Symbols in Intellectual Property Law" in R.M. Hilty, J. Drexl, and W. Nordemann (eds), *Schutz Von Kreativitat Und Wettbewerb* (2009) 242.

IV. NICHE-MARKETS, PRODUCT QUALITY, AND PRODUCER ACCOUNTABILITY: ECONOMIC BENEFITS OF GEOGRAPHICAL INDICATIONS OF ORIGIN

As supporters of GIs have argued, even though GIs do not incentivize innovation or development in the same terms as other intellectual property rights, they offer unique economic benefits.[56] In particular, GI protection has generally been accepted on the basis that GIs prevent consumer confusion in the marketplace by providing information about the geographical origin of the GI-denominated products.[57] In addition, GIs aim at motivating a group of regional producers to meet particular production standards and, in turn, at creating and maintaining social capital for the entire group of producers that operate within the GI-denominated region.[58] As a result of GI protection, GI beneficiaries can capture the value that consumers – at the local, national, or international level – place on a product because of the product's geographical origin.[59] To fully capture this value, however, GIs necessitate that consumers associate the GI-denominated products with the respective GI-denominated regions.[60] The stronger this association, the higher the value that GI beneficiaries could derive from the exclusive use of GIs. Hence, under the current level of protection adopted under Article 22 of TRIPs GIs are only protected against confusing or misleading uses, whereas inaccurate but not confusing uses are tolerated.[61] Only GIs identifying wine and spirits are also protected in the absence of

---

[56] *See, e.g.,* M Agdomar, "Removing the Greek From Feta and Adding Korbel to Champagne: The Paradox of Geographical Indications in International Law" (2008) *Fordham Intell. Prop. Media & Ent. L. J.* 541, 577–80.

[57] The same has been acknowledged by scholars in the United States. *See, e.g.*, J. Hughes, "Champagne, Feta, and Bourbon: the Spirited Debate about Geographical Indications" (2006) 58 *Hastings L. J.* 299, 305 ("[G]eographical indications … communicate a product's geographical source and non-geographic qualities of the product that are related to its geographic origin.").

[58] *See* Rangnekar, *supra* note 25, at 15–16. *See also* Gangjee, "GIs and Cultural Heritage," *supra* note 20, at 94–5 (noting that "[t]hese geographical signs exhibit features of club goods, whereby the right to exclude is enjoyed by all members of the club").

[59] D.J. Gervais, "Traditional Innovation and the Ongoing Debate on the Protection of Geographical Indications" in P. Drahos and S. Frankel (eds), *Intellectual Property & Indigenous Innovation* (ANU EPress, 2012) 4.

[60] Rangnekar, *supra* note 25, at 9–10; Agdomar, *supra* note 56, at 578–80. *But see* Raustiala and Munzer, *supra* notc 25, at 352–4, 361–64.

[61] TRIPs, *supra* note 1, art 22.

consumer confusion – that is, GIs identifying wines and spirits enjoy higher (Lisbon-like) protection under Article 23 of TRIPs.[62] As several scholars have noted, there is no logical reason (beyond specific corporate interests) for such double standards, and TRIPs Members should consider extending the anti-usurpation protection currently granted by Article 23 to all GIs, as TRIPs negotiators had originally planned, and as was repeated in the Doha Development Agenda.[63] As I elaborate below, the shift towards a system of enhanced GI protection for all GIs could produce unique market benefits, namely the creation of niche-markets; the reduction of the information asymmetries between consumers and producers; and the establishment of a system of geographical accountability for local producers.

The argument that GIs promote the establishment of GI-denominated niche-markets within the general market for the type-level products is, in particular, one of the staple arguments in support of enhanced GI protection. Undoubtedly, GIs facilitate the conservation or the establishment of these markets, which frequently specialize in higher quality goods compared to the type-level generic products[64] by allowing consumers to mentally associate GI-denominated goods with the GI-denominated territory from which the products are originating.[65] In other words, GIs capitalize on people's desire to choose products with a known geographical identity[66] – ham from Parma, olives from Kalamata, tea from India, coffee from Bali, and so on – and, in turn, promote the dissemination of authentic products. As consumers seek products with a geographical identity for a variety of reasons – e.g., to have knowledge about the means of production, capture the romance of a location, avoid mass production, purchase sustainably produced products, etc. – GIs additionally offer consumers the means to identify the origin of the products and thus fulfill their need of information in all these various respects. Accordingly, a shift towards an anti-usurpation level of protection for all GIs would permit GI beneficiaries to better capture the value

---

62 Ibid., art 23.

63 Ibid., art 24. *See also* E.C. Creditt, "Terroir vs. Trademarks: The Debate over Geographical Indication and Expansions to the Trips Agreement" (2009) 11 *Vand. J. Ent. & Tech. L.* 425, 427.

64 Ibid.

65 Rangnekar, *supra* note 25, at 13.

66 Ibid. *See also* J. Black, "The Geography of Flavor" *Washington Post* (22 August 2007); Gangjee, *Relocating GIs*, *supra* note 11, at 266. ("Since consumers are willing to pay more for such goods, this encourages framers to invest in making the transition from producing un-differentiated bulk commodities, towards producing higher quality niche products.")

associated with GI-denominated goods by preventing free riders from capturing some of this value by producing similar versions of the authentic products. Furthermore, as regional producers bear the cost of developing and maintaining the reputation of GI-denominated products, they are vulnerable to free riders who piggyback off this reputation and identify their product by unduly evoking the authentic products. Ultimately, free riders are not part of, and do not contribute to, sustaining the GI-denominated markets.[67] Yet, should GI beneficiaries not be able to prevent free riders from using GIs to identify free riders' non-authentic products, free riders could make subpar products with little concern regarding the impact that these lower standards could have on the reputation of the GI-denominated markets.[68] This, in turn, could tarnish the reputation of the GI-denominated goods and negatively impact the market for the authentic products. Moreover, the availability of non-authentic products bearing the GI terms (even in ways supposedly non-confusing) may lead consumers to become less interested, or not interested at all, in the authentic GI-denominated products – either because the imitations are frequently less expensive than the original products, or due to the fact that such imitations dilute their appeal and make them less unique, and thus less interesting.[69]

Besides incentivizing the creation and conservation of niche-markets, GIs also provide consumers with a unique set of information about the products that are identified by the GIs,[70] namely with respect to the physical location and the methods of production of the GI-denominated

---

[67] M. Ritzert, "Champagne is from Champagne: An Economic Justification for Extending Trademark-Level Protection to Wine-Related Geographical Indicators" (2009) 37 *AIPLAQJ* 191, 212-–20.

[68] *See* Agdomar, *supra* note 56, at 586–7.

[69] Ritzert, *supra* note 67, at 212–20. Against this argument, however, the argument has been made that non-authentic versions of GI-denominated products frequently increase the demand for the authentic products, as consumers of the imitations successively purchase, or desire to purchase, the original products coming from the GI-denominated region.

[70] Agdomar, *supra* note 56, at 586–7. The argument is that asymmetrical information places the consumer in a weaker position because the consumer cannot optimize his choices due to the lack of a full set of information. Methods of improving communication include advertising, quality signs and authenticity certificates. Thus, geographical indications could be a solution to this problem as they signal quality and expertise and enable consumers to distinguish between premium-quality products and low-end products.

products.[71] Specifically, GIs offer additional information about the quality and safety of a product by informing the consumer about the origin of the natural substance and the practices which go into making the products.[72] Further, GIs offer a method of identifying how much a product is tied to the land or the "naturalness" of a product. This set of information can assist in addressing consumers' health issues or simply their concerns regarding highly processed foods, for example by assisting consumers in identifying less processed and potentially healthier foods or artefacts made with traditional or environmental-friendly manufacturing techniques. In this respect, a shift towards protecting all GIs against usurpation where third parties cannot use similar or identical terms even in non-confusing contexts – for example, Darjeeling tea for tea that does not originate from Northern India or Ceylon tea for tea that does not originate from Sri Lanka in countries where consumers are not aware that Darjeeling tea originally comes from Northern India and Ceylon tea comes from Sri Lanka – could directly protect the ability of GIs to continue to provide correct information to the benefit of both GI beneficiaries and consumers. In contrast, a weaker GI protection could lead, in the long term, to GI genericide, or the erosion of the ability of a GI to signal the origin of the GI-denominated products. Simply put, Darjeeling or Ceylon would become generic terms for certain types of teas, no different than Earl Gray or Jasmine tea, which simply identify the types of tea and not their geographical origin. In turn, this would deprive consumers of important information about the qualities that are associated with the geographical origin and manufacturing process of the products.[73] Furthermore, free riders could lead consumers into believing that their non-GI-denominated products share, in part, the original product's authenticity, even though this is often not accurate – to turn to a controversial example, many consumers in the US may believe that the American champagne sold by Korbel is made with the same method used to produce *champagne* in France.

Finally, because of the incentives that GIs create for local producers to invest in high quality products, GIs play an important role in providing information about the impact of the manufacturing and other practices on the environment, public health, labor practices, and even the respect of human rights. Specifically, by acting as identification links between

---

[71] Rangneckar, *supra* note 25, at 13–14.
[72] Agdomar, *supra* note 56, at 587–8.
[73] Ricolfi, *supra* note 55, at 239.

GI-denominated regions and GI-denominated products, GIs can contribute to reward those producers who adopt environmental, health, and labor-related friendly policies. Likewise, GIs can contribute in holding accountable those producers who create environmental, public-health-related, and other types of damages to a region, country, or larger communities. Ultimately, by tying producers to the land, GIs assist in placing the "cost" of the damages that the producers may cause also on the producers, and not solely on consumers[74] – simply put, consumers will easily know how to avoid the products coming from GI-denominated regions with health-related or other type of problems.[75] Yet, GI-denominated regions will be rewarded if producers make wise production choices. In other words, GIs motivate producers to create environmentally sustainable production methods and maintain the physical region of production – the land, water, and air. Since GIs force producers to remain in that particular physical location and use the local land and the local (or relocated) human factor to produce the GI-denominated products, the long-term health of the land and its resources is crucial for the long-term success of the producers operating in the GI-denominated region.[76] GI protection can also promote biodiversity conservation, as GIs clearly facilitate *in situ* conservation.[77] Moreover, GIs may assist in reducing possible "contagion effects" due to negative incidents in a given geographical market – for example, consumers could avoid contaminated "mozzarella di bufala" cheese from Campania when toxic waste was found to contaminate the cheeses in the region in 2008.[78] Similarly, GIs can shield from the negative consequences of "contagion" (primarily withdrawal of demand for the

---

74 Agdomar, *supra* note 56, at 588.

75 Ibid. This includes, for instance, "the 'costs' of industrialized agriculture in terms of environmental damage from overuse of carbon-based fertilizers, misallocation of water, and land stress due to concentration of certain production processes."

76 Ibid. at 4, 8. *But see* Sarah Bohen, *Embedding Local Places in Global Spaces: Geographical Indications as Territorial Development Strategy*, 75(2) RURAL SOCIOLOGY, 209, 211 (2010) (comparing two GI systems – Tequila in Mexico and Comté in France – and finding that the GI for Tequila "has largely failed to benefit the local population and environment" whereas the Comté GI benefitted the local economy).

77 *See* Gangjee, *Relocating GIs*, *supra* note 11, at 279.

78 *See* M. McCarthy and J. Phillips, "Italy's Toxic Waste Crisis, the Mafia – and the Scandal of Europe's Mozzarella" *The Independent* (22 March 2008), <http://www.independent.co.uk/news/world/europe/italys-toxic-waste-crisis-the-mafia-ndash-and-the-scandal-of-europes-mozzarella-799289.html>.

products) producers of the same types of products that are made in non-affected geographical regions[79] – for example, consumers could still safely purchase "mozzarella di bufala" made outside the Campania region in the aftermath of the toxic waste scandal.

V. CULTURAL HERITAGE, CULTURAL IDENTITY, AND CULTURAL DIVERSITY: CULTURE-BASED BENEFITS OF GEOGRAPHICAL INDICATIONS OF ORIGIN

In addition to the argument that GIs can create economic benefits, another argument has been brought forward in recent years to justify GI protection. Notably, the argument has been raised that GIs are important tools to protect the cultural identity of local and regional communities, which in turn can contribute to promoting cultural diversity.[80] The cultural protection argument parallels the market diversity argument and is based on the assumption that providing exclusive rights as a reward for local production not only encourages economic benefits, but also provides a platform for a multitude of cultural products to enter the market.[81] Against this argument, however, some scholars have pointed out that the current intellectual property system is not well formulated to serve such social functions, as this system has been created primarily to

---

[79] *See, e.g.,* L.H.P. Lang and R.M. Stulz, "Contagion and Intra-Industry Effects of Bankruptcy Announcements" (1992) 32 *J. Financial Econ.* 45, 46.

[80] In this respect, *see, e.g.*, B. Hazucha, "Intellectual Property and Cultural Diversity: Two Views on the Relationship Between Market and Culture", (2010) 28 *Intell. Prop. L & Policy J.* 39; A. Kamperman Sanders, "Incentives for Protection of Cultural Expression: Art, Trade and Geographical Indications", (2010) 13 *JWIP* 81; T. Kono, "Geographical Indication and Intangible Cultural Heritage", in B. Ubertazzi and E.M. Espada (eds), *Le Indicazioni di Qualità Degli Alimenti* (Guiffrè, 2009) 289; C. Antons, "Intellectual Property Rights in Indigenous Cultural Heritage: Basic Concepts and Continuing Controversies", in C.B. Graber, K. Kulprecht, and J. Lai (eds), *International Trade in Indigenous Cultural Heritage: Legal and Policy Issues* (Edward Elgar Publishing, 2012) 144. *See also* the various contributions to the following collective works, Graber, Kulprecht, and Lai, above; T Kono (ed.), *Intangible Cultural Heritage and Intellectual Property: Communities, Cultural Diversity and Sustainable Development* (Intersentia, 2009).

[81] *See also* J. Gibson, "The Cultural Diversity in Biodiversity" (2003) 2 Situation Analysis 46 <http://ssrn.com/abstract=1426562> [hereinafter Gibson, "Diversity"].

respond to economic-centered concerns.[82] Still, despite these criticisms, several countries have already turned to intellectual property law to protect cultural knowledge. For example, the Philippines enacted a *sui generis* system that grants property rights to indigenous communities over their traditional knowledge, including "controlling access to ancestral lands, access to biological and genetic resources and to indigenous knowledge related to these resources."[83] Similarly, Canada has extended copyright, industrial design, and GI protection to grant property rights for domestic and foreign cultural works such as "tradition-based creations including masks, totem poles and sound recordings of Aboriginal artists."[84] The growing importance of culture-related concerns led to the adoption of the Convention for the Safeguarding of the Intangible Cultural Heritage[85] under the patronage of the United Nations Educational, Scientific and Cultural Organization (UNESCO) in 2003. Entered into force in 2006, the Convention refers to "intangible cultural heritage" as "the practices, representations, expressions, knowledge, skills – as well as the instruments, objects, artifacts and cultural spaces associated therewith – that communities, groups and, in some cases, individuals recognize as part of their cultural heritage."[86]

Under this framework, GIs seem well suited for the protection of culture-based interests. In particular, GI-denominated products frequently

---

[82] For an exhaustive discussion of this aspect, *see* C. Oguamanam, "Local Knowledge as Trapped Knowledge: Intellectual Property, Culture, Power and Politics", (2008) 11 *JWIP* 29, 31–2. *See also* T. Broude, "Taking 'Trade and Culture' Seriously: Geographical Indications and Cultural Protection in the WTO," (2005) 26 *Univ. Pa. J. Int'l Econ. L. U* 623 [hereinafter Broude, "Culture"].

[83] *See* Indigenous Peoples' Rights Act of 1997 of the Philippines (Republic Act No. 8371 of 1997), <http://www.wipo.int/wipolex/en/details.jsp?id=5755>. *See also* Commission on Intellectual Property Rights, *Final Report,* Chapter 4: *Traditional Knowledge and Geographical Indications* (2002) 79, <http://www.cipr.org.uk/papers/pdfs/final_report/Ch4final.pdf>. The Commission is a forum set up by the British Government to examine the relationship between, and the integration of, intellectual property rights and development policies. *See* <http://www.cipr.org.uk/home.html>.

[84] Commission on Intellectual Property Rights, *supra* note 83, at 79 (including additional national examples).

[85] UNESCO Convention for the Safeguarding of the Intangible Cultural Heritage, 17 October 2003, in force 20 April 2006, 2368 U.N.T.S. 1 <http://unesdoc.unesco.org/images/0013/001325/132540e.pdf> [hereinafter UNESCO Cultural Heritage Convention].

[86] Ibid. art. 2(1). *Cf.* T. Voon, "UNESCO and the WTO: A Clash of Cultures?" (2006) 55 *Int'l & Comp. L Q.* I 635.

embody a cultural component, which relates to local and traditional knowledge of the region where the products are made.[87] The protection of GI-denominated products could thus serve to promote the continuation of traditional manufacturing techniques, which could otherwise succumb to the competition of mass production techniques.[88] In addition, by encapsulating the uniqueness arising from the interplay between producers and the land where products are grown or made, GI protection can contribute to a system that rewards communities for their contributions to local culture. In other words, by promoting the name of GI-denominated localities and products, GIs simultaneously promote the culture that is associated with those localities and those products. The potential of GIs as promoters of culture-related interests expands beyond agricultural products and frequently concerns non-agricultural goods, namely handicrafts, local artworks, and so forth. In recent decades, for example, countries like India have resorted to GI registrations to protect numerous locally made textiles[89] and handicrafts.[90] Similarly, Mexico has maintained valuable GI protection for Olinalá, a specific type of lacquered product, which uses an intricate technique that was developed and perfected over centuries in the Mexican city of Olinalá.[91]

Generally, the most relevant benefit that GI protection can offer to cultural knowledge is that GIs directly contribute to reinforcing local identities by again promoting the making and selling of local products.[92] As some scholars have suggested, this may promote greater product diversity in an economy where products would be otherwise increasingly

---

[87] *See, e.g.*, T.W. Dagne, "Harnessing the Development Potential of Geographical Indications for Traditional Knowledge-based Agricultural Products" (2010) 5 *J. Intell. Prop. L. & Practice* 441, 447.

[88] *See* T. Cottier and M. Panizzon, "Legal Perspectives on Traditional Knowledge: the Case for Intellectual Property Protection", (2004) 7 *J. Intell. Econ. L. J* 371, 380.

[89] India has resorted to GI protection for Indian silk, for example. *See* GI Registration, Central Silk Board, Ministry of Textiles – Government of India <http://www.csb.gov.in/gi-registration/>.

[90] In general, for a complete list of the GIs that have currently been granted in India, see *Registration Details of GI Application*, *see* <http://ipindia.nic.in/girindia/treasures_protected/registered_GI_29March2012.pdf>.

[91] *See* S. Scafidi's remarks in J. Hughes, L. Beresford, A. Kur, K. Plevan and S. Scafidi, "That's a Fine Chablis You're Not Drinking: the Proper Place for Geographical Indications in Trademark Law" (2007) 17 *Fordham Intell. Prop. Media & Ent. L.J.* 933, 958 [hereinafter "Fine Chablis"].

[92] *See* Kamperman Sanders, *supra* note 80, at 82–4; Gangjee, "GIs and Cultural Heritage," *supra* note 20, at 99.

similar due to the globalization of trade and the de-localization of product manufacturing (frequently to save costs in manufacturing, assembling, and packaging the products). In this respect, the role of GIs is even more relevant as the outsourcing of product manufacturing has increasingly blurred local boundaries by focusing instead in promoting mass production, mass distribution, and uniformity of products across various countries and internationally. Professor Broude summarized this very well when he wrote: "[I]t is often asserted that the devastation of local cultures is the product of a triumph of cultural hegemony or cultural imperialism on the ideological battleground of culture. The result of which … is westernization or 'Americanization.'"[93] Though the effects of the "Americanization" theory may have been exaggerated in many circles,[94] it seems clear that "globalization … does produce changes in local cultures and traditions"[95] due to economic pressures of efficiency and maximum exploitation. GIs, however, contrast this business model of uniformity and standardization. As expressions of local *terroir*, GIs offer incentives for the preservation of culture as embodied in the traditional methods of production, which stem directly from the use of the natural resources and the traditional yet evolving knowledge of the geographical region that is identified under the GI in question. In other words, because GIs protect the *terroir* and its link with the GI-denominated products and manufacturing techniques, GIs promote the epitomic opposite of globalization, namely cultural diversity, by recognizing and incentivizing preservation of local cultural practices and local knowledge.[96]

Specifically for this reason, European countries have resorted to GI protection in order to identify and protect their cultural traditions – primarily but not exclusively with respect to agricultural and culinary products – against the misappropriation and confusing use of the names defining these traditions.[97] Besides European countries, a growing

---

[93] Broude, "Culture," *supra* note 82, at 634–5.

[94] *See* T. Broude, "Conflict and Complementarity in Trade, Cultural Diversity and Intellectual Property Rights" (2007) 2 *Asian J. WTO & Int'l Health L. & Policy* 345, 348–9.

[95] Broude, "Culture," *supra* note 82, at 635.

[96] *But see* T. Voon, "Geographical Indications, Culture and the WTO" in Ubertazzi and Espada, *supra* note 80, 300.

[97] In the European Union (EU), the notion of *terroir*, and its relevance as a qualifier for GI protection, is often referred to as the *goût du terroir* – taste of earth. In order to promote GI-denominated foods, the European Commission defined *le goût du terroir* as

number of developing countries has also embraced GI protection and demanded higher protection for their GIs at the international level.[98] For example, countries such as Kenya, Nigeria, South Africa, Egypt, Mexico, Peru, Cuba, India, Pakistan, Mauritius, and Sri Lanka have demonstrated significant interest in GIs and implemented various levels of GI protection at the national level.[99] This growing interest and participation in the GI debate additionally reflects the growing role of GIs as a tool to protect not only niche-markets and economic interests, but also to safeguard traditional methods of production and other cultural aspects of national cultural heritage. This, of course, is not without problems, as GIs can become a double-edged sword and lead to inconsiderate exploitation of the GI-denominated region, which may result in dire consequences for the environment, sustainable development, and so on. In this respect, developing countries may be more susceptible to this risk – an indicative example is the case of "Phu Quoc," which was recently registered as a GI for fish sauces in Vietnam, but has been overexploited since, with unwelcome results for the local environment.[100] Still, when carefully managed, GIs can contribute to the conservation and promotion of traditional and cultural knowledge, local identities, and cultural diversity, both of developed and developing countries. Yet, to achieve these goals, GIs should be protected against commercial forces that threaten to

---

> a distinct, identifiable taste reminiscent of a place, region or locality. … Foods and beverages that evoke the term *terroir* have signature qualities that link their taste to a specific soil with particular climate conditions. Only the land, climate and expertise of the local people can produce the product that lives up to its name.

See Raustiala and Munzer, *supra* note 25, at 344.

[98] Despite the traditional opposition to GIs by the US, some scholars in the US have also emphasized this point. *See* D. Giovannucci, E. Barham, and R. Pirog, "Defining and Marketing 'Local' Foods: Geographical Indications for US Products" (2010) 13 *JWIP* 94.

[99] *See also* Doha Declaration, *supra* note 12.

[100] For an overview of the development of the problems related to "Phu Quoc" fish sauce, *see* <http://talkvietnam.com/ 2012/08/part-1-the-storm-rushes-down-in-the-phu-quoc-fish-sauce-craft-village/#.UbRtmfkwdsk>. For a detailed discussion on the "Phu Quoc" registration process, *see* T.B. Vu and D.H. Dao, "Geographical Indication and Appellation of Origin in Vietnam: Reality, Policy, And Perspective" *Institute Of Policy And Strategy For Agriculture And Rural Development – MISPA Project* (2006) <http://www.fao.org/fileadmin/templates/olq/documents/documents/GI%20and%20AO% 20in%20Vietnam.pdf>.

compel homogenization and obliterate local cultures of production.[101] This may include protecting GIs against the usurpation of the GI names, that is, beyond confusing uses of the GIs and by applying the same standards that are currently applied to GIs identifying wines and spirits to all GIs.

VI. MOVING THE GEOGRAPHICAL INDICATIONS OF ORIGIN AGENDA FORWARD: LEGITIMATE CRITICISM, COUNTERARGUMENTS, AND THE FUNDAMENTAL ROLE OF THE *TERROIR*

In light of the above, GIs clearly provide unique benefits both in terms of economic incentives to local communities, as well as with respect to the protection and promotion of the cultural identity of the same communities. In particular, both producers of GI-denominated products and consumers looking for authentic goods can directly benefit from GI protection. GI protection additionally benefits society as a whole by increasing the public's awareness of the differences between the authentic and non-authentic products – in terms of geographical origin and related quality and characteristics. Based upon these considerations, it is thus important that WTO Members reopen the international debate on GI protection and possibly agree on the adoption of an enhanced protection for all GIs as has been advocated by GI supporters in many countries. As I have elaborated in Parts IV and V, the result of the adoption of such a system of enhanced GI protection would translate in GI beneficiaries being finally able to control the use of the terms that are identical or similar to existing GIs also when these terms are used in non-confusing settings – under the current system, GI beneficiaries can only prevent misleading and confusing uses of GIs. Should a system of enhanced GI protection be adopted, GI beneficiaries could be able to capture a higher value for the use of GIs, as no competitor could refer to the geographical terms to identify competing products. Ultimately, such exclusive use could also facilitate the (socially relevant) process of educating the public – at the national and international level – about the existence of the GI-denominated products and the difference existing between these authentic products and their imitations – for example, that authentic Parma ham comes only from the Italian region of Parma, authentic

[101] *See* Broude, "Culture," *supra* note 82, at 651–2 (highlighting the advantages and disadvantages of this position).

Darjeeling tea only comes from the Indian State of West Bengal, authentic Ceylon tea comes only from the Sri Lankan region of Ceylon, and so on. Better educated consumers would become more aware of, and perhaps more sensitive to, the characteristics and qualities that are embodied in the authentic GI-denominated products. Equally important, better educated consumers would become able to distinguish between authentic products and the imitations of these products that are made outside the GI-denominated territory – this, in turn, would prevent GIs becoming generic terms for the type-level product identified by the GIs as consumers would be able to mentally associate GIs not with types of products, but with the localities from which GI-denominated products originate. Furthermore, by increasing consumer awareness, GIs could increase the demand for authentic GI-denominated products in local, national, and international markets – consumers could seek authentic Parma ham, or Darjeeling or Ceylon tea rather than imitations of these products. On a general level, consumers would have better information upon which to make better-informed choices while purchasing GI-denominated products, or alternative products in the marketplace.

Enhancing GI protection for all GIs, however, would not come without some inherent costs. In this respect, I acknowledge that an enhanced level of protection for all GIs may affect market competition.[102] As I noted above, GI protection undoubtedly represents a barrier to entry in the group-level products' market – the market for red wine, for example, with respect to the Chianti-denominated products. Accordingly, the benefits of a shift toward a generalized system of enhanced protection against usurpation should be weighted carefully, and such a system should be adopted with specific limitations that would still guarantee the functioning of a competitive marketplace.[103] In particular, a system of enhanced protection of GIs against non-confusing use of GIs should be reserved, in my opinion, to GI-denominated products that effectively derive from the GI-denominated territory because they are grown or manufactured therein. This is consistent with the historical normative underpinning of protection of GIs (and appellations of origin before GIs). Only when this territorial linkage is adequately safeguarded can GIs fulfill their function of providing consumers with accurate information regarding the GI-denominated products and, in turn, promote the creation of local niche-markets and benefit local producers. Likewise, only when GI protection is based upon this linkage with the *terroir* can GIs effectively

---

[102] *See, e.g.*, Raustiala and Munzer, *supra* note 25, at 352–9.
[103] *See* Calboli, *supra* note 16, at 200–3.

raise producers' accountability with respect to the GI-denominated territory. This may also provide a contractarian normative basis to protect GIs because consumers are more likely to benefit when those conditions are present, an argument that has been made also with respect to trademarks.[104] Should this linkage be loosened, however, the argument that GIs are an unnecessary regional subsidy would become more relevant, and the very rationale for GI protection – signaling the geographical origin of the products – becomes weaker.[105] Without a strong territorial linkage, the use of GIs could even lead to consumers being given misleading information about the actual origin of the products, or their ingredients. A strict interpretation of the territorial requirement for GI protection is also compatible, as I noted above, with Article 22 of TRIPs. Even though Article 22 refers to products that "essentially" derive their qualities from the GI-denominated region, rather than "exclusively or essentially," as stated in the Lisbon Agreement, the wording "essentially" in TRIPs can, and should, be interpreted as only "exclusively." In other words, also under TRIPs, the "essential" elements of a GI-denominated product – that is, the core elements, the essence, of that product – should come "exclusively" from the GI-denominated region, the relevant *terroir*.

Hence, when GI protection is based upon or linked to a strict enforcement of the underlying *terroir* requirement, GI protection does not seem untenable in a competitive economy, including at the enhanced level of protection. In particular, contrary to the argument supported by GI opponents, GI protection does not "stifle competition"[106] as it does not affect competition within the type-level products that GIs identify – competitors are still entitled to produce the same kind of products, they are "merely prohibit[ed] [from using] the same nomenclature."[107] For example, under the current system of enhanced GI protection for wines

---

104 *See* J.N. Sheff, "Marks, Morals, and Markets" (2013) 65 *Stan. L. Rev.* 761.

105 *See* Broude, "Culture," *supra* note 82, at 666–7 (reconstructing the history of the Chianti recipe and highlighting the abandonment of the original requirement to include white grape varieties into the wine due to market pressures and the need to achieve "higher quality that conforms to internationally accepted tastes and standards" but which nonetheless diluted the traditional wine recipe). *See also* T. Josling, "The War on Terroir: Geographical Indications as a Transatlantic Trade Conflict" (2006) 57 *J. Agric. L.* 337 (describing the fact, due to the existence of the GI Chianti, Italian wine producers could not market a "modified" Chianti wine, but had to resort to a "Super Tuscan" designator, which also became very popular with those seeking a less expensive similar wine).

106 Agdomar, *supra* note 56, at 590.

107 Ibid., at 591.

and spirits, no wine maker is prevented from producing sparkling wine simply because the sparkling wine coming from the Champagne region in France has the exclusive right to be identified with the "Champagne" GI – instead, all sparkling wine producers can produce sparkling wines under their own trademarks but simply cannot call the products "Champagne." Ultimately, GI protection could even result in "stimulat[ing] competition and innovation" with respect to the type-level products, as the recognition of GIs forces outside producers "to develop innovative techniques to improve upon a product to compete vis à-vis the [GI-denominated] product category."[108] In addition, GI protection does not interfere with the competition that always exists between producers that operate in the GI-denominated region.[109] To use an additional example from the wine industry, the "Chianti" region in Tuscany, the recognition of "Chianti" as a GI does not eliminate competition between the local producers of Chianti wine. By contrast, producers of Chianti wine still compete for market share against other local producers and generally turn to their particular brand names – Marchesi Antinori, Marchesi de Frescobaldi, and so forth – to identify the specific Chianti wines that they produce within the GI-denominated market.

Still, as GI opponents have highlighted, a shift towards an enhanced system of protection for all GIs could nevertheless create an absolute right over geographical names, including unauthorized use of these names for descriptive and comparative purposes. In particular, some scholars in the US have expressed concerns that developing strong usurpation protection for GIs would not pass the test established by the Supreme Court in the *Central Hudson* case,[110] which protects non-misleading commercial speech.[111] Along the same lines, EU scholars have speculated that strong anti-usurpation level GI protection might be challenged by the principle of free speech embodied in Article 10 of the

---

[108] Ibid.

[109] *See* D.E. Long, "Branding the Land: Creating Global Meanings for Local Characteristics" in I. Calboli and E. Lee (eds), *Trademark Protection and Territoriality Challenges in a Global Economy* (forthcoming 2014) (on file with author).

[110] *Central Hudson Gas & Electric Corp. v Public Service Commission*, 447 U.S. 557 (1980).

[111] H.N. Niska, "The European Union Trips Over the U.S. Constitution: Can the First Amendment Save the Bologna That Has a First Name?" 13 *Minn. J. Global Trade* 413, 440–1.

European Convention on Human Rights.[112] As I have argued before, a possible solution in this respect could be to permit the unauthorized uses of GI-related terms for comparative and descriptive purposes.[113] In other words, competitors should be left free and should be able to identify and refer to their products using GI terms accompanied by the terms "style," "like," or "type," as long as the GI terms are not used misleadingly or to engender consumer confusion as to the origin of competitors' products – in other words, cheese producers of mozzarella made with buffalo's milk outside the Campania region should be able to refer to their products as "made with buffalo's milk like the 'mozzarella di bufala Campana.'" Even though TRIPs directly excludes the use of "style," "like," or "type" with respect to GIs identifying wines and spirits,[114] the argument could be made that an enhanced anti-usurpation protection for all GIs may require the revision of this exclusion, and eliminate this exclusion for all GIs, including for GIs for wine and spirits. Such a change would thus permit comparative and descriptive unauthorized uses of all GIs as long as consumers are not confused and the comparisons and descriptions at issue are not misleading.[115] Naturally, a change in this direction, including a change in the current text of Article 23 of TRIPs, would be strongly opposed by GI beneficiaries. Yet, this approach could resolve the competition and linguistic-related concerns that have been raised, with valid reasons, with respect to enhanced GI protection. Ultimately, the adoption of such a more compromising approach could offer an even stronger argument in support of enhanced GI protection – it would be more difficult to categorize such protection simply as a monopoly or a

---

[112] Convention for the Protection of Human Rights and Fundamental Freedoms, art 10(1), 4 November 1950, 213 U.N.T.S. 222 ("Everyone has the right to freedom of expression. This right shall include freedom to hold opinions and to receive and impart information and ideas without interference by public authority and regardless of frontiers. This article shall not prevent States from requiring the licensing of broadcasting, television or cinema enterprises."). *See* also comments by Kur, "Fine Chablis," *supra* note 91, at 968.

[113] Calboli, *supra* note 16, at 202.

[114] TRIPs, *supra* note 1, art 23. Equally relevant, comparison between GI-denominated products and non-GI-denominated products is also excluded under the system of comparative advertising that has been adopted in the EU with the Comparative Advertising Directive. *See* Council Directive 97/55, art 3a(1), 1997 O.J. (L 290) 18, 21 (EC) ("Comparative advertising shall, as far as the comparison is concerned, be permitted when … for products with designation of origin [the comparison] relates in each case to products with the same designation.").

[115] Calboli, *supra* note 16, at 202.

subsidy for GI-denominated region – and could contribute to effectively moving forward the international debate on GI protection.

Lastly, besides the impact of GI protection on competition, some concerns have been raised as to the ability of GIs to effectively act as tools to promote and protect cultural heritage. A cultural approach to justifying GIs would basically amount, some scholars have argued, to disguising economic protectionism with culture-related interests.[116] In addition, other scholars have underscored that incorporating heritage and culture narratives into intellectual property rights poses the danger of oversimplifying the notion of culture.[117] Even supporters of cultural protection have warned that "'[a]ssimilation' of the value of intellectual property within Western notions of property is an inadequate and often destructive means by which to protect traditional knowledge."[118] Scholars have also questioned the ability of GIs to preserve cultural heritage since "local traditions and cultures of production … change when markets cause them to, and remain constant when markets cause them to."[119] As a response to these critiques, however, it should be pointed out that, like production requirements, cultural practices also naturally evolve. Notably, as recognized in the UNESCO definition of intangible cultural heritage,[120] culture is a dynamic rather than a static concept, and GIs can facilitate the protection of cultural knowledge also in a dynamic context, where natural changes may prompt product variations – for example, sweeter wine due to changes in the quality of the local grapes due to warmer seasons, different colors used for traditional saris, and so forth. Here again, however, these critiques may be on point if GIs are used to identify products that are not made with ingredients and labor coming entirely from the GI-denominated region. In these instances, GI protection would lack the essential connection with the *terroir* and thus have

---

[116] *See, e.g.,* Voon, *supra* note 96, at 311 (arguing that "the cultural justification for GI protection is largely subsumed within the broader purposes of preventing unfair competition and consumer confusion" and that a cultural argument would essentially be reduced to protectionism interests). *See also* the well-reconstructed discussion in this respect by Gangjee, "GIs and Cultural Heritage," *supra* note 20, 100–1.

[117] J. Gibson, "Knowledge and Other Values – Intellectual Property and the Limitations for Traditional Knowledge" in G. Westkamp (ed), *Emerging Issues in Modern Intellectual Property: Trade, Technology, Market Freedom, Essays in Memory of Herchel Smith* (Edward Elgar Publishing, 2007) 309, 312.

[118] Ibid.

[119] For a further discussion on counter arguments to the "cultural heritage rationale" for GI protection, *see* Broude, "Culture," *supra* note 82, at 663.

[120] UNESCO Cultural Heritage Convention, *supra* note 85, art 2(1).

weak or nonexistent normative grounds. In particular, whereas GI protection for locally made products does promote local culture and preserve local cultural heritage, such protection becomes less justifiable when the products are not made with local ingredients and not *in locus*.

VII. CONCLUSION

Almost two decades after the enactment of TRIPs, countries across the globe continue to prove deeply divided on GI protection. The spectrum of controversies spans from the rationale and justification for protection to the format under which GIs should be protected, the creation of a GI registry, or the suitability of extending the anti-usurpation protection currently available to wines and spirits to all GIs. In this chapter, I attempted to highlight the unique benefits of GI protection, and I considered whether an enhanced protection against GI usurpation for all GIs may be desirable to further these benefits. Namely, I underscored that GI protection may promote the development of niche-markets, incentivize investments in high quality products, and contribute to creating a mechanism of rewards and accountability for producers, thus supporting more sustainable development. I also stressed that, besides purely economic benefits, GIs may serve to protect culture-related interests. Specifically, GIs can promote local products and their associated knowledge as cultural expressions. In this respect, GIs not only can contribute to preserving cultural heritage and existing traditions – they can also lead to (re)affirming cultural identities and promoting these identities nationally and internationally. Ultimately, GIs can provide "rural areas with a new vitality" and "right owners with the opportunity to get benefits," which may "translate into an equitable distribution of value and benefits to the owners of geographical indications and their communities."[121] This, in turn, can benefit society as a whole.

GI protection does not come, however, without costs. In this chapter, I have also suggested that the inherent costs of GI protection in aggregate do not outweigh the unique benefits that GIs bring both to the communities operating in the GI-denominated territory as well as to consumers and the rest of society. This is particularly true where GI protection is limited to products that are grown or produced entirely in the GI-denominated territory. To the contrary, should this territorial

121 *See* Zografos, *supra* note 13, at 12.

linkage be loosened, GI protection could easily turn into an anti-competitive, and unjustifiable, subsidy in favor of local producers. Moreover, GIs could become a source of misinformation for consumers who rely on GIs as an indication of authenticity and local origin. Hence, as I have supported in this chapter, GI protection for authentic and genuinely local products can contribute to stimulating competition and innovation within local and regional niche-markets. Most frequently, these markets produce higher quality products compared to the type-level mass-produced goods. Under the same conditions, GIs may contribute to the conservation of local and regional cultural knowledge, taking into account that culture changes over time and adapts to external factors, as noted also in the definition of intangible cultural heritage offered by the 2003 UNESCO Convention for the Safeguard of Intangible Cultural Heritage.

Based upon these observations, I conclude this chapter by advocating for the re-opening of the GI negotiations at the WTO (and elsewhere) with a view to seriously considering the adoption of an enhanced protection for GIs, with the limitations that I advocated for in Part VI, namely the possibility that competitors and third parties use GIs for descriptive and comparative purposes. Unquestionably, countries will continue to quarrel over the details of the implementation of such protection. Controversies and debates in this respect are expected to continue. Hence, WTO Members should considering moving forward the GI protection agenda, which continues to be gridlocked and dominated by special interests. As I have highlighted in this chapter, the key element to justify GI protection, both at the anti-confusion as well as anti-usurpation levels, remains and will always be the territorial linkage between the GI-denominated territory and the products, either because products are grown or are made therein. WTO Members, countries' delegates, supporters, and opponents of GIs should keep this in mind while negotiating the details of the GI Development Agenda: *in territorio veritas.*

Index